Frank Schoonmaker's

ENCYCLOPEDIA OF WINE

Frank Schoonmaker's
Encyclopedia
OF
WINE

Revised and Expanded by
JULIUS WILE

HASTINGS HOUSE • PUBLISHERS

New York

Second Printing, October 1980
Third Printing, April 1981

FOREIGN EDITIONS
In Danish: SPEKTRUM, Copenhagen, Denmark
In French: ANDRÉ GERARD & CO., Verviers, Belgium
In England: A. & C. BLACK, London, England
In German: FISCHER TASCHENBUCH VERLAG GmbH,
    Frankfurt am Main, Germany
In Italian: U. MURSIA & C., Milan, Italy
In Swedish: ALBERT BONNIERS FORLAG, Stockholm, Sweden

Library of Congress Cataloging in Publication Data

Schoonmaker, Frank, date
    Frank Schoonmaker's Encyclopedia wine.

    1. Wine and wine making — Dictionaries. I. Wile,
Julius. II. Title. III. Title: Encyclopedia of wine.
TP546.S47   1978   641.2'2'03   78-9563
ISBN 0-8038-1947-1

Published simultaneously in Canada by
Saunders of Toronto, Ltd., Don Mills, Ontario

Printed in the United States of America

Designed by Al Lichtenberg

Contents

Introduction

I first met Frank Schoonmaker in 1944 in Algiers. He was an intelligence legend, having recently been ousted from Spain for organizing a successful underground railway to return allied air personnel to active duty. The older and more sophisticated members of our OSS team knew him as "the American wine expert", but it took me almost 15 years to realize what a golden opportunity had slipped through my fingers, for I had the privilege to be with the most erudite international wine writer of our time. Except for our acquisition of a rather remarkable cellar for the officers' mess in Algiers, I doubt if we ever discussed wine.

I did not see Frank again until after I had read most of what he had written and was in awe of my old war-time buddy who had not only endless erudition, but also an ability to write on wine with elegance and ease that marked him as a poet amongst pedestrian writers. He had opened America's eyes to the world of wine. He made his mark on French, German, and American wines and to a lesser degree on wines from Iberia and Italy. There was no end to his knowledge, no limit to his ability for expression.

We were friends, but at a distance. Our age and our professional life separated us. It was only in his last years that I began to urge him to bring his major works, *The Wines of Germany* and the *Encyclopedia*, up-to-date. I felt that time was running out and he owed all of us a final word and judgment. Unfortunately, though he wanted to, he was not given the time. Walter Frese, his publisher, asked me shortly after Frank's death to suggest an editor for the *Encyclopedia*.

Bringing a classic up-to-date was not only a problem of updating information but also of conserving the original style and elegance. This task required both infinite knowledge and perspicacity. Without

vii

hesitation I suggested Julius Wile, who had just retired as the chief operating officer of one of the most prestigious wine and spirit importers in America, a company founded by his grandfather in 1877. For over 40 years he had the intimate international associations and training in every facet of the wine business. More importantly he had throughout his career given his time unstintingly to the commonweal. Still young and dynamic enough to take on a challenge; he could also understand the immense responsibility of editing a classic, somewhat like bringing the *Encyclopaedia Britannica* up to date, a job with which he was also familiar.

I was delighted to hear from the publisher that Julius had accepted the challenge, a little less delighted when he started to impose on my time and brains to help with an entry here and an entry there. I can attest from first hand experience that he left no stone unturned in order to make this the most exact and up-to-date work of its kind in the Western World, without losing its conciseness and literate value. He has given the wine consumer, wine merchant and wine writer the most important source of information, making an essential book an indispensable one. I am delighted to attest in this latest edition to the perfection of the information and the charm and style.

As in all good encyclopedias you will find yourself looking up one thing and ending up browsing and learning a lot more than you bargained for. It is indeed what the meaning of the word implies: a "general course of instruction". I am sure it will be as essential a part of your library as it will be of mine.

PETER SICHEL

Preface

Editing Frank Schoonmaker's Encyclopedia has been like writing a second New Testament. A book which has appeared in six languages is not lightly tampered with, yet, as a viable reference, it had to be updated.

New wine laws in Germany and Italy, a greater public awareness of lesser known wines, expansion of wine making in the United States and the continuing enormous interest in wine have dictated a twenty percent increase in the size of this volume.

I have tried for a good "cuvée" to conserve and implement the "sève" of Frank Schoonmaker without showing any rough edges or obvious patches. His style and acerbity were unique.

JULIUS WILE

Acknowledgements

Acknowledgement must be given and thanks expressed to all those who contributed time, thought and assistance during the year it took to refresh this book:

Special Recognition

For her support, interest and cooperation Mrs. Frank Schoonmaker, New York, N.Y.
For her encouragement, patience and understanding Ruth M. Wile, Scarsdale, N.Y.

Maps

For his constructive, painstaking and artistic efforts in revising old and creating new maps William Lembeck, New York, N.Y.

In and for France

Marquis Jacques d'Angerville, Clos de Ducs, Volnay
G. Canard, Union Interprofessionale des Vins du Beaujolais
Christian Bizot, Champagne Bollinger, Ay-Champagne
Pierre Bréjoux, I. N. A. O., Paris
A. Devletian, I. N. A. O., Paris
Jean-Pierre Gachelin, French Embassy, New York, N.Y.
Pierre Gouttier, Le Comité National des Vins de France, Paris
Francois Gugenheim, Food & Wines from France, New York, N.Y.
La Journée Vinicole
Irving Smith Kogan, New York, N.Y.
Jacques Lamblin, Maison Henri Lamblin, Maligny (Près Chablis)
Robert Lemercier, French Embassy, New York, N.Y.
Philippe Marion, Chanson Père et Fils, Beaune
Jean LePechoux, Food & Wines from France, New York, N.Y.
Edmund Penning-Rowsell, Woburn, England
Bruno Prats, Prats Frères, Bordeaux

In and for Germany

Alan Olson, German Wine Information Bureau, New York, N.Y.
Peter M. F. Sichel, H. Sichel & Sons, Inc., New York, N.Y.
Hanns Christof Wegeler, Deinhard & Co., Koblenz-am-Rhein

In and for Italy

Marquis Piero Antinori, L & P Antinori, Florence
Lucio Caputo, Italian Trade Commission, New York, N.Y.
Mary Mulligan, Italian Trade Commission, New York, N.Y.
Margaret L. Stern, Schieffelin & Co., New York, N.Y.

In and for U. S. A.

Leon D. Adams, Sausalito, California
Gerald Asher, "21" Brands, Inc., San Francisco, California
William Bonetti, Souverain Vineyards, Sonoma County, California
John De Luca, Wine Institute, San Francisco, California
Dr. Harold P. Olmo, Department of Viticulture and Enology, University of California, Davis
Dr. Willard B. Robinson, Institute of Food Science, New York State Agricultural Experiment Station, Geneva, N.Y.
Brian St. Pierre, Wine Institute, San Francisco, California
Philip M. Wagner, Boordy Vineyards, Riderwood, Maryland
Professor A. Dinsmoor Webb, Department of Viticulture and Enology, University of California, Davis

Concerning Sherry

Arthur Humbert, Williams & Humbert International, Ltd., London

Vintage Information

Kenneth Onish, Chateau and Estate Wines, New York, N.Y.

Labels and Food Affinities

Harriet Lembeck, New York, N.Y.

Research and Typing

Marjorie M. Finn, Larchmont, N.Y.

List of Maps

Frank Schoonmaker's
ENCYCLOPEDIA OF WINE

A

ABBOCCATO — (Ah-bo-*kah*-toe) — Italian word which, when applied to wine, means sweet or semi-sweet. It is the equivalent of the French *moelleux,* and is used particularly in connection with the wines of Orvieto (*see*), which are customarily classified as either *secco* (dry) or *abboccato* (semi-sweet).

ABFÜLLER — (Ab-few-ler) — German for Bottler or ABGEFÜLT, Bottled.

ABOCADO — (Ah-bo-kah-doe) — Term to describe a medium-sweet sherry.

ABRUZZO and MOLISE — (Ah-broot-zo Mo-lee-seh) — Adjacent regions on the mid-Adriatic coast of Italy; their best known wines are Montepulciano d'Abruzzo and Trebbiano d'Abruzzo.

ACESCENCE — High volatile acidity due to excess acetic acid, vinegariness, not at all desirable in wine.

ACHAEA — (Ah-*key*-ya) — Greek province, forming the southern shore of the Gulf of Corinth in the Peloponnesus; produces a considerable quantity of red and white table wine, particularly in the neighborhood of Patras.

ACID — All wine, like lemonade, has a certain amount of acid — if too little, it is flat and insipid and unappetizing. But a wine that can be described as "acid" has too much. If this is the natural tartaric and malic acid of the grape (like lemonade in which one has put too much lemon juice) the wine is better described as "tart." If there is the taste or odor of vinegar (acetic acid) the wine is spoiled or sour. The two kinds of acidity are easy to tell apart — one

1

sniff is enough. A tart wine may not be to one's taste; a spoiled or sour wine is not fit to drink.

ACID, ACETIC — The acid of vinegar, CH_3COOH. It is invariably and exclusively the result of a second, *acetic* fermentation in an already fermented and generally potable liquid such as beer, cider or wine. If these did not exist, neither would vinegar; the word comes directly from the French *vin aigre*, sharp or sour wine, and some purists have claimed that it should therefore never be used for cider or malt or even pineapple vinegar. This, of course, is nonsense. Traces of acetic acid are present in all wines, especially old wines, but generally cannot be detected by taste or smell unless over one part per thousand, or .1%. White wines with over .12% and red wines with over .14% of acetic acid must be labeled "substandard" according to American law. This limit is arbitrary, possibly unfair in some instances, but on the whole, sound. Acetic fermentation can only take place in the presence of air, and is produced by a microorganism called the Acetobacter, or mycoderma aceti. The chemical formula is as follows:

Alcohol + Oxygen   Acetobacter   Acetic Acid   +   Water

$CH_3CH_2OH + O_2$ $\longrightarrow$ CH_3COOH H_2O

An excess of acetic acid in a wine is almost always evidence of poor or careless cellar-work, and is completely inexcusable in a wine under five years old, providing, of course, that the wine has been properly stored since leaving the winery. Even wine with an excess of acetic acid will usually not become vinegar (*see*) unless "mother of vinegar" (a concentrate or culture of Acetobacter) is present. "Volatile acidity" (*see*) is the term generally (and accurately) used by wine experts and technicians in reference to acetic acid; a wine that has too much of it is often described as "spoiled" or "sour" or "gone." Wine almost never turns to vinegar in the bottle.

ACIDITY, FIXED — The expert's term for the normal fruit acids which a wine contains — tartaric, malic, citric, lactic, etc.

ACIDITY, REAL — This is a layman's term for what a chemist would call the pH of a wine, the *intensity* of the acidity it contains. Without attempting to be at all technical, it is possible to say that some acids are more intense than others, so that wines may have the same fixed or same total acidity and yet a quite different pH. In general, liquids with a pH of 7 are neither acid nor alkaline, but neutral; those with a pH of 5 or less will turn litmus paper red (acid) and those with a pH of 8 or over will turn litmus paper blue (alkaline). The lower the pH of a wine, therefore, the more intense its acid. A Folle Blanche grown in a cool district in California may have a pH of 2.80, for example, and a Muscat from a warm district a pH of 3.95. These are extremes; the first will taste very tart, and the second extremely neutral and flat.

ACIDITY, TOTAL — Fixed acidity plus volatile acidity in a wine. A technician's term.

ACIDITY, VOLATILE — Acetic acid (*see*). The acid of spoiled wine. Easily detected, even by a beginner, if as much as $1/7$ of 1% is present in a wine.

2

ADEGA — (Ah-*day*-gah) — A wine warehouse or cellar, though generally above ground, in Portugal. The equivalent of a *chai* in France or a *bodega* in Spain.

ADIGE — (*Ah*-dee-jay) — Important river of northern Italy, draining the picturesque and interesting vineyard district of the Italian Tyrol (*see*) as well as Valpolicella (*see*), running through Verona and emptying into the Adriatic south of Venice. *See* also Alto Adige, Bolzano, Trentino.

ADULTERATED WINE — Wine which has been treated with unauthorized material or excessive amounts of permitted substance.

AESTIVALIS — Native American grape species widespread through the central southern states; *Vitis Aestivalis* is widely used in hybridization for its vigor and disease resistance.

AFFENTHALER — (*Ah*-fen-tah-ler) — German red wine from the Black Forest foothills near Baden-Baden. It is made mostly from the Spätburgunder or Pinot Noir grape, but is light in color, almost a *rosé,* and its quality is hardly more than passable. Its odd name has nevertheless given it a certain notoriety, like Zeller Schwarze Katz and Kröver Nacktarsch: *Affe,* in German, means ''ape'' or ''monkey,'' and an Affenthaler is therefore a wine from ''monkey valley.'' What is shipped to America often has a plastic gold-colored monkey wrapped around the bottle, but the wine, needless to say, is made no better by this gimmick.

    ALSO, a red-wine grape widely grown in Württemberg, though generally interplanted with the Trollinger or other varieties. Its wine is undistinguished.

AFRICA — This vast continent produces wine only in its northern and southern extremities, in the Temperate Zones. *See* Algeria, Morocco, Tunisia, South Africa.

AFTER TASTE — Sensation which remains in the mouth after expectorating or swallowing.

AGEING OF WINES — All wines, if properly stored, tend to improve somewhat with age, but, generally speaking, there has been too much emphasis placed on age, as if age itself were a virtue. It can be, but often is not. Every wine has its natural life span, its youth, its prime, its old age, and this pattern varies just as wines vary. Many wines are better when young, and all table wines (light, unfortified wines) lose their freshness and fruit and become ''withered'' and unattractive if kept too long in cask; all table wines and a few rare exceptions among fortified wines (Vintage Port, for example) improve in bottle even more than in wood, although some of them for only six or eight months, and some for 50 years. In general, 75% of the wine produced in the world is as good when a year old as it is ever likely to be, and will only deteriorate, not improve, after its third birthday. Wines that should generally be consumed by the time they are three years old, and certainly before the age of five, include:

    All *vins rosés,* or pink wines, whether from California or France, or elsewhere.

3

All California white wines except a few made from the Chardonnay, Chenin Blanc, Pinot Blanc, Sauvignon Blanc and Johannisberg Riesling.

Most white Burgundies, the exceptions being those from the finest vineyards in unusually good years. Most of the dryer wines of the Loire and those of Alsace. Almost all Italian wines, the exceptions being a small, select company of reds made from the Nebbiolo grape (Barolo, Gattinara, Barbaresco, Valtellina), a few rare Chiantis, and a handful of others, as Aglianico del Vulture. All German wines except estate-bottlings of good producers, superior vineyards and great years. Many dry Graves.

Most Beaujolais, and most of the lesser red wines of France. Most California Zinfandels, Gamays and even some Pinot Noirs.

AGLIANICO (Ah-lee-*ah*-nee-co) — Remarkable red wine, made from the Aglianico grape in the Italian province of Potenza, east of Naples. The better vineyards are planted entirely on the volcanic soil of Monte Vulture; in this isolated and rather backward district, well-equipped cellars are few, and genuine, well-made, unblended Aglianico del Vulture is not easy to come by. However, it is worth looking for — full-bodied, fine, with a notable bouquet. There are few red wines as good, and none better, in central or southern Italy.

AGRAFE — (Ah-grahf) — Metal clip used to secure cork during first bottle fermentation of Champagne (*see*), to a large extent replaced by a crown cap.

AHR — (Are) — Small river in Western Germany which joins the Rhine north of Koblenz and gives its name to the second smallest of the eleven Anbaugebiete (*see*). Its hillside vineyards, the northermost in Germany, planted largely in Pinot Noir (here known as Blauer Spätburgunder), Frühburgunder and Portugieser, produce some of the best of Germany's not particularly distinguished red wines. They are rarely exported. The 1,200 planted acres consist of 1 Bereich, 1 Grosslage and about 40 Einzellagen. The principal wine producing towns are Ahrweiler, Bad Neunahr and Walforzheim. For map, *see* Germany.

AIGLE — (Aygl) — Swiss white wine of superior quality produced from the Fendant (Chasselas) grape in the Canton of Vaud east of Lake Geneva.

AISNE — (Ayne) — French *département* north and east of the Marne, a portion of which is legally part of the Champagne Country and produces some wine used in the making of Champagne (roughly 660,000 gallons a year), most of it of second-rate quality.

AIX — (Eks) — *See* Coteaux d'Aix.

ALAMBRADO — (Ahl-ahm-*bra*-doe) — Spanish term meaning a bottle enclosed in open wire netting (*alambre*); a form of packaging often used in Spain for wines of better than ordinary quality.

ALAMEDA — (Al-ah-*me*-da) — County in northern California, on the east side of San Francisco Bay. One of the North Coast Counties (*see*), its principal vineyards are in the Livermore Valley, southeast of Oakland. These are planted with Sauvignon Blanc, Semillon, Pinot Blanc, Chardonnay and other

4

superior varieties, almost all white; their white wines are among the most appreciated and best of California.

For Map, *see* CALIFORNIA.

ALBA — (*Ahl*-bah) — Important town south of Turin in the Italian region of Piedmont; famous for its white truffles; one of the principal centers of fine wine production in northern Italy. Barbaresco (*see*) is some four miles to the east, Barolo (*see*) about eight miles to the southwest.

ALBANA — (Ahl-*bahn*-ah) — Dry or semi-sweet white wine, rather high in alcohol, made from the grape of this name in the region of Emilia, Italy. The best of it comes from the village of Bertinoro, near Forli.

ALBANELLO — (Ahl-bahn-*nel*-lo) — White Sicilian wine made from the grape of this name in the province of Syracuse. High in alcohol, somewhat reminiscent of Marsala, it can be either dry or quite sweet.

ALBANO — (Ahl-*bahn*-no) — Dry, pleasant, inexpensive white wine from the Alban Hills, southeast of Rome. *See* Castelli Romani.

ALBARIZA — (Al-bar-*reath*-ah) — The extraordinary and typical white chalky soil in the vineyards round Jerez in the Sherry Country of Spain, producing the highest grade Fino Sherries and Manzanillas. There is some similar soil in the Montilla district (*see*).

ALCOHOL — The colorless, volatile spirit, ethyl alcohol, C_2H_6O, is formed by the activity of enzymes secreted by living microorganisms known as yeast cells. These convert the sugar in grape juice into approximately equal parts of alcohol and carbon dioxide gas. This process is fermentation (*see*). Table wines contain from about 8 to 16 percent of alcohol by volume, although the legal minimum is fixed at 10 per cent in California, and the legal maximum at 14 per cent by U.S. Federal regulations; fortified wines, i.e., wines to which more alcohol (in the form of brandy or high-proof neutral spirits) has been added, generally contain from 17 to 22 per cent.

ALEATICO — (Ahl-leh-*aht*-tee-co) — Italian grape and the wine, almost always red and generally sweet, made from it. The grape is of the Muscat family and the wine has an unmistakable and often pronounced Muscat flavor. The best of it comes from the island of Elba, and sometimes carries the name of Portoferraio, Elba's principal town.

ALELLA — (Ah-*lel*-ya) — An agreeable white wine from the village of Alella, just north of Barcelona in Spain. One of the most popular table wines of Catalonia, it is generally shipped in tall, slender brown bottles, like those in which Rhine wines go to market; is usually semi-sweet and rather heavily sulphured.

ALGERIA — (French, *Algérie*) — Former French colony, now an independent country on the Mediterranean coast of North Africa, bounded on the east by Tunisia and on the west by Morocco. Beginning about a hundred years ago, vast areas were planted in vineyard by French settlers, over 800,000 acres in

5

all, and by 1959 the annual production was nearly three times that of the United States, roughly 400 million gallons a year. About two-thirds of this huge output was regularly shipped to France — some six times the total gallonage of all French wine exports put together — and nearly a third of the entire Algerian labor force (of course largely Mohammedan and therefore not wine-drinking) was engaged in grape-growing and wine-making. Most of the production was rather common red table wine of 11-14% alcohol; blended with the wines of the Midi (*see*), it formed the base of France's *vin ordinaire*. Leading grape varieties are the Cinsault, Carignan and Alicante Bouschet (*see*). In addition enormous quantities of *mistelle* (*see*) were produced and shipped to France as a base for vermouth and apéritif wines.

The superior wines of Algeria were quite another matter, and some of them of surprising quality, particularly the reds and a few *rosés* from what the French called "delimited zones of superior quality" (*see* V.D.Q.S.) in the former *départements* of Oran, Alger, Mostaganem and Tlemcen. There were about a dozen such zones, with a total of some 65,000 acres under vineyard and an annual production of about 12 million gallons. The best vineyards are planted in mountainous country, generally from 30 to 50 miles back from the coast, at altitudes ranging from 1,500 to 2,500 feet. From east to west, the leading quality areas are as follows: Aïn-Bessem Bouira (s.e. of the city of Algiers); Medea and Côtes du Zaccar (s. and s.w. of Algiers); Haut-Dahra (near the coast, some hundred miles to the west); Mostaganem and Mostaganem-Kenenda (near the coast, e. of Oran); Aïn-el-Hadjar, Mascara and Coteaux de Mascara (s.e. of Oran); Monts du Tessalah, including Oued-Imbert, M'Silah, Crêtes des Berkèches, Parmentier (s. of Oran) and the Coteaux de Tlemcen (s.w. of Oran, not far from the Moroccan border). The red wine varieties most widely planted include the Carignan, Cinsault, Grenache, Cabernet, Morastel, Mourvèdre, Pinot, etc., with the Faranah, Clairette, Ugni Blanc and Aligoté dominating among the whites.

It is difficult to predict with any degree of confidence, let alone assurance, what will be the future of all this, for years so essential a part of Algeria's economy. A considerable proportion of French *colons* — land owners and technicians — have left the country; many large estates have been taken over and divided, and it is at least somewhat doubtful whether the new owners have the knowledge, organization and technical skills necessary for so major an enterprise. It is an unprecedented problem, to say the least, and, if the Algerians succeed, it will surely be one of the few times in human history that a people manages to produce, in world competition and on an enormous scale, something that they are unwilling, on account of religious scruples, to consume. Some of the vineyards have already been replanted in table grapes and other agricultural products.

ALICANTE — (Ah-lee-kahn-tay) — Wines from the province of this name, south of Valencia, on the Mediterranean coast of Spain. Most of these are sweet red wines, but there is a good deal of sound red Alicante produced which is passable, inexpensive table wine, bland, rather low in acid, made principally from the Grenache grape, (itself often called the Alicante in southern France).

ALICANTE-BOUSCHET — (Ah-lee-kahn-tay Boo-shay) — One of a number of heavy-bearing, rather common red-wine grapes developed in the 19th century by L. & H. Bouschet, who were seeking a hybrid with deep color and high sugar content for the production of cheap bulk wine in the Midi district of southern France, and in Algeria. Unlike almost all other red wine varieties, it has red juice, being a cross of Teinturier du Cher x Aramon x Grenache. Widely planted in California during the Prohibition years as a "juice grape" for home wine-makers, it ranks fifteenth in acreage among California wine grapes; it definitely has no place in any fine wine vineyard.

This variety should by no means be confused with what is called the Petit Bouchet in the Bordeaux country, a familiar local name for the Cabernet Sauvignon, nor with the Gros Bouchet, a similar local name for the Cabernet Franc.

ALIGOTÉ — (Ah-lee-go-tay) — Productive white wine grape of secondary quality, widely grown in Burgundy, where it yields an undistinguished, very agreeable, short-lived white wine — an excellent *vin de carafe* if drunk when young. White Burgundies made from the Aligoté grape must be so labeled, as "Bourgogne-Aligoté"; they are rarely exported, but nearly a million gallons are produced in an average year.

ALMADÉN — (Al-ma-*den*) — The original or "home" vineyard is on the western rim of the Santa Clara Valley, some sixty miles south of San Francisco; first planted in 1852 by two Frenchmen, Etienne Thée and his son-in-law, Charles Lefranc, it is the oldest producing vineyard in California, and takes its name from the famous quicksilver mine in the Santa Cruz Mountains nearby; this in turn was so called by early Spanish explorers after the greatest quicksilver mine in the world, at Almadén, southwest of Madrid, in Spain: the word is Moorish, and *al madén* means "the mine."

The Almadén vineyards (for what is left of the original plot is now hemmed in by housing developments and subdivisions) today include wide holdings in good districts less harassed by progress: over 7,000 cool upland acres at Paicines and La Cienega, in the Gavilán Mountains in San Benito County, directly south, major plantings in the Livermore Valley and especially in Monterey County (*see*).

ALOXE-CORTON — (Ahl-ohss Cor-taw) — Famous wine-producing *commune* of the Côte d'Or, Burgundy, and the northernmost important village of the Côte de Beaune. Unique in the fact that its red wines and white are almost equally celebrated, although the best of these do not carry the name Aloxe at all, and are sold as Corton (*see*), Corton-Charlemagne, Corton Clos du Roi,

ALOXE-CORTON

APPELLATION ALOXE-CORTON CONTROLÉE

TOLLOT-BEAUT & FILS

PROPRIÉTAIRES-RÉCOLTANTS A CHOREY-LES-BEAUNE (COTE D'OR)

MISE EN BOUTEILLES AU DOMAINE

Corton Bressandes, etc. Certain wines from two nearby villages, Ladoix-Serrigny and Pernand-Vergelesses, are also legally entitled to these names, and are produced on adjacent portions of the same impressive, steep, vineyard-covered hill. All of the above must come exclusively from the Pinot Noir or the Chardonnay grape. The red Cortons of great years are probably the best, certainly the longest-lived wines of the Côte de Beaune, magnificent Burgundies of wonderful breed and texture: silky, well-balanced and fine. The white Cortons and Corton-Charlemagne are fully the equals of the best Meursaults, and in the opinion of many experts are even better. Wines marketed as Aloxe-Corton (with or without the name of a specific vineyard) are of a substantially lower class, lighter in body and alcohol, delicate and attractive but maturing early and comparatively short-lived.

ALSACE — (Al-zass) — Ancient French province (although most Alsatians speak a dialect of German among themselves) bordering the Rhine north of Switzerland, and comprising the modern *départements* of Haut-Rhin and Bas-Rhin. The vineyards, which cover the lower slopes of the Vosges Mountains from near Mulhouse on the south to near Strasbourg on the north, are among the most beautiful in the world, and the small vineyard towns are exceedingly picturesque. White wines are produced almost exclusively (some 23 million gallons, in 1976, from 33,000 acres of vineyard), but there is a small amount of *vin rosé* and *vin gris,* the best of it made from the Pinot Noir grape plus, quite often, some Pinot Meunier, and sold as Pinot Rosé. The predominant white grape varieties, more or less in order of quality, are Riesling, Gewürztraminer — or Traminer (*see*), Pinot Gris (Tokay d'Alsace), Pinot Blanc (Klevner), Muscat Ottonel, Sylvaner, Knipperlé, Chasselas.

The following, from north to south, are the more important vineyard towns, which have given their names to their surrounding districts: Marlenheim (largely *vin rosé*), Molsheim, Obernai, Goxwiller, Barr, Mittelbergheim,

9

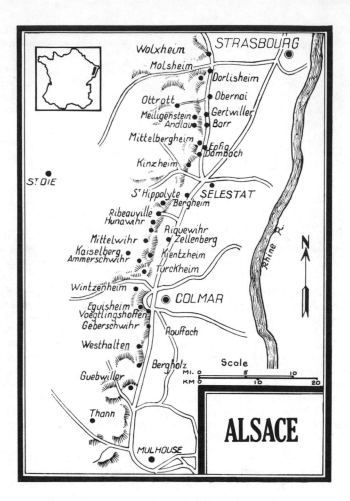

Dambach, Bergheim, Ribeauvillé, Hunawihr, Riquewihr, Beblenheim, Mittelwihr, Sigolsheim, Ammerschwihr, Kientzheim, Kaysersberg, Turckheim, Eguisheim, Husseren-les-Châteaux, Voegtlinshoffen, Pfaffenheim, Guebwiller. However, there are many others, 92 in all, entitled to the name "Alsace" or "Vin d'Alsace," according to the new *Appellation Contrôlée* regulations, recently published. Specific vineyard names (as Kaeferkopf, Kanzlerberg, etc.) are sometimes, though on the whole rarely, used; these should not be confused with brand names which are much more common.

Alsatian wines are generally named after the grape or grapes from which they are made, principally those listed above, but often carry their village name as well; the word Zwicker means a blend (usually one with a Chasselas base), and Edelzwicker, a blend of superior, or "noble" varieties. The words

10

"Grand Vin," "Grand Cru" and *"Grande Réserve"* may only be used on wines of superior varieties containing no less than 11% of natural alcohol by volume.

Shipped in slender *flutes* — tall, green bottles like those used in the German Moselle Valley nearby — not too high in alcohol (10-13%), exceedingly fragrant and on the average quite dry, Alsatian wines have achieved a great and merited popularity since World War I, not only throughout France, but in Great Britain and America.

ALSHEIM — (Ahls-heim) — German vineyard town between Oppenheim and Worms in Rheinhessen; some 600 acres of vineyard, largely planted to Sylvaner.

ALTAR WINES — Wines of whatever origin or type made to be used in the ceremony of the mass, and produced in accordance with the strict church regulations governing purity, naturalness and alcoholic content.

ALTO ADIGE — (*Ahl*-toe *Ah*-dee-jay) — The northern or upper portion of the Adige basin, in Italy, forming the modern province of Bolzano (*see*) and extending to the present Austrian frontier. The fertile valleys and hillsides of this mountainous Tyrol country have been famous for their wines since the days of Rome, and they produce today some 14 million gallons a year of light, fragrant, eminently agreeable, often excellent table wine, more than half of which is exported, in bulk, to Switzerland, Austria and Germany. The finer grades rank among Italy's best wines, and each of these will be found, with additional information concerning it, in its proper alphabetical place in this volume. *See,* therefore, Caldaro, Kuechelberger, Lagrein Rosato, Lago di Caldaro, Santa Giustina, Santa Maddalena, Terlano, etc. There are over 15,000 acres of vineyard in the province, the vines for the most part trained on superb, high "pergolas," which are a unique and charming feature of the lovely Tyrolean countryside. Grape varieties include such regional specialties as the Schiava, Lagrein and Blatterle, but there are plantings, as well, of Gewürztraminer, Sylvaner, Riesling, Pinot Blanc, Pinot Noir, Cabernet, Merlot, etc. Wines from these latter are usually marketed under their varietal name. Most of the Alto Adige wines mature early, and few improve greatly with age: the vines are cultivated and trained, and the wines are made with precisely this end in view; in the freshness of their youth they are among the most delightful table wines in the world.

ALTO DOURO — (*Ahl*-toe - *Du*-roe) — The classic zone of fine Port wine production. The mountainous area north and south of the Douro River upstream and east of Oporto, in Portugal.

AMABILE — (Ah-*ma*-beel-ay; Italian, "sweet or pleasing") — Used to describe a wine which, while sometimes or even usually dry, is in this special instance quite sweet.

AMARONE — (Ah-ma-*roe*-nay) — Long lived type of Italian red wine from Piedmont and Veneto. Made from late picked grapes often stored indoors on racks after the harvest to become almost like raisins with little water content and much sugar. The wine is not made until December or even later.

AMBOISE — (Ahm-bwaz) — Picturesque little town and celebrated Renaissance château on the Loire River near Tours: also a number of fresh, fruity and engaging lesser wines produced nearby and entitled to the appellation "Touraine-Amboise." The whites, which resemble Vouvray, are made from the Chenin Blanc grape; the reds and *rosés* come from the Malbec, or Cot, the Gamay and occasionally the Cabernet Franc. Most of them are consumed locally, but there are some 250,000 gallons a year.

AMBONNAY — (Ahm-bo-nay) — One of the best wine-producing villages of the Montagne de Reims in the French Champagne Country. Its vineyards are planted to the Pinot Noir.

AMELIORATION — Wine-maker's term, often too broadly used, to cover cellar practices some of which are entirely necessary and some of which are illegal; these include the adding of sugar to the juice or must before fermentation, the "correcting" of its acidity, the addition of water to reduce acidity or to compensate for overripe grapes etc., etc. Strict laws cover such matters in most wine-producing lands. *See* — Chaptalization, Gallisation, Water.

AMERICANO — (Ah-mehr-ee-*kah*-no) — Name given by the peasant wine-producers of Italian Switzerland (round Locarno and Lugano in the Ticino, or Canton of Tessin) to the American vines which many of them planted when their original vineyards were destroyed by mildew and by the phylloxera (*see*). Unfortunately, most of these vines are of the variety called Isabella, an inferior, heavy-flavored cousin to the Concord, quite incapable of yielding good wine under any conditions. The other local wine, called Nostrano (literally, "ours"), comes from European vinifera vines and, while rarely distinguished, is a great deal better.

ALSO, a refreshing drink made of sweet Italian vermouth, Campari bitters, plus, usually, a dash of soda.

AMERICAN WINES — According to U.S. law and regulations, any and all wines produced in the United States. Prevailing trade usage is somewhat different; California wines may be called American but are rarely so labeled, nor are the unblended wines of New York or Ohio. The term is commonly employed only on blends of California and Eastern, as "American Sherry." In another and narrower sense, American Wines are those made entirely from native American grapes, such as Concord, Delaware, Catawba, Elvira and others, whether grown on the West Coast or in the East. *See* Grape, New York.

AMMERSCHWIHR — (Ah-mair-schveer) — Important wine-producing village in Alsace, almost totally destroyed in the last war, now largely rebuilt; its best vineyard, known for Rieslings and Gewürztraminers of top quality, is the Kaeferkopf.

AMONTILLADO — (Ah-mone-tee-*yah*-doe) — A superior type of Spanish Sherry, generally fairly dry and paler than the average, although not as pale and light nor generally as dry as a Fino or Manzanilla. Its name comes originally from the place-name Montilla, a village and district south of Cordoba, this type of Sherry supposedly similar to Montilla wine. Literally it means a Sherry of the Montilla type, a "Montilla-fied" wine; by usage a wine of finesse, breed and superior origin, that has acquired some color and increased body through age.

AMOROSO — (Ahm-o-*ro*-so) — A name seldom used anymore for a sweetish, velvety Oloroso Sherry (*see*).

AMPELOGRAPHY — Study of vines and grapes, publication and classification of such by text and illustrations.

AMPHORA — Ancient earthenware container for wine or oil, usually with two handles and pointed end.

AMPUIS — (Ahm-pwee) — Small village on the right bank of the Rhône River, south of Lyon. Its vineyards, dating from Roman times, produce the celebrated red Côte Rôtie (*see*).

AMTLICHE   PRÜFNUMMER — (Am-tlish-e   Prewf-noomer) Qualification number which appears on German Qualitätswein labels. Its ten digits show the following:
        1st — Examination Board
        2nd-4th — Location of Vineyard
        5th-8th — Bottler's Identification
        9th-10th — Year of Tasting (not vintage year)

AÑADA — (Ahn-ya-da) — Used in Spain of wines that are of one specific vintage and at least a year old, as *vino de añada*.

ANBAUGEBIET — (Ahn-bow-ge-beet) — The term for a specified wine growing region for quality wines under the 1971 German Wine Law, same as Gebiet — a short form of the word. There are eleven regions: Ahr, Mosel-Saar-Ruwer, Mittelrhein, Rheingau, Nahe, Rheinhessen, Rheinpfalz, Hessiche Bergstrasse, Franken, Württemberg, and Baden. All the Anbaugebiete have subdivisions: Bereiche (district), Grosslage (general site), and Einzellage (individual site — i.e. specific vineyard). All of these names and terms are separately listed and explained.

ANDALUSIA — Famous, fertile and beautiful region, comprising most of the southernmost fourth of Spain; its best known wines are Sherry, Málaga, Montilla (*see*).

AÑEJO — (Ahn-*yea*-ho; Spanish, "aged") — Largely meaningless term except in its proper and original sense, which is, roughly, "at least a year older than the youngest wine in the cellar."

ANGELICA — One of the poorest and cheapest of American fortified wines, often little more than a blend of sweet, white grape juice and high-proof brandy. It is said to take its name from the city of Los Angeles; if so, it is something of which Angelinos have no reason to feel proud.

ANGÉLUS — (Awn-shay-luhs) — One of the sixty-three vineyards in the St. Emilion district now legally entitled to the rank of Grand Cru Classé. Sometimes listed simply as L'Angélus, but more often as Château L'Angélus, it produces some 13,000 cases a year of soft, pleasant, rather early-maturing, very popular red wine.

ANGLUDET, Château — (Awn-glu-day) — Important and good vineyard of Cantenac-Margaux in the Haut-Médoc, ranked as a *Cru Bourgeois Exceptionnel*. About 6,000 cases a year.

ANJOU — (Awn-shoe) — Historically, a province in west-central France. As far as wines are concerned, principally the *département* of Maine-et-Loire, on both sides of the Loire River, west and downstream from Touraine; the numerous and extremely diverse wines which this province produces. These include some of the best sweet white table wines of France, made from the Chenin Blanc grape (also called the Pineau de la Loire, although it is not a Pinot); dryer white wines that are fruity and good, though less distinguished, some from the Chenin and some from the Melon grape; a few excellent light reds from the Cabernet Franc, and some less good from the Cot, Grolleau, or Groslot, etc.; a vast amount of *rosé*, generally not absolutely dry and ranging all the way from fine to poor in quality. A great deal of sparkling wine is also produced, most of it by the Champagne process, in and around Saumur.

The more important districts that produce, from late-picked grapes in good vintage years, the extremely fruity, rich, delicate dessert wines for which Anjou is above all famous, are the Coteaux du Layon (*see*), the Coteaux de la Loire (*see*), and the Coteaux de Saumur. These, like some of the lesser areas (the Coteaux du Loir, the Coteaux de l'Aubance, etc.), have their dry wines as well, and a little Muscadet is made along the western edge of Anjou.

By all odds the best red wines are those from around Saumur, Champigny (*see*) especially; and many of the finer *rosés,* also made from the Cabernet grape, are from this same area, although some from a little farther west, near Tigné and Brissac — they can be admirable. What is ordinarily shipped as "Anjou Rosé" is of a lesser class and made from the Grolleau or Groslot — really nothing more than a sound, inexpensive carafe wine, light, rather fruity, a bit on the sweet side.

For Map, *see* LOIRE.

APAGADO — (Ah-pa-*gah*-do) — Literally, in Spanish, *apagar* is to put out, or extinguish, a light, or fire. Applied to wine, or more properly to *mosto* (must) before fermentation, it means fresh grape juice to which some 16-18% of alcohol has been added, so that no fermentation can take place. The resulting, raw, alcoholic product is called *vin muté* or *mistelle* in French, and is used in Spain to sweeten the cheapest grades of Sherry; it is not far from what is sold as Angelica (*see*) in this country, but is hardly ever consumed unblended and at this stage of its development either in France or Spain.

APÉRITIF (French) — (Ah-pair-ee-teef) — A very broad term, meaning almost any drink taken before a meal as an "appetizer." A cocktail is an apéritif, so is Sherry, so is a glass of Champagne or white wine, if so consumed. The most popular apéritifs in France include Vermouth, both sweet and dry; Port; various fortified and flavored wines, prepared according to some special formula and often sold under proprietary names such as Byrrh, Dubonnet, St. Raphaël, Cap Corse; stronger drinks, usually taken with water or soda, as Pernod, Pastis, Suze, Clacquesin, Amer Picon, etc. Almost all of these are more or less sweet and few of them, to the American palate, seem truly appetizing.

In France they are drunk without food of any kind — food comes later. From the wine expert's perhaps biased point of view, the best apéritifs are Champagne, dry Sherry, and Sercial Madeira. According to U.S. Federal regulations, however, these three cannot be called apéritifs at all — the term being reserved for "flavored wines" (the French Academy, M.M. Larousse and Littré-Robert, please note).

A.P.No. — *see* Amtliche Prüfnummer

APPELLATION CONTRÔLÉE (French) — (Ah-pell-ah-see-awn Cawn-troll-ay) — Two words that now appear, often in small type, on the vast majority of French wine labels. They are the consumer's principal protection and his best friend, and of enormous value to all honest producers as well. All of the finer French wines except Champagne should carry this designation (*see*, however, V.D.Q.S.). Literally, it means that the name that the wine bears is one officially recognized and legally defined by governmental decree: the wine *must* come from the specific district, or township, or, in some instances, vineyard, from which it takes its name; from certain established varieties of grape and no others, and from grapes that have achieved a specified minimum of ripeness; it must have been made according to the traditional and proper usages of its district. It must, in other words, be genuine; this is not, of course, to say that it must be good. This admirable system of controls has largely been set up since 1935; standards have been established for over 200 different wines and the controls are rigidly enforced, violators being punished with extremely heavy fines, and in some instances, by imprisonment as well.

APPELLATION D'ORIGINE (French) — (Ah-pell-ah-see-awn Dor-re-gene) — A wine's name, in geographical terms — its place or origin, whether a whole district, as Burgundy; an American county, as Napa; a river valley, as Mosel or Moselle; a township, as Vosne-Romanée; an estate, as Château d'Yquem; or a single small parcel of vines, as Richebourg. Such names have been given wines since Biblical and Greek and Roman days, and most modern laws concerning labeling are based on this immemorial practice. There have of course been many abuses and there still are, but regulations on the whole are far more strict than they were a hundred or fifty or even twenty years ago.

In France, *Appellations d'Origine* are considered to fall into three categories, regulated officially by an admirable organization called the *Institut National des Appellations d'Origine des Vins et Eaux-de-Vie* (I.N.A.O., for short). The highest rank is the *Appellation Contrôlée* (*see*), often abbreviated to "A.O.C."; in this class are practically all of the famous wines of France.

In a highly honorable second category are what are known as the *Vins Délimités de Qualité Supérieure* (V.D.Q.S. — *see*), the Delimited Wines of Superior Quality. These, no less strictly regulated, make up what has been called a sort of "second team" of French wines; they carry a government seal on the label, and their number includes a good many dozens of excellent if less famous and less expensive local wines, produced throughout France.

In 1973 the third category *Appellation d'Origine Simple* was discontinued to bring French law into line with the regulations of the European Common Market. The replacement category is *Vin de Pays*. The wines must come from

15

specific areas, may not be blended with wines from elsewhere and must meet grape variety and other technical criteria under the general *Appellation Controlée*.

Lastly, at the bottom of the ladder, are wines with no geographical appellation at all, sold simply, for example as *Vin Rouge 12°* or *12%*, or under a trade name, or brand. These of course may be blends of anything not found objectionable under the French pure food laws, and they need not be French wines at all unless they bear the words "Product of France" or the equivalent. There is nothing inherently objectionable about them (they are all cheap and some quite passable) providing the consumer knows exactly what he is getting. The address of the shipper on such wines has nothing whatsoever to do with the wine's origin: a bottle labeled "Vin Rosé, Durand-Dupont et Cie., Bordeaux, France," need not contain a single drop of Bordeaux wine.

APPETIZER — Anything taken in the way of food or drink to sharpen or whet the appetite; by contrast, the more exact French term, *apéritif* (*see*) means a pre-prandial drink, exclusively. It is common American usage to describe as "appetizer wines" the dryer fortified wines generally taken before a meal (most Sherry and Madeira, for example) and as "dessert wines" (*see*) the sweeter, fortified wines (Port, Muscatel, etc.) generally consumed afterwards.

APRE — (Ah-pr') — Harsh. French wine taster's term, most often used to describe rough young red wines of high tannin content.

APULIA — (Ap-*poo*-lee-ah) — Region in southeast Italy (Puglia), the "heel" of the Italian "boot." Generally first in total wine production among Italian "regions," with an average of some 275 million gallons a year. Most of this is very common *vino di taglio* (blending wine), with deep color, high alcohol and low acid. There are a few dessert wines of better than average quality and in recent years the table wines have improved.

ARAMON — (Are-ah-mawn) — A common and immensely productive grape, widely planted in the French Midi. The red wine it yields is deficient in color and generally of poor quality.

ARBOIS — (Are-bwah) — Village and wine district in eastern France, near the Swiss border, forming part of the Côtes-du-Jura, in the ancient province of Franche-Comté. Red and *rosé* wines of superior quality are produced from the Poulsard, Trousseau and Pinot Noir; dry white wines from the Savagnin (Traminer) and Chardonnay (some of them made sparkling by the Champagne process) and two unusual and special wines, Vin Jaune and Vin de Paille (*see*) by special methods. Some *rosé* is exported.

ARCHE, Château d' — (Shot-toe Darsh) — 2nd Classed Growth of Sauternes, now divided into two separate small properties, both entitled to the name. The best is château-bottled, and is an excellent sweet Sauternes.

ARCINS — (Ar-san) — Tiny wine-producing village in the Haut-Médoc, north of Margaux. Wines of secondary quality.

ARENA — (Ah-ray-nah) — sandy soil constituting about 17% of the vineyards in the Sherry Country. Easily tillable and produces coarser wines than Albariza and Barro.

ARGENTINA — By a wide margin, the largest wine-producing and wine-consuming country of the Western Hemisphere. Exporting very little and importing even less, Argentina drinks her own wines, almost entirely table wines, at the rather astonishing rate of 600 million gallons a year, some 120 bottles per capita. Most of this is sound, inexpensive, quite ordinary, the red better than the *rosé* or white; it comes from the states of Mendoza and San Juan, and the vineyards are planted along the foothills of the Andes, not far from the Chilean border. There are some 850,000 acres under vines.

ARGOL — The crude tartar (*see*), or potassium bitartrate — cream of tartar being its refined form — which forms as a crystalline deposit in wine vats, during and after fermentation, and even sometimes, as a sediment, in bottled wine. In large wineries it is an important by-product, and is sold mostly to manufacturers of baking-powder. Also known as wine stone (German, *Weinstein*).

AROMA — Very different from bouquet (*see*), the aroma of a wine is more pronounced and more distinctive when the wine is young, being directly related to the odor of fresh fruit. Certain varieties of grape (the Gewürztraminer, the Malvasia, the Muscat and the Concord, to cite a few extreme examples) can be identified, blindfolded, by their scent alone. Much of this aroma disappears during fermentation, and bone-dry wines rarely have as much aroma as those that have retained a certain amount of their natural grape sugar; aroma tends to diminish further as a wine is aged, and bouquet takes its place. The word is also used with a modifying adjective to describe a special, characteristic, fruity odor which certain wines possess, as "aroma of quince," or "apple," or "raspberries," or "blackberries."

AROMATIC — Character of wine related to certain grapes with high aroma such as Muscat (*see* Aroma).

AROMATIZED — Flavored wines such as vermouth, apéritifs and May wine are aromatized wines.

ARRIÈRE-CÔTES — (Arry-air Coat) — Name given to a series of slopes in Burgundy, west of and roughly parallel to the Côte d'Or proper, producing wines, both red and white, of second quality, usually marketed as Bourgogne Rouge, Bourgogne Blanc, Passe-Tout-Grains, Aligoté, etc., but more often as Hautes-Côtes de Nuits and Hautes-Côtes de Beaune, (*see*).

ARRIÈRE-GOUT — (Arry-air Goo) French for After Taste (*see*).

ARROBA — (Ah-*ro*-ba) — Spanish measure, approximately 16 liters, or just over four U.S. gallons and equivalent to 25 pounds of grapes.

ARROPE — (Ah-*ro*-pay) — Grape concentrate, used as a sweetening and coloring agent in Sherries. It is produced by boiling down unfermented grape juice to its "quintessence," or one-fifth of its volume, whereby it acquires a deep brown color and a burnt-sugar, or caramel, flavor. *See* Sherry.

ARSAC — (Ar-sack) — Wine-producing *commune* of the Haut-Médoc now entitled to the appellation Margaux: one 5th Growth vineyard, which produces some 10,000 cases a year, Château du Tertre (*see*) plus several *crus bourgeois*.

ARTISAN — (Ar-teas-zah) — One of the minor classifications into which Bordeaux wines are traditionally divided. A *Cru Artisan* is a less good vineyard than a *Cru Bourgeois* (*see*), barely above a *Cru Paysan* in rank; such wines are the *ordinaires* of Bordeaux, almost always blended, rarely carrying a vineyard name, hardly ever château-bottled.

ASCIUTTO — (Ah-shoot-toe) — Italian word which, when applied to wine, means dry, the opposite of sweet.

ASPRINIO — (Ahs-sprin-nee-o) — Dry, pale, rather agreeable, light white wine, produced just north of Naples, in Italy.

ASSEMBLAGE — (Ah-some-blahge) — act of making a cuvée (*see*).

ASSMANNSHAUSEN — (Ahs-mans-how-zen) — Village on the Rhine immediately north of Rüdesheim, producing what is probably the best and certainly the most famous red wine of Germany. Made from the Pinot Noir grape (known in Germany as the Spätburgunder) this is, at its best, comparable to a light, mediocre Burgundy, often somewhat sweet.

ASTI — (Ahs-tea) — Important wine-producing town south of Turin, in the Piedmont region of Italy; famous particularly for its rather sweet sparkling wine, Asti Spumante, Italy's best known and most popular. It is also a major center of the Vermouth trade, and the hilly surrounding country produces a great deal of light white Muscat wine, largely from the Moscato di Canelli grape, and much red of good quality from the Barbera, Freisa, Grignolino and Nebbiolo.

ALSO a town in the northern part of Sonoma County, California, home of the Italian-Swiss Colony, and also famous for its red table wines.

ASTRINGENT — Wine tasters' term, applied to wines that make the mouth pucker, generally because of an excess of tannin. Many excellent red wines are astringent when young; providing they are not bitter, this is not a serious flaw, for they will soften and mellow with age. In a young red wine, astringency is often, but not invariably, an indication that the wine will be long-lived.

ASZU — (Ahs-zoo) — A special, superior quality of sweet Tokay (*see*).

AUBANCE — (Oh-bawnss) — Small river, tributary of the Loire, in the old French province of Anjou. The adjoining hillsides, "Les Coteaux de l'Aubance," produce good quality, semi-dry white wines from the Chenin Blanc grape, and very creditable *vins rosés,* the best of these made from the Cabernet Franc, around Brissac. The overall production of the delimited area is in the neighborhood of a half million gallons a year.

AUBE — (Ohb) — French *département,* e. of Paris, forming the southern and secondary part of the Champagne Country, with some 9,000 acres of vineyard.

AUDE — (Ode) — French *département,* second only to the Hérault (*see*) in total wine production, with some 300,000 acres of vineyard. Part of what is known as the Midi, its most important towns are Carcassonne and Narbonne; most of

18

what it produces is simply *vin ordinaire* but two districts, Corbières (*see*) and the Minervois (partly in the Hérault) yield what are perhaps the best of the common table wines of France.

AURORE — (Aw-roar) — French hybrid, early standard in Finger Lakes and Chatauqua vineyards; makes good quality white table and sparkling wines.

AUS EIGENEM LESEGUT — (Ouse I-gennem Lay-zeh-goot) — German for Grower's Own Harvest, equivalent to Estate Bottling.

AUSLESE — (Ouse-lay-zeh) — German, "Selection." A German wine, whether from the Moselle, the Rhine, Franconia or elsewhere, of a very special and superior sort, considerably sweeter and a great deal more expensive than others made by the same producer in the same year. At the time of the *Lese,* or grape harvest, the especially ripe and perfect bunches, and those most affected by the Noble Mold, Botrytis (*see*), are put aside and pressed separately; the resulting wine is Auslese, and it rarely amounts to over 10-15% of a vineyard's production, even in favorable years. Auslese wines, until the new German wine laws became effective, in 1971, were often further graded, especially on the Moselle, and given such ratings as *feine* Auslese, *hochfeine* Auslese, and *feinste* Auslese; all wines labeled Auslese should properly be sweeter and more expensive than the Spätlese (*see*) from the same cellar in the same vintage; an Auslese of a great year, especially from the Palatinate or Rhine, should properly be classified as a desert wine. *See* also Beerenauslese, Porriture Noble, Trockenbeerenauslese.

AUSONE, Château — (Oh-zone) — Famous Great 1st Growth vineyard of St. Émilion, in the Bordeaux Country; with Château Cheval Blanc (*see*), it ranks

19

officially as the best of the St. Émilions, and its wines bring as high prices as the most celebrated Médocs — Lafite, Latour, Margaux, etc.; many of them, especially prior to World War II, were of truly astonishing quality. The average production is some 2,500 cases a year. Ausone takes its name from the Latin poet and wine-lover, Ausonius, who had an estate and vineyard somewhere in the neighborhood, though almost certainly not on the actual site of Château Ausone.

AUSONIUS — Roman man of letters, born in Bordeaux *circa* 310 A.D., eventually made consul by the Emperor Gratian, whose tutor he had been. He had a well-loved vineyard near what is now St. Émilion, though probably not on the site of Château Ausone which is nevertheless named after him; he also wrote a celebrated poem in praise of the Moselle River, its landscapes and its wines.

AUSTRALIA — Although there are no indigenous native vines in Australia, the history of viticulture and wine-making there rather closely parallels that of the United States, especially of California. The first grapes were planted near Sydney in 1788, and in 1830 a Mr. James Busby (the Australian prototype of California's Colonel Haraszthy) was sent to Europe to select and bring back superior grape varieties; he returned with 20,000 cuttings of over 600 sorts. As in California, the wines were given what the producers felt to be their appropriate European appellations — Sherry, Burgundy, Claret, Sauternes, etc. (although, on account of a British-Portuguese treaty, the Australian "Port" was called "Port type"); many of the early vineyards were devastated by the phylloxera, then replanted on American roots; again, as in California, great progress has been made in the way of quality and improved wine-making technique in the past two decades. Many Australian wines are surprisingly good today, the *flor* Sherries especially, and varietal table wines made from the "Rhine Riesling," the Cabernet and the "Shiraz" or Syrah. Their increasing popularity in England and in Canada is fully justified.

The vine was first introduced in New South Wales, but this state has long since been surpassed in viticultural importance by its neighbors, Victoria and especially South Australia. There are over 175,000 acres of vineyard, and it is interesting to note that the best of these are about as far from the equator as San Francisco, between 34° and 38° south latitude.

AUSTRIA — To a far greater extent than Germany, Austria is by tradition a wine-drinking country; it was of course even more so in the high old days of the Austro-Hungarian Empire, when the best vintages of what is now the Italian Tyrol, of Hungary, Czechoslovakia and Yugoslavia all found their way to Vienna. But even today the annual consumption is over 9½ gallons per capita, and far more wine is imported (largely from Italy) than exported.

Almost all of the better Austrian wines are white, and in character they tend to resemble those of the Italian Tyrol and of southern Germany, especially Baden (*see*); they are mostly shipped in tall, slender, green or brown bottles; many of them carry varietal grape names, as Riesling, Gewürztraminer, Sylvaner, Müller-Thurgau, plus such local favorites as Veltliner and Rotgipfler; some bear designations of superior quality, as *Spätlese* and *Auslese,* but are less sweet than their German counterparts. As a whole, they can be described

20

as rather low in alcohol, fruity, refreshing, fairly dry, with good bouquet, and soon ready to drink.

Many of the most agreeable of all are produced practically in Vienna itself, and sold (as "open" wine, in the outdoor cafés of Grinzing and the Vienna suburbs) as Wiener, Nussberger, or Grinzinger, sometimes plus a vineyard name. Gumpoldskirchener (*see*), from vineyards some fifteen miles south of Vienna, enjoys an even higher rating and is perhaps the best known Austrian wine today. A third district, also excellent, forty miles west of Vienna on the steep Danube hillsides, yields Loibner, Kremser and Dürnsteiner.

The red wines, of little consequence and rarely seen outside Austria, are mostly made from the Pinot Noir, or Spätburgunder grape.

AUVERGNE — (Oh-vairn) — Famous old province in central France, near the headwaters of the Loire. Although of ancient reputation, its vineyards are of little consequence today, and names such as Chanturgues, Châteaugay and Corent are now hardly wine-names, in the real sense of the word, at all. These wines were largely made from the Gamay, or in rare instances from the Pinot Noir or Chardonnay; certainly they were and are much less remarkable than Auvergnats all over the world have led us to believe. Nevertheless, wines bearing the following appellations are entitled to the V.D.Q.S. seal: Côtes d'Auvergne, Côtes du Forez, Côtes Roannaises, Saint-Pourçain-sur-Sioule.

AUXEY-DURESSES — (O-say Dew-ress) — One of the good secondary wine-producing villages of the Côte de Beaune, in Burgundy, set down in a little side-valley northwest of Meursault. Both white wines and red of good quality are produced, from the Chardonnay, Pinot Blanc and Pinot Noir, the former comparable to the lesser Meursaults, the latter not unlike Volnays, albeit without as much body and class. Being little known, they are often excellent values.

AVENSAN — (Ahv-on-sawn) — Wine-producing *commune,* just west of Margaux in the Haut-Médoc: one *cru exceptionnel,* Château Citran.

AVIGNON — (Ah-vee-nyaw) — Historic and interesting little city on the Rhône River, in southern France, seat of the Papacy from 1309 to 1377. An important center of the trade in the wines of the lower Rhône Valley — Châteauneuf-du-Pape, Tavel, Lirac, Gigondas, etc.

AVIZE — (Ah-veez) — Major wine-producing village in the Champagne Country of France, south of Épernay and the Marne; with Cramant, it is the most important *commune* of the Côte des Blancs, rated 100% in the official classification; its wines, produced entirely from the Chardonnay grape, have extraordinary finesse and class. *See* Champagne, Blanc de Blancs.

AY — (Eye) — Village in the Champagne Country, near Épernay, on the north or right bank of the Marne; its admirable hillside vineyards are planted almost entirely to Pinot Noir, and in the official rating, Ay is one of seven townships accorded the highest rating, 100%. *See* Champagne, Blanc de Noirs.

AYL — (I'll) — Important wine-producing village on the Saar, in Germany. Ayler Kupp and Herrenberg are the best vineyards.

AZAY-LE-RIDEAU — (Ah-zay-le-Ree-doe) — Charming little town and lovely little town and lovely Renaissance château west of Tours in the Château Country; also a pleasant, fruity white wine, somewhat like Vouvray, produced there from the Chenin Blanc grape, and legally entitled to the appellation ''Touraine Azay-le-Rideau.''

B

BACCHUS — Another name for Dionysus (*see*), the Greek and Roman god of wine.

BACHARACH — (*Bach*-ah-rach) — Small and picturesque town of the Mittel-Rhein (*see*), between Bingen and Coblenz. Once an important center of the German wine trade, still produces a certain number of Rhine wines of second quality, of which Bacharacher Posten and Bacharacher Wolfshöhle are perhaps the best known.

BACO — (Bah-co) — French hybridizer who has given his name plus a serial number to several of his successful hybrids (*see*). Baco No. 1 is a red wine grape now in production in several vineyards in the eastern United States, under the name Baco Noir. Baco No. 22A may now legally be used in the making of Armagnac, in France, though whether it is as good as the traditional Picpoul (*see*) certainly remains to be demonstrated.

BADACSONYI — (Bahd-ah-chon-y) — Celebrated Hungarian appellation of origin, used in conjunction with the name of a grape variety on a number of Hungary's finest table and dessert wines, as Badacsonyi Rizling (Riesling), B. Furmint (*see*), B. Muskotaly (Muscatel), etc.

BADEN — (Baad'n) — Large province in southwestern Germany, bounded on the south by Switzerland and on the west by Alsace. The Black Forest is its most important physical feature, and most of its extremely diverse and numerous vineyards are planted along the Black Forest foothills and overlook the Rhine Valley. The wines, mostly white, in general very agreeable and in a few rare cases of high quality, are almost all consumed locally and are not generally exported. Baden is one of the eleven Anbaugebiete or Specified Wine Regions of Germany yielding one-eighth of the total harvest. It comprises seven Districts (*see* Bereich) from north to south as follows: Badisches Frankenland, planted in Müller-Thurgau grapes and shipped in Bocksbeutel (*see*); Badische Bergstrasse/Kraichgau, which includes the ancient university town of Heidelberg; Ortenau, clothing the edge of the Black Forest directly across the Rhine from Strasbourg and producing occasionally distinguished white wines and the red Affenthaler (*see*); Breisgau; Kaiserstuhl-Tuniberg, odd sorts of "islands" of volcanic tufa producing good and interesting growths in the middle of the Rhine Valley west of Freiburg; Markgräflerland, principally planted in Gutedel (or Chasselas) grapes; and Bodensee (Lake Constance) noted for Seeweine and Weissherbst (*see*). In the seven Bereiche are 16 Grosslagen and over 300 Einzellagen. For Map, *see* GERMANY.

BAD DÜRKHEIM — (Baad Dirk-heim) — Small resort town in the German Palatinate or Pfalz, important for its vineyards, of which it has the largest acreage of any township in Germany, and for its wines, both red (fair) and white (very good). *See* Dürkheim.

BAD KREUZNACH — (Baad Kroytz-nahch) — *See* Kreuznach.

BAKING — Process to induce maderization (*see* Estufa, Maderise) on the island of Madeira and in America and other countries to approximate the taste of sherry.

BALANCE — Wine-taster's term, a little difficult to explain. Essentially, a well-balanced wine is one completely harmonious in its make-up, with nothing overly pronounced and no striking deficiency in its bouquet, flavor or aftertaste. If light, it will be delicate; if full-bodied, it will have a corresponding amount of flavor and character. A well-balanced wine may not be great; it is exactly what it should be in its type and class, and the term is high praise.

BALATON — The Plattensee, lake in Western Hungary the waters of which temper the climate of Badacsony, center of white wine production.

BALESTARD-LA-TONNELLE, Château — (Bahl-less-tar la Toe-nell) — One of the better Grands Crus Classés of St. Émilion, sturdy, but with considerable breed; there are some 6,000 cases a year. It is famous above all for a poem which François Villon wrote five hundred years ago in its praise, describing it as . . . *"ce divin nectar, Qui porte nom de Balestard."* The complete poem now appears on the label.

BALLING — Hydrometer and scale generally used in the U.S. for measuring the sugar content of unfermented grape juice, and therefore the probable alcoholic content of the finished wine. Balling readings are in terms of grams of sugar per 100 grams of juice and roughly the Balling reading multiplied by .55 will give the wine's future alcoholic content by volume, e.g. juice of 22° Balling should give a 12% wine.

BALTHAZAR — An oversize Champagne bottle, holding sixteen ordinary bottles. Son of the last King of Babylon, capital of Chaldea.

BANDOL — (Bahn-dawl) — Pleasant, lesser wines, white, red and above all *rosé*, produced on the Mediterranean Coast of France, round the twin resorts of Bandol and Sanary-sur-Mer, near Toulon. Although coming from the general region of the Côtes de Provence (*see*) these, like Cassis, but unlike most of the others, have been given an *appellation contrôlée* (*see*) although this is not by any means to say that they are better than Provence wines that carry instead the V.D.Q.S. seal (*see*). The reds and *rosés* are mostly from the Mourvèdre grape, plus Grenache and Cinsault; the whites from the Clairette and Ugni Blanc.

BANYULS — (Ban-yulz) — The most famous and perhaps the best of French dessert wines, somewhat comparable to a light Tawny Port; it is classified either as a *Vin Doux Naturel* (a sad misnomer since it is fortified) or, more correctly, as a *Vin de Liqueur*. By law, it must have at least 15% of alcohol by volume, but often runs much higher; it is russet-brown in color, quite sweet, and with age acquires a special bouquet and flavor known as *rancio* (*see*). Banyuls is made largely from the Grenache grape in a picturesque little district known as the *Côte Vermeille,* where the Pyrénées come down to the Mediterranean along the Spanish border. The tiny fishing port of Banyuls is the center of the trade, and the other villages of the zone, beloved of artists and summer tourists, are Collioure, Port-Vendres and Cerbère. The vineyards are terraced on steep, sun-drenched hillsides, and the grapes are picked late; even if unfortified, the wine would tend to be strong and sweet, but it receives the addition, before, during or after fermentation, of from 5% to 10% of high-proof brandy.

BARBACARLO — (Bar-ba-*car*-lo) — Italian red table wine of good quality, from southern Lombardy. Like two other oddly named wines, Buttafuoco and Sangue di Giuda (*see*), it is produced in the townships of Broni and Canneto Pavese, from various grape varieties including the Ughetto, Croatina, Moradella, etc.

BARBARESCO — (Bar-bar-*ess*-co) — Justly celebrated red wine of Piedmont, northwestern Italy, made from the Nebbiolo grape in two townships (Barbaresco itself, and Neive) within a few miles of the district which produces, from the same Nebbiolo grape, the very different and even more remarkable wine called Barolo. Lighter than Barolo, shorter lived, maturing more quickly and acquiring, after two or three years in bottle, the brownish, autumn-leaf color which the French call "pelure d'oignon" (*see*), it is a wine of true distinction and great class, certainly one of Italy's ten best. Became one of the first D.O.C.G. (*see*) in 1978.

BARBERA — (Bar-*bear*-ah) — A red wine grape grown principally in the region of Piedmont (northwestern Italy) and to a large extent in California; the wine made from this grape, deep-colored, full-bodied, full-flavored, somewhat lacking in distinction, very agreeable with Italian food and at its best when young.

BARBERONE — (Bar-bear-*own*-eh) — Literally, a "big Barbera" (*see*). Term rarely if ever used in Italy, sometimes applied to heavy red wines in California, usually without any justification or excuse, since few such wines are made, even in part, from the true Barbera grape.

25

BARDOLINO — (Bar-doe-*lean*-o) — Excellent light red wine produced round the village of the same name, on the eastern shore of Lake Garda, in northern Italy. Like Valpolicella, which is grown on a very different soil some ten miles further east, Bardolino is made mostly from Corvina, Negrara and Molinara grapes; hardly darker in color than a dark *rosé*, at its best when from one to three years old, rarely over 11% alcohol, fruity, charming, never great, it is one of the most delightful wines of the province of Verona, and a perennial favorite in Switzerland as well.

For Map, *see* ITALY.

BARET, Château — (Bah-ray) — Vineyard in the *commune* of Villenave-d'Ornon in the Graves District, near Bordeaux. Red and white wines of good quality, some 2,000 cases a year of each.

BAROLINO — (Bar-o-leen-o) — Wine name without any standing or legal meaning formerly applied to lesser wines made in the environs of Barolo (*see*).

BAROLO — (Bar-*oh*-lo) — Perhaps the best red wine of Italy, very full-bodied, slow-maturing, comparable to the great French wines of the Rhône Valley, such as Hermitage or Côte Rôtie. It is made from the Nebbiolo grape in Piedmont, south of Turin, in a small, strictly delimited, hilly district of which the village of Barolo is the center and which includes as well the townships of Serralunga, Castiglione, Grinzane, Monforte, La Morra, Sommariva Perno, Verduno. Generally kept at least three years in wood before bottling (in ''Burgundy'' bottles), it deserves and almost requires additional ageing in bottle before being drunk, although it often throws considerable sediment. Powerful, deep-colored, long-lived, it is definitely a great wine and, at it's best, a quite extraordinary one. Became one of the first D.O.C.G. (*see*) in 1978.

For Map, *see* ITALY.

BAROSSA — Valley in South Australia near Adelaide. Australia's largest wine district and possibly the best, producing white wines primarily.

BARR — (Bar) — Important wine-producing town in northern Alsace; its Rieslings and Gewürztraminers are among the best of the *département* of Bas-Rhin.

BARREL — As far as the wine trade is concerned, a wooden (preferably oak) container of any size in which wine is stored, aged and sometimes shipped. A barrel is readily movable; a cask, in many cases, is not.

BARRIQUE — (Bah-reek) — One of many French words meaning barrel, used particularly in the Bordeaux Country (*pièce* being the Burgundian equivalent) to designate the oak casks of 225 liters (roughly 60 U.S. gallons) in which Bordeaux wines are commonly stored and often shipped. A *barrique* is supposed to yield 24 cases of finished wine.

BARRO — (*Barr*-roe) — Spanish word meaning clay soil, used particularly in connection with the vineyards in the Sherry Country. The finest of these are planted on white, chalky soil, *albariza;* the less good (which give a heavier and coarser wine) on clay, *barro;* the poorest of all on sandy soil, *arena.*

BARSAC — (Bar-sack) — The northernmost and, after Sauternes itself, the most famous of the five townships of Sauternes. It is some twenty-five miles southeast of Bordeaux, and its vineyards are on low, rolling hills that overlook the Garonne River. All Barsacs, legally, are Sauternes, made by the same methods and from the same grape varieties. They are all rather sweet, though often somewhat less sweet than other Sauternes, and with a special delicacy and fruit. Château Climens and Château Coutet are the outstanding vineyards, but there are many smaller good ones; all the best of them château-bottle their production except in very poor vintage years.

For Map, *see* SAUTERNES.

BASILICATA — (Bah-zee-lee-*cah*-tah) — Region in the "arch" of the Italian "boot"; not very important viniculturally except for Aglianico del Vulture produced in the province of Potenza (*see* Aglianico).

BASKET — *see* CRADLE

BAS-MÉDOC — (Bah-May-dawk) — The northern, flatter, sandier and less fine portion of the Médoc (*see*). Its wines are entitled to the appellation "Médoc" (although of course not "Haut-Médoc") and most of the wine sold simply as "Médoc" comes from its vineyards. These are red Bordeaux of fairly good quality though no great distinction. There are no Classed Growths in the Bas-Médoc, but in general the best wines come from the villages of Bégadan, St. Christoly-de-Médoc, Valeyrac, etc.

BAS-RHIN — (Baa-Ran) — The northern of the two *départements* into which Alsace (*see*) is divided. On the whole, its wines are of less distinction than those of Haut-Rhin, but a first rate *vin rosé* is made from the Pinot Noir grape at Marlenheim, and other vineyards, planted along the Vosges foothills, yield good Rieslings, Traminers, etc., at Obernai, Goxwiller, Barr, Mittelbergheim, Dambach, etc.

BASSERMANN-JORDAN — Distinguished wine-producing family, with a great estate (including most of Forster Jesuitengarten) at Deidesheim, in the German Palatinate, or *Pfalz*. Among wine-lovers, the name is one of the most respected of Germany, and the label one of the most familiar as well as most beautiful. The late Dr. Friedrich von Bassermann-Jordan was considered the dean of German wine-producers; he was the author of a number of scholarly books on the history of the vine, and created in his home a sort of remarkable wine museum.

BASTARD — Sweet red or white wine from the Iberian Peninsula, popular in England in Elizabethan days, and mentioned by Shakespeare (*Measure for Measure, Henry IV*). It may be presumed to have got its name from the Bastardo grape, one of the principal varieties used in the making of Port (*see*) and used also in Madeira.

BASTO — (Baas-toe) — Spanish term meaning coarse or common, the opposite of *fino*. Applied to a Sherry of no breed and poor quality.

BATAILLEY, Château — (Bat-tie-yea) — 5th Classed Growth of Pauillac, in the Haut-Médoc, now divided into two separate properties, Château Batailley and Château Haut-Batailley (*see*). The first produces some 20,000 cases of good quality claret a year, the second about one-third as much.

BÂTARD-MONTRACHET — (Bat-tarr Maw-rah-shay) — One of the best and most celebrated white-wine vineyards of Burgundy, consisting of 29.24 acres half in Puligny-Montrachet and the remainder in Chassagne-Montrachet, with an annual production of some 4,000 cases. Generally ranked third (after Montrachet itself, and Chevalier-Montrachet) among the Montrachet vineyards, it has consistently produced, at least since World War II, better wines than its reputed superiors. These, made exclusively from the Chardonnay grape, are pale gold in color, comparatively high in alcohol (13-14%), dry without being excessively so, and have a quite extraordinary wealth of bouquet and flavor. The best are estate-bottled. (*See* Montrachet.)

For Map, *see* PULIGNY, CHASSAGNE.

BÉARN — (Bay-arn) — Old French province, consisting of most of the modern *département* of Basses Pyrénées; its capital is Pau. Its best known wine is the rather sweet white Jurançon (*see*); but some more than passable *rosé* and dry white wines are also produced and sold as Rosé de Béarn, Rousselet de Béarn (a white wine made at least in part from the grape of that name) or simply as Vin de Béarn.

BEAUJEU — (Bow-zhuh) — Small town on the western edge of the Beaujolais Country, long considered the capital of the little district though today far over-shadowed by Villefranche-sur-Saône. The Hospices de Beaujeu is a charity hospital, organized somewhat along the lines of the Hospices de Beaune (*see*) in that a large part of its endowment consists of vineyards; the wines from these (in Fleurie and other good *communes* of the Beaujolais) are usually labeled "Hospices de Beaujeu," but carry the name of their village of origin as well.

BEAUJOLAIS — (Bow-zhow-lay) — One of the most popular and best-loved wines of France, nearly always red (an insignificant amount of *rosé* and white is produced and legally entitled to the name); also the district from which it comes, in southern Burgundy, just north of Lyon. The vineyards make up a rather small, compact area of vine-covered hills west of the main Paris-Lyon-Riviera railway line and road. Although traditionally part of Burgundy, its wines are very different from those of the great Côte d'Or, being made from a different grape, the Gamay, rather than the Pinot Noir; its prevailing soil, fur-thermore, is clay and granite rather than limestone. Only a few Beaujolais wines may legally be labeled "Bourgogne" (Burgundy) — these are admit-tedly the best; they come from nine specific villages or vineyard slopes: Brouilly, Côte-de-Brouilly, Chénas, Chiroubles, Fleurie, Juliénas, Morgon,

Moulin-à-Vent, St. Amour. Any one of these names on a bottle of Beaujolais is an indication, almost a guarantee, of superior quality; few such wines are ever sold as "Burgundy" or "Bourgogne," even though entitled to the name, being more saleable and worth more under the appellation of their village of origin. Ordinary Beaujolais is a light, agreeable, fruity, eminently drinkable red table wine; it is usually served at the temperature of the cellar rather than that of the dining room; it should be inexpensive, and is at its best when under two years old. Beaujolais Supérieur is a slightly better grade, with a somewhat higher minimum alcoholic content — 10%, rather than 9%, for the red; Beaujolais-Villages (or a wine labeled Beaujolais plus the name of a town) is of a higher class, and must come from one of 39 designated villages or *communes*, of which those listed above (Fleurie, etc.) are particularly outstanding. Even these wines should generally be served cool and drunk young — only exceptional bottles of great years improve appreciably after their third birthday, and many French gourmets prefer them when their age can still be counted in months, not years. Few wines go so wonderfully well with good food, and fine Beaujolais is unquestionably among the most agreeable red table wines in the world, fruity, full-bodied, with a special, almost spicy flavor and no trace of harshness. (*see* page 441 in the appendix.)

BEAULIEU — (Bowl-yuh) — One of California's most famous vineyards, at Rutherford, in the Napa Valley. Founded by the late Georges de Latour in 1900, it remained a family property for some 65 years when, like Inglenook, its next door neighbor, it was taken over by the Heublein Corporation. For almost forty years until his retirement and later as a consultant, the legendary André Tchelistcheff was enologist and winemaker at Beaulieu and pioneered the production of Cabernet Sauvignon wines in the United States and particularly in the Napa Valley.

BEAUMES DE VENISE — (Bome-d'Ven-ease) — Sweet Muscat wine (*see*) made in the French *département* of Vaucluse.

BEAUNE — (Bone) — The principal center of the Burgundy wine trade, a picturesque little city of some 17,000, famous both for its wines and for its ancient buildings, among them the Hospices de Beaune (*see*), an extraordinary charity hospital dating from 1443. Beaune has given its name to the southern half of the Côte d'Or (Côte de Beaune) as well as to the wines, almost all red, produced by its own 1,350 acres of hillside vineyard, west of the town. The best of these are of extremely high quality, remarkable for their distinction, balance and grace, comparable to the better wines of Pommard, the township which directly adjoins Beaune on the south. Leading vineyards include Les Grèves, Les Fèves, Les Cent Vignes, Les Marconnets, Bressandes, Cras, Champs-Pimont, Clos de la Mousse, Clos des Mouches, Clos du Roi,

Beaune

VIGNES FRANCHES

APPELLATION BEAUNE CONTROLÉE

Louis Latour

MAISON FONDÉE EN 1797

NÉGOCIANT A BEAUNE (COTE-D'OR)

ROUALET BEAUNE

Teurons, Avaux, Aigrots, etc. The best known white, not unlike a Meursault in character, is Clos des Mouches. (*See* also Côte de Beaune.)

BEAUREGARD, Château (Bow-reh-gar) — 1st Growth vineyard of Pomerol, one of the fifteen or twenty best of this little district, producing some 6,500 cases a year. A number of other Bordeaux châteaux also bear this name, but their wines are of little interest or consequence.

BEAUSÉJOUR, Château — (Bow-say-zhur) — Excellent 1st Growth of St. Émilion, presently divided into two properties with different owners, both entitled to the name. Together they produce some 6,000 cases a year. There are other chateaux of the same name in Montagne-St. Emilion, Puisseguin-St. Émilion, St. Estèphe in the Médoc, etc., but their wines are by no means of the same class.

BEERENAUSLESE — (Bearen-ouse-lay-zeh) — German, "Berry-selection." A German wine of an exceedingly rare, special and expensive sort, made from individual grape berries selected for their over-ripeness at the time of the *Lese,* or picking. In the production of Auslese (*see*) the most perfect and ripest bunches are set aside and pressed separately; here the selection is in terms, not of bunches, but of chosen, single grapes, cut from the bunches with tiny scissors. Beerenauslesen are produced by leading growers in all of the more important German wine districts only, with rare exceptions, in years ranked as good or great, and, with no exceptions at all, more as a matter of prestige than profit. Quite sweet though not at all cloying, with an almost indescribable wealth of bouquet and fruit and flavor, properly served only with dessert or after dinner, they are among the most remarkable white wines in the world, fully worth the fabulously high prices they bring.

BEESWING — Light sediment, sometimes floating, found in very old bottled red wines, usually port. The name comes from its appearance.

BELAIR, Château — (Bay-lair) — One of the very best Premiers Grands Crus Classés of St. Émilion, directly adjoining Château Ausone (*see*) and owned by

33

the same family. Annual production is just under 4,000 cases. Incidentally, there exist, in the Bordeaux Country, some fifteen properties, all producing wine, called Château Bel-Air (so spelled), and at least one vineyard called "Bélair," though without mention of a château. These should not be confused with the original, which is, by a long way, the best, although one Château *de* Bel Air in Lalande-de-Pomerol (*see*) and another Château Bel-Air in Pomerol both produce good red wine.

BELGRAVE, Château — (Bel-grahv) — 5th Classed Growth of St. Laurent, Haut-Médoc. Annual production, some 12,000 cases. Should not be confused with many lesser known vineyards also bearing the name "Château Belle-grave."

BELLET — (Bel-lay) — Popular and agreeable *vin rosé* (also occasionally a white wine) produced near Nice, on the French Rivera. There are only about fifty acres of vineyard entitled to the name, and the annual production amounts to some 50,000 bottles, promptly and happily consumed by the Niçois themselves and by thirsty tourists.

BELLEVUE, Château — (Bel-vu) — Grand Cru Classé of St. Émilion. Best known of literally dozens of châteaux so named, both in the Bordeaux Country and elsewhere. Some 3,000 cases a year.

BENICARLÓ — (Ben-nee-carl-*lo*) — Town on the Mediterranean Coast of Spain, north of Valencia, known for its heavy, deep-colored blending wines.

BENTONITE — *See* Fining.

BERCY — (Bear-see) — Section along the Seine in Paris where a large part of the city's common table wine is received, handled and distributed.

BEREICH (Bair-rysh) — German word meaning "region" or "area." Under the new German Wine Law the name given to a sub-region of one of the major winegrowing regions (such as the Rheingau, Rheinhessen, Mosel-Saar-Ruwer, etc.). A Bereich encompasses many winegrowing villages in a given region and covers extensive vineyard areas. Bereich Johannisberg, for example, includes the entire Rheingau with the exception of Hochheim, and Bereich Bernkastel includes the whole *Mittelmosel* region from just below Trier almost down to Zell. A Bereich wine will never carry a vineyard name and will generally correspond in quality to a French regional wine. An appellation of *Médoc,* for example, means that the wine may come from anywhere in the Médoc region without mention of a specific vineyard or township. A simple *Côtes-du-Rhône* would also roughly correspond to the German use of Bereich, since the wine could come from any number of villages in the Rhône Valley. Wines from a Bereich are usually of perfectly satisfactory quality, just as are regional wines from France, though neither category will ever attain the distinction of a wine from a single vineyard in a superior winegrowing area.

BERGERAC — (Bear-shair-rack) — Town of 28,000 on the Dordogne River, east of Bordeaux, center of a large wine-producing area, with an annual yield of over 8 million gallons. Most of this is white and of only fair quality at best. (*See* Monbazillac.)

BERG — (Bairg) —German, mountain. When part of a vineyard name indicates location on a hill.

BERGHEIM — (Bairg-hime) — One of the best wine-producing village of Alsace, in the *département* of Haut-Rhin. Renowned for its Rieslings, Gewürztraminers, etc; its leading vineyard is called the Kanzlerberg.

BERGSTRASSE — (Bairg-strah-suh) — See Hessische Bergstrasse.

BERINGER — Famous old California vineyard, founded in 1876 at St. Helena in the Napa Valley by Frederick and Jacob Beringer, originally from the German Rhineland; it was well known in pre-Prohibition days as "Los Hermanos," and remained a family business until quite recently. The winery has over 1000 feet of impressive tunnels, cut with picks by Chinese labor into the adjoining hills, now used for ageing wines.

BERNKASTEL — (Bairn-cast'l) — Wonderfully picturesque and world-famous little town in the heart of the Moselle wine country; its finer wines (those that carry a specific vineyard name and are estate-bottled) have always been rightfully considered among the best of all Germany and are certainly among the most expensive. Under the German Wine Law of 1971 Bernkastel became a Bereich, one of the largest, stretching southwest from just below Zell to the Ruwer. It encompasses 10 Grosslagen and 215 Einzellagen (individual sites); therefore, instead of its former limited connotation it now indicates a sizeable geographic area. The most famous vineyard by all odds is Bernkasteler Doktor, originally but 3.5 acres of the highest priced vineyards in Germany. To meet the new minimum Einzellage area it must be increased. The exact size and boundaries are not yet fixed since the three original owners—Deinhard,

Thanisch and Lauerberg have taken the matter to court. Other fine vineyards are Lay, Bratenhöfchen, Matheisbildchen and Graben.

BESTES FASS — (Bestess Fahss) — Literally, "the best barrel." Term sparingly and traditionally used by the estate-bottlers of Rhine wines to designate the very best cask of a given vintage usually a Beerenauslese (*see*) or Trockenbeerenauslese (*see*). It is no longer permitted under the new German Wine Law. The equivalent on the Moselle was *Bestes Fuder*. Neither term was ever abused, and wines so labeled were great rarities and invariably fabulously expensive. Both designations have been outlawed by the new German wine regulations and we shall never, alas!, see such wines again so labelled. Probably nothing short of a personal acquaintance with a grower or an estate owner will make it possible for one to know about and buy these special bottlings from the "best barrels" in vintages from 1971 onwards.

BESTIMMTE — (Be-*shtim*-te) — German word meaning "designated" — a Bestimmte Anbaugebiet is a designated specified wine growing area.

BEYCHEVELLE, Château — (Baysh-vell) — Well-known vineyard, and the fine red Bordeaux wine (15,000 cases a year) which it produces, at St. Julien, in the Haut-Médoc. Officially classified in 1855 as a 4th Growth, Château Beychevelle now brings a higher price than many 2nds, and is notable for its texture, delicacy and breed. The present elaborate château, dating from 1757, overlooks the estuary of the Gironde; its name is said to be derived from the French, "baisse-voile," or "lower sail" — a gesture of respect which all passing ships paid to the Duke of Épernon, one-time owner of the estate and Grand Admiral of the French Fleet.

BÉZIERS — (Behz-yea) — City of some 80,000 in the *département* of Hérault, southern France, in the heart of what is known as the Midi wine district, and an important center of the trade in *vin ordinaire*.

BIANCO — (Bee-*ahn*-ko) Italian, "white". — The common word for white in Italian; a *vino bianco* is any white wine. *See*, however, *Rosso*.

BIARNEZ — (Be-ar-nes) — 19th century French poet and wine-lover who published, in 1849, a remarkable description and eulogy, in verse, of the wines of Bordeaux.

BIENNE — (Be-en) — Lake in the Canton of Berne, Switzerland. Its steep northern shore is one long terraced vineyard and gives (largely from the Fendant grape) a number of light, good-quality white wines —Twanner, Schafiser, Daucher, Inser, etc.

BIENVENUE-BÂTARD-MONTRACHET — (Be-eh-vay-noo Bat-tarr Mawrah-shay) — Small northern portion of the already small Bâtard-Montrachet vineyard, in Burgundy, whose admirable, golden, fairly dry, full-bodied wines, among the best of France, must henceforth carry this rather clumsy name. Until quite recently they were sold as Bâtard-Montrachet, and there are few experts, if indeed any, who could distinguish between them. The total yield is about 1,100 cases a year. (*See* Montrachet.)

BIG — A wine with more than the average amount of body, alcohol and flavor; not necessarily either fine or great, quite possibly a wine without much distinction. A too "big" wine has a tendency to be heavy and coarse.

BIKAVÉR — (Beek-ah-vair) — Deep-colored, full-bodied Hungarian red wine, made in and around the village of Eger, from the Kadarka grape, plus (it is said) several French varieties including the Cabernet and Gamay.

BINGEN — (*Bing*-en) — Important wine town (720 acres of vineyard) of Hessia, in Germany, overlooking the confluence of the Rhine and Nahe, and directly across the Rhine from Rüdesheim. Back of it rises the celebrated Scharlachberg, or "scarlet hill," one of the most famous vineyard sites of Hessia, although the color of its soil is much more dark brick-red than scarlet. The township of Bingen now includes the adjacent vineyards of Büdesheim and Kempten, and all of these produce, from the Riesling, Sylvaner and Müller-Thurgau grape, white wines of excellent quality, surpassed in Hessia only by those of Nierstein, Nackenheim, and perhaps Oppenheim. The best vineyards are Scharlachberg, Pfarrgarten, Kappellenberg, Kirchberg, Osterberg, Rosengarten, Schelmenstück. Corkscrews, in German, are sometimes jokingly referred to as "Bingen pencils", the idea being that citizens of Bingen are more likely to have corkscrews than pencils in their pockets.

BINNING — The laying away of bottled wine for ageing (*see*). In the case of table wines and sparkling wines, the bottles should invariably be stored on their side, lying down, so that the wine is in contact with the cork. Temperature and other factors are important. (*See* Cellar.)

BISCHÖFLICHES KONVIKT — (Bish-*huff*-lish-ess Kon-vikt) — A Catholic refectory for students at Trier, on the Moselle; a large part of its endowment is in the form of vineyards in Piesport, Ayl, Eitelsbach, Kasel, etc. The wines have been sold since 1970 by a centralized church management known as the "Verwaltung der bischöflichen Güter."

BISCHÖFLICHES PRIESTERSEMINAR — (Bish-*huff*-lish-ess *Priest*-ter-semme-*narr*) — A Catholic seminary at Trier, on the Moselle, with important holdings in many of the better vineyards of the Moselle, Saar and Ruwer. Now a part of the combined church properties in Trier (*see above*).

BISHOP — One of the many versions of Mulled Wine (*see*), and not the best. Most recipes call for a bottle of Port (not a good one, let us hope), an unpeeled orange, stuck with cloves and halved, and a few spoonfuls of sugar, heated together in an enamel saucepan.

BITTER — A wine-taster's term. Bitterness is generally perceptible only in the aftertaste of a wine. It is a fault sometimes due to the variety of grape (the Sauvignon Vert in California, for example), sometimes to climate (an overly dry year, in most cases), and sometimes to unskillful cellar work. Occasionally in red wines but hardly ever in white, it is a flaw that will disappear with age.

BLACK FOREST — *See* Baden.

BLACK ROT — A fungus disease to which grape vines are subject, particularly in moist areas and in periods of exceptional humidity. It attacks both the leaves and the grapes themselves, and copper sulphate is commonly used as a preventive.

BLACK VELVET — Famous tipple of Victorian days, half Champagne, half stout. There is practically nothing that can be said in its favor except that it is obviously better than BROWN VELVET, which is half Champagne, half Port.

BLAGNY — (Blan-yee) — Tiny hilltop village of the Côte de Beaune, Burgundy. Classified as a *hameau* (hamlet) rather than a *commune* (township), it sits astride the line dividing Meursault (*see*) from Puligny-Montrachet and has vines in both. Its excellent red wines and even better whites are therefore sold under a confusing multiplicity of names — the reds, which are delicate, fine, comparable to the lighter Volnays, as "Blagny-Côte de Beaune"; the whites most often as "Meursault-Blagny" or, more rarely, "Puligny-Montrachet, Hameau de Blagny."

BLANC DE BLANCS — (Blaw d' Blaw) — A white wine made from white grapes. A term originally and properly used in the Champagne district of France to describe wines made entirely from the white Chardonnay grape, as distinguished from other white wines made from the Pinot Noir (Blanc de Noirs, *see*) or blends of the two. Blanc de Blancs Champagnes are made mostly in the villages of Cramant, Le Mesnil and Avize; they are remarkable for their delicacy, pale green-gold color, lightness and bouquet. Of late years the term has become widely used in other districts (Provence, the Loire Valley, etc.) where it is entirely meaningless, since, in these districts, *all* white wines are made from white grapes, *none* from black.

BLANC DE NOIRS — (Blaw d'Nwar) — A white wine made from black grapes; especially a Champagne produced entirely from black grapes of the Pinot Noir variety. A few such are made, largely by small producers or *manipulants,* in the villages of Ay, Bouzy, Verzenay, Mailly, Hautvillers, etc.; they are rather full-bodied, soft, pale, but with a trace of very light brown in their color, rather than the greenish tinge of Blanc de Blancs.

BLANC-FUMÉ — (Blaw-Foo-may) — Name given locally to the Sauvignon Blanc grape in and around the town of Pouilly-sur-Loire (*see*). A Pouilly-Fumé, or Pouilly-Blanc-Fumé, is therefore a wine made from the Sauvignon Blanc grape in this district, and thus distinguished from the common wines of the same district, made from the Chasselas grape, which are sold as "Pouilly-sur-Loire." The origin of the term "fumé" (literally, "smoked") is uncertain. California has recently adopted this varietal name, which is in fact Blanc-Fumé (and *not* Fumé Blanc) for some lighter and fruitier wines made from the Sauvignon Blanc, especially in Napa and San Benito counties.

BLANCHOTS — (Blaw-show) — One of the seven Grand Cru vineyards of Chablis (*see*).

BLANQUEFORT — (Blawnk-for) —Southernmost *commune* of the Médoc; its little tidal stream, the Jalle de Blanquefort, forms the official boundary between the Médoc district and that of Graves. Few wines of any consequence.

BLANQUETTE DE LIMOUX — (Blawn-kett duh Lee-moo) — Sparkling white wine, generally decidedly on the sweet side, produced round the town of Limoux, near Carcassonne, in southern France. Non-sparkling wines of the region may carry the name "Limoux nature."

BLAYE — (Bly) — Town and large wine-producing area in the Bordeaux Country, north of Bourg and opposite the Médoc, on the right bank of the Gironde estuary. Its annual production is in the neighborhood of 4 million gallons, about nine-tenths of it white and, on the whole, of mediocre quality. The red — fruity, soft and rather full-bodied — is somewhat better. The superior grades, both red and white, are entitled to the appellation "Premières Côtes de Blaye"; the commoner sorts are sold as "Blaye" or "Blayais," or, perhaps more frequently, as just Bordeaux Blanc or Bordeaux Rouge, although not all of the whites are entitled even to this modest name.

BLENDING — Practice of mixing or "marrying" wines of somewhat different characteristics, or origin, or age, for any one of many diverse reasons, some wholly proper and honorable and some much less so. All Sherries, including the best, are blends; so are most but not all of the best Champagnes. On the other hand, the finest table wines of the world are emphatically not blends, and they would be much less interesting and less good if they were. The legitimate reasons for blending are largely these: (1) to produce a wine of consistent quality and character, year after year, which a consumer may buy with confidence under a familiar name or label; (2) to produce something better in the way of a wine than any of its component parts; (3) to render a wine acceptable which would otherwise be much less so, or not acceptable at all. Not even a purist could object to such blends, *providing, of course,* that the final product is honestly labeled, does not pretend to a vintage which is not its own, nor to be a wine of specific origin when it contains an admixture of others, and, finally, that it has not wholly lost its individuality and character in becoming something acceptable, perhaps, but basically uninteresting, and "standard." Unfortunately, not all blends, by any means, fulfill these conditions.

BLIND — Lack of clarity and transparency in wine, caused by a fine cloudiness which does not settle.

BLUE FINING — *See* Fining.

BÖCKELHEIM — (*Beck*-el-heim) — *See* SCHLOSS BÖCKELHEIM.

BOCKSBEUTEL — (*Bawks*-boy-tel) — The squat, flat-sided, green flagon in which the German wines of the Franken region and also the Badischer Frankenland, the northernmost District of Baden, are traditionally shipped. It presumably gets its name from its fancied resemblance to a goat's scrotum. Before 1971 most German wines shipped in Bocksbeutel were labeled Steinwein (*see*). A somewhat similar bottle is widely used in Chile and Portugal.

BOCKSTEIN — (*Bawk*-stein) — One of the best vineyards of Ockfen, on the Saar, in Germany. Its light white wine, of admirable quality in good vintage years, is sold as Ockfener Bockstein. Like all Saar wines, it is classified, in general, as a Moselle.

BODEGA — (Bo-day-ga) — A wine storage room or "cellar" in Spain, usually above ground. Also a winery, with its installations.

BODENHEIM — (*Bo*-den-heim) — Wine-producing town in the German province of Rheinhessen, south of Mainz. Its wines (Bodenheimer) are generally made from the Sylvaner grape unless specifically labeled "Riesling"; while less distinguished than the neighboring Niersteiners, for example, they are among the better Hessian wines, soft, well-balanced and attractive. Best vineyards include Burgweg, Hoch, Kapelle, etc. Leading producers are Oberstleutnant Liebracht and the Hessian State Domain.

BODENSEE — see CONSTANCE

BODENTON — (Beau-den-tohn) — A special, unique, unmistakable and disagreeable flavor, called *goût de terroir* in French, and often *Bodengeschmack* in German, which certain wines possess, due to the fact that they were produced on heavy clay or alluvial soil.

BODY — A wine-taster's term, often misused. Body means substance. A full-bodied wine is not necessarily high in alcohol, but it is the opposite of watery or thin; it gives an impression of weight, rather than lightness. Full body is not always a virtue — in many white wines and in some red it can be a fault, for only in rare instances and in very great wines does it go hand in hand with delicacy and finesse and distinction. A very full-bodied Moselle or Riesling or Chablis or Champagne or Beaujolais is a wine that lacks balance, and probably lacks fruit and charm. On the other hand, a great Burgundy or a fine Cabernet, let alone a superior Barolo or Châteauneuf-du-Pape, must have body and plenty of it.

BOLZANO — (Boll-*zahn*-no) — Capital of the Italian Tyrol, an attractive little city on the Adige River, not far from the Brenner Pass, and Austria. The province of Bolzano (like that of Trento, immediately to the south) was part of Austria until 1918, and Bolzano was known as Bozen. It is an important center of the wine trade; the hills to the northeast and northwest are covered with pergola-vineyards, and a number of admirable and well-known wines (Santa Maddalena, Santa Giustina, etc.) are produced just outside the city limits. For additional information concerning these and other wines of the Tyrol, *see* Tyrol and Alto-Adige.

BOMMES — (Bumm) — One of the five townships, or *communes,* which constitute the Sauternes district of France, the others being Barsac (*see*), Preignac, Fargues and Sauternes itself. Bommes numbers, within its boundaries, such great estates as Château La Tour-Blanche, Ch. Lafaurie-Peyraguey, Ch. Rayne-Vigneau, Ch. Rabaud-Promis and Ch. Rabaud-Sigalas, all of them officially ranked as 1st Growth vineyards.

BONARDA — (Bo-*nar*-da) — Italian red wine grape widely grown in Piedmont, especially in the provinces of Alessandria and Asti.

BONNES MARES — (Bunn Mar) — Celebrated Burgundian vineyard, producing what is unquestionably one of the dozen finest red wines of the Côte d'Or. It consists of 38½ acres of vines, of which some 34 are in the *commune* of

40

Chambolle-Musigny, the remaining 4½ in Morey-St. Denis. Its maximum legal yield (hardly ever attained) is approximately 5,000 cases. Situated about half way between Chambertin and Musigny, its wine has some of the characteristics of both of its illustrious neighbors — the power and great class of Chambertin, somewhat attenuated; the incomparable finesse of Musigny, though to a less remarkable degree.

For Map, *see* MOREY, CHAMBOLLE.

BONNEZEAUX — (Bunn-zo) — One of the best small vineyard areas in the French province of Anjou, part of the Coteaux du Layon (*see*). Some 250 acres of the Chenin Blanc (Pineau de la Loire) variety yield white wines that are quite sweet, distinguished by their fruitness and bouquet.

BONTEMPS — (Bunn-taw) — Shallow wood bowl used primarily for beating egg whites for the collage (*see*), used in cellars in the Bordeaux Country. As such it has become the emblem of a well-known confratcrnity of wine-lovers, that of the Médoc.

BOORDY — Interesting and unusual small vineyard at Riderwood, Maryland, near Baltimore. It was founded and developed by Philip and Jocelyn Wagner first more or less as a hobby, then as an experimental nursery of Franco-American hybrid vines, and more recently as a commercial winery with an annual output of some 3,000 cases, approximately one-third red, one-third white and one-third *rosé*. Mr. Wagner, until his retirement, was editor of the Baltimore Sun, and has written a number of books on viticulture and wine-making. He was one of the first to introduce the superior, modern hybrids (*see*) and has done more, perhaps, than any one individual to popularize them in the Eastern states, where they have acquired greatly increased importance.

The Boordy wines are American *vins de pays* in the truest sense of the word, and it is to be regretted that the pattern set by their production has not been more widely followed, as it well could be, in scores of other areas all the way from New York to Nebraska and from Michigan to Texas. Made from carefully chosen varieties, well-vinified, with definite character but none of the

41

pronounced "Eastern grape" taste and aroma, the Boordy wines have grown steadily in popularity, and the entire production is now sold and consumed locally, in Baltimore, Washington, etc.

BORDEAUX — (Bore-doe) — Seaport and city of 220,000 on the Garonne River in southwestern France. A few miles north of the city, the Garonne is joined by the Dordogne to form the broad estuary of the Gironde; this has given its name to the *département* which comprises the entire Bordeaux wine country; its 175,000 acres of Appellation Contrôlée produce some 85,000,000 gallons of wine a year.

All of this wine is entitled to the name "Bordeaux," and this appellation is a sort of catch-all, or lowest common denominator. "Bordeaux Supérieur" is very little better — the wine must have slightly more alcohol (10½% as against 9¾%) and its maximum legal production per acre is somewhat lower. Both wines may and generally do come from inferior portions of the Bordeaux Country — if they came from the Médoc or St. Émilion or Graves or Sauternes they would be so labeled. In general, they are mass-produced and blended.

The better districts in the Bordeaux Country have been defined and delimited with characteristic French precision: each one produces wine of a somewhat different character or class. Thus, north of the city, forming the left or west bank of the Gironde estuary, are the low, gravelly hills of the incomparable Médoc, producing red wines almost exclusively, and many of the greatest red wines of the world. West and south of Bordeaux is the wide district of Graves, with white wines ranging from dry to semi-sweet, and many excellent reds. Along the southern edge of Graves, in turn, are the five little villages (including Barsac) which alone are entitled to the famous name Sauternes. Across the Garonne, beyond the intervening hills and the Dordogne, are the vineyards of St. Émilion and Pomerol — this is red wine country, second only to the Médoc in quality. Lesser wine districts include Côtes de Bourg, Fronsac, Lalande-de-Pomerol, Montagne-St. Émilion, Néac, etc.; white wine districts of less importance and less fame are Entre-Deux-Mers, Côtes-de-Blaye, Ste. Croix-du-Mont, Loupiac, Cadillac, Premières-Côtes-de-Bordeaux, Cérons (actually part of Graves), Graves-de-Vayres (not part of Graves), etc.

The red wines of Bordeaux have been known as "Claret" in English-speaking countries ever since the three-hundred-year occupation of the region by the English (1154-1453); the French term *Clairet* has an altogether different meaning and is used to designate a sort of *vin rosé*. Ordinary Claret is simply a pleasant table wine, but the very best Claret is second to no other red wine in the world, fine Burgundy being its only real rival; it is made principally from the Cabernet Sauvignon grape, plus a good deal of Cabernet Franc and Merlot, often a little Malbec, Petit Verdot and Carmenère; while lighter in alcohol than Burgundy, it is generally deeper in color and even longer-lived — certain Médocs of great vintages have been known to hold up, and even to improve, for fifty, sixty and even eighty years.

White Bordeaux is a whole family of wines, some quite dry, some extremely sweet, though all made from grapes of the Sémillon and Sauvignon Blanc varieties, plus an occasional minor admixture of Muscadelle. Graves, Sauternes and Barsac are known, like Claret, the world over.

What goes to market as "Bordeaux Blanc" is a rather common wine, golden, ranging from dry to semi-sweet. The superior grades have, of course, their superior, and more limiting, appellations.

The finer Bordeaux wines, both red and white, invariably carry either (a) the name of one of the better districts (as Médoc, Graves, St. Émilion, Sau-

43

ternes) or, more specifically, (b) the name of a village in one of these districts (as St. Julien, Margaux, Pauillac), or, most specifically of all, (c) the name of the actual vineyard or château, where the wine was made. As a general rule it may be said that the more specific the name, the better the wine. The finest Bordeaux, both red and white, carry, without exception, the name and label of a particular château, plus the statement that they were bottled at the château where grown, as *mise du château,* or *mis en bouteilles au château. See —* Classed Growth, Classification.

BORDEAUX MIXTURE — Our name for what the French call *bouillie borde-laise,* a fungicide spray made of copper sulphate and slaked lime, widely used in Europe against oidium and mildew. It is this (or some quite similar, related product) that so often gives the French and German vineyards their character-istic blue-green tinge in summertime.

BOTA — (Bow-ta) — Spanish for Butt (*see*) also a leather wine pouch.

BOTRYTIS CINEREA — (Bow-treat-iss Sin-eh-ray-ah) — The ''noble rot,'' called *Edelfäule* in German and *pourriture noble* in French. A highly benefi-cient mold which in certain districts (notably the Rhine Valley and the Sau-ternes District) forms on the skins of the ripening grapes of certain varieties, bringing about a concentration of sugar and flavor and a vast improvement in the quality of the resulting wine. The same mold prior to maturity results in *grey rot,* a deterioration of the grapes.

BOTTLE — The ordinary European wine bottle, whatever its form, generally contains ¾ U.S. quart, or a little less; the precise reason for this size is un-known, but some have declared it to be the proper ration of wine for a good trencherman at one sitting. American wine bottles, those used for California and N.Y. State wines, are a little larger, of $^4/_5$ quart capacity; half bottles, in all cases, generally contain one-half as much. On the other hand there are many exceptions, and fortunately American law requires that the actual net contents be stated on the label, or blown into the glass. A bottle's shape and its color are useful but by no means infallible clues to a wine's origin and type: the straight-sided, high-shouldered ''Bordeaux bottle'' is used, in green glass, for all red Bordeaux, and in clear glass for nearly all white, but the same or a very similar bottle is used in almost all other wine-producing coun-tries, and sometimes for very dissimilar wines. The slope-shouldered ''Burgundy bottle'' is also that of the Rhône Valley, of many Italian and Spanish wines, and, in a somewhat heavier version, that of Champagne. The slender, tapering ''Rhine bottle'' is brown on the Rhine, but green in Alsace and on the Moselle, and a colorless *''flute''* of nearly the same form serves for many *rosés.* Italy provides us with all sorts of straw-covered bottles, of various shapes and sizes, and both Germany and Chile have their stumpy flagons. Actually, the form of the bottle makes no difference at all, providing, of course, that it can be easily binned. All wines, however, age more quickly in small bottles than in large, and a half-bottle of a given vintage will always be readier than a full bottle, and both readier than a magnum of the same wine. Champagne is an exception, since Champagne is normally fermented and stored in the most popular size bottles and loses something by being decanted into Jeroboams, Nebuchadnezzars, and all the rest. All wines are somewhat affected by light, and all last longer, except under absolutely ideal cellar conditions, when in green or brown bottles, and the possibly less attractive brown bottle, in the author's experience, seems to be the best.

The best known oversize bottles of France are these: Magnum — 2 bottles; Double-Magnum or Jeroboam — 4 bottles; Rehoboam — 6 bottles; Imperial or Methusalem — 8; Salmanazar — 12; Balthazar — 16; Nebuchadnezzar — 20. In the United States new Standards of Fill for both American and imported wines effective January 1, 1979 are stipulated as follows:

New Standard	Equivalent U.S. fl. oz.	
3 Liters*	101	
1.5 "	50.7	
1 "	33.8.	*Larger sizes in exact liters are permitted
750 milliliters	25.4	up to 18 liters i.e.
375 "	12.7	4.75 Gal.—608 fl. oz.
187 "	6.3	
100 "	3.4	

BOTTLE AGE — Development of wine after bottling; after the initial bottle sickness (see) wines will mature in bottle, reach a plateau and finally gradually deteriorate as any other living thing. The length of life and height of development are functions of grape, soil, wine making skill and practice, vintage and storage conditions.

BOTTLE SICK — Unhappy condition in which a wine generally finds itself immediately after bottling. All wines are badly shaken and "numbed" by passing through the filtration which normally precedes bottling, the bottling-machine, etc. If sound, they invariably recover from this bottle-sickness, but sometimes only after ninety days or more. Somewhat the same effect is produced, especially in old or delicate wines, by rough handling, even long after bottling — it is for this reason that fine wines should be "rested," at least for a week or two, before they are opened.

BOUCHES-DU-RHÔNE — (Boosh-dew-Rone) — French *département,* that of Marseille, Aix-en-Provence, Arles and the Rhône delta. Its best wines are the white Cassis (see), a perennial favorite with bouillabaisse; the white and *rosé* wines of Palette, some of the Côtes de Provence, the Coteaux d'Aix, etc., none of them, to be truthful, very distinguished.

BOUCHET — (Boo-shay) — Local name given to the Cabernet Franc grape in the St. Émilion district of Bordeaux. Under no circumstances should it be confused with the Bouschet hybrids, so called after their creator, Henri Bouschet, mostly mass-production grapes of high yield and low quality, grown in the French Midi district and to some extent in Algeria and California.

BOUCHONNÉ — (Boo-shon-nay) — French for corky (see), from *bouchon,* cork.

BOUGROS — (Boo-gro) — One of the seven Grand Cru vineyards of Chablis (see).

BOUQUET — The complex of diverse, interesting and pleasing odors which a good, mature wine gives off once it is opened; everything that such a wine says to the nose (as distinguished from the palate); one of a fine wine's greatest attractions and greatest charms. On the basis of bouquet alone, many experts can determine a fine wine's origin, its grape variety, its approximate age, its condition, its class and value. Young wines may have aroma or odor or perfume or "fruit" or "flower"; bouquet is distinct from all these, may include all of them, but comes mainly from esters developed by the slow oxidation of certain elements in the wine, including alcohol but above all fruit acids. Wines with high acid, coming from northern vineyards, almost invariably have more bouquet than those with lower acid, from sunnier zones; similarly, wines from chalky, stony and, on the whole, less fertile soil, have more bouquet than others, as do wines made from grapes that have matured slowly, in a temperate climate, without excessive heat. One does not have to be any sort of expert to like and appreciate the bouquet of a fine wine.

BOURG — (Bourg) — Name shared (in most instances with some suffix) by at least twenty towns and villages in France. The one of interest to wine-drinkers, neither the largest nor the most beautiful of the lot, has no suffix and is in the Bordeaux Country, on the Gironde estuary, directly across from the Médoc. The area of which it is the center produces some 4 million gallons of wine annually, a little over a sixth of it white wine of mediocre quality not entitled to the Appellation Contrôlée, the rest red, and much of it far from bad. Apart from the general appellation, "Bordeaux Rouge" (under which most of it is sold), it is entitled, when red, to the names "Bourg," "Bourgeais," and "Côtes de Bourg," but these are rarely seen on wine labels outside France. Full-bodied, well-balanced, made largely from the Cabernet grape, it is a red wine that deserves to be better known than it is.

BOURGEOIS — (Boor-zjwah) — One of the main categories of Bordeaux wine, qualitative rather than geographical, however, as in the expressions *"cru bourgeois,"* or "bourgeois growth." In the whole Bordeaux Country there are well over 5,000 separate vineyards; less than 200 of these constitute what might be called the aristocracy, the "classed growths" (*see*) of the Médoc, Sauternes, St. Émilion, etc. In highly honorable second place comes a whole collection of others, smaller and less famous châteaux, some but not all of which practice château-bottling; known as the *"crus bourgeois"* and *"crus bourgeois supérieurs,"* these often produce wines as good as those of their reputed superiors, and their labels are worth looking for. A partial list of such châteaux has been included in the appendix. It is important to note that a bourgeois growth of a good vintage is not by any means an ordinary wine, and may be a truly excellent one.

BOURGOGNE — (Boor-gon-yuh) — French for the province of Burgundy (*see*) and its wine.

BOURGOGNE MOUSSEUX — (Boor-gon-yuh Moo-suh) — French for Sparkling Burgundy (*see*).

BOURGUEIL — (Boor-goy) — Village in the old French province of Touraine, in the Loire Valley, long famous for its red wines, made from the

Cabernet Franc (known locally as Breton) and Cabernet Sauvignon grapes, although the best of these generally carry the appellation St. Nicolas-de-Bourgueil (*see*), and come from an adjacent township, higher up on the Loire hillsides. One of the most agreeable lesser red wines of France, Bourgueil should be drunk fairly young, preferably at cellar temperature. It is rather light (rarely over 12%), delicate, fruity, fresh, of a brilliant light ruby color. Total production amounts to something over one and a half million gallons a year. Students of French literature will recall that it was at Bourgueil that Rabelais situated his "Abbaye de Thelème" and that it was here that Ronsard met his "*belle Angevine,* Marie," whose charms he celebrated in some of the greatest lyrics of the French Renaissance.

BOUSCAUT, Château — (Boose-ko) — One of the most important and best-tended vineyards of the Graves District, south of Bordeaux. It is in the township of Cadaujac, and produces some 10,000 cases of good quality Claret and about one fifth as much good dry white Graves, per year. Invariably château-bottled.

BOUTIQUE — (Boo-teek) — A word loosely applied, and some think condescendingly, in the U.S. to small wineries producing less than 25,000 cases of varietal or unique wines, also applied to the wines produced.

BOUZY — (Booz-ee) — Major wine-producing village in the Champagne, Country of France, rated as one of the best. *See* Champagne.
   ALSO an extremely pleasant red still wine made in the same village from the Pinot Noir grape and, for the most part, consumed locally.

BOXBEUTEL — *see* BOCKSBEUTEL

BOYD-CANTENAC, Château — (Boyd-Cawnt-nack) — 3rd Classed Growth of Cantenac-Margaux, Haut-Médoc. Some 5,000 cases a year.

BRACCHETO — (Bra-ket-toe) — Red Piedmontese wine, generally *frizzante* (*see*), made from the grape of this name.

BRANAIRE-DUCRU, Château — (Brahn-air Dew-crew) — 4th Classed Growth of St. Julien, Haut-Médoc, directly adjoining Beychevelle and accorded the same rank in 1855. Its wine (some 14,000 cases a year) hardly deserves such rating today, although there has been considerable recent improvement, thanks to a change in ownership.

BRANE-CANTENAC, Château — (Brahn Cahnt-nack) — 2nd Classed Growth of Cantenac-Margaux, Haut-Médoc, with an annual production of about 20,000 cases of good quality Claret. While hardly one of the best of the 2nds today, its wine is dependable, generally not too expensive, and almost always a good value, well-balanced and sound.

BRAUNEBERG — (Brown-uh-bairg) — Famous wine-producing village on the Moselle, in Germany; long considered, even by such discerning tasters as Thomas Jefferson, the Moselle's best; formerly known as Dusemond (from the Latin *mons dulcis,* "sweet mountain" — supposedly because of the excellence and sweetness of its wines). Today these wines, less fashionable, are no less admirable, quite comparable to those of Wehlen and Zeltingen, full-

bodied, fine and rich. The best vineyards are Brauneberger Juffer, Klostergar-
ten, Hasenläufer, Kammer, Juffer-Sonnenuhr. The leading producers include
Haag, von Schorlemer, the St. Nikolaus Hospital, the Brauneberger Winzerverein, etc.

BRAZIL — Only the very southernmost corner of Brazil, the state of Rio Grande
do Sul, is sufficiently far from the equator and temperate enough in climate to
provide proper growing conditions for the vine. There are some 165,000 acres
of vineyard, a good part of them producing table grapes; the wine is undistinguished.

BREATHING — Rapid oxidation taking place during decanting or by opening
bottles in advance of use. Much pretentious nonsense is written about breathing. It can be of some help in rounding out sturdy young wines and a few
powerful northern Italian wines. It can presage the death of older delicate
wines.

BREED — An expression for high quality, and elegant delicacy.

BRILLANTE — (Bree-yantay) — White, slightly sweet, Spanish table wine.
This, like Diamante, is a trade name.

BRILLIANT — Term applied to a wine impeccably clear, as all good wines
should be.

BRISTOL — City and major seaport in the west of England, long famous for its
trade with France, Spain, the West Indies, etc. Several important British wine
merchants (Avery, Harvey) have their home offices in Bristol; the latter now
markets in the United States two popular Spanish Sherries under the names
"Bristol Milk" and "Bristol Cream."

BROCHON — (Broh-shaw) — Village directly north of Gevrey-Chambertin, on
the Côte d'Or, in Burgundy. All of its better vineyards, about 125 acres,
produce red wines legally entitled to the name Gevrey-Chambertin, and one
rarely, if ever, sees a bottle labeled "Brochon."

BROLIO — (Brol-yo) — Perhaps the most celebrated castle and wine-estate of
the Chianti Country: a famous fortress in the Medieval wars between Siena
and Florence. There was an old saying that "when Brolio growls, all Siena
trembles," and one of the battles around its walls was so bloody that Dante
said that it "colored the Arbia red" (the Arbia being a small river nearby). For
over 800 years, Brolio has been the property of the Ricasoli family; Bettino
Ricasoli, in the 19th century was the first Premier of reunited Italy after
Cavour. (see Chianti)

BROUILLY — (Brew-ye) — One of the best and most famous wine-producing
districts of the Beaujolais (see). Like Moulin-à-Vent, it is not a township, but
a strictly delimited zone, and consists of portions of the communes of Odenas,
St. Lager, Cercié, Quincié and Charentay, all surrounding the celebrated Côte
de Brouilly (see), a hill crowned by a chapel which is the site of an annual pil-
grimage. As a wine, Brouilly, or Beaujolais-Brouilly, is one of the most typical and most attractive of the Beaujolais, especially when young; fruity, full-

bodied, full-flavored, sturdy, yet soon ready and, as compared with other Beaujolais (Moulin-à-Vent, Morgon, etc.) relatively short-lived, it is among the most agreeable red table wines in the world.

BROUSTET, Château — (Brew-stay) — 2nd Classed Growth of Barsac, producing some 4,000 cases a year of white wine, a little less sweet than most Barsac but of considerable distinction and breed.

BRUNELLO — (Brew-*nell*-o) — Deep colored red wine, slow maturing and long lived, produced in Montalcino near Siena in Tuscany and made from the Brunello grape, a variety of Sangiovese. One of the first Italian wines to be classified D.O.C.G. (*see*) beginning with the 1978 vintage.

BRUT — (Brute) — French term applied to the dryest Champagnes and other sparkling wines, dryer than "Extra Dry." Properly it means, in this instance, "unmodified" — a Champagne to which no *dosage,* or sweetening, has been added. Actually, all *brut* Champagnes, or practically all, do contain some *dosage;* this is not supposed to exceed 2% at most, but in many instances does. Most Champagne houses ship their best wines, both vintage and non-vintage, as *brut,* but the term alone is no guarantee of quality. *See* Champagne.

BUAL — (Also BOAL) — Name of one of the leading grape varieties of Madeira (*see*) and the sweet, fine, golden wine made from it.

BUCELLAS — (Boo-sailas) — White Portuguese table wine, produced near Lisbon.

BÜDESHEIM — (Bew-des-heim) — *See* Bingen.

BUENA VISTA — (Bway-na Vee-sta) — Historic California vineyard, at Sonoma, north of San Francisco. It was founded, not long after the Gold Rush, by an extraordinary Hungarian nobleman, Count (a title which he later abandoned in favor of the more democratic one of "Colonel") Agoston Haraszthy (*see*), who has not incorrectly been called "the father of modern California viticulture." Famous from Civil War days until its cellars were largely destroyed by the San Francisco earthquake, it got off to a fresh start when purchased by Frank Bartholomew (later president of United Press-International) in 1943, and is today once more a producer of premium wines.

BUGEY — (Bew-zhay) — Little district in the *département* of Ain, northeast of Lyon, producing a variety of very light but often agreeable and refreshing wines, red, white and *rosé,* entitled to the V.D.O.S. seal (*see*). Most of these are sold as *Vins du Bugey* or *Roussette du Bugey,* plus, in some cases, one of the village names as Montagnieu or Virieu.

BÜHLERTAL — (Buel-ler-tahl) — Small vineyard district near Baden-Baden, in southwestern Germany. Pleasant red and white wines of little more than local interest. *See* Baden.

BULGARIA — Balkan country with some 460,000 acres of vineyard and an annual production of some 80 million gallons of wine, about two-thirds of it red. A substantial amount is exported, mainly to the Soviet Union, Czechoslovakia and Eastern Germany.

BULK PROCESS — Method of making sparkling wine, considerably less expensive and less slow than the true Champagne process, never as good. The wines are not fermented in bottle but in large sealed tanks, and drawn off into bottle under pressure. No wine so made may be called Champagne (*see*) in France; in the United States such wines must carry the words "Bulk Process" or the equivalent, on their labels.

BURDIN — (Buhr-dan) — One of the better known French Hybridizers. (*See* Hybrid.)

BURGER — Productive white wine grape of poor quality, known in Germany and Alsace as the Elbling (*see*) or Kleinberger; it may no longer be used in the making of wines with an Appellation Contrôlée in France.

BURGUNDY (French, Bourgogne) — Old French province southeast of Paris, long an independent Duchy; the world famous wines, red, white, and in rare instances *rosé,* from this region, which is generally considered to comprise the *départements* of Yonne (the Chablis district), Côte d'Or (area of the greatest Burgundies, both red and white), Saône-et-Loire (Mâcon, Pouilly-Fuissé, etc.) and part of Rhône (Beaujolais).

However, by no means all of the wines produced in these four *départements* are entitled to the name "Burgundy" (or "Bourgogne"); French law reserves this name for wines made from certain superior grape varieties, grown in certain specific townships, and all true Burgundies are therefore better-than-average wines of some well-defined type and some known, established origin. The total production is only about one-third that of Bordeaux — it amounts to 2% of the wine produced in France. This percentage has declined sharply in the last hundred years — vineyard acreage in Burgundy is now less than half of what it was in 1870.

Truly fine Burgundy is therefore something of a rarity and always will be; it is produced only on a few narrow, especially favored hillsides, in a country of generally unfavorable climate, principally from two grape varieties which yield very little to the acre. A few additional figures may serve to make this even clearer:

In the five years 1972-1976, the wine production of Burgundy amounted to 2% of that of France, or to some 42 million gallons. In 1976 48% was Beaujolais; 9% was Mâcon or Mâcon *Supérieur;* 1% was what is called "Bourgogne *grand ordinaire"* (the lowest legal grade, and what most Sparkling Burgundy is made of); 3% was Bourgogne Aligoté (*see*), a white carafe wine made from a second-rate grape; 3% was Passe-tout-grains (an inexpensive blend of Gamay and Pinot, rarely exported), and about 6% was simply called Bourgogne, honest wine, no doubt, but of no special quality.

Out of the remaining 32% (seven-tenths of 1% of the total wine production of France) came the world's supply of all those wines beloved of gourmets in all countries: Chablis, Pouilly-Fuissé, Meursault, Montrachet, Chambertin, Clos de Vougeot, Nuits-Saint-Georges, Corton, Beaune, Pommard, and all the others. For these, *see* each, in its proper alphabetical place, in this volume. *See,* also, Beaujolais, Passe-tout-grains, Gamay, Pinot, Chardonnay, Mâcon, Côte d'Or, Sparkling Burgundy, etc., as well as the listing of Burgundian towns and vineyards in the Appendix.

DIJON

CÔTE DE NUITS
FIXIN
BROCHON
GEVREY-CHAMBERTIN
MOREY-ST-DENIS
CHAMBOLLE-MUSIGNY
FLAGEY-ECHEZEAUX
VOUGEOT
VOSNE-ROMANEE
NUITS-ST-GEORGES
PREMEAUX
CORGOLOIN
COMBLANCHIEN
PERNAND
VERGELESSES
ALOXE-CORTON
SAVIGNY-LES-BEAUNE
CHOREY-LES-BEAUNE
BEAUNE
POMMARD
MONTHELIE
VOLNAY
AUXEY-DURESSES
MEURSAULT
CÔTE DE BEAUNE
ST-ROMAIN
ST-AUBIN
PULIGNY-MONTRACHET
CHASSAGNE-MONTRACHET
SANTENAY
CHAGNY

RULLY

MERCUREY

CÔTE CHALONNAISE
GIVRY

MONTAGNY

MACONNAIS

MACON
POUILLY-
FUISSE
POUILLY-LOCHE
POUILLY-VINZELLES
JULIENAS
ST-AMOUR
CHENAS
FLEURIE
MOULIN A VENT
CHIROUBLES
MORGON
CÔTE DE BROUILLY
BROUILLY

BEAUJOLAIS

VILLEFRANCHE-
S.-SAONE

BURGUNDY

N

SCALE

MI. 0   5   10
KM. 0   5   10   15   20

Drawn by W. Lembeck

With a handful of exceptions — Chablis, perhaps Pouilly-Fuissé, and a few rare, outstanding Beaujolais — all of the wines that have made Burgundy's international and enduring fame come from one extraordinary strip of hillside vines. This, the "Côte d'Or," or "Golden Slope," extends from near Dijon to well south of Beaune and faces south of east over the wide plain of the Saône, beyond which the Alps are occasionally visible in clear weather. All of these wines are made either from the Pinot Noir or from the Chardonnay grape, and all of them carry either the name of the *commune,* or township, from which they come (as Pommard, Beaune, Nuits-Saint-Georges, Chambolle-Musigny), or the name of some specific vineyard plot, or *climat,* which produced them (as Richebourg, Musigny, Bonnes Mares); often they carry both (as Pommard Épenots, Beaune Grèves, Meursault Perrières, etc.). These vineyard plots are very small, rarely over forty acres in extent and often much smaller, usually divided among many different owners, some of whom estate-bottle their production, while others sell their grapes, still on the vine, or their wine soon after the vintage to a shipper, or *négociant.* Such wines, when both genuine and good (and unfortunately, despite all the controls, there are some which are neither) are unsurpassed in the world: the reds have a warmth and fruit and vigor and bouquet, a combination of power and finesse, matched by no other wines; and of all the white wines in the world, the white Burgundies are those that most true gourmets would prefer to drink with their meals.

The word BURGUNDY, alas, in a great many countries, including the United States, is considered a generic term applicable to red wine, however and wherever produced, even to sweet red wines made from Concord grapes in New York State or in Michigan or Ohio. There is possibly a little more justification for the use of the name in California, where wines so labeled are at least made from European grape varieties, but as contrasted with the very strict French controls, which even govern pruning methods and maximum yield per acre, there are almost none, and it is common practice to bottle "Burgundy" and "Claret" out of the same tank. The name, so used, has become meaningless, and those interested in finding an honorable American counterpart of a French Burgundy will do better to look for bottles labeled Pinot Noir, Chardonnay, Pinot Blanc and Gamay-Beaujolais — these are true cousins, and in some cases quite distinguished cousins, to the real Burgundies of France.

BUTT — Large barrel or cask, especially of the sort and size in which Sherry is traditionally aged and shipped. It holds just over 132 U.S. gallons (500 liters).

BUTTAFUOCO — (Boo-ta-fwo-co) — Derived from "spatters like fire", one of the three oddly named and rather agreeable red wines (the others being Barbacarlo — or "Charles' Beard" — and Sangre de Giuda — or "Blood of Judas") produced near Pavia (Lombardy), in northern Italy. The vineyards are in the township of Broni.

BUTYRIC — Rancid odor sometimes found in certain spoiled wines.

BYRRH — (Beer) — Well-known French apéritif, with a wine base, made in the town of Thuir, Pyrénées Orientales.

C

CABERNET FRANC — (Cab-air-nay Fraah) — see Cabernet Sauvignon

CABERNET ROSÉ D'ANJOU — (Cab-air-nay Rose-A Dahn-zhoe) — Legally a *rosé* wine made from the Cabernet Franc grape in a clearly defined area in the Loire Valley in western France, an area more or less comprising the old province of Anjou (*see*). Several *appellations contrôlées* are involved, since Rosé de Cabernet is made almost everywhere in Anjou — round Saumur and on the Coteaux de l'Aubance (perhaps the best), the Coteaux du Layon, the Coteaux de la Loire, etc., etc. The variations in quality are nevertheless not as great as all this complicated terminology would lead one to believe: the wine, while much better than the ordinary Rosé d'Anjou, made from the Grolleau (or Groslot) grape, is pleasant, inexpensive, usually a little sweet, by no means extraordinary.

CABERNET SAUVIGNON — (Cab-air-nay So-veen-yaw) — Superb red wine grape, responsible in large part for the great Clarets of Bordeaux, and, in the North Coast Counties of California, for what are rightly considered America's best red wine. The name Cabernet, or Cabernet Sauvignon, on a California wine label, is therefore an indication, almost a guarantee, of superior quality, and it is under this name that America's finest "Clarets" are sold. Actually, there exist two Cabernet grapes, distinct but closely related: the smaller and less productive Cabernet Sauvignon predominates in the Médoc and in California, and gives a longer-lived slower-maturing wine, with more tannin; the Cabernet Franc is the leading variety in the St. Émilion district and produces Chinon, Bourgueil, Champigny, and many excellent *rosés* in the Loire Valley.

53

Both Cabernets are planted in Chile and the best red wines of South America generally carry this name. The so-called "Ruby-Cabernet," rather widely planted in California during the past decade, is not a true Cabernet but a very productive, recently developed métis (*see*) of Carignane with Cabernet Sauvignon — it is not, on the basis of present evidence, a really superior wine grape, and, in any case, has no established right to this name.

CABINET — (Cab-ee-*net*) — Since 1971 written Kabinett. A term employed in Germany, originally in the Rheingau district, to designate a superior grade or special reserve of natural (i.e. unsugared) wine, usually estate-bottled. Originally *Kabinettweine* were those which the vineyard owner put aside for his own use, but the term had come to be more and more loosely used, and, until 1971, many proprietors designated as Cabinet wines any lots which brought more than a certain minimum price, per bottle or per cask, when sold. This minimum varied considerably from one producer to another, and even from one vintage to the next. In general, all wines labeled Auslese (*see*) or Spätlese (*see*) were ranked as Cabinet wines, but so, in many cases, were others of less distinguished class. The term was somewhat differently used at Schloss Johannisberg (*see*). Today, a Kabinett wine ranks just below Spätlese in quality and is usually the driest of a given producer's wines. If it is also an Erzeugerabfüllung (*see*) it corresponds to the former designation of Original-Abfüllung (*see*).

CABRIÈRES — (Cab-ree-air) — *Vin Rosé,* made from Carignan and Cinsault grapes, near Lodève, in southern France. It is one of the better wines of the Midi, and entitled to the V.D.Q.S. seal.

CADILLAC — (Cad-dee-yak) — Picturesque little town in the French Bordeaux Country, facing Graves and Sauternes across the Garonne river and forming part of the district called "Premières Côtes de Bordeaux." Its rather sweet white wines are not unlike Sauternes, but of lower quality and less class.

CAHORS — (Kah-or) — Interesting, excellent, almost legendary red wine, produced round the old city of this name, north of Toulouse in central France. It is made principally from the Malbec grape, but vinified in the ancient, traditional way, and it is perhaps the most deeply colored of fine French red wines, its dark crimson tinged, one might almost say, with black, like certain of the best wines of Valtellina, in northern Italy. Slow-maturing, remarkably long-lived, firm but not harsh, it has unmistakable distinction and a special cachet of its own, some affinity with a good, full-bodied red Graves. Those interested in wine "discoveries" will do well to seek it out, although the best is not easy to come by, and it is pleasant to be able to report that instead of being ranked as a V.D.Q.S. wine, it has at last been accorded the *Appellation Contrôlée* which it obviously deserves.

CAILLOU, Château — (Ky-you) — 2nd Classed Growth of Barsac, and definitely one of the best of these, its production not far from 9,000 cases a year. Not to be confused with many other Bordeaux châteaux bearing quite similar names.

CAIRANNE — (Kay-rahn) — One of the better wine-producing villages of the lower Rhône Valley, in France, some twenty-five miles northeast of Avignon. Its red, white and *rosé* wines are among the best of those sold as Côtes-du-Rhône, and carry the special appellation Côtes-du-Rhône-Cairanne.

CALABRIA — (Kah-*lah*-bree-yah) — Region in the "toe" of the Italian "boot"; noted for a robust red wine called Cirò (*see*)

CALDARO — (Kahl-*dar*-o) — Picturesque little vineyard town some ten miles southwest of Bolzano, in the Italian Tyrol. The surrounding hillsides are covered with vines trained on their characteristic pergolas, and produce a remarkably diverse collection of fresh, light, eminently agreeable table wines, both red and white. Many of these, notably those made from the Traminer *aromatico* (Gewürztraminer), the Riesling, Silvaner (Sylvaner), Pinot *bianco* (Pinot Blanc), Moscato Giallo and Pinot *nero* (Pinot Noir) are marketed under these varietal names. What is sold as Caldaro or Caldaro Collina is a rather tart red wine, light in body and color but fruity and appetizing, made from a grape known as the Schiava (*see*). A somewhat finer but very similar wine is called Lago di Caldaro (*see*) and comes from the steep shores of a little lake three miles to the south. In Austrian days Caldaro was called Kaltern, and the lake wine was known as Kaltererseewein; in Switzerland and Austria, where both wines are still great favorites, they are often still so listed and so sold.

CALIFORNIA — America's one major vineyard country, producing in 1976 71% of the wine consumed in the United States, as against about 16% of imports and some 13% from the other states. There are over 630,000 acres under vines and the crop varies between 3.8 and 4.0 million tons of grapes a year; more than half of this is made into wine, most of the rest being marketed as table grapes or raisins. In 1976, the state's 285 bonded wineries (there were over 600 in 1936) produced a total of 300 million gallons, compared with an average of 68 million gallons in the years 1936-1940 and an average of 181 million gallons in the years 1966-1970.

At present, four-fifths of California's output is table wine, whereas for many years after the repeal of Prohibition in 1933, it had been fortified wine, rather than table wine which predominates in almost all other wine-producing lands, Australia being an odd exception. Since repeal these wines (Sherry, Port, Angelica, Muscatel, etc.) have been called dessert wines in the U.S. even though many are dry and are consumed before meals.

Thus, in the early years of repeal, California produced only one-eighth as much table wine as Spain, but over three times as much Sherry, and only one-fourth as much table wine as Portugal, but nearly ten times as much Port. With a few rare and notable exceptions, most of this was mass-produced for a mass market, sold and consumed when less than a year old; it was poor stuff, drunk because it contained 20% of alcohol by volume, and was cheap.

In the past twenty-five years, and particularly in the past ten, however, the producers of superior wine in California have made extraordinary progress, especially in the field of table wines. The cheaper California reds and whites are, on the average, quite as good as the *vin ordinaire* of France or Italy or

Drawn by W. Lembeck

56

Spain, and the finer ones, the varietal wines (*see*) can stand comparison with all but the rare, truly great wines from European vineyards. The plantings of fine European grape varieties (Cabernet, Pinot, Riesling, Sémillon, etc.) have greatly increased; in equipment and technique, California's best wineries are now on a par with those of Germany and France.

Grapes are grown in 33 of California's 58 counties (there are bonded wineries in 34), but the major wine districts are two: the cool North Coast area, centered round San Francisco, producing principally table wines; and the much warmer interior valleys, where most of the fortified wines are made. The North Coast area includes the counties from north to south, of Mendocino, Lake, SONOMA, NAPA, Solano, Contra Costa, Alameda (the LIVERMORE Valley), SANTA CLARA, Santa Cruz, SAN BENITO and MONTEREY, to which must be added San Luis Obispo and Santa Barbara (those in caps being the more important). In the interior valleys there are vast irrigated areas where raisin and table grapes predominate and where cheap dessert wines are made, often from culls — over 40% of the grapes used for wine in California are not "wine grapes" but "raisin grapes" or "table grapes". The counties where these are grown, in the San Joaquin and Great Central valleys, are, from north to south, Amador, Glenn, Sacramento, San Joaquin, Stanislaus, Merced, Madera, Fresno, Tulare, Kings and Kern.

A third district, directly east of Los Angeles, San Bernardino (the largest county in the United States) and Riverside have some 12,000 acres of wine grapes, and produce wines comparable to, and in general superior to, those of the French Midi.

Several species of grape vine grow wild west of the Rockies including the economically valueless *Vitis californica* and *Vitis arizonica,* but *Vitis vinifera,* the "wine-bearing" grape of Europe, was brought to California by Franciscan monks, who established a chain of missions from what is now the Mexican border all the way to Sonoma, north of San Francisco, before 1840. The original grape introduced, now known as the Mission, is a hardy variety giving on the whole poor wine; it has been largely replaced, and now ranks only twelfth among red wine grapes, in acreage. During Prohibition (1919-1933) the first action of the winegrowers was to remove vines but they soon realized that there was a ready sale for grapes and grape juice which by "accident", if not kept sterile, would turn into wine after the consumer brought it home. Almost overnight grape prices multiplied ten fold to a record one hundred dollars per ton and so a new planting boom was on. This time high yield black grapes which were hardy enough to ship all over the country were grown and the better wine grapes were almost forgotten. With the usual perversity of American businessmen, there was great overplanting and the boom burst in 1925. The vines remained, however, with a constant surplus of grapes which, except for the world War II period, lasted until 1971.

The mass-production red grapes are: Zinfandel (of uncertain origin but the closest thing to an indigenous grape, productive, giving a rather common but agreeable wine, fruity, not too heavy, fair — and in superior mountain vineyards, quite good); Carignane (the "old dependable" of the French Midi and of Algeria — rather coarse, full-bodied wines, no real quality but not too bad); the Alicante Bouschet (an inferior hybrid, which has no possible virtue

57

except the deep color of the wine it yields); the Grenache (in the proper location, and *only* there, an admirable grape for *rosé*, elsewhere, a passable variety for Port-type wine); the Mission; the Mataro (a common, coarse, productive grape from Spain); the Petite Sirah (an aristocrat in France, the grape of red Hermitage; very probably *not* the same variety in California, possibly the Duriff, yielding very full-bodied wines without any trace of distinction or breed).

The roster of mass-production white "wine-grapes" is much shorter, since by far the largest part of inexpensive California white wine is made from the Sultanina, or Thompson Seedless, a vastly productive raisin grape which gives a neutral, almost flavorless, pale white wine. The true wine grapes are the Palomino (excellent for Sherry, almost worthless for table wine); the Sauvignon Vert, definitely no better, and today total plantings are less than 1,000 acres; the Burger, so poorly thought of in its native Alsace that it has not even been "tolerated" in the better Alsatian vineyards since 1965.

Nevertheless, on the whole, the inexpensive table wines of California are good quaffing wines. When they are sold under honest American names, and presented with no great fanfare, the reds are quite acceptable; the whites (as is very often the case with *ordinaires*) somewhat less so.

Since the repeal of Prohibition, a vast amount of experimentation and development, primarily at the University of California in Davis, has produced new varieties and improvements of existing varieties — some by clonal selection, some by hybridization, a loose term which includes true hybrids (cross-pollination of several species, i.e. vinifera x rotundifolia) and métis (cross-pollination in the same species, i.e. vinifera x vinifera). Some of these new grapes are successful enough to be used as new varietals (*see* Hybrid). In addition the growers and wine makers have found that a few of the mass production grapes such as Zinfandel and Petite Sirah when grown in the right places, vinified carefully and aged properly produce quite spectacular wines.

When it comes to better table wines, California has little to be ashamed of and in fact much of which we can be proud. These increasingly tend to go to market under their "varietal" names — the name of the variety of grape from which they are made — and no one could devise a more honest system of labeling. This, plus the name of a respectable vineyard and a good district, is about all that a wine-buyer can ask in the way of a guarantee, and those who know California wines ask for Cabernet Sauvignon, Pinot Noir, Gamay Beaujolais or even Petite Sirah and Zinfandel when they want good red wine, and Chardonnay, Johannisberg Riesling, Pinot Blanc, Sauvignon Blanc, Chenin Blanc, etc., when they want fine white. Their quality is at least as good as many European wines in the same price bracket, and their production is increasing as more people come to appreciate this fact.

Traditional quality grapes and some of the new ones have been extensively planted beginning about 1967. Cabernet Sauvignon now ranks third in red grape acreage while Chenin Blanc and Chardonnay rank second and third respectively in the whites. Conversely, Alicante Bouschet, formerly second, was eleventh in 1976, in the reds and Burger has become eleventh in the whites.

The following list of California varietal wines is complete except for a few oddities which are of no great interest and not widely available.

WHITE WINES

Rank by Acreage	Variety	Quality	Nearest European Equivalent
3	Chardonnay (or Pinot Chardonnay)	Excellent	Pouilly-Fuissé or Chablis
4	Johannisberg Riesling (or White Riesling)	Excellent	Dry Rhine Wines
6	Sauvignon Blanc (or Blanc Fumé)	Excellent	Superior Dry Graves, Pouilly-Fumé, Sauternes
2	Chenin Blanc (or White Pinot)	Very Good	Vouvray or Saumur
9	Gewürztraminer	Very Good	Alsatian
13	Pinot Blanc	Very Good	Lesser White Burgundy-Mâcon Blanc
14	Sylvaner	Good	Lesser Rhine Wines
7	Sémillon	Good	Dry Graves, Sauternes
1	French Colombard	Fair	Vin Blanc
8	Emerald Riesling	Fair	Lesser Moselle Wines
—	Fólle Blanche	Fair	Vin Blanc Supérieur
10	Gray Riesling	Fair	Vin Blanc
—	Green Hungarian	Fair	Vin Blanc
12	St. Emilion (or Ugni Blanc)	Fair	Vin Blanc

RED WINES

Rank by Acreage	Variety	Quality	Nearest European Equivalent
3	Cabernet Sauvignon	Excellent	Red Bordeaux
13	Merlot	Excellent	Red Bordeaux
14	Gamay Beaujolais	Very Good	Beaujolais
9	Pinot Noir	Very Good	Lesser Burgundy
4	Barbera	Good	Italian Barbera
2	Carignane	Good	Côtes du Rhône
7	Petite Sirah	Good	Côtes du Rhône
10	Gamay	Fair	Lesser Red Mâcon
1	Zinfandel	Fair	Vin Rouge Supérieur
17	Carnelian		
20	Centurion	yet to be proven	
8	Rubired		
6	Ruby Cabernet		

ROSÉ WINES

Rank by Acreage	Variety	Quality	Nearest European Equivalent
5	Grenache	Excellent	Tavel
10	Gamay	Fair	Vin Rose
—	Grignolino	Fair	Italian Grignolino

(Almost any red grape can also be used for Rosé Wine.)

59

The numbers in the left hand column represent the position of each grape in relation to total acreage planted. Red and white grapes are positioned separately. Missing numbers represent grapes not used as varietals.

All of these grape varieties will be found, described in much greater detail, in their proper alphabetical place in this volume; and additional details concerning them in the Appendix.

The California producers who have undertaken the difficult and often unprofitable and thankless job of turning out this country's best wines and marketing them under honest but relatively unknown varietal names, deserve well of all wine drinkers and of their country. They are, of course, not very numerous, but they are the elite of California, and most of them are in the North Coast counties. Most of them, and their plant managers and wine makers as well, have a genuine love of good wine and an inextinguishable enthusiasm for it, and rarely willingly deviate from the path that leads toward better quality.

California also produces a substantial amount of sparkling wine, entitled to the appellations California Champagne and California Sparkling Burgundy. However, in our laws there are no restrictions (like those that exist in France) as to the grape varieties that can be used and only a few, especially honorable, top producers conform voluntarily to what are the legal minimum standards abroad. The best California Champagnes are made, and well made, by the authentic French process, largely from the Chardonnay, Pinot Blanc, Chenin Blanc, Folle Blanche and they are extremely good sparkling wines, better, in the opinion of many experts, than those of New York State, and among the best produced in the world outside the Champagne District of France. But there is a large amount of California sparkling wine, most of it labeled Champagne, which is a long way from fine.

In the field of California Sherry and Port, the situation is even worse: hardly a half-dozen producers follow the classic and costly solera method which is normal practice in Spain, but what these producers make is remarkably good. Most California Sherry and Port is a sort of by-product of the raisin and table-grape industry, and the average age of California Sherry and Port, when it reaches the consumer is under eighteen months.

In addition to all the above, California produces about 70% of the vermouth (*see*) made in the U. S. and 95% of the flavored wines, also known as "other special natural wines," "pop" wines and "refreshment" wines most of which are sold under fanciful trade names and many of which have a wine base other than grapes.

A discriminating public of wine-drinkers (and their numbers are increasing daily) certainly help make of California one of the very good, possibly great, wine districts of the world. There is still a long road ahead and the good producers need all the encouragement they can get.

CALON-SÉGUR, Château — (Cal-awn Say-gour) — 3rd Classed Growth of St. Estèphe, Haut-Médoc. Produces some 20,000 cases a year of outstandingly good claret, full-bodied, yet soft and fine. One of the best 3rd Growths today.

CALUSO — (Cahl-loos-o) — Town north of Turin, in the Piedmont region of Italy, and the unusual, rather sweet white wine which is its specialty. This is

made from grapes of the Erbaluce variety, left to partially raisin (*see Passito*) indoors over the winter, and pressed and fermented in the spring.

CAMENSAC, Château — (Cam-ah-sack) — 5th Classed Growth of St. Laurent, Haut-Médoc. Some 3,500 cases a year.

CAMPANIA — (Cam-*pan*-ee-ah) — Italian district south of Rome, including Naples, Capri, Vesuvius, etc.; source, in Roman days, of what were then considered the world's best wines, as Falerno (*see*). Now produces some 90 million gallons of table wine, of varying quality, a year. The finer wines of Campania include Lachrima Christi, Capri, Gragnano, Ischia, Falerno.

CAMPARI — (Cam-*par*-ree) — Pink, bitter-sweet, popular Italian apéritif (though incidentally *not* a flavored wine), used in the Americano cocktail, and the Negroni, more often drunk simply with a twist of lemon peel and soda.

CAMPIDANO DI CAGLIARI — (Comp-pi-*don*-no dee *Cal*-yar-ee) — Important wine-producing district near the city of Cagliari, on the island of Sardinia. Pale white and red wines, rather high in alcohol.

CAÑA — (*Cahn*-ya) — Small, slender tumbler with a heavy bottom out of which Manzanilla is usually drunk in southern Spain. The *venencias,* or long-handled little dippers, used for taking samples of Manzanilla from the cask in Sanlúcar de Barrameda, are generally made of *caña*, or bamboo (instead of whalebone and silver, as in Jerez), and these probably gave the glass both its unusual shape, and its name.

CANADA — Canada's two main wine-growing areas are in British Columbia and the Niagara peninsula between Lake Erie and Lake Ontario. The wines from the latter district much resemble those of New York State, being made mostly from the same varieties of grape — Concord, Catawba, Niagara, Delaware, etc. However, experiments with some of the new French hybrids (*see*) have been very encouraging, as have plantings of such Vinifera vines as the Chardonnay and Pinot Noir. There has been much improvement in the overall quality of Canadian wines in recent years, and the efforts currently being made there seem to give promise of far better quality in the not-too-distant future. In British Columbia, many new wineries have been developed in recent years in the Okanagan Valley, and although the eastern grape varieties and the French hybrids predominate, there are many who feel that some Vinifera varieties could be planted there successfully. At any rate, it is interesting to note that the annual production of the Dominion, of all types of wine, is now in the neighborhood of 20 million gallons, well over double that of a decade ago.

CANARY — Canary Island wines, celebrated in England in Elizabethan times, have almost ceased to exist commercially, the vineyards having been repeatedly devastated by insects and fungus diseases brought in from overseas (*see* Oidium). A good deal of red and white wine is made (some 1½ million gallons a year), a little exported — mainly to South America, it is said — but the once-famed "Canary Sack" is a thing of the past.

CANELLI — (Kahn-*nell*-lee) — Important vineyard town not far from Asti, in Italian Piedmont. Famous above all for a special variety of Muscat grape to which it has given its name, Moscato di Canelli, and for the light, often sweet, very fragrant wine made from it, widely used in Asti Spumante (*see*) and also in Italian Vermouth.

CANON, Château — (Can-aw) One of the best of the Premiers Grands Crus Classés vineyards of St. Émilion, producing about 8,000 cases a year of sturdy, full-bodied, generally long-lived red wine.

CANON-FRONSAC — *See* CÔTES-CANON-FRONSAC.

CANTEMERLE, Château — (Cahnt-mairl) — 5th Classed Growth of Macau, Haut-Médoc. Produces some 7,500 cases a year of very good Claret, notable for its admirable balance and bouquet. One of the best of the 5th Growths today, yet not far, in character, from the finer red Graves.

CANTENAC — (Cahnt-nack) — Major wine-producing *commune* in the Médoc, adjoining Margaux on the south. Its Clarets, very similar to those of Margaux and of substantially equal quality, have been, since 1954, officially entitled to this name which was traditionally theirs. Leading vineyards include Château Brane-Cantenac, Palmer, Kirwan, d'Issan, Cantenac-Brown, Boyd-Cantenac, Prieuré-Lichine, etc.

CANTENAC-BROWN, Château — (Cahnt-nack Brown) — 3rd Classed Growth of Cantenac-Margaux, Médoc, which, unlike some others, still deserves its 1855 rating. Produces about 9,000 cases a year of honorable red wine which has the typical breed and finesse of its district.

CANTENAC-PRIEURÉ, Château — (Cahnt-nack Pre-oo-ray) — One of the 4th Classed Growths of Cantenac, in the Haut-Médoc, now known as Prieuré-Lichine (*see*).

CANZEM — (Kahnt-zem) — *See* Kanzem.

CAPRI — (Cop-pree) — Dry white wine, one of the best of southern Italy, produced on the island of Capri, near Naples. The quality of Capri varies considerably from one shipper to another and much of what is exported is by no means first rate.

CARAFE — Clear glass bottle or decanter for holding wine and serving it at table. Young, inexpensive, "open" wines are generally served *en carafe* in France, and a *vin de carafe* is any wine of this sort, so served. Carafes are also used for decanting (*see*) old red wines that have thrown sediment in bottle. A small carafe or decanter is sometimes called a *carafon*.

CARBONATED — As far as wine is concerned, one made sparkling, like "club soda" and most popular soft drinks, not by the ancient and costly *méthode champenoise*, nor even by the faster, cheaper, but passably good "bulk process" (*see*), but simply by the addition, under pressure, of CO_2 (carbon dioxide). Such wines tend to lose their sparkle rapidly, and have large bubbles very unlike the creamy *mousse* of good Champagne. According to American law they have to be labeled "carbonated" and according to French law "gazéifié": there are no good ones, certainly none worth what they cost, considering the high tax they pay.

CARBONNIEUX, Château — (Car-bahn-yuh) — Important vineyard of Léognan, in the Graves district of Bordeaux, producing some 7,500 cases of good red wine a year, and about 8,000 cases of even better white; it is the latter wine, pale, racy, dry, one of the half dozen best Graves, which has made the name famous. According to a possibly apocryphal story, it was once consumed in vast quantities at the teetotal court of the Sultan of Turkey and known there, on account of the Koran's strict prohibition of wine, as *Eau Minérale de Carbonnieux* or "Carbonnieux mineral water."

CAREMA — (Car-*eh*-ma) — Superior red wine made from the Nebbiolo grape (*see*) north of Turin, in northwestern Italy. Rarely exported.

CARIGNANE — (Car-reen-yan) — Productive red wine grape, widely planted in southern France, Spain, Algeria and California (where it is second only to the acreage planted in Zinfandel). While by no means of highest quality, it yields a quite satisfactory, ordinary table wine in many districts.

CARMENÈRE — (Car-men-air) — Secondary grape variety of the Bordeaux Country, probably related to the Cabernet.

CARMIGNANO — (Car-mean-*ya*-no) — Important wine-producing town in the Monte Albano district northwest of Florence; once famous in its own right, its wine now usually goes to market as Chianti.

CARMINE — New California red grape variety first planted commercially in 1977, a métis of Ruby Cabernet and Merlot, more productive and earlier ripening than Cabernet Sauvignon.

CARNELIAN — Métis of Carignane, Cabernet Sauvignon and Grenache first planted commercially in 1973. Produces red wine of relatively high acidity in California's Central Valley.

CARRASCAL — (Car-rahs-*cahl*) — One of the largest and best vineyards of the Sherry Country and after Macharnudo perhaps the most famous. It is planted on white, chalky, *albariza* soil northwest of the town of Jerez and produces some three or four thousand butts a year of fine, rather full-bodied wine.

CARRUADES — (Car-roo-odd) — Name formerly given to the secondary wine of Château Lafite (*see*) in the Haut-Médoc, generally those cuvées (usually from younger vines) considered not quite worthy of the famous Lafite label, being lighter, with less depth and less class; château-bottled, the wine was nevertheless very good, the equal of many third and fourth classed growths, and of some seconds. It was sold as Carruades de Château Lafite, was less expensive, and sooner ready to drink. Not made since 1967.

CASCADE — Very early ripening hybrid making agreeable red and rosé wines.

CASK — Wooden container, generally with round or oval heads, in which wine is matured and stored; oak is by all odds the best wood, chestnut (in Europe) and redwood (in California) being barely passable substitutes. Casks of widely varying shapes and sizes are used for different wines. The following list includes the most important:

64

District	Name	Liters	U.S. Gallons	Cases ‡
Chablis	Feuillette	136	36	15
California	Barrel	188	50	21
Champagne	Queue	216	57	24
Beaujolais	Pièce	216	57	24
Bordeaux	Barrique*	224	59	25
Burgundy	Pièce†	228	60	25
Sherry	Butt	500	132	55
Port	Pipe	522.5	138	58
Rhine	Halbstück	600	158	67
Moselle	Fuder	960	253	107

* A *Tonneau,* in Bordeaux, is the equivalent of 4 Barriques, but there is no standard cask of this size. In today's commerce a tonneau is considered to be 100 cases
† A *Queue,* in Burgundy, is the equivalent of 2 Pièces.
‡ Approximate cases of locally used bottles.

CASSE — (Cass) — Disease to which wines are subject, the symptoms of which are a persistent cloudiness and an off taste. The cause is usually an excess of metallic salts, and even brief contact with copper or iron can bring about *casse* in an otherwise sound wine. There are a number of remedies, but none effective once the wine is bottled.

CASSIS — (Cas-seece) — Picturesque little fishing village on the Mediterranean some 20 miles east of Marseille; its dry white wine, pleasant, made principally from the Ugni Blanc grape, pale gold, traditionally the wine to drink with bouillabaisse. Some 20,000 cases a year are produced, plus a certain amount of less good red and quite good *rosé* also entitled to the name.

ALSO, a syrup made from black currants, (*cassis,* in French), as deep purple in color and as sweet as blackberry jam, though generally with 10-16% of alcohol. Widely used to sweeten and flavor mixed apéritifs, including dry vermouth and white wine, it is a Burgundian specialty and the best of it is produced in Dijon. There is also a popular apéritif made with cassis syrup and white wine, known as a Kir. It is named for Canon Kir, the one-time mayor of Dijon, whose favorite apéritif it was.

CASTEGGIO — (Cahs-*tedg*-jo) — Italian wine-producing town, in southern Lombardy, center of a small, hilly district overlooking the Po Valley, in which the Pinot Noir and Pinot Blanc, transplanted from France, have been successfully cultivated for many decades. Much of the wine from these (and a good deal of the pale, light, local Moscato wine as well) is shipped to Piedmont and made into *Spumante* (*see*), or sparkling wine. A little of it, surprisingly good, is bottled as still wine in Casteggio, and some of this is even exported, notably under the brand name "Frecciarossa," which means "Red Arrow" in Italian.

CASTELL — (Cahz-tell) — Wine-producing town on the Main River near Würzburg, in Franconia. Its wine is of course shipped in the traditional *Bocksbeutel,* and its best vineyard is the Schlossberg.

CASTELLI DI JESI — (Cahs-*stel*-lee dee *Yay*-zee) — Wine district in east-central Italy, in the foothills of the Apennines some twenty miles from the Adriatic port of Ancona, which produces one of the lightest, most popular and best white table wines of Italy. This is made from the Verdicchio grape (*see*) in some half-dozen villages of which Cupramontana is the most important; it is usually exported in a special, slender, amphora-like bottle, and often sold simply as "Verdicchio." Dry, pale, with a freshness and breed rare in white wines from so far south, it deserves its international acceptance and increasing fame.

CASTELLI ROMANI — (Cahs-*stel*-lee Ro-*mahn*-nee) — The popular, common, inexpensive, and often quite agreeable table wine of Rome, produced round the villages of the Alban Hills, southeast of the city, and not far from Anzio. The best of this (for there are many sorts) is a dry white wine with an almost amber tinge, usually served in carafe and drunk young, rather coarse and lacking in distinction but by no means unpleasant with good Roman food. It comes principally from the villages of Frascati (*see*), Marino, Grottaferrata, Genzano, Albano, Ariccia, Rocca di Papa, Velletri, etc.

CATALONIA — (Spanish, Cataluña — Cat-ah-*loon*-ya) — Large region of northeastern Spain, bounded on the north by France and on the east by the Mediterranean, generally considered to comprise the provinces in which Catalan is spoken: Barcelona, Gerona, Lerida, Tarragona. These produce a remarkably diverse collection of wines, ranging all the way from the sweet, heavy Priorato (which was formerly known as "Tarragona Port") to the light, pale, white wines of the Panadés (which, when made to sparkle by the Champagne process, were formerly known as "Spanish Champagne"). There are many good, though never great, table wines as well, all relatively inexpensive. *See* Tarragona, Priorato, Alella.

CATAWBA — (Ca-*taw*-ba) — Native American grape of somewhat uncertain origin, believed to be an accidental hybrid of wild, indigenous varieties (it is of the species *labrusca*) probably first found growing in the woods along the Catawba River, in the Carolinas. In any case, in the 1820s, it was being cultivated in Montgomery County, Maryland, and in the District of Columbia, where it found a champion in the person of a Major John Adlum, who once hopefully stated that, "in bringing this grape into public notice, I have rendered my country a greater service than I could have done had I paid off the national debt" (then $84,000,000). Time has perhaps proved him wrong, but for the better part of a century the Catawba was the leading wine grape of America; it was the basis of Nicholas Longworth's famous sparkling wine, produced along the banks of the Ohio, near Cincinnati; it is still widely grown, both in Ohio and in the Finger Lakes district of New York State. It is a light red grape, highly productive, giving a white wine with a pronounced native or "foxy" flavor. Much of this is used in New York State Champagne, and is found good by those who do not object to its assertive taste; some passable non-sparkling Catawbas have been made, generally quite tart but with the same basic fault. There also exists an amber horror, a 16% or 18% fortified Catawba, foxy and sweet, of which it would be impossible to say anything favorable. Few people, in any case, today, would agree with what Longfellow wrote when he received a gift of Sparkling Catawba from Nicholas Longworth:

Very good in its way
Is the Verzenay,
Or the Sillery, soft and creamy;
But Catawba wine
Has a taste more divine,
More dulcet, delicious, and dreamy.

CAUDALIE — (Code-ah-lee) — French technical term for measure of persistence of aromatic flavors after tasting; one caudalie = one second of persistence.

CAVE — (Cah-v) — The French word for cellar. This can mean, as in English, a storage space underground, or simply a collection of bottles. Commercially, it is just as meaningless as in English — a term to be regarded as suspect on a wine label unless a good deal of sound information follows it directly. Thus *"mis en bouteille dans nos caves"* does NOT mean estate-bottled; *"Les Caves de Chablis"* can be just a brand; a *caviste,* however, is unequivocally a "cellar-man."

CELLAR — Storage space for wine and, by inference, the wine it contains; traditionally, but by no means necessarily, below ground. There are few underground cellars in the Bordeaux Country, few in California, almost none in Spain. Whether underground or no, a wine cellar should be cool, with as even a temperature as possible throughout the year, free from vibration, and dark. A somewhat damp cellar is likely to be cooler than one absolutely dry; some ventilation is essential. The ideal cellar temperature is between 55° and 60°, with 45° and 70° as perhaps permissible extremes; within these limits, the cooler the cellar, the more slowly wines will develop and the longer they will live.

Apart from one's current requirements, the wines that should be laid away in a cellar (the bottle horizontal, of course, so that the wine covers the cork) are those most likely to increase in value and improve with age; many wines (*see* Ageing) do neither. A carefully kept record, or cellar-book, will be found a most useful and helpful guide: it should show at least, for each wine, where purchased, when purchased, price, when served, to whom, with what food, and tasting notes.

CENTURION — Métis of Carignane, Cabernet Sauvignon and Grenache first planted commercially in California's Central Valley in 1974. Produces red wine with darker and fuller flavor than Carnelian (*see*).

CÉPAGE — (Say-pahj) — Variety of grape vine. Thus one may say that the Pinot Noir and Chardonnay are the leading *cépages* of Burgundy. *Cep* means an individual vine or vine-stock.

CÉRONS — (Say-raw) — Village in the Bordeaux Country, once officially part of Graves, adjoining Barsac and the Sauternes district. Its golden, rather sweet

67

wines, fairly high in alcohol but with a good deal of fruit, bouquet and breed, are more like Sauternes than Graves. The official Cérons district includes as well the townships of Illats and Podensac.

CHABLAIS — (Shab-lay) — Wine-producing district in the Canton of Vaud, in southern Switzerland. The vineyards, planted to the Fendant or Chasselas grape, extend from Villeneuve, at the eastern tip of Lake Geneva, southeast along the upper Rhône Valley. The wines are all white, fairly full-bodied, and some of them, as Yvorne and Aigle, rank among the best Swiss wines.

CHABLIS — (Shab-lee) — Little town southeast of Paris, in the *département* of Yonne, and the surrounding district, which produces some of the most famous of all white Burgundies (*see* also the Appendix, Page 440). Chablis may be made only from the Chardonnay grape, and the zone entitled to the name is strictly delimited, comprising only certain areas of chalky soil in a total of 20 small *communes*. The average annual production, including Chablis Grand Cru and Chablis Premier Cru, is roughly 1,240,000 gallons; in addition, some 170,000 gallons of ''Petit Chablis'' are made, also from the Chardonnay, from less fine vineyards in the same 20 *communes*. Petit Chablis is a lighter wine, of less distinction and class, shorter lived and soon ready — much of it is drunk up as carafe wine in Paris restaurants when less than a year old. The finest Chablis, that called Grand Cru, must come from a single slope with 125 acres of vines consisting of seven tiny vineyards: Vaudésir, Les Clos, Grenouilles, Valmur, Blanchots, Preuses, Bougros (*see,* however, Moutonne); such wine generally carries the vineyard name in addition to the words ''Grand Cru''; a good deal of it is estate-bottled, and only some 40,000 cases are produced; crop failures on account of frost are frequent. Chablis Premier Cru, too, quite often carries a vineyard name, and in good years is a wine of almost equal quality; the 1st Growth vineyards (*Climats Classés Premiers Crus*) cover some 860 acres and include: Montée de Tonnerre, Monts-de-Milieu, Vaulorent, Vaucoupin, Fourchaume, Côte-de-Léchet, Vaillons, Mont-

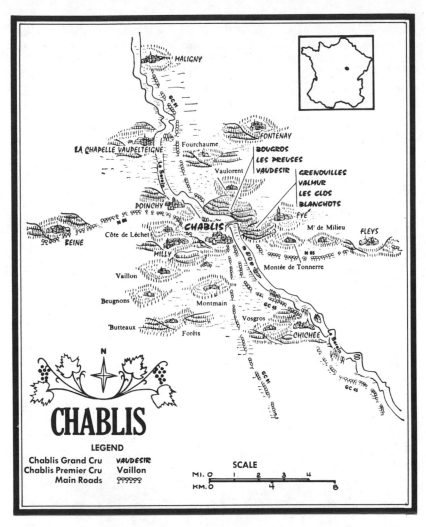

mains, and some dozen others. Wines labeled simply Chablis, without vineyard name or designation as to growth (*cru*), may be assumed to be from
1,600 acres of less good vineyards, although they are of a higher class than
Petit Chablis. The quality of Chablis varies enormously from one vintage to
another, that of poor years being often disagreeably thin and tart. At its best, it
is a dry, almost austere wine, pale straw in color (sometimes with a hint of
green), remarkably clean on the palate, with a delicate, fleeting bouquet, and a
characteristic flavor often described as "flinty." In other countries the name is
loosely used and is largely meaningless; in the United States (as formerly in

69

Spain, Chile, etc) any white table wine, wherever made and of whatever grapes, may call itself "Chablis" — or even, it is shameful to report, "pink Chablis" (actually a rosé). Those interested in finding a California counterpart of this fine French wine should look for bottles labeled "Chardonnay," or "Pinot Chardonnay."

CHAI — (Shay) — Building used for wine storage in France, generally above ground, as distinguished from a *cave,* or true cellar. Commercially, the two terms are largely interchangeable.

CHAINTRÉ — (Shen-tray) — One of four townships in Burgundy producing white wines entitled to the name Pouilly-Fuissé (*see*).

CHALON — (Sha-law) — *See* Côte Chalonnaise.

CHAMBERTIN — (Shawm-bair-tan) — Remarkable and famous vineyard of the Burgundian Côte d'Or, consisting of 32 acres of Pinot Noir vines, and producing one of the very greatest red wines of the world. One directly adjoining vineyard, the 37-acre Clos de Bèze (*see*), is also entitled to the name, although its wines are more often sold as Chambertin-Clos de Bèze. The total production of both *climats* together averages 8,800 cases, and an authentic Chambertin of a good vintage is invariably expensive. It may be added that it is worth what it costs, for there is no better red Burgundy and a few as good — powerful, long-lived, with astonishing class and breed, it is a "noble" wine, in the true sense of the word. The vineyard has been celebrated since about the year 600 A.D., and its reputation has never waned: its wine was the favorite of Napoleon, and of it Alexandre Dumas wrote that "nothing makes the future look so rosy as to contemplate it through a glass of Chambertin." Today the 69 acres are divided among numerous growers, a majority of whom estate-bottle. Many other nearby vineyards, of excellent but somewhat less exalted class, produce wines that carry the name Chambertin, in various specific combined forms, rigidly controlled by the French government. Thus the entire *commune* is now known as Gevrey-Chambertin (*see*), and the less good wines of the *commune* are marketed under this regional name; of a

70

higher grade are those that carry the appellation Gevrey-Chambertin, plus a vineyard name; while the plots closest to Chambertin itself, both geographically and in quality, are classified as Grands Crus (great growths) and each has a special name of its own: Latricières-Chambertin, Mazoyères-Chambertin, Charmes-Chambertin, Mazis-Chambertin, Griotte-Chambertin, Ruchottes-Chambertin and Chapelle-Chambertin (*see* each of these, in its proper alphabetical place, in this encyclopedia).

For Map, *see* GEVREY.

CHAMBÉRY — (Sham-bay-ree) — Small city in the French *département* of Savoie, east of Lyon, known especially for its pale, light, dry vermouth, which many wine experts consider one of the best apéritifs.

CHAMBOLLE-MUSIGNY — (Shahm-boll Moos-een-ye) — Celebrated wine-producing township of the Côte d'Or which, like many another Burgundian

Chambolle-Musigny

village, has added the name of its finest vineyard (Musigny) to its own original village name (Chambolle). There are some 420 acres under vines, all, except for a tiny portion of Musigny (*see*) producing red wines exclusively, and some of the most charming, delicate and fragrant of all Burgundy. Musigny and Bonnes Mares (*see*), the two best, are sold under these names without mention of Chambolle; the next highest in quality, ranked as Premiers Crus and often truly admirable, go to market as Chambolle-Musigny plus a vineyard name, as Les Amoureuses, Les Charmes, etc.; what is labeled simply Chambolle-Musigny comes last of all, is often rather light, but generally makes up in finesse for what it may lack in body.

CHAMBOURCIN — Mid-season hybrid making good quality red wine.

CHAMBRER — (French; Shahm-bray) — To warm a red wine, from the temperature of the cellar to that of the dining-room. The only proper way to do this is to bring the bottle to the dining room an hour or more ahead of time, and let it stand. No wine worth drinking should be set near an open fire or plunged into hot water — common practices, alas, both of them. *See* Serving, Temperature.

CHAMPAGNE — (Sham-pain) — Strictly speaking, Champagne means French Champagne: a specific wine made by a specific process, from only certain varieties of grape, in a legally delimited part of France. The Champagne Country lies east of Paris, and consists principally of the *département* of the Marne (plus portions of the Aube, and Aisne); the total area under vines (some 50,000 acres) is less than 1% of the vineyard land of France, and far less than 1% of French wine is therefore Champagne. The better vineyards are planted along a series of chalky hillsides south of the old cathedral city of Reims, and on slopes overlooking the Marne Valley nearby, north and south of Épernay. There are three main districts that produce superior wine: (1) the *Montagne de*

Reims

VILLEDOMMANGE
SACY
MONTAGNE DE REIMS

MAILLY
VERZENAY
VERZY

VALLÉE DE LA MARNE

HAUTVILLERS
BOUZY
AMBONNAY

AY
MAREUIL-SUR-AY

Epernay

CRAMANT
AVIZE
OGER
LE MESNIL

COTE DES BLANCS

VERTUS

Drawn by W. Lembeck

N

CHAMPAGNE

LEGEND
Grand Cru   ● MAILLY
Premier Cru   ● OGER

SCALE
MI.   0   2   4
KM.   0   4   8

REIMS
CHATEAU THIERRY
EPERNAY
CHALONS-S-MARNE

Delimited Regions of Champagne

Reims, yielding, from the Pinot Noir grape, its "wines of the Mountain," notable for their body and power; (2) the *Vallée de la Marne,* just north of Épernay, producing, also from the Pinot Noir, its "wines of the River," particularly soft and round; and (3) the *Côte des Blancs,* which gives, almost entirely from the Chardonnay grape, its *blanc de blancs,* outstanding in delicacy and finesse. Within these three districts, the various *communes* have been officially ranked and rated according to the average of excellence of the wines they yield. Thus Verzenay, Mailly, Bouzy, Ambonnay (all on the *Montagne de Reims*), Ay (in the *Vallée de la Marne*) and Avize and Cramant (on the *Côte des Blancs*) are rated 100%, or *"hors classe."* Only 13 of the 250 vineyards are rated 100% but many other *communes* (Mareuil-sur-Ay, Dizy-Magenta, Hautvillers, Le Mesnil, etc., etc.) are very nearly as good and rate 90-98% or 80-89%. Most Champagnes are blends of wines from various *communes* in all three districts, and the proportions often vary according to the individual character of each vintage. Champagne made exclusively from vineyards rated 100% may legally be called "Grand Cru" and those from vineyards 90% or higher "Premier Cru."

The Champagne vineyards are the northernmost of France and, as might be expected, there is a wide variation, from one year to another, in the quality of the wine they yield. The more expensive and best French Champagnes carry a vintage, which means that they were made *in large part* from wines produced in a single, particularly favorable year. Non-vintage Champagnes are almost invariably blends of less good *plus* good years, for alone, the former would hardly be salable.

However, the matter of vintage years on labels is notoriously one difficult to regulate and control. The method set up for Champagne is both practical and effective, allowing the producer some latitude and discretion while protecting the public against large-scale fraud. Briefly, no producer may sell, as the wine of a given vintage, over 80 per cent of his actual production for that year: in other words, what is sold as 1966 Champagne cannot exceed four-fifths of what was produced in that particular year.

At the same time, a producer who finds, for example, that his 1969, unblended, is too heavy and too alcoholic (as was often the case), may, if he sees fit, blend in some 1968 or 1970 and still call his wine "1969." But by doing so he will not increase, by as much as a single bottle, what he can legally sell as 1969.

In addition, Vintage Champagnes must be submitted to an interprofessional committee of experts, for tasting and approval, before they are shipped, and no Champagne may be shipped, carrying a vintage, until it is three years old.

Since virtually all Champagnes are blends, Champagne is one of the very few wines (perhaps the *only* French wine) on which a brand is more important than a vineyard or district name. The larger and better-known French producers are listed below. However, a small amount of interesting and often excellent Champagne is sold under the name of its *commune* of origin, as Cramant, Avize, Le Mesnil, Ay, Mailly, etc. This is made, generally, by small producers or cooperative cellars and is unblended.

The shippers below are listed alphabetically and represent the 25 houses (out of a total of 163) which lead in exports. Among them are the famous brands which have made the reputation of Champagne throughout the world, plus a few names not known at all to the general public since they ship under an assortment of labels:

Ayala	Moët et Chandon
Bollinger	Mumm
Canard Duchêne	Perrier Jouet
Charbaut	Piper Heidsieck
Charles Heidsieck	Pol Roger
Deutz et Geldermann	Pommery
De Venoge	Ruinart
Heidsieck Monopole	S. A. M. E.
Krug	Taittinger
Lanson	Trouillard
Louis Roederer	Veuve Clicquot
Marne et Champagne	Veuve Laurent Perrier
Mercier	

The Pinot Noir (and to a much lesser extent the Pinot Meunier) and the Chardonnay are the grape varieties cultivated to the virtual exclusion of all others; the first two of these, of course, are black grapes, but pressed as soon as picked they give white wine (or, in rare instances, a pink or *rosé*).

The still wines of the Champagne Country (*see Champagne Nature*) are made sparkling by a special, laborious and expensive process, imitated the world over but known the world over as the *méthode champenoise,* or Champagne Process. A carefully predetermined amount of sugar is added (about 3⅓ oz. per gallon to produce a pressure of six atmospheres), plus yeast, to the still wine, to bring about a second fermentation; the wine is then bottled and corked or sealed immediately, and the bottles are stacked away. The second fermentation takes place *in bottle,* over a period of months or years, and gives of course a small amount of additional alcohol, plus CO_2, or carbon dioxide; this, unable to escape, remains dissolved, under pressure, in the wine. But sediment is also formed in the wine during fermentation, and this must be got rid of; in order to accomplish this, without sacrificing the wine's sparkle, the bottles are placed individually, neck down, in inclined perforated racks, or "pulpits," then shaken and turned daily, by hand, over a period of months. The sediment finally slides down against the cork, and is then ejected, by a process known as "disgorging." At this point, all Champagnes (and all sparkling wines made by the Champagne process) are absolutely bone dry; before the bottle is finally recorked, therefore, it receives what is known as its *dosage* — generally a sugar syrup with an old wine base, sometimes plus a little brandy. It is this *dosage* and only this which determines the dryness or sweetness of the finished wine. In theory, but rarely in practice, the various designations of dryness are supposed to indicate the precise degree of *dosage,* as *Brut,* up to 1½%; *Extra Dry,* up to 3%; *Dry,* or *Sec,* up to 4% or more. *Nature* is supposed to mean, but rarely does, a Champagne that has received no *dosage* at all. Once "dosed" and given its final, wired-down cork, Champagne is ready to market; despite much nonsense that has been written to the contrary, Champagne improves in bottle, *after* disgorging, hardly at all; most

75

very old Champagnes found to be in good condition — and they can be superb — have been aged in the original cellars *before* disgorging, with the sediment still in the bottle. French law requires non-vintage champagne to have one year minimum bottle age and vintage champagne can not be shipped until at least three years after the crop. The better champagnes all exceed these minimums.

A great many countries have finally recognized, by treaty or trade agreement, that Champagne is an appellation of origin, and belongs to its French originators; they have adopted other names for their own sparkling wines, as *Sekt*, in Germany, *Spumante*, in Italy, and even *Xampán*, in Catalonia. However, in the United States, any sparkling wine, even red wine, may be called Champagne provided, (1) it is made by the same bottle-fermented process as French Champagne, and, (2) that it bears on its label in easy-to-read type its geographical origin, as "California," "American," "New York State," etc. There are no legal restrictions as to the grape varieties that may be used, nor the areas of production, and the less expensive domestic Champagnes are perhaps comparable to French *vins mousseux* (*see*) but certainly not to French Champagne. On the other hand, a number of reputable producers in California and in the Finger Lakes district of New York State are attempting to produce and indeed producing Champagnes that are comparable in quality to all but the best French. Such producers, especially in California, are tending to use a large proportion of Chardonnay or other superior grapes, and the increasing popularity of their wines is the best proof of this improved quality.

Sparkling wines can, of course, be made in a variety of other, less expensive ways. *See* Bulk Process, Carbonated Wine, etc.

CHAMPAGNE NATURE — (Shahm-pain Nah-tuhr) — In general usage, the still white or red wine of the Champagne Country: the white, formerly a favorite carafe wine in Paris restaurants, is not unlike an especially fresh, light Chablis, the red, like an extremely delicate Burgundy. The official name is now *"Coteaux Champenois"* (*see*). Very little is exported.

CHAMPIGNY — (Shahm-peen-yee) — Village southeast of Saumur in the Loire Valley; its light, tender, fragrant red wine, somewhat resembling Chinon, made from the Cabernet Franc grape, and properly considered the best red wine of Anjou. It is often listed and sold as Saumur-Champigny, and is said to have been the favorite wine of Clemenceau.

CHANCELLOR — Early mid-season heavy producing hybrid making dark, full-bodied solid red wine.

CHANTEPLEURE — (Shahnt-plurr) — Rather fanciful name given to the spigot of a wine-barrel, generally made of box-wood, and inclined to squeak ("sing") when opened; thus it "sings" (*chante*) and "weeps" (*pleure*) as the wine runs out. The wine confraternity of Vouvray, one of the many in France, is known as the Confrerie de la Chantepleure. In other parts of France the same word is often used to designate a glass pipette, or "thief," used to take a sample of wine out of the bung hole of a barrel.

CHANTURGUES — (Shahn-teerg) — Almost mythical red wine, produced (in infinitesimal quantities) not far from Clermont-Ferrand, near the headwaters of the Loire, in what was once the old province of Auvergne. Although loyally described by Auvergnats the world over as the world's best, it is in truth a small, pleasant Gamay, a hard-to-find *vin de pays*.

CHAPEAU — (Shap-O) — Literally "hat" in French, the solid parts of grapes skins, pips, stems, etc. which rise to the top of the must during red wine fermentation; it is broken frequently to distribute the yeasts, allow air to enter and promote color extraction from the skins.

CHAPELLE-CHAMBERTIN — (Sha-pell Shahm-bair-tan) — Excellent Burgundian vineyard comprising 13 acres directly adjoining the Clos de Bèze (*see*), and producing less than a thousand cases a year of red wine of admirable quality. *See* Chambertin.

CHAPITRE — (Sha-peet-truh) — French for chapter-house; name often given in France to a vineyard adjoining, and. presumably or formerly connected with, an important church. *See* Clos du Chapitre.

CHAPTALIZATION — (Shap-tally-zah-see-aw) — The special process, widely decried but often helpful and in some instances necessary in wine-making, of adding sugar to the must, or grape juice, before fermentation. It takes its name from, and was presumably invented by, Chaptal, Napoleon's Minister of Agriculture (although honey, for precisely the same reason, has been used in wine-making for centuries). It is properly resorted to in cooler countries and in poor years when the grapes do not have enough natural sugar of their own to produce an acceptable wine; it can be, and often is, abused. Its purpose is not to make a sweet wine, but one with a proper minimum alcoholic content; *nor does it involve adding water as well as sugar to the must*. It is authorized rarely, and only in very poor years, in Bordeaux; always, but within very strict limits, in Burgundy; not at all in California, where it is illegal and considered unnecessary. The cheaper German wines at present (never those marked "Kabinett" or "Spätlese") and many in New York State and Ohio are made with the addition of sugar *and* water; this not only brings the alcoholic content up to par, but also reduces the wine's final total acidity, which might otherwise be excessive. It also, of course (as the producers are quite aware), greatly increases the amount of wine that can be made from a given tonnage of grapes. Truly superior wines are never so made. The use of water is completely forbidden in Germany after 1979.

CHARACTER — Wine tasters' term. A wine with character is one, whether passable or good or outstanding, that has definite and unmistakable qualities, whether due to its geographical origin, its grape variety, or something else. A wine without character is dull and uninteresting.

CHARBONO — (Shar-bo-no) — Wine grape, of unknown origin, which produces a rather agreeable, somewhat rough, full-bodied red wine in California, especially in the Napa Valley.

CHARDONNAY — (Shar-doe-nay) — One of the very finest of all white wine grapes, rivaled only by the true Riesling. In France it produces all of the great white Burgundies, including Chablis, Montrachet, Pouilly-Fuissé, etc., and it is the white grape of the Champagne Country. In California, in spite of its ex-

77

tremely small yield per acre, it has been widely planted; ranking third among the whites; its wine is perhaps the best white table wine made in the United States, and comes generally from the North Coast Counties (*see*). Although often called the "Pinot Chardonnay," not only in America but in French statutes, it is not, in the opinion of the most competent botanists and ampelographers, a true Pinot at all, nor related to the Pinot Noir, Pinot Blanc, etc.

ALSO, a small village in the Mâconnais district of France.

CHARENTE — (Shar-ont) — District north of Bordeaux producing much thin and acid wine with little alcohol. This is the wine from which all Cognac is distilled, however not all is made into Cognac; some is consumed as wine and most of the excess is exported, primarily to Germany, for distillation into brandy.

CHARLEMAGNE — (In French, Sharl-main) — King of the Franks, and Emperor (742-814 A.D.). Said to have been responsible for the planting of the first vines around what is now Schloss Johannisberg (after observing, from his palace at Ingelheim, across the Rhine, that snow melted on this slope earlier than elsewhere); he seems also to have had a vineyard at Aloxe-Corton (*see*) in Burgundy, with which his name is still associated — Corton-Charlemagne; in the year 775 he conveyed a portion of this domain to the Abbey of Saulieu.

Until quite recently there existed a white Burgundy wine called simply "Charlemagne," made partly from the inferior Aligoté grape (*see*), as distinguished from Corton-Charlemagne, made exclusively from the Chardonnay. These Aligoté vines have now been pulled out, and the difference between the two appellations has ceased to exist; a "Charlemagne" is now a Corton-Charlemagne.

CHARMAT PROCESS — (Shar-mah) — Another name for the Bulk Process (*see*), used in the making of sparkling wines.

CHARMES — (Sharm) — Burgundian vineyard name, designating certain specific plots in the *communes* of Meursault (*see*), Chambolle-Musigny (*see*) and Gevrey-Chambertin.

CHARMES-CHAMBERTIN — (Sharm Shawm-bair-tan) — Officially a *Grand Cru* it consists of 31 acres, separated from Chambertin itself only by a narrow vineyard road; it produces admirable red wines, only slightly inferior in body and distinction to those of its incomparable neighbor to the west. Adjoining it to the south is Mazoyères-Chambertin whose wines may also be legally labeled Charmes-Chambertin and usually are.

CHARNU — (Shar-noo) — French, for rich in substance, meaty, full bodied wine.

CHARPENTÉ — (Shar-pahn-tay) — French term for well balanced wine, high in alcohol and flavor.

CHASSAGNE-MONTRACHET — (Shass-anya Mon-rasch-shay) — Important wine-producing township, near the southern end of the Côte d'Or, in Burgundy. There are some 900 acres of vineyard, and the average annual production is in the neighborhood of 100,000 cases, 40% of it white wine of

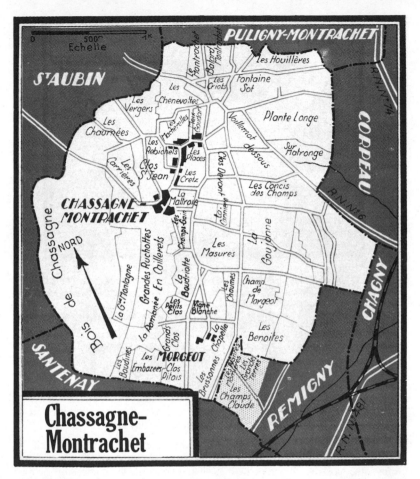

Chassagne-Montrachet

extremely high quality, the balance red, often very good but rarely of absolutely top class. Within the communal limits of Chassagne lie major portions of Montrachet and Bâtard-Montrachet, as well as Criots-Bâtard-Montrachet (*see*) in its entirety — three of the greatest dry white-wine vineyards of France; wines from these, however, do not carry mention of Chassagne-Montrachet on their labels, and are sold simply under the vineyard name alone. However, of almost equal excellence, and magnificent white wines by any standards, are Chassagne-Montrachet Les Ruchottes, Caillerets, Chenevottes, Morgeot, and a few others, while white wines labeled simply Chassagne-Montrachet are almost always good and sometimes quite remarkable. Many of the lesser red Chassagnes have an easily recognizable and not unpleasant earthy taste, or *goût de terroir;* the finer ones are marketed as Chassagne-Montrachet plus a vineyard name, as Clos St. Jean, La Boudriotte,

79

La Maltroie, Morgeot, etc., and there are few better values on the market, in the way of red Burgundies, than these. *See* Montrachet.

CHASSELAS — (Shahss-la) — Productive and hardy white grape (occasionally pink) of which many sub-varieties exist. Several of these are justly famous as table grapes; none can be considered a truly superior wine grape, since, except in extremely cool regions, their wines have a tendency to be low in acid, flat, very short-lived. Nevertheless, in Switzerland, where it is known as the Fendant, the Chasselas is by all odds the leading wine grape, as it is in Markgräflerland, in southern Baden (*see*), where it is known as the Gutedel. It is also widely cultivated round Pouilly-sur-Loire (*see*) and, as a mass production grape, in Alsace. In California it has never yielded any wine of consequence or interest, but has sometimes been confused with the Palomino.

CHASSE-SPLEEN, Château — (Shass Spleen) — Superior vineyard and its red wine, of Moulis, in the Haut-Médoc. Originally rated as a *Cru Bourgeois Supérieur*, it has enjoyed the rather rare rank of *Cru Exceptionnel* since 1932, and its wine is better than many of the lesser classed growths. Some 12,000 cases a year.

CHÂTEAU — (Shot-toe) — As far as this wine encyclopedia is concerned, and properly, as in France, a house attached, both by proximity and ownership, to a specific vineyard. Many "châteaux," especially in the less renowned sections of the Bordeaux Country, are simply country homes or small farmhouses, whose owners cultivate their own vines and make their own wine. According to French law, the word "château" may not appear on a label, as part of the name of a wine, unless a *bona fide* vineyard exists and has produced it and has some traditional right to the name.

Of several hundred such châteaux, or vineyard properties, listed in this volume, almost all will be found alphabetically listed under their own name (as Château Lafite under "L," Château d'Yquem under "Y," etc.). The exceptions, below, are those where the word "château" forms an integral part of the name and does not refer to an individual vineyard property.

CHÂTEAU-BOTTLED — A wine bottled on the property which produced it, by the vineyard owner, especially in the Bordeaux Country (the equivalent in most other areas is "estate-bottled"). Château-bottling is practiced by the vast majority of the owners of better vineyards in Bordeaux, in all except the poorest years, and often even then. It is a definite guarantee of authenticity, to a much lesser extent of quality. Wines château-bottled are invariably so marked, usually on a branded cork but in any case on the label. *"Mise du Château"* and *"Mis en bouteilles au Château"* are the terms customarily used.

CHÂTEAU-CHALON — (Shot-toe Shah-law) — Unusual and rare white wine of the Jura, not the product of a château, but of a tiny, hilltop village that bears this name. Among French wines it is an exception to all rules, much closer in character to an unfortified Sherry or Montilla from southern Spain than to any other wine from French vineyards. Its grape variety is the Savagnin, said to be a sort of Traminer, although Château-Chalon has no resemblance to any other Traminer in bouquet or flavor, even when young. It is the only French wine (except Fitou —*see*) which, legally, has to be stored in cask for a specified period (in this instance, six years) before bottling, and it has its own special bottle, the *clavelin* (*see*). Actually, it is a sort of unique, accidental French version of Sherry, and it matures in casks that are not kept full, under a layer of *flor* yeast, just as Fino Sherry and Montilla do in Spain. Higher in acid than these and lower in alcohol (the legal minimum is 12%), it is much less good, and its fame is based more on its uniqueness than on its quality.

CHÂTEAU GRILLET — (Shot-toe Gree-yay) — Remarkable tiny vineyard (5 acres — its production is the smallest of any French wine having its own *Appellation Contrôlée*) on the west bank of the Rhône River south of Lyon. It is the property of the Gachet family, and like Condrieu nearby, its grape is the Vionnier (or Viognier). The total output is generally under 600 cases a year, and the wine is as unusual as it is rare: golden, dry, full-bodied, rather high in alcohol, with a unique, spicy bouquet and flavor.

CHÂTEAUNEUF-DU-PAPE — (Shot-toe-nuff dew Pop) — Celebrated sturdy wine of the Rhône Valley, from the village of this name, some dozen miles north of the old papal city of Avignon, in southern France. The *"château neuf"* (new castle), now a ruin, was the summer home of the Avignon Popes in the 14th century; the vineyards are planted on an extraordinary, high, stony tableland, dominating the Rhône and the surrounding fertile plain; the soil consists of the coarsest sort of gravel and small boulders on which it seems impossible that vines should grow. As a district, Châteauneuf-du-Pape is the most important of the Rhône, some four miles by five in extent, and its annual production (99% red, about 1% white) is in the neighborhood of two million gallons. About a dozen different grape varieties are grown and most of the wine contains some admixture of most if not all of these; more or less in the order of their importance, they are: Syrah, Grenache, Cinsault, Mourvèdre, Clairette, Picpoul, Terret Noir, Counoise, Roussanne, Muscardin, Vaccarèse, Picardan and Bourboulenc. The wine is deep crimson in color, full-bodied, generous, fairly high in alcohol (usually 13-14%); it is softer and matures more quickly than Hermitage and Côte-Rôtie, being quite drinkable when about three years old and generally (for there are exceptions) at its best between the ages of five and ten. The best of it is estate-bottled, and the finer vineyards include the Domaine de Mont-Redon, Cabrières-les-Silex, La Solitude, Château Fortia, Château de la Nerthe, Château des Fines Roches, Château Rayas, Château de Vaudieu, etc.; the district produces as well, as might be expected, a great deal of sound but more ordinary wine.

For Map, *see* RHONE.

CHÂTILLON-EN-DIOIS — (Shot-tee-yaw on Dee-wah) — Red, *rosé* and white wines produced along the eastern edge of the Rhône Valley, near the little town of Die (*see*). Unlike Clairette de Die (*see*) they are not sparkling. The amount produced is very small, and little if any is likely to be exported. Became an Appellation Contrôlée in 1975.

CHAVIGNOL — (Shahv-een-yawl) — One of the better *communes* of the district of Sancerre (*see*) in the upper Loire Valley of France. Also famous for its small, round cheeses, made of goat's milk, and known as *crottins de Chavignol.*

CHEILLY-LES-MARANGES — (Shay-ye lay Mar-ronj) — Village south of Santenay, at the extreme southern end of the Côte d'Or in Burgundy. Produces a little red wine of only passable quality.

CHELOIS — (Shell-oy) — Red hybrid grape grown in New York's Finger Lakes, Washington and Idaho. Makes good light Burgundy type wine.

CHÉNAS — (Shay-nass) — Township in the very heart of the Beaujolais Country of France, bounded on the north by Julienas and on the south by Fleurie. About half of the vineyards entitled to the name "Moulin-à-Vent" lie within its communal limits (the others in Romanèche-Thorins, to the east). The finer wines of Chénas are therefore almost invariably marketed as Moulin-à-Vent, but what remains and is called simply Chénas, should not by any means be disprized — less rounded and less fine than Moulin-à-Vent and maturing more quickly, it is a typical Beaujolais and an extremely good one.

CHENIN BLANC — (Shay-nan Blaw) — White wine grape of excellent quality, sometimes known as the Pineau de la Loire, though it is not one of the true Pinots, nor related to them. In the French provinces of Touraine and Anjou it is the predominant white variety, almost to the exclusion of all others, and is solely responsible for Vouvray, Saumur, Coteaux du Layon, Savennières and other ancient and famous wines. In northern California and cooler Central Valley it is being successfully and more and more widely grown, now second among the whites, for it is highly productive and yields a fresh, pale, early-maturing wine of considerable finesse and breed. Unfortunately it is sometimes confused with the Pinot Blanc and even more frequently referred to as the White Pinot; it is neither, and deserves to be known by its own proper and proud name.

CHERIBITA — (Chair-ee-*be*-ta) — Pidgin Spanish-English for Sherry-and-bitters, an old English morning favorite that has managed to make itself known, through Jerez and Gibraltar, in southern Spain.

CHEVAL BLANC, Château — (Shev-al Blaw) — Celebrated and remarkable vineyard of the St. Émilion district, generally rated at least on a par with Ausone, as St. Émilion's best. In great years its wines have extraordinary distinction, softness and bouquet and are among the finest of all Clarets; they bring as high prices as those of Lafite and Margaux, perhaps mature more quickly. The vineyard normally produces some 13,000 cases a year but was gravely damaged early in 1956 by a cold wave of unprecedented severity; its yield is just now back to what it was before.

CHEVALIER, Domaine de — (Shev-al-yay) — Excellent vineyard in the Graves district, *commune* of Léognan. Its white wine, something of a rarity, is outstanding, perhaps the finest of dry white Graves; its red is comparable to the 2nd classed growths of the Médoc. There are some 4,500 cases a year, two-thirds red.

CHEVALIER-MONTRACHET — (Shev-al-yay Mon-rah-shay) — Tiny Burgundian vineyard, consisting of only 17½ acres of sloping and stony soil, which produces some 1,500 cases a year of one of the very best dry white wines of France. It lies directly west of, and uphill from, Montrachet (*see*), entirely within the communal limits of Puligny (*see*), and its wine, as might be expected, is a great rarity, expensive but of memorable quality.

CHIANTI — (Key-*ahnt*-tee) — A wonderfully agreeable, and in some cases quite distinguished, red Italian table wine, made from Sangiovese and Canaiolo grapes, plus a small amount of white Trebbiano and white Malvasia. Sprightly and appetizing, it has acquired some, at least, of its world-wide fame thanks to the attractive straw-covered bottle (*fiasco*) in which it is customarily shipped. In Italy, it is the common red wine of Tuscany, usually and properly drunk young, often as a carafe wine, in the restaurants of Florence. Inexpensive, refreshing, almost a little piquant (as the result of a special method of fermentation — *see Governo*) it goes admirably with Italian food. The annual wine production of Tuscany is in the neighborhood of 100 million gallons, one quarter of which is Chianti.

Much of this, of course, is rather poor stuff, with little except its name, its price, and its straw-covered bottle to recommend it. Actually, however, this fancy straw-wrapped *fiasco* (*see*) is gradually dying out. The assembly of the woven straw wrapper and the glass, round-bottomed flask is a cottage industry and today's more modern Italian woman will not do such work for a pittance and many are not interested at all. As a result, the *fiasco* is becoming a "fiasco" in true sense in that it is now not only more costly than a normal bottle, but often is more valuable than the wine it contains. In addition to its cost disadvantage, the *fiasco* cannot be used for bottle ageing since the straw wrapper would deteriorate.

Chianti *Classico* is a wine of an altogether different and much superior sort — well-balanced, firm, improving considerably with age in bottle, one of Italy's best. This is made in a delimited area between Florence and Siena comprising four townships (Greve, Radda, Castellina and Gaiole) plus portions of six others; the total yield is about 4 million gallons a year. Chianti *Classico,* unless bottled outside its zone of production, is entitled to the seal of the "private" producers' association, the *Marca Gallo* — a black target with a cock in the center and varying color borders — red indicating at least one year of ageing, silver two years and gold three years. However, the use of the seal is not mandatory and is not a guarantee of quality. As a result, some of the more famous producers are now discontinuing its use since they feel that the new D.O.C. law (*see*) is in itself a guarantee of origin. Chianti *Classico* often carries the name of a vineyard owner or a specific estate, as Barone Ricasoli (Brolio), Conte Serristori (Machiavelli), Marchese Antinori (Villa Antinori), and Santa Cristina etc.

However, a good deal of excellent Chianti is produced in Tuscany outside this classic zone. There are six other legally defined areas, of which Rufina (*see*) and Montalbano rank as very good, the Colli Fiorentini and Colli Pisani as good, but with small production; most of the very cheap Chiantis shipped abroad come from the Colli Senesi and Colli Aretini, both of them mediocre. A number of the better producers outside the classic zone have formed a separate association and taken as their "seal" a white *Putto*, which resembles a Della Robbia angel.

Chiantis of fine grades are aged in bottle, bear a vintage date and are shipped in straight-sided Bordeaux style bottles. If they are two years old they may be labelled "vecchio" (not allowed in the U.S.A. since it means *old*), if three years of age, they may be labelled "Riserva."

The white wines from Tuscany, made mostly from the Trebbiano grape (*see*), are dry, golden, rather full-bodied wines, agreeable but of no great distinction. Formerly known as "White Chianti," they are now sold as "Vino Bianco di Toscana", or simply "Vino Bianco Toscano"; however, because of over-production of white grapes and a burgeoning demand for white wines, there are rumblings about a new D. O. C. "White Chianti" or "Chianti Bianco".

Counterparts and imitations of Chianti have been produced outside Italy in most countries where Italians have settled, including Argentina and California. Rarely made from the same grape varieties, these rarely resemble Chianti, although some of them are very good, even excellent, red table wines.

For Map, *see* ITALY.

CHIARELLO — (Key-are-*el*-lo) — *See* Chiaretto.

CHIARETTO — (Key-ah-*ret*-toe) — *Rosé* wine, certainly one of Italy's best, produced round the southern end of Lake Garda, between Milan and Verona. Light, fresh, pale, low in alcohol (10-11%), it is never as good as when drunk young, as *vino aperto,* or "open" wine, on the lakeside terraces of the villages where it is made. However, some is now being bottled for export and, if properly handled and *not too old,* this can be very pleasant. The best Chiarettos come from the village of Padenghe, Moniga, Manerba, and the Polpenazze, all in the province of Brescia, and are made from the local red wine grapes, the Gropello, Schiava, Marzemino. Equally good, but somewhat different in character, are the *rosés* from the eastern shore of Garda, in the province of Verona; these are generally sold as Chiarello rather than Chairetto, although the terms are virtually interchangeable; their producing grape varieties are basically those of Bardolino (*see*) and in distinction and flavor they are very close to the lightest Bardolino reds.

CHICLANA — (Chee-*clah*-nah) — Small town at the southern end of the Sherry Country, near Cadiz. Its wines are of second quality.

CHILE — The oldest and, after Argentina, the most important wine-producing country of Latin America. Wine was being made in Chile before 1600; now with a population of less than five and one-half million, Chile produces about half as much table wine as the United States. Much of this is of surprisingly good quality, from superior grape varieties and well made, but it is only fair to add that most of the Chilean wines shipped to the United States since World War II have been bought by our importers only because they were cheap, and were far from outstanding and far from their country's best.

As might be expected, the vine flourishes in Chile only in the central, temperate zone of this 2,600-mile-long country, and on account of the cold Humboldt current in the Pacific, somewhat closer to the equator than in Europe or in California — generally between 30° and 40° south latitude. Most of the best vineyards are in the fertile central valley, not far from Santiago, and the majority of them are irrigated.

The modern history of wine in Chile dates from about 1850, when for the first time expert French vintners and cuttings of the finer French vines were brought over from Europe; since then, Chilean viticulture and wine-making have largely followed French methods and tradition, though of course in a vastly different climate and on very different, largely volcanic soil.

By all odds the best Chilean wines, those truly fit for export, are made from the "noble" grape varieties and quite often carry a varietal name, as Cabernet, Sémillon, Riesling (the last usually shipped in a squat, local version of the German *Bocksbeutel*); others, like their California compeers, are sold as Sauternes (in this case with a final "s"), Chablis, Borgoña (Burgundy), Rhin (Rhine wine), etc. These may or may not come from the original European varieties, but are rarely made from heavy-bearing, mass-production grapes, and Chile has a surprisingly large acreage of Pinot, Sauvignon, Folle Blanche (here called *Loca Blanca*), Merlot, Malbec, etc. Some quite good sparkling wine is made, much of it sweeter than it should be. Superior grades of still wines are usually labeled *Reservado* or *Gran Vino* and these designations are subject to government control.

CHILL — To cool a wine for better enjoyment, in an ice bucket, the refrigerator or even outdoors in winter. (*See* Temperature).

CHINON — (She-naw) — Birthplace of the immortal Rabelais; picturesque and historic little town in the old French province of Touraine, famous for its red wine, the *"bon vin breton"* of Rabelais' chronicles, and for the fact that it was here that Joan of Arc first met the Dauphin, later crowned King of France at Reims. The wine, made entirely from the Cabernet Franc grape, is *"bon et frais"* as it was in Rabelais' time — fresh, light, best when young and served at cellar temperature, one of the most delightful of the lesser red wines of France. The annual production rarely exceeds 800,000 gallons, most of it consumed locally; it is not often exported.

CHIPIONA — (Chip-pee-*o*-nah) — Little summer resort and wine-producing town, on the Atlantic Coast of Spain, near Jerez. It is in the Manzanilla zone, just west of Sanlúcar de Barrameda, but the Moscatel from its sandy vineyards is better known than its dry wine.

CHIROUBLES — (Shee-roubl) — Village in the Beaujolais Country and its excellent red wine, fruity, racy and charming. Most of the annual production (roughly 300,000 gallons) goes early to market and is soon consumed, gains less by ageing than other Beaujolais from nearby villages such as Chénas, Morgon, etc.

CHOREY-LES-BEAUNE — (Shor-ray lay Bone) — Wine-producing village in Burgundy, directly north of Beaune. There are some 300 acres of vineyard, mostly planted on flat land.

CHRISTIAN BROTHERS — Catholic Order, originally founded shortly after 1700 by St. Jean Baptiste de La Salle, in France. Its official name in English is "Brothers of the Christian Schools" and it is primarily a teaching Order. In the United States, the Christian Brothers are now one of the largest wine producers in the North Coast County area of California, with important vineyards at Mont La Salle on the edge of the Napa Valley, and a large ageing cellar, formerly known as the Greystone Winery, in St. Helena. They are also a major producer of California Brandy.

CHUSCLAN — (Shuss-clah) — Pleasant and palatable *rosé* wine of the Côtes-du-Rhône; the zone of production consists of five townships on the right bank of the Rhône, north of Tavel and west of Orange, Chusclan itself being the most important of the five.

CINQUETERRE — (*Chink*-waeh-ter-eh) — Italian white wine produced in five villages (whence, presumably, its name), on the Ligurian coast between Genoa and Spezia; of these Riomaggiore is the most important. Rather high in alcohol, golden in color, occasionally dry but more often somewhat sweet, with a pronounced and unusual bouquet, it is an interesting wine but one that will hardly appeal to all palates.

CINSAULT — (San-so) — Superior red-wine grape, giving a firm, full-bodied, deep-colored wine of definite character and good class. Although rarely vinified alone, it plays an important albeit minor role in Châteauneuf-du-Pape, in Tavel, and in many of the better red and *rosé* wines of the French Midi.

CIRÒ — (Chee-ro) — Italian red wine, high in alcohol and usually somewhat sweet, from the region of Calabria. Should not be confused with Girò, a somewhat similar wine made in Sardinia.

CISSAC — (See-sack) — Wine-producing *commune* of the Haut-Médoc, adjoining St. Estèphe: many good *bourgeois* growths.

CLAIRET — (Clair-ray) — Old French term (whence the English word Claret) applied centuries ago to the then rather light red wines of Bordeaux; revived since World War II, it is now the name given to certain specially vinified red Bordeaux wines, soon ready to drink and without much color or tannin. These resemble full-bodied *vins rosés,* although deeper in color than most such wines; they are usually served at cellar-temperature or chilled, and may be passably agreeable or quite good, depending on where they were made, by whom, and on the grape varieties used.

CLAIRETTE — (Clair-ette) — Productive, good quality, white wine grape, widely grown in southern France and, though not very extensively, in California. Although white, it is used in the making of red Châteauneuf-du-Pape and the *rosé* of Tavel. Alone, it gives a pleasant, well-balanced, rather neutral wine without much bouquet or fruit; one produced near Montpellier in the Midi, has astonishingly and absurdly enough, been granted an *Appellation Contrôlée* — Clairette du Languedoc, and another from near Nîmes, Clairette de Bellegarde, shares the same honor. Neither remotely merits it.

CLAIRETTE DE DIE — (Clair-ette d' Dee) — French sparkling wine, generally rather sweet and with a pronounced Muscat flavor, produced round the town of Die, in the *département* of the Drôme, along the eastern edge of the Rhône Valley. It is made principally from the Clairette grape, from which it takes its name, but with enough Muscat to give it its special character and bouquet. Surprisingly enough, over 300,000 cases are produced per year.

CLAPE, La — (La Clop) — Red, white and *rosé* wines produced just east of Narbonne, in southern France. Made from the commoner varieties of grape (Carignane, etc.), they are hardly outstanding but carry nevertheless the V.D.Q.S. seal.

CLARET — Loosely and widely used term, meaning, in most countries other than England, a light red wine. Thus, in the U.S., any and all red table wines may be labeled "claret," whatever their origin, character or type; it is a catchall term, and hardly one that inspires confidence on a wine label. The name has no meaning and no legal status in France, nor has Clarete (*see*) in Spain or

88

Chile. Traditionally (although not legally) in England, the word means red Bordeaux, but red Bordeaux wines are almost never so labeled.

CLARETE (Spanish) — (Clar-*ate*-tay) — Term used in Spain, especially in the Rioja district, to describe any red wine which is rather light both in body and color.

CLASSED GROWTH — Used in this encyclopedia to designate wines of a specific vineyard or estate or "growth" (particularly those of Bordeaux) that have been officially classed, or classified. The first such official grading was the famous Classification of 1855 (*see*), and almost all mentions of "Classed Growth" in this volume, have direct reference to, and are based on, this.

CLASSICO — *see* Chianti.

CLASSIFICATION OF 1855 — In preparation for the *Exposition Universelle,* held in Paris in 1855, a committee of experts and wine brokers officially classified the leading wines of two great Bordeaux districts, the Médoc and Sauternes. Their ratings were largely based on the opinions and prices then prevailing, and despite many changes in ownership, etc., the classification remains surprisingly accurate, after over a hundred years. However, only 60 wines of the Médoc, 22 of Sauternes and 1 of Graves, were ranked; it is greatly to be regretted that St. Émilion, Pomerol, and most of Graves, plus all of the lesser districts, were not included in the committee's assignment. The 60 "Classed Growths" of the Médoc, it should be clearly understood, represent only the extreme elite of nearly a thousand estates, all producing wine of above average quality. The 1855 Classification is given in the appendix, and all of the châteaux will be found, in their alphabetical places, in this volume; it is essential to remember that a 3rd Growth or 4th Growth wine is by no means a third- or fourth-rate wine, but a noble wine indeed — a duke, if you wish, compared to the kingly Firsts. All of the Classed Growths may fairly be considered as great vineyards; many others, called *Crus Bourgeois* or *Crus Bourgeois Supérieurs,* also produce admirable wine.

CLAVELIN — (Clahv-lan) — Special sort of stumpy bottle, holding 62 centiliters or about 20½ ounces, used in the Jura district of France for Château-Chalon and for certain *vins jaunes*.

CLEAN — Essentially, a clean wine is a sound wine, one without any "off" aroma or taste, palatable, agreeable, refreshing. It is a term that can quite properly be applied to a young wine as well as an old one, to an inexpensive wine as well as a very great one. A wine that is not clean is bad, generally not fit to drink.

CLERC-MILON, Château — (Clair Me-law) — 5th Classed Growth of Pauillac, Haut-Médoc. Some 5,000 cases a year.

CLIMAT (French) — (Clee-ma) — Used in connection with wine, means, especially in Burgundy, a specific, named vineyard, whether owned outright by a single proprietor, or split up among many.

CLIMENS, Château — (Clee-mah) — One of the two best vineyards and perhaps the greatest wine of Barsac, generally regarded as second only to Yquem in the hierarchy of Sauternes (Barsac being of course part of the Sauternes district). Sweet, luscious, golden, with extraordinary fruit and breed, it more than merits its rank as a 1st Classed Growth, and is one of the truly incomparable dessert wines of the world. There are some 8,000 cases a year.

CLINET, Château — (Clee-nay) — One of the better Growths of Pomerol. About 3,000 cases a year.

CLONE — A plant reproduced asexually therefore retaining identical genetic characteristics of the parent.

CLOS — (Clo) — Originally, in France, a walled or otherwise enclosed vineyard, as Clos de Vougeot. The term today is much more loosely used, but may not appear on a French wine label, as part of the name of a wine, unless such a Clos, or vineyard, genuinely exists, and actually produces the wine in question.

CLOS, Les — (Clo) — Celebrated *Grand Cru* vineyard of Chablis (*see*), one of the best of the seven so classified.

CLOS DE BÈZE — (Clo d' Bezz) — Celebrated Burgundian vineyard, consisting of 37 acres directly adjoining Chambertin (*see*) on the north; its magnificent red wines are legally entitled to the name Chambertin, but more often sold as Chambertin-Clos de Bèze. They are fully the equals of other Chambertins, and some experts consider them even better.
For Map, *see* GEVREY.

CLOS BLANC — (Clo Blaw) — One of the better vineyards of Pommard, in Burgundy, rated as a Première Cuvée, and giving a red wine, despite its name.

CLOS DU CHAPITRE — (Clo dew Shap-peet-truh) — Name given to several French vineyards, notably two: one in the village of Fixin (*see*), at the northern end of the Côte de Nuits, which produces a red Burgundy of outstanding quality and breed; the other in the village of Viré (*see*) north of Macon, which yields an excellent dry white wine, made from the Chardonnay grape, and one of the best of the Maconnais.

CLOS DES CORVÉES — (Clo day Cor-vay) — Perhaps the best vineyard of Prémeaux, near the southern end of the Côte de Nuits, in Burgundy. Its excellent red wine, full-bodied, round, with a rather agreeable trace of earthiness, is entitled to the appellation Nuits-Saint-Georges and is invariably estatebottled. The adjoining and hardly inferior Clos des Argillières is part of the same domain.

CLOS FOURTET — (Clo Foor-tay) — Premier Grand Cru Classé vineyard of St. Émilion; its red wine, sturdy, full-bodied and long-lived. Its production amounts to some 6,000 cases a year.

CLOS DES GOISSES — (Clo day Gwass) — Extraordinary and unique vineyard at Mareuil-sur-Ay in the Champagne district of France. It consists of one extremely steep hillside overlooking the Marne, and is planted to both Pinot Noir and Chardonnay grapes. The resulting wine is fairly full-bodied, but with outstanding quality and class. It is about the only French Champagne which carries a specific vineyard name, and in good years is usually shipped as "nature," completely unsweetened.

CLOS DES LAMBRAYS — (Clo day Lahm-bray) — Superior vineyard classified as a *Premier Cru* (1st growth), in the township of Morey-Saint-Denis (*see*), in Burgundy. Its red wine is one of the heaviest, fullest-bodied and longest lived of the Côte d'Or.

CLOS DES MOUCHES — (Clo day Moosh) — Well-known vineyard of Beaune, in Burgundy, producing an attractive, fine-textured red wine and, curiously enough, a perhaps even better white. This latter, Beaune's only white wine of any consequence, is comparable to a Meursault.

CLOS DE LA MOUSSE — (Clo d'la Moose) — One of the good vineyards of Beaune, in Burgundy. Not to be confused with the preceding, it gives only red wine.

CLOS DE LA PERRIÈRE — (*Clo* d' la Per-ry-air) — Burgundian vineyard and its excellent red wine. *See* Fixin, Perrière. The CLOS DES PERRIÈRES is one small, especially renowned portion of the Perrières vineyard in Meursault (*see*), giving a white wine of remarkable balance and breed.

CLOS DE LA ROCHE — (Clo d'la Rosh) — Distinguished Burgundy vineyard, officially classified as a *Grand Cru* (great growth) in the *commune* of Morey-Saint-Denis. It produces, from 38 acres of vines, approximately 3,900 cases of red wine a year — wine which, at its best, is one of the truly great Burgundies, quite the equal in power and depth, if not always in class and breed, of Chambertin.

CLOS DU ROI — (Clo dew Rwah) — Two quite distinct vineyards in Burgundy, both producing red wines of excellent quality. The finer and more famous of the two is in the township of Aloxe-Corton, and its wines are sold as Corton-Clos du Roi (*see* Corton); the other is in Beaune (*see*) and produces Beaune-Clos du Roi.

CLOS ST. JEAN — (Clo San Zhahn) — Excellent vineyard in Chassagne-Montrachet (*see*). With Les Boudriottes and La Maltroie, it produces about the best red wines of this celebrated little Burgundian town.

CLOS SAINT-DENIS — (Clo San Den-nee) — Leading Burgundy vineyard, one of the best of the *commune* of Morey, or Morey-Saint Denis, and officially ranked as one of the 23 *Grand Crus* (great growths) of the Côte de Nuits. Its 16 acres yield some 1,800 cases a year of a particularly sturdy well-knit red wine, long-lived and slow to mature.

CLOS SAINT-JACQUES — (Clo San Zhock) — Excellent vineyard in the township of Gevrey-Chambertin (*see*), in Burgundy, officially ranked as a *Premier Cru,* and perhaps the best of those so ranked. Its red wine is outstanding, full-bodied, fine, and brings nearly as high a price as Chambertin itself.

CLOS DE TART — (Clo d'Tarr) — One of the great vineyards of Morey-Saint-Denis, in Burgundy, officially classified as a *Grand Cru*. Its 18 acres make up a single property, and yield annually about 1,700 cases of very full-bodied, long-lived red wine.

For Map, *see* MOREY.

CLOS DE VOUGEOT — (Clo d'Voo-zho) — World-famous Burgundian vineyard, the largest (126 acres) of the Côte d'Or, created on what had been, until then, waste land, by Cistercian monks in the 12th century. Its average annual production is now in the neighborhood of 15,000 cases, but 66 producers own portions, some obviously much larger than others, of the Clos, and a Clos de Vougeot of a given year is therefore not one, but 66 different wines, some estate-bottled, some not, some fuller-bodied than others and some better. The finest wines are traditionally those that come from the upper part of the vineyard, which here is bounded by Musigny (*see*) and Grands Échézeaux (*see*), but the entire Clos produces red Burgundy of classic quality, distinguished perhaps more for its breed and bouquet than for its body and power. The picturesque and venerable Château de Vougeot, with its massive, ancient winepresses, is now the property of the Burgundian wine confraternity, the Che-

92

valiers du Tastevin. A little red wine is produced called simply Vougeot, but not Clos de Vougeot, and a white wine of first-rate quality, the Clos Blanc de Vougeot. *See* also Vougeot.

CLOUDY — A wine that is not clear or brilliant. No sound and good wine is ever cloudy, but the term should NOT be applied to a clear wine which has thrown sediment (*see*) in bottle.

COARSE — A wine lacking in finesse, common, heavy, with plenty of body and not much else. Cheap California Burgundies are usually coarse, and so is most of the red *vin ordinaire* that the average Frenchman drinks every day.

COBBLER — Old-fashioned American mixed drink, really a sort of julep, although generally made with wine. There are dozens of recipes, but always involving shaved ice in a tall glass, sliced fruit and/or a sprig of mint and sugar. Over this one pours three or four ounces of red or white table wine, or even Sherry or Port.

COLARES — (Co-*lar*-rays) — Interesting Portuguese red wine, produced north of Estoril and west of Cintra along the dunes and sandy foothills of the Atlantic Coast. The predominating vine is the Ramisco, planted in ditches or pits in the clay subsoil which underlies ten feet or more of sand. Rather full-bodied and "fleshy," somewhat lacking in subtlety but improving with age, Colares has definite character, but not all wine-drinkers will find it deserving of the extremely high regard in which it is held in England.

COLD DUCK — Pink sparkling wine made by any method; theoretically a mixture of champagne and sparkling burgundy. The name is a translation of the German *Kalte Ente* — "Cold Duck" which was originally *Kalte Ende* "Cold End," a combination of all unused open wine at the termination of a banquet, saved for subsequent drinking. Cold Duck was wildly successful in the late 1960's, served as an introduction to wine for many beginners and today is a minor inexpensive sparkling wine.

COLLAGE — (Call-ajh) — French term for fining (*see*), or clarifying wine, through the addition of any one of many different substances or products to the wine before bottling. An essential step in wine-making.

COLLI EUGANEI — (*Cohl*-lee Eh-oo-gahn-*nay*-ee) — Chain of vineyard-covered hills near Padua, some thirty miles southwest of Venice; the diverse, rarely outstanding wines (the Venetians' *vin ordinaire*) from this district, both red and white.

COLMAR — (Call-mar) — City in the *département* of Haut-Rhin, France; an important center of the Alsatian wine trade.

COLOMBARD — (Call-awm-bar) — Productive, good quality white wine grape, grown principally in the Cognac district of France, but to some extent in the northern fine table wine district of California. It is sometimes called the *Colombar* or *Colombier* in France. In California its official name is "French Colombard" and it is the most widely planted white wine grape, some 26,000 acres in all. In France, it gives an agreeable, not very distinguished, dry white wine, fuller-bodied and higher in alcohol than the *Folle Blanche,* but also rather high in acid and therefore suitable for distillation. In California, its wine is well-balanced, pale, fresh, rather tart, and widely used in California "Chablis" and in the lesser grades of California Champagne.

COLOBEL — Hybrid used as a *teinturier* for deep red color in blends.

COLOR — An expert can tell a great deal about a wine, particularly a white wine, by looking at it in a clear glass, tilted either against a white tablecloth or against the light, or in a silver *tastevin,* in the Burgundian fashion. A good wine in any case should be clear and brilliant. Dry white table wines from cooler districts should be somewhere between the color of pale straw and that of gold, with a distinct greenish cast; white table wines from Bordeaux, and Italy, and some (though rarely the best) from California, may be as gold as ripe corn with almost no green at all; in practically all white table wines a trace of amber or brown is either a tell-tale sign of age, or, in a younger wine, an indication that the wine is slightly "maderisé" (*see*) and will probably be short-lived. Sweeter white wines should be gold, never at all brown unless very old. Red wines have their own range from purple (generally a very young wine, almost always a heavy coarse one) to a sort of autumnal reddish brown, like oak leaves in the fall. This last, which the French call *pelure d'oignon,* or onion skin, comes invariably to fine red wines as they grow older — it can best be noted along the edge of the wine in a tilted glass. *Rosé* wines, too, have their variations — from the color of a strawberry almost to that of an orange; both extremes are bad, and a *rosé* too orange is generally too old, one too pink generally no good to begin with. All of these graduations of color are very subtle and it is hard to remember and recognize and judge them except after long experience. They are more for the wine expert than for the novice.

COLTURA PROMISCUA — (Col-*too*-rah Pro-*mees*-coo-ah) — Italian method of growing grapes with other crops; vines that are interplanted with potatoes or "married" to trees, or strung over random pergolas, or against walls, or in cabbage patches — hardly what one would call vineyards at all. This old fashioned system is now becoming obsolete allowing for modern vineyard care and machine cultivation.

COMBLANCHIEN — (Caum-blah-she-an) — Tiny village far more famous for its marble quarries (which supplied much of the stone for the Opéra in Paris) than for its wine; it lies south of Nuits-Saint-Georges and Prémeaux, near the southern end of the Côte de Nuits, and was the only town of the Côte to be badly damaged in World War II.

COMMANDARIA — *See* Cyprus.

COMMON — Applied to a wine, means about what it does when applied to a person. Perhaps not disagreeable, perhaps sound and clean, perhaps an ordinary table wine adequate for everyday use. Nothing that can be called fine.

COMMUNE (French) — (Caw-mune) — A township; a small administrative unit in France, consisting of a village and its surrounding land. Often used in this encyclopedia, and always in this sense.

CONCORD — Blue-black, slip-skin American grape of the *labrusca* species, by far the most widely planted of the "native," Eastern varieties. It takes its name from Concord, Massachusetts, where it appeared as a seedling in the garden of Mr. Ephraim Bull, in 1843. It is doubtless a cross of two *labrusca* varieties, perhaps one of them the Catawba; hardy and productive, a good table grape, and a wholly satisfactory variety for jelly and unfermented grape juice, it rapidly became both popular and famous. It is responsible today for most of the sweet, so-called "Kosher" wine, where its pronounced "foxy" flavor is apparently not considered objectionable. As a true wine grape, however, it has almost nothing to recommend it: it can hardly be made into wine at all unless heavily sugared, and a dry Concord table wine is assertive in flavor and extremely common. It is nevertheless the dominant variety in a good deal of New York State "Burgundy" and much New York State "Port."

CONDRIEU — (Cawn-dree-uh) — Interesting and unusual white wine of the Rhône Valley, produced some thirty miles south of Lyon, on 17 acres in the three communes of Condrieu, Vérin and St. Michel and four others. Its terraced vineyards, planted to the Viognier (or Vionnier) grape, are as steep as those of Côte Rôtie nearby, and their output is small, averaging less than 2,000 cases a year. Almost all of this is consumed locally in Lyon and in the famous Restaurant de la Pyramide (Point) at Vienne, where it is a favorite specialty. Condrieu is something of a changeling of a wine: it can be fairly dry or moderately sweet, depending on the vintage and the producer; it is often faintly *pétillant* or sparkling when young; golden in color, fruity, it has a special and distinctive bouquet.

CONEGLIANO — (Cawn-el-*ya*-no) — Small city north of Venice, known for its important wine school and viticultural station, but even more for its white wines, among the best of northern Italy. These are of several types, of which the most engaging is perhaps the extremely light, dry, pale green-gold wine sold as Verdiso; the somewhat sweeter Prosecco is also a superior quality, however, and there are some good sparkling and semi-sparkling sorts as well.

95

CONSEILLANTE, Château La — (Cawn-say-yahnt) — Excellent vineyard of Pomerol, in the Bordeaux Country, separated from Château Cheval Blanc (this, of course, a St. Émilion) only by a winding country road. Its red wine is outstanding, velvety, rich and full; there are some 3,500 cases a year.

CONSTANCE — One of the largest lakes of Western Europe, bounded on the south by Switzerland, on the east by Austria and on the north by Germany. The Rhine, rising in Switzerland, empties into and runs out of Lake Constance, just as the Rhône into and out of Lake Geneva. Lake Constance is known in German as the Bodensee, and a few wines, almost all of them consumed locally, are produced along its northern shore, and known as *Seeweine;* of these the Ruländer or Pinot Gris is perhaps the best, but there is an interesting oddity known as *Weissherbst,* an exceedingly pale *rosé* made from the Pinot Noir.

CONSTANTIA — South African wine from near Cape Town which, during most of the 19th century, enjoyed a fame and vogue in England and the Low Countries and even France such as no other non-European wine has even approached. It came from a vineyard called Groot Constantia (now State-owned), originally planted by the Dutch governor, Simon van der Stel, before 1700, and named after his wife, Constance. Huguenot refugees from France played a large role in the establishment of the vineyards, and the predominating vine seems to have been the Muscadelle du Bordelais. The estate is still producing wine today, as are also Klein Constantia and High Constantia, which adjoin it. Their wines, while often of good and even superior quality, are far indeed from deserving the international rank which our great-grandfathers accorded them. Future students of the history of wine may explain this, like the decline of Falerno (*see*), it is for the moment a mystery.

COOKED — Flavor resulting from must or wine having been heated, more pronounced when heated in presence of air, resulting in oxidation (*see*).

COOKING WINE — Inexcusable term, since it would lead one to believe that something not good enough to drink could be good enough to eat. The truth is that the only two major elements which bad wines and good have in common — water and alcohol — are largely dissipated in cooking by evaporation (the alcohol, being more volatile, almost completely) and what remains is the flavor — quality is no less important in the saucepan than in the wine glass. There are a few reservations, none the less. What is left in the bottom of a wine bottle (if there is no sediment), can certainly be kept overnight and used for cooking the next day, or even, if kept in the refrigerator, two or three days later. A wine loses its bouquet, so kept, and picks up a little of what experts call "volatile acidity"; in cooking, this is no disadvantage since the bouquet is evanescent anyway and volatile acidity, within reason, is an asset in the kitchen. Let skeptics prepare the same dish using Madeira, Sherry and Marsala, for example — Madeira will be found the best, nine times out of ten, simply because it is far higher in volatile acid. The French have known this for a long time, which is why they have so many distinguished dishes *à Madère,* and ordinarily leave Sherry to the Spaniards, and Marsala to the Italians.

96

COOPERAGE — General term applied to a totality of wooden casks or vats or barrels (i.e. those made by a cooper) used for storage in a given cellar or winery. Thus "100,000 gallons of cooperage" means a storage capacity of 100,000 gallons, whether used or not; "new cooperage" means unused casks or barrels, etc. By a long margin the best wood for wine storage is oak; redwood (in California) and chestnut (in Europe) are acceptable substitutes, although wines stored in these do not develop in the same way, or as rapidly. The use of glass-lined concrete or metal tanks, especially for white and *rosé* wines, is increasing both in Europe and in America.

COOPERATIVE — A winery or cellar owned and operated jointly by a number of small producers; there are hundreds of such in Europe and a good many in California, some of quite modest size and others that rank among the largest wineries and cellars in the world. They have come into being primarily because the small grower, except in districts of famous and expensive wine, cannot afford alone the machinery and cellar equipment he needs to make and bottle properly and market profitably his own wine.

CORBIÈRES — (Cor-be-air) — District of vineyard-covered, rolling hills, southeast of Carcassonne, in what is known as the Midi of France. This, in general, is the homeland of *vin ordinaire*, but Corbières, while inexpensive and produced on a large scale, belongs in a somewhat higher category — it is recognized as an *appellation d'origine* and has been accorded the V.D.Q.S. seal. Legally, it can be red, *rosé* or white; the sturdy red is by all odds the best, and is made mostly from the Grenache, Carignan, Terret and Cinsault varieties of grape. Corbières Supérieur is a superior grade, and Corbières du Roussillon comes from a zone a little farther south, in the *département* of Pyrénées Orientales.

CORBIN, Château — (Cor-ba) — 1st Growth vineyard of St. Émilion, one of a number of châteaux that bear, in various combined forms, this ancient name; all of them produce good wine and all were part of a single feudal domain. Thus we have, in addition to Château Corbin, Château Corbin-Michotte, Château Grand-Corbin, Château Corbin-Despagne, Château Grand-Corbin-David, and several others, all in the section known as Graves-St. Émilion — the gravelly plateau which adjoins the *commune* of Pomerol, and boasts, as its most famous wine, Château Cheval Blanc.

CORGOLOIN — (Cor-go-lwa) — Southernmost village of the Côte de Nuits, in Burgundy. Its wines are of secondary quality, and one encounters them only as blends, as *"Côte de Nuits-Villages"* or simply as *"Bourgogne"*.

CORKAGE — Fee paid to a restaurant for the privilege of having one's own wine, purchased elsewhere, served there with a meal or for a party. If not too high, this is a legitimate charge, and anything up to 40% of the value of the wine (unless it is an expensive rarity) is fair. If Corkage is not charged, one has been done a favor, and the wine waiter should be very liberally tipped.

CORKS — Plastic "corks" are more and more tending to replace those made of the bark of *Quercus suber* (the cork oak) in sparkling wine, not only in

America but in Europe; most of the Sherry and Port produced in this country is now shipped with a screw-cap or some such "closure," and even many inexpensive table wines in both France and Italy are sent to market with some simple, ingenious cap which does not require a corkscrew. All this greatly alarms the traditionalists, but they are wrong. Common wine (at least 95% of the world's production) is made to be consumed almost as soon as bottled, and providing its container is sanitary, cheap, and gives no bad taste to the wine, there can be no legitimate objection to it, and it is certainly better than the goatskins, leather flasks, re-used bottles, and all the picturesque paraphernalia of the wine business of a century ago. The same thing, precisely is true of the "closures."

On the other hand, precisely the opposite is true of wines capable of ageing and improvement in bottle. For these, the elite, corks are still irreplaceable and indispensable. They permit the slow evaporation and eventual slight oxidation of the wine which give it bouquet and distinction.

A cork's length, and even its quality, should be in relation to the expected life span of the wine it is supposed to protect, for longer corks last longer. Thus, a Beaujolais may legitimately have a much shorter cork than a great Burgundy, and a Rhine wine a shorter cork than a great red Bordeaux.

Normally, even the best corks have a life of not much over twenty years, even in the best cellars, and have to be replaced after about two decades.

The fact that a cork is "loose" rather than "tight" in its bottle, is usually an indication that the wine has been poorly stored, upright rather than on its side. A cork that is dry and hard to pull means usually that the wine has been kept in too dry a cellar, but has nothing to do with its quality. That the top of a cork, beneath its capsule, should be moist or even black with mould, means nothing at all. Unless a wine is frankly corky, it is impossible, even for an expert, to say more of a cork until he tastes the wine.

CORKSCREW — Device for pulling corks: in its simplest, traditional form, a wire spiral attached to some sort of handle. But there are literally hundreds of diverse and ingenious modifications today, some admirably efficient, some wholly worthless.

A wine-drinker, in choosing a corkscrew, should keep in mind that the screw itself, or worm or *mèche,* is far more important than all the elaborate, silver-plated or wooden levers or double-levers, or reverse helixes, which are supposed to bring out the cork with a minimum of effort. All are pretentious and ridiculous unless the screw itself is properly designed. A good one is easy to recognize: it is not a gimlet, but an open spiral, in which one can easily insert an old-fashioned kitchen match, and of which the outside diameter is between $5/16$ and $3/8$ of an inch. The screw itself should be thin and tapered, (few are) with a sharp point, which follows the spiral and is not centered. Those of drawn steel, rectangular or oval in cross section rather than round, are the best, but hard to come by. Under no circumstances should a good corkscrew have a sharp cutting edge on the outer side of its spiral. It is *essential,* if it is to be used for fine wine, that the screw be from 2¼ to 2¾ inches long.

This said, a wine lover may suit his fancy, but it is certainly a fact that a corkscrew with some sort of lever or double screw arrangement is vastly to be preferred when one is dealing with long corks, old bottles, and, above all, with wines that one wishes to open in a pouring basket, or cradle.

Another type of cork-puller, with nothing much to recommend it, consists of two parallel, thin, flexible blades, attached to a handle and separated by about the diameter of a wine cork. Inserted on each side of the cork. these blades permit one, after a good deal of maneuvering and twisting and pulling, to bring out the cork unpierced, and presumably reusable. This may be of some interest in a commercial cellar, but is hardly of importance in the home.

In recent years, an entirely new type of cork extractor has come on the market, of which the essential elements are a hollow needle and a cartridge of compressed air or CO_2 or freon gas, which is injected into the space between the lower end of the cork and the wine itself, so that the cork is actually pushed, rather than pulled out of the bottle. This ingenious idea offers many advantages. They are particularly effective when one is dealing with an old, friable cork, likely to crumble or break; the air or gas injected has no effect whatsoever on the wine. Unfortunately, in most cases, the needles of these instruments are too short to transpierce the long corks used in the finest wines.

CORKY — Many people say "corked" when they mean "corky." All bottled wines (except those with screw-caps or other such "closures") are corked; a corky wine is one that has the definite and disagreeable odor and flavor of a bad cork. Such bottles come along occasionally, even from the best of cellars; the odor and off-flavor are due to some invisible flaw in what appears a perfect cork; generally the cork, when pulled has the same scent of rotten wood to a pronounced degree. There is nothing to do with such wines except pour them down the drain; fortunately, they arrive only about one time in a thousand, or less.

CORNAS — (Cor-nahss) — Sturdy, agreeable, though not particularly distinguished red wine of the Rhône Valley, made from the same Syrah grape as Hermitage (see) a dozen miles further south and on the opposite (or west) bank of the Rhône. Total production amounts to some 15,000 cases a year; the wine often has a rather marked goût de terroir, especially when young, but ages well.

CORONATA — (Cor-o-na-ta) — Good white wine produced on the hills back of Genoa, Italy.

CORPS — (Core) — French for "body." See Corsé.

CORSÉ (French) — (Cor-say) — Full-bodied. The noun is corps.

CORSICA — (In French, Corse) — Large Mediterranean island, one of the départements of France. The production of wine on Corsica has increased tenfold in the last 15 years or so, and there are now more than 12,000 acres of vines on the island. Not all of the wines are of high quality, however, and the two best are Patrimonio and Ajaccio, both of which are entitled to an Appellation Controlée.

CORTAILLOD — (Cor-tie-yo) — Pale red wine, fruity and agreeable, but often almost rosé or oeil de perdrix in color, produced round the village of this name, on Lake Neuchâtel, in Switzerland. Its grape is the Pinot Noir of Burgundy.

CORTESE — (Cor-*teh*-zeh) — Italian white wine grape of superior quality, grown mostly in Piedmont, where it yields a fresh, light, pale, short-lived wine, eminently agreeable, usually sold as Cortese though sometimes under a town name such as Gavi. The principal zone of production is some thirty miles north of Genoa. The word *cortese*, incidentally, means "courteous" in Italian, just as *soave* (*see*) means "suave."

CORTON — (Cor-taw) — Generally and rightly regarded as the greatest red wine of the Côte de Beaune (*see*); also a white wine of the very highest class. Both are produced in the Burgundian village of Aloxe-Corton (*see*), plus small portions of two adjoining *communes*, Ladoix-Serrigny and Pernand-Vergeles- ses. The lighter and less distinguished (although very good) wines of these *communes* are marketed simply as Aloxe-Corton or Pernand-Vergelesses; the finer as Corton, or as Corton plus the name of a vineyard — e.g., Corton Bressandes, Corton Clos du Roi (both red) or Corton-Charlemagne (white). The vineyards entitled to these proud names have been most carefully delimi- ted; they produce in an average year, some 27,000 cases of red wine and some 11,000 cases of white (the latter, except for a small fraction, all Corton- Charlemagne). Several of the best *cuvées* of the Hospices de Beaune (*see*) are in fact Cortons. Corton Château Grancey is not a vineyard, but a none-the-less excellent and authentic Corton, bottled at Château Grancey, in Aloxe-Corton. For Map, *see* ALOXE.

CORVINA — (Cor-*vee*-na) — Red wine grape widely grown in northern Italy, especially in the districts that produce Bardolino (*see*) and Valpolicella (*see*). Unknown or at least unidentified in most other wine countries.

CORVO DI CASTELDACCIA — (Cor-vo dee Cas-tel-*datch*-cha) — One of the better known table wines of Sicily, usually white although some red is pro- duced. The vineyards are just east of Palermo and form part of the estate of the Dukes of Salaparuta.

COSECHERO — (Co-say-*chay*-ro) — Literally, in Spanish, a harvester (*cose- cha*, harvest); in wine parlance, a vineyard-owner.

COS D'ESTOURNEL, Château — (Cawss Dess-tour-nell) — Outstanding vine- yard of St. Estèphe, in the Haut-Médoc, one of the best of the 2nd Classed Growths. The facade of the château is a sort of Victorian version of a pagoda, and the vines face, across a little tidal stream and its salt meadows, those of Château Lafite. The wine is consistently excellent, full and sturdy, yet soft and fine. There are some 20,000 cases a year.

COS LABORY, Château — (Cawss La-bo-ree) — 5th Classed Growth of St. Es- tèphe, Haut-Médoc. Directly adjoins Cos d'Estournel, but produces a lighter and less distinguished red wine. A very respectable 5th Growth, none the less, with a production of some 4,000 cases a year.

COSTIÈRES-DU-GARD — (Caws-tee-yare dew Gahr) — Red, *rosé*, and white wines produced on the hills along the River Gard, or Gardon, in the *dépar-*

100

MIS EN BOUTEILLE AU CHATEAU

COS D'ESTOURNEL
APPELLATION SAINT-ESTÈPHE CONTROLÉE
1975
SOCIÉTÉ DES DOMAINES PRATS PROPRIÉTAIRE A SAINT-ESTÉPHE (GIRONDE)
PRODUCE OF FRANCE 730 ml

VIN DE BORDEAUX
PRODUCED AND BOTTLED IN FRANCE
CONTENTS
24.5 OZS
PRATS ALCOHOL 12 % BY VOL.
PRATS FRÈRES NÉGOCIANTS-ÉLEVEURS, SAINT-ESTÈPHE (GIRONDE) FRANCE

tements of Gard and Hérault, in southern France. Although entitled to the seal of V.D.Q.S. (*see*), they may legally come from any one of 18 varieties of grape, few of them of any real quality; the wine is common, at best a superior sort of *vin ordinaire.*

CÔTE, La — (Coat) — Large wine-producing district in Switzerland, the steep northern shore of Lake Geneva (or Lac Léman) between Geneva and Lausanne, in the Canton of Vaud. The wines, all white and made from the Fendant or Chasselas grape, are light, fresh, reasonably pleasant carafe wines, nothing more.

COTEAUX D'AIX — (Coat-toe Deks) — Pleasant and popular wines, red, white and *rosé,* produced round the fine old university city of Aix-en-Provence, in southern France. They are classified as *Vins Delimités de Qualité Supérieure,* or V.D.Q.S. (*see*) and the better of them carry the V.D.Q.S. seal.

COTEAUX DE L'AUBANCE — *See* Aubance.

COTEAUX CHAMPENOIS — (Coat-toe Sham-pen-wa) — Non-sparkling table wine made in the Champagne country under the same limits of grape variety and production as Champagne; actually a still Champagne but since it does not effervesce, it is not nor can it be labeled Champagne (*see* Champagne Nature).

COTEAUX DU LAYON — (Co-toe dew Lay-oh) — The banks of a small river, tributary of the Loire, in western France; in both quantity and quality by far the most important wine-producing district of the province of Anjou, with over

101

10,000 acres of vines (Chenin Blanc) and an annual production of well over a million gallons of white wine entitled to this name. The district also produces a very substantial quantity of white wine from less good vineyards, this sold simply as Anjou, and a great deal of *rosé* (from the Cabernet Franc and Grolleau, or Groslot) marketed either as Rosé de Cabernet or Anjou Rosé. The fine white wines of the Coteaux du Layon range from fairly dry to very sweet, depending on the vineyard and the year; at their best they are rich, golden wines of astonishing texture and breed, quite comparable to the finer Sauternes and Barsacs and the great Auslesen of the Rhine. The two most famous vineyard areas are Bonnezeaux and Quarts de Chaume and from a quality standpoint the leading wine-producing villages are Rochefort-sur-Loire, Beaulieu-sur-Layon, St. Aubin-de-Luigné, Rablay, Faye, Chavagnes, etc.

For Map, *see* LOIRE.

COTEAUX DU LOIR — (Co-toe dew Lwahr) — Minor wine-producing district north of Tours, in France. Not to be confused with the Loire, of which it is a tributary, the Loir runs westward along the extreme northern limit of the cultivation of the vine; there are some 1,500 acres of vineyard (largely Pinot Noir and Chenin Blanc) which yield red and white wines of quite remarkable quality, though only in exceptionally good years. The most celebrated wine is that of Jasnières (*see*).

COTEAUX DE LA LOIRE — (Co-toe d'la Lwahr) — Literally, the Loire hillsides, and, in general, the wines produced along the Loire River, in France; legally and specifically, however, two delimited districts, one directly south of the city of Angers, capital of the old province of Anjou, the second farther west, round the town of Ancenis, near Nantes. Wines from the latter zone are made from the Melon grape and are sold as Muscadet (*see*) des Coteaux de la Loire. Wines from the former are labeled Anjou-Coteaux-de-la-Loire; made from the Chenin Blanc, here harvested very late, they are rather sweet white wines of outstanding quality, fruit and bouquet. Savennières (*see*) is the most important wine-producing village.

COTEAUX DE SAUMUR — (Co-toe d'So-muhr) — *See* Saumur.

COTEAUX DE TOURAINE — (Co-toe d'Tour-rain) — General name given to a vast variety of pleasant local wines, still and sparkling, red, white and *rosé,* produced along the Loire River, and its tributaries, the Cher and Indre, in the old French province of Touraine, round Tours. The finer of these have their own, more restrictive appellations, as Vouvray, Montlouis, Chinon, etc.

CÔTE CHALONNAISE — (Coat Shall-lone-nays) — Vineyard district in Burgundy, south of the Côte d'Or but north of Macon; produces a number of good red and white wines from Pinot Noir and Chardonnay grapes, of which the best known are Mercurey, Rully, Givry and Montagny (*see*). It takes its name from the town of Chalon-sur-Saône, near its southern end.

CÔTE DE BEAUNE — (Coat d'*Bone*) — The southern half of the celebrated Burgundian Côte d'Or (*see*), that long, narrow belt of hillside vineyards which is responsible for almost all of the greatest Burgundies. Unlike the northern half, known as the Côte de Nuits (*see*), the Côte de Beaune produces white wine (Montrachet, Meursault, Corton) fully as famous as its red (Pommard,

Volnay, Beaune, Corton, etc.). These latter, for all their wonderful refinement and softness and charm, are less great, less extraordinary than those of the Côte de Nuits; they mature more quickly and are generally shorter lived.

A wine labeled "Côte de Beaune" without any mention of town or vineyard, is a regional wine, often of secondary quality, from the township of Beaune itself; it is less good than a wine labeled simply "Beaune." A wine labeled "Côte de Beaune-Villages" is a wine or a blend of wines from a township or townships of the Côte de Beaune other than Beaune; it, too, is a regional, rarely of top class. A wine, however, that carries the appellation

"Côte de Beaune" *preceded by the name of a village* (as Monthélie-Côte de Beaune, Saint-Aubin-Côte de Beaune, Santenay-Côte de Beaune, etc.) must come from that specific village; such wines, although generally inexpensive, are in many cases excellent. (*See also* Hautes-Côtes De Beaune.)

CÔTE DE BEAUNE-VILLAGES — (Vee-lahj) — *See* above.

CÔTE DE BROUILLY — (Coat d'Brew-ye) — Excellent vineyard district in the Beaujolais Country of France, consisting of portions of four *communes* (Odenas, St. Lager, Cercié and Quincié), and producing some 300,000 gallons a year of fruity, full-bodied red wine, rather high in alcohol (13-14%) and, surprisingly best drunk young. It is a heavier and bigger wine than Brouilly (*see*) but not always a more agreeable one. The vineyards are on the steep slopes of an extraordinary round hill called Mont de Brouilly; the name comes from a tiny village, the Hameau (hamlet) de Brouilly.

For Map, *see* BROUILLY.

CÔTE DE NUITS — (Coat d'Nwee) — The more northerly of the two main sections of the Burgundian Côte d'Or (*see*); perhaps the greatest red wine district in the world, the Médoc of the Bordeaux Country being its only real rival. An insignificant amount of white wine is produced (*see* Musigny, Clos de Vougeot, Nuits-Saint-Georges) but the reds include most of those responsible for Burgundy's world-wide reputation. The area takes its name from Nuits-Saint-Georges, its principal town, and extends from Fixin on the north to Corgoloin, where the Côte de Beaune (*see*) begins, on the south; its narrow hillside vineyards are hardly a mile wide, but they produce Chambertin, Bonnes Mares, Musigny, Clos de Vougeot, Échézeaux, Richebourg, Romanée-Conti, Nuits-Saint-Georges and many others almost equally illustrious. Such wines, however, never carry the appellation Côte de Nuits, but are sold under the far more specific *commune* or vineyard names. A wine labeled Vin Fin de la Côte de Nuits, or one that carries the new appellation Côte de Nuits-Villages, is a regional Burgundy, perhaps good but not outstanding in quality, quite possibly a blend. (*See also* Hautes Côtes de Nuits.)

CÔTE DE NUITS-VILLAGES — (Vee-lajh) — *See* above.

CÔTE DES BLANCS — *see* CHAMPAGNE

CÔTE D'OR — (Coat Door) — Literally, in French, "golden slope"; *département* in the heart of the old province of Burgundy (*see*), southeast of Paris, taking its name from this same "golden," vineyard-covered hillside, on which most of the great Burgundy wines are grown. The slope in question extends from near Dijon, to Santenay, south of Beaune, faces southeast over the wide, flat, fertile valley on the Saône, and parallels for some thirty-five miles the main railway line and one of the main roads from Paris to Lyon, Marseille and the Riviera; the vineyards form a sort of mile-wide band along the hillside, between the rocky outcroppings and trees near the crest, and the fertile farmland below. There are a few other vineyards, of vastly less interest and fame, on parallel slopes farther west, the Arrière-Côtes (*see*), but this single hillside is the true kernel of the Burgundy wine country. It consists of three well-defined sections, each one of which is named after its principal town —

CÔTE DE NUITS

LEGEND

Major wine-producing towns	**VOUGEOT**
Secondary wine-producing towns	*FIXIN*
Commune boundaries	– – – – –
Main roads	ççççççç

SCALE

MI. 0   1   2   3   4
KM. 0   2   4   6   8

FIXIN
BROCHON
GEVREY-CHAMBERTIN
MOREY-St-DENIS
CHAMBOLLE-MUSIGNY
FLAGEY-ECHEZEAUX
VOSNE-ROMANEE
VOUGEOT
NUITS-St-GEORGES
PREMEAUX

Drawn by W. Lembeck

the Côte de Dijon, the Côte de Nuits (*see*) and the Côte de Beaune (*see*). The Côte de Dijon has no vineyards of importance: its best wine is an agreeable *vin rosé,* made from Pinot Noir grapes in the village of Marsannay-la-Côte; all of the great wines come from the other two sections. Côte d'Or, incidentally, is *not* a wine name — no wine may legally be sold under this appellation.

For Map, *see* BURGUNDY.

CÔTE RÔTIE — (Coat Roat-ee) — Celebrated red wine of the Rhône Valley, produced near Vienne, and some twenty miles south of Lyon. The vineyards, which overlook a great bend in the river and face almost due south, are incredibly steep, and consist really of a series of narrow terraces, held up by

105

retaining walls, or *murgeys,* and of necessity worked by hand. Their cultivation is therefore expensive and their production small, rarely over a total of 16,000 cases a year. There are 52 officially listed *quartiers,* or vineyard areas, but the two main divisions are the Côte Brune and Côte Blonde, the former with somewhat darker soil and producing a somewhat sturdier, longer-lived wine. According to legend, a noble lord of the district, one Maugiron, once bequeathed the Côte Blonde to his blonde daughter and the Côte Brune to her dark-haired sister. The main grape is the Syrah, here interplanted with from 10% to 20% of white grapes of the Viognier variety, which produces Château Grillet and Condrieu *(see)* nearby. A fine Côte Rôtie of a great year is truly admirable wine, deep-colored, full-bodied, long-lived, yet with great distinction and class; certain experts claim to detect in it the scent of violets and raspberries. It has been famous since the days of Rome.

CÔTES D'AGLY — (Coat Dah-lyee) — A district producing sweet, full-bodied, fortified wines, not far from the Spanish border, in southern France; as in nearby Rivesaltes and Banyuls *(see),* the principal grape varieties are the Grenache, Muscat and Malvoisie, and the wines must contain a minimum of 15% of alcohol by volume. *See* Roussillon.

CÔTES DE BERGERAC — (Coat d'Bair-shair-rack) — Rather common red and white wines produced around the town of this name, east of Bordeaux, in southwestern France.

CÔTES DE BLAYE — (Coat d'Bly) — *See* Blaye.

CÔTES DE BORDEAUX — (Coat d'Bor-doe) — Name given to two adjoining vineyard districts in the Bordeaux Country, both on the rather steep right bank of the Garonne river, southeast of Bordeaux itself. Correctly, the northern and more important of the two is called the Premières Côtes de Bordeaux; it produces some rather ordinary red wine, plus a great deal of good, fairly sweet and sometimes very sweet white wine, recalling that of the Sauternes district (directly across the river) but of less remarkable quality. Cadillac *(see)* is the best known of the various village names. The southern area is called Côtes de Bordeaux-Saint Macaire, and only white wines may be so labeled; most of these, too, are sweet, but a few dryer ones are now being made, some of them of good quality.

CÔTES DE BUZET — (Coat d'Bew zay) — Red and white wines of not much interest except locally, produced southeast of Bordeaux, in France.

CÔTES-CANON-FRONSAC — (Coat Ca-naw Fraw-sack) — One of the best of the less-known red wines of Bordeaux, coming from a small, strictly delimited area just west of St. Émilion.

CÔTES DE DURAS — (Coat d'Dew-rahs) — Red and semi-sweet white wine (the latter somewhat like Monbazillac) produced east of Bordeaux, in France.

CÔTES DE FRONSAC — (Coat d'Fraw-sack) — Good red wine produced on hillside vineyards near the town of this name, west of St. Émilion in the Bordeaux Country. Less fine than Côtes-Canon-Fronsac *(see).*

CÔTES DE MONTRAVEL — (Coat d'Maw-tra-vel) — *See* Montravel.

CÔTES DE PROVENCE — (Coat d'Pro-vahnce) — The red, *rosé* and white wines coming from the hilly country along the Mediterranean coast between Marseille and Nice. Early-maturing, fairly light, pleasant, and on the whole inexpensive, these have long been popular among visitors to the Riviera; they are now being shipped, in increasing quantity, to other parts of France, and even exported. The *rosés*, fresh, rather light in color, generally sold in special amphora-like bottles, are perhaps the best of them; the whites (predominantly made from the Ugni Blanc and Clairette) are often marketed as *Blanc de Blancs* (*see*), are pale gold, dry, agreeable, not especially distinguished; the reds (from the Grenache, Cinsault, Mourvèdre, Carignan, and two locally known varieties, the Pecoui-Touar and the Oeillade) are soft, garnet rather than crimson, low in tannin, although quite high in alcohol, soon ready. The heart of the production zone is the *département* of the Var. The Côtes de Provence was promoted from V.D.Q.S. to Appellation Contrôlée on October 24, 1977.

CÔTES DE TOUL — (Coat d'Tool) — Red, white and *rosé* wines (the last usually called *vin gris*), light, agreeable, extremely low in alcohol, produced near Toul in the old French province of Lorraine. Although made mostly from Pinot and Gamay grapes, they are really nothing more than good *vins de pays,* and are rarely exported, if indeed ever. They nevertheless carry the V.D.Q.S. seal.

CÔTES DU JURA — (Coat dew Zhu-ra) — Literally, the Jura hillsides; the general, regional name under which most Jura wines (other than Château-Chalon, Arbois and L'Étoile) are sold. The vineyards are due east of the Burgundian Côte d'Or, more or less parallel to the Franco-Swiss frontier, and they are planted along the foothills and lower slopes of the Jura Mountains. Red, white and *rosé* wines, and some sparkling wines, too, are entitled to the appellation. They are rarely much above the level of good *vins de pays,* and are rarely exported.

CÔTES DU LUBÉRON — (Coat dew Lew-bay-raw) — Red, white and *rosé* wines, of which the last are by a wide margin the best, produced in the hilly district east of Avignon and north of the Durance River, in southern France.

CÔTES DU MARMANDAIS — (Coat dew Mar-mahn-day) — Red and white wines entitled to the V.D.Q.S. seal but of purely local interest, produced round the town of Marmande, on the Garonne River, in southwestern France.

CÔTES-DU-RHÔNE — (Coat dew Rone) — General name given to the wines produced in the Rhône Valley between Vienne, south of Lyon, and Avignon, a distance of 120 miles. The finer of these, of course, are all sold under more specific village or district names, from north to south, as follows: Côte Rôtie and Condrieu (part) in the *département* of the Rhône; Château Grillet and the rest of Condrieu in the *département* of the Loire; Hermitage and Crozes-Hermitage in the Drôme; Cornas, St. Péray and St. Joseph in the Ardèche; Tavel and Lirac in the Gard; Châteauneuf-du-Pape, Rasteau and Muscat de Beaumes-de-Venise in the Vaucluse (*see* all of these). The remainder, amounting to over 30 million gallons in favorable years, less than 1% of it white, is called Côtes-du-Rhône. This, however, is further subdivided and classified by law, and the superior grades generally carry a village name as well; the village names used most frequently are Cairanne, Chusclan, Laudun

LYON

COTE ROTIE
CONDRIEU
CHATEAU GRILLET
VIENNE

CROZES-HERMITAGE
SAINT JOSEPH   HERMITAGE
TAIN
TOURNON

Isère

CORNAS
SAINT PERAY   VALENCE

N

Drôme

CÔTES DU RHÔNE
LEGEND
Towns   AVIGNON
Rivers   *Rhône*
Major Vine yards   HERMITAGE
Lesser Vine yards   CORNAS   VIOLES
SCALE
MI. 0   10   20
KM. 0   20   40

Rhône

CAIRANNE

ORANGE
RASTEAU
CHUSCLAN
LAUDUN   VIOLES   GIGONDAS   Mt Ventoux
VACQUEYRAS
LIRAC   CHATEAUNEUF DU PAPE
TAVEL   AVIGNON   BEAUMES DE VENISE

Luberon

NIMES

Durance

ARLES

E. B. Eshman

CAMARGUE

MEDITERRANEAN SEA

MARSEILLE

108

and Vacqueyras (*see*). These better grade wines may also be labeled Côtes-du-Rhône-Villages. Twenty different grape varieties are authorized, the more important being the Syrah, Grenache, Mourvèdre, Cinsault, Clairette, Roussanne, Marsanne, Viognier. Côtes-du-Rhône *Rouge* is a pleasant, soft, rather inexpensive table wine, sound and good but without any claim to greatness; Côtes-du-Rhône *Rosé* resembles a rather light and somewhat common *rosé* of Tavel; the white, often lacking in finesse and fruit, is generally the least good of the three.

CÔTES DU RHÔNE-VILLAGES — (Vee-lajh) *See* above.

CÔTES DU ROUSSILLION — (Coat dew Roo-see-aw) — Red and white wines produced in the Pyrenees-Orientales, better qualities can be labeled Côtes du Roussillon-Villages, Côtes du Roussillon-Caramany and Côtes du Roussillon-Latour de France. These were the first wines to be promoted (March 3, 1977) from V.D.Q.S. to Appellation Contrôlée.

CÔTES DU VENTOUX — (Coat dew Vawn-too) — *See* Ventoux.

COUDERC — (Coo-dair) — French grape hybridizer, several of whose crosses, carrying his name plus a serial number, are now being grown with some success in the eastern United States. *See* Hybrids.

COUHINS, Château — (Coo-anse) — Well-known vineyard in the township of Villenave d'Ornon, Graves district. Produces a little red wine but about 3,000 cases a year of good quality, dry white Graves.

COULANT — (Coo-law) — Literally, in French, "running," as of a stream of water. As a wine taster's term it means easy to drink, and is applied to light, fresh, tender wines, low in tannin and alcohol.

COULÉE DE SERRANT — (Cool-lay duh Sair-rah) — *See* Savennières.

COULURE — (Coo-luhr) — One of the many afflictions of the vineyard owner, the disastrous result of persistent rain or very cold weather during the flowering season of the vine — some blossoms are never properly pollinated; the embryo grapes never develop and eventually fall off. This has no effect on quality but may reduce the crop by as much as half, and occasionally even more. A less severe version of the same thing is called, in French, *millerandage* — a few flowers in each bunch are only partially pollinated and result in tiny, seedless grapes, called *millerands,* or "shot berries." Since these are generally very sweet, they can bring about an actual improvement in the quality of the resulting wine, though of course at the sacrifice of volume.

COUPÉ — (Coo-pay) — French word which, when applied to wine, means "cut," or blended. A *vin de coupage* is a blending wine.

COUR-CHEVERNY — (Coor Shev-air-nee) — Pleasant white *vin de pays* produced near Blois, in the French Chateau Country. It is entitled to the V.D.Q.S. seal.

COURTIER — (Coor-tyay) — French wine broker, very important in Bordeaux and other districts; the courtiers are local expert intermediaries between the numerous small growers and the shippers. Sometimes they work exclusively for a shipper but many are independent entrepreneurs and pass their skills and secrets on from one generation to another.

COUTET, Château — (Coo-tay) — One of the two great vineyards of Barsac (Climens being the other), officially and correctly ranked as a 1st Growth; some 6,000 cases a year. Its wine is the prototype of classic Barsac; golden, rich, but not cloyingly sweet, racy, fruity, with a fine bouquet, great distinction and breed.

ALSO, a 1st Growth vineyard of St. Émilion which produces, of course, red wine exclusively.

CRACKLING — Term meaning slightly sparkling — natural, induced or pumped in. If pressure does not exceed one atmosphere (15 pounds per square inch equivalent to 0.3922 grams of carbon dioxide per 100 milliliters) and the wine is not packaged as a sparkling wine, the lower table wine taxes apply; in this case the term "crackling" can not appear on the label. (*see* Frizzante)

CRADLE — Wire, wicker or straw basket (French, *panier*) made to hold a bottle of wine in nearly the same horizontal position it occupied in the cellar, thus permitting it to be brought from storage to a place where the wine will be opened and decanted (*see*). To use a cradle for table service of a wine that has no sediment at all, is pure chi-chi and demonstrates one's lack of wine knowledge.

CRAMANT — (Cram-maw) — Important wine-producing village in the Champagne Country, south of Épernay, rated as one of the very best. Its wines, all made from the white Chardonnay grape, are remarkable for their delicacy, bouquet and breed, and are among the rare Champagnes quite often sold unblended and under the village name (i.e., as Cramant), rather than a brand. *See* Champagne, Blanc de Blancs.

CREAM — Generic name for smooth, sweet oloroso sherry.

CRÉMANT — (Cray-mauw) — French term, literally "creaming," applied to wines which are mildly sparkling — between *pétillant* and *mousseux*. Should not be confused with Cramant (*see*), which is a place name. A *Crémant de Cramant* actually exists — it is a light, most agreeable Champagne from the town of Cramant, with less pressure and less sparkle than most Champagnes.

CRÉPY — (Cray-pee) — Pleasant little white wine produced in the Haute-Savoie, France, not far from the southern shore of Lake Geneva. It is marketed in tall, slender bottles, like Alsatian wines, but made from the Chasselas (or Fendant) grape, and much resembles the light white wines of Switzerland. Annual production amounts to some 20,000 cases.

CRESZENZ — (Cress-zenz) — German wine-term meaning "growth," or "production of," properly followed by the name of the vineyard owner. No longer allowed on German labels under the new 1971 Wine Law, this word indicates, on older vintages, that the wine is a natural (i.e. unsugared) wine but is not estate-bottled. It was most often used by German hotels and restaurants for wines which they purchased in barrel and then bottled themselves. Although such wines were not estate-bottled, they nevertheless could come from a top-ranking vineyard or grower, and the term *Creszenz,* or *Wachstum (see),* in conjunction with the grower's name was permitted on the label as a guarantee of quality and authenticity of the wine.

CRIADERA — (Cree-ah-*dair*-ah) — Literally, in Spanish, a nursery. As applied to wines (rather than children or plants) its use is confined to the Sherry Country, where wines are aged and blended in *soleras (see).* The *criadera,* in Jerez, is the section in which young wines are cared for, selected and graded before being admitted to what might be called their university, the *solera* proper. The word may, however, be correctly used to include all of the stages of the *solera* itself, except of course the lowest and final one.

CRIOTS-BÂTARD-MONTRACHET — (Cree-oh   Bat-tarr   Mon-rah-shay) — New appellation, created in 1937, under which some four or five hundred cases a year of superlative white Burgundy are now sold. The vineyard, in the township of Chassagne-Montrachet *(see),* consists of a small prolongation, to the south, of Bâtard-Montrachet *(see).* The wines from the two plots are both of very high quality and can hardly be told apart, even by an expert.

CROIZET-BAGES, Château — (Crwah-zay Bahj) — One of the less distinguished of the 5th Classed Growths of Pauillac, Haut-Médoc. Annual production about 6,000 cases.

CRÖV — (Kruhv) — Usually spelled Kröv *(see).*

CROZES-HERMITAGE — (Crows Air-me-tahj) — Comparatively new appellation, used since 1952 to designate the red and white Rhône wines produced in 11 townships north, east and south of the one extraordinary hillside which alone yields Hermitage *(see).* Until then many of the better red wines of this district had been sold as "Crozes" and some excellent whites as "Mercurol," village names both, and both now part of the Crozes-Hermitage zone. The reds are made exclusively from the Syrah grape and the whites from the Roussanne and Marsanne; they are not unlike Hermitage but rather more common, with less distinction and less bouquet. About 93% of the production is red, 7% white, and the total is about six times that of Hermitage itself, not far from 560,000 gallons a year.

CRU — (Crew) — French word meaning "growth." When applied to wine, a specific vineyard and the wine it produces; by implication, one of superior quality, as *vin de cru.* The word is not, as some writers in English have supposed, the past participle, *crû,* of the verb *croître,* to grow, but a quite separate noun, written without the circumflex. Most classifications of French wines divide the various wines and vineyards into *crus,* as *Grand Cru, Premier Cru, Deuxième Cru, Cru Classé, Cru Bourgeois Exceptionnel,* etc.

CRU CLASSÉ — (Crew Class-A) — *See* Classed Growth.

CRUSTED — Term applied to an old red wine, usually a vintage Port, which has thrown a heavy sediment, in the form of a film, or "crust," over the inner face of the bottle. Such wines should generally be carefully decanted before serving.

111

CUIS — (Quee) — Wine-producing village of secondary importance in the Champagne Country of France. South of Épernay and part of the Côte des Blancs, it is nevertheless one of the villages in which both white grapes (Chardonnay) and black (Pinot Noir) are grown.

CULTIVAR — Cultivated variety, vine selected for planting from thousands of wild varieties and hybrids.

CUSSAC — (Cew-sack) — Small wine-producing town of the Haut-Médoc, between Margaux and St. Julien. Secondary red wines.

CUVAISON — (Cew-vay-zahn) — Practice, essential in the making of red wine, of allowing the juice and skins to ferment together, thereby giving color and additional tannin to the wine. CUVAGE is the length of time this process lasts, a mere matter of hours in the case of *vins rosés,* generally from four or five days to two weeks for red wines.

CUVÉE — (Cew-vay) — From the French *cuve,* vat, tank or cask, especially a large one, in which wines are fermented or blended. Therefore a specific lot or "batch" or blend of a given wine, possibly different from others that may carry the same or a quite similar label. The term is loosely and not always accurately used. Thus the "English cuvée" of a given Champagne house will be a blend presumably made for the English market, but quite possibly on a vast scale, far more than any vat or *cuve* could contain; the "Tête de Cuvée" of a château or domain will be its best lot of that vintage, whether from one cask or ten; a "Première Cuvée" (a term once widely used in Burgundy but now fortunately tending to disappear) simply means one of the best wines of a given *commune.*

CYNAR — (Chee-nar) — Odd Italian apéritif made from artichokes. It has no legitimate place in a wine dictionary, but some people have thought it a flavored wine, and the truth may as well be told.

CYPRUS — Large island of the eastern Mediterranean, with over 90,000 acres of producing vineyard, and a wine tradition dating back to the Crusades. Richard Coeur de Lion celebrated his marriage to Queen Berengaria (in the year 1191) in Cyprus wine, and the golden Commandaria, first produced round Limassol by the Knights of the Order of the Templars and St. John, was famous throughout Western Europe. Most of the Cyprus wine now exported is sweet, fortified, somewhat comparable to Madeira, and it has enjoyed a recent vogue in England. The best is still usually sold as Commandaria.

CZECHOSLOVAKIA — Has some 100,000 acres of vineyard, mostly round Melnik, in the Elbe Valley north of Prague, and in the vicinity of Brno (Brunn) in the province of Moravia. The wines, almost all consumed locally, are not outstanding.

D

DALMATIA — (Dal-*may*-she-ya) — The mountainous, picturesque and charming eastern shore of the Adriatic Sea, a province of Yugoslavia, between Trieste and the Albanian border. A great deal of wine is produced, although little of outstanding quality. Those generally considered the best include a full-bodied, rather dry white from near Mostar, called Žilavka; a red, labeled Dingać and pronounced "Dingatch"; and a somewhat sweet red, high in alcohol, called Prošek; lastly, and almost everywhere, a pleasant *rosé* called Ružica, "little rose." Many wines are now shipped under the brand name "Adriatica" by the State, sometimes with a varietal name as well.

DAMBACH — (Dahm-bach) — One of the better small, wine-producing villages of Alsace, not far from Sélestat, in the *département* of Bas-Rhin.

DAME BLANCHE, Château La — (Dahm Blawnch) — One of the rare Médoc vineyards producing white wine exclusively, about 5,000 cases annually; it is situated only a few hundred yards north of the legal boundary of Graves, at Le Taillan, near Blanquefort. Its wine, being white, is not entitled to the appellation Médoc, and is rated a Bordeaux Supérieur.

DAME JEANNE — (Dahm Zhahn) — This is the French term from which the English *demijohn* is derived; literally "Lady Joan," it means about the same thing as in English, an oversize bottle of no fixed capacity, which may or may not be covered with straw or wicker, or set in a wood frame. Much *vin ordinaire* is so shipped in France, but very large Bordeaux bottles (jeroboams, impériales, etc.) are often called *Dames Jeannes,* as well.

113

DÃO — (Da-o) — One of the best Portuguese table wines, produced round the town of Viseu in a hilly country half-way between Lisbon and Oporto. The reds, deep colored, rather full-bodied, extremely fruity, somewhat lacking in breed, are made primarily from the same grape varieties as Port — the Tourigo, the Tinta, the Alvarelhão, the Bastardo. The whites are rather high in alcohol, golden, full-bodied, and these, too, are made mostly from white Port varieties — the Arinto, etc. Now shipped to the United States, Dão has become more and more popular in recent years.

DAUZAC, Château — (Doe-zack) — 5th Classed Growth of Labarde-Margaux, Haut-Médoc. Some 10,000 cases a year of good quality, rather delicate red wine.

DAVID — Author of the Psalms (circa 150 b.c.) in the 104th of which is written: "Wine maketh glad the heart of man."

DEBOURBAGE — (Day-boor-baj) — Practice, highly beneficial in the making of white wine, of delaying the fermentation of the newly pressed juice for some twenty-four hours, until it has had a chance to clear and can be drawn off its gross lees, or original coarse sediment. To accomplish this worthy end, the juice must either be held at a very low temperature or treated with metabisulphite and then (usually) set to ferment with a culture of selected yeast. These processes are all accepted parts of modern wine technique, but there are still more than a few famous European cellars which would greatly benefit by their introduction.

DEBRÖI HÁRSLEVELÜ — (Da-brewie Hahrsh-lav-a-loo) — Dry white Hungarian table wine, officially ranked as a *grand cru*.

DECANT — To transfer a wine from its original bottle to another vessel — carafe, bottle or decanter — usually for serving. The purpose of decanting is to separate the clear wine from any sediment which it may have thrown: this is almost never necessary in dealing with white wines, or red wines that have been less than five years in bottle, but old Rhône wines, many old Clarets and even some old Burgundies are better when decanted than when served, no matter how carefully, in a cradle. Wines should be decanted if possible, in the cellar; the bottle is first placed as gently as possible in a cradle, the cork drawn, and the wine poured slowly into the carafe against a lighted candle until the first sign of sediment appears.

DECANTER — Glass carafe into which old wines are decanted, and in which young, inexpensive wines are often served. Also, the rather more elaborate vessels, usually of cut crystal, in which Sherry, Madeira and even Port are sometimes kept on the sideboard.

DE CHAUNAC — (Duh-Shawn-ack) — Red hybrid grape grown in Northeast and Middlewest United States and in the Canadian Niagara Peninsula, valued for hardiness and general reliability.

DECIZE-LES-MARANGES — Day-seez lay Mar-ronj) — Tiny village near the southern end of the Côte d'Or, in Burgundy. Its passable red wine is usually sold at Côte de Beaune-Villages (*see*).

DEIDESHEIM — (*Die*-des-heim) — Famous and picturesque little town in the German Palatinate, or Pfalz; with the adjoining villages of Forst, Ruppertsberg and Wachenheim, it produces the best of the Palatinate's white wines. There are nearly a thousand hillside acres under vines, over 60% Rieslings, and the finer Deidesheimers invariably carry the word "Riesling," as well as a specific vineyard name, on their label, as Deidesheimer Hohenmorgen Riesling, etc. The leading vineyard sites located in three *grosslagen* include: Hohenmorgen, Grainhübel, Kieselberg, Leinhöhle, Kalkofen, Paradiesgarten, Mäushöhle, Nonnenstück, Herrgottsacker, and Langenmorgen. The village is quaint and charming, with fine old patrician houses in red sandstone, a venerable Rathaus, or Town Hall, and dozens of winding narrow streets and walled gardens green in summer with apricots and figs. The wines are full-bodied, with great bouquet, and range all the way from dry to very sweet; they have remarkable distinction, the Rieslings especially, and fully deserve their international reputation.

DEKELEIA — (Day-kel-lay-ah) — Red and white table wines, of no special distinction, from near Marathon, in Greece. The name has somehow found its way into almost all existing wine dictionaries and is included here for tradition's sake, and for no other reason.

DELAWARE — One of the best and most widely planted of our native American varieties, almost unique in that it yields excellent table grapes which are also excellent for wine. Its precise ancestry and origin are unknown; some botanists feel that it is an accidental cross of the wild Labrusca vine of our Northern woods and the wild Southern Aestivalis or Bourquiniana of the Carolinas; others believe it has some European Vinifera blood. It first was noted in 1850 in a vineyard at Frenchtown, New Jersey, whence it was transplanted to Delaware, Ohio, and it therefore takes its name from this small town, rather than from the river or the state.
   A pink grape, it has white juice and yields white wine, fresh, pale, well-balanced but rather high in acid, with the definite but not too oppressive native-grape or "foxy" flavor and aroma of its Labrusca ancestors. It is widely used in Eastern Champagnes and until the arrival of the new French hybrids (*see*) was consistently responsible for the best white table wines of New York State and Ohio.

DELICATE — Wine tasters' term, properly applicable to wines that are light, rather than full or big; subtle, rather than coarse or sturdy; fine and elegant, rather than great.

DELICATESSEN — This familiar word which, in its original German, means "delicate viands" or "fancy foods," is also the name of a grape, an American hybrid developed by the late T. V. Munson, of Denison, Texas. It is said to give a deep-colored red wine of good quality, but it is no longer grown on any commercial scale.

DEMI, DEMIE — (Dem-mee) — These, in French, are the masculine and feminine forms of the same word, and both mean "half"; oddly enough, beer (*bière*), which is feminine, takes the masculine form, and wine (*vin*), which is

115

masculine, takes the feminine. This is less illogical than it seems: *une demie* means a half-bottle of wine (half of *une bouteille*); *un demi* means, or should and used to, a half-liter (half of *un litre,* roughly a pint) of beer, but French beer glasses have grown smaller year by year, and today when you order *un demi* you get about seven ounces.

DEMIJOHN — A large, squat, round bottle or jug, generally wicker-covered, holding anywhere from one to ten gallons. In French it is called a *bonbonne* or *Dame Jeanne.*

DEMI-SEC — (Dem-mee-seck) — Literally, in French, "half-dry"; actually, when applied to Champagne or other sparkling wines, it means sweet, and now that it is no longer fashionable to label Champagnes, even the sweetest of them, *"doux,"* the demi-secs are about the most heavily dosed, or sweetest, on the market, containing anywhere from 5% to 7% of sugar syrup or liqueur, as against about half as much for wines marked *"sec."* The term is rarely used of still wines, and has no precise meaning in this connection, other than vaguely "on the sweet side."

DENOMINAZIONE DI ORIGINE CONTROLLATA — (Deh-nom-ee-*natz*-ee-o-neh Dee Ori-*jean*-eh Con-trol-*lah*-ta) — Abbreviated D.O.C. Wines meeting certain standards of origin, grape variety, yield and quality are so labeled under the Italian Wine Law of 1963.

DENOMINAZIONE DI ORIGINE CONTROLLATA E GARANTITA — (Deh-nom-ee-*natz*-ee-o-neh Dee Ori-*jean*-eh Con-trol-*lah*-ta Ee Gar-ahn-*tee*-ta) — Abbreviated D.O.C.G. Wines meeting even more restrictive and higher quality standards under the Italian Wine Law of 1963 are so labeled. The first D.O.C.G. wines should be the 1978 vintages of Barbaresco, Barolo, Brunello and Vino Nobile di Montepulciano.

DENOMINAZIONE DI ORIGINE SEMPLICE — (Deh-nom-ee-*natz*-ee-o-neh Dee Ori-*jean*-eh Sem-*plee*-cheh) — Abbreviated D.O.S. Under the Italian Wine Law of 1963, a geographic indication of wines made according to local usage from grapes typical of the production area.

DÉPARTEMENT — (Day-par-te-maw) — Administrative unit in France, more or less the equivalent of an American county. There are 95 of them. Term often used in this volume, in giving the location of certain villages and vineyards.

DEPOSIT — (French, *dépôt*) — Sediment which many red wines and some white tend to throw in the course of their normal evolution in bottle. In the case of white wines this generally takes the form of colorless crystals of tartaric acid, harmless and tasteless; but red wine sediment, containing tannin and pigment, is usually bitter and always disagreeable — it should be left behind in the bottle when the wine is poured.

DESMIRAIL, Château — (Day-me-rye) — Classed in 1855 as a 3rd Growth of Margaux, Haut-Médoc. No longer exists as an independent vineyard. The property was bought by the owners of Château Palmer (*see*), its production incorporated into that of the latter château and the name Desmirail no longer is used.

DESSERT WINE — Rather confusing term, since it is used, on the whole correctly, in two widely different senses. In California it means a fortified wine, generally, but by no means always, a sweet one; it is perhaps worth noting that the word "sweet" has also come to have precisely this same special meaning, and a "sweet wine producer," in California, may be a person with a sour disposition who manufactures nothing but the dryest of dry Sherry. A dessert wine, in perhaps more sensible and better usage, is a wine that one might properly serve with dessert, whatever its alcoholic content: for most tastes, Sauternes would fall into this category, together with sweet Sherry, Port, Banyuls, and even the Beerenauslesen and Trockenbeerenauslesen of the Rhine.

DETZEM — (*Dets*-em) — Ancient little wine-producing village on the Moselle, in Germany. Ten Roman miles from Trier, on the old Roman road to Mainz, it took its name from the tenth milestone (*ad decimum lapidem*); its wines are of no real quality or importance.

DÉZALEY — (Day-za-lay) — One of the best dry white wines of Switzerland, produced on steep, terraced vineyards overlooking Lake Geneva, east of Lausanne in the Canton of Vaud. Although made from the Fendant or Chasselas grape, it has considerable distinction and its reputation on the whole is deserved. *See* Lavaux.

DHRON — (Drone) — Vineyard town on the Moselle, between Trittenheim and Piesport. Its wines are of good, not extraordinary quality, but with fine bouquet — the best is Dhroner Hofberger and other superior vineyards include Engelgrube, Grosser Hengelberg, Roterd, Laudamusberg and Rosengärtchen. Since 1971 the wines are sold as Neumagen-Dhron.

DIAMOND — *See* MOORE'S DIAMOND.

DIE — (Dee) — Town east of the Rhône Valley, known for its sparkling wine, Clairette de Die (*see*).

DIENHEIM — (*Dean*-heim) — Wine-producing town in Rheinhessen, on the Rhine south of Nierstein and Oppenheim, where the escarpment of the *Rheinfront* falls away to the alluvial plain toward Worms. The Dienheimer wines are soft and pleasant but a bit common, with some *Bodenton*, the coarse taste of heavy soil. Best vineyards include Falkenberg, Herrenberg, Herrengarten, Tafelstein. The leading producer is the Staatsweingut, the Hessian State Domain.

DIJON — (Dee-jaw) — Principal city (Pop. 157,000) of Burgundy, in the French *département* of Côte d'Or, although less important in the wine trade than Nuits-Saint-Georges and Beaune. There is a saying to the effect that Dijon is the capital of La Bourgogne (the province) and Beaune (*see*) the capital of Le Bourgogne (the wine). The Côte de Dijon begins at the city's southern edge; it is the northernmost and by far the least important of the three vine-

117

yard slopes that make up the celebrated Côte d'Or (see). A major tourist center, Dijon is also known for its mustard, made with a white wine base, and for its great annual Gastronomic Fair.

DIONYSUS — In Greek mythology, a nature god, especially of the vine and of wine, the son of Zeus and Semele, the earth goddess. He was also called Bacchus and his symbol was the thyrsus, a staff wreathed with ivy and grape leaves and surmounted by a pine cone.

DISGORGING — From the French *dégorgement*, one of the essential, final steps in the making of Champagne (see), by which the sediment is removed from the bottled wine before it receives its *dosage*, or sweetening, and its final cork.

DISTINGUISHED — Used by a wine expert, this is the highest sort of praise, almost the equivalent of the German word *edel*, and reserved for wines of truly extraordinary balance and class. The quality of such wines is immediately obvious, even to a beginner.

DIZY — (Dee-zee) — One of the better wine-producing towns of the French Champagne Country, directly across the Marne from Épernay. Its vineyards are almost entirely planted to Pinot Noir, and are officially rated 95%, which means its grapes bring 5% less, per kilo or per ton, than those from the adjoining town of Ay, rated 100%.

D.O.C. — See Denominazione di Origine Controllata.

D.O.C.G. — see Denominazione di Origine Controllata y Garantita.

DOISY-DAËNE, Château — (Dwah-zee Day-en) — 2nd Classed Growth of Barsac, Sauternes, properly considered one of the best of these, lying, as it does, between Coutet and Climens; 3,000 case output. Recently the owners have been pioneers in the production of a dry white wine from this district, sold, not as Barasac, but as "Bordeaux Sec de Doisy-Daëne"; of excellent quality, racy, light and fine, this is already acquiring the acceptance it deserves.

DOISY-DUBROCA, Château — (Dwah-zee Dew-bro-ca) — Originally one of the classified 2nd Growths of Barsac, in France, it is now a part of Château Climens.

DOISY-VÉDRINES, Château — (Dwah-zee Vay-dreen) — 2nd Classed Growth of Barsac, Sauternes, originally part of the same vineyard as Doisy-Daëne. Some 5,000 cases a year.

DOLCETTO — (Dohl-*chet*-toe) — Italian red wine grape of good quality, widely grown in Piedmont, especially on the higher slopes in the provinces of Alessandria and Cuneo. Precocious and productive, it gives a rather soft red wine, short-lived, soon ready to drink, usually sold under the varietal name.

DÔLE — (Dole) — Generally considered the best red wine of Switzerland, produced in the high, rocky, upper valley of the Rhône, in the Canton of Valais. It is made from the Pinot Noir grape plus, quite often, a good deal of Gamay, is full-bodied, deep-colored, quite high in alcohol, long-lived. In character it perhaps is closer to Côte Rôtie than to the Burgundies of the Côte d'Or.

DOM — (Dawm) — In German, the word for Cathedral: as far as wine is concerned, especially the Hohe Domkirche, or Cathedral of Trier, on the Moselle, which has a few important vineyards as part of its endowment. The finest include part of the Scharzhofberg, at Wiltingen on the Saar, and vines at Trier. The Cathedral's wines are estate-bottled but by no means better than wines made by laymen in adjacent vineyards. *See also* Dom Pérignon.

DOMAENE — (Doe-may-nuh) — German for the French word *domaine* or English "domain" — as far as wine is concerned, a vineyard property. In Germany it is often and almost exclusively applied to the state-owned vineyards, or Staatsweingüter, which are numerous and justly famous, in the Rheingau, in Hessen, and on the Nahe, Moselle and Saar.

DOMAINE — (Doe-main) — Vineyard holdings or vineyards making up a single property or estate, although these vineyards may or may not be widely separated in different *communes* or townships, and bear entirely different names. A single Burgundian *Domaine* might, for example, comprise vines in Chambertin, Clos de Vougeot, Corton and Montrachet; the wines from these will of course be kept scrupulously separate, and will be marketed under the various vineyard appellations, with the name of the *Domaine* appearing only as the producer, not as the name of the wine. Many Domaine wines are estate-bottled (*see*) although by no means all; those that are, carry on their labels the words *Mise du Domaine* or *Mis en Bouteilles au Domaine*.

The word is quite differently used in the Bordeaux Country and in Provence where it is practically synonymous with Château, e.g., Domaine de Chevalier, Domaine de la Croix, etc.

DOM PÉRIGNON — (Dawm Pay-reen-yaw) — Cellar-master at the Abbey of Hautvillers, in the Champagne Country, from 1670 to 1715; this is a singularly gracious old building and commands an incomparable view of the vineyards and of Épernay and the Marne Valley. It was here, according to well-publicized tradition, that Dom Pérignon "invented" Champagne, and made his celebrated remark, on first tasting it, "I am drinking stars." Actually, of course, no one "invented" Champagne, and the old monk never claimed to have done so. He was, like his contemporary, Dom Oudard, one of the most competent and imaginative wine technicians of his day, and there is no doubt that he was one of the first to experiment with cork closures, then rare in France, and to make what is now known as a *cuvée* by blending wines of different origins and of both black grapes and white. But modern Champagne owes fully as much to half a hundred nameless and forgotten experts as to him.

The Abbey of Hautvillers is now the property of the great Champagne house of Moët et Chandon, and a statue of Dom Pérignon has been set up in the courtyard. The name "Dom Pérignon" has been given to Moët's best and most expensive wine, shipped in the sort of slender-necked, low-shouldered bottle used for all Champagnes a hundred years ago. However, it was found necessary to discontinue the use of corks tied down with string instead of wire, and sealed with wax instead of foil (all Champagnes came this way, and in wicker hampers, in our great-grandfathers' days) for there is, after all, a limit to archaism. The wine does not always merit its great present reputation, but is generally of outstanding quality.

DOMTAL — (Dawm-tahl) — Originally the name of a vineyard in Nierstein, on the Rhine, literally "cathedral-valley"; this has now become a *Grosslage* (*see*) and is called "Gutes Domtal." It includes about 15 small wine-producing villages (none of outstanding quality) and even one vineyard (Pfakkenkappe) in Nierstein itself. Much abused as an appellation of origin in the past, the name is somewhat more restricted in use since the new law went into effect in 1971, but even now a bottle of "Niersteiner Gutes Domtal" will never be a top quality wine from Nierstein and will in all probability not even be a wine from the village of Nierstein at all.

DORDOGNE — (Dor-doyn) — Important river of southwestern France, joining the Garonne just north of Bordeaux, to form the tidal estuary of the Gironde; also a *département* farther east, bordering the Bordeaux Country and producing a good deal of rather common wine, mostly white and somewhat sweet, sold as Monbazillac (*see*), Montravel, etc.

D.O.S. — *See* Denominazione di Origine Semplice.

DOSAGE — (Doe-saj) — All Champagne is absolutely bone dry up to the moment when it is "disgorged" and receives what is known as its *dosage*. This consists of anywhere from a teaspoonful to two ounces of syrup, or *liqueur d'expédition,* and the amount determines whether the wine is Brut, or Extra Dry, or Sec, or Demi-sec. There exist various formulas for the syrup, but generally there are three parts of sugar to two of old wine.

DOUBLE MAGNUM — see Jeroboam.

DOURO — (Doo-row) — One of Portugal's three great rivers, all of which rise in Spain and change their spelling and their nationality before they empty into the Atlantic: the Tajo becomes the Tejo, the Duero, the Douro, and the northernmost is the Spanish Miño on its northern bank and the Portuguese Minho on its southern. For wine lovers, all three are relatively undistinguished in Spain, but the Douro, once it crosses the border, becomes the spinal column and even the principal highway of one of the world's great wine countries. *See* Port.

DOUX — (Doo) — Simply means "sweet" in its ordinary French sense, but applied to wine it becomes much more complicated. The good, natural, not-quite-dry table wines are more properly described as *moelleux* — the best Graves for example; another adjective, *liquoreux,* is applied to the naturally sweet wines, such as the great Sauternes and the finer white wines of Anjou; a *vin doux* is generally a wine possessing a sweetness not entirely normal — one only partially fermented and heavily sulphured, as the *vin doux de Gaillac;* or a sweet fortified wine, as the so-called *vins doux naturels* of the eastern Pyrenees; or the very sweetest and on the whole the poorest of Champagnes. The term, in brief, is one rarely applied to good, let alone outstanding, wines.

DRACHENBLUT — (Drak-en-bloot) — Literally, in German, "dragon's blood." So-called, usually with a wink, it is a pale, watery red wine, of poor

120

quality at best, produced on a hill known as the Drachenfels, on the east bank of the Rhine, near Bonn.

DRÔME — (Droam) — French *département* on the left bank of the Rhône south of Lyon; that of Hermitage, Crozes, Mercurol (*see* all of these).

DRUNKARDS' LINE — An affectionate name given to the single track railway which prior to the canalization of the Moselle River in the 1960's used to follow the winding Moselle Valley from Trier to Bullay in Germany; the *Saufbähnchen*. Its timetable read like a wine-list, but there was no club car and no dining car, nor hardly a wine which ran as high as 11% alcohol produced along its route; its average of passenger sobriety was certainly higher than that on the Super-Chief. Unfortunately, at the time the locks were built for the new Moselle barge canal, the expense of relocating the track was considered too great and the *Saufbähnchen* no longer exists.

DRY — As far as wine is concerned, the opposite of sweet is not sour, but dry; and even an extremely dry wine is no more necessarily sour than unsugared coffee is sour. Practically all of the widely used table wines of the world are dry rather than sweet, as are many apéritif wines such as Fino and Amontillado Sherry, Sercial and Rainwater Madeira, and some Marsalas.

In California, the word has acquired a somewhat different connotation and, colloquially at least, is synonymous with unfortified. Thus, in California — in wine parlance — wines under 14%, even if sweet, are "dry wines." Similarly, dry Sherry is often referred to as "sweet" (i.e., fortified).

DRY SAUTERNE — Only in America could this happen. The name Sauternes, recognized in most countries as a specific geographic area in France which by law can only produce sweet wines bearing the Appellation Controlée Sauternes, was appropriated (without the final "s") in the 19th Century for dry wines made in this country. Dry Sauterne therefore is a complete anomaly (*see* Sauternes).

DUBONNET — (Due-bawn-nay) — Excellent, popular, widely-advertised French apéritif made, according to a proprietary formula, of sweet, red, fortified wine, quinine and various herbs. It is used as an ingredient in many cocktails but more often, in France at least, served straight or with ice and soda. Dubonnet is also manufactured under license in California, and theoretically according to the same formula, but the basic wine is of course not the same and the end product is somewhat different.

DUCRU-BEAUCAILLOU, Château — (Dew-crew Bow-ky-you) — 2nd Classed Growth of St. Julien, Haut-Médoc; some 15,000 cases a year. *"Caillou"* in French means pebble, and *"beau,"* of course, means beautiful; the vineyard is just north of Beychevelle and extends down to the river on gravelly soil, as its name indicates. The wines in the past were rather hard, slow to mature, and brought prices below some of tthe other 2nd Growths; there has been a striking improvement since the early 1940's.

DUHART-MILON-ROTHSCHILD, Château — (Dew-har Mee-law Rawt-sheeld) — 4th Classed Growth of Pauillac, Haut-Médoc, adjoining Lafite to which it now belongs, producing some 7,000 cases a year of good claret, full-bodied, slow-maturing, better than some châteaux that have a higher official rank.

DULCE — (Dool-they) — Literally, in Spanish, means "sweet." Applied to wine, in a special sense, it means a sweetening agent, any one of many, added to the dry wines of the Sherry Country to make them more acceptable abroad. Most of these are very sweet wines from sun-dried grapes, others are concentrates — *see* Pedro Ximénez, Arrope, Apagado, Sancocho.

DULL — A dull wine is like a dull person — perhaps honorable and sound, but not very interesting and certainly not much fun. Such a wine may be dry, full-bodied and have other qualities; it should certainly be cheap.

DUMB — A tasting term for wine with a potential promise but not yet developed enough to show its character.

DUR — (Dewr) — Literally, "hard," in French. As a wine-tasters' term it has almost exactly the same meaning and connotation as its English equivalent. *See* Hard.

DURAS — *See* Côtes de Duras.

DURBACH — (Door-bak) — German wine-producing town in Baden, almost directly across the Rhine from Strasbourg. Many of the wines, Rieslings, Traminers and Ruländers (Pinot Gris), are far from bad and some of them occasionally quite remarkable, but most of them are drunk up by the local gentry and by thirsty tourists before they are two years old.

DURFORT-VIVENS, Château — (Dear-for Vee-vah) — Classed in 1855 as a 2nd Growth of Margaux, Médoc. The château itself is now owned by Pierre Ginestet, former owner of Château Margaux, and the vineyard is owned by Lucien Lurton, the owner of Château Brane Cantenac, who makes the wine from this property. The average production is about 6,000 cases of wine a year.

DURIFF — (Dew-reef) — Rather common red wine grape, grown to some small extent in the Rhône Valley. It bears a superficial resemblance to the Syrah of Hermitage, but does not have the Syrah's unfortunate tendency to drop its fruit before maturity (*see* Coulure); for this reason, it used to be known to the peasant *vignerons* of the district as the "Syrah-*que-ten*," which could perhaps be translated as the "Holdfast-Syrah"; it is nevertheless not a Syrah at all and its wine is of poor quality. It seems very probable that the so-called "Petite Sirah" of California, which is one of the most widely planted of red wine grapes there, is in fact the Duriff, rather than the illustrious vine whose name it has assumed.

DÜRKHEIM — (*Derk-heim*) — Usually called, except of course on wine labels, Bad Dürkheim (on account of its mineral springs) this happens to be the largest wine-producing township in all Germany, with nearly 2,000 acres of vineyard. It is an agreeable small town, with the wooded hills of the Mittel-Haardt sheltering it on the west, and its many hotels overlook a mile or so of sloping vineyards, and then the flat and fertile Rhine Valley. There is a good deal of red wine, mostly quite poor and made from the Portugieser grape, a large amount of fair, and a little very good white wine: the best is Riesling, and is so labeled, plus a vineyard name, as Herrenmorgen Riesling. Spielberg, Hochbenn, Steinberg and Rittergarten, are other well-known *Lagen*.

DUTCHESS — A native American grape variety of high quality, like the Delaware, but scarcer and more difficult to grow.

E

EARTHY — This is perhaps the best English translation of what the French call a *goût de terroir* and the Germans a *Bodengeschmack,* a rather odd, special flavor which certain soils tend to give to the wines they yield. If too pronounced, this can be highly disagreeable, and is usually the mark of a coarse wine produced, often from the best of grape varieties, on heavy, alluvial soil. It is easy to recognize, almost impossible to describe.

EAST INDIA — Old term, less used now than formerly, to designate Oloroso Sherries of a particular brown, sweet, full-bodied sort. Originally such wines were supposed to have received additional ageing in the holds of sailing vessels, in the course of a voyage to the East Indies and back.

EBERBACH — (Eh-bear-bach) — *See* KLOSTER EBERBACH.

ECCLESIASTICUS — A book of the Apocrypha (about 180 B.C.) in which is written: "Wine drunk with moderation is the joy of the soul and the heart."

ÉCHÉZEAUX — (A-shay-zo) — Important Burgundian vineyard of the Côte de Nuits, between the Clos de Vougeot and Vosne-Romanée, 74 acres in all, with an average production of some 9,700 cases a year. Lying mostly on the gently-sloping, lower half of the *Côte,* it gives a wine more remarkable for its subtlety than its power, rather light in color and body, but racy and fine.

EDEL — (Eh-dell) — German word meaning "noble," or, in a wider sense, "superior" or "fine." Thus *Edelfäule* mean the "Noble Mold" or *pourriture noble; Edeltraube* a superior variety of grape; *Edelbeerenauslese,* now obso-

NOTE: All of the wines of Flagey-Échézeaux are entitled to the village appellation "Vosne-Romanée."

lete, a particularly good wine of this exalted class; and *Edelzwicker,* in Alsace, a wine made from a blend of superior grapes. The Alsatians sometimes treat the word *Gentil* (as in *gentilhomme,* or gentleman) as another French equivalent of *Edel,* and this word is sometmes used on Alsatian wine labels, although rather loosely.

EDELFÄULE — (Eh-del-foy-luh) — *See* BOTRYTIS CINEREA.

EDELGEWÄCHS — *See* GEWÄCHS, EDEL.

EDELZWICKER — (A-del-zvick-er) — Alsatian wine term, meaning a blended wine made from superior grape varieties. *Edel* is the German word for "noble," although in Alsace usually translated as *Gentil (see),* and the *Edeltrauben* or *plants nobles* are considered to include the Riesling, Gewürztraminer, Traminer, Pinot Gris, Pinot Blanc, Muscat and Sylvaner. An Edelzwicker may be a blend of any or all of these, often grown in the same vineyard and picked together. *See* Zwicker.

EGER — (A-gair) — Important Hungarian wine-producing town, set in mountainous country some 120 miles northeast of Budapest, and especially famous for two red wines, Egri Bikavér ("bull's blood") and Egri Kadarka (which is the name of a grape). These are grown in Eger and some dozen surrounding villages, and were much appreciated in Austria, Germany and even the United States in happier and more tranquil days. Both are full-bodied, deep-colored, long-lived, the Kadarka made from the grape of that name, the Bikavér from a number of different varieties including the Kadarka but also the Gamay, the Cabernet Franc, and others.

125

ÉGLISE — (A-gleeze) — Means church in French. The Clos l'Église, Clos l'Église-Clinet and Domaine de l'Église are well-known vineyards of Pomerol, each producing some 2,000 cases a year of very full, soft, good quality claret. In addition there are at least three other properties in Bordeaux with Église as part of the name.

EGRAPPAGE — (Eh-grah-pahj) — Process, essential in the making of all good wine, of removing the grapes from their stems prior to pressing and/or fermentation. In the old days this procedure was less strictly observed for red wines, some stems being left to ferment with the skins; the resulting wines were harsher, higher in tannin, slower to develop, but unquestionably longer-lived.

EGRI BIKAVÉR — see EGER.

EGUISHEIM — (Eh-gwish-heim) — Good wine producing village in Alsace, just south of Colmar in the *département* of Haut-Rhin.

EINZELLAGE — (Eyn-zell-la-guh) — German term for a single vineyard. Under the new German Wine Law, which went into effect in 1971, the term *Einzellage* is used to refer to a single vineyard with strictly-defined boundaries and a legally approved name. An *Einzellage* must be at least 12 acres in size and because of the consolidation of many small vineyards into large vineyards, a number of previously well-known single vineyard names have now disappeared, apparently forever. Under this new arrangement, it is obvious that many of the best vineyards in Germany have increased their acreage at the expense of the less known (and, of course, less good) vineyards which adjoin them. For example, the vineyard of Wieshell in the village of Rauenthal in the Rheingau has been absorbed into the more highly-regarded vineyard of Baiken. This will have the result of increasing the amount of wine from the Rauenthaler Baiken vineyard while at the same time possibly lowering the over-all quality of this famous wine. The German wine industry has been making a serious effort since the end of the Second World War to eliminate the unwieldy number of individual vineyard names in all winegrowing areas. This in itself is praiseworthy and would certainly benefit the consumer, but to limit vineyard names by incorporating many secondary vineyards into two or three highly-regarded vineyards in each town or village seems to undermine the striving for quality which is the aim of all reputable winegrowers everywhere.

EISWEIN — (Ice-vine) — Rare oddity in the way of German wine — it could almost be called an accidental Auslese — made from the first pressing of frozen grapes. The vintage, or grape harvest, comes very late on the Moselle and Rhine, and severe night frosts are not uncommon: perhaps once in a decade temperatures as low as 20° Fahrenheit are recorded, and when the pickers go back in the vineyards the next morning they find the less ripe grapes, with lower sugar content, frozen solid, but the over-ripe grapes with sweeter juice only partially frozen. They must nevertheless be harvested, and are brought to the *Kelterhaus*, put in a hydraulic press and subjected to pressure, sometimes after but often without a preliminary effort to break or crush the individual berries. The first run of juice therefore comes almost entirely from the ripest berries, and this, if fermented separately, is Eiswein. The term Eiswein may be used as applicable on any of the Prädikat classes of quality.

126

EITELSBACH — (I-tells-bach) — Tiny town on the Ruwer, a tributary of the Moselle, in Germany; most of its renowned, steep, splendid vineyards once belonged to a Carthusian monastery, but have been, for over a century, the property of the Rautenstrauch (now Tyrell) family, although still called Eitelsbacher Karthäuserhofberg, or "Carthusians' Hill." This, some seventy acres in all, is divided into a number of vineyard-plots, or *Lagen* — Kronenberg, Sang, Burgberg, etc. — and one of these names, too, appears on the crowded little label, which is almost in the nature of a pretty collar around the bottle's neck; there is a joke to the effect that the German wine with the longest name has the smallest label. The wine is nevertheless worth looking for and remembering, for it is one of the very best of the Mosel-Saar-Ruwer, especially in good vintage years — very light, rather austere, with a bouquet of incredible floweriness and distinction. Authentic Eitelsbachers have been made by a few other producers, but Rautenstrauch-Tyrell's is, by a wide margin, the best.

The new German wine regulations, promulgated in 1971, may bring an unfortunate end to all this charming tradition: the name Eitelsbacher may cease to exist and be replaced by *Trierer* Karthäuserhofberg, though the subdivisions (Burgberg, Sang, Kronenberg and Orthsberg) will still be used. (*See* Trier.) Litigation is still in progress, however, and we may hope that the Eitelsbach name will still be retained.

ELBA — (*El*-ba) — Island in the Tyrrhenian Sea, a dozen miles off the west coast of Italy. Produces a substantial amount of red and white table wine, most of it rather common and high in alcohol, and (especially around Portoferraio) one red dessert wine that is internationally famous. This, made from the Aleatico grape (*see*), is somewhat on the order of a light Port, with a pronounced, unmistakable Muscat bouquet and flavor.

ELBLING — (L-bling) — Productive German wine grape of poor quality, known in California as the Burger and in Alsace sometimes as the Eisling. Giving a flat, dull wine low in acid, it is planted in the less good German districts and its wine, in Germany, generally goes into cheap sparkling wine, or *Sekt*. In Alsace and in Lorraine, it has no longer been a legal wine grape since 1965. In California it is no better.

ELDERBERRY — Shrub of the genus *Sambucus* which grows wild in many parts of Europe and the United States. Its cream-colored flowers have a rather pronounced odor, and in the bad old days, were often used (or so they say) to

127

give additional bouquet to Moselles and Rhine wines; the dark purple berries have undoubtedly yielded wine of a sort in Europe and America for centuries, but require a great deal of added sugar to produce anything at all potable. Elderberry juice has often been used (illegally, and, let us hope, no longer) to give added color to light red wines, especially Port.

ELECTROPHORESIS — A laboratory technique for analyzing enzymes to assist in identifying grape varieties; thus isozyme "finger printing" has linked Duriff to Petite Sirah, Syrah and Shiraz, and Zinfandel to Primativo de Gioia of south east Italy.

ELEGANT — Wine taster's term, applied to light wines which have finesse and breed.

ÉLEVEUR — (A-lev-err) — French, the raiser of the wine as against the winemaker, one who buys newly made wine and cares for it during maturation, bottles and ships it. Most negociants are also éleveurs.

ELTVILLE — (Elt-vila) — Major wine-producing town of the Rheingau, the easternmost except Hochheim of those that are well-known, with nearly 500 acres of vines, giving wines which are rarely remarkable but consistently sound and good. The best vineyards are Sonnenberg, Langenstück, Taubenberg, Sandgrub. A number of famous producers have their cellars in Eltville, including Freiherr Langwerth von Simmern and the Verwaltung der Staatsweingüter, or Hessian State Domain. Eltville is also an important center for sparkling wines, Matheus Müller and many others.

ELTZ — (Eltz) — One of the great vineyard-owning families of Germany. Since 1976 Schloss Eltz, a lovely old Renaissance manor-house on the Rhine in Eltville and their vineyards became property of the government.

ELVIRA — One of the better and better-known native white Eastern grapes, closely resembling and perhaps identical with what is called the "Missouri Riesling." It is of course not a Riesling at all, but a Labrusca x Riparia cross. It was first noted and popularized by Jacob Rommel in Missouri in 1869; it is a cousin to the Noah, but better in quality. Its wine, especially from the Finger Lakes district, is fresh and attractive, with a rather pronounced native-grape or "foxy" aroma, but considerable distinction nonetheless.

EMERALD RIESLING — One of the métis (see) developed at the University of California, Davis. It has no riesling character but has good acidity and high production. Introduced in 1948, thirty years later there were some 15 wineries producing it as a varietal wine.

EMERSON, Ralph Waldo (1803-1882) — American essayist, who wrote, "Give me wine to wash me clean of the weather-stains of cares."

EMILIA-ROMAGNA — (A-meal-ya Row-*mah*-nya) — North Italian region. Bologna, Ferrara and Ravenna are its principal cities, and it is justly celebrated for its food, less for its wines. Few of these are of much distinction. The best known is probably Lambrusco (see), especially that produced round the town of Sorbara, west of Bologna.

128

EMPTY — Lacking in character and substance; wine with bouquet and promise but without sufficient body.

ENFER — (En-*fair*) — One of a number of rather unusual and interesting dessert wines, made from grapes that have been partially dried or raisined (*see Passito*) in the Valle d'Aosta, in the extreme northwestern corner of Italy. These, produced in very small quantity, are almost without commercial interest; they include, as well as the Enfer of the village of Arvié, and the somewhat better known *Caluso* (*see*), a Malvasia from Nus, a Moscato from Ciambave, etc.

ENGLISH WINE — Never a factor in international trade, English wines have been made at least since the Middle Ages. Some interesting white wines are made today.

ENKIRCH — (*En*-keersh) — Little vineyard town at the northern or downstream end of the Mittel-Mosel, in Germany. Steffensberg, Herrenberg, Battereiberg and Monteneubel are the best *Lagen*.

ENOLOGY (Also OENOLOGY) — The whole science of wine — its production, its care and handling. The name is derived from Oeneus, the legendary Greek king of Calydon and originally a wine god.

ENTRE-DEUX-MERS — (Awn-truh Duh Mair) — Literally, "Between-Two Seas." One of the major divisions of the Bordeaux wine country, comprising almost one-fifth of the whole Gironde *département*. Geographically, it consists of a triangle of rather lovely, rolling hills between the two confluent rivers, Garonne and Dordogne, and should perhaps more logically be called Entre-Deux-Fleuves. Portions of it (Côtes de Bordeaux, Loupiac, Ste. Croix-du-Mont, Graves de Vayres and Ste. Foy-Bordeaux) are considered separate districts under French wine law; what remains produces a vast amount (not far from 2 million gallons a year) of rather common and inexpensive white wine. Red wines are not entitled to the appellation, and are sold as Bordeaux or Bordeaux Supérieur.

Until quite recently, Entre-Deux-Mers wines were generally somewhat on the sweet side. Faced with a declining demand, the growers made a courageous and intelligent decision, and set out to produce dry wines exclusively. They adopted the amusing slogan, *"Entre deux huîtres* (between two oysters) — *Entre-Deux-Mers"*; the quality of the wines has improved and is still improving; they are today good values in their price class, though hardly distinguished.

For Map, *see* BORDEAUX.

ÉPERNAY — (A-pear-nay) — One of the two main centers of the French Champagne trade, Reims being the other; a rather pedestrian modern town on the Marne River east of Paris, under which extends a veritable rabbit-warren of cellars and tunnels, doubtless 200 miles and more of them in all. South of the town and sometimes called the Côte d'Épernay, is what is more properly known as the Côte des Blancs, with Cramant, Avize and other famous *crus;* across the Marne are Ay, Hautvillers and the equally celebrated villages of the Côte des Noirs. *See* Champagne.

ÉPLUCHAGE — (A-ploosh-shaj) — Operation of picking over, by hand, the newly harvested grapes before they are crushed or pressed, so as to eliminate defective bunches and berries. This is normal procedure in wineries interested in superior quality.

ÉQUILIBRÉ — (A-key-lee-bray) — French term for a well balanced wine where bouquet, acidity, taste and other characteristics are in harmony.

ERBACH — (Air-bach) — Justly famous little vineyard town on the Rhine, producing some of the Rheingau's most distinguished wines. The incomparable Marcobrunn (*see*) is mostly in Erbach, and the other celebrated plots include Steinmorgen, Honigberg, Siegelsberg, Hohenrain, Schlossberg, and Michelmark, all yielding rather hard, firm wines, long-lived and obviously of great class.

ERBALUCE — (Air-ba-*loo*-chay) — White wine grape cultivated in northern Italy, especially used in the making of the *passito* of Caluso (*see*).

ERDEN — (*Air*-den) — Tiny, wine-producing village on the Moselle near Zeltingen. Its vineyards are among the steepest of Germany, as the name of one of them, Treppchen ("little stairway") would indeed indicate, and the spicy, delicate wines they produce are among the best of the Moselle. The better plots include, in addition to Treppchen, Busslay, Prälat and Herrenberg.

ERMITAGE — (Ehr-me-taj) — Variant spelling of Hermitage (*see*), no less correct but less widely used. Also a white wine from the Canton of Valais, in Switzerland, made from the Marsanne grape.

ERZEUGERABFÜLLUNG — (*Air*-tzew-ger-*ahb*-fue-lung) — Bottled by the producer, similar to "Estate Bottled". Prior to the 1971 German Wine Law, the most widely used term was Original-Abfüllung (*see*).

ESCHERNDORF — (*Esh*-shern-dorf) — Important wine town in Franconia, after Würzburg one of the very best. Its wine, made from the Sylvaner or Riesling (the label generally tells which) are of course shipped in the traditional stumpy flagon, or Bocksbeutel. The best vineyards — there are some 200 acres in all — include Lump, Fürstenberg, and Berg.

ESPUMOSO — (Es-spoo-*mose*-o) — Spanish word for sparkling.

ESSENZ — see ESZENCIA

ESTATE-BOTTLING — Practice whereby vineyard owners bottle the unblended product of their own vines. Like Château-Bottling and *Erzeugerabfüllung,* which are virtually the same thing, Estate-Bottling is always a guarantee of authenticity and to some extent an indication of superior quality; it has been standard procedure in the finer Bordeaux and German vineyards for many decades and has become increasingly general in Burgundy, the Côtes-du-Rhône, the Loire Valley, etc. Many wines, unfortunately, appear to be estate-bottled when they are not, and carry basically meaningless statements on their labels, calculated to deceive the unwary. Some such statements are quite factual, yet mean that the wine was bottled by the shipper (by no means the same thing as the producer) rather than by the restaurant where served or the retail store were sold. The following terms, for example, have nothing to do with Estate-Bottling:

Mis en bouteilles dans nos caves	*Mis en bouteille dans nos chais*
Mise de l'origine	*Produced and bottled by* (in English, on a French wine)
Mis en bouteille au vignoble	*Mis en bouteilles à Beaune* (etc.)

Those who are interested in getting the real thing will be well advised to give their preference to wines and labels which conform with the following generalizations:

1. Statements having to do with Estate-Bottling should be on the main label, not a strip. If in English (as "Estate-Bottled"), the statement should also appear on the main label in one of the various forms (see below) in French.

2. The label should state that the wine comes from someone who is a vineyard owner, not just a shipper, although a person may be and is often both. Thus *négociant* means "shipper," *éleveur* more or less the same thing; but *propriétaire* means "vineyard owner," *récoltant* a grower who harvests his own crop, *viticulteur* and *vigneron* mean "wine grower."

3. It should be stated unequivocally that the wine was bottled by the person who made it, or at least on his premises. The following terms are those generally used to indicate this fact:

Mise du Domaine	*Mise au Domaine*
Mis en bouteilles au Domaine	*Mise du Propriétaire*
Mis en bouteilles par le Propriétaire	*Mise à la Propriété*

In the United States, too, the term "Estate-bottling" has come to have a specific new meaning, and can only be used on California and other wines made *exclusively* from grapes grown by the producer himself.

EST! EST!! EST!!! — Light, semi-sweet white wine, made from the Moscatello grape round the villages of Montefiascone and Bolsena, north of Rome. It owes its curious name (which of course in Latin means, "It is, It is, It is") to the often-told story of the wine-loving German bishop who, on his way to Rome, sent his servant ahead as a scout and taster. The latter was instructed to write the word "Est" on the walls of every tavern where he found the wine especially good. On reaching Montefiascone he wrote, not "Est", but "Est! Est!! Est!!!," and the bishop, on his arrival, proceeded to drink himself to death. His tomb, with an inscription in Latin which tells the story, has been piously preserved.

ESTERS — The fruity and sweetish flavors in the bouquet (*see*) are esters formed during maturation by the combination of certain acids and the alcohol in the wine.

ESTOURNEL — *See* COS D'ESTOURNEL.

ESTUFA — (Ess-*too*-fa) — Portuguese term meaning either a hot-house for the cultivation of plants and flowers, or, in the special case of wine, a room in which Madeira, for example, is held when first made, at a high temperature, thanks to which it acquires its special "Madeira" flavor and changes from purplish red to dark amber.

ESZENCIA — (Ess-zen-cee-ah) — An extraordinary Tokay (*see*) made from juice of unpressed Trockenbeeren; a rare and extremely long lived wine, some have lasted over 200 years.

ÉTAMPÉ — (A-tahm-pay) — French wine shipper's term, largely meaningless, sometimes used to describe Bourdeaux or other wines which are not Château- or Estate-Bottled, but which nevertheless carry a vineyard name. It has no precise legal meaning under French law, but indicates, more or less, that the shipper gurantees its authenticity and quality.

ESTREMADURA — Portuguese province near Lisbon producing large quantities of red, white and fortified wines.

ÉTOILE — (A-twahl) — Still, or occasionally, sparkling white wine produced round the village of this name in the French Jura.

ETNA — (*Et*-na) — Famous active volcano in Sicily, sometimes spelled Aetna in English, rising to 10,758 feet from the sea south of the Straits of Messina. A large portion of its eastern slope is planted to vines. The higher of these, round the villages of Nicolosi, Trecastagni, Zafferana, etc., at over 2,000 feet, produce red and white wines of exceptional quality and breed, with good acidity and not too much alcohol. They are the best table wines of Sicily and are sold as Etna.

EVANGILE, Château de l' — (Eh-vaw-geel) — One of the best vineyards of Pomerol. In a normal year some 4,500 cases of excellent red wine.

EYQUEM — (A-kem) — The Château d'Eyquem is a rather large vineyard near Bourg (*see*) in the Bourdeaux Country, produces ordinary red wine, plus a little semi-dry white of second quality. The Clos d'Eyquem, at La Brède, Graves district, is a small property giving rather undistinguished red and dry white wine. Neither should be confused with Château d'Yquem (*see*), greatest of Sauternes and one of the most celebrated white wines of the world.

F

FAIBLE — (Feh-ble) — French term for weak, without much character, anemic.

FALERNO — (Fah-*lair*-no) — The most celebrated wine (Falernian) of ancient Rome, praised in the most extravagant fashion by Pliny and Horace, and considered "immortal," amphoras of certain vintages having been opened and found good after over a century. It was produced near Formia, on the coast north of Naples, and the identical hillsides are planted in vines today. What they now yield is rather good but by no means extraordinary, sound red and dry white wines that are pleasant but a long way from immortal. They have nothing in common with the Falerno of antiquity except their geographical origin and their name.

FALKENSTEINER HOFBERG — Famous German vineyard in the Saar Valley, owned entirely by the Friedrich-Wilhelm Gymnasium in Trier.

FARGUES — (Farg) — Least important of the five townships of the French Sauternes Country. Its best known vineyards are Château Rieussec (*see*), Château Romer, and Château de Fargues, the last owned by the Lur-Saluces family, of Château d'Yquem. White wines exclusively.

FASS — (Fahss) — German word for barrel, especially the 600-liter *Halbstück* used in the Rheingau. The plural is Fässer, pronounced *Fesser*. See also Bestes Fass.

FAT — Wine with much substance and smoothness but not a lot of firmness; contains natural glycerine; particularly those affected by botrytis cinerea (*see*).

133

FATIGUÉ — (Fah-tee-gay) — French term meaning tired; even fine wines just after bottling and traveling are *fatigué* and recover; an old wine will become *fatigué*, losing its sprightliness and verve.

FAUGÈRES — (Fo-zhare) — Passably good red and white wine produced north of Béziers, in the French Midi. A surprisingly agreeable brandy comes from the same production zone and is distilled in Bédarieux.

FAVERGES — (Fa-vairzh) — Pale, dry white wine from the district known as Lavaux, on the north shore of Lake Geneva, in Switzerland. It is made from the Fendant or Chasselas grape and the vineyard is owned by the Canton of Fribourg. Pleasant, hardly remarkable.

FAYE — (Fie) — Important wine-producing town on the Coteaux du Layon (*see*), in Anjou. Sweet white wines of top quality and a few good *rosés*.

FEEBLE — Wine lacking character, color and distinction; the result of an indifferent vintage.

FEINE, FEINSTE, HOCHFEINE — German puffery adjectives — no longer permitted on labels under the 1971 Wine Law.

FENDANT — (Fawn-daw) — Name given in Switzerland to the Chasselas grape, which is by a wide margin the leading variety in this happy and thirsty small country. It is, on the whole, a far from remarkable grape for wine, but in the Cantons of Vaud, Valais and Neuchâtel it yields a great many fresh, often fine and almost invariably agreeable white wines.

FERME — (Fairm) — French, firm wine with body and strength, will improve with age.

FERMENTATION — Process by which sugar is transformed into alcohol (*see*) plus carbon dioxide, and by which grape juice becomes wine. Although fermentation had been observed since the dawn of history, it was thought to be a wholly spontaneous phenomenon until Pasteur, in 1857, showed it to be work of living organisms — more specifically, of zymase, the enzyme of yeast. Modern technical knowledge goes much farther, and in most good cellars and wineries today fermentation is no longer left to chance but is carefully controlled, above all as regards the temperature of the fermenting must: the fermenting-rooms are often warmed in Champagne and Burgundy where, because of the northern location, the vintage is late and the rooms are too cold for spontaneous fermentation, and the must is generally cooled in areas such as Bordeaux and California where the ambient temperature is higher. Other practices go much farther, and involve the sterilization of the juice with sulphur dioxide and the introduction of special strains of yeast; in some instances white wines are now fermented. Red wines are fermented very slowly over a long period and at low temperatures to retain the fresh fruitiness of the grapes, with their skins, white wines without (*see* Cuvaison). Fermentation normally continues until all, or practically all, of the grape sugar has been converted; it can be stopped at any time, as in the making of Port, by the addition of brandy or high-proof spirits (*see* Fortified Wine), and even without such addition, it will tend to slow down and stop as soon as 14% or 15% of alcohol by volume has been attained.

FERMENTATION, MALO LACTIC — Secondary fermentation which takes place in many table wines, either shortly after the original fermentation or, more normally, in the spring following the vintage. Through its action, much of the malic acid which wine normally contains, and which is the acid of unripe fruit, is transformed into milder lactic acid, rendering the wine, to the palate, less green, less harsh and less tart and simultaneously releasing additional carbon dioxide. Formerly thought to be a continuation of the original fermentation brought about in spring or summer by the change of season, it is now known to be a bacterial fermentation. It can be induced by inoculation of the proper bacteria and/or maintaining warmth in the fermentation room after the alcoholic fermentation has ceased. White wines, because of stem and skin removal, undergo little malolactic fermentation compared to red wines.

FERRAN, Château — (Fair-rah) — Good secondary vineyard of Martillac in the Graves district. Some 1,000 cases a year of red wine, plus an equal amount of dry white.

FERRAND, Château de — (Fair-rah) — Large Grand Cru St. Émilion vineyard, producing some 15,000 cases a year of sound, agreeable claret.

FERRIÈRE, Château — (Fer-ry-air) — 3rd Classed Growth of Margaux, Haut-Médoc. Very small production — some 1,500 cases a year.

FEUILLETE — (Feh-yet) — Small oak barrel, of 136-liter or about 36-gallon capacity, in which the wines of Chablis were traditionally stored. Such barrels have largely been replaced by the conventional Burgundian *piéces,* holding 228 liters, and the change is all for the better.

FIASCO — (Fee-*ask*-ko) — This word simply means "flask" in Italian; the plural is *fiaschi* (fee-*ask*-key). The *fiasco* used for wine, especially but not exclusively for Chianti, is round-bottomed, often hand-blown; thin and light, it would be extremely fragile without its straw-covering, and of course would not stand up on a table. The straw is woven on before the *fiaschi* are filled. Properly speaking, a true *fiasco* traditionally holds two liters, but they come today in all sorts of sizes and shapes.

FIEUZAL, Château — (Fee-oo-zahl) — One of the best vineyards of Léognan, in the Graves District, now ranked as a *Cru Classé*. Some 3,000 cases a year of superior red wine, and 1,500 cases of less good dry white.

FIGEAC, Château — (Fee-zhack) — One of the largest and best vineyards of the St. Émilion district, a Premier Grand Cru Classé adjoining Cheval Blanc. Its soft, sturdy wines (some 15,000 cases a year when in full production) are not far inferior to those of its illustrious neighbor, and fully merit their 1st Growth rank. A half dozen other nearby vineyards, all good but somewhat less famous, also carry the name Figeac but in a combined form: Châteaux La Tour-du-Pin-Figeac, La Tour-du-Pin-Figeac-Moueix, La Tour-Figeac, Grand Barrail-Lamarzelle-Figeac, Yon-Figeac, Cormey-Figeac, Petit Figeac etc.

FILHOT, Château — (Fee-yo) — Justly famous Sauternes vineyard, owned by the Countess de Lacarelle, née Lur-Saluces, and sister of the late owner of Yquem. Although officially ranked as a 2nd Classed Growth, its wine, a shade dryer than most Sauternes but of great distinction and breed, generally sells for a higher price than many 1sts. There are some 6,000 cases a year.

FILLETTE — (Fee-yet) — Literally, in French, a young girl. The word is used in the Loire Valley, especially in Touraine, to mean a half-bottle of wine.

FILTERING — The clarifying of a wine, prior to bottling, by passing it through any one of many different types of filter. Too heavy or severe a filtration can "numb" a wine and destroy many of its finer qualities, and many of the very best wines of the world are never filtered at all. It is by no means, however, a practice that should be condemned, for, if not carried to extremes, it is usually helpful and often necessary, particularly these days, now that the public is reluctant to accept wines that are not absolutely brilliant and have a minimum of sediment, or none. Many white wines are now "sterile-filtered," all bacteria thus being removed; this process permits earlier bottling and and fresher fruitier wines.

FINE — Wine taster's term, rather loosely used. It is properly applied to any wine that has an inherent, unmistakable superiority, whether due to its origin, its grape variety, or other factors. (*See* Fining)

FINESSE — Breed or class or distinction, rendering a wine out of the ordinary. A full-bodied wine that has finesse can often be described as great; without finesse it would be simply heavy or common.

FINGER LAKES — The principal wine-producing district of New York State; after California, the most important of the U.S. The long, narrow lakes,

136

southeast of Rochester, are four in number, roughly parallel, and, on a map at least, they look rather like imprints left by four enormous fingers, whence their name. Only two of them, Keuka and Canandaigua, are known for their vineyards, (Seneca and Cayuga having other claims to fame); the first grapes were planted here in 1829, and wine has been produced on a commercial scale since Civil War days. Until recently, almost all of the grapes were of the native, Eastern varieties (Delaware, Catawba, Elvira, Niagara, Isabella, Iona, Concord, etc.) but many of the newer hybrids and a few viniferas have been planted and the results are very promising. There are six major wineries — Pleasant Valley (Great Western), Urbana (Gold Seal), Bully Hill, Vinifera Wine Cellars and Taylor's, on Lake Keuka; and Widmer's, at Naples on Lake Canandaigua. A great deal of Champagne, or sparkling wine, is produced, as well as fortified wines and table wines; most of these carry, in addition to the required words, "New York State," the common European appellations, as Sherry, Port, Burgundy, Sauterne, etc.; many of them are blended with California wines brought in by tank car. A few, and generally the best, bear varietal names, especially Delaware, Elvira, Riesling (see), or that of one of the French-American hybrids — Baco, Couderc, Seibel, or Chelois.

FINING — Traditional method of clarifying wine (collage, in French) known since Roman days, whereby certain substances are added to the wine in barrel and gradually settle, carrying down, in the form of sediment or lees, the suspended particles and leaving the wine clear. White of egg, isinglass (from the bladders of sturgeon), gelatine, casein and fresh blood have all been used in this way, as have many types of clay including Bentonite (aluminum silicate) from Wyoming and tierra de Lebrija from southern Spain. Various chemical products are also employed when specific problems arise, as potassium ferrocyanide ("blue fining") when the wine contains an excess of iron or copper; this last has the odd and disturbing property of turning the wine pale blue, but this is only temporary; a great many German wines and quite a few from California are so treated.

FINO — (Fee-no) — Type of Sherry: the palest, lightest, most delicate, generally the dryest and, in the opinion of many experts, the best. It has a wholly distinctive and memorable bouquet, the result of the flor (see) under which it passes a good deal of its life in cask, and of course partially derives its quality from its blending and ageing in soleras (see). Served chilled, it is one of the best of apéritifs.

FITOU — (Fee-too) — One of the best red wines of the French Midi, produced (largely from Grenache and Carignane grapes) just south of Narbonne, in the district known as Hautes-Corbières. Full-bodied if somewhat common, it is inexpensive, often a good value. According to law it has to be aged two years in wood before bottling; it carries an Appellation Contrôlée.

FIXIN — (Feex-an) — Northernmost village of the Côte de Nuits, in Burgundy; its red wines, too little known, are often among the best values in the way of fine Burgundy that can be found, comparable, in character and quality, to the better Gevrey-Chambertins. There are six outstanding vineyards; Les Herve-

137

Fixin

NOTE: The *Clos Napoléon,* a fairly recent appellation, was formerly called "Aux Cheusots" and is so shown on this old map. It was granted this new name in honor of a remarkable and famous Memorial, "Napoléon's Awakening," the work of the sculptor, Rude (who was also responsible for the Arc de Triomphe, in Paris), in the pine woods directly above and behind the vineyard.

lets, Clos de la Perriére (*see*), Clos du Chapitre, Les Arvelets, les Meix-Bas and Clos Napoléon (formerly named Aux Cheusots).

FLAGEY — (Flah-jay) — Village north of Vosne-Romanée on the Côte de Nuits, in Burgundy. Its official name is Flagey-Échézeaux; both Échézeaux and Grands Échézeaux (*see*) lie within its communal limits, but both wines are invariably sold under their vineyard name, usually without any mention of Flagey. The lesser wines of Flagey are entitled to the appellation Vosne-Romanée.

For Map, *see* ÉCHÉZEAUX.

FLAT — Applied to Champagne or other sparkling wines, one that has lost its sparkle; to still wines, one too low in acid, unattractive, neutral, dull.

FLAVORED WINE — Wine specialty consisting of a neutral wine base (not necessarily or always grape wine) combined with natural flavors resulting in a beverage resembling fruit punch, well known soft drinks or fanciful new taste sensations. They are usually sweet and cater to the young and uninitiated who fortunately, from a gustatorial view, are switching to more classic wines.

138

From a peak of 20% of total U.S. wine production in 1973, there is a rapid and accelerating shift away from these wines.

FLESHY — Wine of substance, a proper mouthful harmoniously combining flavor, alcohol and smoothness.

FLÉTRI — (Flay-tree) — Swiss wine term. A *vin flétri,* in the Canton of Valais, is a sweet wine made from grapes either picked late, when almost raisins, or left on straw mats in the sun, like a *vin de paille* (*see*), or *passito* (*see*). There is no *pourriture noble* (*see*) in this dry, mountain country and a *vin flétri* is very different from a Rheingau Auslese or a French Sauternes. The grape, although here known as the Malvoisie, seems actually to be the Ruländer, or Pinot Gris.

FLEURIE — (Fluh-ree) — Little town in the very heart of the Beaujolais Country; its attractive, fruity, fragrant red wine, one of the Beaujolais' most typical and best. (*See* Beaujolais).

FLEUR-PÉTRUS, Château La — (Fluhr Pay-truhss) — Small but good Pomerol vineyard, producing about 3500 cases a year.

FLIERS — Small tasteless particles which float in wine; they are harmless and if produced by exposure to cold weather during shipping will ordinarily disappear in time.

FLINTY — Used to describe a dry, clean, hard, almost austere white wine (such as Chablis) which has a special bouquet recalling the smell of flint struck with steel. The French call it *pierre-à-fusil,* which is the same thing.

FLIP — Mixed drink made either with spirits or with wine, or both, having as its ingredients shaved ice, sugar, bitters, plus an egg and wine, or wine and brandy.

FLOR — (Flore) — The Spanish word for "flower"; in connection with wine, it means an unusual and special yeast, native to the Sherry Country. This is also called "film yeast" in California, where it has recently been introduced (as in South Africa and Australia). Naturally in Spain and through inoculation in other lands, it forms a white film or "flower" on the surface of certain wines soon after fermentation, the casks being only three-quarters full and the wine exposed to the air. It lives and multiplies there, gradually forming a layer as much as half an inch thick, looking not unlike cottage cheese, and it radically affects the bouquet and flavor of the wine. Oddly enough it only forms and prospers on the lighter wines and these, thanks to its working, become Finos and Amontillados (*see*). The *flor* is also native to the Manzanilla and Montilla districts (*see*) and to Château Chalon (*see*) in France. Its use has greatly improved the quality of the better dry California Sherries and done equally good service in South Africa and Australia. (*See* Sherry).

FLORAISON — (Floor-eh-zoh) — French term for flowering (*see* Flower).

FLOWER — Like all fruit-bearers, grape vines have their flowers; these are a good deal less spectacular than those of the cherry, the peach, the orange and the apple, to mention but four, but they are no less necessary antecedents to the fruit, and either a succession of rainy days or a period of cold weather dur-

139

ing the blossoming season can and often does bring about a disaster, especially in the form of *coulure* (*see*). The critical flowering period is called *floraison* in French, and to the French wine-grower it is often a week or fortnight of sleepless worry.

FLOWERY — Special term of high praise applied to the bouquet of certain wines, more particularly white wines, which to the nose recall the scent of flowers. The finer Moselles have this quality to a pronounced degree, but a few other wines, particularly those produced on stony soil from the Riesling grape and in cool districts, share this special excellence.

FLUTE — Name given, in French, to a special form of bottle, like that used in Alsace and on the Rhine. Many *rosé* wines are now shipped in flutes. Also a rather attractive, traditional glass, often used in France for Champagne, in the shape of a slender V, sometimes with a stem.

FOCH — see MARÉCHAL FOCH.

FOGARINA — (Fo-gar-*een*-na) — Red wine of rather low alcohol and high acid, produced in the province of Reggio Emilia, northern Italy.

FOLLE BLANCHE — (Fall Blawnch) — Variety of white grape, widely grown in France under a confusing multiplicity of names, and to some small extent in northern California. Fairly productive, it gives a pale, light wine, not distinguished but fresh, clean and very high in acid; unfortunately, its tightly packed bunches are fatally vulnerable to mildew and mold, and in many districts it is being replaced for this reason. It is unquestionably the best of all grapes for brandy, but, unhappily, in the calcareous soil of the Cognac Country, it has not done well since the phylloxera, when grafted on American root stocks, and is gradually being supplanted by the less good if hardier Ugni Blanc (*see*); in Armagnac, too, where it is known as the Piquepoule or Picpoul, various other mediocre grapes are being planted, including even one of the Baco hybrids. Round Nantes, at the mouth of the Loire, it is called the Gros Plant and gives a tart but otherwise rather neutral white carafe wine, which has lost out in popular favor to the Muscadet. As Picpoul, it is extensively planted in the French Midi, but yields nothing of any real consequence. In California, its wine is occasionally but rarely bottled under the varietal name, more often used in California "Chablis," to which its higher acid brings a welcome and refreshing tartness, and, for this same reason, in many of the better California Champagnes.

FOREZ — (For-ez) — Red and *rosé* wines of no great interest, made from the Gamay grape in Auvergne, near the headwaters of the Loire.

FORST — (Forst) — Justly celebrated little town, of well under a thousand inhabitants and some 500 acres of vines, which produces what are certainly among the best and perhaps, all things considered, the best white wines of the German Pfalz, or Palatinate. The vineyards are 70% planted to the Riesling grape and the wines, while quite full-bodied, have extraordinary elegance and bouquet, said to be due to outcroppings of a special sort of black basalt in the vineyards. All of the leading Palatinate producers have vineyard holdings in

RHEIN PFALZ

Weingut Dr.Bürklin-Wolf
WACHENHEIM/WEINSTRASSE

Forster Pechstein
Riesling Kabinett
Erzeugerabfüllung · A. P. Nr. 5 142 043 21 73

QUALITÄTSWEIN MIT PRÄDIKAT

Forst, in the seven named vineyard sites, or *Lagen:* Kirchenstück, Jesuitengarten, Ungeheuer, Pechstein, Elster, Musenhang and Freundstück.

FORTIFIED — Old British euphemism for wines that have been "spiked," or liberally laced with brandy or other spirits somewhere between the vineyard and the bottle, as Port, Sherry, Muscatel (in almost all cases), Madeira, Marsala, etc. Our Federal authorities have seen fit to forbid the use of the term on labels and in advertising, no doubt for good and sufficient reason, since it is an obvious truism that people should not be induced to drink certain wines on account of their higher alcoholic content; the simultaneous suppression of the term "unfortified" is a good deal harder to explain. American vintners seem to have accepted these restrictions without complaint, and they now apply to precisely the same wines, the perhaps more genteel terms "appetizer wines" and "dessert wines." The French are as bad as we are — *see* Banyuls.

FOUDRE — (Food-dre) — French term for a large cask of indefinite size.

FOURCHAUME — (Foor-showm) — One of the largest and best first-growth vineyards of Chablis.

FOURTET, Clos — (Foor-tay) — Picturesque and famous vineyard of St. Émilion, lying practically in the town itself. Its wine (some 6,000 cases a year) is exceptionally sturdy, long-lived, slow to mature.

FOXINESS — Foxes have had to do with vineyards since Biblical days, generally as consumers, but many of the early settlers in America called the wild, native grape the "Fox grape" and in many Eastern states it is still so called (to "fox," of course, means to intoxicate as well as to trick); its pronounced special aroma is unmistakable, whether as a grape or its juice or the wine made from it, and all native varieties share the characteristic, especially the red or black ones, as Concord, Isabella, Ives, etc., but to a definite degree the whites as well — Delaware, Catawba, Elvira. The French, who began to import American grape cuttings at the time of the phylloxera (*see*), and who were the first hybridizers of American and European varieties, called this special aroma or taste *"queue de renard"* or *"fox's tail"* for no well established reason, and it is still so called. Wines having this wholly American tang are usually found either delicious or undrinkable by those who taste them for the first time, but this is wholly a matter of personal preference, and no field for an expert.

FRAGRANT — Of a wine, one that has an especially pronounced and agreeable bouquet, or aroma.

FRAIS — (Fray) — French word for "fresh." It also means cool, however, and *servir très frais* on a French wine label means "serve well chilled."

FRANCE — France has been called the world's vineyard. One fifth of all the wine of the world is produced in France, and French wine is the universal standard by which wine is judged. Yet, out of an annual production of some nine billion bottles a year, less than 10% has any real claim to superior quality, and at least four-fifths is nameless — called *vin rouge, vin blanc, vin rosé, vin ordinaire,* and is simply a staple, like potatoes or milk. Frenchmen drink it with their meals not because the water in France is bad (it isn't — they have less typhoid than we do) but because this sort of wine is cheap, goes well with food, is cheering and pleasant and (drunk thus) hardly more intoxicating than beer; they like it better than coffee or tea or sweet carbonated drinks, and in the opinion of many doctors (including, of course, Pasteur, who said so) it is a healthier mealtime beverage for adults than milk. It is interesting to note that there were nearly five million acres under vines a century ago. The average annual production, however, in the 1870's was almost 30% less than during the period 1970/74. This is of course due to increased regional specialization and more efficient agricultural methods, as with wheat, corn, etc., in the U.S.A. They like it, so much that France imports far more wine than she exports, consumes more than her own three million acres of vineyard can provide.

All of France, including the Riviera, is farther north than Buffalo or Boston, and nearly a third of France lies beyond the northern limit of commercial viticulture, its climate too sunless and cold, or too rainy and undependable for wine-growing. The line has been clearly drawn by a dozen centuries of trial and error; it begins on the Atlantic Coast near Nantes, in southern Brittany, parallels the Loire some fifty miles to the north, sweeps up to include the Champagne Country east of Paris, and runs on east to the border of Luxembourg on the Moselle. South of this line, except in a few mountainous districts, it is safe to say that there is hardly a French farm on which the vine has not been planted at one time or another and where wine has not been made. About two-thirds of the 95 *départements* of France have commercial vineyards.

France is a country of small vineyards rather than large: there are few, if indeed any, that comprise as much as 500 acres under one ownership. Modern cooperatives, increasingly well run, in some districts permit operations on a larger scale, but most French wine is produced by artisans and peasant farmers, who are quite content to be so called and who take a true artisan's pride in what they make. Most of them now send their young wines, for analysis and constructive criticism, to their local, well-staffed government stations, and willingly accept the technical advice they receive.

For in no other country is wine produced according to such strict rules as in France, and the rules have been established, it is important to remember, by the growers themselves, and simply ratified by the State. The whole precise, immensely complicated classification of districts and townships and *crus* comes from the producers, and no better proof could exist of their deep interest in the quality of what they make. Clear lines of demarcation have been drawn, with the accord of all concerned, between the great wines and the good wines and the *vins ordinaires*.

Most of the very best French wines have been given a special legal designation, *"Appellation Contrôlée"* (*see*), and these words appear on the label except in the case of Champagne (where they are considered unnecessary). They mean that the French Government guarantees the origin of such wines, and their right to the name they bear; violations are considered fraud, and are severely punished. These words are also, to some degree, an assurance of quality, since they may only appear on wines made from specified, superior varieties of grape, in delimited districts, and according to rules which forbid over-production, improper blending, and everything else which is not in keeping with local tradition and good cellar practice.

In all, there are some three hundred of these *Appellations Contrôlées* (all listed in this encyclopedia), plus scores of variant and combined forms (as "Beaujolais," "Beaujolais Supérieur," "Beaujolais Villages," for example): some, such as "Bordeaux," cover a whole district producing millions of gallons annually, while others, such as "Château-Grillet" or "Montrachet," are restricted to the output of a tiny vineyard or a single farm. Sixteen *vins mousseux*, or sparkling wines, plus Champagne, have been accorded this rank, and about the same number of fortified wines, most of these from the Mediterranean Coast and the eastern Pyrénées; the rest are table wines, and they include all of the best and practically all of the well-known wines of France — the Burgundies, the Bordeaux, the wines of the Rhône Valley and of the Loire, and a scattering of others from the Jura, Provence, etc., etc.

Below these in rank, forming what might be called a sort of "second team," or "junior varsity," come some fifty others, officially known as V.D.Q.S., *"Vins Délimités de Qualité Supérieure."* These (listed in their alphabetical place in this volume and in the Appendix) are also controlled, though less stringently, by the French Government, and carry the V.D.Q.S. seal, which looks rather like a postage stamp, on their label. Many of these are exported, and some are of good, even excellent quality, and may well become increasingly interesting in periods of rising wine prices. As time goes by and the wines attain stricter standards of quality they are promoted to Appellation Contrôlée; examples are Côtes de Forez, Côtes de Provence.

In a still lower, less official category come the *vins de pays*, the little "country" wines, usually consumed locally, often interesting and charming,

143

The Vineyard Districts of **FRANCE**

Drawn by W. Lembeck

144

often sold under the name of their village or *département* in the local inns and taverns.

The lowest grade of all, of course, is *vin ordinaire:* this, in France, must be marked with its alcoholic content, (as 12°, or 12%), but carries no designation of origin; it may be and usually is blended, but may not be watered; it is strictly covered by the French equivalents of our pure food regulations, but by not much else in the way of controls. When sold under a brand name, as Vin du Postillon, Vin des Rochers, Pampre d'Or, Prefontaine, etc., it is called a *Vin de Marque,* the word *marque* meaning "brand" in French.

Not far from one-third of the space in this whole encyclopedia is devoted to French wine, properly and appropriately, for if most French wine is admittedly common or mediocre, the best is simply incomparable: there are no red wines and no sparkling wines on earth as good as the best French, and few white wines better — none, surely, except perhaps the rarest and finest estate-bottlings of the Moselle and Rhine.

Of all of the fruits of nature and man's skill that have, over the centuries, given delight and comfort to people of good taste in all countries, the wines of France are easily first, and by a wide margin. Our whole literature is full of their praise, and a roster of the enthusiastic lovers of French wine in the past five hundred years would read like a Who's Who of the Western World.

FRANCONIA — English word for Franken (*see*).

FRANKEN — (Frahn-ken) — one of the eleven Anbaugebiete or Specified Wine Regions of Germany yielding 4% of the total crop from 4 Bereiche, 15 Grosslagen and some 135 Einzellagen. Located in the upper valley of the Main, east and west of Würzburg, the leading wine town along with Escherndorf, Iphofen, Randersacker, Rödelsee and others, the region grows primarily Müller-Thurgau followed closely by Sylvaner. Franken wines are shipped in flat flagons called Bocksbeutel (*see*). Prior to 1971 many Franken wines were labeled Steinwein but this is now obsolete; however, the name persists in common but inaccurate usage. About half the wines are marketed by nine grower-cooperatives, or Winzergenossenschaften; other producers are the German State, several charitable endowments and a half dozen noble families.

For map, *see* Germany.

FRANKEN RIESLING — Name sometimes given to the Sylvaner grape (*see*), although it is emphatically not a true Riesling. As a result of this misnomer, wine made from the Sylvaner may legally be labeled Riesling in the United States.

FRAPPÉ — (Frah-pay) — Used of a wine, means very, very cold. A liqueur served *frappé* is poured over shaved ice.

FRASCATI — (Frahs-*caht*-ee) — An attractive little town in the Alban Hills, southeast of Rome. Its white wine is one of the best of the Castelli Romani (*see*), a great favorite in Rome, and more often bottled for export than most of the others. Dry, golden, full-bodied, generally about 12% alcohol, it is an agreeable table wine, though hardly a distinguished one.

145

FREDONIA — Native American grape; an early ripening Concord used for red wines.

FREE RUN — Grape juice which collects during destemming and crushing prior to pressing — sometimes fermented separately, other times combined with press juice.

FRECCIAROSSA — (*Fraitch*-cha-*roas*-sa) — Brand name (it means "red arrow") of a popular and good table wine from Lombardy, Italy. *See* Casteggio.

FREISA — (*Fray*-sa) — Superior Italian red wine grape and the wine made from it, notably in that hilly part of Piedmont lying between Turin and Casale Monferrato; the Freisa of Chieri is particularly famous. Two quite different wines, however, are made: the one more likely to appeal to the average wine drinker is a dry red wine, fruity, often a little tart and rough when young, but quite ready to drink and possessing a special and remarkable bouquet by the age of three; even more popular in Italy, but rarely exported, is the Freisa that is both *abboccato* (*see*) and *frizzante* (*see*) — bottled early, slightly sweet and slightly sparkling, it is not a wine that will please all palates, despite its bouquet and fruit. A few plantings of the Freisa grape exist in California, but it is not possible, as yet, to give any sort of judgment as to what it is capable of producing. The name is often misspelled Fresia in California, and pronounced "*free*-si-a," like the flower.

FRENCH COLOMBARD — *See* COLOMBARD.

FRESH — Despite the fact that many people have been led to believe that an old wine is necessarily better than a younger one, this is by no means the case — the majority of wines are at their best when young. Most white wines, all *rosés,* and a good many lighter reds have an engaging freshness in their youth which they tend to lose after their third or fourth birthday, if not sooner. A fresh wine is one which has not lost this early charm.

FRIBOURG — (Free-boorg) — Canton in western Switzerland, producing a few red and white wines of no great value. *See* Faverges.

FRIEDRICH WILHELM GYMNASIUM — (*Free*-drich *Vil*-helm Gim-*nah*-zee-um) — Famous secondary school in Trier, on the Moselle, in Germany. Thanks to gifts and bequests over the years, its endowment now includes extensive vineyards in many of the best townships of the Moselle and Saar, including Trittenheim, Graach, Zeltingen, Mehring, Oberemmel and Ockfen. The wines, always estate-bottled, carry the Gymnasium's label and name. The two Saar vineyards of Jesuitengarten and Falkensteiner Hofberg are owned entirely by the Gymnasium.

FRIULARO — (Free-oo-*lahr*-ro) — Red wine grape and the wine made from it in the province of Padua, near Venice, Italy. Undistinguished, but popular in Venice as ordinary table wine.

FRIULI-VENEZIA GIULIA — (Free-*oo*-lee Vay-*net*-zee-ah *Joo*-lee-ah) — Northeasternmost region of Italy; produces good wines bearing varietal names: Pinot, Cabernet, Tokai, Riesling, Merlot, etc.

FRIZZANTE — (Freez-*zahn*-tay) — Italian wine term meaning slightly sparkling, or *pétillant*, or crackling, usually as the result of a minor secondary fermentation in bottle. Many Italian wines, even red wines, are deliberately bottled before their original fermentation is entirely complete, while they still contain some sugar from the grape. Eventually such wines become a little "prickly" or "fizzy" and even foam up briefly when poured; most of them remain a little sweet. *Frizzante* wines of this sort are much prized in northern Italy, though to an educated palate they appear merely oddities, and hardly wine at all. Lambrusco (*see*) is generally *frizzante* since revised U.S. regulations classify *frizzante* as table wine.

FRONSAC (Fraw-sack) — Small red-wine district in the Bordeaux Country, which deserves to be better known than it is. The little town of Fronsac, from which it takes its name, is on the Dordogne just west (downstream) from St. Émilion and Libourne, and the vineyards are on steep hills overlooking the verdant and singularly beautiful river valley. The best are in a zone entitled to the name Canon-Fronsac, but Côtes-de-Fronsac is an appellation of only slightly lower class. Both produce extremely robust, deep-colored wines, what the French call "fleshy," and soft, somewhat recalling the Pomerols but with less breed. They have long been popular in northern Europe and are good values. Total production amounts to some 1,200,000 gallons a year.

FRONTIGNAN — (Fraw-tee-nyaw) — Town on the Mediterranean Coast of France, near Sète, and its sweet, golden Muscat wine; this is the best French wine of its type, a *vin doux naturel* of considerable distinction and real class. These qualities, rare in Muscatels, it owes to the fact that it is made from a special, much superior variety of grape, the Muscat-doré-de-Frontignan. Usually fortified, it must legally contain a minimum of 15% alcohol by volume. The same grape has been transplanted to other countries, and is grown to some small extent in California's Napa Valley, where it gives a much dryer and quite different wine.

FRONTON — (Fraw-taw) — Red and *rosé* wines of purely local interest, produced round the town of this name, some twenty miles north of Toulouse, in southern France. They are sometimes sold as Côtes de Fronton.

FROST — Of the many anxieties that beset the vintner and cause him sleepless nights, none is as bad as frost. And since most of the best table wines and sparkling wines of the world are produced fairly close to the nothern limit of the vine, frost is a worry shared by most good wine growers. Even California is not exempt, and the Napa Valley vineyards were grievously damaged in April, 1964. Theoretically, the danger exists in French and German vineyards for about six weeks — roughly from the first of April until the days of the Ice Saints (*see*) are past, on May 15th — yet the vines of Pouilly-Fumé, on the Loire, were severely hurt on May 28, 1961, by the latest damaging frost in the history of the French Weather Bureau. Similarly, vines are supposed to be safely dormant during the winter, but St. Émilion and certain other sections of Bordeaux suffered a veritable disaster in February, 1956, when sub-zero weather arrived after a period of warm days, and many thousands of vines were killed outright. In 1977 Bordeaux, especially Sauternes, was badly hit.

Even three or four degrees of frost, during the critical weeks can mean the partial or total loss of the year's crop, and in some cases the damage is more lasting, and the following year's vintage, as well, is impaired. A few progressive growers in some of the northern districts, notably Champagne, Chablis, the Moselle, the Loire, now set out smudge-pots or little fuel-oil or gas stoves in their vineyards, and these, while not 100% effective and yet very expensive, have proven enormously helpful — in Chablis, in 1960 and in several years since then, *only* the growers with stoves in their vineyards produced wine worth harvesting.

Other anti-frost measures have been no less successful, both in America and abroad: these include infra-red heaters overhead, enormous fans and even helicopters to keep the air circulating, and sprinklers to coat the vines with a protective layer of ice, where adequate water supplies are available.

FRUITY — Said of a wine which has the definite and attractive aroma and flavor of fresh fruit, though not necessarily and certainly not to a pronounced degree, that of grapes (*see* Grapey). Almost all fine young wines are fruity, few poor ones are, and almost no old wines, however good. California Zinfandels have this charming quality when young; so have all better *vins rosés,* which is why they are so popular in America; so has Beaujolais; so have the Alsatian wines, almost all German wines, and to a lesser degree the best Rieslings, Sylvaners and Pinots of California.

FUDER — (Foo-der) — Oak cask in which Moselle wines are stored, in Germany. Its standard capacity is 960 liters (253 U.S. gallons), or 106 cases of finished wine. In other areas fuders vary from 900 to 1,000 liters.

FUISSÉ — (Fwee-say) — One of the four townships in which Pouilly-Fuissé (*see*) is made, west of Mâcon, in southern Burgundy.

FULL — Wine-taster's term, related to Body (*see*), and no less often wrongly defined and wrongly used. Its proper place is in the tasting-room, not the laboratory, and it has only the vaguest connection with alcoholic content or specific gravity. Heavy cream weighs less than light cream and both weigh much less per quart than skimmed milk; a wine expert, if induced to taste them, would describe heavy cream as full-bodied, and skimmed milk as thin and light. Alcohol weighs less than water, and a quart of 20% dry Sherry less than a quart of 9% Moselle; gallon for gallon, the Moselle may well weigh more than the sturdiest Châteauneuf-du-Pape, with 14% of alcohol by volume. Yet no competent taster would ever describe the Moselle as the "fuller" wine of the two. On the other hand, he would almost certainly say that the Châteauneuf-du-Pape was "fuller" than the dry Sherry.

FUMÉ — see BLANC-FUMÉ.

FUMÉ BLANC — A corruption of Blanc-Fumé (*see*) used to identify some wines made of Sauvignon Blanc in California.

FUNCHAL — (Foon-shal) — Port and principal town of the island of Madeira, in which most Madeira wines are stored and aged and whence they are shipped.

148

FURMINT — (Foor-mint) — Celebrated white wine grape of Hungary, the principal and informing variety of Tokay. Many other Hungarian wines, however, are made from the Furmint, and these are generally so labeled, so Somloi Furmint, Badacsonyi Furmint, Pécsi Furmint, etc., the first word in each case indicating their district or town of origin.

FÛT — (Foo) — French word meaning barrel.

G

GAFFELIÈRE, Château La — (Gaf-fe-l'yair) — Premier Grand Cru Classé of Saint-Émilion. Until 1964 known as La Gaffelière-Naudes, this fine property lies just below Château Ausone and in recent years its increasing fine quality has been much appreciated by connoisseurs. It produces 9,000 cases from 50 acres of vines.

GAILLAC — (Guy-yack) — White wine produced round the town of this name, on the River Tarn, some thirty miles northeast of Toulouse, in southern France. Sometimes dry but usually a little on the sweet side, it is widely drunk in France as a *vin de comptoir,* or ''bar wine,'' by the glass. Pale, low in acid, often heavily sulphured, rather bland and without much character or class, made from a grape known locally as the Mauzac, it is rather ordinary at best. Much of it is converted into a fairly sweet, inexpensive *Mousseux,* or sparkling wine. Total production of Gaillac, Premières Côtes de Gaillac and Gaillac Mousseux is in the neighborhood of 1½ million gallons a year.

GAILLAT, Domaine de — (Guy-ya) — Small vineyard in the Graves district near Langon, yielding a pleasant, pale, dry white wine.

GALLISATION — The adding of water and sugar to grape juice before fermentation in order to reduce the acidity and increase the alcoholic content of the finished wine — and of course, incidentally, to increase its volume. This practice is outlawed in many wine countries, including most of France, Portugal and California. It is permitted within strict limits in the eastern United States, in Germany and in certain other of the colder wine producing countries of the

HEARTY BURGUNDY.

OF CALIFORNIA

*We are often told by knowledgeable people that they are
delighted in having discovered a great wine in Hearty
Burgundy. Its rich, full-bodied flavor—from extremely
fine varietal grapes—will surprise you. Alc. 12.5% by vol.
Made and bottled by the ®Gallo Vineyards of Modesto, Ca.*

world. In Germany, before 1971, growers were allowed to add up to 25%
water and sugar to wines of poor vintages. This process was known as *Nass-
verbesserung* in German. Under the new German Wine Law which went into
effect in 1971, this percentage has been much reduced and by 1980 *Nassver-
besserung* will be entirely eliminated.

GALLO — The brothers Ernest and Julio Gallo have fashioned by far the largest
wine business in the United States supplying about one-third of total consumption including imports. To say this is due to mass production, distribution and
marketing without mentioning quality would be an injustice. They have pioneered in strict laboratory research and scientific control from the growers
through to the final bottling of their numerous, well-conceived and well made
products.

GALLON — The old American saying, "a pint's a pound the world around,"
leaves out of consideration the British Empire, where a pint is 20 ounces, and
there are 100 pence but only 16 ounces, in a pound. The British, or Imperial
Gallon is of 160 ounces, or $1^1/_5$ times the U.S. Gallon of 128 ounces (our
ounces being slightly larger). The same proportions hold, of course, for pints
and quarts. There are 3.785 liters to the U.S. gallon, and a liter is 1.057 U.S.
quart.

GAMAY — (Gam-may) — Excellent red wine grape, grown to the virtual exclusion of all other varieties in the Beaujolais Country of France, where, on
prevailingly clay and granitic soil, it yields a better wine than even the Pinot
Noir. Farther north in Burgundy, where the soil is predominantly calcareous
(as on the Côte d'Or) the Gamay does much less well, is ranked as an inferior

grape, and cannot legally be planted in the better vineyards, where the Pinot Noir's supremacy remains unchallenged. Wines (*see* Passe-tout-Grains) are occasionally made from the two varieties crushed and fermented together.

The true Gamay, or Gamay Beaujolais, of which some 4,400 acres are planted in California, especially in Santa Clara, San Benito, Monterey, and Napa counties yields a remarkable wine, often superior to any Pinot Noir from the same vineyard. Usually this is sold as Gamay Beaujolais, and it should by no means be confused with the ordinary California wine called simply "Gamay," made from a much inferior and far more productive grape which is possibly not a Gamay at all.

GAMAY BEAUJOLAIS — *see* GAMAY

GARD — (Gahr) — French *département* extending from the lower Rhône Valley well into what is called the Midi, third among French *départements* (after the Hérault and the Aude) in total wine production, its output of table wine being about 75% of that of the United States. Most of this, of course, is nothing but *vin ordinaire* (*see*). Some of the best *vins rosés* of France, however, are produced in the Gard, along or near the Rhône, notably Tavel, which is internationally famous, and Lirac (*see*).

GARDA — (*Gar*-da) — The largest and one of the most beautiful of the Italian Lakes, noted for its mild climate (lemons are grown even commercially in certain sheltered corners); its northern tip extends into what was, prior to 1918, Austrian territory, and the low hills round its wide southern end are largely covered with vineyards. These produce quite a collection of different wines, red, white and *rosé,* all of which, oddly enough, seem to have a certain family resemblance: they are all low in alcohol, rarely reaching 12%, and therefore easy to drink; they are delightfully fresh and fruity when young, and improve practically not at all with age; they are, in other words, wonderfully good carafe wines, among the best such wines in the world. Most of them are drunk up, gratefully and promptly, by the North Italians themselves and their Swiss neighbors, with the enthusiastic help of a good many thirsty tourists. Unquestionably, the best of the reds is Bardolino (*see*) — and incidentally the village called Garda adjoins Bardolino, and its wines are entitled to this name; the best white is probably Lugana (*see*), made at the southern end of the lake from the Trebbiano grape (*see*); the *rosés* are called Chiarello or Chiaretto (*see*). However, there are many others, from Moniga, Padenghe, Polpenazze, and other villages, and they are worth investigating.

GARGANEGA — (Gar-gahn-*eh*-ga) — White Italian grape, largely responsible for the excellent white wine of Soave (*see*), but generally blended with Trebbiano.

GARONNE — (Gar-*rawn*) — Largest river of southwestern France, rising in the Spanish Pyrenees near Luchon, flowing by way of Toulouse to Bordeaux, just north of which it is joined by the Dordogne, to form the wide estuary of the Gironde (*see*). It is navigable as far up as Bordeaux, and the vineyards of Sauternes, Graves, Cadillac, Ste.-Croix-du-Mont, etc., overlook its valley.

GASSY — Wines having an excess of carbon dioxide.

GATTINARA — (Gaht-ee-*nah*-ra) — Splendid Italian red wine, easily one of Italy's half dozen best, made from the same distinguished Nebbiolo grape as Barolo (*see*) and Barbaresco (*see*), but in an altogether different part of Piedmont, round the village of this name, northeast of Turin and soughwest of Lake Maggiore. Full-bodied, slow-maturing, long-lived, with a fine bouquet and great depth of flavor, it is a great wine by any standards and can readily hold its own against the best reds of the French Rhône Valley.

GAUDICHOTS, Les — (Go-dee-show) — Famous old Burgundian vineyard in the heart of the best portion of Vosne-Romanée: some thirty years ago practically its entire acreage was officially reclassified and made part of La Tâche (*see*), thereby quadrupling the extent and production of that even more prestigious parcel of vines. Although Les Gaudichots has therefore practically ceased to exist as a separate entity, its name still often appears in current articles on Burgundy and books on wine. Formerly it bounded La Tâche on the north and west, and was separated from Romanée-Conti only by another narrow, celebrated vineyard plot, La Grande Rue.

GAY LUSSAC — (Gay Lew-sack) — French wine chemist whose name is synonymous with percent by volume — i.e. 14 degrees G.L. = 14% by volume.

GAZÉIFIÉ — (Gah-zay-eef-ee-yay) — French for artificial carbonation; i.e. making a sparkling wine by the injection of carbon dioxide.

GAVI — (*Gah*-vee) — Dry white wine, one of Italy's best, made from the Cortese grape (*see*) round the little town of Gavi in Piedmont. It is generally shipped in tall, slender, green bottles like the wines of Alsace; pale, fresh, light, it should be consumed when still young.

GAZIN, Château — (Ga-zan) — One of the fine large vineyards of Pomerol, ranked as a 1st Growth. Some 8,000 cases a year of full-bodied, good quality red wine. There is also a Château Gazin of considerably less importance at Léognan, in the Graves district.

GEBIET — (Ge-beet) — Same as Anbaugebiet (*see*).

GEISENHEIM — (Guy-zen-heim) — Important wine-producing town in the Rheingau, with nearly 500 acres of vineyard, almost entirely Riesling. In great years (as 1945, 1953 and 1971) the Geisenheimers are of absolutely top quality, with great fruit and breed, and the better Lagen include Rothenberg, Mäuerchen, Fuchsberg, Kilzberg, Kläuserweg, Mönchspfad, Klaus and Schlossgarten. It is the location of the State Viticultural Research Center — one of the great training schools known throughout the wine world.

GEMEINDE — (Ge-mind-eh) — In Germany, a wine community, identical to the political community.

GÉNÉREUX — (Shay-nay-ruh) — French wine-tasters' term, applied to a big, hearty, warming wine, as Châteauneuf-du-Pape or Chambertin.

GENERIC — Wine name or designation of class unrelated to the wine's origin, as *vin rosé*, sparkling wine, apéritif wine, *pelure d'oignon*, etc. The question of what are known in the United States as ''semi-generic'' names is much more thorny. Most of these are old, traditional, geographical place names that now have been declared, at least to some extent, in the public domain. They are names that were in wide general use before today's strict rules regarding appellations went into effect, and it is an unquestioned fact that wines from New York State and Ohio and California (not to mention Australia, South Africa and Chile) were being sold as "Sherry," "Port," "Rhine wine," "Burgundy" and the like, well over a hundred years ago. In most cases no fraud was intended, and the wine was simply given the existing wine name that seemed to fit it best. All this is of course now highly displeasing to the Spaniards who regard the name "Sherry," to the Portuguese who regard the name "Port," and to the French, who consider "Burgundy," "Sauternes," "Chablis" and "Champagne," as part of their national patrimony. There is much to be said on both sides, but a majority of countries have come to accept the French-Spanish-Portuguese-German point of view, and have renounced the use of these place names by international accord. The U.S. Government has so far refused, and has considered that it would work a grave injustice on California vinters, for example, to deprive them of appellations which have come to have substantial trade value and which their grandfathers, often born abroad themselves, were allowed to use freely. A not too unfair compromise seems to have been worked out; the number of such "semi-generic" appellations is limited and will not be extended (an American wine may be labeled Sauterne but not Barsac, Chablis but not Pouilly, Rhine Wine but not Rüdesheimer); such wines, furthermore, must show their origin, (as California, New York State, or American) in type substantially as large and readable as the foreign appellations they have assumed.

GENEVA — (French, Genève) — Largest city of French-speaking Switzerland; there are a few small vineyards in the canton of this name, yielding a white wine on the order of a light Neuchâtel.

GENTIL — (Jawn-tee) — Alsatian wine-grower's term, meaning a superior grape variety, or plant noble. Wines so labeled are generally blends of several such varieties, often grown and picked together. See Edelzwicker.

GERMANY — Despite the wholly merited and centuries-old fame of its Rhine wines and Moselles, Germany can hardly be called either a major wine-producing or a true wine-drinking country. As in America, wine is treated there more as an occasional and festive beverage than as a daily necessary. Germany's vineyard acreage is less than one-third that of Portugal, and the average German drinks one-half as much wine as the sober average Swiss.

Nevertheless, Germany manages to export more white wine to the United States than even France, and at least three times as much as any other country; experts agree that the finest German wines are of astonishing quality, quite possibly the best in the world, and even the sound, less expensive ones have their special character and charm: they are light, refreshing, easy to drink, fruity, fragrant, unfailingly agreeable, and their popularity is not at all surprising. Of course, it must be kept in mind that in Germany, as in all other wine-producing lands, there is more, much more, mediocre and common wine than good, but Germany's average of quality is perhaps the highest of all.

All German wines of any real consequence are white; with rare exceptions they are low in alcohol (8% to 11% is the normal range), usually with a trace or more of pleasing sweetness as well. Those ranked as the best and, in any case, the most expensive, are very sweet indeed. They are shipped for the most part in tall, slender bottles (brown for Rhine wines, green for Moselles) and some in stumpy, flat-sided flagons called Bocksbeutel.

The very southernmost German vineyards are as far north as Newfoundland, and many of them at the latitude of Labrador. Grapes can only be grown commercially on south-facing hillsides along river valleys (the Rhine and most of its tributaries) and only a few, hardy varieties of grape can be successfully cultivated; fortunately, almost all of these yield superior white wine. In order of quality they are: the Riesling, the Gewürztraminer (rare), the Sylvaner, the Ruländer (rare), and the Müller-Thurgau plus a few others. These names often appear on German wine labels; if they do not, it may be assumed that more than one variety has been used in making the wine.

The 1971 German Wine Law delineates five table wine districts (*see* Tafelwein) and eleven Specified Regions for quality wines (*see* Anbaugebiet), and reduced the vineyard sites allowed on labels from 25,000 to less than 3,000.

The vineyards of the Rhine Valley proper are divided into three minor and three major Anbaugebiete. That called the Rheingau is acknowledged the best, faces due south over the Rhine between Wiesbaden and Rüdesheim, and includes such celebrated wine towns as Hochheim, Johannisberg, Rüdesheim, etc. Reinhessen is on the west or left bank of the Rhine south of the Rheingau and of Mainz: it produces, in addition to most of the world's supply of Liebfraumilich, such perennial favorites as Niersteiner, Oppenheimer, etc. Rheinpfalz, or the Palatinate, still further south, is also on the left, west bank of the Rhine and borders Alsace; its best vineyard towns are Forst, Deidesheim, Wachenheim, Ruppertsberg. The three minor regions are: first, the so-called Mittelrhein, in the Rhine gorge between Rüdesheim and Koblenz; and stretching north from Koblenz almost to Bonn: then, on the Black Forest foothills, facing Alsace, the scattered and not-too-important vineyards of Baden, and finally, the Hessische Bergstrasse beginning north of Heidelberg and running north toward Frankfurt.

The Rhine's most important tributary, in terms of water but even far more in terms of wine, is the Moselle. Here wines are produced fully equal to the Rhine's best in quality, although very different, and the Moselle, in turn, has its tributaries, the Saar and Ruwer, hardly less distinguished. This entire area is the region named Mosel-Saar-Ruwer.

Two other river valleys, on account of their considerable acreage and because of the distinctive character of the wines they grow are also Anbaugebiete. One, Nahe (*see*) takes its name from the river Nahe that joins the Rhine at Bingen, directly opposite Rüdesheim; it produces many wines of high quality some fifteen miles upstream, to the southwest, round Bad Kreuznach and Schloss Böckelheim. The other, Franken (*see*) or Franconia in English, is the easternmost region. The Main, before joining the Rhine near Mainz, cuts its winding way through the vine-covered hills of Franconia; the most famous of its Frankenweine come from Würzburg and a half dozen other villages

155

GERMANY

N

SCALE

MI. 0   5   10   15   20   25   50
KM. 0   25

RHEINPFALZ
WACHENHEIM—WORMS
HEIDELBERG
BAD MERGENTHEIM
HEILBRONN
STUTTGART
WÜRTTEMBERG
FORST
DEIDESHEIM
MANNHEIM
KARLSRUHE
BADEN-BADEN
OFFENBURG
BADEN
STRASBOURG
RHEIN RIVER
Kaiserstuhl
IHRINGEN
FREIBURG
MÜLLHEIM
BASEL
MEERSBURG

nearby, and are shipped in a special sort of stumpy flagon called Bocksbeutel (*see*).

Finally there are two more regions, also tributaries, which are of little importance in international commerce. The Ahr, from the river of the same name, is the second smallest Anbaugebiet and the northernmost; it produces more red wine than white. Württemberg is widespread along the Neckar river system and lies to the east of the Rhein below Franken.

German wine labels are very specific and must contain the following information:

Quality category	Tafelwein, Qualitätswein bestimmter Anbaugebiete (QbA) or Qualitätswein mit Prädikat which last must also indicate Kabinett (lowest fine quality) through Spätlese, Auslese, Beerenauslese and Trockenbeerenauslese (highest fine quality). Eiswein is a special category which may be applicable to any of the Prädikat wines; Sparkling wines in order of quality — Schaumwein (if carbon dioxide is added — mit zugesetzter Kohlensäure), Sekt or Qualitätsschaumwein, and Prädikatssekt.
Geographic area	for Tafelwein, "Deutscher" and color of wine when grapes come from more than one district, otherwise only name of the district; for Qualitätswein, name of specified region.
Bottler	name and address.
Amtliche Prüfungsnummer	A.P. Nummer for short — the certificate number for Qualitätswein.
Optional information	may be added when applicable as follows: Vintage, Proprietary or trade name, type of grape, alcoholic content, estate bottling (Aus eigenem Lesegut or Erzeugerabfüllung), specific geographical information — name of Bereich (district), Gemeinde (community), Grosslage (general site), Einzellage (individual site or vineyard).

As might be expected wines labeled Spätlese and Auslese are more expensive and generally sweeter, those labeled Beerenauslese and Trockenbeerenauslese even more so. Estate-bottling is a complete guarantee of authenticity; an indication, but not a guarantee, of superior quality. The vintage year is extremely important, perhaps even more so than in France: oddly enough, the less expensive, sugared wines are often better in poor years than in good, although this is of course not true of wines that are natural and unsugared. Sugar may be used in fermenting Tafelwein and QbA only.

Liebfraumilch is a special case — the 1971 law defines it as a Qualitätswein which may come from and be a blend of Rheingau, Rheinhesse, Rheinpfalz and Nahe.

The cost of producing wine in Germany's basically unfavorable northern climate is higher than in any other country in the world: it follows that very cheap German wines are almost always poor (far less good than comparably priced wines from California); the medium priced ones, if carefully selected, are both good wines and good values; the best are extraordinary, always expensive and sometimes fabulously so — rare bottles often bring as much as several hundred dollars and sometimes more. To the true wine lover they are worth it, for they are incomparable and unique.

GEROPIGA — (Jair-o-*pea*-ga) — Fresh grape juice reduced by evaporation to a concentrate or syrup, used to give added sweetness and body to the less fine grades of Port.

GERS — (Jair) — *Département* of southwestern France producing, in the way of wine, little of interest except what is distilled into Armagnac. There are a few agreeable white and *rosé vins de pays* but none really worth exporting.

GEVREY-CHAMBERTIN — (Jev-ray Shawm-bair-tan) — World-famous wine-producing town, eight miles south of Dijon, in Burgundy; red wines exclusively. Like many other villages of the Côte d'Or (*see*) Gevrey has added to its name the appellation of its most famous vineyard, Chambertin (*see*). The finest wines of this extraordinary *commune* do not, however, carry the town name: what is sold as Gevrey-Chambertin is a sound, secondary, almost regional Burgundy, from the less good vineyards; of a distinctly higher grade are those that are labeled Gevrey-Chambertin ler Cru, or Gevrey-Chambertin plus the name of a vineyard, as Gevrey-Chambertin, La Combe aux Moines. Still better, and very great wines by any standards, are the Grands Crus: Latricières-Chambertin, Mazoyères-Chambertin, Charmes-Chambertin, Mazis-Chambertin, Griotte-Chambertin, Ruchottes-Chambertin and Chapelle-Chambertin. It is perhaps worth noting that Gevrey-Chambertin, Clos St. Jacques, although not officially a Grand Cru, is rated at least on a par with these. Of course, what is called simply Chambertin, or Chambertin-Clos de Bèze, is the best of all.

GEWÄCHS — (Ge-*vex*) — Means "growth" in German, and on a wine label or wine list was usually followed by the producer's name. It was usually but not invariably an indication of estate-bottling. (*See* Wachstum, Originalabfülung). Under the new German Wine Law, this term is no longer permitted on any German wine label.

GEWÜRZTRAMINER — (Ge-vertz-tram-me-ner) — Excellent and unusual wine grape, formerly applied to a selection of Traminer but now replacing the word Traminer entirely. It is widely planted in Alsace, and to some extent in Germany and in the Tyrol; a shy bearer, it is pinkish in color and gives a highly special, extremely spicy, rather soft white wine, which some wine-drinkers find almost too heavily perfumed; it nevertheless brings a higher price than even the Riesling in its native Alsace. There are some important new plantings in California, and the wine runs true to type, although its spiciness (the name, in German, means "spicy Traminer") is on the whole less pronounced.

GHEMME — (*Ghem*-eh) — Very good red wine, made from the Nebbiolo grape (*see*) round the village of this name, south of Lake Maggiore in Italian Piedmont.

GIEN — (Jhan) — Little town on the Loire, upstream from Orléans and directly south of Paris; it is more famous for its pottery and faïence than for its wine, but some agreeable, light *vins de pays*, red, white and *rosé*, are produced on the nearby hillsides called the Côtes de Gien, and carry, when bottled, the V.D.Q.S. seal.

GIGONDAS — (Jhe-gone-dah) — Red and *rosé* wine of the Rhône Valley, produced round the village of this name at the foot of the Mont-Ventoux (*see*) northeast of Avignon. The red on the whole is better than the *rosé* — full-bodied, rather high in alcohol (often 13%), yet surprisingly soft, not unlike a lesser Châteauneuf-du-Pape; the *rosé* is pleasant enough when young but has a marked tendency to maderise (*see*). The proper name of both used to be Côtes-du-Rhône-Gigondas; they have just been accorded a separate, special Appellation Contrôlée of their own. Both are often sold in a stubby, long-necked, square-shouldered bottle, recalling the bottles sometimes used for Port.

GINGER WINE — Very popular in England, a flavored wine made both at home and commercially.

GIRÒ — (Gee-*ro*) — Red dessert wine, on the order of a light Port, produced near Cagliari, on the Italian island of Sardinia.

GIRONDE — (Jhe-rawnd) — The *département* of Bordeaux (*see*), as such the most important of France in the field of fine wine, since practically the entire Bordeaux wine district lies within its borders.

ALSO, the river, or tidal estuary, formed by the Garonne and Dordogne rivers which meet north of the city, and thanks to which Bordeaux is a seaport. Most of the better Médoc vineyards overlook the Gironde, as do those of Bourg and Blaye.

GISCOURS, Château — (Shees-coor) — 3rd Classed Growth of Labarde-Margaux, Haut-Médoc, producing some 27,000 cases a year of fine, rather delicate Claret. Somewhat neglected for a period of years, Giscours is rapidly regaining its former high place.

GIVRY — (Jhe-vree) — One of the good, less known wine-producing *communes* of the Côte Chalonnaise (*see*). More red wine than white.

GLACIER — (Gla-see-A) — An odd, rather agreeable but almost bitter white wine produced in a high Alpine valley near Sierre, in the Swiss Canton of Valais.

GLASSES — Proper wine glasses play an extremely important role in the tasting and appreciation of fine wine. From a taster's standpoint, the best glasses are stemmed, made of thin, clear crystal, more-or-less tulip-shaped, very large; 6 ounces should be considered minimum capacity, 8 or 10 ounces greatly to be preferred; of course they are never filled much over one-third full. This is not a matter of mere fancy nor of fashion, for fine wines taste better in such glasses: the wine's color can be seen and judged, and the tulip-shaped glass serves as a sort of chimney, concentrating the wine's bouquet and channeling it upwards to the nose.

A number of wine districts — the Moselle, Champagne, Vouvray, Anjou, and even Manzanilla, for example — have their special regional glass, and still other shapes are traditional in other regions. All such glasses can and often do provide amusement and interest to the hobbyist and specialist, though whether any of them is as good or better than the basic, simple tulip-shape, is doubtful, to say the least. (*see* Appendix 7 for illustrations.)

GLÖGG — (Glewg) — A traditional Swedish cold-weather drink, a special type of hot spiced wine. It is usually made with aquavit or brandy added just before serving in cups or glasses containing a few almonds and raisins.

GLORIA, Château — Relatively new property in Saint-Julien, Haut-Médoc, created by combining bits and pieces of various highly rated châteaux. It produces 12,000 cases of well made wine from its 106 acres.

GLYCERINE — One of the many alcohols produced during fermentation; a colorless, tasteless and slippery liquid which imparts smoothness and oiliness to wine. The legs (*see*) are some indication of the presence and quantity of glycerine.

GOLDEN CHASSELAS — same as Palomino.

GOULEYANT — (Goo-lay-ah) — French for wines that are easy to drink, light agreeable wines which go down nicely.

GOÛT — (Goo) — In French, simply means taste. In connection with wine, when applied to Champagne, it is a rather undependable indication of sweetness, as *Goût Américain* (fairly sweet); or *Goût Anglais* (quite dry); of other wines it is used, plus an adjective or descriptive phrase, for wines that have a special or unusual flavor, either agreeable or (more frequently) disagreeable. Thus *Faux Goût* means an "off" (literally "false") taste; *Goût de Bois* means Woody; *Goût de Bouchon* means Corky; *Goût de Cuit* that a wine tastes sugared or "cooked"; *Goût de Ferment* or *de Lie* means Yeasty; *Goût de Terroir* (*see*), the rather special taste of wines grown on heavy soil. On the other side of the ledger, there are *goût de Noisette*, which means Nutty; *Goût de Violette, de Framboise*, etc., applied to wines which, to some enthusiastic tasters, appear to have the scent of violets, the flavor of raspberries, and so on.

GOVERNO — (Goh-*vehr*-no) — Name given, in Italian (sometimes *Governo alla Toscana*), to a special method of vinification widely used in the Chianti Country, and which often plays a major part in giving Chianti its special flavor and character. Some 10% of the grapes harvested — usually of the rarer varieties, Cannaiolo, Mammolo, Colorino, etc. — are not pressed, but put aside to raisin on straw trays. They are then crushed and set to ferment in late November and, once fermentation is under way, they are added to the already fermented Chianti wine; the vats are then sealed, with a bubble-valve to allow

CO_2 to escape, and so left until spring. A slow, slight, secondary fermentation of course takes place, and the final result is a wine that is faintly, almost imperceptibly sparkling, with an attractive freshness and a bit of "prickle" on the tongue.

COXWILLER — (Gawks-vee-lehr) — Village in northern Alsace, producing good wines and some altogether remarkable fruit brandies — Kirsch, Mirabelle, Framboise, etc.

GRAACH — (Grack) — Famous little town of the Mittel-Mosel, it is on the right bank of the river between Bernkastel and Wehlen, and its 240 acres of vineyard form part of the same incomparable steep hillside as those of its even more illustrious neighbors. The Graacher wines are admirable — sprightly and fragrant, perhaps a bit lighter and less overpowering than the Wehleners, but of equal distinction.

The best plots include Himmelreich, Domprobst and Abstberg, plus the Josephshof, a single property adjoining Wehlen and belonging to the Kesselstatt family: the wines from this are sold as Josephshöfer, not Graacher.

GRAFTING — A method by which vinifera grapes can be grown on American rootstock to control phylloxera (*see*).

GRAGNANO — (Gran-*yah*-no) — A soft, light, red wine, fruity and pleasing, not absolutely dry, produced not far from Pompeii, southeast of Naples, in Italy.

GRAND CRU — (Graw Crew) — French indicating great growth or great vineyards, particularly in Burgundy (*see* Appendix 3).

GRAND CRU CLASSÉ — (Graw Crew Clah-say) — This phrase applies to the Bordeaux wine classifications of 1855, 1953, etc. (*see* Appendix 3).

GRAND ORDINAIRE — (Grawnd Or-dee-naire) — A superior grade of *vin ordinaire* entitled to some sort of geographical appellation protected by French law; the wine, while better than average, need not be in any way exceptional. An example is "Bourgogne Grand Ordinaire" (the cheapest legal Burgundy), etc.

GRAND PONTET, Château — (Graw pawn-tay) — One of the many 1st Growth St. Émilion vineyards; about 5,000 cases a year.

GRAND-PUY-DUCASSE, Château — (Graw Pwee Dew-cass) — 5th Classed Growth of Pauillac, Médoc. Some 8,000 cases a year of very sound, pleasant red wine.

GRAND-PUY-LACOSTE, Château — (Graw Pwee La-cost) — 5th Classed Growth of Pauillac, Médoc. One of the most dependable and consistent of the 5th Growths, 11,000 cases a year.

GRAND ROUSSILLON — (Graw Roo-see-yaw) — One of a number of appellations (Côtes d'Agly, Côtes de Haut-Roussillon, Maury, Rivesaltes — but Grand Roussillon is the broadest term of all) given to the sweet, fortified wines produced in the *département* of Pyrénées Orientales, near Perpignan.

163

These must contain a minimum of 15% alcohol by volume, but generally run higher; they are made principally from the Grenache, Muscat and Malvoisie grapes and somewhat resemble a rather light Port. *See* also Banyuls, Rancio.

GRAND VIN — (Graw Van) — Literally, in French, "great wine," although the term has not legally been defined and is rather freely used. Not a reliable indication of superior quality.

GRANDE RESERVE — (Grawnd Ray-zairv) — Only in Alsace does this term have any official or legal standing; elsewhere it is used by many producers, bottlers and shippers, supposedly to designate a superior grade of what they sell, but how much it means depends on the producer's commercial policy, or his whim. However, Alsatian wines may not carry this designation unless they are made from grapes of one of the "noble" varieties that have attained a fixed minimum of ripeness; the result is a rough equivalent of a German *Spätlese*.

GRANDE RUE, La — (Grawnd Roo) — Extraordinary little vineyard forming what is almost a three-acre corridor (or street, as its name would indicate) from east to west through the very kernel of the best vineyard land of Vosne-Romanée. Its wine is of truly superlative quality, quite comparable to those of its illustrious neighbors, Romanée-St.-Vivant and La Tache.

GRANDS ÉCHÉZEAUX — (Grawnz A-shay-zo) — Great Burgundian vineyard and its splendid red wine. Lying just above the Clos de Vougeot and a short distance below Musigny on the north, its 23 acres could hardly be more superbly placed, and what they yield is a classic Burgundy, far fuller, richer and more distinguished than what is called simply Échézeaux (*see*), and certainly one of the 20 best red wines of the Côte d'Or, annual production averages 3,000 cases.

For Map, *see* ÉCHÉZEAUX.

GRAPE — In all probability (leaving out of consideration the original apple of the Garden of Eden) the first fruit cultivated by man. Grape seeds, resembling those of our present-day wine grapes, have been found in Egyptian tombs and in the remains of lake dwellings dating from the Age of Bronze. Noah is said to have planted the first vineyard, but the arts of vine-dressing and wine-making are far older than the beginnings of recorded history.

All grapes belong to the genus *Vitis;* there are some forty species, all native to the temperate zone. The most important of these, by an immense margin, is *Vitis Vinifera,* the *"wine-bearer,"* which, apart from some native American sorts and recent hybrids, is the only species grown commercially to any real extent in the world. There are of course an almost limitless number of varieties of *Vinifera* — botanists and ampelographers have recognized and classified several thousand, and at least several hundred have recognizable characteristics and are cultivated. These are propagated by planting cuttings, or by grafting, for they do not remain true to type if grown from seed. Grapes grown from seed are called seedlings and it is usually impossible to determine their precise ancestry, except in experimental vineyards, under controlled conditions.

164

Different varieties have their special uses and advantages: some give particularly good table grapes, others produce the best raisins; some are extremely productive and give common wine, others, shy-bearers, yield the best; some will do well under almost any conditions, others require a specific sort of soil and climate. There are apparently only about twenty, and certainly less than forty, capable of yielding outstanding wine.

GRAPEY — A wine should taste like wine, not like fresh grapes. But certain grapes always seem to impart their special flavor to wines made from them — the Muscat is one such grape and the Concord another (to a lesser degree, so are many of the other Eastern varieties). Lacking in subtlety, too pronounced in flavor, such wines are never highly regarded by an expert. One soon tires of them.

GRAS — (Grah) — French term for soft, full wines with a fair amount of glycerine.

GRAVES — (Grahv) — The word in French simply means gravel, or gravelly soil, and is used in a combined form in connection with several districts of the Bordeaux Country (*see* below). Alone, it means a specific, defined area on the left bank of the Garonne River, largely west and south of the city of Bordeaux. Total production in a normal year is in the neighborhood of 3 million U.S. gallons, of which about 48 per cent is red wine, the rest white. The appellation Graves Supérieures is restricted to *white* wines of at least average quality or better, despite the fact that the finest red Graves consistently bring higher prices than the finest white; most of these reds, however, do not carry the name Graves but are sold under the label of a specific château. Ignored, with the single and notable exception of Château Haut-Brion, by those responsible for the Classification of 1855, the Graves châteaux have now been officially classified, at least in part, though how competently is perhaps open to question: the official classification will be found in the Appendix.

The best red Graves come from the *communes* of Pessac, Léognan, Martillac, and include Châteaux Haut-Brion, La Mission-Haut-Brion, Pape-Clément, Haut-Bailly, Chevalier, Malartic-Lagravière, Smith-Haut-Lafitte, etc. In character they are closer to the Médocs than to the St. Émilions, Pomerols, etc.; they age well, but with rare exceptions have a little less distinction, are a little less "classic" than their Médoc compeers, and someone has quite properly said that they are like soft, as compared with glossy, prints from the same negative, less distinct and less clean.

The finest white Graves come principally from the *commune* of Léognan, plus a few exceptions from Talence, Pessac, Martillac, Cadaujac, etc.; these are dry wines, although with a trace of *moelleux,* or softness — they are often better, being lighter and dryer, in years rated fair or poor than in years rated great, although this is by no means true of the reds. The best are: Domaine de Chevalier, Laville-Haut-Brion, Carbonnïeux, Olivier, Bouscaut, etc., but many others of less fame produce good wines too, including several near Langon, at the extreme southern end of the Graves district. The rare white wine of Château Haut-Brion, at least in the author's opinion, is often too high in alcohol and often surpassed in quality by several of those listed above.

Officially the Graves district used to include three townships (Cérons, Podensac and Illats) which adjoin Barsac and produce rather sweet, golden wines, of excellent class but far nearer Sauternes than what one expects from a wine labeled Graves. These wines are usually marketed as Cérons (*see*).

The white Graves are made largely from Sauvignon Blanc and Sémillon grapes, and where the former predominates the quality is better. Red Graves comes from the Cabernets (*see*), plus some Merlot, Malbec, Petit Verdot, etc.

Further information may be found under the names of the *communes* and châteaux listed above, the grape varieties, etc.

GRAVES-ST. ÉMILION — (Grahv Sant A-*me*-lee-on) — Not an appellation according to French law, but a term widely and properly used in connection with a large part of the official St. Émilion district, to designate the gravelly upland plain, behind the north of the steep hills that look down on the Dordogne Valley. The wines of Graves-St. Émilion are at least as good: they include Châteaux Cheval Blanc, Figeac, Grand Corbin, etc.

GRAVES DE VAYRES — (Grahv duh Vair) — Secondary Bordeaux district, geographically part of Entre-Deux-Mers, on the left bank of the Dordogne River, not far from St. Émilion. The dry white wines are passable, the reds less good.

GRAY RIESLING — Misnamed and mediocre white grape (since it is not a Riesling and has none of the characteristics of one) rather widely planted in California, especially in the Livermore Valley. It has also been called the Grey Dutchess (another misnomer, since it is unrelated to the Dutchess grape of New York State); its true name is the Chauché Gris and in its native France — it comes from the district round Poitiers — it is so poorly thought of that it is not used in any French wine having an appellation. In California it gives a mild, soft wine (spelled Grey Riesling), not disagreeable but without much character; it is hard to explain its present vogue, for it is much less good than the less popular Sylvaner.

GRAY ROT — Botrytis Cinerea (*see*). The same as the "noble rot"; however, when the mold attacks prior to maturity of the grapes it occasions serious deterioration.

GREAT — Great wines, like great novels and great men, do not come along every day, and the term should be reserved for those extraordinary ones that are head and shoulders above their fellows — certainly less than 1% of the world's production. A great wine should have no flaws, perfect balance, real distinction. Such bottles are never cheap, but they are worth whatever one pays for them.

GRECO DI GERACE — (*Gray*-co de Jer-*ratch*-chay) — Famous white wine, not always up to advance billing as far as quality is concerned, produced at the extreme Calabrian "toe" of Italy, not far from the Straits of Messina.

GREECE — In no ancient civilization, so far as we can judge, did wine play such a major role as in that of Greece; in the Greek art and Greek literature that have come down to us, the vine, the grape and wine are omnipresent, perhaps even more so than in the Bible. Clearly, they were a familiar part of everyday common living; they were even the basis of a religious cult, that of Dionysus (*see*).

It is hard therefore not to come to the conclusion that the Greek wines of antiquity were better than what Greece produces today. Greece is an important wine-growing country, with twice the production of Germany; she exports a vast tonnage of excellent raisins (mostly what are known to the trade as "currants" — actually the sun-dried berries of the Black Corinth grape) and a good deal of sweet fortified wine, principally in barrel to Switzerland, Malta and Northern Europe. Some of these — the Muscat of Samos, and those made

167

from the Mavrodaphne grape in various districts — are of fairly good quality; there are no outstanding wines at all.

Some Greek table wines are flavored with resin (*retsina*) which renders them wholly unacceptable to a wine-drinker not yet accustomed to this highly special, turpentine taste. Tourists can nevertheless find some quite passable wines from the Peloponnesus (Achaia, Arcadia, Messenia) and from the islands — Cephalonia, Leukas, Corfu, Zante, Santorin, etc. As might be expected in this southern latitude and warm climate, most of them are rather high in alcohol, lacking in finesse and breed.

GREEN — Wine taster's term meaning raw, harsh, with a disagreeable acidity; lacking softness, roundness and maturity. This is not necessarily a matter of age, though young wines are more often green than older ones.

GREEN HUNGARIAN — Productive white grape of uncertain origin, grown to a limited extent in some of the better California districts. It gives a pale, fairly agreeable but rather neutral wine, which is more often used in blends than sold under this name.

GRÊLE — (Grell) — French word for hail: like frost, one of the major natural hazards of a wine-grower's life. Hail storms are by no means infrequent in most vineyard countries, and if heavy they can be nothing short of catastrophic; an entire crop is often destroyed in a matter of minutes and the vines so gravely damaged that even the following year's vintage is affected. Even light hail can take its toll during the ripening season, for the bruised berries give a wine (red wine, especially) that has what the French call a *goût de grêle,* or "hail taste," readily recognizable by an expert, as a faint overtone of rot in an otherwise sound wine.

GRENACHE — (Gre-nahsh) — Very productive but good quality wine grape, widely planted in southern France, where it is often called the Alicante, in the Rioja district of northern Spain (where it is known as the Garnacha) and in California. It is one of the varieties used in Châteauneuf-du-Pape, and, differently vinified, gives the sweet, heavy dessert wine of Banyuls, as well as a superior grade of California Port. On the whole its best wines, however, are *vins rosés,* notably Tavel (*see*), and others in the Rhône Valley, and the excellent Grenache Rosé of California. A white variety of Grenache also exists, but is less widely grown.

GRENOUILLES — (Gre-new-ee) — One of the seven Grand Cru vineyards of Chablis (*see*).

GREY RIESLING — Name of California wine made from the Gray Riesling grape (*see*).

GRIGNOLINO — (Green-yo-*leen*-no) — Excellent Italian red wine grape; also the wine made from it, notably in a hilly district known as the Monferrato (*see*), north of the town of Asti, in Italian Piedmont. When genuine and of good quality, Grignolino is an interesting and unusual wine, with a quite special character and flavor; in color it tends to be what the French call *tuilé,* with a hint of orange in its crimson; it gives an impression of lightness, although it is often high in alcohol (13-14%); its bouquet is almost unmistakable.

There are some plantings of Grignolino in California, in Napa, Santa Clara and Tulare, where it has been made into a very passable *vin rosé* and some red wine as well.

GRILLET — *See* CHÂTEAU GRILLET.

GRINZING — (*Grint-*zing) — Suburb of Vienna, producing some of the most pleasant of the pale, dry, fruity white wines of Austria. The principal grape varieties are the Veltliner, the Riesling and Sylvaner, and although some superior Grinzingers are bottled and even exported, far more is consumed as open wine in the little local taverns when under a year old.

GRIOTTE-CHAMBERTIN — (Gree-ott Shawm-bair-tan) — One of the Grand Cru vineyards adjoining Chambertin (*see*), 14 acres in all; a great red Burgundy wine.

GROLLEAU — (Gro-lo) — New and presently preferred spelling of the Groslot grape (*see*).

GROOT CONSTANTIA — *See* CONSTANTIA.

GROPELLO — (Gro-*pel*-lo) — Italian wine grape, used in making some of the lesser red wines of Garda (*see*) as well as in Chiaretto (*see*).

GROSLOT — (Gro-lo) — Productive red wine grape of fair quality widely grown in the Loire Valley of France, where it yields most of the rather common, less expensive, semi-sweet *Rosé d'Anjou* (when made from the far superior Cabernet, this is invariably labeled *"Cabernet Rosé d'Anjou"*). Farther east, in Touraine, the Groslot gives some rather more than passable carafe wines.

GROS PLANT — (Gro Plah) — Name given to the Folle Blanche grape and the fresh, light, tart white wine made from it round Nantes, near the mouth of the Loire. It is entitled to the V.D.Q.S. seal.

GROSSLAGE — (Gross-la-guh) — Literally, "large vineyard." Under the 1971 German Wine Law, a Grosslage is a general site where geography, soil and exposure combine to produce wines of similar quality and character, therefore every Einzellage, or individual vineyard, with few exceptions will be part of a Grosslage. Variances in Grosslagen are enormous — from 125 to 3,700 acres, often irregular in shape but not in terrain, and include from a very few to more than seventy-five Einzellagen. When the name of a Grosslage appears on a label an Einzellage may not be stated. This can be utterly confusing since, for example, Niersteiner Pfaffenkappe is a wine from a particular vineyard and Niersteiner Gutes Domtal applies to any wine from that part of the town of Nierstein which lies within the Grosslage Gutes Domtal. To complicate matters further Nierstein has also given its name to a Bereich (*see*) and there are labels reading Bereich Nierstein.

GRUAUD LAROSE, Château — (Grew-oh La-rose) — 2nd Classed Growth of St. Julien, Haut-Médoc. One of the very largest Bordeaux vineyards, with an average annual production of 25,000 or more cases. Gruaud Larose for many years (in fact until just before World War II) consisted of two separate domains, Gruaud-Larose-Sarget and Gruaud-Larose-Faure. Reunited at last, their wine is one of the most popular and best of the St. Juliens.

GRUMELLO — (Groo-*mel*-lo) — One of the best red wines of Valtellina (*see*) made from the Nebbiolo grape near Sondrio, Italy, not far from the Swiss Border.

GUEBWILLER — (Gewb-vee-lehr) — One of the better wine-producing towns of southern Alsace.

GUIRAUD, Château — (Jhee-roe) — 1st Classed Growth of Sauternes: about 10,000 cases a year. Major vineyard, not far from Yquem, and producing a very comparable although somewhat less distinguished wine.

GUMPOLDSKIRCHEN — (*Goom*-poldz-keerk-en) — Certainly the best known wine-producing town of Austria and, with those of the Wachau district (Loiben, Krems, Dürnstein), doubtless the best. Its light, pale, fragrant, fruity white wines have been Viennese favorites for generations, and the vineyards are less than a half-hour's drive from Vienna, to the south. Most Gumpoldskirchners sold in bottle carry a grape name, as Veltliner, Riesling, Gewürztraminer, Rotgipfler, etc.; some of them a designation such as Spätlese or Auslese, and occasionally a specific vineyard name as well. Few of them could be described as extraordinary, but almost all of them are fresh and clean and attractive, and good values.

GUNTERSBLUM — (*Goon*-terz-bloom) — Major vineyard town in Rheinhessen, with nearly a thousand acres under vines producing wine of good but not distinguished quality, for the most part sold as Liebfraumilch.

GUTEDEL — (Goot-*eh*-del) — German name for the productive but mediocre Chasselas (or Fendant or Sweetwater) grape — an exaggeration if there ever was one, since the white wine it yields is a long way from *edel* (noble) and by no means always *gut* (good). It is the principal variety of Markgräflerland (*see*) in southern Baden, where it gives a quite passable, mild *Schoppenwein,* and is also sometimes called by this name in California, where it is responsible for something equally innocuous and uninteresting.

GUTSVERWALTUNG — (Goots-vehr-vahl-toong) — German estate management company which oversees vineyard and wine-making operations — or other farm products.

GYPSUM — *see* PLASTERING

H

HAARDT — (Hart) — Chain of hills in the German Rheinpfalz or Palatinate, their lower slopes covered with the vineyards that have made this district's fame. Overlooking the wide, fertile Rhine Valley, like a northern prolongation of the French Vosges, these extend from Schweigen, on the French frontier, northward for nearly fifty miles. All of the finer Pfalz wines come from the central portion, the so-called Mittel-Haardt, which embraces such famous wine towns as Deidesheim, Forst, Ruppertsberg, Wachenheim, Dürkheim, etc.; the Ober-Haardt, to the south, and the Unter-Haardt, the northern section, are districts of large production and relatively common quality.

HAIL — *See* GRÊLE.

HALBSTÜCK — (*Hahlb*-shtick) — Six hundred-liter cask in which Rheingau wines are generally stored and aged. The word *Stück* means "piece," and 1,200-liter casks of this sort do exist, but are rare. When Rhine wines are sold in barrel, a Halbstück is assumed to yield 800 bottles or 66 cases of finished wine.

HALLGARTEN — (*Hahl*-gar-ten) — Important wine-producing town of the Rheingau, with some 370 acres of vines. Like Rauenthal and Kiedrich, this is an upland village, set well back from the river, and its best vineyards (Schönhell, Würzgarten, Hendelberg, Jungfer) are only about a stone's throw from the famous Steinberg. The Hallgartner wines, especially in good years, are fine and forthright and sturdy — often the fullest-bodied of the whole Rheingau.

HARASZTHY, Agoston — (Har-*ras*-thee) — Often and quite fairly called the "father of California viticulture," a talented, impetuous Hungarian count who changed his title into the more democratic one of "Colonel" when he immigrated to this country. He founded a town in Wisconsin and gave it his name (later changed to Sauk City), moved west, was the first sheriff of San Diego, a member of the State Assembly, planted vineyards. The most famous and successful of these was Buena Vista, in Sonoma County. In 1861 he was officially sent to Europe by California's Governor Downey and returned with cuttings of some 300 different grape varieties, thereby laying the foundation of California's wine industry: the report of this trip, which he wrote on his return to Buena Vista, is a minor masterpiece, readable, informative, overflowing with the Colonel's unquenchable optimism and enthusiasm. Soon thereafter he was struck by a series of misfortunes — financial difficulties, problems brought on by the Civil War, phylloxera in his vineyard, a disastrous fire — and went to Nicaragua in an effort to recoup his fortunes through the distillation of rum. There, in 1869, he disappeared; it is believed he fell into a river infested with alligators.

HARD — Wine taster's term, meaning austere, without much charm or suppleness. Many excellent wines, however, are hard in their youth and come round splendidly with time. Hardness, unless accompanied by greenness, is not necessarily a fault, but can be an indication of probable long life. The wines of Chablis and those of the Saar are almost always a little hard; so, in their youth, are the great Clarets of Pauillac.

HARMONIOUS — Good balance; when appearance, bouquet and flavor are in harmony the wine must be tops in its class no matter in what price category or type.

HARO — (Ha-ro) — Brown little city on the upper Ebro River, in Spain, principal center of the Rioja wine trade. During the final decades of the last century, when the phylloxera had devastated Bordeaux but had not yet crossed the Pyrenees into Spain, over a hundred French families settled in Haro: many of the town's *bodegas,* much of its viticultural tradition and its wine-making methods date from those briefly prosperous days.

HARSH — In a wine, harshness is hardness carried to an extreme, generally accompanied by astringency. Occasionally, particularly in red wines and providing other qualities are present, this will disappear in time.

HARSLEVELU — (Hahrsh-lava-loo) — White Hungarian wine grape, used with the Furmint and some Muscat, in Tokay.

HATTENHEIM — (*Hot*-ten-heim) — Charming old village in the Rheingau, producing outstanding wines. Its 475 acres of vineyard include a portion of the Marcobrunn (*see*) and the celebrated Steinberg in its entirety, although the wines from these two plots are not sold as Hattenheimer, but under the vineyard name alone. The other distinguished sites, or *Lagen,* giving somewhat lighter wines, almost equally remarkable but more delicate, include: Nussbrunnen, Wisselbrunnen, Mannberg, Engelmannsberg, Heiligenberg, Hassel, Pfaffenberg, and Schützenhaus.

HAUT — (O) — French word meaning "high," or, in certain combinations, "upper" or "higher" or "top." There is rarely any implication of superior quality, only of altitude: Bas-Armagnac, for example, produces far better brandy than Haut-Armagnac. The confusion arises only because, usually, in France and the world over, hillsides and upland districts yield better wines than lowlands and plains. However this is a broad generalization, not a rule.

HAUT-BAGES-LIBÉRAL, Château — (O Bahj Lee-bay-rahl) — 5th Classed Growth of Pauillac, Haut-Médoc. Some 4,000 cases a year.

HAUT-BAILLY, Château — (O Bye-yee) — One of the best vineyards of Léognan, in the Graves district. Produces red wine exclusively, some 5,000 cases a year of very long-lived, generally rather slow-maturing claret. Ranked deservedly as a 1st Growth of Graves.

HAUT-BATAILLEY, Château — (O Bat-tie-yay) — 5th Classed Growth of Pauillac, Haut-Médoc. The 1855 Classification gives only Batailley, but the vineyard has since been divided and both portions are legally entitled to the name and 5th Growth rank. About 7,000 cases a year of sound, good claret.

HAUT-BENAUGE — (O Ben-ohj) — Agreeable dry white wine, produced on the right bank of the Garonne, near the southern boundary of the Entre-Deux-Mers district. One of the better inexpensive white Bordeaux.

HAUT-BRION, Château — (O Bree-aw) — One of the very greatest red wines of Bordeaux, the only wine of Graves officially ranked in 1855, when it was quite properly placed on a par with Lafite, Latour and Margaux as one of the four 1st Classed Growths of Bordeaux. The vineyard, just outside of the city limits of Bordeaux on the west, is now almost surrounded by suburban villas; its extent is approximately 100 acres and its production averages 12,000 cases a year. In good vintages its wine is altogether remarkable and even in poor years far from bad. There is a little white Haut-Brion produced, which carries the chateau label, printed in silver rather than gold: unquestionably a great

1970

CHATEAU HAUT-BRION
PREMIER GRAND CRU CLASSÉ
APPELLATION GRAVES CONTRÔLÉE
MIS EN BOUTEILLES AU CHATEAU

DOMAINE CLARENCE DILLON S.A., A PESSAC, GIRONDE
MARQUE ET BOUTEILLE DÉPOSÉES

wine, this is often almost too full-bodied and too high in alcohol and there are other more distinguished white Graves.

HAUT COMTAT — (Oh *Cawn*-ta) — Red or *rosé* wine produced in six *communes* north of Avignon, in the Rhône Valley, better than average quality, rarely exported.

HAUTES-CÔTES DE BEAUNE — (Oat Coat d'Bone) — Vineyards on the hills behind the Côte de Beaune. Average production — white: 3500 gallons, red: 225,000 gallons.

HAUTES-CÔTES DE NUITS — (Oat Coat d'Nwee) — Vineyards on the hills behind the Côte de Nuits. Average production — white: 3300 gallons, red: 84,000 gallons.

HAUT-GARDÈRE, Château — (Oh Gar-dair) — One of the good vineyards of Léognan in the Graves district, producing mostly red wines.

HAUT-MÉDOC — (Oh May-dock) — The higher, southern and far better part of the Médoc, extending from the northern edge of the city of Bordeaux to beyond St. Estèphe; all of the Classed Growths and all of the wines which have made the Médoc's fame are in this area. Most of the wines commonly sold as Médoc come from the sandy, lowland country farther north, and are much less good. Haut-Médoc is therefore a superior appellation, strictly defined by French law, and a wine so labeled will almost always be better than something called simply "Médoc."

HAUT MONTRAVEL — *See* MONTRAVEL.

HAUT-PEYRAGUEY, Clos — (Oh-Pay-rah-gay) — 1st Classed Growth of Sauternes. One of the very best vineyards of Bommes (*see*); excellent, golden, sweet wine, typical Sauternes. Small production, rarely over 2,500 cases a year.

HAUT-RHIN — (Oh ran) — French *département* comprising the southern and, as far as wine is concerned, the superior half of Alsace. The vineyards are planted along the lower foothills of the forest-covered Vosges Mountains and are strikingly beautiful, with dozens of picturesque little villages, some of them with their medieval walls intact.

HAUT-SAUTERNES — (Oh Saw-tairn) — Wine name widely used but without any legal standing. Commercially, a very sweet Sauternes of superior quality which may (but need not) come from a higher and better vineyard. When a shipper offers Sauternes and Haut-Sauternes, the latter may be presumed to be sweeter, better and more expensive, but the term, basically, is meaningless. It is no less so in California where, without the final "s," it is sometimes similarly used on a sweeter version of a producer's "California Sauterne."

HAUTVILLERS — (Oh-vee-lay) — Village in the Champagne Country, a Premier Cru rated 90%, which means that its grapes bring 10% less per kilogram, or per ton, than those for example, of Ay, next door, rated 100%. Black grapes are grown exclusively. It was in the Abbey of Hautvillers that Dom

BAS-MÉDOC

St SEURIN

VERTHEUIL
St ESTÈPHE

CISSAC

Gironde

St SAUVEUR

PAUILLAC

St LAURENT St JULIEN

CUSSAC

LISTRAC
MOULIS

ARCINS

AVENSAN SOUSSANS

N

Dordogne

MARGAUX
CANTENAC
LABARDE

Garonne

ARSAC

MACAU
LUDON

HAUT-MÉDOC

LEGEND
Major wine-producing towns   MARGAUX
Secondary wine-producing towns CANTENAC
Rivers   Dordogne
Main Roads

BLANQUEFORT

PESSAC
GRAVES
SCALE
ML.0   1   2   3   4
KM.0   2   4   6   8

BORDEAUX

176

Pérignon (*see*) conducted his celebrated experiments, and the Abbey has been called, perhaps with partial justification, "the birthplace of Champagne."

HAZY — Said of a wine that is possibly clear but certainly not brilliant; this is usually the first step on the road to cloudiness. A hazy wine is almost certainly "off," may be "sick." *See,* however, Sediment.

HEAVY — Full-bodied, without delicacy or much distinction. An unfavorable term, but less severe than "coarse" (*see*).

HECTARE — (Hec-tar) — Metric measure of area containing 10,000 square meters — 2.471 acres. Vineyard area in France is commonly expressed in hectares, and yield figured in hectoliters per hectare. Superior vineyards often have, as their maximum legal yield, 30 or 35 "hectos" per hectare — roughly 320 to 374 gallons per acre.

HECTOLITER — Metric system term for 100 liters, the equivalent of 26.42 U.S. gallons, or 22.03 British imperial gallons. Wine production figures in France are usually given in hectoliters (or, colloquially, "hectos").

HÉRAULT — (A-ro) — French *département* on the Mediterranean, half way, more or less, between Marseille and the Spanish border. It is the heart of that vast *vin ordinaire* country known as the Midi, and although not much larger than a large American county, has over 400,000 acres of vineyards and produces nearly twice as much table wine as the United States. Most of this is common, cheap red wine, coarse, made from the most productive varieties, usually light in color and low in alcohol and often blended with the stronger and darker wines of Algeria. The vines stretch in an immense green band along the gently rolling coastal plain for nearly a hundred miles: Béziers, Sète and Montpellier are the main centers of the wine trade. A few wines of superior quality are grown, notably the sweet white Muscats of Frontignan and Lunel, and some more than passable red table wines in a district known as the Minervois, in the hills back of Béziers.

HERBACEOUS — Odor peculiar to some varietals such as Cabernet, but a little goes a long way, and if too strong or strange it is undesirable.

HERMITAGE — (Air-me-tahj) — Deservedly famous wine of the Rhône Valley, produced on a single steep, spectacular, terraced hillside some 50 miles south of Lyon. It is sometimes and not incorrectly spelled Ermitage or L'Hermitage, and the town where it is made is called Tain-l'Hermitage. The vineyards are rock and face due south; they cover an area a half-mile wide and less than two miles long, and their total yield is approximately 40,000 cases a year. About one-third of this is white, made from Roussanne and Marsanne grapes; two-thirds red, made from the Syrah. An insignificant amount of *Vin de Paille* (*see*) is also produced, from white grapes left to semi-raisin on straw mats, and this of course is quite sweet, golden, high in alcohol (often 15%). White Hermitage is a dry, full-bodied, pale gold wine, with definite character and pronounced bouquet; the red is decidedly better, in favorable years, one of the truly great wines of France — deep colored, very long lived, forthright and fine. The late George Saintsbury described one red Hermitage as "the manliest wine" he had ever drunk, and the adjective was well chosen. Many legends exist (most with little or no foundation) having to do with the origin of the vineyards, their name, and the Syrah grape, which some believe to have been brought from Shiraz, in Persia, by a returning crusader, who became a hermit and built a chapel on the hill; others have pointed out that the "crusader" in question, Gaspard de Sterimberg, arrived in 1225, had been fighting in the religious wars in southern France and had never been within a thousand miles of Persia. It is probable that the vineyards existed in Roman days; no one can surely say why they are called Hermitage; and the origin of the Syrah grape is unknown. Officially there are 18 *quartiers*, or vineyard areas, in the Hermitage hillside, all named, but few if any Hermitage labels carry such names, and most of what appear to be vineyard appellations on Hermitage labels are really nothing of the sort, but simply brands. The *quartiers* are as follows: Beaumes, Les Bessards, La Croix, La Croix de Jamanot, Les Diognières, Les Diognières et Torras, Les Greffieux, Les Gros des Vignes, L'Hermite, L'Homme, Maison Blanche, Le Méal, Les Murets, Péléat, La Pierrelle, Les Roucoules, Les Signaux, Varogne.

HESSIA — *see* RHEINHESSEN

HESSISCHE BERGSTRASSE — (Hes-sish-uh   Bairg-strasse-uh) — Smallest of the eleven German Specified Wine Regions or Anbaugebiete (*see*). Its 2 Bereiche, 3 Grosslagen and 20-some-odd Einzellagen are planted over 50% in riesling. Its total production is less than ½% of all wines produced in Germany. For Map, *see* Germany.

HEURIGE — (*Hoy*-rig-guh) — Name generally given to the fresh young wine served in carafe or by the glass in the many cafés round Vienna.

HIPPOCRAS — Medieval (14th Century) wine flavored with cinnamon, ginger, other spices and sugar; an ancestor of liqueurs and cordials.

HOCHHEIM — (Hawk-heim) — Important wine-producing town in Germany, properly considered part of the Rheingau, although it overlooks the Main rather than the Rhine, and is separated from the other vineyards by at least ten miles of farm and orchard land. There are nearly 500 acres under vines, and the better Einzellagen (as Domdechaney, Kirchenstück, Stein, Hölle, etc.) give wines that have the unmistakable Rheingau stamp of character and breed, though perhaps somewhat gentled and softened.

HOCK — The Englishman's general term for Rhine wine, as Claret for Red Bordeaux. It is supposed to be derived from Hochheimer, and in any case has replaced the older "Rhenish" in current British usage; no very good reasons have ever been advanced to explain why Hochheim, almost outside the Rheingau proper, was selected for this honor, instead of, more logically, "Jo," "Hat," or "Rue," for Johannisberger, Hattenheimer and Ruedesheimer. But who are we to carp? It is still legally possible, under American regulations, to manufacture something called California Hock, and indeed New York Hock and Ohio Hock, in the United States.

HOGSHEAD — Common name for half sized barrels of various sorts, i.e. claret — 55 U.S. gals.; sherry — 66 U.S. gals., etc.

178

HOLMES, Oliver Wendell (1809-1894) — American author and physician, who, in addressing the Massachusetts Medical Society in Boston, May 30, 1860, said: "Wine is a food."

HOMER — Greek epic poet of antiquity, who said: "Wine gives strength to weary men."

HONEY — Natural sugar available long before cane and beet sugars; used for sweetening wines; itself, when diluted with water and fermented becomes mead, hydromel and metheglin.

HORACE — (65-8 B.C.) — Roman poet, who wrote: "Who prates of war or want after taking wine?"

HOSPICES DE BEAUNE — (Awss-peace duh Bone) — One of the most beautiful buildings of Europe, a charity hospital (often referred to as the "Hôtel Dieu") in the Burgundian town of Beaune; scene annually, on the third Sunday of November, of what is perhaps the most famous wine auction in the world. Since its foundation in 1443 it has been bequeathed holdings in many of the best vineyards of the Côte de Beaune: these constitute its principal endowment and the wines from these provide most of its revenue. The prices brought at the auction, a most picturesque affair, tend to establish the level of Burgundy wine prices for the vintage in question. Although the wines are sold when still new, and delivered in barrel, the Hospices name is almost never abused; the wines are of superior quality and generally worth the high prices they bring.

The Hospices owns 32 vineyards in all, and produce some 500 to 600 *pièces* (barrels of 228 liters roughly 25 cases each) or 12,500 to 15,000 cases a year (although only 27 *pièces* in 1940 and 871 *pièces* in 1973). The product of each vineyard is auctioned separately, under the name of its *cuvée*, which in most cases is that of its donor, and prices vary widely according to the origin, reputation and quality of each wine. Listed on p. 180 are the various *cuvées*, more or

Hospices de Beaune
1969
BEAUNE

Appellation Beaune Contrôlée

Cuvée Maurice-Drouhin

Acquéreurs : Dreyfus, Ashby & Co
New York, N. Y.

PRODUCT OF FRANCE

Chaque année, le troisième Dimanche de Novembre, a lieu la célèbre vente aux enchères «à la chandelle» des Grands Vins du Domaine des Hospices, constitué tout au long des siècles grâce à de généreuses donations.
Ces grands vins en tonneaux sont pris en charge par les acquéreurs qui ont la délicate mission de les élever et de les mettre en bouteilles.

THE HOSPICES DE BEAUNE Cuvées

Name	Appellation Contrôlée	1977 Pieces	Cases
(Red Wine)			
Nicolas Rolin	Beaune	27	675
Guigone de Salins	Beaune	20	500
Charlotte Dumay	Corton	23	575
Docteur Peste	Corton	27	675
Dames Hospitalières	Beaune	25	625
Dames de la Charité	Pommard	4	100
Blondeau	Volnay	20	500
Brunet	Beaune	22	550
Jehan de Massol	Volnay-Santenots	27	675
Clos des Avaux	Beaune	27	675
Billardet	Pommard	27	675
Gauvain	Volnay-Santenots	17	425
Hugues et Louis Betault	Beaune	35	875
Rousseau-Deslandes	Beaune	18	450
General Muteau	Volnay	18	450
Maurice Drouhin	Beaune	27	675
Boillot	Auxey-Duresses	9	225
Arthur Girard	Savigny-les-Beaune	13	325
Fouquerand	Savigny-les-Beaune	27	675
J. Lebelin	Monthélie	9	225
Forneret	Savigny-les-Beaune	25	625
Rameau-Lamarasse	Pernand Vergelesses	12	300
Madeleine Collignon	Mazis-Chambertin	27	675
(White Wine)			
François de Salins	Corton-Charlemagne	2½	68
de Bahèzre de Lanlay	Meursault-Charmes	18	450
Albert Grivault	Meursault-Charmes	9	225
Baudot	Meursault-Genevrières	18	450
Philippe le Bon	Meursault-Genevrières	8	200
Jehan Humblot	Meursault	12	300
Goureau	Meursault	9	225
Loppin	Meursault	7	175
Paul Chanson	Corton-Vergennes	2½	68
TOTAL		572	14,300

TOTAL REVENUE 1977

Red Wine	5,629,000 francs
White Wine	868,000
Eaux de Vie	147,664

6,644,664 francs at $0.20 = $1,328,933.

less in the order of the prices they regularly bring, together with the origin of each, and (merely as an indication) the quantity sold in 1977.

There is no one standard label for the Hospices wines, but the consumer has the right to expect that the name of the *cuvée* and its *appellation contrôlée* should appear, as well as the name of the bottler; in some instances, each bottle is numbered.

It should perhaps be added that a little *Eau-de-Vie de Marc,* distilled from the grape skins or hulls, is also sold at the same auction, though this of course is always of the preceding vintage.

HOSPICES DE NUITS — (Awss-peace d'Nwee) — Hospital in Nuits-Saint-Georges, in Burgundy, which, like the far more famous Hospices de Beaune, has an endowment in the form of vineyards and sells wines which carry its name. Many of these come from the best *climats* of Nuits, and are of high quality.

HOTTE — (Hot) — French back-pack made of cane, wood, metal or plastic into which pickers dump their hand carried baskets during the vintage. The *hotte* carrier then climbs up and tips his grapes into the vehicle which will carry a large load to the presses.

HUDSON RIVER —Table grapes of native American varieties have long been grown in the Hudson Valley, particularly on the right or west bank below Kingston where the first New York commercial winery opened in 1839; originally called Blooming Grove, it is now the Brotherhood Corporation. Today the area also grows many hybrids (*see*) and a very few vinifera grapes.

HUNAWIHR — (Hoo-na-veer) — Exceedingly picturesque village in Alsace, perched on a vineyard-covered hill northwest of Colmar. Very good wines.

HUNGARY — Hungarian wines have been famous for centuries, Tokay especially, and were well-known and appreciated in America even in pre-Civil War days. Those now being exported are of fair and occasionally good quality, but they are certainly more standardized and less remarkable than in the past — apparently the inevitable fate of wines grown under a Socialist economy. Most of the labels carry a geographic designation — a town or district name, used as an adjective and ending in "i," as *Badacsonyi, Egri, Szekszárdi, Debröi, Soproni, Móri, Somlyói, Pécsi, Gyöngyösi, Balatonfüredi, Villányi,* and of course *Tokaji.* Generally, this is followed by a second name, which is usually but not always that of a grape; the leading white wine grapes, more or less in order of quality, are *Furmint, Hárslevelü, Rizling* (or *Olaszrizling*), *Veltelini, Kéknyelü, Muskotály, Ezerjó* and *Leányka;* for red wine, *Kadarka,* above all, and *Vörös.*

Bikavér, which means "bull's blood," is an exception and Egri Bikavér (from Eger), generally regarded as the best Hungarian red, is a blend of varieties including the *Kadarka* but also a few others of French origin. Similarly, when it comes to Tokay, made from the *Furmint* and *Hárslevelü,* terms such as *szamorodni, aszú, eszencia* and *puttonyos* have to do with methods of vinification, and for these, *see* Tokay.

HUNTER RIVER — One of the oldest and best vineyard districts of Australia (*see*), which produces some highly creditable red and white table wines.

HUSSEREN-LES-CHÂTEAUX — (Who-ser-en lay Shat-toe) — Attractive little wine-poducing town in southern Alsace, remarkable for the three ruined castles on top of its steep, vineyard-covered hill — these constitute a famous landmark and are visible for miles.

HYBRID — In viticulture, the result of a cross of two grape varieties. Botanically, the idea is a fairly new one, less than two centuries old; applied to the grape, it is wholly revolutionary, since the wine-bearing vine has been almost entirely propagated by cuttings rather than seeds since the dawn of human history. The term hybrid includes both true hybrids (cross-pollination of several species, i.e. vinifera x rotundifolia) and métis (cross-pollination in the same species, i.e. vinifera x vinifera). Most hybrids and métis are an attempt to combine the best qualities of two quite different parent vines, or to produce an offspring able to contend with some special problem, such as the phylloxera, without compromising its superiority. Considering the fact that there is hardly such a thing as a pure strain of grape, or one surely able to transmit its specific qualities to its seedlings, this is a monumental problem, and it is surprising that so much definite progress has been made. There is no doubt, for example, that a number of the newer hybrids are capable of giving better wine in our Eastern states than any of the original "native" varieties; hybrids also provide quite passable wine for home in many parts of France. These crosses usually bear the name of the hybridizer, often plus a serial number, in France — as Seibel 5279, Couderc 4401, Baco No. 1, Bouschet, and Müller-Thurgau; in other countries they have a bad tendency, like illegitimate children, to claim the name of their more illustrious parent, however few of his or her characteristics they may possess; as a result, wines are often presented to a somewhat confused public under names that sound familiar but to which the wines have no well authenticated right. Thus we have Goldriesling and Mainrielsing in Germany, Emerald Riesling (*see* Riesling) and Ruby Cabernet in the United States.

Mr. Philip Wagner of *The Baltimore Sun* and of Boordy Vineyard (*see*) has done much to popularize the better hybrids in America. Extensive experiments in hybridizing are being carried on by the University of California's College of Agriculture, at Davis, California, and by similar establishments in several continents and at least a dozen countries. It seems certain that much of benefit to the wine-drinker will eventually come out of all this and a number of hybrids through use have acquired distinctive varietal names (*see* Appendix 2B).

HYDROMEL — Medieval wine made from honey and water, like Mead and Metheglin.

HYMETTUS — Name for red and white table wines made in Attica (Greece) and taking the name from Mt. Hymettus.

ICE — While an acceptable companion to almost all spirits (since it merely replaces the water lost in distillation) ice, like water, is a confirmed enemy of fine wine, and should never be put in fine wine — there is enough mediocre stuff produced to quench the world's thirst for wine-and-soda, sangría, and all the rest.

ICE BUCKET — Except in restaurants, ice buckets seem to be used less and less generally in this day of electric refrigeration; this is to be regretted, for white wines and *rosés* and Champagnes are far better served in a bucket. Prechilling, however useful, does not accomplish the same end; chilled wines lose their freshness and sprightliness and charm as they warm up during a meal, and the last glass rarely tastes as good as the first. Of red wines, particularly if brought to table at slightly below room temperature, the opposite is of course true; they improve as they warm up and taste better and better, as they should.

Many ice buckets are poorly designed, and the wine in the neck of a Rhine or Moselle bottle, for example, never gets chilled at all. In such cases it is perfectly correct procedure to put the bottle in the bucket neck down for ten minutes or so, before the capsule is cut away and the cork drawn.

ICE SAINTS — In German, *Eis Heiligen,* the patron saints of four days in May, the 12th through the 15th, during which danger of spring frost is still considered to exist in German vineyards, especially those of the Moselle and Saar. Their names are St. Pancratius, St. Servatius, St. Bonifacius, and finally *die kalte Sophie,* or cold St. Sophia. Once they are past, the growers breathe easier, and in fact killing frosts after May 15th are almost unknown. *See,* however, Frost.

ICE WINE — *see* Eiswein.

IHRINGEN — (*Ear*-ring-en) — One of the best wine-producing villages of the Kaiserstuhl, near Freiburg, in southwestern Germany. It is particularly noted for its Ruländer, or Pinot Gris, much like a top-grade Alsatian and perhaps the finest white wine of Baden.

IMPERIAL — Oversize bottle, in which Clarets of great years are occasionally laid away, for slower development and longer life. Holds as much as eight ordinary bottles.

INDRE — (An-dr) — Tributary of the Loire, in the French Château Country. Most of the red, white and *rosé* wines produced along its banks are entitled to the appellation "Touraine"; they are really nothing more than sound *vins de pays,* but light and fresh and very agreeable.

INFERNO — (In-*fair*-no) — Perhaps the most famous of the five classic red wines of Valtellina (*see*), produced along the northern edge of the Lombardy region of Italy, not far from the Swiss border.

INGELHEIM — (*Ing*-el-heim) — Picturesque and historic little town in Hessia, facing Johannisberg across the Rhine. Today it produces some rather common red wine, never exported, and a certain amount of even less distinguished white. Its fame comes from the fact that Charlemagne spent a good deal of time in his castle there and, according to tradition, once observed that the snow melted earlier than elsewhere on one especially favored opposite hillside. He therefore ordered that vines be planted in what is still regarded as one of the world's great vineyards, Schloss Johannisberg.

INGHILTERRA — (Ing-gil-*terr*-ra) — *See* Marsala.

INGLENOOK — Famous old California vineyard, at Rutherford, in the Napa Valley. The first vines were planted in 1879 by Gustave Niebaum (or Nybom), a retired Finnish sea captain and one of the first directors of the Alaska Commercial Company, and the impressive stone winery was constructed a decade later. Until the mid 1960s the property still belonged to Captain Niebaum's collateral descendants including John Daniel, Jr., who directed it and had been an important figure in California viticulture since the end of Prohibition. Like Beaulieu, its immediate neighbor, it now belongs to the Heublein Corporation.

IONA — Native, Eastern, pink grape, but giving white wine, rather widely planted in the Finger Lakes district. It takes its name from Iona Island, in the Hudson not far from Peekskill, where it was first grown.

IPHOFEN — (*Eep*-ho-fen) — One of the better wine-producing towns of Franconia, in Germany. Its white wines are shipped in Bocksbeutels, and the top vineyards are Julius-Echter-Berg, Kronsberg, and Kalb.

IRANCY — (Ee-rah-see) — Pleasant, inconsequential red and *rosé* wine, produced round the village of this name, some ten miles southwest of Chablis, in northern Burgundy. It is entitled only to the appellation "Bourgogne"; when made from the Pinot Noir, it is a fresh and delightful *vin de pays*, but all too often it comes, as it may legally, from two far less distinguished grapes, the César and the Tressot, and is wholly ordinary.

IROULÉGUY — (Ee-roo-lay-ghee) — Full-bodied, golden, dry white wine, also a less fine red, produced round St. Jean-Pied-de-Port, not far from Biarritz in the western Pyrenees. Of purely local fame, it is often quite good and, in local cellars, surprisingly long-lived.

ISABELLA — An old, heavy-flavored Eastern grape, an inferior predecessor of the Concord, now fortunately little used for wine except for a passable *rosé* made in the Finger Lakes (*see*). Through sheer stupidity or bad luck, it was planted rather widely in certain parts of southern Switzerland and northern Italy at the time of the phylloxera (*see*) to which it is of course immune. Its almost undrinkable deep-colored wine is there, particularly in the Swiss Canton of Tessin, or the Ticino, known as "Americano" (*see*), hardly the best possible propaganda for the United States.

ISCHIA — (Isk-*key*-ah) — Island facing Capri across the Bay of Naples. Produces a considerable amount of very good, pale, dry, white wine, most of it, until quite recently, marketed, quite legally, as "Capri" (*see*), it being considered that the Capri production zone included both Ischia and the adjoining island of Procida. All this has been changed by the new Italian wine regulations; Ischia now has a well-merited *denominazione controllata* of its own.

ISERA — (Ee-*sair*-ah) — Small town in the Italian Trentino (*see*), not far from Lake Garda. Known for its excellent light red wine and its even better *rosé*, both made from the Marzemino grape, and both sold as Marzemino d'Isera.

ISLAND BELLE — Native red grape of poor quality, also called Campbell's Early, which has unfortunately been widely planted along the Pacific Coast in the State of Washington, and on the islands northwest of Seattle. Its wine has a pronounced "foxy" flavor and is mediocre at best.

ISRAEL — Wine has been made in what is now Israel since the beginning of recorded history — certainly almost everywhere in Biblical days — and then, after a thousand "dry" years (which makes our own American Prohibition seem really no longer than a school recess) again since 1870. Later, with the help of Baron Edmond de Rothschild, vines were planted and a winery constructed in 1866 at Richon Le Zion, southeast of Tel Aviv.

Most of the real progress in modern wine production dates, however, as might be expected, from 1948, when Israel became an independent state; this small land is therefore perhaps the oldest and yet the youngest wine-producing country in the world. Much has been accomplished: there are over 20,000 acres under vines; production in 1976 was in excess of 11 million gallons. Over 10% of this is exported.

The vineyard districts are scattered, the major ones are round Richon Le Zion, near Tel Aviv, and Zichron Jacob, southeast of Haifa; there are small, recent plantings in the Jerusalem corridor, and in the Lachish, Ashkelon and Beersheva areas further south. The grape varieties, selected for this latitude and its generally warm, arid climate, are principally, for red wine, the Ali-

CARMEL

PRODUCE OF ISRAEL

SELECTED ISRAEL
CABERNET SAUVIGNON

IMPORTED

12% ALCOHOL BY VOLUME · 4/5 QUART

PRODUCED & BOTTLED BY
Carmel Wine Growers Cooperative · Richon le Zion · Zichron Jacob

cante, Carignane, Grenache, Alicante Bouschet, and for white wines, the Muscat of Alexandria, the Muscat of Frontignan, and the Clairette; there are, however, plantings of Malbec, Cabernet Sauvignon, Semillon, Ugni Blanc and even Concord.

Since Israel has adhered to the Madrid Convention (unlike the United States), European names such as Champagne, Sauternes, Burgundy, Port, Sherry, etc., no longer appear on Israeli wine labels. There are some twenty wineries, mostly cooperatives, of which a number export; the Carmel Wine Co., or more correctly, the Société Coopérative Vigneronne des Grandes Caves, is the most important.

The wines are increasingly well-made, by competent technicians and with good equipment. Most of them are consumed in Israel, where they are inexpensive, and a large proportion of those shipped to the U.S. are consumed by observant Jews for ritualistic purposes, for which, for obvious reasons, they are often preferred.

While never of exceptional quality, they are honest, good, not overpriced.

ISSAN, Château d' — (Dee-sah) — 3rd Classed Growth of Cantenac-Margaux. One of the better vineyards of Cantenac; some 5,000 cases a year of Claret distinguished for its finesse and breed. The old-fashioned gold label carries the proud devise, *Regum mensis arisque Deorum,* "For the Tables of Kings and the Altars of the Gods."

ITALIA — (Ee-*tal*-ee-ah) — Special type of Marsala (*see*).

ITALIAN SWISS COLONY — Winery in Sonoma County founded in 1880 as a philanthropic farming venture; today it is a tourist haven visited by almost half a million visitors every year and is part of the United Vintners conglomerate, second largest wine shippers in the United States.

ITALY — *Oenotria tellus,* immemorial "Land of Wine," Italy deserves her ancient name as does no other country, perhaps not even France. Every province of Italy produces wine; one acre out of every eight of Italian soil is either given over to vineyard or has, at least, its small quota of vines. Far smaller than California, Italy produces four times as much wine as the United States, 20 per cent of all the wine of the world — 1¾ billion gallons a year.

Most of this, of course, is the most ordinary sort of wine — undistinguished, inexpensive, made to be drunk within a year. On the other hand, between the Alps and Sicily, Italy possesses an extraordinary diversity of climates, soils, grape varieties and viticultural traditions, and almost every province has at least some specialties fit for export. In recent years, Italy has often shipped more wine to the United States than France.

Few Italian wines, can equal in quality the best German and French. However, there are literally dozens of Italian wines that are quite remarkable — interesting, distinctive, and of oustanding excellence, their price considered. Nearly all of these were once classed as *"Vini Tipici"* (*see* Tipico), are under strict government control as to authenticity, and carry the phrase *Denominazione di Origine Controllata.* They are all listed in their proper alphabetical place in this encyclopedia.

It would hardly be possible for anyone except a professional or a specialist to be familiar, even superficially, with all the wines of Italy. But there are at least thirty or forty or fifty worth cultivating and any catalogue of this elite would include at least the following:

Several of the red wines of Piedmont, magisterial BAROLO, full-bodied GATTINARA, and somewhat lighter BARBARESCO, all three made from the Nebbiolo grape, plus a few of their sturdy cousins, BARBERA, FREISA, GRIGNOLINO; the classic VALTELLINA of Lombardy; BARDOLINO and VALPOLICELLA from the province of Verona; two or three red wines from the Italian Tyrol, SANTA MADDALENA, LAGO DI CALDARO, perhaps SANTA GIUSTINA; the characteristic LAMBRUSCO of Emilia (although it will not please everyone); *Classico* CHIANTI, preferably that shipped in ordinary wine bottles rather than in *fiaschi;* GRAGNANO from near Naples, possibly AGLIANICO DEL VULTURE, though this is hard to find.

In the way of dry wines, or semi-dry: the CORTESE of Piedmont, especially that sold as Gavi; the LUGANA of Lake Garda and, of course, SOAVE from near Verona; the pale TERLANO and TRAMINER *aromatico* from the Alto Adige; the VERDISO of Conegliano, near Venice, and the VERDICCHIO from the Castelli di Jesi; ORVIETO, perhaps EST! EST!! EST!!!, and the Castelli Romani wines, such as FRASCATI, CAPRI, ISCHIA, and LACHRIMA CHRISTI from near Naples; and the white ETNA from Sicily.

As *vins rosés,* the CHIARETTO (Chiarello) of Garda, LAGREIN ROSATO from the Italian Tyrol.

Among dessert wines, MARSALA, of course; the ALEATICO of Elba; the VINO SANTO produced both in Tuscany and the Trentino, half a dozen different sorts of MOSCATO, and many others. And, as sparkling wines, ASTI

The Wines of **ITALY**

Drawn by W. Lembeck

SPUMANTE, and, for those who like a dryer wine, the GRAN SPUMANTE made out of the French Pinot grapes of Casteggio.

With hardly any exceptions (Est! Est!! Est!!! being one and Chiaretto another) Italian wines take their names either from their town or district of origin, or from a variety of grape. The labels as a whole are dependable, and the wines honest. It must be admitted, however, that as far as vintages are concerned, this is not altogether the case; Italian wines *do* vary in quality from year to year, but much less than those of Germany and France, and Italians themselves rarely pay any attention to the vintage when ordering wine, and cheerfully accept whatever vintage is currently available. Many Italian wines would not even carry a vintage if it were not for the exigencies of foreign buyers; often such buyers prefer an old vintage, even on wines that are vastly better when drunk young, and many Italian shippers are quite willing to cooperate, feeling that the matter is of little or no importance. Vintage years on Italian wines are therefore largely to be distrusted. As a matter of fact, with at

Drawn by W. Lembeck

189

most a dozen exceptions, all Italian wines are as good when three years old as they are ever likely to be. Those worth ageing are Barolo, Barbaresco, Gattinara, Ghemme, Valtellina (all made from the Nebbiolo grape), Freisa and possibly Grignolino, the better grades of Chianti and a few other Tuscan wines; perhaps Aglianico del Vulture. All of these are red. Dessert wines such as Marsala are aged in wood and are ready to drink when bottled.

IVES — Red, native, Eastern grape, believed to be a seedling, or accidental cross of other varieties, first grown along the Ohio River near Cincinnati in the 1850's. It give a heavy, deep-colored, coarse wine with a pronounced "foxy" flavor, which few except the most confirmed devotees of Eastern wines find acceptable, let alone good; it is used, but hardly ever straight, in many New York State Burgundies, both still and sparkling.

J

JAMES — Native American black grape, of the Southern Muscadine family, and therefore related to the Scuppernong, sometimes used for wine in the Carolinas.

JASNIÈRES — (Zhan-yare) — Small district in the Coteaux du Loir (*see*) producing interesting (although generally not commercial) wines along the northern edge of the French province of Touraine. Principal grape varieties are the Chenin Blanc for white wine and the Cabernet Franc and Pinot Noir for red.

JEFFERSON, Thomas (1743-1826) — Author of the Declaration of Independence, sometime Ambassador to France, and third President of the United States, who wrote: "No nation is drunken where wine is cheap and none sober where the dearness of wine substitutes ardent spirits as the common beverage."

JEREZ — (Hair-eth) — Attractive and prosperous little city in southern Spain, on the main road and main railway line from Seville to Cadiz; the birthplace of Sherry, which is called *Jerez* or *Vino de Jerez* in Spanish. The vineyards that have made the city's fame and its wealth lie mostly to the west and southwest of the town, out of sight of the highway; many of the streets run between the high, white, windowless walls of the bodegas in which Sherry (*see*) is stored and aged.

JEROBOAM — Oversize wine bottle, holding as much as six ordinary bottles, in which Clarets of great years are sometimes laid away. The jeroboam is also used for Champagne, where it equals four bottles, but here the wine, except by some particularly fastidious makers, is fermented in regular bottles and then transferred just prior to shipment; this of course has a tendency to shorten its life.

JEROPIGA — *See* GEROPIGA.

JESI or IESI — (Yay-zee) — Town in central Italy, not far from Ancona. The surrounding villages produce, from the Verdicchio grape, one of the best Italian dry white wines. *See* Castelli di Jesi.

JESUITENGARTEN — (Yez-you-*eat*-en-gar-ten) — Name (literally, "Jesuits' Garden") given to at least four different and widely separated vineyards in Germany; one at Pellingen on the Saar, property of the Friedrich Wilhelm Gymnasium; Winkeler Jesuitengarten, which adjoins Schloss Vollrads in the Rheingau, is even better known; and Forster Jesuitengarten is by far the most famous of all, one of the Palatinate's best *Lagen,* mostly owned by the Bassermann-Jordan family; and Königsbach Jesuitengarten also in the Palatinate south of Deidesheim.

JOHANNISBERG — World-famous little village, and its even more celebrated castle (*see* Johannisberg, Schloss, below) overlooking the Rhine in the heart of the German Rheingau. Its production figures are hardly impressive — there are only 87 acres in the Schloss or castle vineyard (part of these usually non-productive through the rotation of replanting) and only about 200 more under vines in the whole township. These would be hard pressed to supply the whole world's demand for Johannisberger, and commercial wines labeled simply Bereich Johannisberg, with no indication of specific vineyard site, or producer's name, or estate-bottling, may legitimately be looked on with skepticism. On the other hand, the true Johannisbergers, with vineyard name and Erzeugerabfüllung, are of a quality hardly surpassed and not often equaled in the Rheingau, wines of extraordinary grace and breed and bouquet. The dependable *Lagen,* or vineyard names, are: Hölle, Vogelsang, Hansenberg, Mittelhölle, Goldatzel, and Schwarzenstein. Note that Johannisberger Erntebringer is a *Grosslage (see)*.

JOHANNISBERGER RIESLING — Name usually given to the white Riesling grape in California to differentiate it from other varieties which, in fact, are not Rieslings at all — the so-called Franken Riesling (really the Sylvaner), the Grey Riesling (really the Chauché Gris), the Emerald Riesling, the Goldriesling and the Mainriesling, all of which are crosses, giving wine of lesser quality.

JOHANNISBERG, Schloss — Germany's most famous vineyard, 87 acres, spectacularly situated on one of the steepest of the Rheingau's hillsides, commanding an incomparable view over the fertile and busy Rhine Valley. According to tradition, it was the Emperor Charlemagne who first ordered vines planted on its slope (having observed, from his palace at Ingelheim across the river, that snow melted sooner there than elsewhere); by 1100 a Bénédictine abbey had been constructed on the site, and when church properties were secularized in 1801, this became the property of Prince William of Orange. The Congress of Vienna ceded it to the Emperor of Austria, and he bestowed it on Prince Metternich; it is still the property of the Metternich family, and their home.

The present castle, however, is new, the old *Schloss* having been bombed during the last war, and almost entirely destroyed.

The wines are now sold under two quite different labels, with differently colored capsules indicating the various gradations of quality. The more familiar label carries the Metternich *Wappen,* or coat-of-arms, and three wines are so marketed: the *Rotlack,* or red capsule, is the Kabinett, generally a dry wine of decided breed but not outstanding quality; the *Grünlack,* green capsule, is a step higher, and is always a Spätlese; the best, the *Rosalack,* pink capsule, is not produced every year, and is always an Auslese. The alternate label carries an engraving in color of the *Schloss* and vineyard, and is also marketed under three separate capsule colors: the *Orangelack,* or orange capsule, is the Kabinett; the *Weisslack,* white capsule, is the Spätlese; the *Himmelblaulack,* sky-blue capsule, is the Auslese. When a Beerenauslese is made in great years, such as 1971, a portion is sold under the regular label as *Rosa-Goldlack,* a gold capsule with a pink stripe, and the balance is sold with the alternate "Schloss" label as *Blau-Goldlack,* a gold capsule with a blue stripe. Trockenbeerenauslese is always sold as *Goldlack,* gold capsule, and also carries the label with the engraving of the *Schloss* and vineyards. It should perhaps be added that in poor years only a small portion of the wine is estate-bottled, the rest being made into sparkling wine, or Sekt. In 1973, a new color was introduced in the American market: *Gelblack,* or yellow capsule. This color, with a yellow label in the familiar *Wappen* style, is being used for wines which were made with the addition of sugar, and the 1972 vintage was the first one sold to the general public in this manner.

JOHNSON, Samuel (1709-1784) — British author and lexicographer, quoted by his biographer, James Boswell, as saying, "Wine gives great pleasure and every pleasure is of itself a good." He also described Claret as drink "for boys," assigning Port to men and brandy to heroes.

JOSEPHSHOFER — (*Yo*-zefs-hof-er) — Excellent vineyard at Graach on the Moselle, owned in its entirety and for over a century by the Kesselstatt family; both the steeply terraced vines and the picturesque buildings at their foot belonged to the Monastery of St. Martin until 1802, when they were secularized and given their present name. Although in the township of Graach, the Josephshof directly adjoins Wehlen, and its wine, sold as Josephshöfer, is generally more like a Wehlener than a Graacher, rich and full-bodied rather than sprightly, big and fine rather than delicate and charming.

JOURNAL — (Zhoor-nahl) — Old Burgundian measure of area, about five-sixths of an acre.

JUG WINE — Common use word for wines sold in large bottles — gallons, half-gallons, and sizes over one liter.

JULIÉNAS — (Zhule-yea-nahs) — One of the most important *communes* and one of the best wines of the Beaujolais — perhaps less fruity than Brouilly and less engaging than Fleurie, but a firm wine of unusual distinction, balance and fine texture. Total production is close to a half million gallons a year. (*see* Beaujolais).

193

JURA — (Zhew-rah) — Mountain range, *département,* and wine-growing district in eastern France, not far from the Swiss border. The vineyards are strung along the Jura foothills, which run roughly parallel to the Burgundian Côte d'Or, from the town of Arbois southward for some fifty miles, in the old French province of Franche-Comté. Neither in quality nor in quantity are the wines of much consequence — total production, about half of it white, is about 900,000 gallons a year — but the very diversity of the Jura wines makes them rather interesting. The *rosé* wine of Arbois *(see)* is probably the best as well as the best-known, and the only one likely to be found outside of France; the others include a rather more than passable sparkling wine called L'Étoile; a distinct oddity, Château-Chalon *(see)*, which might be called a French version of unfortified Sherry; a small quantity of *vin de paille (see)*; finally, some fairly good reds and whites, the best marketed under the appellation Arbois.

JURANÇON — (Zhew-rahn-saw) — Rather sweet, golden wine, celebrated in history and legend, produced on the Pyrenees foothills south and west of Pau, in southwestern France. It is made from grape varieties unknown in other districts, the Petit Manseng, the Gros Manseng and the Courbu; it has a special, spicy bouquet and flavor which some local enthusiasts have compared to the scent of carnations and the taste of cinnamon or cloves. The individual vineyard holdings are small, and the vines trained high, almost pergola-fashion; surprisingly, the average production is not far from 400,000 gallons a year. Rarely found on wine-lists, even in France, yet well-balanced, interesting and long-lived, Jurançon was of course a favorite wine of King Henry IV (who was born in Pau), and on the whole deserves its reputation.

K

KABINETT — (Cab-ee-*net*) — The designation for the first of the six "quality wines with special attributes" (*Qualitätswein mit Prädikat*) under the German Wine Law. On all German wines of the 1971 vintage and later, the word is equivalent of the no-longer-legal *Originalabfüllung* (*see*), and guarantees an quality, and should always be the driest and least expensive wine from a given vineyard and producer in any vintage. The designation *Kabinett* used in conjunction with Erzeugerabfüllung (*see*) on a German wine label is now the equivalent of the no-longer-legal *Originalabfüllung* (*see*), and guarantees an estate-bottled, unsugared wine.

KADARKA — (*Ka*-dar-ka) — Hungarian red wine grape, widely planted in that once happy country, and responsible for the vast majority of red wines ranked officially there as *Premiers Grands Crus*. These carry the name Kadarka plus a regional appellation of origin on their labels, as Szekszárdi Kadarka, Pécsi Kadarka, Villányi Kadarka, Gyöngyosi Kadarka and Egri Kadarka. It was once thought to be identical with the Zinfandel of California, although the wine it yields is of a far different character; this comforting theory has now gone pretty well by the board.

KAEFERKOPF — (Kay-fer-kopf) — One of the rare wines of Alsace to carry a specific vineyard name. The Kaeferkopf is in the *commune* of Ammerschwihr, and yields admirable Rieslings and Gewürztraminers.

KAISERSTUHL — (Kai-ser-shtool) — Interesting little wine-producing district in Baden, southwest Germany. This consists of an extraordinary "island" of volcanic tufa, rising out of the fertile Rhine Valley between Colmar (in Alsace) and Freiburg-im-Breisgau; its wines are not unlike those of Alsace, and most of the Alsatian grape varieties are grown, but perhaps the best here are made from the Ruländer, or Pinot Gris, and come from the villages of Ihringen, Endingen, Achkarren and Bötzingen.

KALLSTADT — (Kahl-shtat) — One of the better wine-producing villages of the Pfalz, north of Dürkheim, with over 700 acres of vines, including a fairly high percentage of Rieslings. Good vineyards include Kronenberg, Kreidkeller, Steinacker, Annaberg, all in three Grosslagen — one with the extraordinary name of Saumagen, or "sow-belly."

KANZEM — (Kahnt-zem) — Celebrated wine-producing village on the Saar, in Germany, with some hundred precious acres of Riesling vines. In great years its wines are close in quality to those of Wiltingen and Ockfen (there can hardly be higher praise) and its vineyard sites or *Lagen* are Sonnenberg, Altenberg, Schlossberg, and Hörecker.

KARTHAUSER HOFBERG — (Kart-*hoy*-zer *Hawf*-bairg) — Celebrated vineyard on the Ruwer, in Germany. *See* Eitelsbach.

KASEL — (Kah-zl) — The most important vineyard town of the Ruwer, a tributary of the Moselle, producing pale, light, delicate white wines, of great bouquet and charm. Leading vineyards include Nieschen, Kehrnagel, Hitzlay, Herrenberg, Paulinsberg, Timpert, and Dominikanerberg.

KAYSERSBERG — (*Kayz*-zerz-bairg) — Picturesque and justly famous little wine town in Alsace. Its Rieslings and Gewürztraminers are of top quality and it is the birthplace of Dr. Albert Schweitzer.

KÉKNYELÜ — (*Cake*-nyel-eu) — Hungarian white wine grape; the name means "blue-stalked".

KELLER — (Kel-ler) — Simply means cellar, in German; thus *Kellerarbeit* means cellar-work, *Kellermeister* means cellar-master. However, *see* below.

KELLERABFÜLLUNG — (Kel-ler-*ahb*-fil-lung); also KELLERABZUG (Kel-ler-*ahb*-zook) — Literally, the first of these meant "cellar-filling," and the second, "cellar-drawing-off"; for all practical purposes they meant (until 1971) the same thing, Estate-Bottled, when used in conjunction with the word "Original." One or the other, or ORIGINALABFÜLLUNG (the commonest form of all), was always found on the label of a fine German wine, followed by the name of the producer. KELLEREIABFÜLLUNG (Kel-ler-*rye*-ahb-fil-lung) was not at all the same thing, was not at all an indication of estate-bottling, and meant simply "bottled in the cellars of — "; the name that followed was usually *not* the producer's. Under the new German Wine Law Kellerabfüllung may no longer be used. (*See* Erzeugerabfüllung.)

KESSELSTATT — (*Kes*-sel-shtat) — Old titled family with extensive vineyard holdings on the Moselle, Saar and Ruwer, in Germany. These include, in addition to a central cellar in Trier, the entire Josephshofer (*see*) in Graach, considerable acreage in the best *Lagen* of Piesport, vines at Kasel on the Ruwer and at Oberemmel and Niedermennig on the Saar.

KEUKA, Lake — (Q-ka) — One of New York State's Finger Lakes, and perhaps the most important of all, as far as wine is concerned; the little town of Hammondsport is at its southern end, and the three wineries where Taylor wines, Great Western and Gold Seal are produced, are all nearby.

KIEDRICH — (Key-drich) — Little vineyard town of the Rheingau, set back in the hills between Rauenthal and Hallgarten, producing excellent wines which, like the Rauenthalers, deserve to be as well-known abroad as they are in Germany; fruity, racy, spicy, they are truly admirable in good years. There are some 320 acres of vines, and the best plots are: Gräfenberg, Wasserros, and Sandgrub.

KINHEIM — (Kin-heim) — Small, secondary vineyard town on the Moselle near Traben-Trarbach.

KIR — see CASSIS.

KIRWAN, Château — (Keer-wan) — 3rd Classed Growth of Cantenac-Margaux, one of the larger vineyards of this township, of old reputation; some 8,000 cases a year.

KLEVNER — (Klev-ner) — Name given in Alsace and in Germany to the Pinot Blanc grape, less widely grown along the Rhine than the Pinot Gris, or Ruländer, and giving less good wine, but ranked nonetheless as a *plant noble,* or superior variety.

KLOSTER EBERBACH — (Klaws-ter Eh-ber-bach) — Ancient Gothic monastery in the Rheingau, founded by Augustinian monks in 1116 but almost immediately taken over by the Cistercians, under the direction of the same remarkable man who created the Clos de Vougeot on a bare, Burgundian hillside, the wine-loving St. Bernard-de-Clairvaux. Here, as in Burgundy, the Cistercians constructed a wall that still stands around their superb vineyard, the Steinberg, and within a century after its foundation, Kloster Eberbach had become the principal center of German viticulture and the German wine trade, with a branch in Cologne and a fleet of wine ships on the Rhine. Fortunately, although the monastery was secularized in 1801 and is now the property of the German State, most of what the Cistercians created has been preserved; the old buildings, with their great vaulted rooms and venerable wine-presses, are intact and were actually in service until quite recently. Wine auctions are still occasionally held here, and the whole establishment, hidden in a narrow, wooded valley back of Hattenheim and Erbach, is of the greatest possible interest to anyone who likes wine and has a taste for history, or vice versa. It is the home of the German Wine Academy, which conducts five-day seminars for foreigners every summer from May to September.

KNIPPERLÉ — (Nip-per-lay) — Mediocre Alsatian grape, known in Germany and Switzerland as the Räuschling (by no means to be confused with the Riesling); its white wine is of fair quality, better on the whole than that from the Gutedel or Chasselas, and most of it is consumed locally.

KÖNIGSBACH — (Ker-nigs-bach) — One of the best wine-producing villages of the Pfalz, lying well up on the Mittel-Haardt hillsides, just south of Deidesheim. The best plots are Idig, Jesuitengarten, Ölberg and Reiterpfad.

KORBEL — Famous old winery in Sonoma County, California, especially known for its Champagne, one of America's best. Founded in 1886 by three brothers of this name, who had emigrated from Czechoslovakia and made a considerable fortune in lumber, it remained a family enterprise until sold in 1954 to the Heck brothers; the first vines were planted around enormous redwood stumps near Guerneville, in the Russian River Valley, and the stone winery there dates from 1886.

KOSHER WINE — Wine made and supervised under rabbinical law, may be red or white, dry or sweet. Most, however, is exceedingly sweet, made from Concord grapes and produced year round from frozen juice or concentrate. Used at home and in the synagogue for ritual purposes, it is also enjoyed simply as a beverage and it is much in demand by people who are not Jewish and who like sweet heavy wines.

KREUZNACH — (Kroytz-nach) — Also called Bad Kreuznach (it has mineral springs and some modest local fame as a watering-place), this is the center of the Nahe wine region, and lies some ten miles up this lesser stream from Bingen, where the Nahe joins the Rhine. A number of good vineyards (Hinkelstein, Krötenpfuhl, Kahlenberg, Narrenkappe, etc.) are actually within the town limits, and the Kreuznacher wines rank with those of Schloss Böckelheim as the best of the Nahe. There is also an important wine school in Kreuznach, and the filters manufactured in its celebrated *Seizt-Werke* are gratefully used by vintners all over the world.

KRÖV — (Kruhv) — Sometimes written Cröv, a pretty little town on the Moselle near Traben-Trarbach. Its vines yield a fairly ordinary wine which has nevertheless achieved fame and popularity on account of the odd name and comic label under which it is sold. Kröver Nacktarsch literally means "naked behind," and the label shows a small boy being spanked, with his trousers down.

KRUG, Charles — Oldest of the important Napa Valley vineyards, just north of St. Helena, in California. It was planted in 1858 by Charles Krug, who had learned wine-making in his native Germany, and the original stone winery was constructed in 1861. Since 1943, it has been the property of the Mondavi family.

KÜCHELBERGER — (*Kew*-kell-bairg-er) — Light and fragrant red wine of the Italian Tyrol, produced just outside the attractive resort town of Merano, and a great favorite there. It is made from the Schiava meranese grape (*see*).

L

LABRUSCA — One of the principal species of native North American grape, *Vitis Labrusca,* of which the Concord is a typical example and which is distinguished by its slip-skin and musky "foxy" flavor; grows primarily in New York and Washington.

LACRIMA CHRISTI — (*La*-cree-ma *Kris*-tee) — Celebrated white wine (a little red, less good, is also produced) grown on the slopes of Mt. Vesuvius, near Naples. Made from the Greco della Torre grape, pale gold in color, it is a bit softer and less austerly dry than the wine of Capri, produced nearby, and in character and flavor not too far from a fairly dry Graves. The name, of course, means "Tears of Christ" and there are many stories to explain its origin. The lovely Bay of Naples country has been called a "fragment of Paradise," and, according to one account, the Lord, returning to earth, found this heavenly corner of the world "inhabited by demons" (presumably the Neapolitans); touched and distressed, He wept, and where His tears fell there sprung up green vines — the vines of the Lacrima Christi vineyards.

LADOIX-SERRIGNY — (La-dwa Seh-reen-yee) — Village in Burgundy on the Côte de Beaune. *See* Aloxe-Corton.

LAFAURIE-PEYRAGUEY, Château — (La-fo-ree Pay-rah-gay) — 1st Classed Growth of Sauternes. One of the best vineyards of Bommes (*see*) and one of the most impressive châteaux of the Sauternes district. Full-bodied, golden, very sweet wine, typical Sauternes. About 2,500 cases a year.

LAFITE, Château — (La-feet) — In the opinion of most impartial experts, and perhaps in the mind of the general public as well, the *ne plus ultra* of Claret

MIS EN BOUTEILLES AU CHÂTEAU

CHATEAU LAFITE-ROTHSCHILD
1970

DÉPOSE

APPELLATION PAUILLAC CONTRÔLÉE

and the greatest red wine vineyard in the world. Lafite, or Lafite-Rothschild (both names are correct and both have been used at various times on the château label) was ranked first among the 1st Growths in the Bordeaux Classification of 1855, and has maintained its place with surprising consistency over the decades. Its special fame dates from the 17th century, when it was the property of M. de Ségur, and it was purchased in 1868 by Baron James de Rothschild for 5 million gold francs.

There are some 200 acres under vines (Cabernet, Merlot, Petit Verdot) and the annual yield is not far from 20,000 cases. The fermenting rooms, the *chais* and cellars are models of what such installations should be, and the "Library" of bottles extends back, great vintage by great vintage, to before 1800.

The wine of Lafite varies, as all Bordeaux wines vary, from one year to another, although Lafite less than most, but of its best vintages it is hard to speak except in terms of the highest priase. Rarely over 12½% alcohol, they have an astonishing authority, impeccable breed, fruit and fragrance and depth of flavor, all the qualities with which a great Claret should be endowed.

LAFLEUR, Château — (La-flerr) — One of the *Premiers Crus* of Pomerol. An admirable small vineyard, some 1,600 cases a year of excellent claret.

LAFON ROCHET, Château — (Lah-faw Roash-A) — Fourth Growth Médoc in Saint-Estèphe; 10,000 cases annually of typical sturdy wine of that town, yet with an unusual suppleness.

LAGAR — (La-*gahr*) — large square shallow trough for pressing grapes in Jerez and the Port wine region; pressing done by feet with special hob-nailed shoes in Spain, no shoes in Portugal.

LAGE — (La-guh) — In German, a specific, named vineyard, or plot of vines; what the Burgundians would call a *climat,* and the Bordelais a *cru.* The plural is *Lagen. See* also Einzellage and Grosslage.

LAGO DI CALDARO — (*La*-go dee Kahl-dar-o) — Small lake not far from Bolzano, in the Italian Tyrol; the excellent, light red wine produced on the steep, lake-side vineyards to its west and north. Made from the Schiava *gentile* grape (*see*), fragrant, well-balanced, it is superior to the neighboring Caldaro (*see*), and one of north Italy's best.

LAGRANGE, Château — (La-grawnj) — 3rd Classed Growth of St. Julien, Haut-Médoc. One of the less distinguished of the 3rd Growths. Approximately 20,000 cases a year. There are at least three other properties with the same name in other parts of Bordeaux.

LAGREIN ROSATO — (La-*grain* Roas-*sa*-toe) — Delightful *rosé* wine of the Italian Tyrol, produced practically in the suburbs of Bolzano (*see*), and known as Lagreiner Kaetzer when this district was part of Austria, before 1918. It is made from the Lagrein grape.

LAGRIMA — (*La*-gree-ma) — An especially sweet and heavy type of Malaga wine, produced around the city of this name, in southern Spain.

LAGUNE, Château La — (Lah-gewn) — 3rd Classed Growth of Ludon, Haut-Médoc. Southernmost of the classed vineyards of the Médoc, only some seven miles from the northern limit of Graves, La Lagune produces a fine, firm, slow maturing Claret which, in character, is perhaps closer to the better red Graves of Pessac than to the Médoc wines as a whole. The château changed hands in 1957: a most ambitious program of replanting was undertaken, and the new cellar installations are among the handsomest and best of the whole Bordeaux Country. Some 25,000 cases a year.

LALANDE-DE-POMEROL — (La-lawnd-d'Paum-may-rawl) — Secondary Bordeaux district including Néac, adjoining Pomerol on the north. Its wines, all red, resemble those of Pomerol but are less fine. Château Bel-Air and Château de la Commanderie are considered the best vineyards.

LAKE CONSTANCE — *see* Constance.

LAMBRAYS — (Lawm-bray). Burgundian vineyard. *See* Clos des Lambrays.

LAMBRUSCO — (Lom-*bruce*-co) — Unusual red wine, almost always slightly sparkling or *frizzante* (*see*), produced just west of Bologna in northern Italy, especially around the village of Sorbara. Made principally from the grape of the same name, extremely fruity, somewhat sweet, with an intense and extraordinary bouquet, it is a great favorite throughout the region of Emilia and perhaps Italy's best wine of this class. It is not a class likely to appeal to a real wine lover, let alone an expert. However, since there are more wine lovers (fortunately for the trade) than experts, Lambrusco has taken the public fancy and in 1976 there were 4,700,000 cases imported into the United States representing 61% of all Italian table wines shipped here.

LAMOTHE, Château — (La mote) — 2nd Classed Growth of Sauternes. Good quality, sweet white wine; about 2,500 cases a year. There are six other minor châteaux in the Bordeaux Country with this identical name.

LANDES — (Lawnd) — French *département* directly south of Bordeaux; flat, sandy, sparsely populated and largely covered with pine forests, it produces little wine of any consequence, but some Armagnac of fine quality along its eastern edge near Villeneuve-de-Marsan.

201

LANGOA-BARTON, Château — (Lawn-go-ah Bar-taw) — 3rd Classed Growth of St. Julien. One of the best of the 3rd Growths; some 6,000 cases a year of fine claret, a typical St. Julien.

LANGUEDOC — (Lahn-guh-dawk) — Ancient French province, extending along the Mediterranean from the Rhône River to beyond Narbonne; as far as wine is concerned, this is known as the Midi, and produces most of the *vin ordinaire* of France; the three *départements* of Hérault, Aude and Gard rank 1, 2, and 3 in total vineyard acreage and total production among the ninety French *départements*. The vast bulk of this is common stuff, and goes to market simply as *vin rouge,* but there are some excellent sweet Muscat wines produced at Frontignan (*see*) and Lunel, a well-known sparkling wine at Limoux (*see*), and table wines of rather more than passable quality in a number of specific, delimited zones. A few of these have been granted an *Appellation Contrôlée,* and a number of others may carry the V.D.Q.S. seal. *See* the following: Clairette, Fitou, Corbières, Minervois, Cabrières, Rousillon, etc.

LARCIS-DUCASSE, Château — (Lar-see Dew-cass) — Grand Cru St. Émilion. Some 4,000 cases a year. High quality red wine.

LAROSE, Château — (La-Rose) — *See* Gruaud-Larose. There are however two very minor Bordeaux châteaux called Château Larose, two others called Château Laroze, and, finally, the Co-operative Cellar of Pauillac puts out a good, fairly inexpensive, agreeable red wine called La Rose de Pauillac.

LARRIVET-HAUT-BRION, Château — (La-ree-vay Oh Bree-awn) — Good small vineyard of Léognan, Graves. Some 3,000 cases of red wine a year and 500 white.

LASCOMBES, Château — (Lahs-caumb) — 2nd Classed Growth of Margaux. Now one of the better 2nds, giving some 18,000 cases of claret a year.

LA TÂCHE — (La Tahsh) — Celebrated Burgundian vineyard and its great red wine. *See* Tâche.

LATIUM — *See* LAZIO.

LATOUR, Château — (La-tour) — 1st Classed Growth of Pauillac. Admirable and world famous vineyard, legally and properly ranked as one of the four best of the Médoc, a worthy rival of Margaux, Lafite, and Mouton. Its 146 acres are planted on thin, poor, unfertile, gravelly soil, and the yield per acre is extremely low: the resulting wine, some 25,000 cases a year, is one of the most robust and sturdy of clarets, deep-colored, long-lived, astringent when young but obviously of great class, developing a splendid bouquet as it grows older.

There are literally scores of châteaux in the Bordeaux Country having the words Tour or La Tour as part of their name. The most important of these are listed elsewhere, in their proper alphabetical place, in this encyclopedia. They should not, of course, be confused with the one great original Château Latour, which has a stylized tower, surmounted by a lion, on its familiar, old-fashioned label.

GRAND VIN
DE
CHATEAU LATOUR

PREMIER GRAND CRU CLASSÉ

DÉPOSÉ

APPELLATION PAUILLAC CONTROLÉE

LATOUR-POMEROL, Château — (La-tour Paum-may-rawl) — Good 1st Growth vineyard of Pomerol, owned by the owner of Château Pétrus. About 3,000 cases a year of fine, soft Claret.

LATRICIÈRES-CHAMBERTIN — (Lat-tree-see-air Shawm-bair-tan) — Distinguished Burgundy vineyard and its red wine, officially a *Grand Cru* and, after Chambertin and Clos de Bèze, one of the best of this extraordinary little district. Seventeen acres in extent, it directly adjoins Chambertin on the south, shares the same exposure and practically the same soil.

LAUBENHEIM — (Lau-ben-heim) — Small wine-producing town on the Rhine south of Mainz, in Hessia. Its 300 acres of vineyard produce rather soft and common wines of mediocre quality.

LAUDUN — (Lo-duhn) — Village of the lower Rhône Valley, in France, west of the river and north of Tavel and Lirac. Its red, *rosé* and white wines, of which the last are regarded as the best, are marketed as Côtes-du-Rhône-Laudun.

LAUSANNE — (Lo-zahn) — Attractive city on the northern shore of Lake Geneva, itself the owner of two celebrated vineyards nearby, the Clos des Abbayes and the Clos des Moines. Both produce good quality, dry white wines from the Fendant grape.

LAVAUX — (La-vo) — District of extremely impressive terraced vineyards on the northern shore of Lake Geneva, between Vevey and Lausanne, in the Canton of Vaud. It produces some of the best white wines of Switzerland.

LAVILLEDIEU — (La-veal-dee-uh) — Red and white wines of some small local fame, produced northwest of Toulouse in southern France. They are entitled to the V.D.Q.S. seal.

LAVILLE-HAUT-BRION, Château — (La-veel Oh-Bree-awn) — Excellent small vineyard at Talence, on the outskirts of Bordeaux. It produces some 2,000 cases a year of what is certainly one of the very finest dry white Graves.

LAYON — (Lay-oh) — Little river in Anjou, tributary of the Loire, famous for its white wines. *See* Coteaux du Layon.

LAZIO — (Lahtz-ee-o) — The region of Rome, in Italy. Produces over 100 million gallons of table wine a year, almost all of it consumed locally, more white wine than red. Perhaps a third of this total comes from the Castelli Romani (*see*) and is sold as such, or as Frascati, Albano, etc.

LEÁNYKA — (*Lay*-ah-ny-kyah) — Hungarian grape variety meaning "young girl"; makes white delicate table wine.

LEES — Heavy, coarse sediment which young wines throw in barrel before they are ready for bottling. These are left behind when the wine is "racked" or transferred from one barrel to another, and this process is generally repeated two or three times before the wine is bottled.

LEGS — After swirling in a glass, the wine adhering to the inside surface forms tears which slowly descend leaving "legs" in their wake. The spacing, thickness and rate of appearance are indications of the viscosity of the wine and its glycerine content; note however that the legs are affected by the temperature of the wine and often by the soap or detergent used to clean the glasses.

LÉOGNAN — (Lay-own-yaw) — One of the very best wine-producing villages of the Graves district, some seven miles southwest of Bordeaux. Its red wines and its white are equally distinguished and its best vineyards include Domaine de Chevalier, Châteaux Carbonnieux, Haut-Bailly, Malartic-Lagravière, Fieuzal, Olivier, etc.

LÉOVILLE-BARTON, Château — (Lay-oh-veel Bar-taw) — 2nd Classed Growth of St. Julien, Haut-Médoc. A very good 2nd Growth, giving approximately 10,000 cases a year, 86 acres. Originally all three Léovilles were one property, the largest in the Médoc.

LÉOVILLE-LAS-CASES, Château — (Lay-oh-veel Lahss Kahz) — 2nd Classed Growth of st. Julien, Haut-Médoc. Justly celebrated vineyard and its consistently good, well-balanced, fine-textured claret. Usually 25,000 cases a year, 148 acres.

LÉOVILLE-POYFERRÉ, Château — (Lay-oh-veel Pwah-fair-ray) — On the whole the best vineyard of St. Julien, fully meriting its rank as a 2nd Classed Growth. Its excellent red wine, 10,000 cases a year, 89 acres, is perhaps a little fuller-bodied than the other Léovilles, and generally brings a slightly higher price.

LEISTADT — (*Ly*-shtat) — Vineyard town in the German Palatinate north of Dürkheim; white wines of fair quality and a few mediocre reds.

LÉMAN, Lac — (Lay-maw) — What the French and Swiss call what *we* call Lake Geneva; a good part of its northern or Swiss shore is covered with vineyards.

LÉON MILLOT — (Lay-oh Mee-oh) — French hybrid originated in Alsace and planted in short season areas of eastern United States. Related to Maréchal Foch and makes as good or better red wine.

LESSONA — (Less-*sone*-ah) — Superior red wine from the Piedmont region of Italy, made from the Nebbiolo grape in the province of Vercelli.

L'EVANGILE, Château — *See* EVANGILE.

LIBOURNE — (Lee-boorn) — Town on the Dordogne River, some twenty miles east of Bordeaux; an important center of the wine trade, especially the wines of St. Émilion, Pomerol, Fronsac, etc., all produced nearby.

LIEBFRAUENSTIFT — (Leeb-frau-en-shtift) — Twenty-six-acre vineyard surrounding the Gothic Liebfrauenkirche, or Church of Our Lady, in the city of Worms, on the Rhine. There are of course hundreds of churches called Liebfrauenkirche in Germany; this one happens to be, in all probability, the orginal source of Liebfraumilch. The vines are planted on heavy alluvial soil well inside the city and not far from the river, and the wines they produce, while unquestionably authentic, are rather common and a long way from the best of Rheinhessen; they are sold as Liebfrauenstiftswein, not as Liebfraumilch.

LIEBFRAUMILCH — (Leeb-frau-milsh) — In German, this word, which is certainly one of the most universally known of wine names, simply means, "Milk of the Blessed Mother." It was probably originally given to the wine produced by a few acres of vines round the Liebfrauenkirche in Worms, on the Rhine (the Liebfrauenstift (*see*) and by no means an outstanding vineyard), but it has long since turned into a meaningless passepartout of a name, vaguely synonymous with Rhine Wine. The cheapest and poorest wines of Rheinhessen used to be and usually were shipped as Liebfraumilch, and a number of producers in the Palatinate then entered the lists, with Liebfraumilchs of their own. On the other hand, a few shippers have found it advantageous to offer some excellent wines as Liebfraumilch — wines from Nierstein, Nackenheim, Oppenheim, etc., which are properly entitled to these more precise and honorable names. The consumer's best guide to quality (other than such rarely used terms as Spätlese and Auslese) is the name of the shipper. This may or may not be the producer's name, and in most instances is not. Since 1971, Liebfraumilch is defined as a Qualitätswein from Rheinhessen, Rheingau, Rheinpfalz or Nahe and must be made from Riesling, Sylvaner or Müller-Thurgau grapes.

LIESER — (*Leez*-zer) — Little wine town near Bernkastel, on the Moselle; its wines are of good but not top quality, being somewhat heavier than the Bernkastelers, Graachers, etc., with less bouquet and breed. Niederberg-Helden, Rosenlay and Süssenberg are the vineyards.

LIEU-DIT — (Lee-uh dee) — In French, a place name that has no precise official meaning, other than one based purely on tradition and local usage.

LIGHT — According to American law, a light wine is one that contains less than 14% alcohol by volume. It is not in this sense, however, that the word is used by experts — it is the opposite of Full-Bodied but also the opposite of Heavy, and as such can be complimentary. Light wines may have finesse and fruit and charm; only in rare instances can they be called Great.

LIGURIA — (Lee-*goo*-ree-ah) — Region of the Italian Riviera just east of France on the Mediterranean; smallest wine producing area, noted for Cinque-terre (*see*) white and Dolceacqua red wines.

LILLET — (Lee-lay) — Fairly dry French apéritif, made with a white wine base, plus herbs and brandy.

LIMOUSIN — (Lee-moo-zan) — Forest in central France, west of the Charente. Its oak is used for aging Cognac and is highly prized by California wine makers.

LIMOUX — (Lee-*moo*) — Town in southern France, not far from Carcassonne, which produces some white wines of quite considerable local fame. The best known of these is the sparkling Blanquette de Limoux, made by the Champagne process, generally rather sweet; Limoux Nature is a still, dry white wine, pleasant enough but hardly remarkable.

LIMPID — Term meaning absolutely clear and star bright.

LIPARI — (*Lee*-par-ree) — Largest of a group of small islands off the north coast of Sicily; according to Greek mythology, home of Aeolus, god of the west wind. Several of the islands, especially Salina, produce a famous golden, dessert wine, made from the Malvasia grape and usually sold as Malvasia di Lipari.

LIQUEUR — (Lee-kerr) — In common, conventional usage, a sweet after-dinner drink, high in alcohol. Applied to whiskey or brandy, it means, rather vaguely, one of sufficiently fine quality to be consumed straight in this way, although of course not sweet. But the word has other and specific meanings as far as wine is concerned, notably two, with respect to Champagne: the solution of sugar, or rock-candy, in wine, which is added (usually plus a yeast culture) to the young wine before bottling, to bring about a second fermentation in bottle, is called *liqueur de tirage;* the quite similar syrup, added in the form of *dosage* (*see*), to sweeten the bone-dry, already sparkling wine at the time of disgorging, to make it *brut,* or extra dry or *demi-sec,* is called *liqueur d'expédition.*

In addition, liqueur, when applied to the great, naturally sweet dessert wines — those of Sauternes and Anjou, for example — means the sweetness, or unfermented grape sugar, left in the finished wine: thus one can say, of a Château d'Yquem, that it contains 14% alcohol, plus perhaps 4% of liqueur.

However, what is called a *vin de liqueur* is almost always a fortified wine (it would be called a *vin liquoreux* (*see*) if its sweetness were wholly natural and involved no addition of brandy); the term is generally applied in this sense to wines from the eastern Pyrénées, such as Banyuls, Grand Roussillon, etc.; perpared in a slightly different way, these are called *vins doux* (*see*).

LIQUOREUX — (Lee-cor-ruh) — Used in French to describe a sweet, luscious white wine that has retained, without fortification, a good deal of natural grape sugar, or liqueur (*see*).

206

LIRAC — (Lee-rack) — Village immediately north of Tavel, in the lower Rhône Valley; its *rosé* wine, very like Tavel, although sometimes lighter and with less character. The predominant grape is the Grenache.

LISBON — Capital and chief city of Portugal. Also a general term used by the British wine trade to designate the sweet, fortified and table wines, red and perhaps more often white, produced near Lisbon. Carcavelos is the best known of these.

LISTRAC — (Leece-trac) — Village in the Haut-Médoc, producing no wines of great class but a good deal of sturdy, well-balanced, agreeable and inexpensive Claret. Most of this is entitled to the appellation Moulis (*see*), the rest, usually labeled Listrac, carries the designation "Appellation Haut-Médoc Contrôlée." Listrac has long been a favorite wine on French dining-cars. There is a large co-operative cellar.

LITER — Metric measure of volume: 1.057 U.S. quart; .88 British quart. A liter contains 1000 cubic centimeters, and a liter of distilled water weighs one kilogram, or 2.2 pounds.

LIVERMORE — Town in Alameda County, California, some forty miles southeast of San Francisco. The surrounding Livermore Valley has been recognized since the 1880's as one of the best table wine districts of the United States; its rolling, gravelly soil seems particularly well adapted to the production of white wines, and such famous European varieties as the Sauvignon Blanc, Sémillon, Pinot Blanc and Chardonnay are widely planted, as are also the Grey Riesling and Ugni Blanc. The leading producers are Wente Bros. and Concannon.

LJUTOMER — *see* LUTOMER

LOCHÉ — (*Lo*-shay) — Wine-producing village south of Mâcon, in southern Burgundy; it adjoins Vinzelles, Fuissé, Pouilly, etc., and its fresh, agreeable white wine, made from the Chardonnay grape, is sold under the appellation Pouilly-Loché.

LODGE — Ground level warehouse in Oporto and Vila Nova de Gaia for storage of Port wine; same as *chai* in Bordeaux and *bodega* in Jerez.

LOGROÑO — (Lo-groan-yo) — Little city and province on the Ebro River in northern Spain; as a center of the wine trade, the town is less important than Haro (*see*), but most of the celebrated Rioja district is in the province of Logroño and this, of course, produces by far the best table wines of Spain.

LOIRE, La — (La Lwahrr) — The longest and one of the most beautiful rivers of France, traversing, in the course of its 600-mile journey from its source, west of Lyon, to the Atlantic, near Nantes, a whole series of different provinces and viticultural areas. Its wines, sometimes collectively called *Vins de la Loire,* include a most diverse and interesting collection of reds, whites, and *rosés,* ranging all the way in quality from poor to great. All of the more important ones will be found listed, in their alphabetical place, in this volume.

MUSCADET · ANJOU · COTEAUX DU LOIR · COTEAUX DU LOIR ET · TO · COTEAUX DE LA LOIRE · Angers · COTEAUX DE L'AUBANCE · COTEAUX DU LAYON · BOURGUEIL · MUSCADET DES COTEAUX DE LA LOIRE · MUSCADET DE SÈVRE-ET-MAINE · Nantes · COTEAUX DE SAUMUR · CHINO · SAUMUR · ATLANTIC OCEAN · N · SCALE · MI. 0 · 5 · 10 · KM. 0 · 10 · 20

LOIRE

Drawn by W. Lembeck

See Pouilly-Fumé, Sancerre, Quincy, Touraine, Vouvray, Bourgueil, Chinon, Saumur, Anjou, Muscadet, etc., etc.

LOIR, Le — (Luh Lwahr) — Tributary of the Loire, west of Paris. Its best wine is Jasnières (*see*).

LOMBARDY — (Lohm-*bahr*-dee) — Important region of northern Italy; its capital is Milan. Produces between 50 and 60 million gallons of table wine a year, the best of it from three widely separated districts: that of Valtellina (*see*), around Sondrio, east of Lake Como and not far from the Swiss border; second, a hilly area south of Pavia and the Po River, including Casteggio (*see*) and the vineyards of Barbacarlo, etc.; finally, the western and southern shores of Lake Garda (*see*).

LONG — Wine having persistence (*see*). A good wine has echoes of taste after it is swallowed. *See* Caudalie.

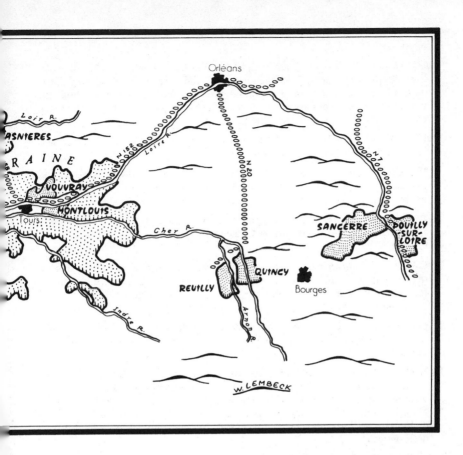

LORCH — (Lorsh) — Town on the Rhine, considered officially as belonging to the Rheingau, although it is actually in the Rhine gorge, north of Assmannshausen; its wines are made in large part from the Sylvaner grape, and, in character and quality, are more like those of the Mittelrhein than those of the Rheingau proper. Pfaffenwies, Bodental-Steinberg, and Krone are considered the better *Lagen*.

LORRAINE — (Lor-rain) — Ancient French province which produces nothing worth exporting in the way of wine, but a few amusing and agreeable *vins de pays;* most of these come from the upper Moselle Valley between Metz and Toul, and the best of them are the so-called *vins gris* (see), small, light, fresh *rosés,* produced around Bruley, Liverdun and on the Côtes de Toul.

LOUCHE — (Lewsh) — French, dull or hazy wine with no perceptible deposit.

LOULOUMET, Clos — (Clo Lu-lu-may) — Small vineyard at Toulenne, near the southern edge of the Graves district, producing a pleasant, soft, fairly dry white wine.

LOUPIAC — Village on the right bank of the Garonne, directly opposite Barsac, in the Bordeaux Country. Although geographically part of the Premières Côtes de Bordeaux (*see*), it forms a distinct district and has its own appellation. Its white wines, decidedly sweet, are heavier and more common than Sauternes, but similarly made and of the same general type.

LOUVIÈRE, Château La — (La Loo-vee-air) — Important vineyard at Léognan, in the Graves district. Both red wines and white.

LUBÉRON — (Lew-bay-raw) — Chain of hills along the northern bank of the Durance River, east of Avignon. Some very good *rosé* wines are produced, and some quite passable reds. *See* Côtes du Lubéron.

LUDON — (Lew-daw) — *Commune* near the southern end of the Haut-Médoc. By all odds its best vineyard is Château La Lagune (*see*), a 3rd Classed Growth.

LUGANA — (Loo-*gah*-na) — Very agreeable dry white wine produced around the tiny village of this name, at the southern end of Lake Garda, in northern Italy. It is made from the Trebbiano grape (*see*), and is generally the best of the white Garda wines.

LUGNY — (Lew-nyee) — One of the more important wine-producing villages of the Mâconnais (*see*); white wines of good quality from the Chardonnay grape.

LUNEL — (Lew-nel) — One of three towns on the Mediterranean Coast of France (Rivesaltes and Frontignan being the others) producing a sweet Muscat wine of justified reputation and high quality. Lunel's vineyard area lies west of Nimes, is much the smallest of the three, and the total production of Muscat de Lunel is well under 10,000 cases a year. The informing grape is the Muscat de Frontignan.

LUSSAC-SAINT-ÉMILION — (Lew-sac Sant A-me-lee-aw) — Secondary wine district, northeast of St. Émilion, and entitled to the name only in this combined form. Its red wines are full, often a bit common, not too expensive. A good deal of white wine is also made but this, not entitled to the appellation, is sold as Bordeaux Blanc.

LUTOMER — (Lyoo-taw-muhr) — Best known wines of Slovenia, northernmost state of Yugoslavia; good quality white wines with varietal labeling and typical characteristics.

LUXEMBOURG — (Lewkes-em-boorg) — The Moselle River, after leaving France, skirts the Grand Duchy of Luxembourg for some twenty miles, and along its northern bank there are over 2,000 acres of vineyard. These produce, mostly from the Riesling grape, fresh, light, rather tart white wines, not unlike small German Moselles. The town of origin and the grape variety appear on the labels, and the leading wine producing villages are Wormeldingen, Remich, Wintringen, Ehnen, Grevenmacher and Wasserbillig. A little sparkling wine is also made.

LYNCH-BAGES, Château — (Lansh Bahj) — 5th Classed Growth of Pauillac. Now one of the better and more popular of the 5th Growth clarets, a deep-colored, powerful, robust wine that brings a higher price than many 3rd and 4th Growths and even than some 2nds. About 15,000 cases in a good year.

LYNCH-MOUSSAS, Château — (Lansh Moo-sah) — 5th Classed Growth of Pauillac. Less well known and less good than the preceding. Some 2,000 cases.

LYON — (Lee-aw) — Third city of France (pop. 535,000), situated at the junction of the Saône and Rhône rivers, famous for the excellence of its food, and for the fondness which its citizens demonstrate daily for the wines of the Beaujolais district, nearby. It has often been said (first said, it would appear, by Léon Daudet) that there are not two rivers in Lyon, but three: the Rhône, the Saône . . . and the Beaujolais.

LYONNAIS — (Lee-aw-nay) — Name given to a few, small, rather nondescript wines produced round Lyon in the *département* of the Rhône. The best of them are like poor Beaujolais, but they are entitled to the V.D.Q.S. seal.

M

MACAU — (Mac-co) — One of the southernmost villages of the Haut-Médoc, but not a wine name or appellation. By all odds its best wine is Château Cantemerle (*see*).

MACHARUNDO — (Mac-ahr-noo-doe) — *see* Sherry.

MÂCHE — (Mahsh) — French term for full flavored wine with good body.

MACHIAVELLI — Illustrious Italian statesman and political commentator, whose books, *The Prince and the History of Florence,* have come to be regarded as classics. Long attached to the Court of the Medici, he wrote these books at his family estate at Sant' Andrea in Percussina, south of Florence. His home — a "national monument" today — is now part of one of the most celebrated estates of the Chianti Country, that of the Conti Serristori, whose best wine is called *Chianti Machiavelli.*

MÂCON — (Mac-caw) — Important town (Pop. 40,000) on the River Saône in southern Burgundy; a major center of the wine trade. As a wine, Mâcon may be red, *rosé, or white; if red or rosé,* it must be made exclusively from Gamay, Pinot Noir or Pinot Gris grapes, or a blend of these; if white, from the Chardonnay alone (although a small admixture of Aligoté is tolerated), being legally sold either as Mâcon Blanc or Pinot-Chardonnay-Mâcon. The average annual production is over 5½ million gallons, about ¾ of it red. Red Mâcon is a pleasant, sound, generally inexpensive wine, less fruity and attractive than good Beaujolais, though somewhat firmer and coarser. In the field of white wines, Pouilly-Fuissé, Pouilly-Loché, and Pouilly-Vinzelles are entitled to the

212

appellation Mâcon, but almost never so sold; most of what is marketed as Mâcon Blanc comes from the less known *communes* of the Mâconnais farther north and is a somewhat similar but less expensive wine, dry, fresh, palatable, but with less notable finesse and breed.

MÂCONNAIS — (Mac-caw-nay) — Large district in southern Burgundy, consisting of much of the *département* of Saône-et-Loire, centered around the town of Mâcon (*see*). Pouilly-Fuissé, Pouilly-Vinzelles and Pouilly-Loché are all in the Mâconnais, as are Viré (*see*), Lugny and Clessé, all three producing superior white wines from the Chardonnay grape. Most of the lesser wines of the Mâconnais, however, are sold simply as Mâcon and Mâcon Blanc.

A new and increasingly important appellation; St. Véran (*see*) has been given official status. The best of it comes from a small constellation of communes surrounding Pouilly-Fuissé.

Incidentally, a little sparkling wine called Dentelle is now being made by the Champagne process and from the Chardonnay grape. It may well prove remarkable.

MÂCON VILLAGES — (Mac-caw Vee-lahj) — Appellation for better quality white Mâcon wines which must come from specified communes.

MADEIRA — (Ma-day-rah) — Portuguese island, far out in the Atlantic, which has been famous for its wines for nearly four hundred years. Oddly enough, these first achieved what might be called international reputation and standing because of the favor they enjoyed in America in colonial days: clipper ships, following the prevailing trade winds, made Madeira a regular port-of-call, taking on water and supplies plus a few casks of wine on their return voyage from Europe to Charleston or Philadelphia, Baltimore or New York or Boston. The sea voyage reputedly improved the wine, and a good many 18th and 19th century Madeiras, bottled in this country, carried on their label the name of the vessel that transported them, and the year of the voyage.

It has often been stated and quite possibly is true that the British taste for Madeira dates from our War of Independence, when returning British officers spoke enthusiastically of the quality of bottles they had tasted in American cellars. In any case, a few decades later, the Madeira trade had followed the pattern set by Port, Sherry and Marsala and was largely in English hands. Like almost all European wine lands, but more severely than most, Madeira was invaded and its vineyards devastated in the late 1800's by two plagues of New World origin — the oidium (a sort of mildew) and the phylloxera. The island's economy never entirely recovered, and it is safe to say that Madeiras of as high quality have never since been made. Nor is America today the principal market for Madeira: France (where it is used principally in cooking), Sweden and Denmark each import three or four times our modest annual total of under 20,000 gallons.

All Madeiras, of course, are fortified wines, brought up to their strength of 18-20% by the addition of high-proof brandy. Although aged and blended in *soleras*, like Sherry (true vintage Madeira hardly exists, if indeed at all), they are made by a quite different process, much like that used for Marsala, and owe their characteristic flavor to the fact that they are kept, for a period of months, in special rooms called *estufas* at a high temperature.

Madeira, it should be kept in mind, is not by any means just one wine but a whole company of wines, ranging from very dry to very sweet, from pale straw (Rainwater) to deep gold (Malmsey) in color, from cheap to very expensive, from mediocre to extraordinary in quality. As cooking wines, even the lesser grades are remarkable and no Sherry or Marsala can replace them. As apéritif or dessert wines, those of exceptional class are quite properly high-priced, and are increasingly hard to find. The nomenclature has become more

214

and more standardized, and most of the old, once-famous export houses have come together and tend, increasingly, to draw their wines from jointly held stocks. The old system of individual vineyard names has pretty much disappeared, like true vintage wines, in Madeira, and is not likely soon to return.

The finest Madeiras, with a few exceptions, take their name from the grape from which they were made. The dryest, called Sercial, is somewhat comparable to a Fino Sherry, but with an altogether special and often extraordinary bouquet and character. One called Verdelho could be described as its cousin, but is now rarely available. Boal or Bual is a good deal sweeter and more golden, almost a dessert wine by modern standards, although our grandfathers drank it with terrapin and shad. Malmsey, deep gold, very sweet, can be entirely remarkable, and it seems too bad that wines such as this, however magnificent, are a little out of fashion today.

Rainwater Madeira, the palest of all, was, it seems, created by an American wine-lover, from Savannah, Georgia, called "Rainwater Habisham," who developed a special system of fining and clarifying to render his family wine the lightest, palest, least colored, and most like rainwater, of all. It has become a name in general and unrestricted usage.

MADERISÉ — (Ma-dare-ee-zay) — French term applied to wine, especially a white or *rosé* wine, which is past its prime, has become somewhat oxidized, has acquired a brownish tinge, plus an aroma and flavor reminiscent of Madeira. Anything but a favorable term; a *maderisé* wine is one that is well on its way to becoming spoiled.

In English, the terms "maderized" and "oxidized" are often used interchangeably, but strictly speaking a maderized wine is one which has acquired this different and special character through a combination of heat, plus contact with the air or with oxygen, whereas when the term "oxidized" is used, there is no implication that the wine has (either accidentally or otherwise) been stored in a warm place, or been "baked."

MADIRAN — (Mad-dee-rah) — Sturdy red Appellation Contrôlée wine produced north of Pau and Tarbes, between Bordeaux and the Pyrenees, in southwestern France.

MAGDELAINE, Château — (Mag-duh-lain) — One of the Premiers Grands Crus Classés of St. Émilion, directly adjoining Ausone and Bélair on the escarpments overlooking the Dordogne Valley. Some 4,000 cases a year of wine that is generally full, soft and fine.

MAGENCE, Château — (Ma-zhawnse) — One of the best of the less-known vineyards of the Graves district of Bordeaux, in the *commune* of Saint-Pierre-de-Mons. About 5,000 cases a year of dry white wines of considerable bouquet and breed, made mostly from the Sauvignon Blanc grape, as well as an equal quantity of red.

MAGNUM — Bottle of double normal capacity. Since wines, red wines especially, tend to develop and age more slowly in large bottles than in small, Clarets and Burgundies of great years are often put up in magnums for laying away. Champagne is fermented in magnums, a process tending to lengthen the wine's life. The use of magnums for lesser wines is in some cases a convenience, more often an affectation.

MAILLY — (Mah-yee) — Red grape growing Champagne village of great repute.

MAIN — (Mine) — River which flows through Franken (*see*) and meets the Rhine near Mainz.

MÁLAGA — (*Ma*-la-ga) — City and province on the Mediterranean, in southern Spain: the sweet, brown, fortified wine produced by hillside vineyards in this district, mostly from Pedro Ximénez and Muscat grapes. The cheaper grades are usually sweetened with *arrope* (a grape concentrate, *see*), the better ones through the addition of a special, so-called PX wine, made from sun-dried Pedro Ximénez grapes. Normally both are aged and blended in *soleras* (*see*).

The Malaga grape of California is a table grape and has no connection whatsoever with Málaga wine, except that California "Malaga" may legally be made from it although it need not be.

MALARTIC-LAGRAVIÈRE, Château — (Mah-lahr-teek La-grah-vyair) — Classed growth in Graves (Léognan) produces 5,000 cases red and 1,000 cases dry white.

MALBEC — (Mal-beck) — Excellent red wine grape, also known as the Cot or Pressac, and widely cultivated in the Bordeaux Country, as well as around Cahors in south-central France. It gives a well-balanced wine of considerable finesse, which matures more rapidly than the Cabernets. Now making an appearance in California and used for blending with Cabernet as in France.

MALCONSORTS — (Mal-caw-sor) — Outstanding small vineyard in the *commune* of Vosne-Romanée, in the heart of Burgundy. It is bounded on the north by La Tâche and on the south by Nuits-Saint-Georges, Les-Boudots. Its 15 acres of vines produce a remarkable red wine, well balanced, distinguished, but often with a faint earthy taste or *goût de terroir*.

MALESCOT-SAINT-EXUPÉRY, Château — (Mal-les-co-Saint-Ex-oo-pay-ree) — One of the better 3rd Classed Growths of Margaux. Some 6,000 cases a year of claret known for its finesse and bouquet.

MALIC ACID — *see* FERMENTATION, MALOLACTIC.

MALLE, Château de — (Shat-toe d' Mal) — 2nd Classed Growth of Preignac, Sauternes. Some 5,000 cases a year of ripe, fine, typical Sauternes. The vineyard and its charming château, an historical monument, have belonged to the Lur-Saluces family (owners of Yquem and Filhot) for over two centuries. A dry wine, not entitled to the *appellation* Sauternes, is now also being produced and a red wine from part of the property which lies in the Graves; neither of these are labeled Château de Malle.

MALMSEY — English for Malvasia (*see*), the sweet, fortified amber wine made from the grape of this name, wherever grown; now principally the island of Madeira, but also Cyprus, Sardinia, Sicily, Lipari and other Mediterranean lands. George, Duke of Clarence (1449-1478), a younger brother of Edward IV, is said to have been drowned in a butt of Malmsey wine.

MALOLACTIC — *see* FERMENTATION, MALOLACTIC.

MALVASIA — (Mal-va-*zee*-ah) — Ancient and famous white wine grape (a red variant exists but is far less important) originally from Greece and the Aegean Islands, transplanted to most other Mediterranean countries, to the island of Madeira, South Africa and California. Its wine, usually called Malmsey in English, is, when fortified in the traditional way, extremely sweet and luscious, heavy in body, golden in color but turning deep amber with age, long-lived, with great bouquet. That of Madeira (*see*) is perhaps the most famous, but another of at least equal quality is produced on a little archipelago of islands off the north coast of Sicily, and sold as Malvasia di Lipari, the most important island of this group. A few wines are made from the Malvasia grape in California — some table wines of undistinguished quality, even a sparkling wine, and a few dessert wines which are hardly remarkable, but better than the rest.

MALVOISIE — (Mal-vwah-zee) — French for Malvasia (*see*), a superior dessert wine grape, widely planted in the *département* of Pyrénées Orientales, where, in conjunction with the Grenache and other varieties, it yields the sweet, amber fortified wines for which this district is known — Banyuls,

Rivesaltes, Maury, Grand Roussillon, etc. It is sometimes known by this name, rather than as Malvasia, in California.

MANCHA, La — (La *Mahn*-cha) — Wide, treeless, rolling, upland country, south of Madrid, in Spain; scene of Don Quixote's exploits. Its vast vineyards, including those of Valdepeñas (*see*) produce much of the better, common table wine of Spain.

MANZANILLA — (Mahn-thahn-*nee*-ya) — Legally, a Spanish Sherry; in fact, a quite different wine, although made on the edge of the Sherry Country, by similar methods, and from the identical varieties of grape. Unless specifically prepared for export, it is a very pale, almost painfully dry wine (although neither fruity nor tart), with between 15% and 17% alcohol by volume, a fine, highly special bouquet, and a flavor which is appetizing, faintly bitter, almost salty: some authorities have claimed, rather fancifully, that this is due to the sea wind which blows off the Atlantic over the vines and through the *bodegas*, for the Manzanilla vineyards are some ten miles west of Jerez, around the little white town of Sanlúcar de Barrameda, on the ocean and not far from the mouth of the Guadalquivir River, whence Columbus sailed for America and Magellan for the Pacific. It is said that the young Manzanillas taken to Jerez to mature will take on the characteristics of a Fino and a Fino *must* aged in Sanlucar will become a Manzanilla.

The word Manzanilla is the diminutive of *manzana*, apple, and means crab-apple in Spanish; it also means camomile, but despite some efforts by wine-loving etymologists, it is hard to see any connection between these and the wine, which is very unlike cider and even more unlike camomile tea. Traditionally, it is the wine of bullfighters, and the favorite wine of Seville, where it is drunk out of small, stumpy, cylindrical glasses called *cañas*. Perhaps on account of its almost excessive dryness, it has never been as popular abroad as in Spain.

It should be added that Manzanilla, like Sherry, becomes darker in color and higher in alcohol as it grows old in barrel; there exist, although rarely for sale, deep brown Manzanillas that have 21% of natural alcohol by volume, and these, remarkable and interesting but not for all palates, are perhaps the dryest wines on earth.

MARC — (Mar) — Grape pressings; the mass of skins and seeds left in the press after the wine (red wine) or juice (white wine) has been extracted. Also the brandy distilled from this, *Eau-de-Vie-de-Marc*. In the Champagne Country, the word has a different, special meaning: 4,000 kilograms (8,800 lbs.) of grapes, the load that one of the standard presses used there can handle at one time; normally four metric, or long, tons yield a maximum of twelve 200-liter barrels of usable wine, some 635 gallons in all, plus some 50 gallons of poorer quality, this last not used by the better Champagne producers.

MARCHE — (Mar-kay) — Central Adriatic coast region of Italy noted primarily for Verdicchio dei Castello di Jesi.

MARCOBRUNN — (Mar-co-bruhn) — Celebrated German vineyard, one of the Rheingau's best. It takes its name from the *Marcobrunnen*, a spring feeding an

218

attractive little fountain in red sandstone which, on the old river road, marks the village boundary of Erbach and of Hattenheim. About half the vines are in each village, although the fountain is in Erbach, and a local poet has written, "Let Erbach keep the water. Give Hattenheim the wine." Wines from the Erbach portion were generally marketed as Erbacher Markobrunn, even before 1971, and those from over the border of Hattenheim simply as Marcobrunner. Today, all must be sold as Erbacher Marcobrunn in order to comply with the new German Wine Law.

Although particularly outstanding in dry years, the Marcobrunners on the whole are unsurpassed by the wines of any other German vineyard — fruity, racy, well-balanced, they have truly astonishing bouquet and breed.

MARÉCHAL FOCH — (Mah-ray-shall Fosh) — French hybrid grape developed in Alsace; has become a standard short season grape in the United States. Has good sugar, moderate acid and makes a good red wine.

MAREUIL-SUR-AY — (Ma-ruy-soor-eye) — Wine-producing village in the Champagne Country of France, rate 98% as against 100% for Ay (see), next door. The vineyards are planted almost entirely to Pinot Noir, but there is a little Chardonnay, as in the Clos des Goisses (see).

MARGAUX — (Mar-go) — One of the best sections of the Haut-Médoc, producing Clarets remarkable for their bouquet, silky texture and great breed. The appellation now covers, in addition to the small township of Margaux proper, most of the neighboring communes — Cantenac, Soussans, Arsac and Labarde. The finest Margaux wines of course carry a château label: Château Margaux, a grand seigneur, and its scarcely less illustrious cousins, Rausan-Ségla, Rauzan-Gassies, Brane-Cantenac, Durfort-Vivens, Palmer, etc.

MARGAUX, Château — (Mar-go) — 1st Classed Growth of Margaux. One of the very greatest of the Bordeaux vineyards, producing a Claret of truly incomparable distinction and class — delicate, velvety, suave, well-balanced and astonishingly long-lived, with a bouquet unsurpassed by any other red wine on earth. The château itself is extremely impressive and the great high *chai* with its round stone columns is hardly less so. The vineyards produce some 15,000 cases of red wine a year, all château-bottled, plus a small quantity of dry white wine, sold as "Pavillon Blanc de Château Margaux"; this last, while pleasant enough, is by no means remarkable. For Label, *see* Page 219.

MARKGRÄFLER — (Mark-grayf-ler) — Mild, undistinguished, fairly agreeable white wine produced south of Freiburg, in Baden, Germany. It is made from the Chasselas grape, here called the Gutedel, and its production zone is called Margräflerland; most of it is consumed young, as *Schoppenwein,* for it is short-lived and hardly deserves bottling.

MARLENHEIM — (Mar-len-heim) — Wine-producing village in northern Alsace, due west of Strasbourg, on the Paris road; it is perhaps the only Alsatian *commune* in which black grapes predominate. From these, mostly Pinot Noir and Pinot Meunier, the growers make the best *rosé* of Alsace and one of the best of France — racy, fruity and delicate. This is sometimes given the local name of *Vorlauf.*

MARMANDAIS — (Mar-mah-day) — District of mediocre, nondescript wines southeast of Bordeaux, round the town of Marmande. For no very good reason its reds and whites have been accorded the V.D.Q.S. seal, and the name Côtes du Marmandais.

MARQUE — (Mark) — Simply means brand, in French; *marque deposée* means registered trademark. A *vin de marque* is a wine sold under a trade name rather than a regional or vineyard name; it can be anything and come from anywhere. No such wine is entitled to an *Appellation Contrôlée,* nor to the V.D.Q.S. seal.

MARQUIS-D'ALESME-BECKER, Château — (Mar-kee-Dah-lem Beck-air) — 3rd Classed Growth of Margaux. About 3,000 cases a year.

MARQUIS-DE-TERME, Château — (Mar-kee duh Tairm) — 4th Classed Growth of Margaux, Médoc. Today one of the best of the 4th Growths, producing about 15,000 cases a year of light, "tender," fine-textured claret.

MARSALA — (Mar-sahl-la) — The best known of Italian fortified wines, 17% to 19% alcohol by volume, amber in color, occasionally dry but more often somewhat sweet, roughly comparable to Sherry. It takes its name from the city of Marsala in western Sicily, around which it is produced, and was originally made during the latter half of the 18th century by a few English families (Woodhouse, Ingham, etc.) in an attempt to create a less expensive substitute for the Spanish and Portuguese wines which were then at the height of their popularity in England. The zone of production is today strictly delimited, and only certain grape varieties (the Grillo, Catarratto and Inzolia) may be used. Like Sherry, Marsala is a dry wine, brought up to 17% or 18% by fortification with high-proof grape brandy, and then to the desired degree of sweetness by the addition of an extremely sweet, concentrated grape juice, called either *sifone* or *mosto cotto,* depending on how it was made.

Marsalas are divided into a number of specific categories, each legally defined, as follows: 1. *"Italia"* (also called *Marsala fini*, or *Italia particolare*, or I.P.), which must contain 17% alcohol and 5% grape sugar — these are the lightest and least expensive; 2. *Marsala superiori* (also S.O.M., Garibaldi Dolce, G.D. or L.P., and formerly *"Inghilterra"*) which must contain 18% alcohol — these may be either sweet or dry, must contain 10% grape sugar if sweet, but little sugar or none if classified as dry; most of the Marsala that is exported falls in this class; finally, 3. *Marsala vergini* (also called *"Solera"*), bone dry, 18% wines, aged and blended in *soleras,* like the Sherries of Spain, and entirely unsweetened. In addition, various apéritifs and "tonic" wines are produced with a Marsala base, *Marsala all' uovo* (with egg), *Marsala chinato* (with quinine), etc. which must contain 18% alcohol and 10% grape sugar.

MARSANNAY or MARSANNAY-LA-CÔTE — (Mar-san-nay) — Village on the Côte de Dijon, in Burgundy; its wine, Rosé de Marsannay, made from the Pinot Noir grape, is one of the lightest, freshest and most delightful *vins rosés* of France. A small quantity of interesting white wine is also produced, and sold under its euphonious varietal name, as Chardonnay-de-Marsannay, and a most agreeable red wine, often labeled Pinot Noir de Marsannay, although its *Appellation Contrôlée* is simply "Bourgogne."

MARTIGNY — (Mar-teen-yee) — Swiss town southeast of Lake Geneva; with Sion, the principal center of the wine trade in the district known as the Valais (*see*).

MARTILLAC — (Mar-tee-yack) — Important wine-producing village in the French Graves district, its red wines on the whole better than its white. These, firm sturdy wines that mature rather slowly, include Châteaux Smith-Haut-Lafitte, Haut-Nouchet, Latour-Martillac, Lagarde, Ferran, etc.

MARTINI, Louis M. — One of the leading producers of premium wine in California; a family business of great integrity whose wine roots go back to the earthquake year of 1906. They are owners of prime vineyards in Napa and Sonoma Counties. The large, modern winery is at St. Helena, in the Napa Valley.

MARYLAND — The state has one interesting winery. See Boordy Vineyard.

MARZEMINO — (Mar-zay-*me*-no) — Superior wine grape, used in northern Italy in the production of red and *rosé* wines. See Isera, Chiaretto.

MASCARA — (*Mosk*-ka-ra) — Extremely full-bodied, deep-colored red wine (legally, but rarely *rosé* and white as well) produced in a delimited district near Oran, in Algeria. On account of its high alcohol (13-15½%), its body, color and softness, it was in great demand as a blending wine, and despite all the regulations forbidding such practices, some of it unquestionably found its way into the cheaper, commercial Bordeaux and Burgundies.

MASSON, Paul — Colorful Frenchman, born in Burgundy, who immigrated to California, married the daughter of Charles Lefranc, the owner and co-founder (1852) of Almadén Vineyards. He later created his own brand of California Champagne, made largely from grapes on his father-in-law's vineyard, planted

Emerald Dry

White Table Wine

PAUL MASSON.

Produced & Bottled by Paul Masson Vineyards

Saratoga, California   Alcohol 11.5% by Volume

additional vineyards, built what he termed his "château" at Saratoga nearby, and after, by all accounts, a merry and fruitful life, died in 1940. His most recently planted vineyard, high up on the hills back of Saratoga, was purchased in 1936, together with the brand name, by a San José stockbroker, Martin Ray; then resold, not long after America's entry in World War II, to the Seagram Company, and finally transferred to its present owners, the Paul Masson Company, now one of the largest premium wine producers of California.

MATARÓ — (Mah-tar-*ro*) — Productive, rather common red wine grape of Spanish or French origin (it is called the Mourvèdre in France, and permitted in Châteauneuf-du-Pape, although not widely grown there). In California, it generally gives a rather coarse wine and ranks hardly on a par with the Carignane. There is also a town of this name just north of Barcelona which is possibly the original home of this variety.

MATEUS — Popular brand of Portuguese table wine which has acquired wide acceptance in America. It is shipped in flagons and is, in fact, a somewhat sweet *rosé.*

MAUPERTUIS — (Mo-pair-twee) — Name formerly given to one particular portion of the Clos de Vougeot, now quite without any legal meaning although the name still occasionally appears on Clos de Vougeot labels.

MAURY — (Maw-ree) — Subdivision of Grand Roussillon (*see*), a vineyard district northwest of Perpignan, in the French eastern Pyrénées; it produces sweet, fortified *vin de liqueur,* made mostly from the Grenache grape.

MAVRODAPHNE — Greek name for one of the best-known red wine grapes of the Balkans and the Eastern Mediterranean, known in other countries by its more common name of Mavroud. The best Greek table wines shipped to the United States and some sweet, Port-type wines as well often carry this varietal name.

222

MAXIMIN GRÜNHAUS — (Max-ee-mean Grune-haus) — Tiny village and famous vineyard on the Ruwer, in the Moselle district of Germany, which produces, though only in good years, white wines of the very highest class. There are 120 acres under vines, most of them forming a single domain, that of the Von Schubert family; the labels usually carry an additional indication of vineyard plot, as Maximin Grühäuser Herrenberg. Bruderberg, etc. In 1921 and again in 1971, the estate produced a collection of Auslesen, Beerenauslesen, and the like, unsurpassed in Germany.

MAYACAMAS — Range of wooded hills, of volcanic origin, running from north to south and separating the Napa and Sonoma valleys, in California. There are many vineyards along the lower slopes, on both sides, and a few high up in the hills — Mont LaSalle (*see*), one called Monte Rosso, planted in the 1880's, the Mayacamas Vineyards, etc.

MAY WINE — Originally a German specialty: a sweetened, light white wine flavored with the aromatic leaves of the herb *Waldmeister,* or woodruff. It is served well-chilled, in a bowl, with spring fruits, traditionally strawberries, floating in it. Very passable May Wine is now made and bottled in the United States.

MAZIS-CHAMBERTIN — (Mah-zi Shawm-bair-tan) — Admirable red Burgundy, and the 31-acre vineyard from which it comes, directly adjoining Chambertin-Clos de Bèze (*see*) on the north; a firm, big wine, slow-maturing but of unmistakable class, not far from Chambertin itself in quality.

MAZOYÈRES-CHAMBERTIN — (Mahz-zoy-yare Shawm-bair-tan) — Largest vineyard (47 acres) of Gevrey-Chambertin, ranked as a *Grand Cru;* its excellent red wine, an outstandingly fine red Burgundy may also be labeled Charmes-Chambertin (*see*).

MEAD — (Meed) — Honey wine, a fermentation of honey and water; known since ancient time; like Hydromel and Metheglin.

223

MÉDOC — (May-dawk) — A long narrow triangle of land, world-famous for its red wines, extending some fifty miles north of Bordeaux, bounded on the west by the dunes and pine forests along the Atlantic, and on the east by the Gironde estuary. The good vineyards overlook or are near the estuary; they cover a strip of gently rolling, gravelly hills from six to ten miles wide, and their average production is not far from 4 million cases a year. This is a red wine district exclusively, and the few whites are entitled only to the appellations Bordeaux and Bordeaux Supérieur.

Wines labeled simply "Médoc" almost invariably come from the lower, sandier, less fine, northern third of the district beginning at Saint-Seurin (called the Bas-Médoc, although this is *not* a wine name); while never great, they are generally well-balanced Clarets of good quality and some breed. The Haut-Médoc (and this *is* an appellation — *see*) produces wines of a far higher class: they are sometimes sold under this name, but more often under one of the celebrated village or *commune* names — Margaux, Moulis, St. Julien, Pauillac, St. Estèphe — but most often of all under the label of a château. Well over half of the great Bordeaux châteaux (Lafite, Latour, Margaux, Mouton-Rothschild, the three Léovilles, the two Pichon-Longuevilles, Cos d'Estournel, Brane-Cantenac, Palmer, etc.) come from the Haut-Médoc, and even the lesser wines are outstanding.

To sum up, Médoc is a red wine appellation well above Bordeaux Rouge or Bordeaux Supérieur in quality, less good, since less limiting, than Haut-Médoc. However, even the least expensive Médoc must, according to French law, come from what is recognized as one of the best red wine districts of France, and be made from grape varieties (the Cabernets, Merlot, Malbec, etc.) second to none. It is or should be, therefore, very definitely a superior wine. The five most important communes, while all producing wines of comparable value, do have their own characteristics—for sheer wine power or vinosity Saint-Estèphe leads the pack followed by Pauillac, Saint-Julien, Cantenac and Margaux, in that order.

MELETO — (Meh-*leh*-toe) — One of the more famous estates in the Chianti Country; also part of the traditional holdings of the Ricasoli family. Its wine is somewhat lighter and earlier-maturing than that of Brolio (*see*).

MELLOW — Mature, soft, ripe; without greenness or harshness. In many instances, somewhat sweet.

MELNIK — (Mel-nik) — Red, white and sparkling wines produced round the town of this name, in Czechoslovakia; hardly ever exported, but considered that country's best.

MELON — (Meh-law) — A white wine grape with a faint muscat flavor, known as the Muscadet (*see*) in the lower Loire Valley of France, where it produces the popular wine of that name. Also cultivated to a certain extent in Burgundy where its wine is of mediocre quality.

MENDOCINO — The northernmost of the so-called North Coast Counties of California. Its vineyards, mostly around Ukiah in the upper part of the Russian River Valley, produce very good wines of all sorts. Mendocino is certainly destined to become increasingly important in the fine wine production of California. It is the home of Parducci and Weibel vineyards, among others.

MENDOZA — (Men-dos-sa) — Largest wine-producing province in Argentina, along the foothills of the Andes, west of Buenos Aires, and not far from the Chilean border.

MÉNETOU-SALON — (May-neh too Sal-law) — Interesting and attractive red, white and *rosé*, Appellation Contrôlée wines produced round the village of this name not far from Bourges, in central France. The red and *rosé* are made from the Pinot Noir, the white from the Sauvignon Blanc; there are about 35,000 cases a year,

MERANO — (Meh-*rahn*-no) — Resort town in the Italian Tyrol, known for its excellent local wines, such as *Küchelberger* (*see*).

MERCUREY — (Mair-coo-ray) — Best known and best red wine (a little less good white is made) of the Côte Chalonnaise, from the village of this name, northwest of Chalon-sur-Saône, in Burgundy. It is made entirely from the Pinot Noir (or the Chardonnay, when white) and comparable to a sound, pleasant secondary Burgundy of the Côte de Beaune. Total production amounts to over 200,000 cases a year, 96% red.

MERCUROL — (Mair-cew-rawl) — Village in the central Rhône Valley and its fine, dry, white wine, formerly sold under the village name, now as Crozes-Hermitage (*see*).

MERLOT — (Mair-lo) — Distinguished red wine grape, nearly as important as the two Cabernets (*see*) in the Bordeaux Country, where it gives softness, fruit, grace and charm to many famous wines that would be less attractive without it. Early ripe and quite productive, yielding wines that are less astringent and sooner ready (if shorter lived) than the Cabernets, it is a variety that presents obvious temptations to the grower, and there are certainly vineyards, and indeed districts, in which it has been too widely planted. This is not true in Pomerol, where it is a principal grape, particularly at Château Petrus where it was planted almost exclusively after the great frost loss in 1956. On the other hand, a judicious admixture of Merlot would certainly improve most, if indeed not all, Cabernet Sauvignons in California and about 5,000 acres are now planted in the major wine-growing areas where some wine is labeled with its proper name.

The Merlot is planted and vinified alone in several of the better districts of northern Italy, especially the Alto Adige (*see*), and in the Ticino or Tessin of southern Switzerland, near Lugano. There it yields a soft, round, eminently agreeable red wine, without much distinction or depth, but with a great deal of bouquet and fruit.

MESLAND — (May-lah) — Fresh, fruity and attractive *vin rosé* made from the Gamay grape in the Loire Valley of France, between Blois and Tours. Its full and proper name is "Touraine-Mesland," the latter being the *commune* from which it comes.

MESNIL, Le — (Luh May-neel) — One of the best wine-producing villages of the Côte des Blancs, in the French Champagne Country, rated 99% (as against 100% for its two superiors, Cramant and Avize). White Chardonnay grapes are grown exclusively and the wine has great delicacy and breed.

METALLIC — Having a particular, acrid, unpleasant taste, not unlike greenness, which white wines sometimes acquire and red wines more rarely, possibly through contact with metal.

METHEGLIN — (Meh-thi-glin) — Similar to Mead (*see*).

MÉTHODE CHAMPENOISE — (May-tode Shahm-pen-wahs) — French term for making sparkling wine by secondary fermentation in the bottle; the "champagne method" which is the only legal way to make Champagne in its country of origin. Minimum bottle requirements are four months for non-appellation wines and nine months for Appellation Contrôlée.

METHUSALEM — Variously spelled, an oversize Champagne bottle, holding as much as eight ordinary bottles.

MÉTIS — (May-tee) — Cross-pollination in the same species; i.e. vinifera x vinifera (*see* Hybrid).

METRICATION — *see* BOTTLE

MEUNIER — (Munn-yea) — Sub-variety of the Pinot Noir, a superior wine grape although far less remarkable than its distinguished cousin; it may no longer legally be cultivated in the better Burgundian vineyards but is still rather widely planted in the Champagne Country, in Alsace, and in California, where it is often confused with the Pinot Noir. The word *Meunier* in French means "miller," and this grape is called Pinot Meunier because the under-side of its leaf is whitish, as if it had been sprinkled with white dust, or flour.

MEURSAULT — (Mere-so) — Ancient wine-producing village of the Côte d'Or, in Burgundy (its name is supposed to derive from the Latin *Muris Sal-*

VIN DE BOURGOGNE

MEURSAULT
St Vincent
APPELLATION MEURSAULT CONTRÔLÉE

Caves Chanson (Ancien bastion du XVᵉ Siècle) à Beaune

CHANSON
PRODUCED, BOTTLED AND SHIPPED BY
CHANSON PÈRE & FILS, NÉGOCIANTS-ÉLEVEURS, BEAUNE (COTE-D'OR) FRANCE
1 PT. 8 FL. OZ.   PRODUCE OF FRANCE   ALCOHOL 12,5 % BY VOL.

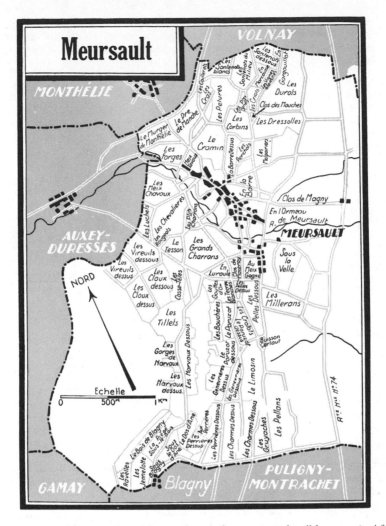

Meursault

tus, meaning Leap of the Mouse, though for no very plausible reason). After Pommard, two miles to the north, its annual production is the largest of any *commune* of the Côte, averaging about 125,000 cases, 95% of it white. The vastly greater part of this is made from the Chardonnay grape, although the Pinot Blanc is also authorized, and the best of it, of course, carries a vineyard name as well as the general appellation Meursault. Leading vineyards, in about this order of quality, include: Perrières (42 acres), Genevrières (42 acres), Charmes (69 acres), Blagny (5 acres), La Pièce-sous-le-Bois (28 acres), Dos d'Ane (7 acres), Poruzot (24 acres), Jennelotte (12 acres), Bouchères (10 acres), Goutte d'Or (14 acres). Even the lesser Meursaults are white Burgundies of high quality and real distinction; the finer ones are surpassed by only a few great rarities among the dry white wines of France. Green-gold in color, full-bodied but racy, rather high in alcohol but well-balanced, dry but not at all austerely so, they are remarkable, and fully merit their fame.

MEXICO — As might be expected, our southern neighbor, Mexico, has a climate poorly suited to table wine-growing, since a good part of its area is actually in the Tropic Zone, and even its northernmost corner, near San Diego, is as far south as Egypt. Vines are nevertheless grown, more for eating grapes than for wine, in many provinces of Mexico, particularly in Lower California and in some of the higher central states where the prevailing weather is somewhat cooler on account of the altitude. The best wines are those produced round the old Spanish Mission of Santo Tomás at Ensenada on the Pacific, just south of the U.S. border. These, today, are well-made, sound, ordinary wines with no real distinction — the reds generally better than the whites. Other grape-growing districts of some importance are in the states of Durango, Coahuila and Chihuahua and more recently Aquascalientes and Quirétaro. Total production of wine from Mexico's 85,000 acres of vines is 41 million gallons, of which 10% is consumed as wine and 90% distilled into brandy.

MICRO-CLIMATE — The local influence of location, altitude, drainage and orientation have been recognized for more than 2,000 years. A perfect combination will produce extraordinary grapes while adjacent vineyards higher or lower, or around the curve of a hill will not reach the same peak of quality.

MIDI — (Me-dee) — In French, means both 12 M., Noon, and, in a general sense, the South — an *accent du Midi* is a French southern accent. It is a rather more specific term when applied to wine: the Rhône Valley is excluded, so are both Provence and the Côte d'Azur. A *vin du Midi* is commonly understood to mean an ordinary table wine (not a dessert wine, in other words) produced along the Mediterranean Coast of France, in the *départements* of Gard, Hérault, Aude and Pyrénées Orientales between Nîmes, Carcassonne and the Spanish border. *See* also Languedoc.

MILAZZO — (Me-*lotz*-zo) — One of the better red wines of Sicily, made around the town of this name, west of Messina, from the Nocera grape.

MILDE — (*Mil*-duh) — German wine taster's term, meaning pleasantly soft, possibly a bit sweet, rather lacking in character.

MILDEW — A grave malady of the vine caused by a virus or fungus; also called the *peronospora* or *mosaic,* and related to the *oidium.* Of American origin, this was introduced into Europe accidentally about the middle of the 19th century and produced almost as serious damage as the *phylloxera* which arrived a few years later. Within limits, it can now be controlled through the use of copper sulphate sprays or flowers of sulphur in powder form. It appears in two related types — downy and powdery.

MILLÉSIME — (Mea-lay-zeem) — French for date or year; vintage, when applied to wine. A wine that is *millésimé* (meal-lay-szee-may) is one marked with its vintage.

MILLOT — *see* LÉON MILLOT.

MINERVOIS — (Me-nair-vwah) — With Corbières, about the best of the not particularly distinguished wines of the French Midi — often an agreeable, full-bodied, well-balanced red table wine, far from bad, deserving the V.D.Q.S. seal which it is entitled to bear. The delimited production zone is the hilly country west and northwest of Narbonne; the authorized grape varieties are the ordinary ones of Languedoc — Grenache, Cinsault, Carignan, etc.; white and *rosé* wines may also be called Minervois, but these are much less good.

MIRASSOU — Fourth and fifth generation wine family, fruit growers and vineyardists in San José and elsewhere, they have since 1966 sold fine wines under their own label.

MISE — (Meeze) — Literally, "putting"; but into bottles, or "bottling," when applied to wine. Thus *Mise du Château* means Château-Bottling, etc.

MISE DU CHÂTEAU — (Meeze due Shato-toe) — *See* CHÂTEAU-BOTTLED.

MISSION — First of the European vinifera vines to reach California, this is a red wine grape of only fair quality at best, brought in during the last half of the 18th century by Franciscan monks and planted around their missions — whence, presumably, its name. It had long been known as the Criolla in Mexico. Although unquestionably of European origin, it has never been further identified and some have believed it to be a seedling, or inadvertent cross. It gives a poor table wine and, when used for Port, a wine often deficient in color; its main use is for Angelica (*see*), which is hardly a recommendation, and it now ranks sixteenth in total acreage among wine grapes in California.

MISSION-HAUT-BRION, Château La — (Me-see-aw O Bree-aw) — 1st Growth of Talence, Graves. Directly opposite Haut-Brion, on the Bordeaux-Arcachon road, La Mission-Haut-Brion is second only to its illustrious neighbor among the vineyards and red wines of Graves. It was created in the 17th century by a religious order, the "Prêchers de la Mission" (whence its name); its 40 acres annually produce some 8,000 cases of wine. This, which generally brings a somewhat higher price than the 2nd Classed Growths of the Médoc, is a truly admirable claret, velvety, generous and fine; long-lived and slow-maturing like Haut Brion, it is in the same noble class.

MISTELLE — (Mee-stel) — Product made from grape juice to which sufficient alcohol is added to prevent fermentation; it is always sweet and is used in making Vin de Liqueur, Madeira, vermouth, apéritifs, etc.

MISURA — (Mee-*zoo*-rah) — Picturesque and attractive Italian wine bottle.

MITTELBERGHEIM — (Mit-tel-bairg-heim) — Important wine-producing village in Alsace, not far from Barr, in the *département* Bas-Rhin. Fairly good wines which should not be confused with the decidedly better ones of Bergheim, in the Haut-Rhin some twenty miles further south.

MITTELHAARDT — *See* HAARDT.

MITTEL-MOSEL — *See* MOSELLE.

MITTELRHEIN — (Mit-tel Rine) — The third smallest of the eleven German Specified Wine Regions or Anbaugebiete (*see*). A narrow ribbon of vineyards stretching 60 miles along the Rhine both north and south of its juncture with the Mosel at Koblenz, it has 3 Bereiche, 11 Grosslagen and some 120 Einzellagen planted 80% in Riesling. This ancient and stunningly picturesque part of Germany produces but 1% of the total output. Very few of its wines are exported. For Map, *see* Germany.

MITTELWIHR — (Mit-tel-veer) — Little Alsatian vineyard town north of Colmar, almost totally destroyed in World War II; completely rebuilt, it is again producing wines of better than average quality.

MOËLLEUX — (Mweh-luh) — French wine tasters' term applied usually to white wines which, while not sweet, are emphatically not bone dry; "mellow" is a poor, imprecise English equivalent — a wine may "mellow" but does not become *moëlleux* with time; essentially, the sweetness of a *moëlleux* wine is the sort of sweetness we mean when we say, "sweet as a nut." Literally, the French word means "marrowy."

MOLDY — Having the unpleasant odor and flavor which mold usually (but by no means always) imparts to grapes and the wines made from them. This is far more likely to be present in red wines than in white, since mold attacks the skins first of all and since, in the making of red wine, the skins are fermented with the juice; it can be the result of hail just prior to the vintage, but more often it is brought on by warm, humid weather during the ripening season: in this case it is practically identical with rot. *See* Pourriture Noble.

MOLINARA — (Mo-lee-*nar*-ra) — Superior Italian red wine grape, used especially in Valpolicella (*see*) and Bardolino.

MOLISE — (Mo-lee-seh) — *see* ABRUZZO and MOLISE.

MOLSHEIM — (Maulz-heim) — Busy, small town near Strasbourg in northern Alsace; wines of superior but not exceptional quality.

MONBAZILLAC — (Maw-baz-zee-yak) — Soft, rather common, sweet white wine, produced east of Bordeaux in the *département* of the Dordogne. It is made mostly from the Sémillon grape, plus a little Muscadelle, and is usually between 13% and 14% in alcohol. The vineyards are on rolling hills south of Bergerac; their total production is not far from 1½ million gallons a year.

MONDAVI — Family of winemakers in California since Repeal and owners of Charles Krug in St. Helena. Robert Mondavi established his own winery in Rutherford in 1966, is producing a fine line of varietals and has done interesting experiments with various types of oak cooperage.

MONDEUSE — (Mawn-duhz) — Superior if not outstanding French red wine grape, widely grown in the Savoie and the upper Rhône Valley east of Lyon, to some small extent in California. It gives a rather fruity wine of definite character, and makes a superior *rosé* (*see* Montagnieu). A less interesting white variety also exists. *See* Refosco.

230

California

RED TABLE WINE

ALCOHOL 12% BY VOLUME

PRODUCED AND BOTTLED BY ·

ROBERT MONDAVI WINERY

OAKVILLE, NAPA VALLEY, CALIFORNIA

A wine for everyday use made entirely of varietal wine grapes. Flavorful and complex in character.

MONFERRATO — (Mahn-feh-*rot*-toe) — Perhaps the finest wine district of Italy, and certainly one of the great wine regions of the world, although few bottles, if any, ever carry the name. It consists of a country of rather steep, rolling hills, some sixty miles by forty, directly south of the wide, fertile Po River valley, in Italian Piedmont: the provinces of Alessandria and Asti, plus part of Cuneo and part of Turin. Almost all of the wines for which Piedmont is famous (Barolo, Barbaresco, Freisa, Grignolino, Gavi, Cortese) come from its hillside vineyards, and its Moscato di Canelli (*see*) is the base of most Asti Spumante and most Italian Vermouth.

MONICA — (Mo-*nee*-ca) — Sweet, red wine, made from the grape of the same name, near Cagliari, on the Italian island of Sardinia. Somewhat on the order of a light Port, generally about 17% alcohol.

MONIGA — (Mo-*nee*-ga) — Village on the southwestern shore of Lake Garda (*see*), producing an excellent fresh *rosé* wine, only occasionally marketed under the village name, usually as Chiaretto (*see*).

MONOPOLE — (Mawn-o-pole) — Term sometimes used on wine labels in connection with a brand name to indicate ownership of the name. It is in no sense related to the wine's origin or its quality.

MONT — (Maw) — Pleasant, fresh dry white local wine, produced not far from the Château de Chambord, in the Loire Valley; sometimes called Mont-près-Chambord, and sometimes Cour-Cheverny, it may carry the V.D.Q.S. seal.

MONTAIGNE DE REIMS — *see* CHAMPAGNE

MONTAGNE-SAINT-ÉMILION — (Maw-tan-ya Sant A-me-lee-aw) — Important wine-producing *commune* adjoining St. Émilion (*see*) on the northeast, also including Saint-Georges-Saint-Émilion and Parsac-Saint-Emilion (although these may also be labeled with their own proper names). Their sturdy red wines are of good quality, and if they lack the distinction and the velvety softness of the St. Émilions proper, they are correspondingly less expensive, and often excellent values. The better known Châteaux include: Roudier, Montaiguillon, des Tours, Negrit, Plaisance, La Bastienne, Moulin-Blanc, etc.

MONTAGNIEU — (Maw-tan-yuh) — *Rosé*, white and (rarely) red wine produced in a district known as the Bugey, in the upper Rhône Valley between Lyon and Geneva. Fresh, light and attractive, often *pétillant*, or slightly sparkling, it had made many friends, especially at the Ostellerie du Vieux Pérouges, near Lyon, where it is featured. As a commercial wine, it hardly exists, but is entitled to the V.D.Q.S. seal.

MONTAGNY — (Maw-tan-ye) — In general, with Rully (*see*), the best white wine of the Côte Chalonnaise, in Burgundy. Made from the Chardonnay grape, dry, fresh, light and clean-tasting, it deserves to be better known.

MONTÉE DE TONNERRE — (Mawn-tay d' Taw-nair) — Perhaps the very best of the *Premier Cru* vineyards of Chablis, giving a wine of great distinction and bouquet which possibly deserves *Grand Cru* rank. The name comes from the road that climbs up and over the hill to the nearby town of Tonnerre, and has nothing to do with thunder.

MONTEFIASCONE — (Mahn-tay-fee-ahs-*co*-nay) — Small town north of Rome, near Lake Bolsena, where the celebrated Moscatello wine called Est! Est!! Est!!! (*see*) is produced.

MONTEPULCIANO — (Mahn-tay-pul-*chan*-no) — *See* Vino Nobile di Montepulciano. Red wine from southern Tuscany, in Italy, produced round the picturesque old hill town of this name. It was extravagantly praised by the English poet, Leigh Hunt, in the early 19th century, as "the king of wines," echoing the earlier opinion of the wine-loving author-physician Dr. Francesco Redi, in his *Bacco in Toscana* and the 1978 vintage will become one of the first D.O.C.G. (*see*). It is not, oddly enough, made from the Montepulciano grape (which is a good red wine variety of southern Italy) but from the Sangiovese and others like Chianti (*see*).

MONTEREY — County south of San Francisco, becoming increasingly important in the production of fine wines. Over 33,000 acres of new vineyards have been planted there, all in wine grapes, putting it in fourth place behind Kern, Fresno and San Joaquin in wine grape acreage. Monterey County is sure to be a very important factor in the production of fine varietal wines as the new vineyards planted in the last decade come into full bearing and production. Many of the major wine producers own vineyards of Monterey.

MONTHÉLIE — (Maw-tay-lee) — Tiny village back of Volnay, on the Côte de Beaune, in Burgundy. Its red wines, usually labeled Monthélie or Monthélie-Côte de Beaune, are among the best of the less known Burgundies, certainly superior to many Pommards, and are worth looking for, since they are generally inexpensive. About 35,000 cases are produced in an average year.

MONTILLA — (Mawn-tee-ya) — Excellent, unusual, and all too little known wine, produced in a district of arid, chalky hills, round the villages of Montilla and Los Moriles, south of Cordoba, in Spain. Part of the production has traditionally been sent to Jerez to form part of the Sherry blends. This is still permitted for limited quantities of sweet wines but not for dry. Amontillado (*see*) which means "in the style of Montilla" has nothing to do with the blending of Montilla wine with Jerez wine. It is a type or style of Sherry. Since 1945 Montilla-Moriles has been the proud possessor of an appellation of its own. Its main difference from Sherry lies in the fact that it is rarely if ever fortified; made from the Pedro Ximénez grape grown on upland vineyards under a relentless sun, it has 15-16% of natural alcohol by volume, and even more when old. Like Sherry, it is made with flor yeasts, stored in ventilated *bodegas,* blended in *soleras.* During its youth, however, it is kept not in wood, but in huge earthenware jars, or *tinajas,* shaped like Roman amphoras, higher than a man. Like Sherry, it has its Finos and its Olorosos, in England these words (and Amontillado) are used only for Sherry. What is ordinarily sold is a very pale, clean, dry wine, possibly with less breed and bouquet than a first-class Fino Sherry or a Manzanilla, but perhaps pleasanter and easier to drink since it has not been fortified. It is served chilled both as an apéritif and as a table wine, especially with *mariscos,* or shellfish; there are those, including the author of these pages, who think it better with clams or oysters than any other wine, including Chablis.

MONT LA SALLE — Principal California vineyard of The Christian Brothers (*see*), high up in the hills northwest of Napa. It takes its name from the founder of the Order, Jean Baptiste de La Salle.

MONTLOUIS — (Maw-lou-we) — Village almost directly across the Loire from Vouvray, in France. Its white wines made, like Vouvray, from the Chenin Blanc grape, were legally sold as Vouvray until 1938 and are of substantially the same quality today; they are usually somewhat cheaper, given equal quality, being less known. Total production amounts to some 265,000 gallons a year.

MONTPEYROUX — (Maw-pay-roo) — Red and *rosé* wine of better than average quality, produced in the hilly country north of Béziers, in the French Midi. It carries the V.D.Q.S. seal.

MONTRACHET — (Maw-ra-shay) — Extraordinary 18½-acre vineyard of the Côte d'Or, in Burgundy, producing the most celebrated and expensive dry white wine of France. Just over half of its area lies within the communal limits of Puligny-Montrachet (*see*), the rest in Chassagne-Montrachet: it has given its name to both villages, as well as to a few specific, small plots of vines which directly adjoin it, notably Chevalier-Montrachet and Bâtard-Montrachet (*see*). Its wine, like all of the finest white Burgundies, is made entirely from the Chardonnay grape, and the total production amounts to a little over a thousand cases a year, though less than two hundred in 1972. The name is said to come from the Latin *Mons rachicensis,* which became *Mont-Rachat,* or "Bald-Hill"; the first "t" is still silent (as well as the last), and the barren hilltop behind the stony vineyards is covered with thin scrub and almost "bald," even today. The vineyard itself is nevertheless probably the most valuable agricultural land in France, despite its small yield per acre, and its wine, rivaled

MONTRACHET

APPELLATION CONTROLÉE

1972 • 1972

DOMAINE JACQUES PRIEUR

Propriétaire à Meursault (Côte-d'Or)

MISE EN BOUTEILLES DU DOMAINE

PRODUCE OF FRANCE

in Burgundy only by that of its immediate neighbors, is wholly remarkable. Pale gold in color, with a hint of green, high in alcohol (rarely under 13%), with tremendous bouquet, flavor and class, dry but with an underlying trace of luscious softness, especially in good years, it is, as someone has said, "not so much a wine as an experience."

For Map, *see* PULIGNY, CHASSAGNE.

MONTRAVEL — (Maw-tra-vel) — Vineyard district in southeastern France and its rather undistinguished, semi-sweet, golden wine. The vineyards are on the north bank of the Dordogne, upstream (east) from St. Émilion, and although the production zone is bounded on three sides by the Bordeaux Country, Montravel is *not* entitled to the name "Bordeaux," and is marketed as Côtes de Montravel, Haut-Montravel, or simply Montravel. Made mostly from the Sémillon grape, it is properly classified as a Vin de Bergerac (*see*), like Monbazillac, Côtes de Duras, etc., which it much resembles.

MONTROSE, Château — (Maw-trose) — 2nd Classed Growth of St. Estèphe, Haut-Médoc. One of the firmest and sturdiest of the great Médoc Clarets, deep-colored, slow-maturing, long-lived; its quality has improved considerably in the last few years. Production amounts to some 14,000 cases a year.

MONTS-DE-MILIEU — (Maw duh Meel-yuh) — One of the very best *Premier Cru* vineyards of Chablis, in the *communes* of Fyé and Fleys; like Montée de Tonnerre (*see*), it is almost deserving of *Grand Cru* rank.

MOORE'S DIAMOND — Native, Eastern white grape, giving a rather spicy, tart, pale wine, developed in the 1860's near Lake Keuka by Jacob Moore, and still planted to some extent in the Finger Lakes vineyards.

MÓR — (Mor) — Town and district in Hungary, not far from Budapest, producing a full-bodied, golden wine from the Ezerjo grape, called Mori Ezerjo.

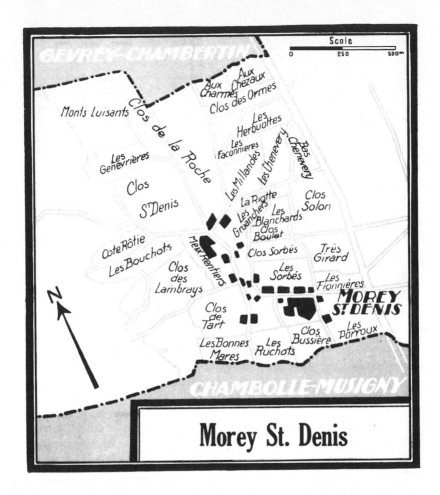

Morey St. Denis

MOREY-SAINT-DENIS — (Mor-ray San Day-nee) — Burgundian village on the Côte de Nuits, producing a number of red wines of the very highest class, firm, sturdy and long-lived. Its best vineyards include a portion of Bonnes Mares, the Clos de la Roche, the Clos St. Denis, the Clos de Tart and the Clos des Lambrays; the wines from these, however, are generally sold under the vineyard, rather than the village, name. What is labeled Morey-St. Denis is of a somewhat less exalted class, often equally full-bodied with less distinction. A little white wine of second quality is also produced in the *climat* known as Monts-Luisants.

MORGEOT — (Mor-jo) — Vineyard or district name, traditionally given to certain excellent red and white Burgundies produced in the southern part of the

235

commune of Chassagne-Montrachet (*see*). The precise area entitled to the appellation is now in dispute and awaiting a final decision by the French courts.

MORGON — (Mor-gaw) — One of the best and yet least typical red wines of the Beaujolais, and the village from which it comes. It is less fruity than other wines of its district, matures less quickly and takes on, with time, an odd, marked resemblance to the Burgundies of the Côte d'Or. Local experts say of any Beaujolais which evolves this way, that "il morgonne," or it is developing like the wine of Morgon. Total production is about 400,000 cases a year. (*see* Beaujolais).

MORILES, Los — (Loze Mo-ree-lace) — *See* MONTILLA.

MOROCCO — Former French Protectorate in North Africa, now is an independent country, producing largely for its European population some 20 million gallons of wine a year. The best of this comes from around Meknes and is a pleasant, ordinary red wine, surprisingly light and good for one grown at this southern latitude. It is rarely, if ever, exported.

MOSCATEL — (Maws-cah-tel) — Portuguese version of Muscat or Muscatel. That produced at Setubal, southeast of Lisbon, ranks among the very finest wines of its type in the world — very sweet, deep amber in color, with an overwhelming fruit and bouquet and flavor. It is of course fortified.

This is also the Spanish spelling, and Moscatels of varying quality are produced in many parts of Spain, those of Sitges and Málaga being perhaps the best.

MOSCATELLO — (Mos-cot-*tel*-lo) — Sub-variety of the Muscat grape. *See* Moscato.

MOSCATO — (Mos-*cot*-toe) — Italian word for Muscat, a variety of grape, or family of grapes (for there are literally dozens of sub-varieties); also, the widely different wines made from these, in all parts of Italy. One of them, the Aleatico (*see*) is red; the others white. They include sparkling wines — Asti Spumante (*see*), for example, many dessert wines, and even a few dry or semi-dry white table wines. They all have, to a greater or lesser degree, a characteristic and unmistakable bouquet and flavor. The better known are as follows: the MOSCATO DI CANELLI, or Moscatello, which takes its name from the village of Canelli, near Asti, where it gives an extremely aromatic, pale, sweet white wine, low in alcohol, used in Asti Spumante and Italian Vermouth; the same or a very similar subvariety produces Est! Est!! Est!!! (*see*) of Montefiascone. The MOSCATO GIALLO of the Trentino and Alto Adige (*see*) is a distinguished, natural white wine, about as sweet as Sauternes, with 13% to 15% alcohol. The true dessert wines (15% to 17% alcohol, extremely sweet) are the MOSCATO DI CAGLIARI (from Sardinia), the MOSCATO DI PANTELLERIA (from a small island between Sicily and Tunisia), the MOSCATO DI SIRACUSA (from Syracuse, in Sicily), the MOSCATO DI TRANI (from near Bari, in southern Italy), etc. There are many others.

MOSEL — (Mo-z'l) — German version of Moselle (*see*). The wine district is officially called Mosel-Saar-Ruwer, and this is the designation that appears on wine labels.

MOSEL-SAAR-RUWER — (Mo-z'l Sahr Roo-ver) — One of the eleven Anbaugebiete (*see*) with 4 Bereiche, 19 Grosslagen and a record number of more than 500 Einzellagen. For details, *see* Moselle, etc. For Map, *see* Germany.

237

MOSELBLÜMCHEN — (*Mo*-s'l-*blim*-shen) — What the Germans, who are the only ones to use it, called a *Fantasie-Name,* a quite meaningless wine name — in English, "Little-Moselle-Flower." Usually a blend of the very cheapest wines of the Moselle Valley, almost always "sugared," never estate-bottled.

MOSELLE — (Mo-zell) — (In German, MOSEL, pronounced *Mo*-z'l) — The Moselle River rises in France, skirts the little Grand Duchy of Luxembourg, and then winds for nearly a hundred miles down one of the most beautiful valleys of western Germany, from Trier to where it joins the Rhine at Koblenz. Even in France there are a few vineyards along its banks (*see* Lorraine), and others of greater extent in Luxembourg (*see*), but those of real consequence and international fame are all in Germany. Officially, the wine district is called Mosel-Saar-Ruwer (the latter being two of the Moselle's small tributaries); there are some 29,000 acres under vines, and the average annual production is not far from 30 million gallons.

Approximately at the latitude of Winnipeg, these are among the northernmost commercial vineyards in the world; they are planted on unimaginably steep hillsides, on unfertile, slate soil, and the Riesling grape is grown almost exclusively. Apart from the wines of the two tributary valleys, the Saar and Ruwer (and these can be admirable), all of the best Moselles come from one central section of the main valley, the Mittel-Mosel, extending from Trittenheim some forty miles to Traben-Trarbach. Thin, tart, even acid in poor vintage years, Moselle wines at their best are perhaps the most delicate, the most fragrant and most distinguished of all white wines. They rarely exceed 11% of alcohol by volume, and often have substantially less; pale, flowery, spicy, with great breed, they are like no other wines on earth.

The finer Moselles carry on their labels, with a few rare exceptions, the name of a village, plus that of a specific vineyard, as Wehlener Sonnenuhr, from the town of Wehlen; Bernkasteler Doktor, from the Town of Bernkastel; Ockfener Bockstein, from the Bockstein vineyard in the town of Ockfen. Most of them are estate-bottled, and their labels so state. The higher grades often carry an indication of special qualities (*see* Auslese, Spätlese, Trockenbeerenauslese).

What follows is a list of the best vineyard towns, with asterisks indicating their respective quality. Each of these towns will be found, together with the names of its best vineyards, in its alphabetical place in this encyclopedia.

Mittel-Mosel: *Trittenheim, *Neumagen, *Dhron, ***Piesport, *Wintrich, **Brauneberg, *Lieser, ***Bernkastel, ***Graach, ***Wehlen, ***Zeltingen, **Erden, **Uerzig, *Traben-Trarbach.

Saar: *Wawern, **Kanzem, ***Wiltingen, **Oberemmel, **Ayl, **Ockfen, *Pellingen.

Ruwer: **Maximin Grunhaus, *Kasel, *Avelsbach.

Under American wine law, Moselle is considered a semi-generic name, and a California Moselle may legally be marketed, even if made from raisin grapes or table grapes. Fortunately, there seems to be little demand for such wines, which of course bear no resemblance to the German original, and the designation is now rarely used in the United States.

MOU — (Moo) — French wine taster's term meaning soft, flat, wholly lacking in character.

MOÛT — (Moo) — Must (*see*) in French — unfermented or fermenting grape juice up to the moment it becomes wine.

MOULIN-À-VENT — (Moo-lah ah Vaw) — Generally ranked as the finest wine of the Beaujolais, and almost always the most expensive; certainly, by a considerable margin, the longest-lived. The vineyards are partly in the *commune* of Romanèche-Thorins and partly in Chénas (*see*); they cover the slopes of a round hill, crowned with the ancient *moulin-à-vent* or windmill, which gave the vineyard and the wine its name. A good Moulin-à-Vent of a good year can almost be classified as a great wine; deep-colored, sturdy, rather high in alcohol (usually over 13%), it "fills the mouth," as the French say, and, at the same time, has undeniable breed and class. (*see* Beaujolais)

MOULINET, Château — (Moo-lee-nay) — Small vineyard in the Pomerol district, little known, but producing an exceptionally good and typical red wine, velvety, round and fine. Some 4,000 cases a year.

MOULIS — (Moo-lee) — Sub-division of the Haut-Médoc (like Margaux, St. Julien, St. Estèphe, etc.) although the least famous and least important of these. It produces hardly any great wine at all, but, on the other hand, much that is good, dependable, well-balanced and not too expensive. The delimited zone comprises the township of Moulis and most of that of Listrac, plus portions of five others nearby, and the better Châteaux include Chasse-Spleen, Poujeaux-Theil, and Dutruch-Grand-Poujeaux, all Grand Cru Bourgeois Exceptionnel. (*see* Appendix 3)

MOUNTAIN — Old English name for Malaga wine.
    ALSO, in California, term used to designate wines from upland or hillside vineyards (some rather low indeed), rather than from irrigated, overly productive vines planted on the flat valley floor. Even if blended, non-varietal, and inexpensive, as "Mountain Red" and "Mountain White," these are on the whole better wines and better values than the common run. Although the word has not yet been strictly defined by law or regulation, an effort is being made by Federal and State authorities to limit its use to wines with some right to this description.

MOURVÈDRE — (Moor-vedr) — Red wine grape. *See* Mataró.

MOUSSE — (Moose) — French term for foam, the "head" on beer and champagne.

MOUSSEUX — (Moo-suh) — French word meaning foaming or effervescent; sparkling, when applied to wine. All French sparkling wines, no matter how produced, whether by the Champagne method, the Charmat process of fermentation in bulk, or even if simply carbonated (*gazéifié*) belong in this category of *Vins Mousseux;* Champagne, despite its obvious *mousse,* or foam, is never so listed or so described, it being considered in a class apart. The following French *mousseux,* and only these, carry an *Appellation Contrôlée* and are therefore certified, as to origin, by the French Government (all other names are brands): Anjou Mousseux, Arbois Mousseux, Blanquette de Limoux, Bordeaux Mousseux, Bourgogne Mousseux (Sparkling Burgundy) which after 1980 must be labeled Crémant de Bourgogne, Clairette de Die Mousseux, Côtes du Jura Mousseux, L'Étoile Mousseux, Gaillac Mousseux, Montlouis Mousseux, St. Péray Mousseux, Saumur Mousseux, Seyssel Mousseux, Touraine Mousseux and Vouvray Mousseux (Sparkling Vouvray), Mousseux de Savoie, Mousseux de Savoie Ayze and one V.D.Q.S. Mousseux de Bugey.

MOUSY — Bacterial infection produced smell and taste, can come from wine too long on its lees.

MOUTON-BARONNE-PHILIPPE — (Moo-taw Bah-run Fee-leep) — Formerly Château Mouton-d'Armailhacq, the name was changed to Mouton-Baron-Philippe in 1956 after its owner Baron Philippe de Rothschild and in 1977 renamed Mouton-Baronne-Philippe in honor of his late wife who will also be remembered by the fine Wine Museum which she created at Mouton-Rothschild. Its production has been deliberately restricted and its wine today is certainly outstanding in its category. One of the very finest of the 5th Classed Growths. Some 15-20,000 cases a year.

MOUTON-D'ARMAILHACQ — (Moo-taw Dar-my-yock) — Original name of Château Mouton-Barrone-Philippe (see).

MOUTON-ROTHSCHILD, Château — (Moo-taw Rawt-sheel) — World-famous Bordeaux vineyard and its magnificient red wine. Classified in 1855 as a 2nd Growth (albeit 1st of the 2nds), Mouton never fully accepted this lesser status, and its proud devise used to read, *"Premier ne puis. Second ne daigne. Mouton suis."* ("I cannot be a First. I do not deign to be a Second. I am Mouton.") For many years its wines have brought prices fully as high as the 1st Growths and it had been a First in all except official rank. Finally on June 21, 1973 it was accorded official First Growth status by the French Minister of Agriculture.

Its wine, perhaps the biggest, most powerful and most robust of the great clarets, is made almost entirely from the Cabernet Sauvignon grape and averages 19,000 cases a year. Often a little astringent and harsh in its youth, it is slow-maturing, exceedingly long-lived, and develops with time an almost unmistakable special character of its own, great depth of flavor, fine balance and a splendid bouquet. It has been called, with Latour, the "manliest" of the red Bordeaux, and it is a superb wine by any standards.

MOUTONNE — (Moo-tun) — Formerly the commercial name under which a popular Chablis, produced by the Long-Depaquit family, is sold; the 4⅔ acre vineyard, part of Chablis Vaudésir, is considered by some equal to a *Grand Cru* in its own name.

MUID — (Mwee) — Old and far from specific French term for a small cask or large barrel, varying in meaning from one district to another — in fact, from 250 to 685 liters.

MULLED WINE — Red wine to which sugar, lemon peel, nutmeg, cloves and occasionally cinnamon have been added; heated and served hot.

Gouache de Marc Chagall réalisée pour le Mouton Rothschild 1970

1970   *1970*

Cette récolte a produit :
315.000 Bordelaises et ½ B^{ses} de 1 à 315.000
7.000 Magnums de M 1 à M 7.000
615 Grands Formats de GF 1 à GF 615
double-magnums, jéroboams, impériales
5000 Réserve du Château marquées R.C.
Ci.

Ph. de Rothschild

Château
Mouton Rothschild

BARON PHILIPPE DE ROTHSCHILD PROPRIÉTAIRE A PAUILLAC
APPELLATION PAUILLAC CONTRÔLÉE
PRODUCE OF FRANCE
TOUTE LA RÉCOLTE MISE EN BOUTEILLES AU CHÂTEAU

MÜLLER-THURGAU — (*Mew*-lair *Tour*-gau) — Most widely-grown, productive German grape variety, one of many Riesling x Riesling crosses (until very recently thought to be Riesling x Sylvaner); yielding wines that tend to be short-lived, low in total acid, pleasing, soft, sometimes a bit flat and dull.

MUNSON, T. V. — American hybridizer from Denison, Texas. He discovered, identified and classified many species of grapes. During the phylloxera epidemic in the late 1800's he provided many of the rootstocks for the re-planting of France's devastated vineyards.

MUSCADELLE — (Mus-cad-del) — White wine grape of the Bordeaux Country, where, however, it is never cultivated or vinified alone. Interplanted with the Semillon and Sauvignon Blanc, in a proportion never exceeding 5% or 10%, it gives a faint hint of agreeable Muscat flavor to most of the sweeter Bordeaux white wines, the Sauternes and Barsacs especially

MUSCADET — (Mus-cad-day) — Light white wine produced round the old Breton capital, Nantes, in the lower Loire Valley of France. The grape from which it comes is also known locally as the Muscadet, although its true name is the Melon, and as such it was brought from Burgundy to the Loire Valley some three centuries ago; a grape of little consequence or quality elsewhere, it

241

yields, in this particular zone, a small, fresh, pale, agreeable, early-maturing wine, dry but generally not green or acid, with good fruit and a faint trace of almost muscat flavor. Up to twenty or thirty years ago it was regarded as little more than a *vin de pays,* a good, inexpensive, local wine; however, particularly since the last war, it has begun to enjoy an extraordinary vogue in Paris, throughout northern France, and even in the export trade. There are two principal producing areas: the so-called "Région de Sèvre-et-Maine," southeast of Nantes and including the important vineyard towns of Vallet, Clisson, Vertou, St. Fiacre, Gorges and Louroux-Bottereau; and the Coteaux de la Loire *(see),* up the river to the northeast. The total production of Muscadet is some 15 million gallons a year, almost all of it made by small peasant growers — although there are some 20,000 acres of vineyard, no single holding amounts to as much as fifty acres.

MUSCADINE — Native American family of vines, considered by most botanists a sub-genus of *vitis.* Wine from the Muscadine, especially from the Scuppernong, its best-known variety, has been made in the Carolinas, Florida and the Gulf States for several centuries, and at one time a single vine on Roanoke Island covered two acres of pergola and yielded 2,000 gallons of wine a year. The two main sorts of Muscadine are technically classified as *Rotundifolia* (on account of its round leaves) and *Munsoniana* (after T. V. Munson, one of the early American writers on grapes and wine). Muscadine wine has a pronounced and special flavor. Its juice requires the addition of a considerable amount of sugar to become wine at all and what it has yielded in the past could more properly be described as a sort of sweet, light cordial, with a pronounced special flavor, than as a proper, normal wine. (*See* Scuppernong.)

MUSCAT, MUSCATEL — Table, raisin and wine grape, of which literally scores of subvarieties exist, ranging all the way in color from pale yellow to blue-black, in quality from excellent to poor, in yield from prolific to shy-bearing; all, to a varying degree, have the special, characteristic, unmistakable Muscat odor and flavor, both as fresh grapes and as wine. Muscats of one sort or another are widely planted in Italy, southern France, Spain, Portugal, Greece, Tunisia, and on almost all of the Mediterranean islands, notably Sardinia, Sicily, Elba, Pantelleria, Cyprus, and the whole Aegean archipelago; also in Alsace, the Tyrol and Hungary; and, of course, very widely, in California where it is called Muscat Blanc or Muscat Canelli.

A catalogue of the various sorts of Muscat would be of more interest to a botanist than to a wine drinker: of those that produce sweet, fortified wine, perhaps the worst is the productive Muscat of Alexandria (and of California); perhaps the best is the Muscat *doré* de Frontignan *(see).* Then there is the Aleatico *(see),* which gives a red dessert wine; the Muscadelle, used in Sauternes; the Muscat Ottonel of Alsace; the Moscatello responsible for Italy's Est! Est!! Est!!!, etc. — but the list is endless. *See* also, in this volume, Moscato, Moscatello, Moscatel, and Muscadelle, as well as under the names of the districts and countries mentioned above.

MUSIGNY — (Mew-seen-yee) — One of the very greatest of red Burgundies, and the 25-acre vineyard from which it comes, directly above and behind the

Clos de Vougeot, in the *commune* of Chambolle-Musigny (*see*), to which it has given its name. The total production is well under 3,000 cases a year (plus from 50 to 100 cases of an excellent dry white wine known as Musigny Blanc). In delicacy, distinction, and that indefinable combination of qualities often called "breed," Musigny is unsurpassed by any other red wine of the Côte d'Or, or indeed of the world, and equaled by few. Lighter and sometimes called "more feminine" than Chambertin, it belongs in the same noble and incomparable class and, especially since World War II, can easily hold its own against even Romanée-Conti.

MUST — Grape juice or crushed grapes in the process of becoming wine.

MUSTY — Disagreeable odor and flavor which wines sometimes possess, generally due to the fact that the casks and the cellar itself have not been kept immaculately clean. It is related to moldy, but comes from a quite different cause, and experts can usually tell the two apart by tasting.

MUTÉ — (Mew-tay) — Unfermented or partially fermented wine, in which fermentation has been arrested, usually through the addition of high-proof brandy. Widely used in the making of apéritifs and also for blending, in order to give sweetness and body to wines that need both.

MYCODERMA ACETI — *See* ACID, ACETIC.

MYCODERMA VINI — *See* FLOR.

MYRAT, Château de — (Me-rah) — 2nd Classed Growth of Sauternes producing some 5,000 cases a year.

N

NACKENHEIM — (Nock-en-heim) — One of the very best wine-producing towns of Rheinhessen, second in quality perhaps only to Nierstein. Its vineyards directly overlook the Rhine south of Mainz; the hillside soil is the color of brick and gives wines, both from the Riesling and Sylvaner, of exceptional fruit and bouquet and breed. Best *Lagen* are Rothenberg and Engelsberg.

NAHE — (*Nah*-ha) — German river, tributary of the Rhine, which it joins at Bingen, opposite Rüdesheim. Further upstream, round Bad Kreuznach and beyond, the steep red sandstone hills are covered with vineyards, and the Nahe gives its name to one of the eleven Specified Wine Regions or Anbaugebiete (*see*) with 10,000 acres of vines yielding 5% of the German crop and consisting of 2 Bereiche, 7 Grosslagen and over 300 Einzellagen. Much of the wine is a long way from mediocre, and the Nahe wines on the whole deserve to be better known. In character they are like the good Niersteiners and Nackenheimers of Rheinhessen, with perhaps greater sprightliness. The most celebrated vineyard area, property of the German State, is Schloss Böckelheim (*see*), but there are others equally good round the valley's principal town, Kreuznach (or Bad Kreuznach) and in the villages of Niederhausen, Norheim, Roxheim, and even one called, rather confusingly, Rüdesheim, which has no connection with its more famous namesake on the Rhine.

For Map, *see* GERMANY.

NAIRAC, Château — (Nay-rack) — 2nd Classed Growth of Barsac. About 3,000 cases a year.

NANTES — (Nahnt) — Chief city of lower Brittany, on the Loire River near its mouth. A wide area of rolling hills nearby, especially to the southeast, produces the increasingly popular dry, white Muscadet (*set*), and another very pleasant, less famous dry white wine called Gros Plant (*see*).

NAPA — Celebrated California wine district, the valley and country of this name, northeast of San Francisco. The valley's lower end, south of the town of Napa, is on tidewater, and touches San Francisco Bay; the 1,800-foot summit of Mt. St. Helena, at its northern end, is often covered with snow as late as March — this, a famous landmark, was so named by a Russian princess after her patron saint, in pre-American days; it is an extinct or at least inactive volcano, and geysers and hot springs in the village of Calistoga at its foot, attest to the fact. The famous and beautiful Silverado Trail, of which Robert Louis Stevenson wrote, runs up the east side of the valley, and vineyards have been planted on the gravelly valley floor and the adjoining foothills since before 1860.

Thus rich in history and tradition, Napa is also a strikingly beautiful bit of country, its vineyards running back into wooded hills, especially on the west, and a number of California's most renowned wineries are strung along or near the main road. These include Inglenook, Beaulieu, Sterling, Louis M. Martini, Robert Mondavi, Beringer, Charles Krug, the so-called Greystone Winery of the Christian Brothers, and many smaller ones of considerable local fame — Mayacamas, Heitz, Schramsberg, Stony Hill, Joseph Phelps, Stag's Leap, Clos du Val, etc. — set back in the hills.

Essentially a district of table wines, Napa produces some of California's best, notably Cabernet Sauvignons that can stand comparison with many of the château wines of Bordeaux, sound Pinot Noirs and good Pinot Chardonnays, interesting wines from the Chenin Blanc, Sauvignon Blanc, Gamay, and many others of the better varieties. Even on lesser and semi-generic wines such as Claret, Burgundy, Chablis and the like, an indication of Napa Valley origin is almost a guarantee of above average quality.

For Map, *see* CALIFORNIA.

NAPA GOLDEN CHASSELAS — Name sometimes given, though for no sensible reason, to the Palomino grape, in California; this of course is not a Chasselas at all, nor does it do particularly well in Napa.

NASCO — (Noss-co) — Superior white dessert wine from the island of Sardinia, produced near Cagliari.

NATURE — (Nah-tewr) — In French, a wine to which nothing has been added — i.e., in its natural state. Applied to Champagne (*see*) it is now practically synonymous with *brut;* until fairly recently, Champagne *Nature* meant still, or non-sparkling, Champagne; but this refreshing and charming dry wine must now legally be offered as Coteaux Champenois. Alas! the complications of modern life.

NATURWEIN — (Nah-*toor*-vine) — One of several terms which, before 1971, on a German wine label, guaranteed that the wine was made *without* the addition of sugar, before or during fermentation. All of the finer German wines

245

were so made, including all estate-bottlings. Synonymous with *Naturwein* were the words: *natur, echt, rein, naturrein, ungezuckerter;* but wines carrying any of the following designations also had to be natural, unsugared, even if the word *Naturwein* did not appear: *Originalabfüllung, Kellerabfüllung, Kellerabzug, Schlossabzug, Wachstum, Crezenz, Gewächs, Cabinet* or *Kabinett, Fass No., Fuder No., Edel, Spätlese, Auslese.* Even under the new German Wine Law the words *Kabinett, Spätlese,* and *Auslese* still denote unsugared wines.

NÉAC — (Nay-ak) — *see* LALANDE DE POMEROL.

NEBBIOLO — (Neb-be-*o*-lo) — The outstanding red wine grape of Italy, one of the world's best. Its name comes from *nebbia* (fog), for it ripens best and gives its finest wine in districts where there is a good deal of morning fog during September, notably the regions of Piedmont and northern Lombardy. Here it produces such splendid wines as Barolo, Gattinara, Ghemme, Lessona, and the admirable Valtellina of Sondrio (*see* all of these); in less celebrated vineyard zones it nevertheless gives a very creditable red wine, this usually sold simply as Nebbiolo, and unfortunately sometimes sparkling. A shy bearer, at its best on steep hillsides, it yields full-bodied, sturdy wines, fairly high in alcohol and almost always requiring a good deal of age; when mature, these have real distinction and great class. There are some small plantings in California's Central Valley.

NEBUCHADNEZZAR — Name, variously spelled, given to a giant Champagne bottle, holding as much as twenty ordinary bottles, or 1⅔ cases. Unwieldy and ridiculous when full, it makes a conversation piece when empty.

NECKAR — (Nek-ahr) — River which flows north through Württemburg and joins the Rhine at Mannheim.

NEDERBURG — An important South African vineyard, at Klein Drakenstein, near Paarl. *See* South Africa.

NÉGOCIANT — (Nay-go–see-ah) — French, a most important link in the chain between winemaker and consumer. The Négociant is not only a wine merchant in his geographical area but is almost always an éleveur (*see*) who buys wine when it is made and "raises" it alone or combined with other wines, gives it the proper attention, bottles it when ready and ships it in proper condition. He works very closely with the local expert brokers. (*see* Courtier).

NEGRAR — (Neh-*grahr*) — Small town in the very heart of the Valpolicella area (*see*), produces some of that district's finest wine.

NEGRARA — (Neh-*grah*-ra) — Superior Italian wine grape, used in Valpolicella and Bardolino (*see*).

NEGUS — Old English tipple, often taken as a nightcap, made of Port, lemon, nutmeg and sometimes sugar and hot water, served warm.

NÉNIN, Château — (Nay-nah) — One of the largest 1st Growth vineyards of Pomerol. Some 10,000 cases a year of excellent Claret, fruity, generous and soft.

NERVEUX — (Nair-vuh) — French wine taster's term, applied to wines that are lively and well-balanced, with character, proper acidity and keeping qualities.

NEUCHÂTEL — (Nuh-shah-tel) — Perhaps the best known, although a long way from the best, white wine of Switzerland. It is produced by some 2,000 acres of vineyard along the northern shore of Lake Neuchâtel, less than twenty miles from the French border; its grape is the Chasselas, here called the Fendant, and it is a small, fresh, pale white wine, agreeable and moderately priced, as indeed it should be. Usually bottled when less than six months old, it is often *pétillant,* or slightly sparkling, in Switzerland, though not when prepared for export. A little red wine is also produced — *see* Cortaillod.

NEUMAGEN — (*Noy-*mah-gen) — Proudly claiming to be the oldest wine town in Germany, perhaps with some justification, since all sorts of Roman relics have been unearthed nearby, Neumagen is a pleasant little Mittel-Mosel village, between Trittenheim and Dhron. Its wines, now labeled Neumagen-Drohn, are hardly of first rank, are fresh, light and charming, notable for their bouquet. The best vineyards, after Hofberger, include: Rosengärtchen, Engel grube, Roterd, Laudamusberg and Grosser Hengelberg.

NEUSTADT — (*Noy-*shtat) — Substantial and prosperous little city in the German Palatinate; it produces no wines of much consequence but is an important center of the trade.

NEW YORK STATE — Although second only to California in total wine production, New York's vineyard districts are neither numerous nor impressively large. Table grapes are grown in the Chautauqua area, southwest of Buffalo on Lake Erie, and to a smaller extent in the Hudson Valley, but no wine of much consequence comes from either zone, and what really remains, therefore, are the Finger Lakes (*see*), especially Keuka and Canandaigua. Although the native varieties such as Delaware, Catawba, Elvira, Ives, Concord (*see* all of these), still make up the greater part of the state's wine production, European vinifera grapes are now growing successfully in several Finger Lakes vineyards, thanks to the efforts of Dr. Konstantin Frank, who has had especially fine results with the Chardonnay and the Riesling grapes. In addition to the vinifera plantings, several New York state producers are planting the French-American hybrids with great success, thus eliminating the "foxy" taste which many wine drinkers find objectionable in wines made from the native American varieties. *See* Hudson River.

NEW ZEALAND — Although producing wine for 150 years, it is only since the 1950's that the industry has become important. Varietal wines, especially the whites, are very well made. Production in 1976 was just short of 7,000,000 gallons.

NIAGARA — White Eastern grape, sometimes used for wine in the Finger Lakes district; what is sold under this name is usually a rather sweet, golden table wine, without much character.

NIAGARA PENINSULA — Part of Canada (*see*) lying between Lakes Erie and Ontario. The climate, tempered by the lakes, is favorable for grape growing, and most Canadian wine is produced in this area.

247

NIEDERHAUSEN — (*Nee*-der-*how*-zen) — One of the best wine-producing towns of Germany's Nahe Valley. Superior vineyards include Hermannshöhle, Hermannsberg, Pfingstweide, etc.

NIEDERMENNIG — (*Nee*-der-*men*-nig) — Little vineyard town of the Saar Valley, in Germany's Moselle district. Quite fine wines, though only in good years; Euchariusberg, Sonnenberg, Herrenberg are the best *Lagen*. The town is now known simply as Mennig, and its wines as Menniger.

NIEDERWALLUF — (*Nee*-der-*vahl*-luf) — Wine-producing town in the Rheingau. *See* Walluf.

NIERSTEIN — (*Neer*-shtein) — One of the very great names in German wine, and easily the foremost wine town of Rheinhessen: first in celebrity, first by far in vineyard acreage, and first in quality as well. Its vines overlook the Rhine south of Mainz, and produce mostly very good quality, a little of it, superb. The best is made from the Riesling grape and so states on its label; the finer vineyard sites, or *Lagen,* are: Hipping, Glöck, Bildstock, Orbel, Kranzberg, Pettenthal, Öelberg, Heiligenbaum, Paterberg and Hölle, and a vineyard name is of capital importance on a bottle of Niersteiner, since under the 1971 German Wine Law there was also created Bereich Nierstein which includes 11 Grosslagen and about 175 Einzellagen. Therefore, a great many wines of Rheinhessen can be sold as Bereich Niersteiner Gutes Domthal (which is not a single vineyard but the name of one of the three Grosslagen in which lie the vineyards of the town of Nierstein). To buy Bereich Nierstein or Niersteiner Gutes Domthal is therefore the equivalent of any old Liebfraumilch; Niersteiner, plus the name of a top vineyard, especially if called Riesling and estate-bottled is a noble wine indeed.

NOAH — Biblical patriarch, ship-builder, friend of animals, mariner, and finally wine-grower for the last three and a half centuries of his life. He is supposed to have found water insupportable as a beverage after the Flood — "it tasted of sinners . . .

Because all things corrupt therein
Both man and beast, were drowned for sin.''

On account of this, and for his undoubted piety, he was vouchsafed the vine, and generations have risen up to be thankful to him.

ALSO, a green, native, Eastern grape, widely planted by despairing growers in Europe at the time of the phylloxera. The quality of the wine it gives would have been enough to discourage Noah himself.

NOBLE — Word used, with considerable justification, of certain grape varieties, certain vineyards and certain wines that seem to possess an inherent and permanent superiority over their fellows and their neighbors. All men may be created equal, but all vines are not, nor all hillsides. A noble variety is one capable of giving outstanding wine under proper conditions, and better-than-average wine almost wherever planted, within reason. A noble vineyard yields wine of some distinction, even in poor years. A noble wine is one that will be recognized as remarkable, even by a novice.

NOBLE ROT — *see* BOTRYTIS CINEREA.

NORHEIM — (Nore-heim) — Important wine-producing town in the Nahe Valley, Germany. Best *Lagen* include Kafels, Klosterberg, Kirschheck.

NORTH COAST COUNTIES — Name given, for lack of a shorter and better one, to California's one truly distinguished district of fine wine, of which the center is San Francisco Bay. Not all the counties in question touch the Pacific, but they share, in general, the cool, coastal climate, and although the area has never been legally defined, it is generally considered to include, from north to south, the following counties: Mendocino, Lake, Sonoma, Napa, Solano, Contra Costa, Alameda (Livermore), San Mateo, Santa Clara, Stanta Cruz, San Benito, Monterey to which must be added San Luis Obispo and Santa Barbara.

For Map, *see* CALIFORNIA.

NORTON — One of the better American red wine grapes, very little foxy flavor.

NOSE — Wine taster's term for bouquet or aroma; this is a neutral sort of word (like taste) and there is no connotation of superior quality.

NOSTRANO — (No-*strah*-no) — Name given by the peasant wine-producers of Italian Switzerland (round Locarno and Lugano in the Ticino, or Canton of Tessin) to the European vinifera vine, and the wine it gives, as compared with what is called Americano (*see*). Literally, it means "ours," and is used in this special sense in parts of northern Italy as well. Most Nostrano wine is made from a variety known as the Bondola, but there are increasingly important plantings in the Ticino of Merlot, Nebbiolo, Freisa and other better red wine grapes.

NOUVEAU — (Noo-vo) — *see* VIN NOUVEAU.

NOVITIATE OF LOS GATOS — Jesuit Seminary founded in 1888 at Los Gatos, on the western edge of the Santa Clara Valley, California; admirably situated hillside vineyards form a good part of its endowment, and wines are made under the supervision of the Jesuit fathers, most of the actual work being done by Jesuit brothers, and novices, or students. A large part of the production is altar wine, available only to the clergy, but some table wines of good quality are sold to the general public under both varietal and generic names, as well as two unusual specialties in the way of dessert wines, a Black Muscat and a Muscat Frontignan.

NU — (noo) — French, naked; i.e. Prix Nu — price of wine without cask or bottles.

NUITS — (Nwee) — *See* CÔTE DE NUITS; also NUITS-SAINT-GEORGES, below.

NUITS-SAINT-GEORGES — (Nwee San Zhorzh) — Celebrated Burgundian town on the Côte de Nuits, to which it has given its name. An insignificant amount of white wine is produced (*see* Pierrière), but the admirable reds, while rarely of the very topmost class, are typical and great Burgundies, generous, sturdy, well-balanced; in certain years those from the less good *climats* (usually sold at Nuits-Saint-Georges, without a vineyard name) often have a characteristic earthy flavor, or *goût de terroir*. The adjoining village of Prémeaux is considered part of Nuits, as far as its wines are concerned. The best vineyards of the two *communes* include the following: Les Saint-Georges, Les Pruliers, Les Cailles, Les Vaucrains, Les Boudots, Clos des Corvées, Les Porrets, Clos des Argilières, Les Perdrix, Château Gris, Clos de Thorey, Les Richemones, Les Murgers, Clos de la Maréchale, Clos Arlot, etc. The terms "Nuits" and "Nuits-Saint-Georges," followed by a vineyard name, mean precisely the same thing and are interchangeable.

NUTTY — Having a flavor and aroma reminiscent of walnuts or, especially, hazel-nuts. Most often applied to Sherries.

O

OAK — The one wood used for barrels, casks, butts, pipes, puncheons and the like (much less commonly for vats, tanks, *cuves* and such larger cooperage) in which wine can almost be counted on to develop and improve; chestnut and redwood are acceptable substitutes, but more neutral and far less good, especially for red wines. All of the fine red wines of the world and most fortified wines owe part of their quality to the oak in which they have been stored. Nearly every wine-producing district has its special and cherished source of supply. New oak barrels are used every year by many of the leading Bordeaux and Burgundy producers in order to give added tannin and other less-easily defined qualities to the new wine. However, if kept too long in oak, new oak especially, these and all other table wines tend to become "withered" or "*sechés*" (*see*), and eventually "woody" or "oaky." In their enthusiasm some California wineries have produced white wines having more the qualities of oak extract than of vinosity, but the tide is turning to a proper balance of flavors.

OBEREMMEL — (O-burr-*em*-m'l) — Little wine-producing village of the Saar, in Germany, adjoining Wiltingen. There are some 200 acres of vineyard, planted in Riesling grapes, and the wines in good and great vintage years are of extremely high quality, light, flowery, somewhat austere. The best *Lagen* include: Hütte, Altenberg, Karlsberg, Rosenberg, Agritiusberg, Raul.

OBERINGELHEIM — (O-burr-*ing*-gel-*heim*) — *See* INGELHEIM.

OBERNAI — (*O*-bair-nay) — Picturesque walled town in northern Alsace,

252

southwest of Strasbourg; its wines are less good than those of nearby villages — Barr, Goxwiller, Mittelbergheim.

OCKFEN — (Awk-fen) — One of the very great white wine villages of the world, in the Saar Valley, near Wiltingen, in Germany. There are some 200 acres of Rieslings, planted on one incredibly steep, slate hillside: in favorable years such as 1953 and 1971 these produce white wines unsurpassed by those of any other German or French vineyard, and therefore in the world. Very light, almost steely, elegant, with a bouquet that can only be called incomparable, they are remarkable, and worth whatever they cost; in secondary years, they are hard and often green and acid. Best vineyard sites are Bockstein, Herrenberg, Geisberg, and Heppenstein.

OECHSLE — (Uhk-sleh) — The usual ·German and Swiss equivalent of our Balling (see) as a measurement of the sugar content of must density, or grape juice before fermentation, and as fairly exact indication of the future alcoholic content of the resulting wine. The *"Grad Oeschsle,"* divided by 8, gives this figure, but it is important to remember that this includes, quite often, the grape sugar, or sweetness, of an Auslese or Spätlese, which is never converted into alcohol and remains in the wine. Thus a great Auslese, of 120° Oechsle, would not end up as a dry wine of 15% alcohol, but as a sweet wine of perhaps 12%, or even less.

OEIL DE PERDRIX — (Oiy d'Pair-dree) — Literally, in French, "partridge-eye," used to describe the color of certain wines made from black grapes which are in fact very light and pale *rosés*. The old term has its charm, and it means a sort of combination of very pale pink and bronze. Few wines have this color any more and almost none are so labeled.

OENOLOGY — *see* ENOLOGY

OENOMEL — (Ee-no-mel) — Old-fashioned beverage made of grape juice and honey, fermented together. The author of these lines has never to his knowledge tasted it.

OENOTHÈQUE — (Ee-no-tek) — French, wine library, bottled wine collection for display, reference and tasting.

OESTERREICHER — (Ay-ster-rike-ker) — Literally, in German, means the "Austrian" — a name often given to the Sylvaner (see) variety of grape in the Rheingau. Whether the Sylvaner is actually of Austrian origin is at least doubtful.

OESTRICH — (Ay-strik) — With some 750 acres under vines, probably the largest wine-producing township in the Rheingau, directly overlooking the Rhine between Hattenheim and Winkel. Most of the vineyards are on fairly flat land and most of the wines are of second quality. Exceptions are those from the best vineyard sites, as: Lenchen, Doosberg and Klosterberg.

OFF — Perhaps the broadest and least specific term of disapprobation which can be applied to a wine. Basically, it means abnormal. An "Off Taste" is a taste which the wine should not have, for whatever reason and from whatever cause. It may be a fault that will soon correct itself due, for example, to the fact that the wine has been shaken up; it may be a real and permanent flaw, like moldiness. "Off" should *not*, however, be used of a wine, however poor, which is simply coarse, or thin, or grapey (because made from a special variety of grape), or earthy. It means abnormal.

OHIO — In pre-Civil War days and, in fact, until the first trans-continental railway was completed, Ohio was by far America's most important wine-producing state, and its wines were rated even more highly than those of the Finger Lakes district of New York. The earliest vineyards were planted by German settlers along the Ohio River, east and west of Cincinnati, where the steep hills overlooking the swift Ohio recalled the landscape of the Rhine, and inspired the most optimistic prophecies concerning the district's viticultural future. Mr. Nicholas Longworth was one of the first pioneers to establish an Ohio wine business national in scope; relying mostly on the Catawba grape, he had, by the 1850's, opened a New York sales agency and was selling his still and sparkling Catawba at prices quite comparable to those which French and German wines then commanded. Some of these wines actually received medals at fairs and expositions in Europe and were widely known.

Somewhat later, grapes began to be planted on a fairly large scale along the southern shore of Lake Erie, west of Cleveland, especially around Sandusky, and on the Lake Erie islands. The lake itself helped to protect the vines against spring and early fall frosts, and a substantial industry existed well into the present century and, in fact, until Prohibition. Although some vineyards are still in production, and Ohio still produces several million gallons of wine a year, its comparative importance in the field of wine has greatly declined; the best-known shipper, accounting for a major proportion of the total volume, is Meiers Wine Cellars at Silverton, Ohio, near Cincinnati. Most of the grapes are still grown near Sandusky and the once celebrated Ohio River vineyard slopes are almost entirely a matter of history today.

OIDIUM — Also called powdery mildew, a fungus, probably of American origin, which attacks the leaves, shoots and tendrils of the vine. It caused enormous damage in European vineyards when it first appeared there, in the mid-19th century, and is still troublesome, although it can now be controlled by the use of Bordeaux Mixture (*see*).

OLIVIER, Château — (O-leave-E-A) — Well-known and popular dry white Graves. About 10,000 cases a year. Château Olivier is in the township of Léognan (*see*) and produces about 2,000 cases of red wine which also carries this name; both red and white are *Crus Classés*.

OLOROSO — (O-lo-*ro*-so) — One of the two basic types of Spanish Sherry, Fino being the other; literally, the word means *"que huele bien,"* or *"*of agreeable odor,*"* and an old, high quality Oloroso possesses in fact as intense, typical and recognizable a bouquet as any wine in the world. Darker in color than the Finos, ranging from dark gold to deep amber, fuller-bodied, generally higher in alcohol (18-21%), Oloroso Sherries are developed and matured without the flor yeasts which give the Finos their special character and quality. Few are shipped in their natural bone-dry state, but are sweetened to please the public palate, and Olorosos can be anywhere from not-quite-dry to luscious and very sweet, as Cream Sherry and "East India." They are mostly properly classified as dessert wines or after-dinner wines, and are conventionally served at room temperature although some prefer them chilled.

OLTREPÓ PAVESE — (Ohl-treh-*po* Pah-veh-seh) — The wine basket of Lombardy, this large area on the south bank of the Pó River provides three quarters of the wine consumed in Milan. All types of wine are produced — red, dry and sweet white, rosé and sparkling wines as well, all under the proper conditions entitled to the D. O. C. Best known wines are Barbacarlo, Barbera, Bonarda, Buttafuoco, Cortese, Sangue de Guida and varietals such as Moscato, Pinot, Riesling, etc.

ONCTUEUX — (Awnk-tew-uh) — French word, of which the literal English translation is "unctuous"; the French sounds better when applied to wine. It is used exclusively to describe full-bodied wines that are quite sweet, soft, "fat," high in glycerine, and of good quality: the great Sauternes are prime examples.

OPORTO — Second city of Portugal, on the Douro River not far from its mouth: it has given its name to what is perhaps the most famous of all dessert wines. Port (*see*), which is produced in a delimited zone up the Douro Valley to the east. According to Portuguese law, all wines called Porto must be shipped either from Oporto or from Vila Nova de Gaia, directly across the river. It is an attractive and picturesque old town, full of the "lodges" and warehouses of the great Porto shippers, a great many of whom are English, as might be expected. (*See* PORTO.)

OPPENHEIM — (*O*-pen-heim) — Important wine-producing town, directly south of Nierstein, in Rheinhessen, Germany. The vineyards lie mostly south of the village, and gently sloping soil that falls away toward Dienheim and the flat plain in the direction of Worms. The wines, although of good class, are well below the Niersteiners in quality, softer and with less breed. The better *Lagen* include: Kreuz, Stackträger, Herrenberg, Gutleuthaus, Schlossberg, etc.

ORANGE — (O-rawnj) — Interesting old town of the lower Rhône Valley, north of Avignon. It was called *Arausio* in Roman days, and still has some exceedingly impressive ruins; its ruling family, the Princes of Orange, eventually became kings of Holland and then of England. It is today the center of an important wine-producing district, with Châteauneuf-du-Pape to its south, and Gigondas, Cairanne, Vacqueras, Rasteau, etc., off to the east and northeast.

ORDINAIRE — (Or-dee-nair) — French for common or ordinary. As applied to wine, one of unknown or unstated origin, sold simply as *vin rouge, vin blanc,* or *vin rosé* but of specified alcoholic content. It would be safe to say that fully half of all French wine consumed in France is so marketed.

ORDINARY — *See* Ordinaire. A rather loose term, in English, never legally defined, applied to cheap, common table wines without special character or fault.

255

ORGANOLEPTIC — Applied to the evaluation or judgment of wines, what can be determined or perceived by the senses (taste, smell and sight) rather than by physical or chemical analysis, in a laboratory. An expert's organoleptic examination will generally give a far better and more exact idea of a wine's marketability, quality and value than the tests of any laboratory technician, however competent.

ORIGINALABFÜLLUNG — (O-rig-ee-nahl-ahb-fue-lung) — Before 1971 the most widely used of several German terms meaning Estate-Bottling. Generally abbreviated to *Orig.-Abfg.*, it was a positive guarantee of authenticity, when followed by the producer's name, and almost never abused. Only *Naturwein* (unsugared, un-chaptalized) could be so labeled and all great German wines carried this designation, or one of its equivalents, on their labels. Replaced in 1971 by Erzeugerabfüllung (*see*).

ORLÉANNAIS — (Or-lay-awn-nay) — Little wine-growing district, principally on the right bank of the Loire, west and therefore downstream from Orléans. Most of the vineyards, important and celebrated a century ago, have disappeared, and the great British expert, P. Morton Shand, has quoted a brief refrain that sounds today like their requiem:

> *"Orléans, Beaugency*
> *Nôtre-Dame-de-Cléry*
> *Vendôme! Vendôme!"*

Once planted in such *cépages nobles* as Pinot Noir, Chardonnay and Cabernet, most of the vineyards that remain are in Pinot Meunier today and some of them produce, especially around Beaugency, a fresh and very agreeable *vin rosé,* excellent as a *vin du pays,* but hardly deserving of wider fame. The rest is history and legend.

ORTSTEIL — (Orts-tile) — German word meaning "part of a community" — a suburb or section. Under the new German Wine Law, which went into effect with the 1971 vintage, several famous vineyards or vineyard estates were granted the right to continue using their own names without any reference to the town or village in which they are actually located. The most famous vineyards with *Ortsteil* status are Schloss Johannisberg, Schloss Vollrads, and the Steinberg, all in the Rheingau, and the Scharzhofberg on the Saar.

ORVIETO — (Or-vee-*eh*-toe) — Famous cathedral town in Umbria, Italy, and its popular, light white wine, occasionally *secco* (dry), more often *abboccato* (slightly sweet). It used to be shipped in squat little straw-covered *fiaschi* called *pulcianelle* but today is mostly in straight Bordeaux type bottles. The Orvieto vineyards are like no others on earth: some of the grapes come from what the Italians call *coltura promiscua* (*see*). The wine, while hardly remarkable, is often, nevertheless, quite good, with its own kind of character and lightness.

OUILLAGE — (We-ahj) — *see* ULLAGE.

OUVRÉE — (Oo-vray) — Old Burgundian measure of area, equal to about one-eighth of a *journal,* or .0428 hectare, roughly one-tenth of an acre.

OXIDIZED — Said of a wine, especially a white wine, which has had too much contact with the air, has lost its freshness and perhaps darkened in color, and is on the way to becoming maderised (*see*). Such wines never recover, and should either be drunk immediately or thrown away.

P

PAARL — (Parl) — River and town in Cape Province, South Africa; the Paarl Valley, directly west of Capetown, comprises one of the best Cape wine districts. *See* South Africa.

PACHERENC DU VIC-BILH — (Posch-a-rank dew Veek-Beel) — Curious, fairly sweet white wine, somewhat comparable to that of Jurançon, produced north of Pau, in southwestern France. Its odd name comes from the local dialect, in which Pacherenc, or *pachet-en-renc,* means ''pickets in rank,'' these vineyards having been the first in this part of France to be planted in the modern fashion, with the vines in regular rows and a picket, or prop, for each vine. Vic-Bilh is the name of a small, hilly district round the village of Portet, south of the Adour River.

PACHINO — (Pa-*key*-no) — A red wine, light purple in color, rather high in alcohol, almost always drunk young, produced (and largely consumed) in the province of Siracusa (Syracuse) in Sicily. Rarely if ever exported.

PADENGHE — (Pa-*deng*-gay) — Village near the southwestern shore of Lake Garda, in northern Italy; produces largely Chiaretto (*see*) plus a few red and *rosé* wines sold under its name.

PAILLE — (Pie) — French word meaning simply ''straw''; a *vin de paille,* however, is a white wine made from grapes that have been allowed to dry and almost become raisins, on straw mats, occasionally in the sun but more commonly indoors. The resulting wine is, of course, sweet, golden, usually quite high in alcohol. The most famous *vins de paille,* produced in extremely limited quantity, are those of Hermitage *(see)*, and the Jura *(see)*. *See also Passito.*

PAJARETE — *see* PAXARETE.

PALATINATE — (Pal-*lat*-teen-ate) — Major German wine-producing district, on the left bank of the Rhine, just north of Alsace *(see* Rheinpfalz).

PALESTINE — *See* ISRAEL.

PALETTE — (Pah-let) — Red, *rosé* and white wine made not far from Aix-en-Provence, near Marseille, in southern France, where it enjoys a certain, hardly merited, local fame. There are only about 8,000 cases produced per year, but the name is an *Appellation Contrôlée.*

PALMER, Château — (Pahl-mair) — 3rd Classed Growth of Cantenac-Margaux. Outstanding Bordeaux vineyard which has consistently produced, since World War II, better wine than most of the 2nd Growths — in 1955, and again in 1961, among the very best of the Médoc. Some 10,000 cases a year of admirably balanced claret, which to quote one French authority, is *"tendre, élégant et bouqueté."* *(see* Desmirail)

PALO CORTADO — (Pah-low Core-tah-doe) — An intermediate classification of Sherry, the lightest of the Olorosos.

PALOMINO — Principal grape grown in Jerez de la Frontera for making Sherry *(see)*; also grown in California to a large extent where it produces good local sherry and very bad table wine.

PALUS — (Pah-loo) — French word meaning originally "swamp" or "marsh," now applied in the Bordeaux Country to the areas of meadowland or reclaimed alluvial soil along the river banks. Little such land is planted to vineyard and most of the *palus* are specifically excluded from the delimited zones of *Appellations Contrôlées.* Vines on such soil are usually extremely productive but never yield wines of any quality.

PANADES — (Pah-nah-*des*) — Region in Catalonia, northeast Spain, which produces fine Moscatel and Malvasia sweet wines as well as red, *rosé* and white table wines of quality. Much sparkling wine (Espumoso) is made, Spain's best, primarily by the *méthode champenoise,* and the largest sparkling wine cellar in the world is in the area.

PANIER À VENDANGE — (Pan-yea ah Vawn-dawnj) — Wicker basket of any one of many shapes and sizes (usually a matter of local tradition) in which grapes are harvested and transported at vintage time.

PANIER-VERSEUR — (Pan-yea Vair-ser) — *See* CRADLE.

PAPE CLÉMENT, Château — (Pahp Clay-mah) — Excellent and ancient vineyard in the *commune* of Pessac, Graves, first planted in 1300 by Bertrand de Goth, Bishop of Bordeaux, who became Pope Clément V in 1305. Some 5,000 cases a year of fine red wine, one of the best of Graves.

PAPE, Le, Château — (Luh Pahp) — Excellent small vineyard of Léognan, in the Graves district of Bordeaux; it produces some 1,500 cases a year of fine red wine, which deserves to be better known, and 1,000 cases of even more remarkable white, hard to come by, but one of Bordeaux's best.

PARISH — In Great Britain (and in Louisiana), a township as well as an ecclesiastical division. Many English writers on wine correctly use "parish" as the equivalent of the French *commune;* this is not general American usage, however, and the U.S., "parish" has the same meaning as the French, *paroisse,* whereas "township" means *commune.*

PARNAY — (Par-nay) — Village on the Loire, east (upstream) from Saumur; its red, white and *rosé* wines are of high quality, entitled to the appellation Saumur under which they are almost always sold. The most famous estate is the Château de Parnay, long the property of Monsieur Cristal, who, during the early years of this century, was among the most celebrated pioneers of modern viticulture in France.

PARSAC-SAINT-ÉMILION — (Par-sack Sant A-me-lee-aw) — One of the less distinguished of the secondary districts adjoining St. Émilion and entitled to the name in this combined form or may be labeled Montagne-Saint-Émilion. Rather full wines that usually lack class; 75,000 cases a year.

PASSÉ — (Pah-say) — French term, applied to a wine which is too old, past its prime, on the decline.

PASSE-TOUT-GRAINS — (Pahss Too Gran) — Red or *rosé* Burgundy wine, rarely from one of the better *communes,* made from Pinot Noir and Gamay grapes crushed together; it must now contain at least one-third of Pinot Noir. Labeled "Bourgogne-Passe-Tout-Grains," it is a rather common wine, generally inexpensive.

PASSITO — (Pass-*see*-toe) — An Italian wine made from grapes that have been partially dried or raisined, whether outdoors or under cover, generally a dessert wine, although such grapes are also used in the making of many Italian dry wines (*see* Governo). Most *Vin Santo* (*see*) is so made, as are many Moscato and Malvasia wines as well, such as Caluso (*see*), Enfer (*see*), etc.

PASSOVER WINE — A type of Kosher wine (*see*) used during the Seder meal, the first night of Pesach or Passover, the Jewish celebration of the sparing of the eldest child during the beginning of the Exodus.

PASTEUR, Louis (1822-1895) — Eminent French scientist, who first determined the true nature of the fermentation which produces wine, and the cause and cure of many of wine's maladies. He gave his name to the celebrated Institut Pasteur in Paris, to the process of pasteurization, and his considered opinion that "wine is the most hygienic and healthful of beverages."

PASTEURIZATION — Process of sterilizing wines and other liquids by heating them (usually to between 130° and 170° F.) so that the microorganisms they contain are destroyed, rendering them stable. This of course cuts short the development and possibility of improvement of a superior wine, and fine wines are rarely pasteurized. There is nothing illegal or wrong about the pasteurization of common table or dessert wines, destined for early consumption.

PASTO — *See* VINO DA PASTO, VINO DE PASTO. In general, means a wine that can be drunk at table, with food, even when applied to Sherry.

PATRAS — One of the better known Greek wines, usually white and fortified; less often, an agreeable red or *rosé* wine from the province of Achaea, near Athens.

PATRIMONIO — (Pah-tree-*mo*-nee-o) — One of the best-known varieties of Corsican wine, produced round St. Florent, on the northwest coast of the island, between Ile Rousse and Bastia. A red (sometimes labeled Cervione), a white and a *rosé* exist, all of good quality, the *rosé*, especially; all three are full-bodied and high in alcohol. They can occasionally be found (outside Corsica) in restaurants in Marseille and on the Riviera and even in Paris.

PAUILLAC — (Paw-yack) — Celebrated little town in the Haut-Médoc, perhaps the most remarkable wine-growing township in the world. Within its communal limits are produced a number of the very greatest red wines of France: Château Lafite, Chateau Latour, Chateau Mouton-Rothschild, and many others of almost equal reputation and class, as Pichon-Longueville, Pichon-Longueville-Lalande, Lynch-Bages, Pontet-Canet, Batailley, etc., etc. All these, of course, carry the words *"Apellation Pauillac Contrôlée"* on their labels, and not much wine is sold simply as Pauillac. The wines of Pauillac, in good years, are "classic" Clarets in every sense of the word; full-bodied, long-lived, with great bouquet and a special, incomparable distinction — at their best they are beyond praise.

PAUL, Saint (d. 67 A.D.) — Apostle who wrote to his friend Timothy: "Drink no longer water, but use a little wine for thy stomach's sake and thine often infirmities."

PAULÉE — (Paul-ay) — End of vintage celebration. Nowadays the only one left is the Paulée de Meursault which is the third of the "Trois Glorieuses" (*see*).

PAVIE, Château — (Pah-*V*) — Large and well-known 1st Growth vineyard of St. Émilion. Some 12,000 cases a year of sound Claret, rarely remarkable but consistently good. Château Pavie-Macquin and Château Pavie-Decesse nearby produce wine of somewhat lesser quality.

PAXARETE or PAJARETE — (Pa-ha-re-tay) — Very dark sweet wine made in the Sherry district of Spain by combining wine with Arrope or Sancocho; no longer consumed as a beverage but occasionally used as a "blending sherry."

PAYS — (Pay-*ee*) — Common, widely used French word, of which the original and basic meaning is "country"; *mon pays* can mean the village where one was born, a district, the city of Paris, France itself. Applied to wine, Vin *de* Pays is the third classification for table wines following Appellation Contrôlée and V.D.Q.S. The labels must show the origin, usually the name of a Départment. The expression vin *du* pays has a different meaning. In an area it refers to the wine produced in that area and can be of any quality from poor to exalted.

PÉCHARMANT — (Pay-char-maw) — Fresh and attractive little red wine produced just outside Bergerac, in southwestern France. The grape varieties (Cabernet, Malbec, Merlot) are those of red Bordeaux, and in character Pécharmant is not unlike a lesser wine of the Médoc. Total production is about 16,000 cases a year.

PEDESCLAUX, Château — (Ped-ess-clo) — 5th Classed Growth of Pauillac, Haut-Médoc. Produces some 7,000 cases a year.

PEDICEL — Botanical name for the short stem which connects the individual grape with the bunch of which it is a part.

PEDRO XIMÉNEZ — (*Pay*-dro He-*may*-nays) — Spanish grape variety, widely grown in the Montilla, Málaga and Sherry districts. According to a highly unlikely story, it was brought to Spain in the 16th century by a German soldier, one Peter Siemens (whence its name), and is in fact the Riesling grape of the Rhine Valley. In Montilla (*see*) where it predominates, it gives a fine, dry wine, somewhat fuller-bodied and higher in natural alcohol than what the Palomino yields round Jerez, and often sold in its unfortified state as a 15-16% wine; in Málaga and the Sherry Country it is differently vinified — grapes are laid out in the sun for two weeks or more and allowed to raisin, then fermented and fortified, so that the resulting wine is very sweet. Well-aged, this becomes what is usually called "P.X.," the best of all sweetening agents for Sherry, and the most expensive; it is sometimes drunk straight, practically as a liqueur.

PEDUNCLE — Botanical term for the stalk by which a bunch of grapes is attached to the vine.

PELLINGEN — (Pel-ling-en) — Small wine-producing village in the Saar Valley of Germany. Its best vineyard is the Jesuitengarten, owned entirely by the Friedrich-Wilhelm Gymnasium.

PELURE D'OIGNON — (Pay-loor Dawn-yaw) — Literally, means "onion skin" in French; with respect to wine, the special russet-brown or tawny tinge which certain red wines acquire as they grow old. Also any light red or *rosé* which has this color.

PERELADA — (*Pair*-ray-*la*-da) — Small wine-producing town on the Spanish side of the Pyrénées, inland from the Costa Brava and just north of Figueras. Its wines include a very acceptable and popular *rosé*, a somewhat less good red and white, and a sparkling wine which was not long ago the subject of a celebrated legal controversy; shipped to London as "Spanish Champagne," its use of the name was challenged in the British courts by the French *Institut des Appellations d'Origine,* which eventually emerged victorious and thereby reconfirmed the exclusive right, under British law, of French Champagne producers to the name "Champagne."

PERFUME — Loosely used tasting term, which properly means fragrance or aroma (qualities which a young wine possesses and which come from the grape) rather than bouquet, which a wine acquires as it matures.

PÉRIGNON — *See* DOM PÉRIGNON.

PERLANT — (Pair-lah) — French term, not legally defined but meaning a wine *very* slightly sparkling (less so than *crémant* or *pétillant*) and almost always naturally and accidentally and temporarily so. The German equivalent is *spritzig*.

PERLWEIN — (*Pairl*-vine) — In German, a slightly sparkling wine, one deliberately so vinified and made — *see pétillant*. Wines in this category have become very popular of late in Germany — they are fresh and agreeable and inexpensive, never outstanding.

PERNAND-VERGELESSES — (Pair-nah   Vair-juh-less) — Small village in Burgundy, just west, up a side valley, from Aloxe-Corton (*see*). Its very finest wines, both red and white, do not carry the village name at all but are sold, quite legally and properly, as Corton, Corton-Charlemagne, and even Aloxe-Corton. What goes to market as Pernand-Vergelesses can nevertheless be very good (at least as good as most of what is labeled Aloxe-Corton or Savigny-les-Beaune) and has the advantage of being not very well-known and therefore relatively inexpensive. One wholly remarkable red wine, not very far in quality from the best of Corton itself, and worth investigating wherever found, comes from a single *climat* in Pernand, called Ile-de-Vergelesses — this, estate-bottled by a good producer in a great vintage, is about the best value in the way of red Burgundy that exists today.

PERRIÈRE — (Per-ry-*air*) — Name, presumably from the French, *pierre,* or stone, given to many stony vineyards, notably four in Burgundy: the Clos de la Perrière in Fixin (*see*), at the northern end of the Côte de Nuits, gives a red wine of real distinction and fine texture; the Perrière vineyard of Nuits-Saint-Georges yields one of the rare white wines of its district; the *climat* of Perrière (or Perrières) in Meursault is perhaps that little town's best and produces one of the finest full-bodied, dry white wines of France; Puligny-Montrachet Perrières fully deserves its rank as a *Premier Cru.*

PERSISTENCE — The lingering and pleasant taste which remains after a wine is swallowed. Good wines are always *long,* their flavor remaining up to half a minute for the greatest sweet whites. The number of seconds of persistence is the caudalie (*see*).

PERU — One of the first South American countries to produce wine. Only about 2 million gallons are produced, much of it Muscat which is distilled into Pisco brandy which in turn is the main ingredient of the Pisco Sour, a fine drink, basically a sour with egg white.

PESSAC — (Pess-sac) — Celebrated wine-producing *commune* just west of Bordeaux, now practically a suburb. Its wines include some of the very finest of red Graves: Châteaux Haut-Brion, Pape Clément, etc.

PÉTILLANT — (Pay-tee-yaw) — French term meaning slightly sparkling, or "crackling," as *frizzante* in Italian and *perlwein* in German. By semi-official international accord, such wines may not have a pressure in excess of two atmospheres (four atmospheres is the *minimum* for wine classified as sparkling, including Champagne) and most of the French ones such as Vouvray, where the term is most commonly used, have far less. French Appellation Contrôlée pétillant wines must have a minimum bottle age of nine months. Despite much that has been written on the subject, by people who should know better, this sparkle is hardly every accidental or natural, but the planned result of special methods of vinification. Such wines are often agreeable and fresh and charming, and it is certainly absurd that they should be compelled to pay in the U.S., on account of this slight effervescence, a tenfold tax as compared with still wines. Because of this tax, few are ever imported.

PETIT — (Peh-tee) — Means "little" or "small" in French, and when applied to wine, is much more unfavorable than its English equivalent. A *petit vin* is a small wine, low in alcohol, deficient in body, of no real value of consequence. Petit Chablis (*see below*) is a rare, accidental exception.

PETIT CHABLIS — (Peh-tee Shab-lee) — Very agreeable, rather short-lived white wine, pale, dry and refreshing, made from the Chardonnay grape in 270 acres of certain parts of the Chablis district and a few *communes* which directly adjoin it, where the soil is less chalky and the exposure less good. It was formerly called *"Bourgogne des Environs de Chablis";* actually, it is, as its name indicates, a small Chablis, interesting only in good vintage years, an excellent lesser wine in its youth.

PETIT VERDOT — (Peh-tee Vair-doe) — Superior red grape of the Bordeaux Country, grown generally on combination with the Cabernets, Merlot, Malbec, etc. It gives a full-bodied, deep-colored, slow-maturing wine, high in tannin.

PETIT VILLAGE, Château — (Peh-tee Vee-lahj) — One of the best vineyards of Pomerol, properly ranked as a *Premier Grand Cru*. Its wines are rather firm and slow to mature, but acquire with time great bouquet and distinction. Some 4,500 cases a year.

PETITE SIRAH — (Peh-teet See-rah) — Name given in California to a red wine grape which is presumed to be the Syrah (*see*) of the Rhône Valley in France. There are some 4,000 acres, in Napa and Sonoma counties and in the Central Valley: it ranks seventh in total acreage among red wine grapes in the State. Until recently it was a satisfactory full-bodied *ordinaire*, deep-colored, rather common, with little in the way of true varietal character or bouquet, and after blending it usually ended up as something called "California Burgundy"; now, however, with special care it is producing some full bodied wines sold as varietals. Far more productive than the true Syrah of Hermitage, Châteauneuf-du-Pape and Côte Rôtie, with none of the distinguished qualities or even the faults of its supposed French ancestor, it is probably not the Syrah at all, but a common variety called the Duriff, which was widely planted in the Rhône Valley a century ago but no longer grown in any French vineyard entitled to an *Appellation Contrôlée* (*see* Electrophoreses).

PÉTRUS, Château — (Pay-trewss) — Without question the best vineyard of Pomerol, now ranked (although unofficially, to be sure) on a par with the great 1st Growth Clarets of the Médoc, with Château Haut-Brion, Mouton-Rothschild and Cheval Blanc. Its production is in the neighborhood of 5,000 cases. The wine is outstanding, soft and good even in mediocre years and, at its best, velvety, *gras*, admirably balanced, with great bouquet and breed. It is planted 95% in Merlot grapes (*see*).

PEYRAGUEY — *See* HAUT-PEYRAGUEY and LAFAURIE-PEYRAGUEY.

PEZ, Château de — (Pez) — Very good *cru bourgeois* in Saint-Estèphe, producing up to 10,000 cases of somewhat softer wine than its neighbors.

PFALZ — (Pfahltz) — *See* RHEINPFALZ.
For Map, *see* RHEINPFALZ.

pH — (P-H) — *See* ACIDITY, REAL.

PHÉLAN-SÉGUR, Château — (Fay-law Say-gour) — Good *bourgeois* growth of St. Estèphe, Haut-Médoc, produces up to 20,000 cases annually.

PHYLLOXERA — (Fill-*lox*-er-ra) — An insect, or plant louse, which is, of all the many enemies of the vine, perhaps the most devastating, whence its Latin name, *phylloxera vastatrix*. It apparently has always existed in the eastern part of the United States, but the native American vines are resistant to it, largely

266

on account of their heavier and tougher roots. It was accidentally introduced into Europe, on vine cuttings brought over for experimental purposes, about 1860, and within two decades it destroyed, in France alone, some 2½ million acres of vineyard, and doubtless as wide an extent in other wine-producing countries, since the *vitis vinifera,* from which almost all the world's good wines are made, is almost fatally vulnerable to its attack. Countless remedies and preventive measures were proposed and attempted; none with any real degree of lasting success until native American vine stocks were brought over and the European vine grafted on these resistant roots. Many varieties of American vine, and innumerable crosses of these, have been planted, *vitis riparia, vitis rupestris, vitis berlandieri,* and many others, and practically all European wines now come from vines grafted on American roots. This is also the case in California, where the phylloxera crossed the Rockies and laid waste the vineyards in the 1880's. At the moment, the insect seems less dangerous, no longer existing in its winged, more infectious form, and a few bold California vintners have planted ungrafted *vinifera* vines, so far successfully, in Monterey County and other places where vines have not grown previously and therefore have no infestation in the soil.

There has been much discussion, pro and con, as to whether the great European wines are as good or have ever been as good, since made from the grapes of grafted vines, as they were before. This is the sort of question that will never find a proper and certain answer, and since pre-phylloxera wines hardly now exist, it is hardly worth arguing about.

267

PICHET — (Pee-shay) — French term for a small jug or pitcher of earthenware or wood, often used in restaurants for serving "open" wine at table.

PICHON-LONGUEVILLE, Château — (Pee-shaw Long-veel) — 2nd Classed Growth of Pauillac. One of the most consistent of the 2nd Growths and one of the best Clarets of Pauillac. The vineyard directly adjoins Château Latour, and is often referred to as "Pichon-Longueville-Baron," to distinguish it from Pichon-Longueville-Comtesse-de-Lalande; it yields some 9,000 cases of wine a year, round, fine, well-balanced, yet fairly full-bodied and long-lived.

PICHON-LONGUEVILLE-LALANDE, Château — (Pee-shaw Long-veel La-lawnd) — 2nd Classed Growth of Pauillac. Just across the road from Pichon-Longueville and equally good, although its wine is of a quite different character and type, being lighter, with more fruit and finesse, due partly, no doubt, to a higher proportion of Merlot and therefore less Cabernet Sauvignon in the vineyard. There are some 15,000 cases a year of this "Pichon de la Comtesse" in a plentiful year.

PICKING BOXES — Instead of the picturesque wicker baskets generally used in Europe at vintage time, American growers more often use wooden boxes, or lugs: these can be stacked on trailers or dumped into gondolas for transportation to the winery.

PICOLIT — (Peek-oh-leet) — White dessert wine from Udine in the north east corner of Italy (Friuli-Venezia Giulia), made from slightly dried Picolit grapes. One of Italy's greatest wines, formerly exported in quantity, it is now very rare due to disease and failure of the vines.

PICPOUL — (Peek-pool) — Name given in the Armagnac Country to the Folle Blanche grape (see) which here, as in the Cognac district, gives a poor, thin, acid wine but an outstanding brandy. It is the only variety used in the best grades of Armagnac.

PIÈCE — (Pea-ess) — French for the oak barrel, roughly the equivalent of the *barrique* of the Bordeaux Country, in which the wines of Burgundy are ordinarily stored and aged. A *pièce* in the Côte d'Or contains 228 liters (60 gallons, or 25 cases of finished wine); in the Beaujolais, 216 liters (57 gallons).

PIED — (Pea-*A*) — One of several French words for a single vine (*cep* and *souche* being two others). Ordinarily and alone, it of course means "foot," but in wine parlance one will often say that a given vineyard has *"3,000 pieds à l'hectare,"* which means 3,000 vines per hectare, or some 1,200 to the acre.

PIEDMONT — (*Italian*, PIEMONTE — P-a-*mawn*-tay) — Most important wine-producing region of Italy, easily first in quality, with a total production of over 100 million gallons a year. Most of the vineyards are on the hills north and south of the wide, upper valley of the Po, in the Monferrato (*see*) especially. The most famous Piedmontese wines are red (Barolo, Barbaresco, Barbera, Freisa, Gattinara, Ghemme, Grignolino, etc.) but many good white table wines (Gavi, Cortese) are also produced, as well as most of the sparkling wines of Italy (Asti, etc.). Turin, the capital of Piedmont, is the principal center of the Italian Vermouth trade.

For Map, *see* ITALY.

PIERRE-À-FUSIL — (Pea-air ah Foo-zee) — French for gun-flint; when applied to wine, a special odor or flavor which recalls the smell of flint struck with steel. Often applied to the wines of Chablis. Flinty.

PIESPORT — (*Peas*-port) — One of the smallest yet deservedly one of the most famous wine-producing villages of Germany's Moselle Valley. Its steep, rocky vineyards, facing due south, produce wines which, at their best, have few equals — wonderfully delicate and fragrant, fruity, with an incomparable distinction all their own. These "Queens of the Moselle," as they have been called, of course carry the name of a ·specific vineyard, as Piesporter Gold-tröpfchen, Schubertslay, Treppchen, Falkenberg, Domherr, or Günterslay, and are estate-bottled by their producers. On the other hand wines labeled simply Piesporter (or even Piesporter Michelsberg) may and often do come from less celebrated townships nearby.

PINARD — (Pea-nahr) — French slang, especially 1914-1918 soldiers' slang, for wine; most often inexpensive, red wine.

PINEAU DE LA LOIRE — (Pee-no duh la Lwahr) — Sometimes, though wrongly, written Pinot. Productive white grape of excellent quality, responsible for most of the best white wines of Touraine and Anjou, in France. Its proper name is Chenin Blanc (*see*), and botanically it is not related to the Pinot Noir, Pinot Blanc, Pinot Gris, etc. It is now quite extensively planted in the North Coast Counties of California, as Chenin Blanc, and gives fresh, fruity, agreeable wines with considerable bouquet; those that are deliberately made somewhat sweet are on the whole less good. It is also, as in Saumur, an excellent grape for sparkling wines, and many of the best California Champagnes contain a good proportion of wine made from it.

PINEAU DES CHARENTES — (Pee-no day Shar-awnt) — or Pineau Charentais. Odd, sweet apéritif, which has achieved in recent years a certain popularity in France. It is actually a *mistelle* or *vin muté* — in other words, new Charentais wine in which the fermentation has been stopped by the addition of Cognac; as such, it has much in common with white Port and with California Angelica (*see*), the difference being that in this case Cognac is used instead of high-proof brandy.

PINOT — (Pee-no) — Perhaps the most distinguished single family in the field of wine grapes, a name second to none in the Almanach de Gotha or Burke's Peerage of the vine. The Pinot Noir alone is responsible for all the great red Burgundies, from Pommard, Beaune and Corton, to Romanée-Conti, Musigny and Chambertin. It also produces over 60% of all French Champagne. The white so-called Pinot Chardonnay or Chardonnay (*see*) is almost certainly not a true Pinot, although it legally may be so called in France; it is the other major grape of the Champagne Country, and the one variety grown, or even permitted, in Montrachet, Chablis, Pouilly-Fuissé. The Pinot Blanc is widely

269

planted in lesser Burgundian vineyards, and another cousin, the Pinot Gris (also called the Ruländer and occasionally, though wrongly, the Tokay) yields excellent wine in Alsace, in Baden, and in northern Italy.

Transplanted to California, the Pinots preserve in general the distinguished characteristics of their French ancestors; they are shy-bearers, and their wines are more expensive than most, but the word Pinot on a California wine label is a pretty good assurance of superior quality. However, those labeled "White Pinot" are generally made from the Pineau de la Loire, or Chenin Blanc (*see*). "Pinot St. George", used mostly by one winery, is not a true Pinot.

In Italy, the Pinot Blanc gives an agreeable, dry white wine round Alba, in Piedmont, often sold as Pinot d'Alba and marketed in tall, slender green bottles; in Lombardy, in the neighborhood of Casteggio, both the Pinot Noir and Pinot Blanc are grown, mostly for sparkling wines; in the Tyrol there are small plantings of both, and especially of Pinot Gris, or Ruländer, which is one of the varieties used in Terlano (*see*).

PINOT BLANC — *see* PINOT above.

PINOT CHARDONNAY — *See* CHARDONNAY.

PINOT GRIS — (Pee-no Gree) — An authentic cousin of the greater members of the Pinot family, sometimes called the Ruländer in Germany, the Auxerrois in certain parts of France and even (wrongly) the "Tokay" in Alsace. Its grapes are a sort of greyish-rose when ripe, and yield wines which are sometimes of considerable distinction, notably in Baden, Alsace, and northern Italy, but often a bit flat, and lacking in acid, freshness and life.

PINOT MEUNIER — (Pee-no Muhn-yea) — Grape variety, almost certainly a Pinot, but of an inferior strain. More productive than the ture Pinot Noir, it is no longer legal in Burgundy but still "tolerated" in Champagne; it is the variety responsible for most of the Pinot Rosé of Alsace and for many pleasant *rosés* produced round Beaugency on the Loire. Its name comes from the fact thst the underside of its leaves is powdery white, almost as if covered with flour, and the word *meunier* means "miller" in French. Grown to some extent in California, it generally passes there for Pinot Noir.

PINOT NOIR — (Pee-no Nwahr) — One of the very greatest of red wine grapes (*see* Pinot, above).

PIPE — Large barrel, customarily of oak and rather sharply tapered toward the ends, in which Port is stored in Portugal and in which it is often shipped. Its size may vary, but is usually 522.5 liters, or 138 U.S. (115 Imperial) gallons. The standard Madeira pipe is considerably smaller — 418 liters, or about 110 U.S. gallons.

PIQUANT — Wine taster's term (*pikant,* in German) used of a fresh, rather tart white wine, attractive and almost spicy.

PIQUÉ — (Pee-kay) — Said of a wine that has begun to go sour, with a trace of acetic acid in its make-up.

PIQUETTE — (Pee-ket) — Derisive term applied to any poor, thin acid wine; correctly to something which is not legally wine at all, made of *marc,* or pomace or grape pressings, plus water and sugar — a sort of "second wine," often served free to cellar workers in Europe.

PLASTERING — The addition of calcium sulphate, or gypsum, to grapes before fermentation: this increases the total acidity and improves the color and clarity of the resulting wine. This is normal procedure in the making of Sherry and certain other wines and is, within specified limits, legal both in Spain and in America.

PLEIN — (Plan) — French for *full*. Applied to wines that are well-balanced, with good body and fairly high alcohol. Applied to people it means inebriated.

PLONK — Marvelous English slang for very ordinary *vin ordinaire*.

PODENSAC — (Po-dawn-sac) — Small town in the Graves district of France producing rather sweet white wines. These are entitled to the appellation Cérons (*see*).

POINTE — (Pwant) — French for "punt" (an English word, although it will not be found in this sense in most dictionaries), meaning the indentation or "push-up" in the bottom of most wine bottles, especially those used for Champagne. A bottle of sparkling wine *mise sur pointe* is one placed neck down, usually for ageing, stacked vertically with the cork of each bottle in the punt of the bottle below. It is thus, after the remuage and *before* disgorging, that the finer Champagnes are aged, and it is only thus that they improve materially in bottle. This system of stacking for ageing is also sometimes called *"en masse,"* and the term *mise sur pointe* is sometimes also used to mean the placing of bottles on "riddling racks" or *"pupitres"* for the turning and shaking which precede disgorging. *See* Champagne.

POINTE, Château La — (Pwant) — Important 1st Growth vineyard of Pomerol. Some 7,000 cases a year of very sturdy, full-bodied red wine.

POLCEVERA — (Paul-chay-*veh*-ra) — Rather good white table wine, often a little on the sweet side, produced near Genoa, Italy.

POLPENAZZE — (Paul-pen-*natz*-zay) — Village and small district near the southern end of Lake Garda (*see*), producing Chiaretto (*see*) and some rather agreeable, light red wines.

POMACE — (*Pum*-mess) — Mass of skins, seeds, stems, etc., left in the fermenting vat or wine-press after the wine or juice has been drawn off. *Marc*, in French.

POMEROL — (Pum-may-rawl) — One of the most interesting and attractive of all Clarets, produced only by some 1,500 acres of vineyard, mostly in a single township, the smallest of the famous districts into which the Bordeaux Country is divided, by tradition and by French law. Some twenty miles east of Bordeaux, it adjoins St. Émilion, runs up to the edge of the little city of Libourne, and its vines are planted on a high gently rolling, rather gravelly plateau north of the Dordogne River.

In average quality the wines sold simply as "Pomerol" are perhaps the best district wines of Bordeaux; they have a winning and generous warmth, great

271

depth of flavor, a color of dark lustrous crimson, and much of that peculiar velvety quality which the French call *"gras."* They mature more quickly than the Médocs, are less subtle, shorter-lived. The best château wines are of course much finer; they include Château Pétrus (almost in a class by itself), Château Certan and Vieux Château Certan, and Châteaux La Conseillante, Trotanoy, Petit Village, L'Evangile, Lafleur, Gazin, La Fleur-Pétrus, Nénin, La Pointe, Beauregard, L'Eglise Clinet, Latour-Pomerol, etc

POMMARD — (Po-mar) — Perhaps the best known and most popular of all red Burgundies, especially in English-speaking countries; the name Pommard alone, unless followed by that of one of the few truly outstanding vineyards of this little *commune,* is anything but a hallmark of quality. The village is just south of Beaune, and bounded in turn on the south by Volnay; its 839 acres of vines produce more than 120,000 cases a year. The estate-bottled wines from outstanding vineyards are not only dependable but fine — soft, gracious, well-balanced, not too deep in color, fruity and attractive, with considerable breed. The best *climats* are Rugiens (which adjoins Volnay and gives a rather full-bodied wine, with a wholly typical and rather agreeable, special *goût de terroir*); Épenots (also spelled Épeneaux) which adjoins Beaune and is remarkable for its finesse and class; then Clos Blanc, Arvelets, Chaponières, Pézerolles, Poutures, Chanlins Bas, Les Croix Noires, La Platière, etc. All of these yield red wine exclusively, but there is an insignificant amount of white produced, by a tiny vineyard known as the Coeur des Dames. Two *cuvées* of the Hospices de Beaune, Dames de la Charité and Billardet, carry the *Appellation Contrôlée* "Pommard" and bring high prices.

272

PONTAC-MONPLAISIR, Château — (Pawn-tack Maw-play-zeer) — Good, small vineyard in Villenave d'Ornon, Graves. Red wine of sound quality and an even better white.

PONTET-CANET, Château — (Pawn-tay Can-nay) — 5th Classed Growth of Pauillac. The largest classified vineyard of the Médoc (40,000 cases a year) and its popular red wine.

POOR — Used of a wine that has not much to it. Not necessarily bad. Mediocre and uninteresting.

POP WINE — Another name for Flavored Wine (see).

PORRÓN — (Pohr-rone) — Portugese glass or ceramic wine vessel with two spouts, a wide funnel-like one for filling and to use as a handle and a narrow pointed one to provide a thin stream of wine for mid-air drinking.

PORT — Certainly the most famous of all dessert wines; originally and properly a sweet, heavily fortified wine from a delimited district in the upper Duoro valley of northern Portugal. In most countries no other wine may be sold as "Port," and even in the United States the name is to some extent protected — the domestic product must be labeled American Port, New York State Port, or California Port. Under a 1968 ruling of the Portuguese government, all Port wines shipped to the United States must be designated PORTO (see). This requirement does not pertain to Port wines shipped to England and was intended solely to distinguish true Portuguese Port from the American varieties made in New York State, California, or elsewhere.

However, both in Portugal and in this country, Port is a wine which owes its sweetness to the high sugar content of the grapes from which it is made. These, crushed, are put to ferment, but at some carefully determined half-way point in their fermentation the juice is drawn off into casks or tanks which contain a predetermined amount of high-proof grape brandy. This, of course, immediately arrests the fermentation, and the result is a wine of 19 to 21 percent alcohol by volume, still quite sweet, the raw material of Port. What it becomes thereafter depends, to a large extent, on the quality of the grapes from which it was made, their variety and their vineyard, and on the cellar care which the crude new wine receives.

Port has been made in this way in Portugal, though of course vastly less well than now, since about 1450, and has been well-known and popular in northern Europe, in England especially, for nearly three centuries.

Various types of Port are now made in Portugal, and they vary widely. The most expensive are VINTAGE PORTS. These are selected lots of wines of exceptionally good years, unblended, bottled young (more often in London than in Oporto). They require anywhere from fifteen to fifty years to reach their peak, throw a heavy sediment or film or crust in the bottle, have to be decanted with great care, and at their best are of quite extraordinary quality. They are regarded with a respect approaching reverence by their devotees. Good recent vintages include 1975, 1970, 1966, 1963, 1960, 1958, 1955, 1950, 1948, 1945. Only the older are considered by connoisseurs as ready to drink.

More generally available is something called "late-bottled Vintage Port." This is a wine bottled after four years in the barrel, instead of the customary two years for regular Vintage Port, and is usually the wine of a year regarded as not fine enough to be "declared" as a vintage. Sooner ready then true Vintage Port, it nevertheless requires decanting and should be handled with the necessary care.

Most of the Port shipped to the United States, however, (some 65,000 cases a year) is aged in wood and ready to drink when shipped. One, properly called RUBY PORT, is fairly young, fruity, attractive, although its quality depends entirely on its shipper and its price. TAWNY PORT has spent more time in oak, thus acquiring a lighter color and a brownish tinge. It is softer, rounder, more mature and usually, quite properly, more expensive. There exists, in addition, WHITE PORT, considerably less esteemed by experts, made precisely as the red is made but from white grapes, principally the Rabigato, Malvasia, Gouveio, etc. The leading red wine varieties include the Touriga, Bastardo, Tinta Francisca, Tinta Carvalha, Tinta Madeira, Mourisco, Tinto Cão, Souzão.

As the result of recent plantings of Tinta Madeira and Tinta Cão grapes, a limited amount of quite good Port is being produced in California, and the word Tinta usually appears on its label. But according to American wine laws and regulations, "Port" may be made anywhere, out of any grapes, including native Eastern varieties, or even table grapes, raisin grapes, or culls. It may be well and properly aged in oak, or it may, and often does, go to the consumer when under six months old. There is no guide to quality other than the rather untrustworthy one of price, and the producer's name or brand.

PORTO — Official designation since 1968 for all Port Wines shipped to the United States. Many brands continue to carry the word "Port" as well, but all must show either the word "Porto," or "Vinho do Porto" somewhere on the label. This ruling does not apply to Port Wines shipped to England nor, of course, can it apply to Port Wines bottled in England and shipped to the U.S. from there. It is very doubtful that the use of "Porto" will ever really catch on in the U.S., since the name Port has a centuries-old tradition of use behind it.

PORTUGAL — When it comes to wine, most people tend to think of Portugal in terms of Port, yet hardly two percent of Portuguese wine is Port, and more than half of this is exported. What the Portuguese themselves prefer, and consume in happy abundance, is table wine. About as large and as populous as Ohio, Portugal produces as much table wine as California and drinks twice as much table wine as the United States, some 25 gallons per capita per year.

Most of this, of course, is simply *consumo,* or *vin ordinaire,* agreeable enough, and cheap. The reds are on the whole more deeply colored and slightly higher in alcohol than their French or California counterparts; the whites are rather coarse and common, as might be expected at this latitude; some of the *rosés* are refreshing and good.

A great deal of progress has been made in methods of vinification and cellar care over the past decades, and a number of superior Portuguese table wines are beginning to find a place in the world market, especially in England and to some extent in the United States. While they can hardly be called distinguished, these are often very agreeable, and good values. Several are sold simply under a brand name (as Lancer's, Mateus, etc.) without any precise indication of origin; others, and increasingly, carry a geographical appellation strictly defined by the Portuguese government.

The more important of these are, 1. what is known as *Vinho Verde* (literally, "green wine," but "green" only in the sense that it is young and fresh and lively), from northern Portugal, red, white, and *rosé;* 2. *Dão,* from a small mountainous district south of the Douro Valley, once again red, white, and *rosé;* 3. *Colares,* a fine, light red wine made from the Ramisco grape, planted in sandy coastal vineyards west of Lisbon; 4. *Bucelas,* rather sweet, white table wine made just north of Lisbon.

In addition to these, Portugal produces one of the most famous muscat wines of Europe, the golden *Moscatel de Setubal,* which is almost a liqueur. And of course Port and Madeira, to round out a truly unique range of great fortified wines. For map *see* page 331.

POSSET — A cold-weather drink made of hot milk, curdled with wine or with beer, sweetened and spiced.

POT — (Po) — Small, very heavy bottle, holding 46 centiliters or about one U.S. pint, in which young "open" Beaujolais is often served, in and around Lyon; in color and shape it is like a slenderer version of the bottle used for Sauternes. The so-called "pots" shipped in recent years to the United States are neither of the same contents nor the same form.

POUGET, Château — (Poo-zhay) — 4th Classed Growth of Cantenac-Margaux. Very small production (under 2,000 cases) of red wine.

POUILLY FUISSÉ — (Poo-ye Fwee-say) — Excellent dry white wine made from the Chardonnay grape in four small *communes,* or townships, just west of Mâcon, in southern Burgundy. Pouilly itself is not a township, but is officially ranked as a hamlet (*hameau*) in the *commune* of Solutré (*see*); the others are Fuissé, Chaintré and Vergisson. The average annual production is not far from 300,000 cases, much of it consumed in Lyon and Paris when still young, the best, usually estate-bottled, is a dry, green-gold, racy, fruity wine, with exceptionally good balance and fine bouquet — perhaps not a great wine but very nearly one, somewhere between Meursault and Chablis in character. Most Pouilly-Fuissés are now bottled before they are a year old, and they do not improve past the age of three. *See* also Pouilly-Loché and Pouilly-Vinzelles. (For Map *see* Mâconnais.)

POUILLY FUMÉ — (Poo-ye Few-may) — Also POUILLY-BLANC-FUMÉ, the terms being interchangeable. Excellent white wine, generally dry though sometimes with a trace of sweetness in great years, produced round the village of Pouilly-sur Loire (*see*). Made entirely from the Sauvignon Blanc (or Blanc-Fumé grape), pale, racy, fruity, usually bottled when less than a year old, it has acquired in the last ten years a great and well merited popularity. The total production, often radically reduced by spring frosts, rarely exceeds 40,000 cases a year.

POUILLY-LOCHÉ — (Poo-ye Lo-shay) — Dry white wine, fresh, pale and attractive, made from the Chardonnay grape in the village of Loché, which adjoins but is not legally part of the Pouilly-Fuissé production zone. *See* Pouilly-Vinzelles.

POUILLY-SUR-LOIRE — (Poo-ye soor Lwahr) — Small town on the Loire River, not far from Nevers, in central France. The wine-producing district of which it is the center includes the adjoining *communes* of Les Loges, St. Andelain and Tracy; there are approximately a thousand acres of vineyard, about one quarter planted to the common Chasselas grape (*see*) and three-quarters to the admirable Sauvignon Blanc, here known as the Blanc-Fumé (*see*) — not the Fumé Blanc, since there is no Fumé Noir. The Pouilly vineyards therefore produce two entirely different wines — that sold simply as Pouilly-sur-Loire is made from the Chasselas; at best it is a fresh, agreeable carafe wine, short-lived, without character or distinction. For the vastly superior wine made from the Sauvignon Blanc, *see* Pouilly-Fumé.

POUILLY-VINZELLES — (Poo-ye Van-zell) — Excellent dry white wine made from the Chardonnay grape in the village of Vinzelles, near Mâcon. Like Loché, Vinzelles directly adjoins the Pouilly-Fuissé district, and its wines, while possibly a little lighter and shorter-lived, are very like the Pouilly-Fuissés, and better than some. They are among the best values in the way of white Burgundies shipped out of France.

POUJEAUX — (Poo-zhow) — High gravelly plateau in the center of the Haut-Médoc, mostly inside the communal limits of Moulis (*see*). Many of the wines here produced have a special character and taste; they are mostly *bourgeois* growths, and the word Poujeaux is often part of their name, as Château Poujeaux-Theil, Poujeaux-Marly, Gressier-Grand-Poujeaux, Dutruch-Grand-Poujeaux, Lestage-Darquier-Grand Poujeaux, etc.

POURRITURE NOBLE — (Poo-ree-tew'r No-b'l) — *See* BOTRYTIS CINEREA.

POWERFUL — High in alcohol and/or assertive in aroma and flavor. A wine of definite character.

PRÄDIKAT — (Pray-dee-cat) — German for attribute (*see* Qualitätswein mit Prädikat).

PRÄDIKATSSEKT — (Pray-dee-cat Zekt) — Highest quality German sparkling wine.

PRÉCOCE — (Pray-cohs) — French term meaning precocious, or early maturing, applied both to grape varieties and to wines. Most grape varieties grown in cool, northern districts are *précoces,* for otherwise they would not ripen, and their number includes almost all of the very best. On the other hand, a *vin précoce,* one soon ready and gaining little if aged, is, however agreeable and charming, rarely much more than that, and hardly ever great.

PREIGNAC — (Preh-nyac) — One of the five *communes* of the Sauternes district in France. Its best vineyards include Châteaux Suduiraut, de Malle, etc.

PRÉMEAUX — (Pray-mo) — Village in Burgundy, directly adjoining Nuits-Saint-Georges on the south; its admirable red wines are legally entitled to the appellation Nuits-Saint-Georges, and are always so sold, usually plus the name of a vineyard. Several of these *climats* yield wines fully equal to the best of Nuits itself, as the Clos des Corvées, Les Perdrix, Les Argillières, and, of a slightly lower rank, the Clos des Forêts, Les Didiers, Clos Arlots, Clos de la Maréchale, etc (*See* map page 250).

PREMIER CRU — (Prem-yay Croo) — French, first growth; term used in classifying Bordeaux wines and Chablis.

PREMIUM WINE — Arbitrary price classification of California table wines; originally meant any wines selling at retail for more than $1.00 per bottle, but times have changed.

PREMIÈRES CÔTES DE BORDEAUX — (Prem-yair Coat d' Boredoe) — Major division of the Bordeaux wine country, consisting of the hilly right bank of the Garonne River between Bordeaux itself and Langon, 30 miles to the southeast. Thus the vineyards face those of Graves, Cérons, Barsac and Sauternes, across the verdant and lovely river valley; they produce some 2 million gallons of white wine, and about half as much red, per year. The latter is generally one of the pleasantest and soundest of inexpensive red Bordeaux; the white ranges from slightly *moelleux* to very sweet indeed, although there have been recent efforts, as in Entre-Deux-Mers, to produce dryer wines. Cadillac and Langoiran are perhaps the two of the best known *communes;* two others, Loupiac and Sainte-Croix-du-Mont (*see*) are geographically part of the Premières Côtes, but have individual *Appellations Contrôlées* of their own.

PRESS — Instrument of many diverse forms used since time immemorial to extract juice from grapes, either before fermentation (white wine) or after (red wine).

PREUSES — (Pruh-z) — One of the best of the seven *Grand Cru* vineyards of Chablis; its wines, often rather hard when young, develop slowly and generally acquire a very special and attractive bouquet and flavor reminiscent of hazel-nuts (*noisettes*).

PRIEURÉ-LICHINE, Château — (Pree-oo ray Lee-sheen) — 4th Classed Growth of Cantenac-Margaux, formerly called Le Prieuré or Cantenac-Prieuré. Some 7,500 cases a year.

PRIMATIVO — (Preem-ma-*tee*-vo) — Remarkable red blending wine produced south of Bari, in the "heel" of Italy, usually shipped and consumed almost as soon as made. The vintage comes early in this hot country, and some Primativo, blended, of course, with older wine, is often being sold and drunk by the 15th of September of the year it is made. The best of it comes from the appropriately named town of Gioia, from the Troja grape, and has about 14% alcohol. The Primativo di Gioia grape has recently been linked to the Zinfandel (*see*).

PRIMEUR — (Pree-merr) — Very young Beaujolais in its first blush of youth, usually *en primeur,* younger than vin nouveau (*see*). Rushed to market on November 15th, first legal day of shipment. By the following spring it should be consumed or dumped.

PRIORATO — (Pree-o-*rah*-toe) — Sweet, full-bodied, onion skin colored dessert wine, sometimes fortified, produced round Tarragona on the Mediterranean Coast of Spain. It is often used in *sangria* (*see*) and other wine punches popular in Spain in summer.

PROHIBITION — The "noble experiment" in the United States. It lasted thirteen years, ten months, nineteen days, seventeen hours, thirty-two and one-half minutes. The cost of enforcing it can never be determined. It has been estimated that, to the government alone, the cost approximated $1,000,000,000 per year, including loss in Federal, state, county and municipal revenues. Actually, appropriations for the Prohibition Bureau ranged from $3,100,000 in 1920 to a high of $14,985,744 in 1930. It is estimated that the American people spent $36,000,000,000 for bootleg and smuggled liquor during the years 1920 through 1933.

PROOF — System of measuring and expressing alcoholic content; there are two scales. According to that used in the U.S., proof is the double of alcoholic content by volume at 60° F.; an 86 proof brandy, for example, will contain 43% alcohol by volume, and a 100 proof bonded whiskey 50% alcohol. In Great Britain, proof spirit contains 57.1% alcohol by volume; liquids containing less are said to be "under proof," and those containing more, "over proof."

PROSECCO — (Pro-*seh*-ko) — Superior white wine grape and the sweeter of two excellent white wines (the other is called Verdiso, also named for its grape) from the town of Conegliano (*see*) north of Venice, Italy. There are several sparkling and semi-sparkling types as well, all with the same, rather striking and special bouquet.

PROTESTANT EPISCOPAL CHURCH — U.S. church, inheritor of the doctrine of the Church of England, which became an independent body within the Anglican communion in 1789, and whose House of Bishops, in Chicago on October 26, 1886, resolved that: "In the judgment of the House of Bishops the use of the unfermented juice of the grape, as the lawful and proper wine of the Holy Eucharist, is unwarranted by the example of our Lord, and an unauthorized departure from the custom of the Catholic Church."

PROVENCE — (Pro-vawss) — Historically and traditionally, an ancient province of France where a separate language, Provençal, by no means just a dialect or patois, was and still is, to some extent, spoken; Aix-en-Provence was its capital, and it was considered to include the modern *départements* of Basses-Alpes, Vaucluse, Bouches-du-Rhône; Var and part of the Drôme; it became part of France in 1487. As far as wine is concerned, its modern boundaries have been somewhat differently defined: Vaucluse, Alpes de Haute Provence and Drôme are outside the limits of viticultural Provence whereas some vineyards in the *département* of Alpes Maritîmes are now entitled to the appellation Côtes de Provence (*see*) although they were not part of France until 1860.

PROVIGNAGE — (Pro-vee-nyahj) — Ancient method of propagating vines by layering or burying the entire vine or a shoot which would then grow new roots. Used in Champagne and discontinued because of phylloxera and the necessity of orderly, well spaced vines for machine cultivation.

PRUNING — Complex agricultural science, which has been the concern of vineyardists and vine-dressers since the time of Noah, by which vines are cut back (in almost all cases during their dormant season) so as to form and train them systematically with some specific end in view. This end may be increased production, higher quality, a longer life for the vine itself, or any combination of these and many other desired results; literally thousands of books have been written on the subject over a period of more than twenty centuries. A capsule condensation of them is impossible and has no place in a volume of this sort.

From the wine-drinker's point of view there are perhaps a few generalizations that may be helpful:

1. Within definite limits, imposed by soil, climate, rainfall (and/or irrigation), almost any grape variety can be pruned so as to produce twice or even five times its minimum.

2. Again within limits, the commoner grape varieties do not yield markedly better wine when pruned to produce less per acre — a wine made from Carignane grapes by a man who harvests three tons per acre is NOT worth twice as much as a wine from his neighbor who gets six tons per acre.

3. The few wine grape varieties which can properly be described as "great" (perhaps a dozen, surely less than twenty) *always* give better wine if severely pruned so as to give their minimum crop, *providing* they are planted in districts suited to them.

279

4. There are many intermediate varieties (Sylvaner, Gamay, Merlot, Grenache) yielding wines best drunk young, which gain nothing and even lose quality if their production is too restricted.

PUGLIA — (*Pool*-ya) — Important wine-producing province in southern Italy. *See* Apulia.

PUISSEGUIN-SAINT-ÉMILION — (Pweece-gah Sant A-me-lee-aw) — Secondary red wine district in the Bordeaux Country, adjoining St. Émilion (*see*) on the west, and entitled to the name in this combined form. Sturdy, full-bodied wines, not too expensive and often good values in a way of claret. There are over a half million gallons a year.

PULCIANELLA — (Pool-chan-*nel*-la) — The small, squat, straw-covered bottle, or *fiasco,* of a special shape, in which the wines of Orvieto (*see*) are sometimes shipped.

PULIGNY-MONTRACHET — (Poo-lean-yee Maw-rah-shay) — Village of the Côte de Beaune, in Burgundy; together with the adjoining village of Chassagne-Montrachet, it produces what are generally and correctly regarded as the finest dry white wines of France. The most celebrated vineyards include Montrachet (about half in Chassagne), Chevalier-Montrachet (all in Puligny), Bâtard-Montrachet (nearly half in Chassagne), Bienvenue-Bâtard-Montrachet

Puligny-Montrachet

(all in Puligny) and Criots-Bâtard Montrachet (all in Chassagne). *See* all of these, which are all sold under the vineyard name alone, with no mention of Puligny or Chassagne. Admirable wines, but of a somewhat less exalted class, are: Le Cailleret, Les Combettes, Les Pucelles, Les Folatières, Clavoillons, Le Champ-Canet, Les Chalumeaux, Les Referts, Sous-le-Puits, La Garenne and Hameau-de-Blagny. There are just over 575 acres under vines, all Chardonnay, except for a small parcel of Pinot Noir, and the annual production is not far from 65,000 cases. Even the lesser wines of Puligny have great breed and class and would rank as extraordinary in any other district.

PULP — The fleshy and juicy part of the grape.

PULPIT — A literal translation of the French, *pupitre,* applied in the Champagne Country to the two-sided perforated racks, hinged at the top and spread apart at the bottom so as to form a shape like the letter A, in which the bottles are placed during their "shaking" or "riddling" and clarification. *See* Champagne.

PUNT — The "push-up" or "kick-up" in the bottom of a wine or Champagne bottle.

PUPITRE — (Poo-pee-tre) — *see* PULPIT.

PUTTONYOS — (Poo-tawn-*yawsh*) — Baskets or hods used during the grape harvest in the Tokay district of Hungary. When a good vintage year permits the making of the superior grade of wine called *Aszu* (the equivalent of a German Auslese), the overripe grapes are picked separately, and a varying number of *puttonyos* of these are added to each cask of normal wine. The number is usually stated on the wine's label, as *"Aszu 2 puttonyos," "Aszu 5 puttonyos,"* etc. Naturally, the more *puttonyos,* the sweeter, fuller-bodied and more expensive the wine.

PX — *see* PEDRO XIMENEZ.

QbA — Initials for Qualitätswein bestimmter Anbaugebiete (Quality Wine of Designated Regions) — same as Qualitätswein.

QUALITÄTSSCHAUMWEIN — (Kval-ee-tates-*showm*-vine) — *See* SEKT.

QUALITÄTSWEIN — (Kval-ee-tates-vine) — Literally "quality wine," this classification of German wines created for vintages which have been sugared or chaptalized (*see*) fills a long felt need in the German wine regulations, which before 1971 did not permit such wines to be sold as estate bottlings. French law has never made any distinction between wines made from sugared musts and those which were not, both being permitted the use of *Mise du Domaine* or *Mis en bouteilles au Château*, if they were in fact estate bottled. The new German Wine Law now permits the use of the new phrase Erzeugerabfüllung on all *Qualitäsweine* which are estate bottled, thus bringing German regulations in line with the French laws.

QUALITÄTSWEIN MIT PRÄDIKAT — (Kval-ee-tates-vine mit Pray-dee-cat) — Under the new German Wine Law, a "quality wine with a predicate" is the designation for the highest quality German wines, all of which carry one of five additional designations in addition to the word *Qualitätswein* (see above). The five "predicates" are: *Kabinett* (now always so spelled), *Spätlese, Auslese, Beerenauslese,* and *Trockenbeerenauslese.* There is also *Eiswein,* but this is not used as a separate "predicate" and will always appear on the label with one of the other five, such as *Eiswein Auslese.* All the wines in these five categories must be made from musts to which no sugar has been

282

added, and a *Qualitätswein mit Prädikat,* which is also an *Erzeugerab-füllung,* is the equivalent of the former *Originalabfüllung* wine of the same estate or producer made before 1971. All *Qualitätsweine,* with or without a *Prädikat,* must be tested by a government control panel and, if found satisfactory, are given an official registration number which must always be printed on the label. The German phrase for this is *Amtliche Prufnummer.* (*See*)

QUART — One-fourth of a gallon: .946 liters in the U.S., 1.136 liters in Great Britain. In French, pronounced *caar,* it again means one-fourth: ¼ liter of open wine, or a quarter-bottle, or "split" of Champagne.

QUARTS DE CHAUME — (Caar d' Shome) — Celebrated vineyard of the Coteaux du Layon (*see*), in the province of Anjou, France. Consisting of 120 acres of Chenin Blanc vines, with an incomparable southern exposure, it produces some of the finest and most expensive of the rich, golden fruity wines for which Anjou is above all famous; average production 20,000 gallons per year.

QUATOURZE — (Kah-tourz) — Red, white and *rosé* wine produced round the town of Narbonne, in southern France, not far from Carcassonne and the Spanish border. Made from the common grape varieties of the Midi, it is a fairly good *ordinaire,* but hardly deserves either its local fame or the V.D.Q.S. seal which it is allowed to carry.

QUEUE — (Keu) — Old French measure of capacity or volume, said to come from the Latin term *culeus.* Until quite recently the wines at the Hospices de Beaune auctions were sold by *Queues* (although invariably lodged in *pièces,* or *demi-queues*) and the Burgundian *queue* is therefore 456 liters; the exact meaning of the word still varies from one French province to another, and a *queue* can be anywhere from 216 to 894 liters. We may well be thankful for the metric system.

QUINCY — (Can-see) — A pleasant, spicy, dry white wine from the village of this name, on the River Cher, not far from Bourges, in central France. Considered a wine of the Loire Valley (the Cher being a tributary of the Loire), made entirely from the Sauvignon Blanc grape, Quincy is not unlike a very dry Sancerre or Pouilly-Blanc-Fumé. There are some 400 acres of vineyard, and about 100,000 gallons of wine in overall per year.

QUININE — Alkaloid drug made from cinchona bark and until World War II the only specific treatment for malaria. Because of its bitter taste it was mixed witl sweet wine and those who took the medicine got to like it. Apéritifs such as Dubonnet, Saint Raphaël and Byrrh were thus developed under the general name of Quinquina.

QUINTA — (Keen-ta) — Portuguese term for a vineyard estate, including vines and buildings, more or less the equivalent of Château, *Domaine, Tenuta, We-ingut,* etc.

R

RABAUD-PROMIS, Château — (Rab-bo Pro-me) — 1st Classed Growth of Bommes, Sauternes. Fine, full-bodied wines, in general quite sweet. For nearly two decades, ending in 1952, Rabaud-Promis and Sigalas-Rabaud formed a single property, known as Château Rabaud. Some 10,000 cases a year.

RABELAIS, François — Celebrated French writer, born near Chinon in the Loire Valley *circa* 1490, who wrote of wine and the joys of wine-drinking with an enthusiasm and eloquence rarely equaled. A collection of quotations from him on the subject would fill pages. In Gargantua I, he says, "There is not a corner nor burrow in all my body where this wine doth not ferret out my thirst."

RABLAY — (Rahb-lay) — One of the best wine-producing *communes* of the Coteaux du Layon (*see*), in Anjou. Sweet white wines of very high quality.

RABOSO — (Rah-*bo*-so) — Interesting and unusual red wine, produced from the grape of the same name in the province of Treviso, north of Venice. Extremely high in acid, it requires some ageing; low in alcohol, a pale, brilliant ruby in color, with a remarkable bouquet, it is, when mature, an extremely pleasant summer wine.

RACÉ — (Rah-say) — term indicating wine with breeding, true to form and elegant.

RACKING — The drawing off of clear young wine from one vat or cask or barrel to another, leaving the lees and sediment behind. This operation, essential in wine-making, is called *soutirage* in French, *Abstich* in German, *travaso* in Italian, and normally involves the loss of 2% or 3% of the wine's volume. All well-made wines are racked at least twice and some of them four times before bottling.

RAINWATER — Odd name given to one of the lightest and palest of Madeiras. In the early 19th century, at least according to tradition, a gentleman and connoisseur of Savannah, Georgia, by the name of Habisham, developed a special and secret method of clarifying and handling his family Madeiras, shipped in cask by clipper ships from Funchal, so as to render them not only excellent but uniquely lightbodied and pale. They soon became famous as "Rainwater Madeiras" and their originator no less famous as "Rainwater Habisham." The word, long since in the public domain, is now used by many Madeira shippers.

RANCIO — (Rahn-see-o) — Special flavor that certain wines, fortified wines especially, acquire as they are aged in wood, akin to maderization but in this case desirable. Madeira itself, like Tawny Port and some Marsala, has this characteristic taste, but it is perhaps most pronounced in the apéritif wines of southern France, such as Banyuls.

RANDERSACKER — (*Rahn*-der-sock-er) — One of the better wine-producing villages of the Main valley, in Franconia, Germany; after Würzburg itself, the most important of all. Its wines are of course shipped in *Bocksbeutel,* the traditional flagon of this part of Germany, and the finer vineyards include Pfülben, Marsberg, Teufelskeller, Sonnenstuhl, and Dabug.

RASTEAU — (Rass-toe) — Sweet, amber, fortified wine, somewhat on the order of a light, white Port, produced in the lower Rhône Valley, northeast of Avignon. Usually about 15% alcohol, occasionally higher.

RATAFIA — (Rah-tah-fyah) — Apéritif made in Champagne and other places by adding alcohol to grape must; similar to Pineau des Charentes (*see*); sometimes considered a liqueur.

RAUENTHAL — (*Rau*-en-tahl) — Small village of the Rheingau, set back in the Taunus hills behind Eltville. Its better vineyards (Baiken, Gehrn, Langenstück, Wülfen, Rothenberg, and Nonnenberg) constitute about the most valuable agricultural land per acre in Germany and, in the opinion of many experts, produce the most distinguished of all Rhine wines. These are especially notable for their "spiciness," fruit and breed, and in good vintages they are truly incomparable. Note that Rauenthaler Steinmächer is a *Grosslage* (*see*) whose wines may or may not come from Rauenthal itself and is in any case never one of the best wines from this village.

RAUSAN-SÉGLA, Château — (Row-sah Say-glah) — Generally considered the best vineyard, after Château Margaux itself, in the *commune* of Margaux; one of the most consistent and distinguished of the 2nd Classed Growths. Some 7,000 cases a year of red wine, *bouqueté* and fine.

285

RAUZAN-GASSIES, Château — (Row-sah Gas-see) — 2nd Classed Growth of Margaux. Perhaps a bit less outstanding than Rausan-Ségla but a good 2nd Growth. About 11,000 cases a year of suave, delicate claret.

RAVAT — French hybridizer whose experiments in crossing native American and *vinifera* vines resulted in some of the best of these hybrids or, as they are called in France, *producteurs-directs*. These carry his name, as Ravat Noir, which gives a light, fruity red wine, somewhat comparable to a Beaujolais, and Ravat Blanc, a superior white-wine grape. Both are grown in the United States.

RAVELLO — (Rahv-*vel*-lo) — Memorably beautiful little town, back of Amalfi and not far from Naples, in southern Italy. Its upland vineyards produce a small amount of white and especially *rosé* wine, of good but not remarkable quality; a good deal of this is exported, much of it consumed, no doubt, by those who find it a nostalgic reminder of hours or days spent in this enchanting little place.

RAYNE-VIGNEAU, Château — (Rain Veen-yo) — 1st Classed Growth of Bommes, Sauternes. One of the most remarkable of the great Sauternes vineyards; golden, sweet wines of extraordinary breed, power and depth of flavor. About 9,000 cases a year.

RAYON D'OR — (Ray-on Door) — French hybrid grown in United States; noted for steady production and high sugar; makes crisp clean white table and sparkling wines.

RECIOTO — (Reh-*cho*-toe) — Celebrated "special" wine of the Valpolicella Country, near Verona, in northern Italy. Made from partially raisined grapes, it is, when not sparkling, a remarkably fruity, highly perfumed, sweet red wine, on the order of an exceedingly light Port. When, which is unfortunately far more often, it is *frizzante,* or slightly sparkling, it remains a remarkable wine in its class, but one not likely to appeal to a confirmed wine drinker, accustomed to dry wines.

RÉCOLTE — (Ray-colt) — French, harvest (verb) or crop (noun).

RED WINE — Wine made from red (or blue, purple or black) grapes, most of which have no red color in the juice. The color in the wine comes from the inside of the grape skin during fermentation or heating. Pink and *rosé* wines are in reality red wines kept light in color by removal of the skins when the desired hue is attained.

REFOSCO — (Reh-*fahs*-co) — Red wine grape of mediocre quality from northeastern Italy, considered by some experts to be probably the Mondeuse (*see*) under a different name. Transplanted to California, notably to the Napa Valley, it somehow became known as Crabb's Black Burgundy. In California, as in Italy, the wine is quite ordinary.

REFRESHMENT WINE — Another name for Flavored Wine (*see*).

REGIONAL — Wine that takes its name from a district or region rather than from a specific town or vineyard, generally inexpensive and generally a blend.

286

Wines labeled "Anjou," "Médoc," "Côte de Beaune," for example, are regional wines.

REHOBOAM — Large size bottle equivalent to six regular bottles.

REICHARTSHAUSEN — (*Rike*-harts-*how*-zen) — German wine-producing estate in the Rheingau, near the town of Oestrich. For some strange reason, the new German Wine Law has seen fit to classify this estate as an Ortsteil (*see*), thus ranking it legally with such famous estates as Schloss Vollrads and Schloss Johannisberg. Such a distinction is hardly deserved and the wines from this estate are usually rather undistinguished.

REIMS — (Ranss) — Famous cathedral city east of Paris; with Épernay, one of the two major centers of the Champagne trade. Underground, it is an ant hill of galleries and vaults and workrooms, cut in the white, underlying chalk, in which the Champagne is stored and aged and processed; these proved an invaluable refuge and shelter during the dark days of World War I.

REINHARTSHAUSEN, Schloss — (*Rhine*-harts-*how*-zen) — Celebrated German wine-producing estate in the heart of the Rheingau, between Erbach and Hattenheim, with some seventy-four acres of vineyard, belonging to the late Kaiser's collateral descendants. The labels of this estate carry the designation, "Erzeuger-Abfüllung Administration des Prinzen Friedrich von Preussen."
Although the castle (never very imposing or attractive) has now been converted into a hotel, the wines are as distinguished as ever and among the Rhine's best. They come from important holdings in Erbacher Markobrunn, Siegelsberg, Steinmorgen, and in Hattenheimer Hassel, and Wisselbrunnen.

REMUAGE — (Ray-mew-ahj) — One of the essential operations in Champagne making: the shaking and turning of the bottles in their racks of *pupitres,* by which the sediment is brought down against the cork, prior to disgorging. This is called *Rütteln* in German, and sometimes "riddling" in California. For all of this, *see* Champagne.

REPEAL — December 5, 1933, when Utah became the thirty-sixth state to ratify the 21st Amendment which repealed the 18th or Prohibition (*see*) Amendment.

RÉSERVE — (Ray-zerv) — Word often found on commercial wine labels. It has no legal or real meaning, except what the producer or shipper sees fit to give it.

RETSINA — (Ret-*seen*-uh) — A Greek wine noted for its pronounced flavor of resin or turpentine, which probably derives from an ancient custom of sealing wine barrels with pitch. The wine is an acquired taste, and most of it is consumed in Greece itself.

REUILLY — (Ruh-yee) — Dry white wine, good but increasingly hard to come by, produced not far from Quincy (*see*) near the Cher river in the upper Loire basin, in France, from the Sauvignon Blanc grape. The vineyards, often grievously damaged by spring frosts, are being gradually abandoned, and it is quite possible that Reuilly will cease to exist within our lifetime.

RHEIMS — *See* REIMS.

RHEIN — (Rhine) — German for Rhine (*see*).

RHEINGAU — (*Rhine*-gow) — In the opinion of many experts, the greatest white wine region in the world. It covers the foothills of the Taunus range, west of Wiesbaden and more or less opposite Mainz, in Germany, and overlooks an extraordinary reach of the Rhine which here, on its way north from Switzerland to the North Sea, makes a great bend and runs slightly south of west for over twenty miles. The vineyards, therefore, strung along the right or generally north bank of the river, have here the most ideal exposure, nearly due south, and they benefit from the warmth of the reflected sunshine off the Rhine. Legally, the wines of Hochheim, east of the Rheingau proper, and overlooking the Main, are Rheingau wines, as are also those of Assmannshausen and Lorch, on the steep slopes of the Rhine gorge on to the north.

The Rheingau is one of the eleven Anbaugebiete (*see*) and consists of 1 Bereich, 10 Grosslagen and almost 125 Einzellagen. Its total production is extremely small by international standards and amounts only to some 6,600,000 gallons a year, 4% of Germany's total, a good part of which is drunk locally. There are about 7,000 acres under vines, well over 75% of them Rieslings, and this variety predominates wherever good Rheingau wine is made. The cheapest wines are generally sugared, to bring their alcoholic content up to the desired minimum, and these often carry just the name of a village on their label, in conjunction with the word *Bereich* (*see*), as Bereich Johannisberg or Bereich Hochheim. Higher quality wine, although still sugared in years when it is necessary, is sold as *Qualitätswein* (*see*). Such wines bear the name of a specific vineyard and are often estate-bottled (*see*). All the best wines are sold as *Qualitätswein mit Prädikat* (*see*) and are nearly always estate-bottled. Assmannshausen produces a few red wines of fair quality and there exist random plantings of red grapes elsewhere, but apart from these all the Rheingau wines are white.

Most of them follow the usual German system of wine nomenclature — a town name plus a *Lagename,* or vineyard name, as Rüdesheimer Bischofsberg, Johannisberger Hölle, Rauenthaler Baiken, Hochheimer Domdechaney. A few vineyard names, however, are so famous that they stand alone: Schloss Johannisberger, Schloss Vollrads, Steinberger, etc. In addition, wines of superior quality always carry such designations as Kabinett, Spätlese, Auslese (*see all of these*); estate-bottling is indicated by the producer's name, plus the term *Erzeugerabfüllung.*

Few, if any, of the world's great vineyard districts can compare with the Rheingau when it comes to the average quality of their wines. There is nevertheless an astonishingly wide variation between the Rheingaus of a poor vintage and those of a great year; and even among the wines of any given harvest. Some sound and authentic bottles can be sold in America for as little as $2, while others may cost $25 or more and be well worth it. The most expensive of all, the Auslesen, Beerenauslesen and Trockenbeerenauslesen, are generally quite sweet, and are truly dessert wines, comparable to the finer French Sauternes, though much lower in alcohol. Those of lesser rank are for the most part fairly but not austerely dry, exceedingly fruity, with a characteristic and memorable bouquet, and rarely contain much over 11% of alcohol by volume. The "big" wines of great vintages are long-lived and rather slow to develop — best, perhaps when from four to ten years old; the smaller, lighter and dryer ones are usually in bottle by their first birthday and quite ready to drink a year or so later.

Between Hochheim on the east and Rüdesheim on the west (and not including Lorch and Assmannshausen) there are fourteen wine-producing villages, nine strung along the river and five set back in the hills; nine or ten of the fourteen are world famous, and all are listed in their proper alphabetical place in this volume. *See,* therefore, **Hochheim, *Walluf, **Eltville, ***Rauenthal, **Kiedrich, ***Erbach, ***Hattenheim, *Oestrich, **Hallgarten, **Winkel, ***Johannisberg, **Geisenheim and ***Rüdesheim. Also Schloss Eltz, Schloss Reinhartshausen, Steinberg, Schloss Vollrads and Schloss Johannisberg.

RHEINHESSEN — (*Rhine*-hess-sen) — The western corner of Hessia, or Hessen, a German state, the Rheinhesse is more politically allied to the Rheinpfalz, its neighbor in the south; as far as wine is concerned one of the eleven Anbaugebiete (*see*) consisting of 3 Bereiche, 24 Grosslagen and about 430 Einzellagen, bounded on the east and north by the Rhine, on the south by the Pfalz, and on the west by the Valley of the Nahe. Mainz is its principal city,

WIESBADEN

MAINZ

MAIN

INGELHEIM

RÜDESHEIM

LAUBENHEIM

BINGEN

BÜDESHEIM

BODENHEIM

GAU-BISCHOFSHEIM

NACKENHEIM

HARXHEIM

NIERSTEIN

N

OPPENHEIM

DIENHEIM

RHEINHESSEN

GUNTERSBLUM

ALSHEIM

SCALE

MI. 0   2   4   6
KM. 0   4   8   12

WORMS

and Rhine Wine is its occupation: there are over 50,000 acres of vineyard, and the average annual production is about 53 million gallons, nearly 90% of it white. The Müller-Thurgau is the leading grape followed closely by the Sylvaner, although the best Hessian wines are made from the Riesling and almost invariably so labeled. Wine is produced in 155 different villages (amusingly enough, 120 of these have names that end in ''-heim'') but all of the truly superior wines come from about ten towns, all strung along the Rhine, rather than from the fertile, rolling country back from the river. These ten, more or less in order of quality, are: Nierstein, Nackenheim, Oppenheim, Bingen, Dienheim, Bodenheim, Laubenheim, Guntersblum, Alsheim and Worms — all of them will be found listed, in their proper alphabetical place, in this encyclopedia; together, they have about 6,000 acres of vines. Practically all the rest of the wine grown in Rheinhessen (and much produced in these ten towns as well) is either sold as ''open'' wine or labeled Liebfraumilch (*see*); this is a general catch-all name, and quite meaningless: *see* also Domtal.

These cheaper Hessian wines have not much except their price to recommend them; mild, soft, often heavily sulphured, without any real character, they reflect credit neither on the Germans who make and sell them, nor on American consumers who seem to buy them in preference to far better Rieslings and Sylvaners from California.

The fine wines of Hessia are another story: made from the Riesling (occasionally the Sylvaner) in the first six of the ten towns listed above, they often have real distinction and many of them can fairly be called great. Less ''classic'' perhaps than the finest Rheingaus, they have great fruit and fragrance, elegance and ripeness and great charm. It goes without saying that the best of them carry a town and vineyard name, and are estate-bottled.

RHEINPFALZ — (*Rhine*-pfahltz) — One of Germany's eleven Anbaugebiete (*see*), in most years first in production, with some 50,000 acres under vines, an average annual yield of better than 60 million gallons and which includes 2 Bereiche, 26 Grosslagen and about 330 Einzellagen. This has been true since medieval days; the Pfalz, or Palatinate, then was known as the ''Wine Cellar of the Holy Roman Empire,'' *propter vini copiam*, on account of the abundance of its wines. Actually both of its current names come from the Latin: Pfalz is a corruption of *Palast*, or palace, and Palatinate, after the ''Palatine'' Hill, one of Rome's seven, where the Roman emperors built their palaces, and from which the word ''palace'' stems. Before long, the person charged with the care of the emperor's palaces acquired the title of *Comes Palatinus*, or Count Palatine, and the title survived in Germany.

The present district is bounded on the east by the Rhine, on the south and west by Alsace-Lorraine, and on the north by Rheinhessen. The vineyards extend along the lower slopes of a chain of hills called the Haardt, a sort of lesser northern prolongation of the Alsatian Vosges, and over a good portion of the fertile plain that extends eastward toward the Rhine, opposite Mannheim and Karlsruhe. Most of all this produces nothing more than very common white and red table wine, with the white predominating by a wide margin.

Such wines as are fit for bottling and for export come almost exclusively from a small central section known as the Mittel-Haardt, between Neustadt and Bad Dürkheim. There is a good deal of ordinary red wine, made mostly from the Portugieser grape, and a great deal more white.

Four especially favored villages produce wine of top class: from north to south, Wachenheim, Forst, Deidesheim and Ruppertsberg (*see* these), but Bad Dürkheim, Kallstadt, Leistadt and Königsbach can all be ranked not too far behind.

The wines have a special character of their own: the lesser ones a

Bodengeschmack, or taste of heavy soil; but the Rieslings from the better vine-yards are truly of the highest quality — fine, fuller-bodied than the Rheingaus but hardly inferior to them. They have considerable bouquet and breed and go better than most other German wines with food. The Beerenauslesen, and Trockenbeerenauslesen, of great vintages are much sought after, and bring astronomic prices.

RHENISH — Old English term for wines of the Rhine, now largely replaced by "Hock" in Great Britain, and by "Rhine Wine" in the United States.

RHINE — 800 mile long river flowing north and west from its Swiss Alpine source through or bordering Switzerland, Lichenstein, Austria, France, West Germany and Holland. On the way, its basin nurtures the great vineyards of Germany, Alsace and Switzerland, primarily producers of white wines.

RHINE WINE — Properly and sensibly, a wine from the Rhine Valley. Unfortunately, under American law, almost any white wine under 14% alcohol may be so labeled, no matter where made or out of what sort of grapes. Those who wish to find some sort of an American equivalent of a German Rhine wine should look to Johannisberg Riesling and Sylvaner from California, or Dr. Konstantin Frank's Johannisberg Riesling from the Finger Lakes district of New York State. For fuller information about the German original, *see* Rheingau, Rheinhesse, Rheinpfalz and Germany.

RHÔNE — (Rone) — One of the great rivers of Western Europe, rising in Switzerland, traversing Lake Geneva, emptying into the Mediterranean west of Marseille. Vines are grown along its banks throughout a large part of its whole length and a great variety of different wines are produced — those of the Valais, the Vaud, Lavaux, and what is called La Côte, in Switzerland; Seyssel, between Geneva and Lyon; and all those known as Rhône wines, or Côtes-du-Rhône *(see)*, between Lyon and the Mediterranean. These include Côte Rôtie, Condrieu, Château Grillet, Crozes, Hermitage, Cornas, Saint Péray, Gigondas, Châteauneuf-du-Pape, Tavel, Lirac, etc. *(see* all of these).
   ALSO, a French *département,* that of the Beaujolais Country and the city of Lyon.

RIBEAUVILLÉ — (Ree-bo-vee-lay) — Important Alsatian vineyard town in the *département* of Haut-Rhin. White wines of exceptional quality.

RICE WINE — Since it is made from a type of grain, rice wine could be considered a kind of beer. It is a specialty of the Far East, especially Japan where it is called Saké.

RICEYS — (Ree-say) — Curious, almost forgotten little corner along the southern edge of the French Champagne Country, in the *département* of Aube, adjoining Burgundy. Its vineyards, planted mostly to Pinot Noir but with some Gamay, a fresh, often quite pleasant, short-lived, non-sparkling *vin rosé,* called Rosé des Riceys. It is something of a collector's item but of no great class.

RICHEBOURG — (Reesh-bourg) — One of the very great red-wine vineyards of Burgundy, just over 19.75 acres, in the township of Vosne-Romanée. It is bounded on the south by Romanée-Conti and La Romanée, and on the east of Romanée Saint-Vivant; its wine (some 2,650 cases a year) is generally somewhat sturdier and fuller, with deeper color, than that of its illustrious neighbors — it is the "biggest" wine of Vosne-Romanée. Until quite recently, a portion of it was still planted to old, non-grafted vines, as in the pre-phylloxera period, and was considered to give an even finer wine. A major part of Richebourg belongs to the Domaine de la Romanée Conti (*see*).

RICHELIEU, Armand, Cardinal de — (1585-1642) — French cardinal and statesman, who asked: "If God forbade drinking would He have made wine so good?"

RICHON-LE-ZION — Location of one of the most important wineries and vineyards in Israel.

RIDDLING — *see* REMUAGE.

RIESLING — (Reece-ling) — One of the very greatest of white wine grapes, apparently a native of the Rhine Valley; it has been grown there since Roman days at least, and no acceptable evidence exists to show that it originated elsewhere. Stories to the effect that it is identical with the Sercial of Madeira and the Pedro Ximénez of Spain are unworthy of credence; in modern times it has been transplanted into many other countries, and has almost always yielded superior wine, in Chile and in California, in Austria and Switzerland and Italy. It gives its best and wholly remarkable wine where it is not asked to produce too much, in cool districts, and on slaty or stony soil.

Thus it is the one variety cultivated in all of the more distinguished Moselle vineyards, and in all the best of the Rheingau; it is widely planted in Rheinhessen and the Rheinpfalz, and immeasurably outdistances all its rivals in quality, if not always in acreage. Its wine is the best of Alsace; it does well in Austria and Switzerland and in the Italian Tyrol. The Chilean "Rieslings" (some of which may well be made from the more productive Sylvaner), shipped in flagons, or Bocksbeutel, are by far the most widely accepted South American white wines in the United States.

In California (and even in New York State) there has been a good deal of confusion, some of it a long way from accidental, with respect to the variety and its name. Here the true variety is known as the "White Riesling" or "Johannisberger Riesling," but wines may be labeled "Riesling" if made from the Chauché Gris ("Grey Riesling") or the Sylvaner ("Franken Riesling"), or the "Emerald Riesling" (a modern hybrid), or even the "Missouri Riesling" (a native American vine, probably the Elvira). The same sort of loose popularization has taken place in Europe, and we have crosses such as the "Main Riesling" and vines such as the *"Wälschriesling"* which have no possible proper right to the name.

In California the true Riesling grape, without the benefit of *pourriture noble* yet grown farther south and under sunnier skies, gives a fine dry white wine of good bouquet and considerable distinction. It is almost always labeled "Johannisberg Riesling."

RIEUSSEC, Château — (Ree-oo-sec) — 1st Classed Growth of Fargues, Sauternes. Lighter than Yquem (*see*) yet full-bodied, deep-colored Sauternes, in general less sweet but more obvious and less fine than most of the other 1st Growths. About 8,500 cases a year.

RILLY-LA-MONTAGNE — (Ree-yee-Lah-Mohn-tahyn) — Secondary wine-producing village of the French Champagne Country, on the Montagne de Reims.

RIOJA — (Ree-o-ha) — The most important and by all odds the best table wine district of Spain. It takes its name from the Rio Oja, a small tributary of the River Ebro, which it joins on the edge of the Basque Country, near Pamplona, not very far from the western Pyrénées and the French border. This is high, cold, upland country, and the bare hills north and south of the valley are often white with snow as late as April; the average altitude of the vineyards is well over 1,500 feet. The wines are therefore anything but fiery and full-bodied (although they have often been called both by writers unfamiliar with them) and on the whole are lighter, lower in alcohol and dryer than those of Bordeaux, to which they bear a certain superficial resemblance.

This kinship (much more marked in the red wines than in the white) is not altogether accidental; when the phylloxera (*see*) arrived and began to devastate the Bordeaux vineyards in the 1880's, several hundred French families from Bordeaux moved south into the still uninfected Ebro valley, and settled in Haro and Logroño, still today the main centers of the Rioja wine trade; they brought with them their Bordeaux methods and their Bordeaux skill. Both, in the light of what we now know about wine production, could stand a little refurbishing, especially as far as white wines are concerned, for Riojas are presently made, operation for operation, almost precisely as Bordeaux wines were made 100 years ago — aged three to five years in oak, and the whites rather liberally sulphured. There is no *pourriture noble* (*see*) in this high arid zone, and therefore no legitimate Rioja counterpart of Sauternes. The dry white wines tend to be dull, neutral and somewhat common; the reds are often quite outstanding and, considering their quality, remarkably inexpensive.

The principal white grapes are the Viura, Maturana, Calgraño and Turrantés (*"ni la comas ni la des — que par vino buena es"* or "don't eat it or give it away — it's good for wine").

295

Most of the red grape varieties, too, are Spanish; none of them are among those properly classified as "noble"; they include the Garnacha (Grenache), Graciano, Mazuela and Tempranillo. Yet, with a very low yield per acre, what they give is surprisingly good: rather light, fine-textured red wines, with a faint earthy flavor and a good deal of breed.

The Rioja district has been officially delimited and there is an excellent, well-staffed government viticultural station in Haro. There are unfortunately no specific vineyard appellations (although many wines are sold under names that appear to be, as "Viña X," etc.) and one has to rely on producers' names, or brands. Vintage years should be generally disregarded and are loosely used. Most producers offer a range of red wines, from *Clarete* (usually the youngest, lightest and cheapest) to *Gran Reserva, Imperial,* and the like, which are always older and generally quite fine. The more reliable shippers include the Marqués de Riscal, the Marqués de Murrieta, Federico Paternina, the Bodegas Bilbainas, the Bodegas Franco-Españolas, La Rioja Alta, etc. The main wine producing towns, apart from Haro, are Elciego, Fuenmayor, Cenicero and Ollauri.

RIPAILLE — (Ree-pie) — Lesser white wine of the Haute Savoie *département* of France, made from Chasselas grapes near Thonon-les-Bains on Lake Geneva, rarely exported and of no great quality.

RIPARIA — The most widespread specie of native American grapes; *Vitis Riparia* is particularly prevalent in the north central states.

RIPE — Wine taster's term and high praise. Applied to a wine that has fruit, no trace of greenness or harshness, generally a white wine that is not bone dry although not necessarily sweet. Sometimes also means a wine ready to drink.

RIQUEWIHR — (Reek-veer) — One of the best wine-producing villages of Alsace and one of the most picturesque of France, its medieval walls and towers and gateways still intact and its narrow streets lined with fine old half-timbered houses. Some ten miles northwest of Colmar, it is set in the vineyard-covered foothills of the Vosges; its Rieslings are particularly famous.

RISERVA — (Ree-sehr-vah) — Legal term in Italy for wines at least three years old.

RIVERO — (Ree-*vair*-ro) — Spanish wine district, in the province of Galicia, along the Portuguese border. Most of the *Vinos de Rivero,* for such is their legal name, are red-purple, very fruity, with a pronounced and highly special flavor which is not likely to appeal to everyone. A fortified sweet wine called Tostado del Rivero is produced in the same district.

RIVESALTES — (Reev-sahlt) — Town north of Perpignan in the French *département* of Pyrénées Orientales. It has given its name to a district comprising over a dozen townships and producing some 12 million gallons a year of fortified dessert wine, about a third of it called Muscat de Rivesaltes, and the rest, principally from Grenache and Malvoisie grapes, sold simply as Rivesaltes or Rivesaltes Rancio. It legally must contain a minimum of 15% alcohol by volume, and is somewhat comparable to Banyuls (*see*), although generally less fine.

ROANNAIS — (Ro-an-nay) — Roanne is a little city west of Lyon in central France, round which are produced a number of pleasant red *vins de pays,* fresh, light, early-maturing, made mostly from the Gamay grape, and sold as Côtes Roannaises (formerly Vins de Renaison). They are entitled to the V.D.Q.S. seal, but few if any are exported.

ROBE — (Rohb) — French term concerning combined color and clarity, a wine should have "une belle robe".

ROBUST — Wine taster's term. Sound, sturdy, full-bodied, not necessarily fine.

ROCHE AUX MOINES, La — (Rawsh oh Mwahn) — One of the best vineyards of Savennières (*see*), which produces some of the most distinguished of the great sweet white wines of Anjou.

ROCHECORBON — (Rawsh-cor-baw) — One of the more important villages of the Vouvray district, just east of Tours, in France.

ROCHEFORT-SUR-LOIRE — (Rawsh-for soor Lwar) — Little town on the Loire, just west of Angers, responsible for some of the very finest white Anjou wines. These, made from the Chenin Blanc grape, rarely carry the town name except as the address of the producer, and are marketed either as Coteaux du Layon (a regional appellation) or as Quarts de Chaume (*see*).

ROMANÈCHE-THORINS — (Ro-man-esh Tor-ran) — Town on the eastern edge of the Beaujolais district, but not the name of a wine. Its vineyards form part of Moulin-à-Vent (*see*) and their wines are marketed under this appellation.

ROMANÉE, La — (La Ro-ma-nay) — Tiny vineyard, barely two acres in extent, producing one of the rarest of red Burgundies. It is in the township of Vosne-Romanée, directly above and west of Romanée-Conti, and its production is rarely much over 300 cases; in recent years it has not often given wines of outstanding quality.

ROMANÉE-CONTI — (Ro-ma-nay Cawn-tee) — Perhaps the most celebrated of all red Burgundies, traditionally the *ne plus ultra* of red wine, often, especially in pre-war years, fully worthy of its extraordinary reputation. The vineyard is of roughly 4½ acres and its average production is about 650 cases, although less than 100 in 1945; previously in old, ungrafted vines (Pinot Noir, needless to say), it was replanted in 1946 and is now producing, from vines grafted on American rootstocks, wines, equal in quality to what it yielded before. It takes its name from the Prince de Conti, its owner from 1760 to 1795, and was acquired in 1869 by M. Duvault-Blochet, the leading vineyard-owner of Burgundy of that day, and direct ancestor of one of the present proprietors, M. de Villaine and M. Leroy. It now forms part of the Domaine de la Romanée-Conti, the most famous single estate of the Côte d'Or; this comprises Romanée-Conti and La Tâche (*see*), both in their entirety, a large part of Richebourg, and important holdings in Échézeaux and Grands Échézeaux. In addition, the Domaine has a long-term lease on the portion of Romanée-St.-Vivant which belonged to General Marey-Monge, and also has a small holding in the famous Montrachet vineyard. All of these, *grands seigneurs* in every sense of the term, are vinified and bottled in the estate cellars and have

SOCIÉTÉ CIVILE DU DOMAINE DE LA ROMANÉE-CONTI
PROPRIETAIRE A VOSNE-ROMANÉE (COTE-D'OR)

ROMANÉE-CONTI

APPELLATION ROMANÉE-CONTI CONTROLÉE

7.220 Bouteilles Récoltées

N°

LES ASSOCIÉS-GÉRANTS

ANNÉE 1974

Mise en bouteille au domaine

PRODUCE OF FRANCE

75 cl

what might be called a certain family resemblance — believed, by certain experts, attributable to some secret of vinification. Romanée-Conti commands the highest price of any of these, and, in most years, the highest price of any red Burgundy. It is a great rarity and a very great wine.

For Map, *see* VOSNE.

ROMANÉE SAINT-VIVANT — (Ro-man-nay San Vee-vaw) — Admirable Burgundian vineyard, directly adjoining Romanée-Conti and Richebourg, in the township of Vosne-Romanée. It takes its name from the Priory of Saint-Vivant, having been conveyed as a gift to the monks of this priory (some three miles west of Vosne) by the Duchess of Burgundy in 1232; it remained their property until the French Revolution. Twenty-three acres in extent, divided among several owners, its average yield is some 2,500 cases. One of the finest of all red Burgundies, full, soft, with great bouquet, it has the incomparable distinction of the Romanées, and there are few if any better wines in France.

ROMANIA — Wine producing country in Eastern Europe, some 200 million gallons yearly, the ninth largest world producer.

ROME — A great wine center in addition to being the capital of Italy (*see* Lazio).

ROMER, Château — (Ro-may) — 2nd Classed Growth of Fargues, Sauternes. Small production (1,500 cases) of good, fairly sweet wine.

RONDINELLA — (Rohn-dee-*nel*-la) — Italian red wine grape of secondary importance, planted to a small extent in the vineyards of Valpolicella and elsewhere.

RONSARD, Pierre de — (Raw-sahr) — Eminent French lyric poet who celebrated the delights of his native Loire Valley, the wines occasionally, but even more the countryside and its lovely girls, in some of the most charming verses ever written.

ROSATO — (Roas-*sah*-toe) — Simply means *rosé* in Italian. Pink wine, of course, can be made anywhere. Italy's best, and they are not very numerous,

298

come from Lake Garda (*see*), and from the Trentino and Alto Adige (*see*). They include Chiaretto and Chiarello, Lagrein Rosato, Marzemino d'Isera (*see* all of these) and Rosato d'Avio, from the lower end of Trentino. There are others, less fine, from the Chianti Country and even from Ravello, near Naples.

ROSÉ — (Ro-zay) — French word for pink, when applied to wine, now pretty much part of the English language, and used in almost every country where wine is produced or drunk. A true *vin rosé* is by no means a blend of red and white wines, indeed this is prohibited in France and some other countries, but a special product, usually made from black grapes alone, and owing its color to the fact that it was neither fermented entirely with the grape skins (like all red wines), nor entirely without (like all white wines). *Rosés* of some sort are produced in almost all wine-growing countries, the best of them from the Grenache, Pinot Noir, Cabernet Franc, Gamay, and several Italian grape varieties: they should be served chilled and drunk young. Excellent *rosés* are made in California; the best French come from Tavel (*see*), Marsannay (*see*), the Loire Valley, the Beaujolais, northern Alsace, and Provence.

ROSÉ DE BEARN — (Ro-zay d' Bay-arn) — Pink or *rosé* wine of fair quality produced (from a number of different grapes) in the *département* of Basses-Pyrénées, near Pau. It carries the V.D.Q.S. seal (*see*).

ROSES — Flowers in the vineyard are weeds to the vigneron — except for roses. These are often grown not for decorative purpose but because they are extremely susceptible to oidium (*see*) and therefore indicate when preventative spraying is required.

ROSETTE — (Ro-zet) — Rather agreeable white wine, not entirely dry, made north of Bergerac in the *département* of the Dordogne. It comes largely from the Sémillon grape, plus some Sauvignon Blanc and Muscadelle.

ROSSARA — (Roà-*sahr*-ra) — Italian red wine grape of superior quality, grown in the vineyards of Bardolino (*see*) and elsewhere.

ROSSO — (*Ross*-so) — Simply means red in Italian, and a *vino rosso* is a red wine, any red wine. The term in recent years has been given a somewhat different meaning in California, and now indicates a red table wine that is not altogether dry; there are many such in Italy, but all of the finest Italian red wines are without any trace of sweetness, and would therefore hardly qualify as *vini rossi* in California.

RÔTI — (Row-tee) — French term for Passito (*see*).

ROTTEN EGG FLAVOR — This is the definite, unmistakable odor of hydrogen sulphide or, as experts prefer to call it, metallic sulphur. It is entirely harmless, extremely disagreeable, inexcusable in wine and fortunately very infrequent. It is the result of bad cellar work and carelessness.

ROTUNDIFOLIA — The muscadine grape which has a powerful fruity flavor; this native American species, *Vitis Rotundifolia,* flourishes in the south central and east coast.

ROUGE — (Roojh) — French word for red and generic use meaning red wine.

ROUGET, Château — (Roo-zhay) — 1st Growth vineyard of Pomerol, producing some 8,000 cases a year.

ROUGH — Astringent (see), full of tannin, lack of mellowness, harsh to the taste. A good big wine will start out this way and soften with time; a poor wine never.

ROUND — Well-balanced, without a major defect, complete. Could never be said of a poor wine but does not necessarily mean either fine or great.

ROUSSANNE — (Roo-sahn) — White wine grape widely cultivated in the Rhône Valley, also called the Roussette, giving, notably at Hermitage, Crozes and St. Péray, a full-bodied white wine of rather pronounced character and considerable distinction.

ROUSSETTE — (Roos-set) — Another name for the Roussanne grape (see). In the higher and cooler upper valley of the Rhône, between Lyon and Geneva, and in the hilly département of Haute Savoie, where it is generally called Roussette rather than Roussanne, it yields a number of fresh, fragrant, extremely agreeable white wines, some made sparkling (see Seyssel), some still. A few of these are sold under the varietal name, as Roussette de Savoie.

ROUSSILLON — (Roo-see-yaw) — Old French province which originally comprised the modern département of Pyrénées Orientales, plus part of the Aude, on the Mediterranean coast, along the Spanish border. Its principal town is Perpignan. In total gallonage this is one of the major wine-producing regions of Europe, with a vast amount of vin ordinaire, a few somewhat better table wines (see Corbières), and more than three-quarters of the fortified wines of France. Roussillon, however, is not a wine name, except in the combined form, "Grand Roussillon" (See Banyuls, Côtes d'Agly, Côtes de Rousillon, Grand Roussillon, Maury, Rivesaltes.)

ROXHEIM — (Rawks-heim) — One of the better wine-producing towns of the Nahe district, in Germany.

ROYALTY, RUBIRED — Both are recent grape varieties developed in California, are grown in the Central Valley and used in blends for their high color.

RUBY CABERNET — Warm climate grape variety developed in California, a métis of Cabernet and Carignane; has no right to the name "Cabernet" alone; fair quality, high production.

RUBY PORT — Standard, wood matured, but not old Port; wine with deep red color and young fruity character.

RUCHOTTES — (Roo-shot) — Burgundian vineyard name, probably derived from ruche, or beehive, on account of the sweetness of the grapes there grown or the special bouquet and flavor, recalling that of honey, of the wine. The Ruchottes vineyard in Chassagne-Montrachet (see) produces one of the very finest white wines of France; Ruchottes-Chambertin (see) is ranked as a Grand Cru.

RUCHOTTES-CHAMBERTIN — (Roo-shot Shawm-bair-tan) — Little 7½ acre plot, ranked as a Grand Cru of Burgundy and one of the Chambertin's distinguished neighbors. Directly above and behind Mazis-Chambertin (*see*), it produces a fine red wine, one of the best of its famous township.

RÜDESHEIM — (*Rue*-dess-heim) — Picturesque and celebrated little town of the Rheingau, in Germany, directly facing across the wide, swift Rhine, Bingen (*see*) and the mouth of the Nahe. It is a major tourist center, and its two main streets, squeezed in between the river and the steep vineyards behind, are crowded all summer long, and no less so in the autumn, the vintage-festival season. There are countless cafés and *Weinstuben,* and a substantial part of the wine that its 650 acres of Riesling vines produce, is beyond question promptly and happily consumed within a few hundred yards of where it is made.

As wines, the better Rüdesheimers are nevertheless outstanding, in poor or fair years often the best of the whole Rheingau, full-bodied and distinguished, although in great years they are sometimes too heavy and too high in alcohol. Their good qualities, like their faults, can be attributed to the steepness of the rocky terraced vineyards, which are gravely affected by drought in dry, hot summers, especially those west of the town itself, on what is called the Rüdesheimer Berg. These carry the word *Berg* as part of their appellation, and names to look for on Rüdesheimer labels are Berg Rottland, Berg Roseneck, and Berg Schlossberg. Also (not from the Berg) Bischofsberg, Drachenstein, Kirchenpfad, Klosterberg, Klosterlay, Magdalenenkreuz, and Rosengarten.

Also a small vineyard town of no great consequence or distinction in the Nahe Valley whose wines are often confused by the unwary with those of the great Rheingau slope described above. If properly labeled, these should carry the designation "Nahe," whereas those of the authentic Rüdesheim will be marked "Rheingau." Rüdesheimer Rosengarten is a wine of the Nahe.

RUEDA — (Rue-*eh*-dah) — One of the good, less-known white wines of northern Spain, produced between Valladolid and Zamora, in the Valley of the Duero.

RUFINA — (Rue-*fee*-na) — Town and small district in Italy's Chianti Country, in the valley of the river Sieve, some twenty miles northeast of Florence. Its wines are now sold, almost invariably, simply as Chianti (*see*) and are among the best of those not entitled to the *classico* designation, full-bodied, deep-colored, with fine bouquet.

RULÄNDER — (Rew-len-der) — German name for Pinot Gris (*see*), also called Grauer Burgunder.

RULLY — (Roo-yee) — Small town in Burgundy, just south of the southern end of the Côte d'Or, and therefore belonging to the Côte Chalonnaise; known in the wine trade for its production of Sparkling Burgundy (*see*). Over three-quarters of the wine actually grown in the *commune,* however, is white, and from the Chardonnay grape, fresh, dry, fruity and very palatable: the fruity red comes from the Pinot Noir, and both are entitled to the appellation Rully.

RUPPERTSBERG — (Roop-perts-bairg) — One of the four best wine-producing towns of the Palatinate, or Pfalz, in Germany. In average quality, its wines are perhaps slightly less distinguished than those of Forst and Deidesheim but they are nevertheless remarkable — full-bodied, ripe, fairly high in alcohol; the finest of them, from celebrated growers, are great wines in every sense of the word. They come from such vineyards as Gaisböhl, Spiess, Nussbien, Reiterpfad, Hoheburg, and Linsenbuch, and are estate-bottled by Bassermann-Jordan, Bürkin-Wolf, von Buhl, and a few others.

RURAL METHOD — Ancient and difficult way of making sparkling wine by filtration of the fermenting must and bottling before completion. The continuation of the fermentation after bottling provides the sparkle. Process still in limited use, particularly for muscat wines. Clairette de Die is sometimes made this way.

RUSSIA — Produces more wine than any other country except France and Italy, almost 860 million gallons in 1976, practically all in the Black Sea, Sea of Azov, Caspian Sea and Caucasus areas. Many of the wines are sweet and some 20 million gallons are sparkling.

RUSSIAN RIVER — Like many California rivers, a not too impressive stream, which nevertheless includes Mendocino County and the northern half of Sonoma County in its basin. It runs north-south for most of its course, then cuts abruptly west through the redwood groves of the West Coast range, to the Pacific, some fifty miles north of San Francisco. Its watershed is important to Sonoma winegrowers (*see* Sonoma).

RUST — (Roost) — Rather sweet white wine from the province of Burgenland, in Austria.

RUWER — (Roo-ver) — Small tributary of the Moselle, which it joins some four miles east of Trier, looking much more like a trout stream than a famous river. It wines are legally Moselles, and carry the regional designation "Mosel-Saar-Ruwer" on their labels; the best of them are among the greatest of all German wines, very close in quality and also in character to those of the Saar. There are only about 500 acres of vineyard in the whole valley, all Rieslings, planted on preposterously steep, black-slate, south-facing hillsides. Two estates, each dominating a tiny village, are internationally known; Eitelsbacher Karthäuserhofberg and Maximin-Grünhauser. Very good, somewhat lighter and lesser wines are made in Kasel further upstream, by a number of growers. See Eitelsbach, Maximin-Grünhaus, Kasel.

S

SAAR — (Sahr) — Small river in Germany, a tributary of the Moselle which it joins at Conz, just west of Trier. It rises in the Saar Basin, famous for its heavy industry; then, farther downstream, near the frontier of France and Luxembourg, runs through a steep valley no less famous for its wines. Legally these are Moselles, and carry the designation Mosel-Saar-Ruwer on their labels; they nevertheless have a special character of their own, being austere, almost "steely," very pale, low in alcohol, remarkable for their bouquet. Made from the Riesling grape in one of the coldest wine-growing areas of the world, they are tart and green in all except good vintage years, and are often converted into *Sekt,* or sparkling wine, but in some years they are altogether extraordinary, fully the equals of any other white wines on earth. The most celebrated vineyard is the Scharzhofberg (*see*), and the leading wine-producing towns are, in about this order of quality: Wiltingen, Ockfen, Ayl, Kanzem, Oberemmel, Wawern, Pellingen, etc.

For Map, *see* MOSELLE.

SAARBURG — (Sahr-boorg) — Picturesque little town on the Saar, in Germany, not far from the French border. Most of its pale, tart white wines end up as *Sekt,* or Sparkling Moselle, and only in rare, especially good years do they, as still wines, achieve any real quality.

SABLES-SAINT-ÉMILION — (Sah-ble Sant A-me-lee-aw) — Small district of red wine, directly adjoining St. Émilion (*see*) on the west. The word *sable,* in French, means "sand" — the sandy and alluvial soil of this little area, on the flat plain running down to the Dordogne River, practically in the town of Libourne, yields no great wines at all, but a few that are fruity, early-maturing, short-lived, highly agreeable. Château Martinet is perhaps the best. Sables-Saint-Émilion has now ceased to exist as a separate appellation, but is included in Saint-Émilion.

SACCHAROMYCES — The yeasts of wine fermentation.

SACK — Term used in Elizabethan England (also "Sherris Sack") to mean Sherry; literally, the verb *sacar* in Spanish means (among other things) "to transfer from one place or country to another," and a *Vino de Saca* then meant, and now means, a wine destined for export. "Dry Sack," however, is a leading brand of Sherry, a good quality dry Oloroso.

SACRAMENTAL WINE — Mass wine or altar wine, made in accordance with the strict church regulations governing purity, naturalness and alcoholic content.

SAGGIA VINO — (Sadj-ja-*vee*-no) — Italian for a *pipette* or "wine-thief," used for taking samples from a barrel.

SAINT AMOUR — (Sant Ah-mour) — Northernmost of the important wine-producing *communes* of the Beaujolais, and officially ranked as one of the nine best; it is directly northeast of Juliénas, and its full name is Saint-Amour-Bellevue (it should not, of course, be confused with the town of St. Amour, off east in the *département* of the Jura). Its wine is popular, perhaps partially on account of its romantic name, but on the whole it deserves its rank and its fame: it is a fruity, tender red wine, soon ready. Some 300,000 gallons a year. (*see* Beaujolais).

SAINT AUBIN — (Sant O-ban) — Wine-producing village of no great importance, back of Puligny-Montrachet and Chassagne-Montrachet, in Burgundy. Most of its better wines are sold as Côte-de-Beaune Villages (*see*) or as Bourgogne-Aligoté.

SAINT DENIS — *See* CLOS ST. DENIS.

SAINT-ÉMILION — (Sant A-me-lee-aw) — Ancient and wonderfully picturesque little town, rich in ruins and medieval buildings, set on the edge of an escarpment overlooking the green Dordogne Valley, some twenty miles east of Bordeaux. It was already famous for its wines in the 4th century, and, with 16,000 acres of vines, its district produces more superior wine today than any other division of the Bordeaux Country. Most of the best vineyards are in the township of St. Émilion itself, but eight adjoining *communes* are also entitled to the appellation, and five more areas, or *communes,* may add the words St. Émilion to their own name on wine labels, as Lussac-St. Émilion, etc. The finest wines come either from the steep, chalky slopes of the escarpment itself (*vins des côtes*), or from the high, gravelly plateau behind (*vins des graves,* or Graves-St. Émilion); among the former, Châteaux Ausone, Bélair, Magdelaine, Canon, Clos Fourtet, Beauséjour, La Gaffelière are perhaps the most famous, with at least 30 or 40 others deserving almost equal rank; of the latter, Château Cheval Blanc is easily first, with Châteaux Figeac, Croque-Michotte, Corbin, etc., not too far behind.

District wines labeled "St. Émilion" often come from the eight adjoining, less distinguished townships, (Libourne, Saint-Christophe-des-Bardes, Saint-Étienne-de-Lisse, Saint-Hippolyte, Saint-Laurent-des-Combes, Saint-Pey-d'Armens, Saint-Sulpice-de-Faleyrens and Vignonet), but even these have a relatively high average quality — they are sturdy, warm, generous, wholly agreeable Clarets, pleasing even when young, and attractive even when not "great"; they have been called "the Burgundies of the Bordeaux Country." The great château-bottlings are, of course, of a far higher class and are by no means inferior to the great Médocs, although their character is quite different.

Wines from the secondary, nearby townships have less breed, and occasionally a *goût de terroir*, or taste of heavy soil, but they are generally inexpensive and often good values. The appellations involved are: MONTAGNE-SAINT-ÉMILION which may include PARSAC-SAINT-ÉMILLION and SAINT-GEORGES-SAINT-ÉMILION (or these two may be labeled with their own names), LUSSAC-SAINT-ÉMILION, and PUISSEGUIN-SAINT-ÉMILION. A little white wine is produced, but is not entitled to any of these names.

ALSO, name given to the Ugni Blanc or Trebbiano variety of grape in the Cognac Country of France. There, known as the St. Émilion, it has almost entirely replaced the somewhat finer Folle Blanche in the making of wine for distillation — it is productive, and yields exactly what is required: a wine low in alcohol and very high in acid. It apparently reached Cognac by way of St. Émilion where, although white, it was planted to some extent in the red-wine vineyards; late maturing, picked when not yet ripe, its grapes supplied a welcome additional acidity to the Cabernets and Merlots in great years.

Incidentally, the name St. Émilion, as applied to the Ugni grape, is considered a localism, not a true grape name, and *no* white wine, whether made from the Ugni or other grapes, may be labeled St. Émilion under French law, although this appears to be authorized in California, where it produces sound, well balanced neutral wines, good but without much character and charm.

SAINT-ESTÈPHE — (Sant Es-teff) — Northernmost of the major wine-producing townships of the Haut-Médoc, directly adjoining Pauillac. Its best wines (Châteaux Cos d'Estournel, Calon-Ségur, Montrose, etc.) are sturdy, full-bodied, generous and attractive; they have perhaps less finesse and breed than comparable Clarets from Margaux, St. Julien and Pauillac, but a sort of forthright, lusty charm instead, which renders them most agreeable. There are many excellent lesser vineyards, *crus bourgeois* and the like, and regional wines labeled "St. Estèphe" are generally good values, although occasionally a bit on the heavy side, and sometimes slightly earthy.

SAINT-GEORGES, Château — (San Zhorz) — The largest vineyard and on the whole the best of the little district known as Saint-Georges-Saint-Émilion (*see*). Its average annual production is 25,000 cases, a figure surpassed, by few other châteaux in the Bordeaux Country. In quality it is both dependable and good.

SAINT-GEORGES-SAINT-ÉMILION — (San Zhorzh Sant A-me-lee-aw) — One of the best of the secondary *communes* adjoining St. Émilion (*see*), entitled to

306

the name in this combined form or may be labeled Montagne-St.-Émilion. A number of its wines are decidedly superior to most of what is ordinarily sold under the more highly rated appellation St. Émilion. The better Châteaux include: Saint-Georges, Saint-Georges-Macquin, Samion, Jacquet, Tourteau, etc.

SAINT-JOSEPH — (San Zho-sef) — A Rhône wine, generally red although a little white and *rosé* is also made and legally entitled to the name, produced opposite Hermitage, on the right or west bank of the Rhône. Its quality is good, but hardly extraordinary.

SAINT-JULIEN — (San Zhoe-lee-eh) — Township in the very center and heart of the Haut-Médoc. Its wines include none of the very highest rank, but practically no poor ones either, and when sold simply as "St. Julien," they are almost invariably the most expensive of the Bordeaux regionals. Sometimes called the perfect Claret for Claret-lovers, St. Julien is a little fuller than Margaux, generally has more finesse and bouquet than St. Estèphe, matures sooner than Pauillac. The more famous Châteaux include: Léoville-Poyferré, Léoville-Barton, Léoville-Las-Cases, Gruaud-Larose, Ducru-Beaucaillou, Beychevelle, Talbot, etc.

SAINT-LAURENT — (San Law-raw) — Township in the Haut-Médoc, west of St. Julien. There are three châteaux officially classed in 1855; Château La Tour-Carnet (4th), Château Belgrave and Château Camensac (both 5ths).

SAINT-MACAIRE — (San Mac-care) — See CÔTES-DE-BORDEAUX.

SAINT MARTIN — (San Mar-tan) — The Patron Saint of wine in the Loire. His celebration on November 11 is a joyous one, what with new wine to be drunk and provisions plentiful for the winter to come.

ST. NICOLAS DE BOURGUEIL — (San Ni-ko-la duh Boor-guh-ee) — Superior red wine made from the Cabernet Franc grape in the province of Touraine, France. *See* Bourgueil.

SAINT PÉRAY — (San Pay-ray) — White wine of the Rhône Valley, more often than not made sparkling by the Champagne process, produced round the village of this name, opposite Valence, on the right or west bank of the Rhône. Coming from the same grapes as white Hermitage, the Roussanne (or Roussette) and Marsanne, it is more golden in color and fuller-bodied than Champagne, but with quite definite, special character — certainly one of the better *vins mousseux* of France. As a still wine, it is a little lighter than white Hermitage, and less fine.

SAINT-PIERRE-BONTEMPS-ET-SEVAISTRE, Château — (San Pea-air Baw-taw ay Sev-ace-tr) — Good 4th Classed Growth of St. Julien, producing a sound, well-balanced claret. It has recently been reunited with its twin and neighbor Château Saint-Pierre-Sevaistre (*see* below), and the property's total output, under the two labels, is in the neighborhood of 7,500 cases a year.

SAINT-PIERRE-SEVAISTRE, Château — (San Pea-air Sev-ace-tr) — 4th Classed Growth of St. Julien. (*See* Saint-Pierre-Bontemps-et-Sevaistre.)

SAINT-POURÇAIN-SUR-SIOLE — (San Poor-san soor See-ole) — Curious and rather rare red (occasionally *rosé*) and white wines from Central France. The red is made from Pinot Noir and Gamay grapes and the white from the Tresallier and others. The light, appley white is bought by Germans for use in sparkling wines. These attractive V.D.Q.S. wines are most enjoyable when young.

SAINT RAPHAËL — (San Rahf-A-el) — Well known French apéritif, red and white, both with quinine plus other flavoring ingredients in the proprietary formula.

SAINT ROMAIN — (San Ro-mah) — Picturesque wine-producing village back of Meursault, in Burgundy. Its red and white wines, of secondary quality, are usually sold simply as "Bourgogne." (*See* Arrière-Côtes.)

SAINT SAPHORIN — (San Saf-fo-ran) — One of the best white wines of Switzerland, dry and pale, made from the Fendant or Chasselas grape on the northern shore of Lake Geneva, east of Lausanne.

SAINT VÉRAN — (San Vay-rahn) — New *Appellation Contrôlée* which, since 1971, has acquired an extraordinary acceptance not only in France, but in many other countries. Actually it rectifies an injustice originally done to a number of *communes,* or villages, which directly adjoin the delimited zone of Pouilly-Fuissé. Several of these make from the same Chardonnay grape, wines scarcely less good and in fact quite as good as all but the best Pouilly-Fuissés.

The zone of production of Saint Véran comprises six villages (Chânes, St. Verand, Leynes, Chasselas, St. Amour and part of Solutré) previously entitled to the appellation *Beaujolais Blanc* and adjoining Pouilly-Fuissé on the south, and two villages (Prissé and Davayé) on the north, formerly entitled to the appellation Macon Blanc, average production 300,000 gallons.

Incidentally, there does exist a village in France called St. Véran, like the wine, but this is at over 7,000 feet altitude in the Hautes-Alpes, where the most powerful telescope in France has recently been installed. It is also a ski resort as well as the highest village in Europe.

SAINT VINCENT — (San Vah-sah) — One of the Patron Saints of wine-growers, particularly in Burgundy, where his holiday is observed January 22nd.

SAINTE-CROIX-DU-MONT — (Sant Crwa dew Maw) — Fruity, golden, full-bodied, extremely sweet white Bordeaux wine, high in alcohol (over 13%), somewhat comparable to Sauternes but heavier and less fine. The hilly and picturesque little district from which it comes lies some twenty miles southeast of Bordeaux, and faces Sauternes and Barsac across the green and fertile Garonne Valley. Total production amounts to about 150,000 cases a year, and the better known châteaux include: Lamarque, Loubens, de Tastes, Grand Peyrot, Coulac, etc. (*See* Premières Côtes de Bordeaux.)

SAINTE-FOY-BORDEAUX — (Sant Fwah Bor-doe) — Small Bordeaux wine district, geographically part of Entre-Deux-Mers (*see*) but quite properly considered a separate entity by French wine law. Its white wines are passably good, semi-sweet, generally inexpensive, somewhat like Monbazillac produced nearby, although the latter is not, of course, a Bordeaux wine. A small amount of inconsequential red wine is also produced and legally entitled to the name.

SAINTE ROSELINE, Château — (Sant Ro-zay-leen) — Popular and pleasant *rosé* wine from Provence. The name is that of a single vineyard property in the village of Les Arcs, near Draguignan, not of a town or district.

SAKÉ — (Sah-kay) — Japanese rice wine usually served warm in tiny cups. Because of its grain base it is sometimes considered a kind of beer. The United States collects import duty as a wine and internal revenue tax as beer (or as wine when alcohol has been added).

SALINA — (Sah-*lean*-nah) — One of the Lipari Islands off the north coast of Sicily; source of most of the well-known Malvasia di Lipari (*see*).

SALMANAZAR — Large size bottle, equivalent to 12 regular bottles (the contents of a normal case).

SALVADOR — *Teinturier* grape grown in California and used primarily to color port wine.

SAMPIGNY-LES-MARANGES — (Sam-peen-yee lay Mar-ranj) — Village at the southern end of the Côte d'Or, in Burgundy. Produces an insignificant amount of passable red wine.

SAN BENITO — County and wine-producing district in California, properly considered one of the "North Coast Counties," although not actually on the Pacific. It lies directly east or inland from Monterey Bay, and the vineyards on the steep hillsides and in the high valleys of its southern half are among the best and coolest of the state. Its total acreage of superior wine grapes has increased substantially in the past few years (largely as a result of Almadén's new plantings at Paicines) and the relative importance of these is certain to increase as housing developments and subdivisions surround and finally overwhelm what were, only a few years ago, some of the best vineyards of the Livermore and Santa Clara valleys. More than half of San Benito's vines are choice French and German varieties — Chardonnay, Pinot Noir, Cabernet, Gewürztraminer, etc. — *planted on their own roots and ungrafted.* This bold experiment seems so far entirely successful, and the predictions of the late, great Professor Frederic T. Bioletti, who foresaw a remarkable viticultural future for San Benito County, seem likely to be fulfilled. Most of the vineyards are in the high country south of the town of Hollister and of San Juan Bautista, which was one of the original Spanish missions, just over a hundred miles due south of San Francisco.

For Map, *see* CALIFORNIA.

SANCERRE — (Sah-sair) — Picturesque hill town, overlooking the upper Loire, in central France; its white wine, pale, fresh, with considerable breed and an engaging fruitness and bouquet, greatly resembling the nearby Pouilly-Fumé (*see*) and made from the same grape, the Sauvignon Blanc. Perhaps on the whole even sooner ready than Pouilly-Fumé, it is bottled when about six months old and will last 4 to 5 years. Sancerre is a great favorite in Paris restaurants and at its best is certainly one of the most agreeable of the lesser white wines of France. The best of it comes, not from the township of Sancerre, but from surrounding villages, of which Amigny, Bué, Champtin, Chavignol, Reigny, and Verdigny are especially noteworthy; the total production varies greatly from year to year, but the average is not far from 500,000 cases. A good deal of excellent *rosé* is produced in the district from the Pinot Noir, and some experts consider it the best *rosé* of France.

SANCOCHO — (San-coach-O) — Sweetening liquid used in making sherry (*see*). Like arrope (*see*) but lighter in color and sweeter.

SANDUSKY — Town on Lake Erie between Cleveland and Toledo. Formerly a center of Ohio wine production, thanks to the vineyards nearby and on the Lake Erie islands.

SAN FRANCISCO BAY — Center of California's fine wine district; its arms and estuaries extend far back into the interior, and since it is tidal, and connected with the cool Pacific by the Golden Gate, its waters act as a sort of gigantic air-conditioning unit for a whole vast country. Thus, it is an odd fact that one can leave the Bay, and travel east, or northeast, or even due north, and find a progressively warmer climate for as much as fifty or a hundred miles. It is thanks to this that Napa, Sonoma, Santa Clara and the other "North Coast Counties" can produce far better wine than vineyards at a comparable latitude (about that of Sicily) abroad.

310

SANGIOVESE — (San-jo-*vay*-zay) — Excellent Italian red wine grape, formerly called the San Gioveto, the dominant variety in the Chianti Country and throughout the whole region of Tuscany. In other districts, Italy's Adriatic provinces, for example, it gives a good but shorter-lived and less distinguished wine. There have been random plantings of it in California, but few if any California Chiantis are made, even partially, from the Sangiovese.

SANGRIA — (Sahn-*gree*-ah) — Refreshing sort of wine punch, popular in Spain in warm weather. Its usual ingredients are red wine, lemon juice, sugar, water or soda water, sometimes plus berries or sliced fruit and various flavorings. Many bottled Sangrias are shipped.

SANGUE DI GUIDA — (*Sahng*-gway dee *Jew*-dah) — Sturdy red wine produced south of Pavia, in the Lombardy region of Italy. The name means "Blood of Judas."

SANKT MARTIN — (Sankt Mar-*teen*) — Secondary wine-producing village in the Pfalz, or German Palatinate. Rather heavy, common white wines. (*see* Saint Martin).

SANKT NIKOLAUS HOSPITAL — (Sankt Nee-ko-*laus* Hos-pi-*tahl*) — Famous charity hospital and home for the aged at Kues, directly across from Bernkastel, on the Moselle. A good part of its endowment consists of vineyards on Graach, Bernkastel, Brauneberg, Lieser, etc.; the wines, generally of high quality, are estate-bottled and are sold at auction. A number of these, from plots bequeathed by Cardinal Cusanus, one of the founders, carry the words "Cardinal-Cusanus-Stiftswein."

SANLÚCAR DE BARRAMEDA — *see* MANZANILLA.

SANSEVERO — (Sahn-say-*veh*-ro) — Good quality white wine, pale, fresh, dry, produced north of Foggia, in southern Italy.

SANTA CLARA — Valley and county at the southern end of San Francisco Bay, taking its name from the old Spanish mission in what is now the town of Santa Clara, near San José. Until not long ago, most of the valley floor was planted in walnuts and prune orchards, and many of the foothills to the east and west were covered with vineyards. As a result of the recent, astonishing increase in population in this part of California, most of these are tending to disappear, and housing developments are taking their place. A number of leading producers (notably Almadén, Mirassou and Paul Masson) have been forced to plant new vineyards in less populous districts further south, and others have simply ceased to exist.

For Map, *see* CALIFORNIA.

SANTA CRUZ — One of California's "North Coast Counties," although never very important as far as wine was concerned; it lies along the Pacific, some fifty to eighty miles south of San Francisco, and directly west of Santa Clara. It is considerably more famous today for its redwood groves and summer resorts than for its vineyards, only a few of which are still in production.

SANTA GIUSTINA — (*Sahn*-ta Juice-*tee*-na) — Fragrant and attractive light red wine, produced in the outskirts of Bolzano (*see*) in the Italian Tyrol.

311

SANTA MADDALENA — (*Sahn*-ta Mah-da-*leh* na) — About the best red wine of the Italian Tyrol, fresh, soft, fruity, appetizing, rather light in color but with adequate body and good balance. It is produced on the northeastern edge of the town of Bolzano, principally from the Schiava grape (*see*), and is quite as well known and fully as popular in Switzerland and Austria as in Italy itself.

SANTA MARIA — Newly developed vineyard area in San Luis Obispo County, and extending into Santa Barbara County. Although much further south than any other fine wine vineyards in California, the Santa Maria area has Region I (*see* Appendix II) growing temperatures and may well become an important producing area in the next few years.

SANTENAY — (Sahn-t'nay) — Southernmost village of the Côte d'Or, in Burgundy. Some very acceptable dry white wines are made from the Chardonnay grape, and others (less good) from the Pinot Blanc; the reds are better. These resemble somewhat the red wines of Chassagne-Montrachet nearby, being rather full and soft, yet with a good deal of tannin and occasionally an earthy taste, or *goût de terroir*. Less expensive than more famous Burgundies, they are often excellent values. The best vineyards are Les Gravières, Clos-de-Tavannes and La Comme.

SAÔNE — (Sone) — French river, a major tributary of the Rhône which it joins at Lyon (*see*), draining the Côte d'Or, the Maconnais and the Beaujolais. The Maconnais district is in the *département* of Saône-et-Loire.

SARDINIA — (*Italian* SARDEGNA — Sar-*den*-ya) — Large island off the west coast of Italy, producing some 60 million gallons of wine a year, most of it quite ordinary table wine, rather high in alcohol (*see* Campidano, Vernaccia). There are a few liqueur or dessert wines of exceptional quality: Monica and Girò, both red, somewhat comparable to Port; Nasco, Moscato di Cagliari, Malvasia di Bosa (*see* all of these).

SARMENT — (Sahr-maw) — French for "cane," the mature shoot of a vine, such as those that bear fruit and are pruned during the dormant season.

SASSELLA — (Sah-*sell*-la) — One of the best red wines of Valtellina (*see*), made from the Nebbiolo grape in northern Lombardy.

SAUMUR — (So-muhr) — Major wine-producing area along the south or left bank of the Loire River, in France, technically part of the province of Anjou although most of its wines resemble rather more those of the adjoining province of Touraine. Saumur itself is an attractive river town, with an old château and a famed cavalry school; the best vineyards are south and southeast of the town, and the total production of the delimited zone is not far from 2 million gallons. Considerably more than half of this is white wine, made from the Chenin Blanc grape; the rest is *vin rosé* and red wine, both of better-than-average quality and both made from the Cabernet Franc. The more productive and inferior grape varieties are hardly grown at all and no wine from them is entitled to the appellations Saumur or Coteaux-de-Saumur. More than half of the production is sparkling wine sold in France and to the export trade as

Sparkling Saumur, or Saumur Mousseux. The still white wines are generally dryer than those from the western part of Anjou, yet with a trace of sweetness; the best of them come from the villages of Montsoreau, Brézé, Bizay, Parnay, St. Cyr, Dampierre, Turquant, Varrains, Epieds and Saix; they improve greatly in bottle and are surprisingly long-lived. The *rosés* are made entirely from the Cabernet Franc grape, and are often too pale, being almost white wines to the eye as well as to the palate, though of good quality; the reds, also from the Cabernet Franc, are somewhat more uneven, but those of good vintage years can be surprisingly fine, somewhere between a light St. Émilion and a Chinon in character, especially those from the village of Champigny.

SAUTERNE — *see* SAUTERNES.

SAUTERNES — (Saw-tairn) — Originally and properly the name of a little French village, set down in a district of vine-covered hillsides some thirty miles south of Bordeaux. The officially delimited Sauternes zone comprises five townships, Preignac, Bommes, Fargues, Barsac and Sauternes itself, and the total annual production is some 250,000 cases; no wine of other origin may legally be sold as Sauternes in France or in most other countries, the United States being, of course, an exception.

True Sauternes (note the final *s,* even in the singular) is a rich, golden wine, high in alcohol (often over 14%) and decidedly sweet; there is no such thing as a "Dry Sauternes" from France. The finest Sauternes are all sold under the names of specific châteaux, and are château-bottled; the leading vineyards include Château d'Yquem (a true *grand seigneur,* and perhaps the most famous single wine in the world), then Châteaux La Tour-Blanche, Lafaurie-Peyraguey, Haut-Peyraguey, Rayne-Vigneau, Suduiraut, Coutet, Climens, Guiraud, Rieussec, Sigalas-Rabaud, Rabaud-Promis, etc. The grapes grown are the Sémillon and Sauvignon Blanc, plus a small amount of Muscadelle; these are picked late, in a series of harvestings, when they are not only ripe but over-ripe, and when their juice has been further concentrated by the action of a beneficient mold, the so-called *"Pourriture noble,"* botrytis cinerea. As a result, Sauternes are among the sweetest of all *natural* wines, and should properly be described as natural dessert wines. At their best they are quite extraordinary, velvety and almost creamy despite their strength, remarkable for their fruit, their breed and their bouquet. The term Haut-Sauternes is a trade designation, generally applied to Sauternes that are particularly sweet, but it has no official meaning, and legally any wine that can be called Sauternes may also be sold as Haut-Sauternes.

In California and generally in the United States, the name "Sauterne" (without the final "s") has practically become a synonym for white table wine. It is made from any and all varieties of grapes, grown no matter where; it is usually dry, and bears little or no resemblance to the French original; it must, however, carry an indication of its American origin in easily readable type on its front label. Many less scrupulous American producers bottle the same wine under the names "Chablis" and "Sauterne," which practice, of course, would be unthinkable and highly illegal in France. The nearest American equivalents of French Sauternes are considerably dryer than the French and are usually sold, not under this *passepartout* name, but as Sémillon or

SAUTERNES

BARSAC

Ch. Coutet ●

Ch. Climens ●

PREIGNAC

Ch. Rabaud-
Promis ●

Ch. Sigalas-
Rabaud ●

Ch.
de Rayne-
Vigneau ●   Ch. Lafaurie-
              Peyraguey

BOMMES

Ch. La Tour-   Ch. Haut-
Blanche ●   Peyraguey

              Ch. d'Yquem ●

Ch. Suduirout ●

● Ch. Rieussec

FARGUES

Ch. Guiraud ●

SAUTERNES

Scale
MI. 0
KM. 0   1   2

Sauvignon Blanc, after the grapes from which they are made. There are a few American sweet Sauternes, but these are made by a process altogether different from that prevailing in the true Sauternes Country of France.

SAVENNIÈRES — (Sav-ven-yair) — Attractive little village some ten miles southwest of Angers, producing the finest white wines of the Coteaux de la

Loire (*see*) in Anjou, France. The two most famous vineyards are the Coulée-de-Serrant (10 acres) and the Roche aux Moines (about 60 acres); other leading estates include Bécherelle, Château d'Epiré, Château de Chamboureau, Château de Savennières, etc.

SAUVIGNON or SAUVIGNON BLANC — (So-veen-yaw) — Splendid white wine grape, perhaps surpassed in quality, among the world's known varieties, only by the Chardonnay and the true Riesling. In the Bordeaux Country, it is the leading variety of Graves and, with the Sémillon, of Sauternes. Again in France, in the upper Loire Valley, where it is also known as the Blanc-Fumé, it yields such charming, fruity and racy wines as Pouilly-Fumé, Sancerre and Quincy. Finally, in the North Coast Counties of California, especially in Livermore, Napa and San Benito, it gives a somewhat fuller-bodied wine, but with the same unmistakable distinction and bouquet and flavor.

SAUVIGNON VERT — (So-vee-nyaw Vair) — White wine grape, not a *Sauvignon,* grown to some extent in California's North Coast Countries; used exclusively for blending in cheap dry wines.

SAVIGNY-LES-BEAUNE — (Sav-veen-yee lay Bone) — Little Burgundian town, set down in a fold of the Côte northwest of Beaune; also its wines, about 95% of which are red. These are light, fresh and what the French call *"tendre"* (supple, fruity and early-maturing); according to an inscription over the cellar door of the Château de Savigny, they are also "nourishing, theological and *morbifuges."* In overall production, Savigny, with nearly 935 acres under vines, is one of the most important *communes* of the Côte d'Or, averaging 9,000 gallons of white wine and 220,000 red; its best vineyards are Vergelesses, Marconnets, Dominode and Jarrons. Never great but generally not too expensive, almost always agreeable and often delicate and fine, the Savignys, both red and white, are among the best and most dependable of the lesser Burgundies.

SAVOIE — (Sah-vwa) — District comprising the modern *départements* of Savoie and Haute-Savoie, south of Lake Geneva and bounded on the east by Italy. Most of the wines are of purely local interest, but Crépy and Seyssel (*see*) are perhaps exceptions.

SAVUTO — (Sah-*voo*-toe) — Good red wine of Calabria in southern Italy.

SCHARLACHBERG — (Shar-*loch*-bairg) — Literally, "scarlet hill" (although its soil is actually dull brick-red in color), the best-known vineyard slope of Bingen (*see*), directly opposite Rüdesheim, on the Rhine. It dominates the confluence of the Nahe and the Rhine and its wines, after those of Nierstein and Nackenheim, are among the best of Hessia.

SCHARZBERG — (Shartz-bairg) — Not to be confused with Scharzhofberg, which it adjoins, the Scharzberg is partly in Wiltingen and partly in Oberemmel on the Saar (*see*), in Germany. A great part of the original vineyard is owned by the Friedrich-Wilhelm Gymnasium in Trier, which is undoubtedly the best producer there. Under the new German Wine Law, Scharzberg has become a *Grosslage* (*see*), and it is likely that we shall see many less-good wines shipped under this name in the future.

SCHARZHOFBERG — (Shartz-hawf-bairg) — One of the very greatest white wine vineyards of the world, consisting of less than thirty acres of Riesling vines, planted on an exceedingly steep, slate hillside, in Wiltingen, on the Saar, in Germany. The Scharzhof is an old manor house that has belonged for several generations to the Egon Müller family; the largest and best part of the vineyard is the property of Egon Müller himself, but his cousins also own a portion, as does the endowment of the Cathedral of Trier (the wines from this last being sold as Dom Scharzhofberger). The wine is called simply Scharzhofberger, without mention of Wiltingen, the village, and few wine names and few labels are accorded such unhesitating respect by wine-lovers in all countries; this is no more than fair for there are few wines as remarkable as a Scharzhofberger of a year like '53, or '71, and even the secondary years such as 1970 and 1972, yield a fine wine of surprising distinction; light, but with great depth of flavor, austere and yet fragrant and flowery, fresh and yet satisfying, the great Scharzhofbergers are not far from perfection.

SCHAUMWEIN — (*Showm*-vine) — General German term for sparkling wine. Legally, it may be made either by the Champagne process, or by the Charmat method of bulk fermentation; it must have a minimum pressure of 4 atmospheres; in addition, it must be made· from European grape varieties (*vitis vinifera*) exclusively, rather than from American varieties or from hybrids.

SCHAUMWEIN MIT ZUGESETZER KOHLENSÄURE — (Tzoo-ge-set-zer Coal-en-soyer) — Carbonated wine, sparkling but in no way comparable to wines made sparkling by secondary fermentation.

SCHIAVA — (Ski-*ah*-va) — Interesting and excellent red wine grape, widely grown in the Italian Tyrol and to some extent along the western shore of Lake Garda; one of the rare fine wine grapes which is a good table grape as well. Generally trained on high pergolas, it gives wines that are rather light in color, low in tannin, fresh, fragrant, early-maturing — *see* Lago di Caldaro, Küchelberger, Santa Maddalena. Three sub-varieties of Schiava exist; the best, with the lowest yield and smallest berries, is the Schiava *gentile* (Kleinvernatch, in the local dialect); somewhat more productive is the Schiavone, or Schiava *meranese;* the Schiava *grigia* is third in importance, though all three are often grown in the same vineyard, at Santa Maddalena, for example.

SCHILLERWEIN — (Shil-ler-vine) — Mediocre pink wine, made in the German province of Württemberg, usually from red grapes and white planted in the same vineyard in haphazard fashion and harvested together. Its name has nothing to do with the poet Schiller, but comes from the German verb *schillern,* which means "shimmer." Rarely exported.

SCHLOSS — (Shlawss) — Literally means "castle," in German. When used of vineyards and wine, it is the equivalent of the French, *château,* and means the entire property, its buildings, its vineyard, and its wine. There are many combined forms, as Schlossberg, or "castle-hill," the name of many vineyards, in Rüdesheim, Zeltingen, etc.; also *Schlossabzug,* which meant castle- or chateau-bottling before the use of this term was forbidden by the new German Wine Law in 1971.

SCHLOSS BÖCKELHEIM — (Shlawss *Beck*-kel-heim) — Perhaps the best vineyard area of the Nahe Valley, upstream and southwest of Kreuznach, owned by the Hessian State. White wines of excellent quality. Unfortunately, under the new German Wine Law, Schloss Böckelheim has also been made a

Bereich (*see*), covering eight or nine different villages on the Nahe. To be sure of getting an authentic Schloss Böckelheimer, it is necessary to buy a wine with a vineyard name such as Schloss Böckelheimer Königsfels or Schloss Böckelheimer Kupfergrube. Slightly less fine, perhaps, are the vineyards of Felsenberg, Heimberg, In den Felsen, and Mühlberg.

SCHLOSS JOHANNISBERG — *See* JOHANNISBERG, SCHLOSS.

SCHLOSS REINHARTSHAUSEN — *See* REINHARTSHAUSEN, SCHLOSS.

SCHLOSS VOLLRADS — *See* VOLLRADS, SCHLOSS.

SCHLOSSBERG — (*Shlawss*-bairg) — Literally, "castle-hill" in German; as such it is a fairly common vineyard name, and has survived in many cases when the "castle" in question is in ruins or no longer exists. Thus, we have Zeltinger Schlossberg, Bernkasteler Schlossberg, and Lieserer Schlossberg on the Moselle, Saarburger Schlossberg on the Saar, Rüdesheimer Berg Schlossberg on the Rhine, etc., etc.

SCHOPPENWEIN — (*Showp*-pen-vine) — German term for *vin de carafe*, or even *vin ordinaire*, of modest but not necessarily poor quality. A "Schoppen" is usually a quarter-liter glass. Schoppenwein is not a legal designation under German law, but is simply a colloquial expression used in Germany to describe any wine served by the glass in a restaurant or purchased in liter bottles in a grocery store.

SCHWARZE KATZ — (Shvar-tse Cats) — *see* ZELL.

SCUPPERNONG — One of the Muscadine grapes (*see*), originally wild, now cultivated to some extent in the Carolinas. It belongs to the subgenus *Rotundifolia* and wine has been made from its grapes since early Colonial days. It is not, however, a proper wine grape and the result, even with the addition of sugar, etc. is rarely better than poor.

SEC — (Seck) — French word for dry, i.e., with respect to wine, the opposite of sweet (although *un pays sec* is a dry country, and *un temps sec* is dry weather). Even the special wine-usage of the word has its complications and exceptions: Champagne (*see*) labeled "Sec" is anything but dry, and not far from the sweetest of the grades regularly marketed. The British statesman Canning is supposed once to have said, "Sir, the man who says he likes dry Champagne, lies." In any case, sweet Champagne has been considered unfashionable for well over a century, and even those who prefer it seem to accept it more readily when it comes to them disguised as its opposite. Nonsparkling French wines have not followed this pattern and, with them, *sec* still retains its original and proper meaning.

SECCO — (*Seck*-o) — Italian word meaning dry; when applied to wine, the opposite of *abboccato* or *amabile* (*see*).

SECHÉ — (Sesh-shay) — French wine-taster's term applied to wines that have lost, often through over-long storage in barrel, their freshness and fruit. Literally, "dried," although "withered" is perhaps a more accurate translation.

SEDIMENT — The deposit, or precipitate of crystals and other solids which most wines tend to throw as they are aged in bottle: it is as natural a part of an old wine as the peel is part of an orange or the shell part of an egg. It should *never* be confused with cloudiness or haziness or lack of clarity, all of which are grave faults, and often indicate that a wine is not fit to drink. *Sediment,* on the contrary, *is not a defect in any sense;* it is a sign of bottle-age, and a fine red wine that claims to be old and has no trace of sediment may well be regarded with suspicion. In the case of white and rosé wines, sediment usually takes the form of colorless crystals of cream of tartar, which is the base of baking powder: these are tasteless and harmless and will often disappear if the wine is shaken and then left for a week or so in a warm room; if white and powdery rather than transparent, some pectins and albumens from the grape are probably also present. Red wine sediment is more copious and more complex, and sometimes forms a mask or crust over the inside of the bottle; it is composed of tannins, pigments and minute quantities of the mineral salts normally present in wine. In any case, sediment should settle fairly rapidly if the bottle is disturbed and should simply be left in the bottle when the clear wine is poured off. Certain very full-bodied red wines (Hermitage and Barolo, for example, in a great vintage) throw so heavy a sediment that they must often be decanted and rebottled, after two or three years' cellar-ageing, before they are shipped. On the other hand, some old red Burgundies throw little sediment.

SEEDLING — Almost all vines are propagated from cuttings which are planted in a nursery and take root. A seedling, on the other hand, comes directly from a grape seed, and except under controlled conditions, its precise ancestry can hardly be known.

SEEWEINE — (*Say*-vine-uh) — Name given to a collection of rather unimportant wines produced along the northern or German shore of Lake Constance (*Bodensee,* in German). These include several whites made from the Ruländer, or Pinot Gris, round the towns of Meersburg and Hagnau, plus one oddity, an extremely pale *rosé,* almost a *blanc de noirs,* from the Pinot Noir, and locally famous as *Weissherbst* (*see*).

SEIBEL — (Si-bel) — One of the better-known French hybridizers — a number of whose phylloxera-resistant crosses have proven successful both in Europe and the United States. (*See* Hybrid.)

SEKT — (Zekt) — German sparkling wine made and matured to certain high standards — same as Qualitätsschaumwein. By international accord the name Champagne, in Germany, is restricted to the French product.

SELLE, Château de — (Sell) — Well-known *rosé* and white wine of Provence, and the vineyard from which it comes, at Taradeau, near Draguignan.

SÉMILLON — (Say-me-yaw) — Excellent white wine grape, widely grown in southwestern France and planted to some extent in California. It gives its best results when interplanted with or vinified with another variety, especially the Sauvignon Blanc, as in Sauternes and Graves. Alone, its wine has definite character and considerable class, but is often too low in acid, lacks freshness and fruit, as frequently in the case of Montravel (*see*) and Monbazillac (*see*), in France, and occasionally in California. On the whole, the best Sémillon wines are those that have at least a trace of sweetness; bone dry, they can be slightly bitter, especially if produced in a warm district.

SERCIAL — (*Sair*-see-al) — An important and excellent white grape variety, producing what are, on the whole, the best dry wines of the island of Madeira. (*See*)

SERPETTE — (Sair-pet) — French name for a special pruning knife with a sharp, hooked tip, used for light pruning and for picking grapes at vintage time.

SERRIG — (Sair-rik) — One of the highest and coldest villages of Germany's Saar valley. Its 250 acres of vineyard yield a few wines of fine quality, but only in exceptionally good years; most of their production, very tart, pale, and low in alcohol, is used for sparkling wine, or *Sekt*.

SERVING — So much pretentious etiquette, not to say ritual, has come to surround the service of wine, that many eager potential wine-drinkers become frightened and discouraged at the start. Most of this is sheer abracadabra and nonsense: rules *do* exist, but it is safe to say that any person of taste would discover these for himself in the course of a month of daily wine-drinking. The real rules are based on common sense, anyway. Thus, the host is served first — principally so that he can sniff or taste the wine and be sure that it is good before it is offered to his guests. Thus, white wines and *vins rosés* are chilled — for the sufficient reason that ninety-nine people out of a hundred find them more refreshing and agreeable when so served. Thus, red wine is traditionally served with red meat — because most people find that the two complement one another. Thus, sweet wines, even as strawberry shortcake and chocolate pudding, belong at the end of a meal, not the beginning.

When several wines are served at a meal, which is not often, these days, the problem is possibly a little more complicated, but here, too, common sense can teach us. A less good wine should precede a better one; a lighter wine should precede a heavier one; a dryer wine should precede a sweeter one. When a meal includes both fish and meat, the fish (with dry white wine) precedes the meat (presumably with red), and so on.

Additional information on this subject will be found elsewhere in this volume; *see,* especially, Decant, Glasses, Temperature, and the Table of Wine-and-Food Affinities in the Appendix.

SET — Vineyardist's term for the crop in prospect once the vine's flowering is over and the grape berries have begun to form.

SÈTE — (Set) — Town on the Mediterranean in the Hérault, center of vermouth and apéritif production.

SETUBAL — (Set-oo-bal) — Town and white wine named after it, near Lisbon, Portugal.

SÈVE — (Sev) — French for sap or vigor as applied to the body and character of a wine.

SÈVRE-ET-MAINE — (Sevr A Main) — District southeast of Nantes in lower Brittany, in which most Muscadet (*see*) is produced. This is legally entitled to the name "Muscadet de Sèvre et Maine" to differentiate it from the perhaps less good "Muscadet des Coteaux de la Loire," produced farther east, on the Loire hillsides.

SEYSSEL — (Say-sell) — Interesting white wine, pale, fresh, light, very dry, produced round the little town of this name on the Rhône River, east (upstream) from Lyon. A large part of the very limited production is made into *mousseux,* and Seyssel Mousseux is one of the very best sparkling wines of France, surpassed, perhaps, only by Champagne.

SEYVE-VILLARD — (Save Vee-yar) — French grape hybridizer whose white wine from the Seyval Blanc grape is being grown in New York State and shows considerable promise for future development in the Finger Lakes district. The wine is sold as a varietal — Seyval-Blanc.

SHAKING — One of the essential steps (*remuage,* in French) in the making of sparkling wine by the Champagne process (*see*). The bottles, on special racks, are shaken and turned daily so as to work the sediment down against the cork, prior to disgorging.

SHERMAT — Short for "sherry material" — the young fortified wine destined to be converted (by any one of several methods) into California sherry.

SHERRY — Originally and correctly, a pale gold or amber-colored, fortified wine from a specific, delimited district in southern Spain, round the little city of Jerez de la Frontera, between Seville and Cadiz. It takes its name from Jerez (which is pronounced, approximately, *Hair-eth* in Spanish) and the word "Sherry" is an anglicized version of this name; it is written Xérès in French. At its best, Sherry is beyond question the finest apéritif wine in the world, deservedly the most famous; and, when prepared for market in a different fashion, it can be an admirable desert wine as well.

Wines called "sherry" have been produced in other countries, especially Australia, South Africa and the United States, for well over a hundred years. A small percentage of these, made, blended and aged as Sherry is in Spain, have made remarkable progress and are surprisingly good. But California alone produces more than twice as much "sherry" as Spain, and only the vaguest sort of regulations cover its origin, its manufacture and its ageing. Most of it is made from raisin or table grapes, then "baked" at a high temperature to give it its special flavor, sweetened with grape concentrate, fortified with high-proof brandy, and sold when less than two years old. It is popular only because it contains a minimum of 17% of alcohol, and because it is cheap.

The Sherry vineyards, which encompass about 51,000 acres and produce over 20 million gallons annually, lie mostly north, west and southwest of the town of Jerez, out of sight of the main road and main railway line from Seville; they can only be reached by local roads across the rolling, arid, generally treeless and empty countryside. The best districts, or *pagos* (the names of which almost *never* appear on Sherry labels) are Macharnudo, Carrascal, Aniña and Balbaina; a few others, no less distinguished, produce Manzanilla (*see*) and are farther west, near Sanlúcar de Barrameda and the Atlantic; commoner wines come from vineyards to the south, overlooking the Bay of Cadiz, and from certain "approved" villages between Seville and Huelva.

The geographical location of the districts, as far as the quality of their wine is concerned, is less important than the precise type of soil on which the vines are grown. The best and least productive is what is known as *albariza* — a hard white chalk very like that prevailing in the vineyards of Chablis and Champagne: this gives wine of exceptional bouquet and great finesse; *barro* (literally, clay) is browner in color, more fertile, and yields larger crops of generally fuller-bodied wine; finally, *arena* (literally, sand) gives the highest gallonage of all per acre, but on the whole wines of less substance and character.

The leading grape variety by far is the Palomino, or Listan, especially in the chalky *albariza* areas whence come the best Finos and Amontillados, but a half dozen others are also quite extensively planted — the Albillo, Perruno, Mantuo Castellano, Mantuo de Pila, Beba and Mollar. The Pedro Ximénez (*see*) is also exceedingly important although not widely grown; its grapes are usually sun-dried before crushing and give an admirable, sweet, heavy wine, used in blending.

The *vendimia,* or grape harvest, normally takes place in the Sherry Country early in September and is eminently worth seeing — there are numerous *fiestas* and the whole operation is very picturesque. Formerly, the grapes were brought to the press-houses on donkey-back, sorted by hand and set out on straw mats to dry for a few hours in the sun; they were then placed in *lagares* (shallow press troughs) and "trodden out" by special workers wearing cleated boots. Once the first free-run juice was drawn off, the pomace, or *marc,* was stacked, wound round with bands of esparto grass, and press. The new modern method substitutes trucks for donkeys and transports the grapes to central press houses where mechanical equipment de-stems, crushes and presses the grapes. The juice, called *mosto,* is of course only the raw material for Sherry, and the finished wine owes most of its character and a good deal of its quality to the various treatments it receives once in barrel. Even before they are pressed, the grapes are liberally sprinkled with chalk or gypsum — the *albariza* soil on which the best of them are grown — and this quite legal addition of calcium sulphate tends to improve both the acidity and the clarity of the wine. For Sherry, like Champagne, Port, Madeira and many others, is basically a "made" rather than a natural wine, far more easily controlled, imitated

323

and even duplicated than, let us say, Montrachet or Scharzhofberger. For example, it could not even exist in its present form, or be called Sherry, without the addition of high proof grape brandy to bring it up from its natural strength of 13-14% of alcohol by volume to the 17-20% which it usually measures when shipped.

Yet many writers on the subject, including several who should know better, have chosen to speak of Sherry-making as if some mystery or deep secret, some accident or vagary of nature were involved. This is, to say the least, an injustice to the makers of Sherry, who are highly skilled professionals and know very well what they are about. Like schoolteachers and horse breeders and gardeners and many other people the world over, they are sometimes disappointed, sometimes surprised and delighted by the evolution of their charges — but rarely, and not even often. Being excellent showmen, they have long since learned that their visitors and guests greatly enjoy deciphering certain cabalistic signs inscribed in chalk on the heads of their oak casks (called *raya, palma, palo cortado,* etc.); these are really abbreviated tasting notes — indications of type and quality — and in Jerez they are chalked up for all to see, rather than discreetly noted down in private cellar books, as in Germany and France.

From the time fermentation begins, which is almost as soon as the grapes are crushed, until the final, blended, finished wine is ready for bottling, Sherry spends most of its life in 158 gallon casks or ''butts'' of American white oak, and it cannot be properly matured or aged in any other way. By December following the vintage, the newly fermented wine is clear and ready for tasting; at this stage it is invariably pale straw in color, and bone dry. Added sweetness and darker color both come later, and neither is in any degree accidental.

The taster's first task, in which the nose is if anything more important than the palate, is to determine into which of two general, broad categories, each butt of new wine falls. Those that are notably clean and light, with fine bouquet are destined to become Finos and Amontillados; they are drawn off into fresh barrels, fortified to about 15½%, and put away to develop *flor*. Fuller-bodied, heavier wines, with less bouquet and no *flor* yeast, are fortified to 17-18%, do not develop *flor,* and will eventually emerge as Olorosos.

This *flor*, or ''film yeast,'' is indigenous only to the Sherry Country, Montilla and the Château-Chalon district of the French Jura. It is essential in the making of fine dry Sherry and almost all of the recent improvement in the California product dates from its introduction there. In appearance, it is at first a sort of white film, becoming a thin, pebbly, white crust on the wine's surface; it has an odd, rather agreeable, appetizing odor, which has been compared to the smell of fresh warm bread, and wines on which it has worked have and retain an altogether special character and flavor. In order to expose the surface of the wine to promote *flor* formation, the butts in a Sherry *bodega* are kept only about three-quarters full.

Once the young Sherries have completed their preliminary development (a year, or two, or more) they are graded once again and enter the *criaderas* or nursery stocks for their appropriate *solera*. And the *solera* (*see*) is another factor without which fine Sherry, as we know it, could not exist.

In its simplest form, a *solera* is a collection of butts or barrels, consisting of three or more sets or stages (usually, but not necessarily, superimposed and arranged in tiers) in which wines of the same type and quality but of different ages are fractionally and progressively blended as they mature. The word is related to the Spanish *suelo,* which means floor or base, and the final stage of the *solera,* from which wines are drawn for bottling or further blending, is invariably the lowest, and on the ground. As a rule, not more than half, and in most cases less than a third, of the wine in this oldest bottom tier is withdrawn in any single year, and it is immediately replaced by wine from the next highest or next oldest stage, and so on, back to the *criadera.* Thus the final wine of a *solera* consists of small fractions of wines of from anywhere from six or seven to a hundred different vintages. There is therefore no such thing as a vintage *solera,* and in practice there is no such thing as a vintage Sherry.

With age, in oak, Sherries have a tendency to become very slightly darker in color, noticeably dryer, and (unlike almost all other wines) higher in alcohol. Manzanillas and Finos of 15½% have been known to reach 21% after fifty or more years in cask; they acquire at the same time an intensity of flavor that makes them almost undrinkable — yet magnificent and priceless as blending wines.

The Sherries of commerce are almost never wines drawn from the final stage of any single *solera:* they are blends of these blends, finished perhaps by the addition of a small amount of precious old reserve, given softness and sweetness and more color in various ways.

The sweetening and coloring agents are called, appropriately enough, *vino dulce* and *vino de color.* Occasionally a single wine will fulfill both functions, but this is rather the exception than the rule.

By all odds the best *dulce* is what is known as "P.X." after the Pedro Ximénez grape from which it is made; when well-aged, this can be one of the most valuable of nectars — the finest Olorosos and Cream Sherries could not be produced without it. In point of fact it is what the French would call a *vin de paille* and the Italians a *passito* — pressed from grapes that have been dried in the sun until they are almost raisins, fermented, fortified, then aged for long years in oak. Much less good is what is called *mosto apagado,* sweet grape juice in which fermentation has been impeded by the prompt addition of high-proof brandy: this, too, requires ageing if it is to lose its original harsh and spirituous character.

There exist two sorts of *vino de color,* both being essences or concentrates of grape juice, reduced very slowly, by boiling, to a fraction of their original volume — *sancocho,* to one-third, and *arrope,* to one-fifth (literally, the "quintessence"). Both acquire some caramel flavor as well as their almost mahogany color in the process.

When it comes to color, Spanish *catadores,* or tasters, divide Sherries into six categories — *muy palido,* very pale, like Manzanilla and most Fino; *palido,* the usual shade of the Amontillado; *ambar,* or amber, as most "medium" Sherries; *oro,* or gold, for the dryer Olorosos; *oscuro,* dark, for the sweeter, luscious Olorosos, or "Creams"; *muy oscuro* for what the English call "brown Sherry." There are of course many subtle gradations within each category.

Wines heavily dosed with *vino de color* are often called Pajarete or Paxarete

325

(after a district in which they were once largely made); a great deal of such stuff used to be shipped to the United States as "blending Sherry" and used by distillers in coloring and softening their whiskey.

Since Sherry, in fact and almost by definition, is a blended wine, and more often than not a blend of blends, and since tastes and preferences and personal budgets vary widely, it follows that there are always at least as many Sherries of any given type as there are blenders. Some of the larger houses, with immense stocks, produce the widest possible range of wines, in type, quality and price; others have only a few specialties and nevertheless seem to do very well. Nearly three hundred firms or individuals own *bodegas* in Jerez; thirty or forty maintain offices or agencies in London; some English companies bring Sherry in bulk from Spain in shipping butts of 132 gallons or in large metal containers, blend and bottle and re-export under their own labels.

Most of the Sherry business in the U.S.A. is done on a brand name basis such as Bristol Cream, Dry Sack, La Ina, etc. These may or may not indicate the type of Sherry in the bottle.

Sherry does not deteriorate once opened. Most dry Sherries (some experts would say *all* Sherries) are best served chilled. All are better served in tulip-shaped glasses of at least 6 oz. capacity, half filled. A proper minimum drink of Sherry is at least 3 oz. Sherry "On the Rocks" is new, fashionable and delicious.

Much additional information on the subject will be found elsewhere in this volume, under such headings as *California, Manzanilla, Montilla, Amontillado, Amoroso, East Indian, Fino, Flor, Oloroso, Pedro Ximénez, Sanlúcar de Barrameda, etc.*

SHORT — Wine lacking persistence (*see*); a good wine is never short and should have some echos of taste after it is swallowed.

SHOT BERRIES — Small, seedless berries often found in a bunch of otherwise normal wine grapes. These are usually the result of incomplete pollenization and are called *millerands* in French. *See* Coulure.

SICILY — (Italian SICILIA, See-*chee*-lee-ah) — Largest island of the Mediterranean, about the size of Maryland, produces some 225 million gallons of wine a year. With a few exceptions (the red and especially the white wines of Etna, Corvo di Casteldaccia, etc.) the table wines are rather common, and are consumed currently and locally. Marsala (*see*) is of course Italy's leading fortified wine, amber, 17-19% alcohol, somewhat comparable to Sherry. There are also a number of Sicilian dessert wines of more than local fame — these, described in their proper place in this volume include: Moscato di Siracusa, Zucco, Malvasia di Lipari, Moscato di Pantelleria, Albanello, etc.

SICK — A sick wine is a bad wine, almost always cloudy, usually with a bouquet which is odd, unfamiliar and unpleasant, a flavor which is definitely "off." Fortunately, very few such wines ever reach the consumer.

SIFONE — (See-*fo*-nay) — Grape juice reduced to about one-third of its original volume, almost to the consistency of syrup. Used as a sweetening agent in Marsala (*see*).

SIGALAS-RABAUD, Château — (See-gah-lah Rah-boe) — 1st Classed Growth of Bommes, Sauternes. About 4,000 cases a year. *See* Rabaud-Promis.

SILKY — Wine-taster's term, applied to wines that are notably smooth and fine-textured.

SILLERY — (See-yair-ree, generally *Sil*-ler-ree in English) — Village in the Champagne Country, southeast of Reims. Its wines, once famous in both France and England, are no longer highly regarded, and the name has almost ceased to exist as an appellation, since Verzenay (*see*) — once considered part of the Sillery zone — produces a much superior wine.

SILVANER — German spelling of Sylvaner (*see*).

SION — (See-aw) — Interesting and picturesque little town, capital of the Swiss Canton of Valais, set down in the high, rocky, narrow, upper valley of the Rhône, not far from its source, in southern Switzerland. The wines made round Sion include the excellent red Dôle (*see*) and red and white Ermitage, the white Johannisberg (legally so labeled, although often made from the Sylvaner grape) and a number of superior grades of Fendant, or Chasselas, notably those of Uvrier, Clavoz, Mont d'Or.

SKIN — The peel or outer covering of the grape; in some English-speaking countries, skins are more commonly called "hulls" or "husks."

SMALL — Wine-taster's term, applied to a wine of not much consequence, not much distinction, let alone body or power — possibly very agreeable all the same. Many "ordinary" wines are small, but there are plenty of us who would prefer them to great wines as a daily diet, as we might prefer good simple cooking to *la grande cuisine*.

SMITH-HAUT-LAFITTE, Château — (Smeet O La-feet) — Excellent, slow-maturing, long-lived red Graves, produced in the commune of Martillac. There are some 15,000 cases a year plus a small quantity of white wine.

SOAPY — Wine-taster's term used of wines that are disagreeably flat, low in acid, and unappetizing.

SOAVE — (So-*ah*-veh) — Excellent dry white wine, among Italy's best, produced just east of Verona, on the southernmost foothills of the Alps. The predominant grape varieties are the Garganega and Trebbiano, plus a little Riesling; the vines are trained high, pergola-fashion, six or seven feet above the ground. In addition to the extremely picturesque little town of Soave itself, the neighboring village of Monforte is considered part of the Soave zone, and a very large part of their local production is crushed by the local cooperative cellar, or Cantina Sociale, one of Italy's most important and best equipped. Shipped in tall, green bottles, like the wines of Alsace, Soave is pale straw in color, light, clean and fresh on the palate, dry without being acid — a most agreeable wine, in short, though hardly a great one. It matures early and should be drunk by the time it is three or four years old.

NET CONTENTS
1 PINT 8 FL. OZS

ALCOHOL 12%
BY VOLUME

SOAVE

CLASSICO · DENOMINAZIONE DI ORIGINE CONTROLLATA

BOLLA

ITALIAN DRY WHITE WINE
PRODUCED AND BOTTLED IN THE CLASSIC ZONE OF
SOAVE · ITALY

BY

FRABO S.P.A. - PRODUTTORI
VERONA · ITALY

SOLE DISTRIBUTORS FOR THE U.S.A. THE JOS. GARNEAU CO. - NEW YORK, N. Y.

SOCIÉTÉ CIVILE — (So-see-A-tay See-veel) — French estate company which owns and manages vineyard and wine-making operations — or other farm products.

SOFT — Wine-taster's term, a generally favorable adjective, although not always so. A soft wine is one neither harsh nor green, although possibly mild and dull. All wines should have some softness — if they have too much they may be flat or even common.

SOLERA — (So-*lehr*-ah) — System by which certain fortified wines, Spanish Sherries above all, are matured and progressively blended; the object is, year after year, to produce wines of perfectly consistent quality that run perfectly true to type. Expert cellar-masters, given a proper range of young wines to work with, can achieve this result to a surprising degree.

The operation of a *solera* has been described in considerable detail under the heading Sherry (*see*). In recent years a number of the more conscientious California producers have set up *soleras,* following the Spanish pattern, and some of these (the ones at Almadén, for example, which contain over a million gallons of wine) are impressively large, even by Spanish standards. It is thanks to such installations and to the introduction of film yeast, or *flor* (*see*) that the finer American Sherries are now able to compete, in quality, with many of the imported.

A very similar system is now rather widely used in the maturing and blending of superior Port.

SOLID — Wine having soundness and ability to last and improve with age.

SOLUTRÉ — (So-loo-tray) — One of the four *communes* of the Pouilly-Fuissé district (*see*), producing somewhat lighter and more delicate wines than the others. The "Rock of Solutré," an extraordinary butte rising directly behind

328

the village, is a famous landmark, visible for miles, and appears on many Pouilly-Fuissé labels.

SOMMELIER — (So-mel-yay) — French term for wine waiter. In French restaurants, the sommelier is usually in charge of some bottling and cellar work as well, and, when serving, wears a traditional uniform, with a chain, cellar keys, a tasting cup, and sometimes an apron.

SONDRIO — (*Sawn*-dree-o) — Town in northern Italy, near the upper end of Lake Como, and only some dozen airline miles from the Swiss border, center of production of the red wine of Valtellina (*see*).

SONOMA — One of the most important wine-producing counties of northern California, and on the whole one of the best. It lies north of San Francisco; its southern edge is on tidewater and overlooks San Francisco Bay. The nearby town of Sonoma owes its origin to the northernmost of the twenty-one Spanish missions established by Franciscan monks, north of what is now the Mexican border, between 1769 and 1823; it was they who brought the vine and viticulture to California. Commercial vineyards were planted near Sonoma before the Civil War.

Like many California counties, Sonoma is almost a little world in itself and has an astonishingly wide diversity of climates and soils and countryside. The interior, from San Francisco Bay and the town of Sonoma northward to Santa Rosa and Guerneville, is as cool as Burgundy in France, and admirably adapted to wine-growing — in this area are located the Sebastiani Winery, right in the town of Sonoma, Buena Vista, Hacienda, the tiny Hanzell Winery, copied after Clos de Vougeot and a fore-runner in producing Pinot Noir and Chardonnay of classic style and others; on the west, the Coast Range, covered with giant redwoods, along the bleak beaches of the cold Pacific, is not wine country at all, far too cold and too humid for the vine; farther north, in the Russian River Valley, from Windsor to Asti and beyond, there are thousands of acres of rolling hills and vineyards, as productive and as warm, as those of central Italy. Here one finds Korbel, Sonoma Vineyards, Simi, Souverain and Italian Swiss Colony to name a few. A number of small and medium size wineries producing very high quality wines have recently come into production in Sonoma, and many once-dormant vineyards are being revived.

For Map, *see* CALIFORNIA.

SOPHISTICATED — Not what one might expect, but a wine "improved" with illegal substances; adulterated.

SORNI — (*Sore*-nee) — Extremely pleasant red wine of the Italian Trentino (*see*); light, soft, well-balanced, made round the village of this name, largely from the Schiava grape, plus some Merlot and Teroldego.

SOUCHE — (Soosh) — French word (*see* also *Cep*) for a grape-stock, or vine. When wines are sold before the grapes are picked, the sale is SUR SOUCHE.

SOUND — Wine-taster's term, used of a wine which is, as the French say, *franc de goût*, clean-tasting, well-constituted, without defects or abnormal qualities.

329

SOUPLE — (Soo-pluh) — Literally, French for "supple," although more properly used of wine than its English equivalent. It means a wine not too high in tannin or acid, smooth, agreeable, ready to drink.

SOUR — In the realm of wine, the opposite of Sweet is *Dry*, not Sour, and a wine with too much natural acidity is Tart or Acid, never Sour. A sour wine is one well on its way to becoming vinegar, spoiled, and not fit to drink.

SOUTH AFRICA — Vines have been grown and wine made in South Africa since early Dutch colonial days, and one of the most famous vineyards, Groot Constantia (*see*) was planted in 1684. There are now some 150 million gallons produced annually, from 300,000 acres of vines all under the aegis of the KWV (Cooperative Winegrowers Association) which officially determines the quantities of wines that are sold and gets rid of the surplus by distillation into some very good brandy and commercial spirits. The leading vineyard areas are all fairly close to Cape Town, between French Hoek and Wellington, in the Paarl Valley, in the Stellenbosch district, and round Wynberg, near Constantia itself. It is interesting to note that these are at almost precisely the same Latitude South as the best vineyards of Chile and Australia. From this Coastal Belt come fine quality table wines and very good fortified wines. The Little Karoo area just to the east grows, under irrigation, hot country grapes yielding a large production of dessert wines and brandy.

SOUTH AMERICA — The vine, being a creature of the Temperate Zones, is truly at home only in the southern and cooler third of this vast continent, and apart from a few vineyards in Peru (all planted at surprisingly high altitudes), wine is only produced well south of the Tropic of Capricorn — in Argentina, Chile, Uruguay, and in the southernmost provinces of Brazil. South America nevertheless produces and consumes more than twice as much wine as North America, almost all of it table wine, imports only an infinitesimal amount, and, apart from Chile, exports practically none at all. Argentina is by a wide margin the largest producer (4th in the world), Chile easily the best.

SOUTIRAGE — (Soo-tee-rahj) — French word for "racking" (*see*), the process of drawing off wine from one tank or barrel to another, leaving the sediment or lees behind.

SPAIN — Accurate statistics are hard to come by, but Spain, almost certainly, has the larges extent of vineyards of any country in the world, over 4¼ million acres in all. Due to the prevailingly arid climate, the average yield per acre is far lower than in France or Italy (let alone California) and the total production of Spanish wine is only about one-third that of France or Italy — it amounts, nevertheless, to the very respectable figure of some 850 million gallons a year.

Only about 2% of this is Sherry, and Sherry, although easily the most famous, is no more the typical wine of Spain than Champagne is the typical wine of France. Most Spaniards have never tasted it, and over 90% of Spain's wine is common table wine, consumed currently and locally.

Travelers in Spain will find such wine available everywhere: it varies widely in quality, but quite often is surprisingly good and it is always inexpensive.

Supposedly of a higher class, yet almost invariably disappointing, are many elaborately labeled local wines which are not exported and not likely to be: higher in alcohol and with more pronounced character than the others of their district, these rarely have any of the freshness and charm of French *vins de pays*.

Except in a few of the better-known districts, wine-making methods are archaic or even primitive in most of Spain and it is a tribute to the producers' care and honesty and their respect for sound tradition that the wines turn out as well as they do, for few can fairly be called bad. Many, if better vinified, would find a ready market abroad, such as the dry white wines of Rueda, in Old Castile; the reds of Toro, not far from Salamanca; and the *rosés* of Yecla, in the uplands west of Alicante.

Drawn by W. Lembeck

On the other hand, the very best Spanish table wines can be quite extraordinary, and remarkably good values, no less in the United States than in Spain.

The best table wines of Spain, especially the best reds, are by a wide margin the Vega Sicilia and the Valbuena from the Duero River Valley (both extremely rare and hard to find), and those of the Rioja district (*see*), in the high valley of the Ebro, west of Logroño and not far from the French border. The finer of these are exceptionally good by any standards, and surprisingly close to the great Bordeaux in quality. In a distinctly lower category come the rather pale, somewhat common red wines of Valdepeñas (*see*), from south of Madrid, and in a still lower class the reds of Alicante; some reds and whites from around Barcelona (Panadés, Alella, Perelada, etc.); and the reds, whites and *rosés* of the Miño Valley, along the Portuguese frontier, such as Ribiera, which is very close to a Portuguese Vinho Verde in character.

Spanish sparkling wine is produced, some of it quite passable but on the sweet side; it is often labeled "Xampán" (pronounced *Champagne*), and comes from the Panadés district, southwest of Barcelona.

It is above all in the somewhat special field of apértif wines that Spain excels, and indeed she has hardly any rival, since the gradual decline of Madeira (both in quality and in public favor) over the past century. Those who are familiar only with a few of the popular, standard brands of Sherry have no idea of the range and variety of wines that make up the Sherry family, and of course Manzanilla (*see*) and Montilla (*see*) are in their limited categories hardly less interesting.

The once famous Spanish dessert wines — Málaga, Tarragona, and the golden Malvasia of Sitges — have almost no commercial importance today, but they are still fine wines in their no-longer-fashionable class.

In a world of rising wine prices and improved technology, Spanish table wines should look forward to a bright future. Sherry, Manzanilla and Montilla will continue to be appreciated and ever more widely known by wine-lovers and true connoisseurs everywhere.

SPARKLING — Term applied to a wine with dissolved carbon dioxide which bubbles and makes a froth or foam when poured.

SPANNA — (*Spahn*-na) — Another name for the Nebbiolo grape (*see*).

SPARKLING BURGUNDY — Burgundy wine made sparkling or *mousseux* (*see*) by any one of several methods; generally red, although some *rosé* and some white are produced. Long popular in the United States and to a lesser degree in England, it is hardly ever drunk in France except by tourists, and does not even appear on the wine lists of most of the better French restaurants. In France it is Appellation Contrôlée "Bourgogne Mousseux" which in October 1980 will change to "Crémant de Bourgogne". The finer grades of still red Burgundy are never used in its manufacture; it is a wine regarded with amused contempt by most real wine-lovers. However, in recent years some quite outstanding sparkling Pinot Chardonnay has come into production and is more than acceptable. American Sparkling Burgundy, whether produced in California or in New York State, is substantially as good as that made in France. (*see* — Crémant, Mousseux).

SPÄTBURGUNDER — (*Shpate*-boor-gun-der) — German for Pinot Noir (*see*).

SPÄTLESE — (*Shpate*-lay-zuh) — German wine term, which literally means "late picking" or "late harvest." On a label it indicates a superior natural (i.e., unsugared) wine, made from grapes picked after the main, normal vintage is over. Such grapes, of course, tend to be somewhat riper than the average, and a Spätlese is therefore fuller-bodied, riper and generally a trace sweeter than other wines of the same vineyard and year; it also usually costs from 30% to 50% more. The German plural is *Spätlesen*. Under the new German Wine Law it is a *Qualitätswein mit Prädikat* (*see*) and ranks just above *Kabinett* in quality.

SPECIAL NATURAL WINE — Table or fortified wine to which natural flavors of any kind are added; Thunderbird, Bali Hai and Silver Satin were the forerunners of these wines in the 1950's.

SPICY — Said of a wine with a pronounced and special aroma or taste, piquant but natural, properly its own and on the whole agreeable. Gewürztraminer is an obvious example, but there are many others.

SPIRITUEUX — (Speer-ee-two-uh) — French word which, as a noun, means "spirits"; applied to wine, as an adjective, it means high in alcohol.

SPLIT — A quarter bottle of wine or champagne, containing about 6 ounces. Ideal for one person and used frequently on trains and airplanes.

SPOILED — Unsound wine; can be from many causes — bacteria, yeasts, poor storage, chemicals, etc.

SPRAYING — The treating of vines with liquid insecticides or fungicides, under pressure. An essential and laborious part of the vine-grower's summer work in all countries.

SPRITZ — Light sparkle produced by voluntary or involuntary second fermentation in bottle. Very pleasant in simple young wines — *German* SPRITZIG.

SPRITZER — Usually one third Rhine wine and two thirds soda, but in general use for a wine highball; most satisfactory and thirst quenching in hot weather.

SPUMANTE — (Spoo-*mahn*-teh) — Italian word which means foaming or sparkling; as applied to wine, a wine that is truly sparkling, as contrasted with one that is *frizzante* (*see*), or only slightly and briefly so. Made in various ways, that called *Gran Spumante* usually by the French Champagne process of fermentation in bottle, most of the others by fermentation in bulk, the "*cuve close*" or "*Charmat*" method.

STABILIZING — The various treatments (including refrigeration and, in extreme cases, even pasteurization) to which many wines are subjected in order to enable them to resist, as far as possible, heat, cold and exposure to light, without losing their clarity and balance.

STAKE — Light post or picket, either of wood or metal, used to support a vine or, in some instances, the wire on which the vine is trained.

STALKY — *See* STEMMY.

STEELY — Wine tasters' term for a wine which is extremely hard, and even tart, without being harsh or green. Austere, possibly remarkable, but unprepossessing.

STEINBERG — (Shtein-bairg) — Celebrated, historic 79 acre vineyard in the heart of Germany's Rheingau district. It was created and the wall around it was constructed in the 12th century by monks of the same Cistercian Order as those responsible for its sister domain, the Clos de Vougeot, in Burgundy; and the same remarkable man, St. Bernard de Clairvaux, oversaw the creation of both. Together with the adjoining monastery, Kloster Eberbach, the vineyard was taken over by the State of Hessia and is now part of the *Staatsweingut*. It stretches over the rolling hills directly behind Hattenheim, and its wines are sold as Steinberger Qualitätswein, Steinberger Kabinett, Steinberger Spätlese, or Auslese, Trockenbeerenauslese, etc. Between these various grades and classes, all estate-bottled, there are of course enormous differences, even in any given year. All of them have, nevertheless, certain family characteristics — full body, authority, great class, power and depth of flavor sometimes at the expense of subtlety; forthrightness sometimes at the expense of charm. They are less good in very dry years than the Marcobrunners, and less attractive in poor years than the riper and fruitier Rüdesheimers; at their best they are simply incomparable.

STEINWEIN — (Shtein-vine) — Name loosely given to German *Frankenweine* as a whole — those, in other words, shipped in the traditional *Bocksbeutel*. Properly, however, a Steinwein was from the town of Würzburg (*see*), grown on its steep slopes overlooking the Main river, and made from Riesling or Sylvaner grapes. Under the 1971 German Wine Law Steinwein became obsolete.

STEMMER — Machine, called an *égrappoir* in French, for separating the newly picked grapes from their stems, prior to crushing and fermentation.

STEMMY — Harsh, green, disagreeable flavor which wines sometimes acquire if fermented with the stems, or stalks. (French, *goût de rafle.*)

STILL — Non-sparkling. If a new wine, one that has finished its fermentation; if an older wine, one that contains no perceptible amount of CO_2, or carbon dioxide. Still Champagne (*see* Coteaux Champenois).

STRAW WINE — *See* PAILLE.

STUCK WINE — Fermentation which has not proceeded to normal conclusion because of excessively high temperature resulting in weakened yeast — a difficult but usually solvable problem.

STÜCK — (Shtook) — German cask containing 1,200 liters (316 U.S. gallons) or 133 cases of finished wine.

STURDY — Wine-tasters' term, perhaps a little less favorable than robust.

SÜFFIG — (*Sue*-fig) — German wine-tasters' word, applied to wines that are light, fresh, palatable, easy to drink.

SUAU, Château — (Su-O) — 2nd Classed Growth of Barsac. There is another and much larger vineyard with precisely the same name in the village of Capian, Côtes-de-Bordeaux (*see*). About 1,500 cases a year.

SUDUIRAUT, Château de — (Sood-we-row) — 1st Classed Growth of Preignac, Sauternes. Splendid château and famous vineyard in the Sauternais, which, after passing through two decades of decline and neglect, is once more producing rich, full-bodied, rather sweet wines (some 10,000 cases a year) worthy of its great name.

SUGARING — French, *chaptalisation;* the adding of sugar (but not water) to must, or fermenting wine, its object being to bring the final alcoholic degree of the wine up to a normal level. It is forbidden in Italy and California, authorized in Germany and the eastern United States, often abused. *See* also Amelioration, Gallisation.

SUGARS — As far as wine is concerned, these are most simply defined as the elements in must or grape juice that can be converted into alcohol through the action of yeast — *fermentable sugars,* in other words. But also normally present in grape juice and most wine are minute amounts of *non-fermentable sugars,* such as pentose; *reducing sugar* is the total of both, determined chemically. *Residual sugar* is the sugar remaining in a wine, for whatever reason, after fermentation.

SULPHITING — The adding of sulphur, in the form of sulphurous acid, sulphur dioxide or sulphites, to grape juice or to wine, with the object of delaying or preventing fermentation. This is common practice in modern wineries: the must, once sterilized, is later re-inoculated with a special chosen yeast culture. But when the same process is used to ''hold'' the sweetness of a light, partially fermented wine, the result, unless great care is exercised, can be most unfortunate — a wine that literally reeks of sulphur, like many cheap Liebfraumilchs and white Bordeaux. *See* Sulphur, below.

SULPHUR — Element properly and widely used in many phases of grape-growing and wine-making. Dusted or sprayed on the vines, it is an efficient safeguard against many of the diseases, funguses and pests to which grapes are subject; in the cellar, it is a standard sterilizing agent for casks, barrels, etc. But (see Sulphiting) it is often used, and often too freely used, to keep a poorly balanced white wine from oxidizing, or to "hold" a certain amount of sweetness in a wine which would otherwise continue fermentation and be completely dry. There is nothing objectionable about this practice, providing the sulphur is not too apparent in the finished wine. To a wine-taster, the presence of even a limited amount of sulphur usually makes itself known by a slight prickling in the nose, and an odd, faintly "pasty" impression on the tip of the tongue.

SULPHURING — See Sulphiting, above. Sulphuring, a quite different process, involves the sterilizing of casks or barrels in the cellar and the treatment of vines in the field. Vineyards are regularly dusted with flowers of sulphur to prevent oidium and mildew during the growing season; sulphur wicks are frequently burned in empty casks to elminate harmful bacteria.

SUPPLE — An attribute of quality wine, smooth, drinkable yet with character and backbone.

SURDO — (Soor-doe) — Portuguese for Mistelle (see) as used in Madeira.

SÜSS RESERVE — (Suce Ray-zerv) — Unfermented grape juice used in Germany to add sweetness to young wine of the same area and quality.

SWEET — Sweetness in a table wine, or a fortified wine for that matter, may be wholly natural or partly natural or not natural at all. In a fine French Sauternes or a Beerenauslese from the Rhineland, it comes from the grapes themselves, which have been allowed to hang on the vines until over-ripe (see, however, *Pourriture noble*) and is wholly natural; due to the difference in climate, a few such natural sweet wines are now being produced in the United States. In many other wines, sweetness also comes entirely from the grape, but remains in the wine because sulphur has been used or brandy added — the former being the case in cheap white Bordeaux and Liebfraumilch, the latter in Port, whether produced in Portugal or in California. Sherry and Marsala are sweet because of heavy, sweet wine or the equivalent of grape syrup added to them. Sweetness, in any case, is not necessarily a virtue, nor is it necessarily a fault; this depends entirely on the character of the wine.

SWITZERLAND — Despite her 32,000 acres of vineyards, Switzerland (half as large as Maine and no more populous than Massachusetts) imports far more wine than she produces. Nearly 90% of this is inexpensive red table wine, shipped in bulk from Italy, Spain and, in much smaller volume, from France. In the way of white wine, Switzerland produces enough to satisfy her own national requirements and even to permit a certain amount of exportation. There are vineyards in over a dozen different cantons, but only four are of any real commercial importance: Vaud, consisting mostly of the northern shore of Lake Geneva, including the wine-producing regions known as Lavaux and Chablais (see); Valais, the upper valley of the Rhône, which here runs parallel to the Swiss-Italian border; Neuchâtel, its vines extending along the northern shore of the lake of that name, in northwestern Switzerland, not far from France; Tessin, or the Ticino, the Italian-speaking region around the lakes of Locarno and Lugano. Much of what the Tessin produces is common red table wine, but some of very good quality is made from the Merlot grape, and is so labelled. A somewhat better red, called Dôle (*see*) is made in the Valais; practically all of the rest is white, and comes mostly from the Chasselas grape, here known as the Fendant — this is often the name under which the wine is sold. Some of the better growths, all listed elsewhere in this volume, are: Dézaley, St. Saphorin, Yvorne, Aigle, Sion and Neuchâtel. *See* also the cantons referred to above.

On the whole, Swiss wines are never great and few of them can even be called outstanding. But they are always well made, generally light, fresh and appetizing. Most of them are bottled when less than a year old.

SWIZZLE STICK — Fiendish implement for undoing in a minute the time, effort and expense of making wines sparkle; those who don't like bubbles should drink still wine.

SYLVANER — (Sil-vah-ner) — Rather productive, superior white wine grape, probably of German or Austrian origin, widely planted in many countries. In Germany, where it is spelled Silvaner, although it gives a lighter, softer, shorter-lived wine than the more distinguished Riesling, it is often used for *Qualitätswein mit Prädikat* and occasionally may yield a wine of even *Beerenauslese* quality. In Alsace it is classed as a "noble" variety, an honor which it scarcely merits, since the wine it yields is really just an excellent *vin de carafe*, fresh, fruity and agreeable. It does well in Austria, and in the Italian Tyrol, especially round Bressanone, and there are some plantings in Switzerland, in California and in Chile. In the course of its travels it has acquired some odd pseudonyms: it is called the *Oesterreicher* (the "Austrian") in the Rheingau, the *Franken Traube* (or "Franconian grape") in the Rheinpfalz, and even the "Franken Riesling" in Franconia itself, where, for once, it approaches the true Riesling in quality. In Switzerland, it is sometimes known as the "Johannisberg," and it even calls itself, quite legally, the "Riesling" in California (*see*). It has been often successfully crossed with the true Riesling.

SYRAH — (See-rah) — Excellent red wine grape, the variety of red Hermitage (*see*) and one of those used in Châteauneuf-du-Pape. It gives a deep-colored, slow-maturing wine, high in tannin, with a distinctive and memorable bouquet. It is almost certainly not the Petite Sirah widely grown in California, which is a far more productive and more ordinary grape, probably the Duriff (*see*).

SZAMORODNI — (Sah-moh-rod-ny) — Dry to fairly sweet Tokay (*see*) made in Hungary, primarily from the Furmint grape.

SZEKSZARD — (Sex-ard) — Hungarian place name, and the red wine of this district.

T

TABLE WINE — Red, white or rosé wine naturally fermented and containing up to 14% of alcohol (occasionally and exceptionally higher) used primarily with or as a part of meals.

TÂCHE, La — (La Tahsh) — One of the very great red Burgundies, produced by a small vineyard in the *commune* of Vosne-Romanée, entirely owned by the owners of Romanée-Conti (*see*) and a part of the domain which carries this name. In the days when wine regulations were less strict, its wines were sometimes labeled "La Tâche Romanée" and the late Christopher Morley gave this name to one of his books, "The Romany Stain," but it is unlikely that Romanée had any connection with gypsies, as he fancied, and it is at least doubtful that Tâche, in this instance, means "stain." Before World War II, the vineyard consisted of about three and one-half acres, between Les Gaudichots and Les Malconsorts (*see* Vosne Romanée, and map); a new decree, during the German occupation in 1943, accorded to a major part of Les Gaudichots, the *appellation* La Tâche, and there are now about fifteen acres entitled to the name. This quadrupling of the vineyard's extent has of course increased its production to some 2,000 cases. The wine has not much suffered (for Les Gaudichots was a very great vineyard) and is velvety, full-bodied, with quite extraordinary bouquet and depth of flavor.

For Map, *see* VOSNE-ROMANÉE.

TACHÉ — (Tah-*shay*) — Literally, "stained." Said of a white wine which has acquired a pinkish tinge, often accidentally, through having been put in a cask previously used for red wine.

338

TAFELWEIN — (*Tah*-fel-vine) — German term meaning "table wine." Under the new German Wine Law, the term Tafelwein has a legal and specific meaning. It ranks below *Qualitätswein* (*see*) in quality, will always be sugared, and will never carry a vineyard name. There are now four officially-recognized regions for Tafelwein, *see* Weinbaugebiete.

Tafelwein is usually bottled in liter bottles, is rarely exported to the United States and can never be anything more than a common *vin ordinaire*.

TAIN L'HERMITAGE — (Tan Lair-me-tahj) — Town on the Rhône south of Lyon, where the red and white wines of Hermitage (*see*) are produced.

TALBOT, Château — (Tal-bo) — Largest vineyard in the township of St. Julien, and one of the best equipped; a 4th Classed Growth, it produces up to 30,000 cases a year of rich, full-bodied claret, deep-colored, rather slow to mature.

TALENCE — (Tal-lawnce) — Commune in the Graves district, now practically a suburb of Bordeaux. Housing projects have overrun most of its vineyards, and there are only three of any real importance that remain: Château La Mission-Haut-Brion, a very great vineyard indeed; Château La Tour-Haut-Brion, producing an excellent, if less celebrated, red wine; and Château Laville-Haut-Brion, one of the very finest of white Graves.

TANK — Large container used for wine fermentation (*see* also vat) or wine storage; if wood, usually in the form of an upright cylinder; if of stainless steel, upright or horizontal cylinder, if of concrete, generally cubical.

TANNIC — Puckery (*see* Tannin).

TANNIN — Technically, a group of organic compounds existing in the bark, wood, roots and stems of many plants; also in wine, red wine especially. To the taste, it is astringent and makes the mouth pucker, as almost always in the better young red Bordeaux wines of good years. It is particularly pronounced in wines that have not been *égrappés*, or separated from their stems before fermentation; some additional tannin is certainly picked up by wines stored in oak barrels, especially new oak barrels, and this often improves them greatly. Tannin forms part of the normal sediment that fine red wines throw as they grow older, and a mature wine has less tannin than a young wine. Some grape varieties give wines far higher in tannin than others, and these generally are the wines which improve with age.

TAP — To insert a spigot or faucet in the bunghole or head of a barrel or cask; also the spigot itself.

TAPPIT-HEN — Old Scottish term for an oversize drinking vessel, or a bottle holding as much as three normal wine bottles, or more.

TARRAGONA — (Tah-ra-*go*-na) — City and province south of Barcelona on the Mediterranean coast of Spain. A great deal of quite ordinary table wine is produced, and a few sweet fortified red wines of somewhat better class, usually known as Priorato in Spain itself, and called Tarragona, and formerly "Tarragona Port," when exported. In recent years a great many so-called "varietal" wines have come out of this area, but this trade has now been restricted by the U.S. Treasury, which requires certificates of authenticity for all wines claiming to be made from one particular variety of grape.

TARRY — Wine-tasters' term (French, *goût de goudron*) used for certain very full-bodied red wines of great vintages; far from disagreeable, it is usually one of the characteristics of a fine red wine made from very ripe grapes, partially raisined.

TART — Said of a wine high, possibly even too high, in acid, but not necessarily either unpleasant or "green."

TARTAR — Tartaric acid is the principal acid of wine made from ripe grapes; some of this is invariably thrown off in the form of crystals of potassium bitartrate, or cream of tartar or wine stone (German, *Weinstein*) as the wine is aged in cask, and sometimes also in bottle. It is harmless and tasteless, and is used in the manufacture of baking powder.

TASSE — (Tahss) — Common French word meaning cup. As far as wine is concerned, a small, shallow saucer, usually of silver with dimpled bottom and sides, in which young wines are tasted. It is part of a wine-waiter's equipment, plus a chain and keys. *See* Tastevin below.

TASTEVIN — (Tat-van) — Flat, shallow, silver wine-tasters' cup widely used in Burgundy for sampling wines, especially young wines. It has given its name to the celebrated Burgundian confraternity of wine, the Confrérie du Tastevin, which has its headquarters in the old château of the Clos de Vougeot, and branches and chapters in many countries, including the United States.

TASTEVINAGE — (Tat-vee-nahj) — System of labeling certain Burgundy wines whereby, once approved by a committee of the Confrérie du Tastevin (*see*) and upon payment of a certain sum per bottle, these wines may carry a special, rather elaborate Tastevin label, on which the shipper's (not always the producer's) name also appears. Such wines are said to be *"Tastevinés."* This is an indication but by no means a guarantee of superior quality.

TASTING — Wine-tasting is both a very simple and an extremely complex art or science or skill: it may quite properly be described as any of these, or a combination of all three. There are two kinds of wine-tastings: one is intended to allow the consumer, whether a novice or a connoisseur, to taste a number of different wines and decide which he prefers and which he likes less well; his own palate is the final arbiter, and there is not, nor should there be, any appeal from his decision. A wine, for him, "is good if it tastes good."

The second sort of wine-tasting involves at least a certain amount of expert knowledge, and only those with wide experience and exceptional "taste memory" are capable of it. There exist quite definite standards as to what can be called quality or superiority in wine, and experts, tasting blind, will rarely vary in their ratings of any given wine, by more than four or five points out of 100. This is a far higher level of unanimity than music critics or art critics or literary critics ever achieve, yet taste and smell are in general the beggars among our five senses, for they have no accurate written language and no permanent record and no past.

Wine-tasters, however, have their own professional jargon, or cant, and although the terms they use often appear bizarre or pretentious or even ridiculous to those unfamiliar with them, they are certainly more precise than the language of music critics (a "lyric" tone, a "warm" voice) or that of painting ("vibrant," "sincere," "well-organized").

Professional wine-tasters do not drink the wines when they taste: they examine them closely for color, either against a white tablecloth or a candle, or against the sky, tilting the glass in either case, to see if there is a trace of telltale brown or gold around the edge of the wine. They shake the wine or spin it in the glass, so as to bring out a maximum of bouquet, then sniff it carefully. They then sip it, wash it around in their mouths, and spit it out, breathing deeply, since the fact is that our nose, rather than our palate, is the best judge.

And then, in their notebooks, they give a fairly detailed verdict. Here are a few of the terms they use; all will be found in their alphabetical place in the encyclopedia, defined as accurately as seems possible:

Acetic	Flinty	Powerful
Acid	Flowery	Rancio
Aromatic	Foxy	Rich
Austere	Fragrant	Ripe
Balanced	Fresh	Robust
Big	Fruity	Rotten Egg
Bitter	Full	Rough
Blind	Gassy	Round
Body	Great	Short
Bouquet	Green	Sick
Brilliant	Hard	Silky
Butyric	Harmonious	Small
Character	Harsh	Soapy
Clean	Hazy	Soft
Cloudy	Heavy	Solid
Coarse	Herbaceous	Sound
Color	Light	Sour
Common	Lively	Spicy
Complex	Maderised	Spiritous
Cooked	Maderisé	Spoiled
Corky	Mature	Steely
Delicate	Mellow	Stemmy
Distinguished	Metallic	Sturdy
Dry	Mild	Subtle
Dull	Moldy	Sulphur
Dumb	Mousy	Supple
Elegant	Noble	Sweet
Empty	Nutty	Tannic
Fat	Off	Tart
Fiery	Ordinary	Thin
Firm	Oxidized	Velvety
Fine	Perfume	Withered
Finesse	Piquant	Woody
Flabby	Pleasant	Yeasty
Flat	Poor	Young

TAVEL — (Tah-vel) — The most famous *rosé* wine of France and probably one of the oldest, since it was said to have been a favorite of François I and was praised by the poet Ronsard. It is made, principally from the Grenache grape, plus a limited but important admixture of Cinsault (*see*) and some Clairette, Bourboulenc, Carignan, etc., round the village of this name, west and across the Rhône from Avignon. The soil in the limited production zone (recently and quite properly enlarged) is, on the whole, rocky, shallow and arid; the yield per acre is small, and the wine has, as a result, more flavor and bouquet and usually more alcohol (12½-14%) than other *rosés* of the Rhône Valley; its one close rival is Lirac (*see*) from a directly adjoining *commune*. The annual output is now not far from 600,000 gallons, well more than half from the large, modern, co-operative cellar. There are a good many smaller producers as well, and many of them estate-bottle.

Many writers on wine, most of them British, have contended that Tavel, is a unique exception among *rosés* and improves with age. This is anything but the opinion of the *vignerons* who themselves produce Tavel, who much prefer their wine when under two years old, and regard a five-year-old bottle as simply a curiosity. Vintage years on Tavel shipped to the United States should generally be distrusted; the youngest is probably the best.

TAWNY PORT — Mature, wood aged Port wine which has lost its deep red color, acquired an amber tinge at the edges, and simultaneously become softer, rounder and usually more expensive.

TEARS — *see* LEGS.

TEINTURIER — (Tan-tew-ree-A) — Literally, in French, "dyer." Term applied to such comparatively rare grape varieties as have red or red-purple juice, rather than white. Some of these, for example the Salvador and Alicante Bouschet, are planted principally for this reason.

TEMPERANCE — Moderation, especially in the use of alcoholic beverages. Its meaning has been corrupted to signify total abstinence, as absurd an idea as that of a Temperate Zone completely without warmth. The evidence of centuries points overwhelmingly to the fact that true temperance is most general in countries where light table wines are the common, popular, daily beverage, and the testimony of most acute observers supports this view. Thus Pasteur called wine (by which he meant table wine) "the most healthful and hygienic of beverages." Adam Smith declared: "The cheapness of wine seems to be a cause, not of drunkenness but of sobriety." And Thomas Jefferson concluded: "No nation is drunken where wine is cheap and none sober where the dearness of wine substitutes ardent spirits as the common beverage."

TEMPERATURE — Wines, especially fine wines, are strikingly affected by the temperature at which they are served; a white wine too warm seems lifeless, flat and dull; a red wine too cold seems numbed, astringent, almost entirely lacking in bouquet. This is not a matter of etiquette but of fact, and anyone who cares to experiment can find it out for himself. Much of what has been written on the subject, particularly by Englishmen and Frenchmen, is entirely irrelevant to wine service in the far different climate of the United States.

"Room temperature" in an English country house or a French château is not the room temperature of a New York apartment, or a New Orleans restaurant in summer. A wine that is best served "cool" in Europe may require considerable chilling to render it fresh and agreeable during July and August in America. Here are a few rules:

1. No wine should ever be served at over 70°, no matter what the temperature of the dining room.

2. Great red wines, particularly old ones, are at their best at 65° to 68°; if they warm up slightly while they are being served and drunk, this will help them rather than injure them.

3. Lesser red wines, the younger ones especially, should be served somewhat cooler, or even slightly chilled in warm weather. 60° is perhaps ideal, which means roughly the temperature of a good cellar.

4. Dry white wines and *vin rosés* should be well chilled, the finer ones and those low in alcohol (as Moselles) to about 55°; the others to 50°.

5. Sparkling wines and most sweet table wines (as Sauternes) should be well chilled to 40°. The great sweet German wines (*Beerenauslesen,* etc.), however, should not be brought to below 55°.

Needless to say, wines can be chilled just as well in an electric refrigerator as in an ice-bucket; the ice-bucket does have the important advantage of keeping the wine cool throughout the meal; its principal disadvantage is that the wine in the neck of the bottle often is not chilled at all, and it is perfectly proper, although a little unorthodox, to put a bottle of white wine neck down in the ice bucket for a few minutes before it is served. On the other hand, don't be frightened by all these numbers to the exclusion of enjoying wine. Most people and restaurants don't have thermometers handy.

TENDRE — (*Tawn*-dr) — French wine-tasters' term, literally "tender," applied to wines that are young, fresh, charming, light, easy to drink.

TENT — Old English term for a red wine from Spain, especially from Alicante. It probably derives from the Spanish *tinto* (*see*).

TENUTA VINICOLA — (Teh-*noo*-ta Vee-*nee*-co-la) — Italian term meaning a major vineyard estate — a "château" or "domaine" with its buildings and vineyards.

TERLANO — (Tair-*lahn*-no) — Most famous and one of the best white wines of the Italian Tyrol, produced round the village of this name in the narrow, deep, spectacular Adige Valley between Bolzano and Merano. Several different varieties of grape are grown in the vineyards — Riesling, Pinot *bianco,* Pinot *grigio,* plus a local variety called the Terlano, or Blatterle; the quality, and even character, of the wine often varies according to the variety which predominates, and it is rarely possible to determine this from the label. In general, Terlano is a soft, well-balanced, dry white wine, pale green-gold in color, not especially pronounced in bouquet and flavor, but delicate and pleasing. It is shipped in tall green bottles like the wines of Alsace.

TERMENO — (Tair-*meh*-no) — Village just south of the Lago di Caldaro (*see*) in the Italian Tyrol; called Tramin in the days, before 1918, when this district was Austrian, and according to tradition, the original home of the Traminer grape.

TERNE — (Tairn) — French word meaning *dull* — specifically, when applied to wine, one that lacks brilliance of color, liveliness and character.

TEROLDEGO — (Teh-roll-*deh*-go) — Agreeable light red wine, fragrant and fresh, made from the grape of this name in the Italian Trentino (*see*), where it is practically the *vin du pays*. Production is centered round the twin towns of Mezzolombardo and Mezzocorona, northwest of Trento.

TERROIR — (Tair-wahr) — Soil or earth, used in a very special sense in French in connection with wine, as *goût de terroir*. Certain wines produced on heavy soil have a characteristic, unmistakable, almost indescribable, earthy flavor, somewhat unpleasant, common, persistent. This is a *goût de terroir,* and the German equivalent is *Bodenton* or *Bodengeschmack.* Superior wines rarely if ever have much of this, which, if once recognized, will not easily be forgotten.

TERTRE, Château du — (Tair-tr) — 5th Classed Growth of Arsac, Haut-Médoc. Near the southern edge of the Médoc, produces some 10,000 cases a year of rather light, pleasant, fragrant Claret.

TERTRE-DAUGAY, Château — (Tair-tr Doe-gay) — A 1st Growth of St. Émilion, good quality, rather small production up to 3,000 cases.

TESSIN — (Tay-sah) — Swiss canton. *See* Ticino.

TÊTE DE CUVÉE — (Tet d' Coo-vay) — Extra special wine put out by some champagne houses, usually extraordinary quality, sometimes *blanc de blancs* or late disgorged, specially packaged and always expensive.

THIEF — Pointed tube of glass or metal, sometimes called *chantepleure* (but more often *pipette*) in French, used for taking samples of wine through the bunghole of a barrel.

THIN — Applies to a wine deficient in alcohol and body; watery, poor.

THOMPSON SEEDLESS — Popular grape variety with the largest acreage of any grape planted in California. With over a quarter-million acres under cultivation, the Thompson Seedless is known as a "three-way grape" (i.e. it can be used for table grapes, for raisins, or for wine). It gives a bland, rather nondescript wine which can be used in blends without imparting any distinctive flavor characteristics of its own. Because of this "neutral" taste, it is rarely used by itself in California wines.

THOUARCÉ — (Too-ar-say) — One of the best *communes* of the Coteaux du Layon (*see*), in Anjou. Sweet white wines of top quality.

TICINO — (Tee-chee-no) — Italian-speaking canton of Switzerland, south of the Alps, with some 4,500 acres of vineyard, producing, for the most part, red wines. The best Ticino wine (and in favorable years about the best red of Switzerland) is called Merlot (*see*), and is made from the Bordeaux grape of that name.

344

TIGNÉ — (Teen-yea) — Village not far from the Coteaux du Layon (*see*) in the Loire Valley, which, with adjoining *communes,* produces perhaps the best *rosé* wines of Anjou. The Château de Tigné and its adjoining property, the Clos du Moulin, are the principal vineyards.

TINAJA — (Teen-*ah*-ha) — Spanish word for the immense, earthenware amphoras in which the wines of Montilla (*see*), and those of Valdepenas, are fermented and first stored.

TINTA — (*Teen*-ta) — Name given in Portugal and in Madeira to a family of red wine grapes, all producing deep-colored, full-bodied red wine, mostly used for Port but some for red table wines such as Dão. They include the Tinto Cão, Tinta Madeira, Tinta Francisca, Tinta Miuda, Tinta Alvarelhão, Tinta Pinhiera, Tinta Carvalha, etc. There exist some plantings of the first two of these mentioned above in California, and they generally give the best California Port, often labeled "California Tinta Port."

TINTA MADEIRA — (*Teen*-ta Ma-day-rah) — *see* above.

TINTILLA — (Teen-*teel*-ya) — Sweet red wine produced in Spain, on the edge of the Sherry Country, especially near the town of Rota.

TINTILLO — (Teen-*teel*-yo) — In Spain, a red wine of little color, almost a dark *rosé*, like many of those of Valdepeñas.

TINTO — (*Teen*-toe) — In Spanish, a *vino tinto* is a red wine. The adjectives *rojo* and *negro* are also used, but more colloquially and less correctly.

TIPICO — (*Tee*-pee-co) — The original Italian equivalent of the French *Appellation Contrôlée:* a *vino tipico* was one defined by law as to origin, grape variety, etc. (*See,* however, Denominazione Controllata.)

TIRAGE — (Tee-rahj) — French word meaning "drawing off," usually from cask into bottle. In the Champagne district (*see*), it means the first bottling of new still wine, plus the sugar syrup and yeast (*liqueur de tirage*) which will make it sparkle after a second fermentation in bottle.

TIREUSE — (Tee-*ruhz*) — In French, a filling or bottling machine, or a woman engaged in this work.

TISCHWEIN — (Tish-vine) — Literally, "table wine" in German, but usually applied only to light wines of no special quality or excellence, as *vin ordinaire. See* Tafelwein.

TOKAY — One of the most famous and, at its best, one of the finest white wines of the world. The best has never been cheap or easy to find, and this has been more than ever the case since World War II, now that the former royal, princely and even papal reserves are presumably consumed by deserving Commissars.

All true Tokay comes from a small district in the Carpathian Mountains of north-eastern Hungary called the Tokaj-Hegyalja, and the wine's name is spelled Tokaji in Hungarian. The principal grape variety is the Furmint, which has never been grown commercially elsewhere, and the total production, of all grades, amounts to aboout 2½ million gallons a year. What is exported is shipped in stubby, long-necked bottles of about 17 oz. (50 centiliter) capacity and the only exporter is the Hungarian Government.

The rarest and finest Tokay, which is truly more of an essence (*see* Eszencia) than a wine, is comparable to a German *Trockenbeerenauslese*. The least expensive and commonest Tokay is a grade called *Szamorodni*, which can be anywhere from quite dry to fairly sweet, depending on the vintage, but is always rather high in alcohol, rarely under 13%.

Considerably better, more expensive and sweeter is what is called *Azsu*, the Hungarian equivalent of a German *Auslese*, which contains a certain fixed proportion of over-ripe grapes, shrunken by the *pourriture noble*, or *Edelfäule*. The quantity of such grapes used per cask in the making of the wine is usually stated on the label in terms of *puttonyos* (*see*), and the more *puttonyos*, the finer, sweeter and more expensive the *Aszu*.

All true Tokays have a wholly distinctive bouquet and flavor; even the lesser ones are often interesting and good values; the best (rarely found) are very great wines indeed.

ALSO, the name often given in Alsace to the Pinot Gris or Ruländer grape, and to wines made from it, although this grape is certainly not of Hungarian origin, is unrelated to the Furmint, and yields an entirely different wine.

ALSO, the name given to a California table grape, properly called the "Flame Tokay," pink, thick-skinned, fleshy, which has no imaginable connection with the Furmint or with true Tokay wine. Wine made from this grape, never good, is legally entitled to the name "California Tokay," and is grown principally around Lodi; most of it is distilled into brandy.

TONNE — (Tunn) — French for a large tank, cask, or tun, of indefinite size.

TONNEAU — (Tun-no) — In general, in French, means practically the same thing as *tonne;* however, in the Bordeaux Country, it means quite specifically four *barriques* or 4 × 225 = 900 liters of wine = 100 cases of 12 bottles; many Bordeaux wines, prior to bottling, are sold in terms of *tonneaux,* although casks of this size hardly exist and are not in general use. The château-owner sells his wine either *frais compris jusqu'à la mise* (charges for racking, fining, filling, etc., up to the moment of château-bottling, included,) as do most of the most celebrated châteaux, or *sans frais,* which means that the buyer must stand the cost of this care, which amounts to 10-20% depending on length of storage. In neither case are bottling charges included and these are usually set at not far from $4.00 per case, to cover the bottles, labels, cases, and the work involved.

TOPPING — The refilling of casks or barrels of young wine, usually carried out weekly, to be sure that there is no ullage, or air space between the wine and the bung. An essential part of good cellar work.

TOSCANA — (Tus-*cah*-nah) — *See* TUSCANY.

TOUL — (Tool) — French town in the province of Lorraine. A few very light and hardly more than passable *vins gris* are produced, largely from the Gamay and Pinot, on nearby slopes entitled to the appellation *Côtes de Toul,* and the V.D.Q.S. seal.

TOURAINE — (Too-rain) — Old, extremely beautiful French province in the Loire Valley, consisting of the modern *départements* of Indre-et-Loire, Loir-et-Cher and Indre; its chief city is Tours, and it makes up most of what has come to be called the Château Country. Its production of *Appellation Contrôlée* wines approaches 7 million gallons a year, a little more than half of it red; the best known names, all listed in their alphabetical place in this volume, are Vouvray, Montlouis, (both white and both sometimes sparkling), Chinon, Bourgueil, Saint-Nicolas-de-Bourgueil (all three red). Lesser wines are marketed as Touraine-Amboise, Touraine-Azay-le-Rideau and Touraine-Mesland, and a great deal of light, pleasant red, white and *rosé* under the general, regional appellation of Touraine. The authorized grape varieties are, for white wine, principally the Chenin Blanc, plus the Sauvignon Blanc, the Pinot Gris and one called the "Arbois"; for red wines and *rosés,* the Cabernet Franc, the Malbec, the Pinot Meunier and the Grolleau (Groslot). Little of what is called "Touraine" is exported; most of it is drunk up, when still less than two years old, by the fortunate inhabitants of this "garden of France," and by thirsty tourists.

For Map, *see* LOIRE.

TOUR BLANCHE, Château La — (Tour Blawnsh) — Celebrated 1st Classed Growth vineyard of Bommes, Sauternes, owned by the French Government, and operated partly as a viticultural school. Its wines are generally a little less sweet and less high in alcohol than the other 1st Growth Sauternes, and are deservedly popular both in France and abroad. Average production is about 5,000 cases a year.

TOUR-CARNET, Château La — (Tour Car-nay) — 4th Classed Growth of St. Laurent, Haut-Médoc. Some 8,000 cases a year.

TOUR-FIGEAC, Château La — (Tour Fee-zhack) — A Grand Cru Classé in the Graves portion of St. Émilion, originally part of Figeac, producing about 10,000 cases of well-made wine a year.

TOUR-DU-PIN-FIGEAC, Château La — (Tour dew Pan Fee-zhack) — Excellent vineyard, directly adjoining Cheval Blanc in the Graves portion of St. Émilion. It is now divided into two separate properties, both producing very sturdy, full-bodied red wine. About 5,000 cases a year. Originally part of La Tour-Figeac.

TOUR-HAUT-BRION, Château La — (Tour Oh Bree-aw) — Small, excellent, classified vineyard of Talence (Graves), practically in the Bordeaux suburbs. Some 1,200 cases a year of first-rate Claret.

TRABEN-TRARBACH — (*Tra*-ben *Trahr*-bach) — Twin towns on the Moselle, in Germany, downstream from Bernkastel and Wehlen but still part of that classic district of great white wine known as the Mittel-Mosel. Traben is on the left bank of the river, Trarbach on the right; between them, they have some 400 acres of vineyard, the best *Lagen* being Schlossberg, Hühnerberg, and Ungsberg.

TRAMINER — *see* GEWÜRZTRAMINER.

TRAUBENSAFT — (Trow-ben-sahft) — German for grape juice, destined to be consumed in its unfermented state, usually white, not red.

TREBBIANO — (Treb-be-*ah*-no) — Good but not especially distinguished white wine grape, of major importance in Italy and to a lesser extent in southern France where, near Marseille, it yields the white wine of Cassis, and is known as the Ugni Blanc (*see*). This is also its name in California, and there is considerable acreage planted to it in the Livermore Valley. In Italy, it is the leading white grape of Tuscany (Chianti); it yields the white wine of Lugana (*see*) on Lake Garda and it is one of the two principal grapes of Soave, the somewhat finer Garganega being the other.

TRENTINO — (Tren-*tee*-no) — District north and east of Lake Garda, south of Bolzano, in northern Italy, forming the province of Trento, Austrian territory until 1918. As far as wine is concerned, it consists almost entirely of the deep, narrow valley of the Adige, and the lower slopes of the 7,000-foot peaks which form the valley walls. The annual production is nevertheless about 20 million gallons, most of it light red carafe wine of rather good quality, although there is some *vin rosé* and some white. Grape varieties include the Teroldego, the Schiava, the Marzemino, and others better known, such as Traminer, Pinot, Merlot, Trebbiano and even Lambrusco (*see* these). A good deal of sweet Vino Santo (*see*) is made; the best wines of the district (all described elsewhere in this volume) include those sold as Teroldego, Marzemino d'Isera, Sorni, Rosato d'Avio, Valdadige and Vallagarina, plus some that carry the varietal grape name. Today the region is referred to as Trentino-Alto Adige and always spoken of together.

TRIAGE — (Tree-ahj) — French word, practically synonymous with *épluchage,* meaning the sorting, or picking over, by hand, of grapes newly harvested, before crushing and fermentation, so as to eliminate the damaged or defective berries. This is standard practice in most wineries interested in the quality of what they make.

TRIE — (Tree) — French term for a special, expensive method of harvesting grapes, involving repeated partial pickings of only the very ripest bunches or individual grapes. The great natural dessert wines of Sauternes and the Rhine, and almost all others where *pourriture noble* (*see*) is involved, are made in this way.

TRIER — (*Tree*-er) — Principal city of Germany's Moselle Valley, not far from the border of Luxembourg. It was already an important city in Roman days, known as Augusta Trevirorum (whence Trèves, as it is still called in French) and its Roman monuments and ruins are still impressive. Many of the leading Moselle wine producers have their cellars·in Trier, and most of the great semi-annual auctions at which fine Moselles are sold take place there.

TRITTENHEIM — (*Trit*-ten-heim) — One of the good but hardly great wine-producing villages of Germany's Mittel-Mosel, with some 225 acres under vines. Its wines are light, engaging and attractive, soon ready; the best vineyard sites include, in about this order of excellence, Apotheke, Altärchen, Felsenkopf, and Leiterchen.

TROCKEN — (*Trawk*-ken) — Literally means dry in German, but as a wine-taster's term it is distinctly less favorable than its English or its French equivalent, *sec*. Except with regard to sparkling wine, it can also mean "withered" (*see*) or *seché,* lacking in freshness and fruit.

TROCKENBEERENAUSLESE — (Trawken-bearen-ouse-lay-zeh) — The highest, sweetest and most expensive of the numerous categories into which fine German wines are divided. Literally the word means a wine made from a selection (*Auslese*) of individually picked grapes (*Beeren*) which have been left on the vine until so ripe as to be practically dry (*trocken*) or raisined. Such grapes are harvested only in great years, and they yield an infinitesimal amount of very sweet, wholly remarkable, and fabulously expensive wine.

TROIS GLORIEUSES, Les — (Trwa Glaw-ree-ehs) — The third weekend in November every year — Saturday an enormous banquet, singing of wine songs, blowing hunting horns and lots of Burgundy at Clos de Vougeot, home of la Confrerie des Chevaliers du Tastevin; Sunday the Vente des Vins (Wine Auction) of the Hospices de Beaune and Monday the Paulée de Meursault celebrating the end of the vintage.

TROJA — (*Tro*-ya) — Extremely productive Italian red wine grape, giving a deep-colored, full-bodied, blending wine, rather high in alcohol; widely grown, especially in Apulia (*see*).

TROLONG-MONDOT, Château — (Tro-lawn Mawn-doe) — 1st Growth of St. Émilion. Some 12,000 cases a year of well-balanced, consistently pleasing red wine.

TROTANOY, Château — (Tro-tan-wah) — One of the best small vineyards of Pomerol. Some 2,500 cases a year of truly outstanding claret.

TROTTEVIEILLE, Château — (Trawt-vee-A) — A Premier Grand Cru Classé of St. Émilion. Wines remarkable for their finesse and breed. About 5,000 cases.

TROUBLE — (Troo-bl) — French word, used of a wine which is hazy or cloudy, for whatever reason, not clear or brilliant.

TUILÉ — (Twee-lay) — French wine-tasters' term, applied to red wines that have a brick-red or roof-tile tinge in their normal crimson, generally the mark of a wine that is already beginning to grow old, and will be short-lived.

TUN — A very large cask or tank or vat, used for wine storage.

TUNISIA — Produces some 20 million gallons of heavy dark, early maturing reds, very dry whites and pleasant *rosés* as well as some quite passable Muscats.

TURSAN — (Toor-san) — Obscure French wine, red, white or *rosé,* produced not far from the Adour River in southwestern France, entitled to the V.D.Q.S. seal.

TUSCANY — (Italian   TOSCANA — Toe-*skaahn*-na) — The   region   of Florence, including the Chianti Country, produces an average of about 100 million gallons a year. Over 99% of this is table wine and practically all of it is red. Twenty five per cent is sold as Chianti (*see*). In addition to Chianti *classico,* which comes from a small, delimited district between Florence and Siena, many Tuscan wines once famous in their own right (Carmignano, Pomino, Rufina, etc.) are now usually marketed under this *passepartout* name, and have largely lost their identity, at least as far as foreign markets are concerned. Much very common wine is also shipped as Chianti, and little red Tuscan wine under any other appellation. However, *see* Aleatico, Brunello di Montalcino, Elba, Vino Nobile di Montepulciano, Vino Santo.
For Map, *see* ITALY.

TYROL — (*Teer*-roll) — Mountainous district, formerly part of Austria, now the Italian provinces of Trento and Bolzano (*see*), in which German is still largely spoken, and which produces many of the most agreeable and best red, white, and *rosé* wines of northern Italy. See Alto Adige, Trentino.
For Map, *see* ITALY.

U

UGNI BLANC — (Oon-ye Blawn) — Productive white wine grape, called the Trebbiano (*see*) in Italy and the St. Émilion in the Cognac Country, rather widely planted in southern France where the best wine it yields is that of Cassis (*see*). It is also grown in California's Livermore Valley, where, as in France and Italy, it gives a sound, well-balanced white wine, agreeable but without any great class.

UKIAH — Town in Mendocino County, California. Many new vineyards have been planted in this region and the climate is well-suited for the production of fine varietal grapes.

ULLAGE — The empty space above the liquid in an incompletely filled wine cask: the amount that it lacks of being full. *Ouillage* is the French term that means the filling or "topping" of such casks; oddly enough, both words come from the Latin *ad oculum* — filling to the "eye" or bunghole of the cask.

UMBRIA — (Oom-bree-ah) — Region in central Italy, north of Rome and south of Florence, by no means a real vineyard country, yet producing about 20 million gallons a year of table wine. Its one wine of more than local fame is Orvieto (*see*).

ÜRZIG — (Ert-zig) — Tiny village on the Mittel-Mosel with some 110 acres of steep, terraced vineyard. Its soil is mostly brick-red (rather than the prevailing black slate of the Moselle Valley) and the wines have a rather special character — a pronounced sprightliness and spiciness — in good years. The best vineyards are Würzgarten, and Goldwingert.

U.S.A. — California is far and away the largest wine producing state (86%), however there is a total of 28 states producing wines. New York is second (10%), Illinois (2%), Virginia (0.6%), South Carolina and Michigan (0.4% each), Georgia (0.3%), Washington, New Jersey, Arkansas and Ohio (0.2% each) and Missouri (0.1%). Total wine production is about 400 million gallons including fruit and berry wines made in 13 states.

USÉ — (Oo-zay) — French word meaning, literally, "worn out," and having not far from the same meaning when applied to wine: a tired wine, definitely past its prime and on the decline.

U.S.S.R. — *See* RUSSIA.

V

VACQUERAS — (Va-kay-ras) — Wine-producing town in the lower Rhône Valley, northeast of Avignon. Usually a red wine, though some *rosé* is made; they are both sold as Côtes-du-Rhône-Vacqueras.

VALAIS — (Val-ay) — Swiss canton producing most of the best red wines of Switzerland and some of the more interesting and better whites. There are nearly 9,000 acres of vineyard strung along the rocky, enormously impressive, upper valley of the Rhône, here only some twenty airline miles from the Italian border but separated from Italy by the highest peaks of the Alps. The vines extend from near Martigny, (*see*) at the foot of Mont Blanc, past Sion, (*see*) Sierre and Visp, almost to Brig, at the northern end of the Simplon tunnel. Among the finer Valais wines are Dôle (*see*), Ermitage, Johannisberg and numerous whites called Fendant after the grape variety out of which they are made.

VALDADIGE — (Vahl-*dah*-dee-jay) — The common, light red table wine of the Trentino (*see*) in Italy. Undistinguished, but usually fresh and pleasant.

VALDEPEÑAS — (Vahl-day-*pain*-yahss) — Name traditionally and loosely given (no longer correctly, however) to the whole vast production of white and red wines of La Mancha, Don Quixote's country, a rolling upland plain south of Madrid. This is the common *vino corriente* of Spain and there are well over a million acres of vineyard (almost twice California's total) in production. Legally, this is now and henceforth to be called Vino Manchego or Vino de la Mancha.

353

The new appellation Valdepeñas is much more limiting, covering only about a million gallons a year, from five villages; of these, Valdepeñas itself, on the main highway south from Madrid to Andalucia, is by far the most important. The wines, furthermore, are supposed to undergo some ageing in oak, and the grape varieties are specified: Arién for white wines, Cencibel, said to be in fact the Tempranillo of the Rioja district, for the reds. It is accepted and common practice, however, to use at least 50% of white Airén in the making of red Valdepeñas, and the wine owes its light color and lack of tannin to this fact.

The white, on the whole, is less good than the red, rather golden and somewhat lacking in sprightliness and bouquet, a sound *ordinaire* which does not improve with keeping. The red, about 13% alcohol, has considerably more fruit and charm, a color not much deeper than a dark rosé, a refreshing lightness and lack of astringency; it can well be served chilled and is best drunk young.

ALSO, a variety of red wine grape, certainly of Spanish origin, and perhaps from the Valdepeñas district (although almost certainly not the Cencibel), of which nearly 2,500 are planted in the warmer districts of California, where it gives a satisfactory, pleasant, undistinguished red wine.

VALLAGARINA — (*Vahl*-la-gar-*ree*-na) — Southern portion of the Trentino (*see*) in Italy. Its vineyards, along the Adige River, produce a good deal of agreeable, rather common, light red wine, and one or two specialties such as Marzemino d'Isera (*see*) that deserve a somewhat higher rating.

VALLE D'AOSTA — (*Vah*-leh *Da-os*-ta) — The northeast corner of Italy, its smallest region — not a great producer of wine but it does have Donnaz and Enfer d'Arvier (*see*).

VALLÉE DE LA MARNE — *see* CHAMPAGNE.

VALMUR — (Val-muir) — One of the seven Grand Cru vineyards of Chablis (*see*); may be labeled either Chablis *Grand Cru*- Valmur, or Chablis Valmur, *Grand Cru*.

VALPANTENA — (Vahl-pahn-*teh*-na) — One of the good lesser red wines of Verona, in Italy, produced just east of the Valpolicella district. It is not unlike Valpolicella, but with less bouquet and class.

VALPOLICELLA — (Vahl-po-lee-*chel*-la) — Admirable red wine, velvety, fragrant, fruity, rather light in alcohol and body but remarkable for its subtlety and breed, produced northwest of Verona, in northern Italy. There are five *communi*, or townships, in the delimited "classic" zone: Negrar, Fumane, Marano, San Pietro Incariano and Sant' Ambrogio; four grape varieties are grown, the Corvina, Molinara, Negrara and Rondinella. The lighter and lesser grades of Valpolicella are usually consumed as carafe wines (and there are no better such wines in the world) when about a year old; those of superior class (Valpolicella Superiore) are bottled after some 18 months in wood, and improve in bottle, but should generally be drunk before they are five years old.

VALTELLINA — (Vahl-tel-*lee*-na) — Vineyard district in northern Italy, at the upper end of Lake Como near the Swiss border; its red wines, which are among Italy's best. The producing grape, known here as the Chiavennasca, is in reality none other than the famous Nebbiolo (*see*) of Piedmont, and here again it gives wines of remarkable firmness, body and class. The best of them come from five little hillside areas just east of the town of Sondrio, called, from west to east, Sassella, Grumello, Inferno, Grigioni and Fracia, the three first being generally considered the finest; in many instances their wines are sold simply under these vineyard names, with no mention of Valtellina at all. They are interesting and unusual wines, their deep crimson color tinged, one would almost say, with black; sturdy, well-knit, almost unattractively firm when young, they develop slowly and well in bottle, and are long-lived. The vineyards are no less extraordinary, for they are terraced along the lower slopes of a great 12,000 foot mountain wall (the Swiss-Italian border) and face, across the narrow, slot-like valley of the Adda, mountains almost equally high, the *Alpi Orobie* of northern Lombardy.

VAR — (Varr) — French *département* on the Mediterranean between Marseille and Cannes. Produces, from scattered vineyards, most of them well back from the coast, a surprising amount of wine, much of it fairly good *rosé* and what is here called *blanc de blancs* (*see*), carafe wines both; the reds are pleasant but undistinguished. A few estates bottle *rosé* wines of superior quality (*see* Côtes de Provence).

VARIETAL (as in "variety") WINE — A wine, in most cases one from California or New York State, which takes its name, not from a town or district, but from the variety of grapes out of which it is principally made. Varietal table wines include most of the best of the U.S., e.g., Cabernet Sauvignon, Pinot Noir, Johannisberg Riesling, Pinot Chardonnay, Grenache, Delaware, Elvira, etc., as distinguished from so-called "generic" wines such as California Claret, New York State Burgundy, etc.

With a few exceptions, notably the wines of Alsace, Switzerland, Austria and the Italian Tyrol, European wines do not carry varietal names; this is due to the fact that the grape varieties grown and used in the fine wine districts abroad are specifically limited and designated, both by tradition and by law. Hence, varietal names for most fine European wines are implicit in the wines' *Appellation d'Origine* — its legally protected geographical name.

VAT — Large container of wood, cement or metal, sometimes open at the top, used for fermentation, blending and storing wine, also used as a verb for making a blend.

VAUCLUSE — (Vo-clews) — French *département* in the lower Rhône Valley, a Papal enclave in the days of the Avignon Popes (1309-1377) and for long thereafter. Its wines include Châteauneuf-du-Pape (*see*), Gigondas, Rasteau, and many pleasant lesser wines, *rosés* and reds especially, often sold as Coteaux du Ventoux, Côtes de Rhône, etc.

VAUD — (Vode) — Swiss canton, first in vineyard area (over 9,000 acres) in the Confederation: white wines almost exclusively, and these made almost exclusively from the Fendant or Chasselas grape. The more important vineyards extend along the northern shore of Lake Geneva, from Nyon to Lausanne (called La Côte) and from Lausanne on eastward to beyond Vevey (called

Lavaux). The district called Chablais (*see*) is also in the Canton of Vaud, as are the Côtes de l'Orbe, near Neuchâtel.

VAUDÉSIR — (Vo-day-zeer) — One of the best of the seven *Grand Cru* vineyards of Chablis. Its wine is outstanding. Moutonne (*see*) is included in the surface of Vaudésir.

V.D.Q.S., or VINS DÉLIMITÉS DE QUALITÉ SUPÉRIEURE — (Van Daylee-me-tay d'Cahl-lee-tay Soo-pay-ree-err) — Category of French wines created in 1949, including many of truly superior quality, which are nevertheless not legally entitled to an *Appellation Contrôlée* (*see*). They are, however, strictly controlled by the French Government as to production zone, grape varieties and yield per acre. When shipped, their labels carry a special stamp with the initials V.D.Q.S. and the words *"Label de Garantie."* The *"garantie"* in question is an official one and the stamp may only appear on wines produced in accordance with the Government's rules, wines, in addition which have been tasted and approved by a committee of impartial experts. There are over fifty such wines as of the present, all listed under their place-name in this volume, and also in the appendix. Some of the better-known ones are: Côtes du Luberon, Côtes de Provence, Costières du Gard, Minervois, Corbières, etc.

VECCHIO — (*Veck*-ee-o) — Italian for "old," not permitted on labels in the U.S.A., but a legal term in Italy for wines aged two years.

VEGA SICILIA — (*Vay*-ga See-*see*-lya) — Rare, interesting and expensive Spanish table wine produced on the banks of the Duero River not far from Valladolid. Its vineyards adjoin those which produce an almost equally rare wine called Valbuena. Surprisingly fine, well-aged, always expensive, hard to find, it is a true collectors' item.

VELOUTÉ — (Vel-loo-tay) — Literally, in French, "velvety"; winetasters' term, applied to wines that are notably mature, mellow, fine textured and soft, as *soyeux,* or "silky."

VELTLINER — (*Velt*-leen-ner) — Good quality white-wine grape, of importance principally in Austria. Its wine somewhat resembles a Gewürztraminer, though with less pronounced bouquet and flavor.

VENDANGE — (Vawn-dawnj) — French for the grape harvest, or vintage, though *never* used of the "vintage" of a particular wine (*see millésime*). The equivalent terms are *vendemmia* (Ital.), *vendimia* (Sp.), and *Weinlese* (Ger.), and these too are applied to the harvest itself, not to the "year" which the wine may carry later on its label.

VENDEMMIA — (Ven-*dehm*-ee-ah) — Italian for grape harvest or vintage, not used of a particular year or vintage.

VENDIMIA — (Ven-dee-me-ah) — Spanish word meaning the grape harvest. Not, however, used in the sense of the word "vintage," nor meaning a specific year.

VENENCIA — (Ven-*nen*-see-ah) — Instrument used (like a *pipette* or "wine thief") in the Sherry and Manzanilla country to take samples of wine through the bunghole of a cask. In its simplest form, it is a strip of bamboo (*caña*)

356

with one cylindrical section left intact at the lower end, so as to form a little cup. This cylindrical cup is now more often of silver, attached to a pliable whalebone rod, with a silver hook to serve as a hanger at its upper end. An expert *bodeguero* in Jerez can use his *venencia* with extraordinary grace and skill.

VENETO — (*Veh*-nay-toe) — The region of Venice, fourth in wine production among Italian regions, some 245 million gallons a year. Much of this is quite ordinary but much, too, is good. Especially notable are the wines of Verona (*see*), Bardolino, Valpolicella, Soave; and those of the province of Treviso, (*see* Conegliano), but there are many others that belong in a somewhat lesser category: Raboso, Friularo, Colli Euganei, etc.

VENTE SUR SOUCHES — (Vawnt suhr Soosh) — In French "sale on the vine" — commercial practice, which has unfortunately become widespread in the Bordeaux district in recent years, whereby the wine of a given vineyard is sold at a fixed price months before the vintage, and long before anything is known of the size of the crop or of its quality. This, which is of course pure speculation, has brought about higher prices and a regrettable tendency on the part of the Bordeaux trade to describe even the most mediocre vintages as "outstanding" or even as "the year of the century."

VENTOUX — (Vawn-too) — Name of a remarkable, isolated, 6,000-foot peak (Le Mont Ventoux literally means "The Windy Mountain," and it is well named) dominating a whole section of the lower Rhône Valley and the *département* of Vaucluse (*see*). Its lower slopes and the surrounding foothills are largely covered with vines and yield much excellent *vin rosé* (usually sold as Côtes du Ventoux), some very good red including Gigondas (*see*), a few white wines that are less interesting and even one sweet liqueur wine called Rasteau (*see*).

VERAISON — (Veh-ray-zoh) — French, stage in ripening when the grapes change color just prior to attaining full sugar content and readiness for the harvest.

VERDELET — (Vair-duh-lay) — French hybrid grown in Western New York and Canadian Niagara Peninsula; suitable for white wine and as table grapes.

VERDELHO — (Vair-*del*-ho) — One of the best grape varieties of Madeira, producing an interesting, fortified wine, generally sold under this name — usually on the dry side and somewhat resembling Sercial, but with a special character of its own.

VERDICCHIO — (Vehr-*dee*-key-o) — Superior Italian white wine grape; also its wine. *See* Castelli di Jesi.

VERDISO — (Vehr-*dee*-zo) — Superior white wine grape and the interesting, dry white wine made from it, round the town of Conegliano (*see*), north of Venice in northern Italy. A sweeter still wine and some sparkling wines as well are made in the same district, and called Prosecco (*see*).

VERGENNES — (Vair-zhenn) — American grape variety, probably a Labrusca seedling, dating from Revolutionary days, named after the then Foreign Minister of France, Comte Charles de Vergennes, who, like Lafayette, was a staunch champion of the cause of American independence.

VERGISSON — (Vair-zhee-saw) — One of the four *communes* producing Pouilly-Fuissé (*see*), perhaps the least important of the four.

VERJUS — (Vair-zhuh) — Juice of unripe grapes, high in acid.

VERMENTINO — (Vehr-men-*tee*-no) — Perhaps the best dry white wine of the Italian Riviera, fresh, pale, tart, excellent with seafood; that produced round Pietra Ligure is outstanding; also produced in Sardinia.

VERMOUTH — (from the German *Wermut,* wormword) — A fortified white wine, flavored with various herbs, barks, seeds, spices, etc. The principal aromatic agent in vermouth consists of flowers of the shrub *Artemisia absinthium,* also known as wormwood; (the far more toxic leaves of the same plant were used in the making of Absinthe). Today, vermouth is used principally as an apértif and as a cocktail ingredient. There are two main types: French and Italian. The French, pale in color, quite dry; the Italian, darker, usually with a base of muscat wine, quite sweet. French type vermouths are, nevertheless, made in Italy, and Italian type vermouths in France. Both are produced in many other countries, including Spain, Argentina and the United States, and are based on similar wines and the same aromatics, including *Artemisia* flowers, bitter orange peel, camomile, aloes, cardamon and anise. The better American vermouths are now substantially as good as the imported.

VERNACCIA — (Vehr-*natch*-cha) — Unusual white wine of Sardinia, dry, rather aromatic, higher in alcohol (sometimes over 17%) than any other natural, unfortified wine in the world. It takes its name from the Vernaccia grape.

VERNATSCH — (Vehr-*nach*) — Local name given to the Shiave grape (*see*) in the Italian Tyrol.

VERONA — (Vehr-*ro*-na) — Charming little city in northern Italy, famous as the home of Romeo and Juliet, and, among wine-lovers, for the wines produced nearby, copiously and joyously consumed by the Veronese themselves, and now exported in increasing quantities. They include Soave, Valpolicella, Valpantena, Bardolino, Chiaretto (*see* all of these).

VERT — (Vair) — French wine-tasters' term, applied to wines that are "green," or unripe, in the same sense as unripe fruit, disagreeably high in acid, and tart. In many cases this is a fault that will correct itself with time, and if the wine is otherwise well-balanced, it can be an indication (though by no means an assurance) of good future development and long life.

VERZENAY — (Vair-zuh-nay) — One of the best villages of the French Champagne Country, on the Montagne de Reims, rated 100% in the official classification. Its vineyards, much fought over in World War I, are planted to Pinot Noir exclusively. *See* Champagne.

VESTE — (Vest-eh) — Italian equivalent of the French word *robe* when applied to wine; a combination of color, clarity and brilliance — *una buona veste* is high praise.

VESUVIO — (Veh-*soo*-vee-o) — Wine, generally a dry, white wine, produced on the slopes of Mt. Vesuvius, near Naples.

VIDANGE — (Vee-danj) — Ullage. The empty space in an improperly filled cask of wine; more rarely, the air space under the cork of a bottled wine. If abnormally great, a danger signal in almost all cases. The word *vide,* of course, means "empty" and *vidanger* means "to drain."

VIEUX — (Vee-uh) — French word for "old" (the feminine is *vielle* — vee-yay), about as loosely used as in English.

VIEUX CHÂTEAU CERTAN — (Vee-uh Shat-toe Sair-tah) — One of the very best vineyards of Pomerol, second perhaps only to Château Petrus. Some 4,000 cases a year of fine, sturdy, velvety Claret, consistently good, improving greatly in bottle.

VIF — (Veef) — French wine-tasters' term, applied to a young wine that is fresh, light, agreeable; perhaps a little more tart than one called *tendre,* and a bit less tart than one called *vivace.*

VIGNE — (Veen-yuh) — In French, an individual vine, or, far more often, a small parcel of vineyard, one man's holding in a *climat* (*see*) or *vignoble* (*see*).

VIGNERON — (Veen-yair-raw) — In French, a vineyardist, or wine-dresser, whether working for his own account or not.

VIGNOBLE — (Veen-yob'l) — In French, a vineyard area, or the vineyards of a district, generally sharing an appellation.

VILA NOVA DE GAIA — (Vee-la No-va day Guy-ya) — Town directly opposite Oporto on the Douro River, in Portugal. *See* Port.

VILLAFRANCA DEL PANADÉS — (*Veel*-ya *Frahn*-ka del Pahn ah-*daice*) — Important center of the wine trade, south of Barcelona, in Spain. Some very passable and surprisingly light white wines are made, a few less good reds, and what are on the whole the best sparkling wines of Spain, mostly fermented in bulk but a few by the authentic Champagne process, especially in the nearby village of San Sadurni de Noya.

VILLAUDRIC — (Veel-lo-dreek) — Inconsequential red and white wine produced round the town of this name in southwestern France.

VILLARD BLANC — (Vee-yar Blah) — Another Seyve-Villard hybrid grown in warmer areas, especially the Southwest, vigorous and productive for white wine.

VILLENAVE D'ORNON — (Veel-nav Dor-naw) — Wine-producing village in the Graves district of France. Its better Châteaux include: Couhins, Baret, Pontac-Monplaisir, etc.

VIN — (Van) — French for wine, legally defined in France (as in the United States) as a beverage made through the partial or complete fermentation of the juice of fresh grapes. Thus, wines made from cherries and other fruits must be labeled "Cherry Wine," "Blackberry Wine," etc.

VIÑA — *(Veen-*ya) — Spanish word for "vineyard," often followed by a proper name.

VINAGRINHO — (Veen-ah-*green-*ho) — Portuguese term for the characteristic flavor of certain old Madeiras and old Ports, akin to *rancio* (*see*) largely the result of partial oxidation and a slight increase in volatile acidity.

VIN BLANC — (Van Blaw) — French for white wine.

VIN BOURRU — (Boo-rew) — French, young unfinished wine, still fermenting and gassy; consumed in this state in various countries.

VIN CUIT — (Van Quee) — French wine tasters' term, said of a wine which appears to have the aroma and taste of concentrate, or wine that has been heated before fermentation so as to reduce its volume and to increase its eventual alcoholic content and its body.

VIN DE L'ANNÉE — (Van d'Lan-nay) — Literally, in French, "wine of the year," used to describe any wine, excellent or mediocre, which is less than a year old.

VIN DE CAFÉ — (Van d'Cafay) — An inexpensive, light-bodied red or *rosé* wine (occasionally but rarely a white wine), made to be consumed as a "bar wine" or *vin de comptoir* in France.

VIN DE GARDE — (Van d'Gard) — French wine taster's term meaning a wine which will improve with keeping.

VIN DE LIQUEUR — (Van d'Lee-keer) — A sweet wine obtained by adding alcohol to unfermented must, thus preserving the sweetness of the natural grape sugar.

VIN DE PAILLE — *See* PAILLE.

VIN DE PAYS/VIN DU PAYS — *See* PAYS.

VIN DE PRESSE — (Van d' Press) — French for wine which is generally not the first "free-run" juice of the crushed grapes, but extracted by a wine press. The first *vin de presse* is usually blended with the "free-run" and gives it more substance, color and tannin, all of which it often lacks. Alone, *vin de presse* is likely to be somewhat harsh.

VIN DE PRIMEUR — (Van d'Pree-muhr) — French term for a wine which matures or at least is drunk when very young; such wines are invariably short-lived.

VIN DE SAVOIE — *See* SAVOIE.

VIN DE TABLE — (Van d'Tahbl) — French, table wine.

VIN DE TÊTE — (Van d'Tet) — Said in French of a wine of outstanding quality, the best of its sort; also a "free-run" wine which has not received the addition of a *vin de presse*.

VIN D'UNE NUIT — (Van dune Nwee) — In French a cheap, light red wine which has been left to ferment on its skins for twenty-four hours or less and which, therefore, has little color and tannin; for all practical purposes, identical with a *vin de café* (*see*).

VIN DOUX NATUREL — (Van Doo Nah-tew-rel) — A higher quality of *vin de liqueur* starting with a must containing more sugar and adding alcohol during the fermentation instead of before it starts. *See* Muscat de Frontignan and Port.

VINÉ — (Vee-nay) — French word meaning "fortified." Wines to which brandy or high-proof grape spirits have been added are *vins vinés*.

VINETTO — (Vee-*net*-toe) — Italian for a small wine, low in alcohol and light in body.

VINEUX — (Veen-uh) — French wine tasters' term said of a wine which is obviously rather high in alcohol — perhaps too much so — and without much finesse. The German is *weinig*.

VINEYARD — A plantation of grape vines.

VINEYARD SITE — The rather clumsy English equivalent of the French word *climat;* the Spanish *pago;* and the German *Weinbergslage,* meaning a specifically named plot of vines.

VIN FIN — (Van Fan) — Loosely used French term meaning, in general, a wine of superior quality; one made from superior grape varieties. Only in rare instances (*see* Côte de Nuits) has it a more specific definition according to French law.

VIN GRIS — (Van Gree) — French term used to describe very pale *rosé* wines, especially those made from black grapes in eastern France, notably Lorraine and Alsace. Some of these are practically white, with an almost imperceptible pink or bronze tinge (*see* Lorraine).

VINHO — (*Veen*-ho) — General Portuguese term for wine.

VINHO GENEROSO — (*Veen*-ho Gen-air-*ro*-so) — Portuguese term reserved for certain fortified wines of superior quality and specific origin.

VINHO DE RAMO — (*Veen*-ho de *Rah*-mo) — Legal Portuguese name for the *consumo* (or table wine) from the Port district, which is sold unfortified for table use, rather than being made into Port.

VINHO DE TORNA VIAGEM — (*Veen*-ho de *Tor*-na Via-jem) — Old Portuguese term applied to wines which had been shipped in casks in sailing vessels to the East Indies and back, which supposedly greatly improved them. Certain Ports and Madeiras were so labeled and they were the Portuguese equivalent of "East India Sherries."

VINHO VERDE — (*Veen*-ho *Vair*-day) — Literally "green wine" in Portuguese. Odd name given to the sprightly, fresh, red, white and *rosé* wines (green only in the sense of being youthful — naturally not in color) produced in northern Portugal, not far from Spanish Galicia. Many of these are very pleasant, a few slightly sparkling, and some are now being exported to England and the United States.

VINICULTURE — General term covering the whole science and business of the growing of wine grapes, the making of wine and the wine's ageing and preparation for market.

VINIFERA — (Vin-*nif*-fer-ah) — One, and by all odds the most important, of the 32 species which make up the genus *vitis*. There are some 60 species which grow in the temperate zones, about 20 native to the United States and the others native to Central and East Asia. Only one, *Vinifera,* "the wine bearer," apart from a few hybrids is responsible for all of the wines of Europe, Africa, South America, Australia and California. There are literally hundreds of varieties, black, purple, blue, red, pink, amber, yellow, green, etc., in this species, which originated in Transcaucasia in pre-historic times.

VINIFICATION — The making of wine from grapes, including its fermentation, treatment, ageing, etc. A very broad term which involves practically the whole process except what goes on in the vineyard.

VINILLO — (Vee-*neel*-yo) — Spanish equivalent of the French *Petit Vin*. A wine of light body, low alcoholic content, generally of poor quality.

VIN JAUNE — (Van zhone) — Odd, special wine produced in the Jura district of France, especially round Château Chalon (*see*) — not far in character from a very light Spanish Sherry.

VIN MOUSSEUX — (Van Moo-suh) — *See* MOUSSEUX.

VIN NATURE — (Van Nah-tewr) — A rather loosely used French wine term meaning, in general, a wine that has not been fortified or sweetened; in some cases, a Champagne which has received no *dosage* or sweetening.

VIN NON MOUSSEUX — (Van Non Moo-suh) — In French, simply means a non-sparkling wine, a still wine.

VIN NOUVEAU — (Van Noo-vo) — Properly applied, in French, it is any wine which has finished its fermentation and is less than a year old and usually still contains some carbon dioxide.

VINO — (*Vee*-no) — The word for wine in Italian and Spanish.

VINO CORRIENTE — (*Vee*-no Cor-ri-*en*-tay) — In Spanish, the equivalent of the French *vin ordinaire;* the young, inexpensive, relatively common wine, currently consumed by most Spaniards, often in carafe.

VINO DA ARROSTO — (*Vee*-no da Ar-*ros*-toe) — Italian for a rather full-bodied red wine, one of better than average quality, properly served with red meat.

VINO DA MESSA — (*Vee*-no da *Meh*-sa) — Italian (French VIN DE MESSE) sacramental or altar wine, made in accordance with strict church regulations governing purity, naturalness and alcoholic content.

VINO DA PASTO — (*Vee*-no da *Pass*-toe) — (Spanish, VINO DE PASTO). In Italian, a table wine as distinguished from apéritif and dessert wines.

VINO DE MESA — (*Vee*-no duh *May*-sa) — Spanish for table wine.

VINO DE YEMA — (*Vee*-no duh *Yay*-ma) — In Spanish, a wine generally of superior quality, made of "free-run" juice or from grapes very lightly pressed.

362

VINO DI LUSSO — (*Vee*-no dee *Lee*-so) — Italian wine term, literally "de luxe wine," a category which includes sparkling wines, fortified wines, etc.

VINO DI TAGLIO — (*Vee*-no da *Tal*-yo) — Italian term for blending wine, usually one having certain special characteristics such as deep color, high alcohol, etc., used to improve wines of lesser quality.

VINO NOBILE DI MONTEPULCIANO — (*Vee*-no *No*-bee-leh Dee Mon-teh-pul-*cha*-no) — Red wine from southern Tuscany, in Italy, produced round the picturesque old hill town of this name. It was extravagantly praised by the English poet, Leigh Hunt, in the early 19th century, as "the king of wines," echoing the earlier opinion of the wine-loving author-physician, Dr. Francesco Redi, in his "Bacco in Toscana"; and the 1978 vintage will become one of the first D.O.C.G. (*see*). It is not, oddly enough, made from the Montepulciano grape (which is a good red wine variety of southern Italy) but from the Sangiovese and others like Chianti (*see*).

VIN ORDINAIRE — (Van Or-de-naihr) — *See* ORDINAIRE.

VINO ROSATO — *See* ROSATO.

VINO ROSSO — *See* ROSSO.

VINO SANTO — (*Vee*-no *Sahn*-toe), also VIN SANTO) — Italian white wine produced principally in Tuscany, but also, to some extent, in the Trentino (*see*), from grapes that have been allowed partially to raisin, either on the vine or indoors. Various grape varieties are used, most often the Trebbiano, and the resulting wine is of course golden in color, quite sweet, bottled generally after two or more years in cask (*see* Passito).

VINOSITY — Word used to denote winy character, wininess.

VINO TINTO — *See* TINTO.

VINO TIPICO — *See* TIPICO.

VIN ROSÉ — *See* ROSÉ.

VIN ROUGE — (Van Rouge) — Red wine, in French.

VIN SUR LIE — (Van Sewr Lee) — French and Swiss term for certain white wines which are drawn off for consumption or bottling before the final racking has taken place; in other words, while there is still some yeasty sediment or deposit in the cask. This is common practice in the Muscadet district of France, to an even greater extent in the Swiss vineyards along Lake Geneva. Such wines have a faint, rather agreeable, yeasty flavor, and an almost imperceptible sparkle.

VINTAGE — Word used in a confusing diversity of senses in English, often practically as a synonym for wine. Properly, however, the vintage is the annual grape harvest and the wine made from those grapes; to this extent, at least, every year is a vintage year and all wines are vintage wines unless they are blended — their vintage is the year they were produced. However, during the 19th century, it became common practice in a few wine-growing districts, notably the Port Country and Champagne, to blend all wines except those of unusually good years, and to allow only the latter to carry a date, or vintage; eventually, in the popular mind, in England and the United States, "vintage year" came to have the meaning of "good year," although it can have no possible such connotation except with regard to Champagne and Port. In Bordeaux, Burgundy, the Rhineland, etc., there are good vintages and bad (the latter, alas, all too frequent) but almost every unblended wine carries its vintage on its label, and is therefore, by any sensible definition, a vintage wine, whether good or bad.

In most wine-producing countries, especially those fairly far north, there is a great difference in quality between the wines of one year and another; vintage years are important, and a reliable vintage chart can be very helpful. This is not so much the case in areas of less variable climate and more consistent sunshine, such as most of California and, to some extent, the lower Rhône Valley, Italy and Spain.

VINZELLES — (Van-zell) — Village in the French Maconnais district, not far from Pouilly. *See* Pouilly-Vinzelles.

VIOGNIER — (Vee-on-yea) — White grape of the Rhône Valley, in France, giving a wine of excellent quality and rather pronounced and special character. Sometimes spelled Vionnier, it is the variety of Château-Grillet and Condrieu (*see*) and is also used to some extent in the red Côte Rôtie.

VIRÊ — (Vee-ray) — Village north of Macon, in southern Burgundy. Its fresh, dry, fragrant white wines, made from the Chardonnay grape, are, with those of Lugny and Clessé, among the best of the Mâconnais. The outstanding vineyard is the Clos du Chapitre (*see*).

VISPERTERMINEN — (Vis-pair-tare-me-nen) — Small, Swiss vineyard in the Canton of Valais, the highest in altitude in Europe, being situated over 4,000 feet above sea level. Its wines, mostly red, are sometimes known as *Païen*, meaning "Pagan."

VITE ALBERATA — (*Vee*-teh Ahl-bear-*ra*-ta) — Vines trained on (or "married to") trees, in the Italian fashion; the tree, in such instances, is often called a *marito,* or husband.

VITICULTEUR — (Vee-tee-cuhl-tehr) — in French, a vine grower, generally one who cultivated his own vineyard; *vigneron* (*see*) is nearly synonymous, but more often used of a skilled employee or share-cropper (*metayer*).

VITICULTURE — That branch of agriculture which involves the science and art of grape-growing; when this has to do with wine production, the proper word is viniculture (*see*).

VITIS — *See* GRAPE.

VIVACE — (Vee-*vahss*) — French wine-tasters' term, applied generally to young wines which are fresh, lively, often a bit tart, likely to keep well and improve.

VOLATILE ACIDITY — *See* ACIDITY, VOLATILE.

VOLLRADS, Schloss — (Vawl-rahdz) — The largest and one of the most famous vineyard estates of the Rheingau, back of the village of Winkel, and just east of Schloss Johannisberg. The castle itself, with a picturesque keep, or central tower, dating from 1355, is a splendid old manor house, and its 91 acres of vines produce an extremely wide range of estate-bottlings, all the way from the light, dry, modest *Qualitätsweine* of secondary years to incomparable *Trockenbeerenauslesen* in great vintages. Wines considered unworthy of the *Schloss* label never are allowed to carry it, but those granted this diploma, with practically no exceptions, have to some degree a certain characteristic elegance, a fine bouquet, a pleasing lightness and fruit.

Of those permitted to bear the name of the owner (Graf Matuschka-Greiffenklau — who is a chess-player) and his coat-of-arms, the least expensive are those that carry the word *Qualitätswein* and a green capsule; those with a green-capsule-with-gold-stripe are of slightly superior class, and occasionally a *Qualitätswein* with a red capsule will also be found. On a higher level are the *Qualitätsweine mit Prädikat*. The *Kabinett* has a blue capsule, and in outstanding years a blue-gold capsule. The *Spätlese* carries a pink capsule, the best barrels of which may be distinguished by a pink-gold capsule. In great years, such as 1971, when wines in the very highest categories are made, the *Beerenauslese* will carry a gold capsule and the *Trockenbeerenauslese* a gold capsule in combination with a special neckband showing a picture of the old medieval tower still standing on the Schloss Vollrads property. When an *Eiswein* is made, such as in 1970, it will also carry this special neckband, and if the wine is an *Auslese,* as was the 1970 *Eiswein,* it will carry the corresponding white-gold capsule.

In vintages before 1971, the word *Kabinett* was used to designate the *Spätlese* quality. It, too, carried a blue capsule, and should not be confused with the *Kabinett* blue capsule of 1971 and later vintages, which is always a dry wine and never a *Spätlese.* Pre-1971 wines assigned the pink capsule to *Auslese* and the white capsule to *Beerenauslese.*

For a few years some confusion is bound to result from the co-existence of two separate capsule-color systems in wine shops, but as older vintages of Schloss Vollrads gradually disappear from wine merchants' shelves, the new capsule colors, together with their quality associations, will certainly be a long-sought-after simplification which will considerably help the consumer in selecting and buying Schloss Vollrads wines.

VOLNAY — (Vawl-nay) — Justly celebrated village of the Côte de Beaune, in Burgundy, its vineyards bounded on the north by those of Pommard and on the south by Meursault's. The average quality of its red wines (the few whites are entitled to and carry the appellation Meursault) is extremely high, certainly above Pommard's, and the Volnays of good years are among the most prepossessing of all Burgundies, wonderfully soft and fine, *bouquetés,* with a special velvety quality, and great breed. The better vineyards include the Clos des Ducs, Caillerets, Champans, Chevret, Fremiets, Pousse d'Or (often, but less correctly, written Bousse d'Or), Clos des Chênes, etc.
    See map on following page.

VORLAUF — (Vor-lauf) — Wine made from the first, gentle pressing of red grapes, usually a pale *rosé.* Name often given in Alsace to the light pink wine there made from the Pinot Noir and Pinot Meunier.

NOTE: What is certainly Volnay's best known vineyard, the *Clos des Ducs,* was inexplicably left nameless on this old map. It consists of the blank section directly above and adjoining the village of Volnay, and is part of the estate of the present Marquis d'Angerville, whose father was largely responsible for the creation of *Appellations Contrôlées* in Burgundy.

VOSGES — (Vojh) — Mountain chain in eastern France, facing Germany's Black Forest across the wide, fertile plain of the Rhine Valley. The wines of Alsace (*see*) come from vineyards planted along the eastern slopes and foothills of the Vosges.

VOSNE-ROMANÉE — (Vone Ro-ma-nay) — Perhaps the most remarkable wine-producing *commune* of all France, though its total production is comparatively small. Within its communal limits are grown some seven or eight truly incomparable red wines, the glories of Burgundy, known around the world: Romanée-Conti, Richebourg, La Tâche, La Romanée, all labeled simply with the vineyard name and no mention of Vosne; then, having Vosne-Romanée as part of their name, Vosne-Romanée La Grande Rue, Les Malconsorts, Les Suchots, Les Beaux-Monts and many others. All of them (even the lesser wine

Vosne-Romanée 1966

APPELLATION CONTROLEE

Ce vin, sélectionné en 1969 par les Jurés-Gourmets de la

Confrérie des Chevaliers du Castevin

a été élevé dans les caves de

Jh. Faiveley

NÉGOCIANT A NUITS-ST-GEORGES (CÔTE-D'OR)

sold simply as Vosne-Romanée) have certain characteristics in common: breed, elegance, exceptional balance, fine bouquet. *See* most of the vineyards listed above in their alphabetical place elsewhere in this volume.

See map on following page.

VOUGEOT — (Voo-zho) — Red Burgundy from a small plot of vines directly adjoining the Clos de Vougeot (*see*), but not entitled to this name. It is definitely of a lesser grade than Clos de Vougeot itself, and often has a certain special *goût de terroir*.

VOUVRAY — (Voo-vray) — The most famous white wine of Touraine, in the Loire Valley of France, and an old American favorite, perhaps due to the fact that AFHQ, in World War I, was set up in Tours, nearby. It is made entirely from the Chenin Blanc grape, and the legally delimited zone of production consists of eight *communes:* Vouvray, Ste. Radegonde, Rochecorbon, Vernou, Noizay, Chançay, Reugny and Parçay-Meslay. A changeling among wines if there ever was one, Vouvray can be (depending on its vintage and its cellar treatment) a fruity, bone-dry wine, somewhat on the tart side; a rich, golden elixir, comparable to a great Sauternes or Rhine wine; a pale and appetizing wine with a slight sparkle (*pétillant*); an out-and-out sparkling wine, and one of the best of France. Despite much that has been said and written to the contrary, Vouvray does "travel"; it is also one of the longest-lived white wines of the world. Total production is in the neighborhood of a million and a quarter gallons a year.

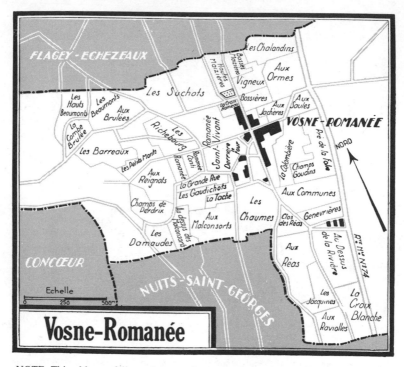

Vosne-Romanée

NOTE: This old map fails to show one important change in appellations which became effective during World War II, whereby a large part of Les Gaudichots became part of La Tâche (*see*).

V.Q.P.R.D. or VINS DE QUALITÉ PRODUITS DANS DES REGIONS DÉTERMINÉES — A European Common Market appellation for quality wines, the use of which is optional, since the traditional wording of member countries may be used. These are specific as follows:

France: Appellation d'Origine Contrôlée, Vin Délimite de Qualité Supérieur, Champagne

Germany: Qualitätswein and Qualitätswein mit Prädikat

Italy: Denominazione di Origine Controlata and Denominazione de Origine Controlata e Garantita

Luxembourg — Marque Nationale du Vin Luxembourgeois.

VULLY — (Voo-ye) — Wine producing district not far from Neuchâtel in the Swiss Canton of Vaud. White wines from the Fendant or Chasselas grape.

W

WACHENHEIM — (*Vahk*-hen-heim) — One of the four best wine-producing towns of the German Rheinpfalz (*see*) or Palatinate. Its wines are a little lighter than those of Forst and Deidesheim nearby, but of the same noble class. The vineyards spread into three Grosslagen. Leading vineyards include: Gerümpel, Böhlig, Rechbächel, Goldbächel, Altenburg and Luginsland.

WACHSTUM — (*Vahk*-stoom) — German wine term meaning "growth," used in conjunction with the name of a specific producer. Although no longer permitted under the new German Winc Law, it may still be seen on labels of older vintages. Such a wine was always *natur,* i.e., unsugared. When used without the word *Originalabfüllung,* it did not guarantee estate-bottling. *See* Erzeugerabfüllung.

WALDMEISTER — (*Vahld*-my-ster) — German name for the wild herb, woodruff (*asperula odorata,* of the madder family) which is the principal flavoring in what is known as May Wine, a popular sort of wine punch in Germany.

WALDRACH — (*Vahl*-drach) — Wine-producing village of secondary importance in the Ruwer Valley near Trier. Its best known vineyards are Doktorberg, Ehrenberg, and Hubertusberg.

WALLUF — (*Vahl*-luf) — The name used on wines of what were previously two separate townships in the German Rheingau — Nieder-Walluf and Ober-Walluf. The best vineyards (87 acres in all) are: Walkenberg, Berg Bildstock, Oberberg, Langenstück, and Fitusberg. The whites, mostly Rieslings, are of

369

fine quality, but have a certain amount of "soil" taste, or *Bodenton;* there are also a few reds made from the Blue Spätburgunder.

WASHINGTON — Northwestern State in which both labrusca and vinifera grapes flourish, particularly in the Yakima Valley.

WATER — One of three substances, the others acid and sugar, which together or separately constitute amelioration (*see*). Such additions, if permitted at all and which are tenable only to correct natural imbalances or deficiencies, are strictly limited by the laws of the producing country.

WAWERN — (Vaa-vairn) — One of the good, lesser wine-producing vineyards of the Saar Valley in Germany. Some 70 acres of Rieslings — best vineyards are: Herrenberg and Goldberg.

WEEPER — One of many terms employed to describe a wine bottle which has shown a tendency to leak or lose wine round its cork. This can be caused either by bad storage conditions or by an inferior cork. It could result in a spoiled bottle but more often appearances are deceiving and if there is no appreciable outage the wine is more likely to be in perfect condition.

WEHLEN — (*Vay-*len) — Little town on the Moselle, between Bernkastel and Zeltingen, now considered by most experts the best of that whole, small but renowned, wine district known as the Mittel-Mosel. A hundred years ago, or even fifty, this was not the case: Wehlen was ranked well below Brauneberg and Bernkastel, and hardly on a par with Graach, Zeltingen and Piesport. The change has been brought about largely through the efforts of a single numerous family called Prüm, whose wines consistently bring the highest prices at the great semi-annual auctions in Trier, where the best Moselles are sold. The village is on the left (here the south) bank of the winding river, and faces the incredibly steep, high vineyard slope in the heart of which, painted on an almost perpendicular outcropping of slate, is the *Sonnenuhr,* or sundial, which has given its name to Wehlen's best wine. This, in good years, has few if indeed any equals: flowery, well-balanced, with an almost supernatural combination of delicacy and richness, it is perfection itself.

Leading vineyard sites, besides Sonnenuhr include, Klosterberg, Nonnenberg and Abtei.

WEIBEL — (Y-bel) —Important family owned California wine producer, especially in the field of less expensive, sparkling wines. The winery is at Mission San Jose, Alameda County, southeast of San Francisco.

WEIN — (Vine) — German word for wine.

WEINBAUGEBIETE — (Vine-bow-ge-beet) — The term for a specified wine growing region for table wines under the 1971 German Wine Law. There are four regions and several subdivisions: 1; Rhein and Mosel (a) Rhein, (b) Mosel; 2- Main; 3- Neckar; 4- Oberrhein, (a) Römetor, (b) Burgengau.

WEINBERG — *(Vine-*bairg) — In German, vineyard or vineyard property.

WEINGUT — *(Vine-*goot) — In German, a vineyard property, generally including the vines themselves, a winery, cellars, etc.

WEINGUTSBESITZER — (Vine-goots-be-sitz-er) — In German, means a vineyard owner — more often than not a fairly prosperous one — who does not himself work in his own vineyard and has at least two hectares (about 5 acres) of vineyard holdings.

WEINSTEIN — (Vine-Shtine) — *see* TARTAR.

WEINSTRASSE — *(Vine-*shtrah-suh) — A road or itinerary which can be pleasantly and profitably followed by tourists in the German wine country. Usually these are marked and designated; Germany's best-known *Weinstrasse* extends south through the Rheinpfalz from Bockenheim west of Worms to Schweigen on the French frontier.

WEISSHERBST — *(Vine-*hairbst) — A vin *rosé* made from Blue Spätburgunder (Pinot Noir) grapes and which must meet Qualitätswein standards. This is a specialty of the little villages strung along the northern shore of Lake Constance, which the Germans call the Bodensee. The best of them comes from the village of Meersburg. It is also made in the Ahr and other regions.

WENTE — Famous California wine-growing family whose vineyards have long produced some of America's finest white wines. Their first vines were planted near Livermore, in Alameda County, southeast of San Francisco, in 1883, and the business has remained a family enterprise ever since.

WESLEY, John (1703-1791) — British preacher and founder of Methodism who wrote in his Journal, September 9, 1771: "Wine is one of the noblest cordials in nature."

WHITE PINOT — California name for the white wine grape more properly called Chenin Blanc (*see*), or Pineau de la Loire (*see*).

371

WHITE RIESLING — *See* RIESLING, JOHANNISBERG RIESLING.

WHITE WINE — Any wine which is not, and has no trace of, red; the color can vary from almost water white, greenish tint, yellow tint, pale yellow, golden, various shades of amber to deep brown, yet all are white wines.

WILTINGEN — (*Vil*-ting-en) — One of the most celebrated and best wine-producing towns of Germany, on the Saar River (*see*), southwest of Trier. Its 330 acres of vineyard are entirely planted in Rieslings and cover a few incredibly steep black-slate hillsides facing south. The best *Lagen* (or vineyard sites) include the incomparable Scharzhofberg (*see*) which many experts regard as the greatest white wine vineyard in the world, and, in addition, Braune Kupp, Rosenberg, Gottesfuss, Klosterberg, Braunfels and Kupp.

The wines from these, in poor years, are often so hard and austere as to be properly called "steely" and in very poor years many of them are sold to be blended and made into sparkling wine. In favorable and great years, however, the best Wiltingers are unsurpassed by any other white wines in Germany or in the world.

WINE — As legally defined in most countries, a beverage made from the partial or complete fermentation of the juice of fresh grapes.

WINE AND SODA — Pleasant summer drink, usually called a spritzer, consisting of ice, wine and soda in a tall glass. German wines, or comparable California wines (Riesling, Sylvaner, etc.) are perhaps best adapted for this purpose on account of their refreshing tartness. "Hock-and-soda" has been famous in England since the days of Byron.

WINE INSTITUTE — An industry California organization whose purpose is the protection and advancement of the interests of California wine producers and the California wine trade.

WINERY — American name for an establishment where wine is made (as brewery, for beer, and distillery, for spirits).

WINE MAKER — According to American usage, the person in charge of production in a winery.

WINE MERCHANT — Commonly, and according to the dictionaries, a person who deals in wine, generally as a retailer. Fifty or a hundred years ago, in most countries, this was regarded more as a profession than as a "trade"; "wine merchants" were expected to have a close, personal knowledge and appreciation of the goods they sold, and their status was not far from that of a trust officer in a bank — a person to whom one looked, with complete confidence, for accurate information and for sound advice. This is far from true today: hardly one retailer in fifty has tasted all the wines displayed on his shelves, and few of their clerks know as much about wine as do the customers they serve. This being the case, wine lovers who want something above the common average will do well to buy from those few special stores whose owners have made an effort to acquire the knowledge which their profession requires, and who may properly be described as "wine merchants." There are not too many of these in the United States, but their number, happily, seems to be increasing year by year.

WINE STONE — *See* TARTAR.

WINE TASTER — Person, either professional or amateur, whose trained palate and specialized knowledge permit him to judge, evaluate and often identify wines organoleptically, or by tasting (*see*).

WINE WAITER — *See* SOMMELIER

WINKEL — (Vink-'l) — Small but important wine-producing town overlooking the Rhine in the heart of the German Rheingau, immediately west of Johannisberg. The word *Winkel* in German means "angle" (as well as "nook" or "quiet corner") and the "angle," looking very much like a carpenter's square, appears in the coat-of-arms of Winkel, and on the wine labels of several of its good producers.

Winkel's leading vineyard is Schloss Vollrads (*see*); others of the better vineyard sites or *Lagen* include: Hasensprung, Jesuitenberg, Gutenberg, Schlossberg, and Bienengarten.

WINO — The slang or colloquial term used, especially in California to describe an alcoholic, generally of limited means, addicted to cheap, sweet, fortified wine.

WINTRICH — (Vint-rick) — One of the good, lesser wine towns of the Mittel-Mosel, in Germany, with about 200 acres of steep Riesling vineyards — better-known ones are: Ohligsberg, Sonnenseite, Grosser Herrgott and Stefanslay.

WINZER — (Vin-sir) — German for wine producer or wine grower, especially one who works in his own vineyard.

WINZERGENOSSENSCHAFT — (Vin-zer-ge-nos-sen-shahft) — An association or cooperative of wine producers in Germany.

WINZERVEREIN — (Vin-zer-ver-rine) — German wine producers' (usually peasant) cooperative or association.

WITHERED — Wine tasters' term, probably the best English translation of the French *seché*. This is properly applied to a wine which has lost its freshness and fruit, either through too long storage in barrel, or through contact with the air, once uncorked.

WOODY — Wine tasters' term for a table wine, particularly one which has been stored too long in oak, and has acquired a woody aroma and flavor.

WORMS — (Vormsz) — Historic little city on the Rhine near the southern edge of the province of Hessia. One of its Gothic churches, the Liebfrauenkirche, is surrounded by some twenty-six acres of vineyard called the Liebfrauenstift, which literally means the Church's endowment. It was this vineyard which gave its name to Liebfraumilch (*see*), and its wine (unfortunately never of very high quality) is sold as *Liebfrauenstiftswein* today. Despite its fame, it is by no means in the same class as the better Hessian wines — Niersteiner, Nacken-heimer, etc.

WÜRTTEMBERG — (*Vur*-tem-bairg) — One of the eleven Anbaugebiete (*see*) consisting of 3 Bereiche, 15 Grosslagen and 200 Einzellagen; its vineyards cover 21,000 acres and it produces one twelfth of Germany's total. This region is known as Swabia and the Swabians are great consumers of their own produce, both liquid and solid. As a result local consumption is three times, the production so that practically none is exported. Much of the wine is red. For Map, *see* Germany.

WÜRZBURG — (*Vurtz*-boorg) — The capital and principal town of the German province of Franconia (Franken); no less famous for its beer, Würzburger, than for its wine, also called Würzburger, produced on the rocky slopes over-looking the Main Valley nearby. This is the original home of Steinwein (*see*) and the leading vineyard is called Würzburger Stein. There are 520 acres of vineyard in all, largely planted in either Sylvaner or Riesling, and apart from Würzburger Stein, the best *Lagen* or vineyard sites are Innere Leiste, Abts-leite, Kirchberg, Pfaffenberg, Schlossberg, and Stein/Harfe.

X–Y

XÉRÈS — (Sair-ress) — Old name for the town of Jerez, or Jerez de la Frontera, in Spain, and for its wine, which we call Sherry. Still used in France, as *vin de Xérès*.

YAKIMA VALLEY — *see* WASHINGTON.

YEASTS — Unicellular microorganisms, some of which (*Saccharomyces ellipsoideus*) bring about fermentation in grape juice, through the agency of an enzyme, zymase (*see*), and turn it into wine; there exist many "selections" or "cultures" of these, some capable of working at lower temperatures than others, or having other advantages or disadvantages, and in most modern wineries the yeast cultures are chosen with great care. Other yeasts (*see* Flor) tend to give a Sherry flavor to wines inoculated with them, whether deliberately or accidentally; still others are responsible for various sorts of wine spoilage.

YEASTY — Wine tasters' term, applied almost exclusively to young wines in barrel, which still have the odor of yeast or fermentation or lees. This is not a grave fault, and indeed some connoisseurs of Muscadet and of Swiss wines consider it a virtue and prefer their wines with this *goût de lie;* in any case, it will usually disappear as soon as the wine has been "racked" (transferred from one cask to another, leaving the sediment, or lees, behind). It is also a characteristic of some champagnes and other bottle fermented sparkling wines.

YIELD — As far as wine is concerned, usually the production of a given extent of vines, expressed in tons of grapes or gallons of wine per acre (see Hectoliter and Hectare for comparable terms in French). It is on this basis that the relative productivity of various grape varieties can be compared, and also that of different vineyards, although of course pruning, irrigation, etc., are all major factors. For a number of the very best French vineyards, the legal maximum is set at about two tons of grapes, or 320 gallons of wine per acre, and few of the finer, shy-bearing varieties ever give over four tons, or some 640 gallons, even when quality is not considered of primary importance. On the other hand, the common, more productive grapes often yield ten or more tons per acre, and far higher figures have been recorded. Needless to say, when yield increases in any such proportions, quality suffers. Yield per acre is one of the basic elements in any comparative rating or classification of superior vineyards and their wines.

YONNE — (Yon) — Northernmost of the French *départements* that make up the old province of Burgundy. Its best known wine by far is Chablis (see), but there are a few others of fair quality, as Irancy (see).

YOUNG — So far as wine is concerned, this is not always a matter of months or years. A four-year-old Cabernet or fine Red Bordeaux is still young, and a six-year-old Vintage Port is still an infant. On the other hand, a three-year-old Muscadet or *vin rosé* or Sylvaner is already middle-aged. Correctly speaking, a young wine is one still not yet at its peak, still improving.

YQUEM, Château d' — (Dee-kem) — The incomparable *Grand Premier Cru* of Sauternes; the one wine, red or white, to be accorded this exalted rank in 1855, a higher classification even than the great Clarets. It is probably the most famous as well as the most valuable vineyard estate in the world, and its superb 15th century château dominates its vine-covered hillsides like a queen. For nearly two hundred years it has been the property of the Lur-Saluces family.

Over a century ago the Grand Duke Constantine of Russia (brother of the Czar) paid the then staggering price of 20,000 gold francs for four barrels of the 1847 vintage, and Yquem has been, ever since, one of the most consistently expensive of all wines; its vineyard, as might be expected, is one of those with the lowest yield per acre — its production of something less than 10,000 cases represents an average of a little more than 100 gallons per acre as compared to twice as much for Château Lafite and three times as much for Chambertin. There are some 225 acres under vines — 80% Sémillon and 20% Sauvignon Blanc. The grapes are picked in successive *tries,* or harvestings, as the *pourriture noble,* or *botrytis* (see) reaches its peak, and the resulting wine is of course high in alcohol (13-16%), very sweet (with from 3% to 7% of unfermented sugar), luscious, almost creamy, with extraordinary fruit and breed.

The Château d'Yquems of great vintages are truly fabulous — the *ne plus ultra* of dessert wines, but even those of lesser years are remarkable, less overpowering, but with classic distinction and finesse.

Until quite recently, much of the wine produced at Yquem in "off" years, which failed to attain its normal degree of alcohol and sweetness, was sold in bulk without the château label, as "Bordeaux Supérieur." About as dry as a medium Graves, with considerable breed and bouquet, this obviously deserved a better fate, and a special name and label have now been created for it — "Y". The letter Y, in French, is called *I-grec* and the wine's name is pronounced, therefore, Château *Ee-greck*. It is produced only in secondary vintages and is of course considerably cheaper than Yquem.

YUGOSLAVIA — *see* DALMATIA and LUTOMER.

YVERDON — (E-vair-daw) — Wine-producing town at the western end of Lake Neuchâtel, in Switzerland. White wines from the Fendant grape, none of outstanding quality.

YVORNE — (E-vorn) — One of the better white wines of Switzerland, made from the Fendant grape in the district known as the Chablais, southeast of Lake Geneva.

Z

ZAHNACKER — (Zahn-ah-ker) — Celebrated Alsatian vineyard in the village of Ribeauvillé, Haut-Rhin.

ZELL — (Tsell) — Little vineyard town in the lower Moselle Valley, well outside the district of superior wine, presumably the original source of what has become internationally famous as Zeller Schwarze Katz. A common, nondescript, commercial Moselle blend (rarely, in fact, from Zell) this doubtless owes its popularity to its odd name and label: *Schwarze Katz* means "black cat," and the familiar cat is always present on the label. Under the 1971 German Wine Law, Schwarze Katz became the Grosslage in which Zell is located, a perfect example of the *Katz* swallowing the canary.

ZELLENBERG — (Zel-len-bairg) — Picturesque little village in Alsace, on the vine-covered Vosges foothills near Riquewihr. Good quality white wines.

ZELTINGEN — (Tsel-ting-gen) — One of the very great vineyard towns of the Mittel-Mosel, first in total production, and easily one of the eight or ten best in average quality. Its 470 acres of Riesling vines from part of the same high, incredibly steep, black slate valley wall as those of Wehlen, Graach and Bernkastel, and have an admirable southwestern exposure; its wines, with those of Brauneberg, are about the fullest-bodied of the fine Moselles. All of the best of them, of course, carry a specific vineyard name and are estate-bottled. Names to look for are Schlossberg, Sonnenuhr, Himmelreich, and Deutschherrenberg.

ZICHRON JACOB — Large winery and vineyards in Israel (*see*).

378

ZINFANDEL — One of the most widely planted red wine grapes (over 30,000 acres) of California. Fairly prolific, although less so than the Carignane, the Mataro, the Mission and even the Grenache, it gives far better red wine than these, and, in the cooler districts, at least, about as pleasant a *vin ordinaire* as one could ask for. It is definitely of the *Vitis Vinifera* family and therefore transplanted from Europe, and wine was being made from it around San Francisco in pre-Civil War days; despite much research, no one has ever been able to determine exactly where it came from in Europe, or its proper European name. It may well have been one of the tens of thousands of cuttings brought to California by Colonel Haraszthy (*see*); it is almost certainly *not* the Zierfandler (a lesser variety of Austria and southern Germany) despite the similarity of name. In recent years persuasive evidence has been obtained which identifies it with the Primativo di Gioia (*see*) in south east Italy (*see* Electrophoresis).

Its wine, unlike that of almost all other "mass-production" grapes, has a definite, and easily recognizable, varietal character, bouquet and flavor, especially when from hillside vineyards in a cool district; it has a fine, bright ruby color, almost as much "fruit" as a French Beaujolais, and what has been called a "bramble" flavor, reminiscent of wild blackberries or dewberries. It gains relatively little by ageing, and is generally best drunk young. Occasionally, however, when made in the classic European manner it can have great body and long life.

ZUCCO — (Zoo-co) — Famous Muscat wine of Sicily, produced near Palermo.

ZÜRICH — (Zur-rick) — Largest city of Switzerland. The canton of this name, at the turn of the century, had over 10,000 acres under vines; there are only some 1,700 today, the best of them southeast of the city, along the northern shore of the Zürichersee. There are both red wines and white, the former mostly from the Pinot Noir, here called the Schwarzer Klevner, the latter from the Rauschling (which shouild not be confused with the Riesling) and Müller-Thurgau (*see*). Some of them are of good quality, but they are almost all consumed locally.

ZWICKER — (*Zvick*-er) — Alsatian white wine, generally made from various grape varieties picked and crushed together: an inexpensive blend, in which the Chasselas usually predominates, though often with some Sylvaner. Bland and rather lacking in character, it is a passable carafe wine when young. *See*, however, Edelzwicker.

ZYMASE — The enzyme of yeast, which produces fermentation and thereby converts grape sugar into alcohol and carbon dioxide.

Appendices

APPENDIX 1

TOTAL WINE PRODUCTION AND WINE CONSUMPTION
OF THE PRINCIPAL WINE-PRODUCING AND WINE-CONSUMING COUNTRIES

As reported to the Office International du Vin in Paris by the various Governments
involved (Figures for 1976 where available, otherwise 1975)

	PROD.[1] '000 Hl.	CONS.[2] '000 Hl.	PER[3] CAP. liters	PROD.[1] '000 U.S. Gal.	CONS.[2] '000 U.S. Gal.	PER[3] CAP. U.S. Gal.
TOTAL — All Countries	323,221	290,152		8,533,034	7,660,013	
France	73,035	53,580	101.27	1,928,124	1,414,512	26.74
Italy	65,850	59,995	107.50	1,738,440	1,583,868	28.38
Russia	32,522	34,000	13.36	858,581	897,600	3.53
Argentina	28,197	21,748	84.76	744,401	574,147	22.38
Spain	27,948	25,600	71.00	737,827	675,840	18.74
U.S.A.	13,383	14,243	6.54	353,311	376,015	1.73
Portugal	9,418	8,636	97.80	248,635	227,990	25.82
West Germany	8,659	14,555	23.60	228,598	384,252	6.23
Romania	7,020	7,012	33.00	185,328	185,117	8.71
Yugoslavia	6,379	6,106	28.60	168,406	161,198	7.55
South Africa	5,966	2,589	9.89	157,502	68,350	2.61
Greece	5,636	3,584	39.80	148,790	94,618	10.51
Bulgaria	5,517	1,740	19.98	145,649	45,936	5.27
Chile	5,143	4,784	47.84	135,775	126,298	12.63
Algeria	5,000	84	0.50	132,000	2,218	0.13
Hungary	4,677	3,500	34.00	123,473	92,400	8.98
Australia	3,770	1,512	11.20	99,528	39,917	2.96
Austria	2,901	2,732	36.30	76,586	72,125	9.58
Brazil	1,970	2,160	2.00	52,008	57,024	0.53
Mexico	1,556	138	0.23	41,078	3,643	0.06
Czechoslovakia	1,388	1,800	12.00	36,643	47,520	3.17
Switzerland	1,194	2,726	42.80	31,522	71,966	11.30
Cyprus	1,100	40	6.20	29,040	1,056	1.64
Uruguay	1,010	768	25.10	26,664	20,275	6.63
Morocco	764	378	2.00	20,170	9,979	0.53
Canada	728	1,525	6.68	19,219	40,260	1.76
Tunisia	604	214	4.20	15,946	5,650	1.11
Israel	430	131	3.75	11,352	3,458	0.99
Turkey	332	215	0.55	8,765	5,676	0.14
Japan	270	274	0.46	7,128	7,234	0.12
New Zealand	265	271	8.77	6,996	7,154	2.32
Luxembourg	128	164	46.16	3,379	4,330	12.19
Peru	80	159	1.00	2,112	4,198	0.26
Great Britain		2,764	4.94		72,970	1.30
Poland		2,517	7.40		66,449	1.95
Belgium		1,443	15.00		38,095	3.96
Holland		1,429	10.46		37,726	2.76
East Germany		1,150	6.60		30,360	1.74
Sweden		709	8.67		18,718	2.29
Denmark		636	12.54		16,790	3.31
Finland		222	4.70		5,861	1.24
Norway		133	3.34		3,511	0.88

[1] In most cases includes wines destined for distillation or for industrial use.
[2] In general, includes only wine consumed as wine, not as brandy, etc.
[3] In many instances does not include wines made by small growers for use at home.

IMPORTS AND EXPORTS OF
THE IMPORTANT WINE TRADE COUNTRIES

As reported to the Office International du Vin in Paris
by the various Governments involved

(Figures for 1976 where available, otherwise 1975)

	IMPORTS [4]		EXPORTS [5]	
	'000 Hl.	'000 U.S. Gal.	'000 Hl.	'000 U.S. Gal.
TOTAL — All Countries	42,457	1,120,865	43,407	1,145,945
Russia	8,520	224,928	720	19,008
West Germany	7,967	210,329	1,096	28,934
France	6,995	184,668	6,724	177,514
Great Britain	3,350	88,440	162	4,277
U.S.A.	1,907	50,345	47	1,241
Switzerland	1,848	48,787	9	238
Belgium	1,541	40,682	92	2,429
Holland	1,460	38,544	—	
East Germany	1,408	37,171	—	
Canada	757	19,985	—	
Sweden	695	18,348	—	
Denmark	645	17,028	11	290
Poland	481	12,698	—	
Austria	428	11,299	187	4,937
Czechoslovakia	343	9,055	14	370
Hungary	297	7,841	1,794	47,361
Italy	216	5,702	12,100	319,440
Spain			6,077	160,433
Algeria			5,500	145,200
Bulgaria			2,294	60,562
Portugal			1,901	50,186
Romania			1,050	27,720
Greece			764	20,170
Yugoslavia			746	19,694
Argentina			452	11,933
Morocco			435	11,484
Tunisia			310	8,184
Cyprus			197	5,201
South Africa			125	3,300
Albania			115	3,036
Luxembourg			79	2,086
Chile			73	1,927
Turkey			69	1,822
Australia			65	1,716
Israel			42	1,109

[4] Includes, in the case of France, wine imported from the former French Colonies in North Africa. In some instances, but not all, includes fruit wines, saké, etc.

[5] Includes in some cases but not all, fruit wines, etc.

COMMERCIALLY PRODUCED WINE ENTERING DISTRIBUTION CHANNELS
IN THE UNITED STATES, BY AREAS WHERE PRODUCED
CALENDAR YEARS 1962 THROUGH 1976

Year (Beginning January 1)	California[1]		Other States[2]		Total U.S. Produced[3]		Imported[4]		All Wine	
	Quantity	Percent of Total	Quantity	Percent of Total	Quantity	Percent of Total	Quantity	Percent of Total	Quantity	Percent Change From Last Year
	1	2	3	4	5	6	7	8	9	10
	1,000 GALLONS	PERCENT	1,000 GALLONS	PERCENT	1,000 GALLONS	PERCENT	1,000 GALLONS	PERCENT	1,000 GALLONS	PERCENT
1962	127,371	75.8	26,670	15.9	154,041	91.6	14,041	8.4	168,082	−2.1
1963	133,991	76.2	27,558	15.7	161,549	91.8	14,368	8.2	175,918	+4.7
1964	143,123	77.1	26,946	14.5	170,069	91.6	15,556	8.4	185,625	+5.5
1965	142,871	75.3	30,520	16.1	173,391	91.4	16,286	8.6	189,677	+2.2
1966	144,192	75.4	29,005	15.2	173,197	90.6	17,979	9.4	191,176	+0.8
1967	148,376	73.0	35,651	17.5	184,027	90.5	19,376	9.5	203,403	+6.4
1968	156,044	73.0	35,403	16.6	191,447	89.6	22,210	10.4	213,658	+5.0
1969	171,679	72.9	39,257	16.7	210,936	89.5	24,692	10.5	235,628	+10.3
1970	195,312	73.1	42,016	15.7	237,328	88.8	30,024	11.2	267,351	+13.5
1971	224,725	73.7	44,340	14.5	269,065	88.2	36,156	11.8	305,221	+14.2
1972	236,884	70.3	53,058	15.7	289,942	86.0	47,043	14.0	336,985	+10.4
1973	240,778	69.3	51,263	14.8	292,041	84.0	55,440	16.0	347,481	+3.1
1974	246,896	70.6	51,175	14.7	298,071	85.3	51,394	14.7	349,465	+0.6
1975	270,229	73.4	48,481	13.2	318,710	86.6	49,319	13.4	368,029	+5.3
1976[5]	269,529	71.6	47,898	12.7	317,427	84.3	58,918	15.7	376,345	+2.3

[1] Shipments of California wine to all markets less estimated shipments to foreign countries.
[2] Total U.S. produced less California.
[3] Taxable withdrawals.
[4] Imports for consumption.
[5] Preliminary.

Sources: Prepared by Wine Institute from reports of the California State Board of Equalization; Bureau of Alcohol, Tobacco and Firearms, U.S. Treasury Department and Bureau of the Census, U.S. Department of Commerce.

UNITED STATES PRODUCED WINE ENTERING DISTRIBUTION
CHANNELS IN THE UNITED STATES, BY TYPES OF WINE
CALENDAR YEARS 1962 THROUGH 1976[1]

Year (Beginning January 1)	Table[2]	Dessert[2]	Vermouth	Sparkling[3]	Other Special Natural			Total OSN	All Wine
					Still Not Over 14 Percent	Still Over 14 Percent	Sparkling OSN		
	1	2	3	4	5	6	7	8	9
				QUANTITY — 1,000 GALLONS					
1962	51,765	80,812	4,153	3,833	[4]	[4]	[5]	13,479	154,041
1963	56,141	83,749	4,275	4,229	[4]	[4]	[5]	13,155	161,549
1964	61,698	84,045	4,689	5,347	[4]	[4]	[5]	14,289	170,069
1965	65,118	81,649	4,846	6,250	[4]	[4]	[5]	15,529	173,391
1966	68,238	77,143	4,862	7,397	[4]		[5]	15,556	173,197
1967	76,573	77,474	5,267	8,753	[4]	[4]	[5]	15,960	184,027
1968	82,791	77,901	4,944	10,285	2,935	12,591	[5]	15,526	191,447
1969	96,978	75,337	5,139	13,702	7,560	12,221	[5]	19,781	210,936
1970	112,747	71,322	5,105	20,299	16,132	11,665	59[5,7]	27,856	237,327
1971	130,127	71,028	4,892	22,005	29,294	11,631	89	41,014	269,065
1972	136,342	70,026	5,127	20,326	46,263	11,823	35	58,121	289,942
1973	145,877	66,382	5,311	18,935	44,560	10,944	32	55,536	292,041
1974	157,213	63,490	5,285	18,009	44,402	9,653	19	54,074	298,071
1975	173,511	64,640	5,282	18,435	45,902	10,918	22	56,842	318,710
1976[8]	182,015	58,002	5,225	19,206	40,975	11,994	10	52,979	317,427

See next page of table for footnotes.

Year (Beginning January 1)	Table[2]	Dessert[2]	Vermouth	Sparkling[3]	Other Special Natural Still Not Over 14 Percent	Other Special Natural Still Over 14 Percent	Other Special Natural Sparkling OSN	Other Special Natural Total OSN	All Wine PERCENT CHANGE FROM LAST YEAR
	1	2	3	4	5	6	7	8	9
					PERCENT OF TOTAL				
1962	33.6	52.5	2.7	2.5	[4]	[4]	[5]	8.8	−3.4
1963	34.8	51.8	2.6	2.6	[4]	[4]	[5]	8.1	+4.9
1964	36.3	49.4	2.8	3.1	[4]	[4]	[5]	8.4	+5.3
1965	37.6	47.1	2.8	3.6	[4]	[4]	[5]	9.0	+2.0
1966	39.4	44.5	2.8	4.3	[4]	[4]	[5]	9.0	−0.1
1967	41.6	42.1	2.9	4.8	[4]	[4]	[5]	8.7	+6.3
1968	43.2	40.7	2.6	5.4	1.5	6.6	[5]	8.1	+4.0
1969	46.0	35.7	2.4	6.5	3.6	5.8	[5]	9.4	+10.2
1970	47.5	30.1	2.2	8.6	6.8	4.9	[6,7]	11.7	+12.5
1971	48.4	26.4	1.8	8.2	10.9	4.3	[6]	15.2	+13.4
1972	47.0	24.2	1.8	7.0	16.0	4.1	[6]	20.0	+7.8
1973	50.0	22.7	1.8	6.5	15.3	3.7	[6]	19.0	+0.7
1974	52.8	21.3	1.8	6.0	14.9	3.2	[6]	18.1	+2.1
1975	54.4	20.3	1.7	5.8	14.4	3.4	[6]	17.8	+6.9
1976[8]	57.3	18.3	1.6	6.1	12.9	3.8	[6]	16.7	−0.4

[1] Taxable withdrawals.

[2] Because of data limitations, the figures for table wine before 1968 are overstated to the extent of the movement of U.S. produced other special natural still wine not over 14 percent alcohol, and the figures for dessert wine before 1968 are understated by the same amount. The amount of such overstatement and understatement is small, probably not exceeding 1 million gallons for the entire United States in any such year.

[3] Figures before July 1970 may include insignificant amounts of other special natural sparkling wine (see footnote 5).

[4] Before 1968 other special natural still wine was not reported by alcohol content categories but such wine is believed to be almost entirely over 14 percent alcohol.

[5] Before July 1970 special natural sparkling wine was not reported separately from other sparkling wine and therefore is not included in the figures reported for total other special natural wine for that period (see footnote 3).

[6] Less than .05 percent.

[7] Quantity entering distribution channels beginning July, 1970 when separate reporting for this item began.

[8] Preliminary.

Sources: Prepared by Wine Institute from reports of the Bureau of Alcohol, Tobacco and Firearms, U.S. Treasury Department.

IMPORTED WINE ENTERING DISTRIBUTION CHANNELS IN THE UNITED STATES, BY TYPES OF WINE CALENDAR YEARS 1962 THROUGH 1976[1]

QUANTITY — 1,000 GALLONS

Year (Beginning January 1)	Table[2]	Dessert	Vermouth	Sparkling[3]	Other Special Natural			All Wine
					Still Not Over 14 Percent[4]	Still Over 14 Percent[5]	Total OSN	
	1	2	3	4	5	6	7	8
1962	7,817	969	3,780	1,036	0	439	439	14,041
1963	8,004	1,014	3,905	1,023	0	423	423	14,368
1964	8,662	1,068	4,190	1,196	6	441	441	15,556
1965	8,963	1,120	4,315	1,436	6	451	451	16,286
1966	10,437	1,153	4,302	1,635	6	452	452	17,979
1967	11,270	1,219	4,475	1,916	42	454	496	19,376
1968	13,002	1,350	5,008	2,228	101	522	623	22,210
1969	15,288	1,392	4,784	2,409	204	614	818	24,692
1970	20,237	1,610	5,124	1,793	580	679	1,259	30,024
1971	24,703	1,929	5,367	1,877	1,553	727	2,280	36,156
1972	33,675	1,838	4,927	1,976	4,066	560	4,626	47,043
1973	39,371	2,129	5,026	2,021	6,384	509	6,893	55,440
1974	35,023	2,317	4,571	1,804	7,130	549	7,679	51,394
1975	35,525	2,120	4,278	1,928	4,999	468	5,467	49,319
1976[7]	45,986	2,561	4,017	2,559	3,426	369	3,795	58,918

See next page of table for footnotes.

					Other Special Natural			All Wine
Year (Beginning January 1)	Table [2]	Dessert	Vermouth	Sparkling [3]	Still Not Over 14 Percent [4]	Still Over 14 Percent [5]	Total OSN	
	1	2	3	4	5	6	7	8
	PERCENT OF TOTAL							PERCENT CHANGE FROM LAST YEAR
1962	55.7	6.9	26.9	7.4	0	3.1	3.1	+15.5
1963	55.7	7.1	27.2	7.1	0	2.9	2.9	+2.3
1964	55.7	6.9	26.9	7.7	[8]	2.8	2.8	+8.3
1965	55.0	6.9	26.5	8.8	[8]	2.8	2.8	+4.7
1966	58.1	6.4	23.9	9.1	[8]	2.5	2.5	+10.4
1967	58.2	6.3	23.1	9.9	0.2	2.3	2.6	+7.8
1968	58.5	6.1	22.5	10.0	0.5	2.4	2.8	+14.6
1969	61.9	5.6	19.4	9.8	0.8	2.5	3.3	+11.2
1970	67.4	5.4	17.1	6.0	1.9	2.3	4.2	+21.6
1971	68.3	5.3	14.8	5.2	4.3	2.0	6.3	+20.4
1972	71.6	3.9	10.5	4.2	8.6	1.2	9.8	+30.1
1973	71.0	3.8	9.1	3.6	11.5	0.9	12.4	+17.8
1974	68.1	4.5	8.9	3.5	12.9	1.0	14.9	−6.8
1975	72.0	4.3	8.7	3.9	10.1	0.9	11.1	−4.0
1976[7]	78.1	4.3	6.8	4.3	5.8	0.6	6.4	+19.5

[1] Imports for consumption.

[2] Includes wine from Japan classified by U.S. Customs Service as "other fermented alcoholic beverages" which is believed to be unflavored fruit wine not over 14% alcohol. Also includes saké (rice wine).

[3] May include small amounts of special natural sparkling wine. Such wine is not reported separately from imports of other sparkling wine.

[4] Figures for 1976 represent wine from Spain classified by U.S. Customs Service as "other fermented alcoholic beverages". Figures before 1976 are estimated on the basis of Spanish Government export statistics. This item is believed to be entirely or almost entirely sangria.

[5] Wine classified by U.S. Customs as "other fermented alcoholic beverages", except that from Spain and Japan. This item is mostly flavored fruit wine from Denmark.

[6] Less than 500 gallons.

[7] Preliminary.

Sources: Prepared by Wine Institute from reports of the Bureau of the Census, U.S. Department of Commerce and Spanish Department of Commerce.

IMPORTS OF WINE INTO THE UNITED STATES
BY TYPES OF WINE AND COUNTRIES OF ORIGIN
CALENDAR YEAR 1976[1,2]

Country of Origin	Table[3]		Dessert		Vermouth		Sparkling[4]		Other Special Natural[5]		Total	
	Quantity	Percent of Total	Quantity	Percent of Total	Quantity	Percent of Total	Quantity	Percent of Total	Quantity	Percent of Total	Quantity	Percent of Total
	1	2	3	4	5	6	7	8	9	10	11	12
	1,000 GALLONS	PERCENT	1,000 GALLONS	PERCENT	1,000 GALLONS	PERCENT	1,000 GALLONS	PERCENT	1,000 GALLONS	PERCENT	1,000 GALLONS	PERCENT
Italy	17,605	38.3	155	6.1	3,288	81.9	1,463	57.2	5	0.1	22,516	38.2
France	10,133	22.0	41	1.6	708	17.6	961	37.6	28	0.7	11,870	20.1
West Germany	8,765	19.1	[6]	[7]	1	[7]	75	2.9	19	0.5	8,860	15.0
Spain	1,518	3.3	1,895	74.0	9	0.2	26	1.0	3,426	90.3	6,874	11.7
Portugal	5,549	12.1	158	6.2	2	[7]	8	0.3	2	0.1	5,719	9.7
Japan	832	1.8	1	[7]	2	[7]	3	0.1	0	0.0	838	1.4
Greece	420	0.9	14	0.5	0	0.0	0	0.0	0	0.0	434	0.7
Israel	342	0.7	4	0.2	1	[7]	10	0.4	16	0.4	372	0.6
United Kingdom	52	0.1	254	9.9	3	0.1	2	0.1	19	0.5	329	0.6
Denmark	1	[7]	3	0.1	0	0.0	3	[7]	246	6.5	253	0.4
Argentina	128	0.3	0	0.0	0	0.0	[6]	[7]	0	0.0	128	0.2
Hungary	106	0.2	0	0.0	0	0.0	0	0.0	0	0.0	106	0.2
Austria	84	0.2	0	0.0	0	0.0	1	[7]	0	0.0	85	0.1

Country	Gal.	%	Gal.	%	Gal.	%	Gal.	%	Gal.	%	Gal.	%
Netherlands	73	0.2	0	0.0	[6]	[7]	2	0.1	8	0.2	83	0.1
Brazil	66	0.1	0	0.0	0	0.0	0	0.0	0	0.0	66	0.1
Yugoslavia	60	0.1	2	0.1	0	0.0	1	[7]	6	[7]	63	0.1
Belgium	51	0.1	[6]	[7]	0	0.0	3	0.1	[6]	[7]	54	0.1
Canada	24	0.1	17	0.7	1	[7]	2	0.1	3	0.1	46	0.1
Chile	34	0.1	0	0.0	0	0.0	[6]	[7]	0	0.0	34	[7]
Australia	23	[7]	1	[7]	0	0.0	[6]	[7]	0	0.0	24	[7]
Iran	20	[7]	0	0.0	0	0.0	0	0.0	0	0.0	20	[7]
Madeira	1	[7]	18	0.7	0	0.0	0	0.0	0	0.0	18	[7]
Rep. of S. Africa	17	[7]	0	0.0	0	0.0	0	0.0	0	0.0	17	[7]
Switzerland	16	[7]	0	0.0	0	0.0	0	0.0	0	0.0	16	[7]
Poland	5	[7]	0	0.0	0	0.0	0	0.0	9	0.2	14	[7]
Other Countries	63	0.1	1	[7]	2	[7]	1	[7]	13	0.3	79	0.1
Total	45,986	100.0	2,562	100.0	4,017	100.0	2,559	100.0	3,795	100.0	58,918	100.0

[1] Imports for consumption.

[2] Sum of components is not equal to total in all cases as a result of rounding individual figures.

[3] Includes fruit wine from Japan and saké (rice wine) amounting to 319,000 and 401,000 gallons respectively. See footnote 5.

[4] May include small amounts of other special natural sparkling wine.

[5] Includes imports classified by U.S. Customs Service as "other fermented alcoholic beverages," except that from Japan which is included in table wine because it is believed to be unflavored fruit wine not over 14 percent alcohol. Wine in this category from Spain is believed to be sangria while that from the remaining countries is believed to be almost entirely flavored still wine over 14 percent alcohol.

[6] Less than 500 gallons.

[7] Less than 0.05 percent.

Sources: Prepared by Wine Institute from reports of the Bureau of the Census, U.S. Department of Commerce.

LIQUID CONSUMPTION TRENDS IN U.S. FROM 1967 TO 1976

(Gallons per capita per year)

	1976[P]	1975	1974	1973	1972	1971	1967
Soft drinks	34.2	31.4	31.6	31.9	30.3	28.7	23.6
Coffee	32.5	33.1	33.8	35.1	35.2	35.3	37.0
Milk	24.5	24.4	24.3	25.1	25.3	24.9	25.3
Beer	21.8	21.6	21.1	20.2	19.4	19.0	16.8
Tea	7.8	7.5	7.5	7.6	7.2	7.1	6.4
Juices	6.2	6.2	6.0	5.7	5.4	5.3	4.7
Powdered drinks	5.8	5.2	NA	NA	NA	NA	NA
Distilled spirits	2.0	2.0	2.0	1.9	1.9	1.9	1.6
Wine	1.8	1.7	1.7	1.7	1.6	1.5	1.0
Subtotal	136.6	133.1	128.0	129.2	126.3	123.7	116.4
Imputed water consumption*	45.9	49.4	54.5	53.3	56.2	58.8	66.1
Total	182.5	182.5	182.5	182.5	182.5	182.5	182.5

*Includes all others. [P] — Preliminary.   NA — Not available

Source: Advertising Age. — July 11, 1977 issue. Copyright, Crain Communications Inc. — 1977.

100 LARGEST UNITED STATES WINERIES — 1977

	TOTAL STORAGE CAPACITY '000 gals.	NUMBER OF PLANTS
E & J Gallo, CA	226,000	3
United Vintners, CA	95,000	8
Guild Wineries & Dist., CA [1]	57,000	8
Vie Del Co., CA ‡	36,000	2
Bear Mt. Winery, CA	32,000	1
Taylor Wine Co., NY [2]	31,367	2
Franzia Bros. Winery, CA †	28,300	1
Paul Masson Vineyards, CA	28,000	4
The Christian Bros., CA	27,483	4
Almadén Vineyards, CA	26,700	4
Sierra Wine Corp., CA	25,900	2
A. Perelli-Minetti & Sons, CA (California Wine Association)	20,000	1
California Growers Winery, CA [3]	15,630	1
Canandaigua Wine Co., NY *	12,000	1

	TOTAL STORAGE CAPACITY '000 gals.	NUMBER OF PLANTS
Giumarra Vineyards Corp., CA	10,500	1
California Mission Wines, CA	9,400	1
Gibson Wine Co., CA	8,500	2
Brookside Vineyards Co., CA	8,000	4
Delicato Vineyards, CA	7,920	1
J F J Bronco Winery, CA	5,750	2
East-Side Winery, CA	5,500	1
Woodbridge Vineyard Assoc., CA	5,100	1
Delano Growers Coop., CA	5,000	1
Mogen David, IL†	5,000	2
Fredonia Products Co., NY	4,750	1
Bisceglia Bros., CA*	4,000	1
Widmer's Wine Cellars, NY	4,000	1
Lodi Vintners, CA	3,600	1
Charles Krug, CA	3,500	1
Monarch Wine Co., NY	3,500	1
Papagni Vineyards, CA	3,500	1
Sonoma Vineyards, CA	3,500	2
Cucamonga Vineyards, CA	3,100	1
Gold Seal Vineyards, Inc., NY	3,000	1
Sebastiani Vineyards, CA	3,000	1
Warner Vineyards, Inc., MI	3,000	1
Del Rey Coop Winery Assn., CA	2,600	1
Liberty Winery Inc., CA	2,500	1
Louis Martini, CA	2,500	1
Meier's Wine Cellars, OH	2,500	1
Beringer Vineyards, CA	2,300	2
Mirassou Vineyards, CA	2,300	1
Wente Bros., CA	2,300	1
Frei Bros., CA	2,200	1
Geyser Peak Winery, CA	2,200	1
The Monterey Vineyard, CA[2]	2,200	1
Napa Valley Coop Winery, CA	2,113	1
Richard's Wine Cellars, VA*	2,000	1
Rio Vista Winery, CA	2,000	1
Ste. Michelle Vintners, WA	2,000	1
San Martin Vineyards, CA	2,000	1
Tenner Bros., Inc., SC*	2,000	1
Selma Winery, Inc., CA	1,836	1
Robert Mondavi Winery, CA	1,800	1
Wiederkehr Wine Cellars, AR	1,750	1
Barengo Vineyards, Inc., CA	1,650	1
Stockton Distillery Corp., CA	1,600	1
Seghesio Winery, CA	1,500	2
Weibel, Inc., CA	1,500	2
Calif. Products Co., CA	1,400	1
Noble Vineyards, CA	1,400	1
Villa Armando, CA	1,350	1
San Joaquin Warehouse, CA	1,274	1
H. Laird & Co., NJ	1,270	1

	TOTAL STORAGE CAPACITY '000 gals.	NUMBER OF PLANTS
Beaulieu Vineyards, CA	1,200	1
Monarch of Georgia, GA	1,200	1
Schenley Distillers, CA	1,200	2
Royal Wine Corp., Bklyn, NY	1,100	1
Parducci Winery, CA	1,030	1
Bronte Champagne & Wines, MI	1,000	1
Foppiano Wine Co., CA	1,000	1
Heublein, Inc., CA	1,000	1
Korbel & Bros., CA	1,000	1
St. Julian & LaSalle Wine, MI	1,000	1
Buena Vista Winery & Vyds, CA	900	1
Bardenheier's Wine Cellars, MO	850	1
J. Filippi Vintage Co., CA	800	1
Novitiate Wines, CA	800	1
San Antonio Winery, CA	800	1
Sonoma County Coop, CA	750	1
Laird & Co., VA	700	1
Cambiaso Winery & Vyds, CA	650	1
Alhambra Wine Co., WA	600	1
Dixie Wine Co., VA	600	1
Simi Winery, CA	587	1
J. Pedroncelli Winery, CA	530	1
Oakview Plantations, SC	520	1
Brotherhood Corp., NY	500	1
Frontenac Vineyards, MI	500	1
Emilio Guglielmo Winery, CA	500	1
Hammondsport Wine Co., NY*	500	1
Lakeside Vineyard, MI	500	1
Milan Wineries, MI	500	1
Renault Winery, NJ	500	2
Rutherford Hill Winery, CA	500	1
Post Winery, AR	490	1
Concannon Vineyards, CA	430	1
Tribuno Wines, NJ†	410	1
Schapiro Wines, NY	400	1
Soda Rock Winery, CA	400	1
Sterling Vineyards, CA [2]	400	1

[1] Includes Cresta Blanca, a wholly-owned subsidiary.
[2] Owned by Coca-Cola of Atlanta.
[3] Includes 3.1 million gals. brandy storage.
*Owned by the Canandaigua Wine Co.
†Owned by Coca Cola Bottling of New York.
‡Includes 16,500,000 gals. brandy storage.

Source: *Wines & Vines,* (The Authoritative Voice of the Grape and Wine Industry, May 1977.)

APPENDIX 2

A TABLE OF VINEYARD TEMPERATURES

Vineyard temperatures are recorded in various countries in various ways: either for the seven-month cycle that extends from the first spring leaf to the latest harvest, or for the four months that generally elapse between the flowering of the vine and a normal vintage. For widely varying climates, the second system is thought by many European experts to give a fairer picture. Both, in any case, are based on a minimum daily temperature of 50° Fahrenheit, or 10° Centigrade (which the vine requires for its growth) and what follows is known as "heat summation". One takes, for example, the mean daily temperature for the month of June; if it happens to be 60°, there results a credit of 10° a day for June's 30 days, or 300 "degree days" for the month. A grand total of these monthly totals, whether for the seven months of April through October or for the four months, June-September, gives the temperature index. Here, based on the four-month cycle, are some figures for the great European districts and for California's most important ones.

District I — 62-65 daily average
District II — 65-68 daily average
District III — 68-70 daily average
District IV — 70-74 daily average
District V — 74-80 daily average

District	EUROPE	Heat Summation (over 50° F) June-July-Aug.-Sept.	Daily Average for these 4 months
I	Geisenheim (Germany — Rhine)	1495	62.3°
I	Trier (Germany — Moselle)	1525	62.5
I	Auxerre (France — Chablis)	1572	62.9
I	Châlons-sur-Marne (France — Champagne)	1644	63.5
II	Bordeaux (France — Gironde)	1971	66.2
II	Beaune (France — Burgundy)	2002	66.4
III	Asti (Italy — Piedmont)	2416	69.8
IV	Florence (Italy — Chianti)	2917	73.9
IV	Palermo (Italy — Sicily)	2936	74.0
V	Algiers (Algeria)	3600	79.5

District	CALIFORNIA	Heat Summation (over 50° F) June-July-Aug.-Sept.	Daily Average for these 4 months
I	Salinas (Monterey)	1482	62.1
I	Paicines (San Benito)	1601	62.6
I	Sonoma (Sonoma)	1682	63.8
I	Oakville (Napa)	1707	64.0
II	Hollister (San Benito)	1923	65.8
II	Los Gatos (Santa Clara)	2046	66.8

District	CALIFORNIA	Heat Summation (over 50°F) June-July-Aug.-Sept.	Daily Average for these 4 months
II	King City-San Lucas (Monterey)	2046	66.8
II	Healdsburg (Sonoma)	2164	67.7
III	St. Helena (Napa)	2214	68.1
III	Livermore (Alameda)	2305	68.9
III	Ukiah (Mendocino)	2360	69.3
III	Calistoga (Napa)	2419	70.0
IV	Lodi (San Joaquin Valley)	2499	70.5
V	Fresno (Central Valley)	3423	78.1
V	Bakersfield (Southern California)	3582	79.4

It should be definitely kept in mind that county lines, in California, and regional lines in Europe, do not precisely correspond to the various temperature zone indications given in these pages. Thus parts of Napa County are in Region III and others in Regions I and II, and in far more than half of Burgundy's total area, the vine cannot be successfully cultivated at all. Nor are accurate temperature records of this kind kept in more than a tiny proportion of villages either in California or abroad. What these tables are intended to convey is nothing more than a rough overall picture of the climate prevailing in a few major viticultural areas.

APPENDIX 3

UNITED STATES

EQUIVALENTS

1 U.S. Gallon	3.785 Liters	
1 Liter	0.264 U.S. Gallon	33.79 Fluid Ounces
1 Hectoliter	26.4 U.S. Gallons	
1 Hectare	2.471 Acres	
1 Acre	2½ to 5 Tons of Grapes	

Tons of Grapes	Approximate U.S. Gallons	Approximate Cases
1	150	63
2	300	125
2.5	375	155
3	450	190
3.5	525	220
4	600	250
4.5	675	285
5	750	315
5.5	825	345
6	900	375

CALIFORNIA

TABLE WINE

VINTAGE — 6-9 weeks: end of August into October.

FERMENTATION — Red wines are fermented on the skins 6-7 days at 70-80 deg. F. White and Rosé wines are kept in contact with the skins for 4-8 hours prior to fermentation. Rosé wines are fermented with the skins until the desired color is attained, then separated from the pulp to continue the fermentation. White wines are separated from the pulp and fermented for a little over 3 weeks, cold at a temperature of 40-50 deg. F.

STORAGE — Bulk storage is either in small cooperage or in large wooden tanks, or a combination of both, for red wines. White wines may have some wood storage plus stainless steel or glass lined storage.

BOTTLING — White wines are bottled prior to the following vintage. Red wines are bottled after two years in wood. After bottling there is an average of 5 months additional storage prior to shipping.

VINEYARD ACREAGE OF LEADING CALIFORNIA COUNTIES IN 1976
AS REPORTED BY THE CALIFORNIA DEPARTMENT OF AGRICULTURE

County	Raisin grapes	Table grapes	Wine grapes	Total
Alameda	—	—	1,936	1,936
Amador	15	—	922	937
Butte	—	50	988	1,038
Contra Costa	—	—	897	897
Fresno	146,235	6,072	35,322	187,629
Glenn	—	—	1,436	1,436
Kern	21,986	10,129	39,372	71,487
Kings	2,343	5	1,096	3,444
Lake	—	—	2,477	2,477
Madera	29,668	487	27,915	58,070
Mendocino	—	2	8,887	8,889
Merced	3,006	116	12,918	16,040
Monterey	—	—	33,143	33,143
Napa	5	8	23,710	23,723
Placer	1	1	301	303
Riverside	2,744	5,014	2,997	10,755
Sacramento	—	44	3,103	3,147
San Benito	—	1	4,575	4,576
San Bernardino	61	205	9,392	9,658
San Diego	19	18	431	468
San Joaquin	457	19,286	34,651	54,394
San Luis Obispo	—	1	4,172	4,173
Santa Barbara	—	1	5,967	5,968
Santa Clara	1	1	2,123	2,125
Solano	—	—	1,638	1,638
Sonoma	—	25	24,360	24,385
Stanislaus	3,597	42	19,613	23,252
Tulare	32,863	24,101	16,282	73,246
Yolo	—	5	485	490
Yuba	—	—	697	697
Other Counties	10	26	844	880
State Total — 1976	243,011	65,640	322,650	631,301
State Total — 1966	261,700	86,050	141,690	489,440
Change Since 1966	−7.1%	−23.7%	+127.7%	+29%

GRAPES CRUSHED FOR WINE AND BRANDY PRODUCTION, 1975
IN THE LEADING CALIFORNIA DISTRICTS AS REPORTED BY THE WINE INSTITUTE

District	Raisin grapes TONS	Table grapes TONS	Wine grapes TONS	Total TONS
Southern California	0	0	31,145	31,145
Los Angeles, Orange, Riverside, San Bernardino, San Diego and Santa Barbara Counties				
Southern San Joaquin	69,698	30,464	192,987	293,149
Kern, San Luis Obispo and part of Tulare Counties				
Central San Joaquin	552,966	59,621	451,769	1,064,356
Fresno, Kings, Madera and part of Tulare Counties				
Escalon — Merced, Modesto	45,794	56,785	281,517	384,096
Stanislaus, Toulumne and part of San Joaquin Counties				
Lodi — Sacramento	11,277	66,807	105,162	183,246
Amador, Butte, El Dorado, Placer, Sacramento, Yolo and part of San Joaquin Counties				
North Coast — North Bay, Humbolt,	130	0	129,969	130,099
Marin, Mendocino, Napa, Solano and Sonoma Counties				
North Coast — South Bay	967	664	80,715	82,346
Alameda, Contra Costa, Monterey, San Benito, San Francisco, San Mateo, Santa Clara and Santa Cruz Counties				
All Districts — 1975	680,832	214,341	1,273,264	2,168,437
All Districts — 1966	671,091	299,378	614,700	1,585,169
Change since 1966	+1.5%	−28.4%	+107.1%	+36.8%

Name of Grape Variety	Where Grown in Europe	Comments	Where Grown in California
Aleatico	Italy, notably the island of Elba.	Produces a sweet red dessert wine, on the order of a light Port, with pronounced Muscat flavor.	In San Bernardino County.
Alicante Bouschet	Midi district of France.	A *"teinturier"* (which means "dyer") — one of the rare grapes with dark red juice, and grown largely for this reason. Common and coarse.	Practically every-where, but mostly in the warmer dis-tricts.
Barbera	Northern Italy, espe-cially Piedmont.	Gives a lusty, full-bodied, deep-colored wine, a bit astringent, lacking in delicacy and class; nevertheless with plenty of charac-ter, excellent with Italian food.	In Sonoma, Napa, and recently, on a very large scale, in the warmer districts around Fresno.
Cabernet Franc	Widely in Bordeaux, especially St. Émilion and Pomerol. Also the Loire Valley — Chinon.	Slightly more productive than Cabernet Sauvignon; its wine is softer, rounder, sooner ready. Also called the Breton and Gros Bouchet (*not* Bouschet).	Hardly anywhere, unfortunately.
Cabernet Sauvigon	In all of the better Bordeaux vineyards, predominates in the Médoc.	One of the two best red wine grapes of the world. Yields a superb, long-lived wine, of incomparable balance and class.	In all of the better North Coast Country vineyards.
Carmine	Nowhere.	Variety developed in California.	Widely adaptable.
Carignane	Everywhere in the Midi district, in Algeria, widely in Spain.	One of the better mass production grapes; in some few districts gives sound, agreeable wine, never dis-tinguished.	Practically everywhere.
Carnelian	Nowhere.	Variety developed in California.	Central Valley.
Centurion	Nowhere.	Variety developed in California.	Central Valley.
Charbono	Uncertain; perhaps in French Savoie and Italian Piedmont.	Possibly a variety called Charbon-neau or Douce Noire in Europe.	Napa.
Gamay	Widely in France.	There are many sub-varieties of Gamay, some good, some medi-ocre. Also called Napa Gamay.	Napa, Monterey and other North Coast countries.

400

RED WINE GRAPES IN CALIFORNIA

1976 Acreage in California	California Wine Type and How Usually Sold	Comments
350	So far, used in blends.	Could be interesting and deserves varietal status.
5,800	In the cheapest blends baptized "Burgundy" or "Claret".	Has no place in any respectable vineyard and should be eliminated.
11,000	Usually under its proper varietal name.	In Sonoma and Napa often produces better wine than in Italy — perhaps California's outstanding "Italian type" wine.
75	Generally blended with Cabernet Sauvignon, as in the Bordeaux Country.	Helps, softens and improves Cabernet Sauvignon; should be more widely planted and used.
27,000	Invariably as Cabernet or Cabernet Sauvignon.	America's best red wine, and a remarkably good one; those from the good North Coast County vineyards can hold their own against all but the very finest clarets of Bordeaux.
under 100	Not yet sold — first planted commercially in 1977.	Métis of Ruby Cabernet and Merlot, more productive and earlier ripening than Cabernet Sauvignon.
27,600	Mostly just as "Burgundy" or "Claret" or "Red Wine"; rarely, when it comes from Sonoma or Mendocino, under its varietal name.	A Carignane from Sonoma is an excellent *ordinaire,* by no means to be despised. What comes from the warmer districts is pretty common but certainly at least as good as what the French Midi produces.
2,800	Not yet sold — first planted commercially in 1973.	Métis of Carignane, Cabernet Sauvignon and Grenache. Wine of relatively high acidity.
1,400	Not yet sold — first planted commercially in 1974.	Métis of Carignane, Cabernet Sauvignon and Grenache. Wine darker and fuller flavor than Carnelian.
100 (?)	For no very good reason, under this undistinguished and unknown name.	Pretty common and coarse, even in the best vineyard districts.
6,000	Generally as Gamay or Gamay Rosé.	Very productive. Gives a wine without much fruit or character, though light and agreeable if well vinified.

Name of Grape Variety	Where Grown in Europe	Comments	Where Grown in California
Gamay Beaujolais	The splendid red wine grape of the Beaujolais. Sub-varieties elsewhere all over France.	On the proper soil gives one of the most agreeable and justly popular wines of France — fruity, tender, early ready; sometimes, from the best vineyards and in good years, wines of true distinction and great class, improving with age.	Now widely in the North Coast counties: San Benito, Monterey, Napa, Sonoma, Mendocino.
Grenache	Almost everywhere in southern France and northern Spain.	An extraordinarily adaptable variety; depending on climate and soil, an admirable rosé (Tavel), good dessert wine (Banyuls), sound but undistinguished short-lived reds.	For rosé in the North Coast Counties; widely elsewhere for common table wine and Port.
Grignolino	Italian Piedmont.	Yields an interesting, often fine red wine, light in color, rather high in alcohol.	Mostly in Santa Clara and Napa.
Malbec	Bordeaux; also around Cahors, in central France.	Also called the Cot, or Pressac; usually blended, gives a red wine of good color, excellent quality.	Experimentally.
Mataro	Widely in southern France and Spain.	Also called the Mourvèdre; just a fairly good mass-production grape except in a few rare districts.	Widely in the warmer districts.
Merlot	Everywhere in Bordeaux, also in southern Switzerland and northern Italy.	Usually blended with the Cabernet, at almost all of the great chateaux. Very high quality, yields a soft, well-balanced wine, soon ready.	Important new plantings in Monterey and other Northern Coast Counties.
Mission	Unknown.	—	Very widely in the warmer districts.
Nebbiolo	Italian Piedmont.	Italy's greatest red wine variety — responsible for Barolo, Barbaresco, Gattinara, etc., etc.	Hardly at all.
Petite Sirah	?	This is almost certainly NOT the true and noble Syrah of Hermitage, Cote Rotie, etc., but a common Rhone Valley grape called the Duriff.	Napa, Sonoma and Northern Central Valley.

402

1976 Acreage in California	California Wine Type and How Usually Sold	Comments
4,400	Almost invariably under its proper and proud name.	Produces remarkable wine in the North Coast counties, all the way from Mendocino to Monterey — often quite as good as Pinot Noir, but somewhat earlier ready and shorter lived. Comparable to the best Beaujolais of France.
19,200	Mostly just as red wine, some as Port. That from the cooler coastal areas as perhaps California's finest *vin rosé*.	Yields one of the best of *rosés*, fresh, clean and fragrant when made in the cooler parts of California; also a rather ordinary red wine in the San Joaquin Valley, and better than average California Port.
150	Principally used for *rosé*, quite often under the varietal name.	Gives a far less good red wine than in Italy; the *rosé*, when properly vinified, has considerable character and is by no means bad.
375	With Cabernet, as in France.	Surely excellent. Deserves more attention.
1,500	Common red table wine — ''Burgundy'' or ''Claret.''	Less good on the whole than the Carignane, has little except its productivity to recommend it.
4,575	Under its proper name and with Cabernet, as in France.	A judicious admixture would certainly improve all California Cabernets.
5,050	Largely in cheaper blends of Angelica and Port.	Despite its distinguished history (planted by the Franciscan Fathers; first *vinifera* grape in California), an extremely poor variety that has never produced good wine; deficient in color, it cannot even yield, alone, a passable California Port.
400	In blends or not at all.	Might or might not do well in the arid California climate. Certainly deserves a try.
14,200	Under its varietal name, and in the better grades of California ''Burgundy''.	Gives a deep-colored, sturdy wine, well-balanced and sound; certainly superior to the *vin ordinaire* of France and Italy.

Name of Grape Variety	Where Grown in Europe	Comments	Where Grown in California
Pinot Noir	The one and only great variety of Burgundy; also Champagne, Germany, spottily in Alsace and the Loire Valley.	Incomparable quality, very small yield. Ranks with the Cabernet Sauvignon for red wine but also gives superb *rosé*, excellent white wine, nearly ⅔ of all French Champagne.	Sonoma, Napa, Monterey, Santa Barbara, San Benito, Mendocino.
Pinot St. George	?	NOT a Pinot	North Coast Counties.
Refosco or Mondeuse	Northern and central Italy. Also in Savoie in France.	Productive, undistinguished.	Napa.
Royalty	Nowhere.	Variety developed in California.	Central Valley.
Rubired	Nowhere.	Variety developed in California.	Central Valley.
Ruby Cabernet	Nowhere.	Variety developed in California.	Increasingly in the warmer counties.
Sangiovese	The Chianti Country and elsewhere in central Italy.	By far the most important variety for Chianti. In quality, fair to very good.	Hardly at all.
Salvador	Nowhere.	A hybrid and as such not permitted in any European wine that carries an appellation.	Extensively in the warmer districts.
Tinta Madiera	Portugal.	One of the better grapes of the Port Country.	Mostly in the warmer districts.
Valdepeñas	Spain?	Certainly NOT the leading grape of Spain's Valdepeñas district, which is the Cencibel or Tempranillo.	Warmer districts.
Zinfandel	Unknown.	Certainly a Vinifera grape of European origin but still not positively identified.	First in total acreage in California.

1976 Acreage in California	California Wine Type and How Usually Sold	Comments
10,100	Invariably under its varietal name.	Excellent, although not as outstanding in California as the Cabernet, nor as close, in character and bouquet, to its French counterpart; its wine is lighter, dryer, less velvety and less complex, with less depth of flavor than good, authentic French Burgundy. Nevertheless always, when genuine, a truly superior wine and fully as fine as any French Burgundy in the same price class.
650	Usually, and of course wrongly, as Red Pinot.	Yields a rather thin, characterless red wine, pleasant, a bit astringent.
200	Probably, most often, as "Burgundy" or in blends.	Before it was definitely identified was called Crabb's Black Burgundy in the Napa Valley. Sturdy, rather common red wine.
3,000	In blends.	Used for its high color.
11,300	In blends.	Used for its high color.
18,300	Properly only as RUBY Cabernet. It has no right to the name "Cabernet" alone.	A métis of Cabernet and Carignane, developed in California. Fair quality. Productive.
100 (?)	Supposedly in a few better California Chiantis.	Perhaps because differently vinified, seems to have little recognizable Chianti character.
3,000	Solely in blends, to give added color to Port and other red wines which would otherwise be too pale.	Has no possible value except as a coloring agent, or dye; can hardly be called a wine grape.
1,250	In the best California Port which is sometimes given the varietal name of Tinta.	Gives something enormously better than the run-of-the-mill California Port. Considerable fruit and bouquet.
2,350	In blends of less expensive red wine.	A sound, very productive variety giving a pleasant, if somewhat common, light table wine.
30,600	The best, from the North Coast Counties, as Zinfandel, or in light, agreeable blended wines labeled "Mountain Red", etc. Also widely in California Claret and even (much less successfully) in California Port.	An admirable, useful and productive grape, which yields, except in the warmest districts, about the most typical and best *vin ordinaire* of the United States — fruity, with a characteristic berry flavor, not too deeply colored, early ready and short-lived. In the irrigated San Joaquin Valley it does much less well. Occasionally, when vinified in the classic European manner, it has great body and long life.

Name of Grape Variety	*Where Grown in Europe*	*Comments*	*Where Grown in California*
Burger	Alsace and Germany.	Very productive; poor quality; no longer permitted in better vineyards.	Nearly everywhere.
Chardonnay	Burgundy, Chablis, Champagne.	Highest possible quality, small yield; sometimes called *Pinot Chardonnay* in France, but not a true *Pinot*.	North Coast Counties.
Chenin Blanc	Central Loire Valley — Vouvray, Saumur, Anjou.	Also called (correctly) *Pineau de la Loire,* and (incorrectly) *Pinot.* Productive, very good quality.	North Coast Counties and cooler Central Valley vineyards.
Emerald Riesling	Nowhere.	A variety developed in California.	North Coast and Kern Counties.
Folle Blanche	Cognac, Armagnac, lower Loire Valley, Midi, etc.	Productive; gives a fresh, tart wine, excellent brandy. Also known as *Piquepoul* and *Gros Plant.*	North Coast Counties.
French Colombard	Cognac district.	Productive; gives a passable table wine, excellent brandy.	North Coast Counties and cooler Central Valley vineyards.
Gewürztraminer	Alsace, northern Italy, Germany	Also called *Traminer,* fine quality, special flavor.	North Coast Counties.
Gray Riesling	Perhaps, under a different name.	Not the true *Riesling* nor related to it. On labels spelled *Grey Riesling*.	North Coast Counties.
Malvasia Bianca	Madeira and Mediterranean Countries.	Malmsey in Madeira.	Mainly Central Valley.
Muscat Blanc	Northern and central Italy, southern France.	Called the *Moscato di Canelli* or *Muscat de Frontignan*. Good quality.	North Coast Counties.
Palomino	Sherry district of Spain.	The principal grape used in Sherry.	Widely, but especially in the warmer districts.

1976 Acreage in California	California Wine Type and How Usually Sold	Comments
1,700	Used in cheaper, blended white wines, sold as California Chablis, Rhine, or Sauterne.	Yields a passable, neutral wine in cooler districts; elsewhere something both coarse and common. Immensely productive.
11,400	Only as Chardonnay or Pinot Chardonnay, also in the best California Champagnes.	Highest quality, very small yield. Its wine is dryer, softer, lower in alcohol than in France, perhaps with less bouquet, but remarkable.
20,200	Most often, these days, under its proper varietal name, though sometimes as *White* Pinot, or in Champagne.	Productive but excellent quality; pale, fresh, attractive wine with good bouquet; occasionally (and less successfully) somewhat sweet.
2,850	Sometimes so labeled, but often in wines called simply *Riesling*.	Productive, fairly good quality. Agreeable bouquet but no true *Riesling* character.
375	Occasionally marketed as *Folle Blanche*; more often, since its wine is fresh, light, tart and pale, used in the best California Chablis and Champagne.	Does better here than in France, though only in the cooler districts. Deserves to be better known.
26,500	Most often as California Chablis, but increasingly in California Champagne.	Very productive. Its wine usually lacks distinction and has an underlying bitterness, pronounced flavor, but good acidity.
2,550	Either as *Traminer* or *Gewürztraminer*, both names being legal and proper.	To a remarkable degree, in cooler districts, the wine develops in California the same extraordinary character and spicy bouquet that it has in Europe.
1,900	As *Grey Riesling*.	Can have considerable finesse and is gaining in popularity.
950	In blends of table and sparkling wines.	Undistinguished quality.
825	As *Muscat de Frontignan* or blended.	Used only as a flavoring for dry white wines.
4,600	Almost entirely for Sherry. Used to be called the *Golden Chasselas*, although it is not a *Chasselas*, and does better in warmer districts than in Napa.	For Sherry, no less outstanding in California than in Spain. Gives a poor, coarse, heavy table wine, and should never be used for this.

Name of Grape Variety	Where Grown in Europe	Comments	Where Grown in California
Pinot Blanc	Burgundy.	Good quality but much less fine than the *Chardonnay*.	North Coast Counties.
Saint Émilion	Cognac district, southern France, northern Italy, Chianti district.	Same as *Ugni Blanc* and *Trebbiano*. Productive, fair quality; good brandy.	Central Valley Counties.
Sauvignon Blanc	Graves and Sauternes, upper Loire Valley.	Very high quality, character, great class, small yield. Also called the *Blanc-Fumé*.	North Coast Counties and cooler Central Valley vineyards.
Sauvignon Vert	?	Not a *Sauvignon*.	North Coast Counties.
Sémillon	Graves and Sauternes, Monbazillac.	Yields soft wines of very good quality.	North Coast Counties and Central Valley.
Sylvaner	Rhineland, Franconia, Alsace, northern Italy.	Same as *Franken Riesling*; Productive, good quality.	North Coast Counties and cooler Central Valley vineyards.
White Riesling	Rhine, Moselle, Alsace, Austria, northern Italy.	Highest possible quality, small yield; sometimes confused with *Sylvaner* (*see*).	North Coast Counties.

1976 Acreage in California	California Wine Type and How Usually Sold	Comments
1,450	Invariably under its varietal name, since it is in great demand; occasionally, however, the best California Champagne.	Gives better wine in California than in France; requires more bottle ageing than the Chardonnay but the end results of nearly equal quality. Fine bouquet, real distinction.
1,600	Almost always in blends.	Produces a very sound, well-balanced, neutral wine, good, but not much character and charm.
3,800	Usually under its varietal name; occasionally blended to give distinction to a California Dry Sauterne. Sometimes as *Blanc-Fumé,* or even wrongly *Fumé Blanc.*	Maintains in California the character and high quality which it brings to the finest French dry Graves. At its best in the cooler areas, sometimes too pronounced in too warm a climate.
825	Happily, only in blends sold as cheaper California Chablis and Sauterne.	A small, harsh, bitter wine, no credit to the name of *Sauvignon.*
3,025	Most often as *Sémillon,* but widely used in the very best California Sauterne, both dry and sweet.	Gives a dryer wine in the dry climate of California than in France; soft, definite varietal bouquet and flavor; very good but not top quality.
1,375	Usually as *Riesling,* its legal California name; sometimes as the best grade California Rhine wine; most properly, of course, as *Sylvaner* or *Franken Riesling.*	Quite productive, and very, very good. Its wine has more fruit than most in California; it is pale, fresh, light, with nice bouquet, early ready, short-lived.
8,600	As *Johannisberger Riesling,* to distinguish it from *Grey Riesling* and also from *Sylvaner,* which can legally be labeled *Riesling* in California. Sometimes called *White Riesling.*	Highest quality, small yield. In California, its wine is dryer and yet less tart than the German Rhines and the Alsatians; less assertive and with less bouquet, yet of exceptional balance and class.

OTHER STATES

HYBRIDS IN THE UNITED STATES OTHER THAN CALIFORNIA
RED HYBRIDS

Variety	Seedling No.	Origin	Use	Comments
*Baco Noir	Baco No. 1	Bordeaux	Short season areas	First hybrid commercially planted. High sugar and acid. Will age.
Bellandais	Seibel 14596	Rhône	Long season areas	Potential for Southwest.
†Cascade	Seibel 13053		Very early ripening	Agreeable red or *rosé*, blends well.
Chambourcin	Joannès-Seyve 26205	Rhône	Mid-season	Well established, good quality.
†Chancellor	Seibel 7053	Rhône	Early mid-season. Heavy producer	Full-bodied solid wine.
Chelois	Seibel 10878		Standard in New York State and on west to Washington. Broad climatic tolerance	Good wine, light Burgundy type.
Colobel	Seibel 8357		*Teinturier* for color	Dark red blending wine.
De Chaunac	Seibel 9549		Northeast and Middle-west and Canadian Niagara Peninsula	Hardiness and general reliability.
Florental	Burdin 7705			Like Gamay Beaujolais.
Garonnais	Seyve-Villard 18283	Garonne		Potential for Southwest.
Landal	Landot 244			Beaujolais style.
*Léon Millot	Kuhlmann 194-2	Alsace	Short season areas	Cousin of Foch-wine as good or better.
*Maréchal Foch	Kuhlmann 188-2	Alsace	Standard in short season areas.	Good sugar, moderate acid, good wine.
*Ravat Noir	Ravat 262	France		Pinot parentage.
Villard Noir	Seyve-Villard 18315	Rhône	Mid-season	Solid wine.

WHITE HYBRIDS

Variety	Seedling No.	Origin	Use	Comments
*Aurore	Seibel 5279	France	Early. Standard in Finger Lakes and Chatauqua	Good quality still and sparkling.

410

Variety	Seedling No.	Origin	Use	Comments
*Ravat Blanc	Ravat 6	France	Difficult to grow	Chardonnay cross, wine very like white Burgundy.
*Rayon d'Or	Seibel 4986	France	Steady production	High sugar, crisp, clean still or sparkling.
Seyval	Seyve-Villard 5276		Early mid-season, much planting	Marketed as Seyval Blanc.
† Verdelet	Seibel 9110		Western New York and Canadian Niagara Peninsula.	Suitable both for table grapes and wine.
Vidal	Vidal 256	Charente	Wide possibilities	Very similar to Ugni Blanc.
† Vignoles	Ravat 51		Champagne in Finger Lakes.	Chardonnay hybrid.
Villard Blanc	Seyve-Villard 12375		Warmer areas especially Southwest	Vigorous and productive.

Notes: These tables and information in the alphabetized text were derived from Philip M. Wagner's "Grapes Into Wine" — A Guide to Winemaking in America — Alfred A. Knopf, New York, 1976 — with kind permission of the author and the publisher.

*Names which arose naturally in France.
†Names coined in 1970 by the New York Finger Lakes Wine Growers Association.
Names not marked were coined by a French official body several years ago.

NATIVE AMERICAN GRAPES

The wine grape species, *Vitis vinifera,* originated in the Middle East and thence spread to Europe. It was subsequently transported to all other major wine growing areas of the world. In the United States and Canada many other species of grapes, native to the New World, have been interbred with each other and with the imported *vinifera* species. From the resultant crosses, some man-made, others natural, hybrid grape varieties have been selected for wine making.

There are four major American species that have contributed to the American varietal situation: *Vitis labrusca,* the slip-skin grape which grows in the Northeast, particularly New York, is distinguished by a musky, "foxy" flavor; *Vitis rotundifolia,* the muscadine grape which flourishes in the south central and east coast sections, has a powerful fruity flavor; *Vitis riparia* is the most widespread geographically and particularly prevalent in the north central states; *Vitis aestivalis* is widespread through the central southern states, and widely used in hybridization for its vigor and disease resistance.

Most of the resultant American hybrid grapes, compared to *Vitis vinifera,* are low in sugar and high in acid, and usually require addition of sugar and often neutralization to obtain proper alcohol and acid balance.

NATIVE AMERICAN GRAPES

	GRAPE COLOR			WINE					EATING		Predominant
	Black	Pink	Green	Red	Rosé	White	Spkl.	Dessert	Table	Juice Jelly	Species Character
Bacchus	x			x							Riparia
Buffalo	x			x							Labrusca-Vinifera
Campbell's Early	x			x							Labrusca
Catawba		x				x		x			Labrusca
Champanel	x			x							Labrusca
Clinton	x			x							Riparia
Concord	x			x					x	x	Labrusca
Cynthiana	x			x							Aestivalis
Delaware		x				x	x		x		Aestivalis-Vinifera
Diamond			x			x					Labrusca
Diana		x				x					Labrusca
Dutchess			x			x	x				Aestivalis-Vinifera
Elvira			x			x	x				Riparia
Eumelan	x			x							Aestivalis-Vinifera
Fredonia	x			x							Labrusca
Iona		x				x					Labrusca
Isabella	x				x	x	x				Labrusca
Ives	x			x							Labrusca
James	x			x							Rotundifolia
Lenoir	x			x							Aestivalis
Missouri Riesling			x			x	x				Riparia
Moore's Diamond			x			x					Labrusca
Muscadine			x			x				x	x	Rotundifolia
Niagara	x					x				x	Labrusca
Noah			x			x					Riparia
Norton	x			x							Aestivalis
Ontario			x			x			x		Labrusca
Portland			x			x					Labrusca
Ripley			x			x					Labrusca-Vinifera
Scuppernong			x			x					Rotundifolia
Steuben	x			x	x						Labrusca-Vinifera
Vergennes			x			x					Labrusca
Westfield	x			x							Labrusca

APPENDIX 4

FRANCE

FRENCH WINE PRODUCTION IN 1976

(The following table originally appeared in *La Journée Vinicole* and is here reproduced by special permission.)

Despite its apparent dullness, this table gives in fact an extraordinarily vivid and accurate picture of French wine production — of the difference between *grand vin* and *vin ordinaire*, of how and where and why both are grown in France. Please note, therefore:

1. The numbers in the extreme left-hand columns are the official French département numbers: this system even extends to the French equivalent of Zip Codes and even to car licence plates: a car from Paris (Seine) invariably has a license number ending with 75; one from Bordeaux (Gironde) a number ending with 33, one from the Côte d'Or a number ending with 21, etc.

2. Vineyard owners are required by French law (strictly enforced) to report their total acreage of producing vineyard and their production in hectolitres. In 1976 there were 1,205,493 hectares (2,978,773 acres) of vineyard which yielded 73,035,424 hectolitres (1,928,135,194 gallons) of wine. This amounted to 60.6 hectolitres per hectare (647 gallons per acre).

3. A total of 905,750 vineyard owners reported (which means that about one French family out of ten was actively engaged in wine production). Comparing this with the total acreage, it is obvious that the average French vineyard owner has just 1⅓ hectares (3.29 acres) of producing vineyard. Only in ONE département, the Gironde (Bordeaux), is the average holding over eight acres.

4. Out of 1,205,493 hectares (2,978,773 acres) of vineyard in production, less than one-quarter 274,918 hectares (679,322 acres) produced wines entitled to an Appellation Contrôlée. This production amounted to 13,019,122 hectolitres (343,704,820 gallons) in all, or 506 gallons per acre, as compared with 647 gallons per acre for French wines as a whole or 689 gallons per acre for non-Appellation Contrôlée wines.

5. It is interesting to note that 69% of the total production of wine in France in 1976 was either red or rosé and only 31% white, whereas 45% of Appellation Contrôlée wines was red or rosé and 55% white.

413

	Département	Number of Vineyard Owners Reporting	Total Vineyards in Production	Vineyards Entitled to Appellation Contrôlée
			Hectares	Hectares
1	Ain	10,534	2,319	64
2	Aisne	997	1,248	1,234
3	Allier	8,973	2,716	—
4	Alpes (Basses-)	3,683	2,467	—
5	Alpes (Hautes-)	2,290	1,147	—
6	Alpes-Maritimes	3,625	779	29
7	Ardèche	21,344	20,299	542
8	Ardennes	78	6	—
9	Ariège	3,407	1,162	—
10	Aube	4,392	3,523	3,236
11	Aude	41,039	119,103	4,098
12	Aveyron	11,393	3,833	—
13	Bouches-du-Rhône	15,633	25,519	203
14	Calvados	—	—	—
15	Cantal	255	39	—
16	Charente	23,233	48,183	—
17	Charente-Maritime	32,840	60,870	—
18	Cher	7,989	3,220	1,355
19	Corrèze	5,096	1,296	—
20	Corse	2,236	27,194	5,733
21	Côte-d'Or	9,752	7,746	6,594
22	Côtes-du-Nord	—	—	—
23	Creuse	1	—	—
24	Dordogne	19,746	23,374	9,010
25	Doubs	542	70	—
26	Drôme	17,089	17,914	10,673
27	Eure	—	—	—
28	Eure-et-Loir	32	3	—
29	Finistère	1	—	—
30	Gard	36,612	93,843	8,652
31	Garonne (Haute-)	13,512	11,065	418
32	Gers	17,638	34,459	135
33	Gironde	28,630	104,668	70,844
34	Hérault	63,260	158,846	1,401
35	Ille-et-Vilaine	2	—	—
36	Indre	15,397	4,011	40
37	Indre-et-Loire	20,075	13,792	5,240
38	Isère	19,615	4,444	91
39	Jura	5,012	1,778	984
40	Landes	15,564	10,729	—
41	Loir-et-Cher	14,670	13,500	1,640
42	Loire	8,958	3,068	18
43	Loire (Haute-)	2,352	542	—
44	Loire-Atlantique	33,568	23,116	9,081
45	Loiret	3,711	1,013	—
46	Lot	9,412	7,485	901
47	Lot-et-Garonne	14,531	13,366	1,423

| Appellation Contrôlée Wines Produced | | Total Production Including Appellation Contrôlée, V.D.Q.S., Vin de Pays, and Vin Ordinaire | | |
White	Red or Rosé	White	Red and Rosé	Total
Hectolitres	Hectolitres	Hectolitres	Hectolitres	Hectolitres
2,928	325	19,427	77,112	96,539
85,891	689	89,669	1,748	91,417
—	—	10,287	76,841	87,128
—	—	3,616	69,246	72,862
—	—	352	33,531	33,883
183	329	772	18,347	19,119
2,149	20,887	8,963	933,939	942,902
—	—	16	248	264
—	—	6	29,809	29,815
197,224	5,161	205,665	15,252	220,917
75,681	44,348	107,424	7,560,794	7,668,218
—	—	1,062	89,082	90,144
3,041	2,280	56,149	1,326,340	1,382,489
—	—	—	—	—
—	—	55	1,354	1,409
—	—	3,661,441	190,251	3,851,692
—	—	5,442,647	299,150	5,741,797
51,201	10,779	56,490	61,777	118,267
—	—	88	34,017	34,105
5,763	127,178	14,866	1,818,148	1,833,014
62,665	226,625	71,466	313,121	384,587
—	—	—	8	8
186,980	144,118	514,240	436,669	950,909
—	—	295	1,883	2,178
33,397	435,500	35,491	756,303	791,794
—	—	—	—	—
—	—	8	123	131
—	—	—	5	5
5,301	381,001	35,772	7,061,280	7,097,052
—	17,041	1,745	385,006	386,751
213	7,518	2,234,257	525,295	2,759,552
1,064,804	2,456,901	2,519,641	2,996,064	5,515,705
38,269	—	580,449	11,501,759	12,082,208
—	—	3	8	11
715	514	5,612	128,004	133,616
115,655	105,989	182,850	411,261	594,111
3,848	1,219	21,448	148,310	169,758
20,484	19,906	25,249	41,873	67,122
—	—	510,620	169,431	680,051
41,604	46,272	249,943	463,527	713,470
210	269	1,474	74,826	76,300
—	—	289	14,586	14,875
591,269	1,450	1,115,409	559,432	1,674,841
—	—	1,701	32,474	34,175
—	50,516	595	285,123	285,718
19,908	33,357	197,969	461,602	659,571

Département	Number of Vineyard Owners Reporting	Total Vineyards in Production	Vineyards Entitled to Appellation Contrôlée
48 Lozère	1,137	183	—
49 Maine-et-Loire	20,320	23,188	14,714
50 Manche	—	—	—
51 Marne	23,491	18,482	18,459
52 Marne (Haute-)	1,854	257	—
53 Mayenne	5	1	—
54 Meurthe-et-Moselle	2,685	356	—
55 Meuse	425	73	—
56 Morbihan	15	2	—
57 Moselle	1,303	126	—
58 Nièvre	4,026	1,142	483
59 Nord	—	—	—
60 Oise	5	1	—
61 Orne	—	—	—
62 Pas-de-Calais	—	—	—
63 Puy-de-Dôme	12,257	3,217	—
64 Pyrénées (Basses-)	9,414	4,401	1,029
65 Pyrénées (Hautes-)	6,302	2,556	47
66 Pyrénées-Orientales	23,802	61,101	26,812
67 Rhin (Bas-)	12,160	4,872	4,077
68 Rhin (Haut-)	8,524	7,075	6,757
69 Rhône	16,320	20,136	17,920
70 Saône (Haute-)	1,782	288	—
71 Saône-et-Loire	18,162	10,431	8,025
72 Sarthe	3,164	771	21
73 Savoie	9,936	2,579	843
74 Savoie (Haute-)	1,698	389	132
75 Paris	—	—	—
76 Seine-Maritime	1	—	—
77 Seine-et-Marne	413	41	7
78 Yvelines	84	6	—
79 Sèvres (Deux-)	13,490	3,905	545
80 Somme	—	—	—
81 Tarn	16,552	22,777	911
82 Tarn-et-Garonne	11,896	12,820	194
83 Var	26,815	55,960	470
84 Vaucluse	23,279	54,041	27,834
85 Vendée	37,508	9,587	27
86 Vienne	20,569	7,814	185
87 Vienne (Haute-)	506	85	—
88 Vosges	1,721	205	—
89 Yonne	5,351	2,926	1,787
91 Essonne	36	2	—
92 Hauts-de-Seine	5	1	—
93 Seine-St-Denis	—	—	—
94 Val-de-Marne	3	—	—
95 Val-d'Oise	15	1	—
Totals	905,750	1,205,493	274,918

| Appellation Contrôlée Wines Produced | | Total Production Including Appellation Contrôlée, V.D.Q.S., Vin de Pays, and Vin Ordinaire | | |
White	Red or Rosé	White	Red and Rosé	Total
—	—	—	6,212	6,212
246,519	504,641	373,613	913,971	1,287,584
—	—	—	—	—
1,264,179	27,654	1,333,778	29,130	1,362,908
—	—	158	9,021	9,179
—	—	—	13	13
—	—	73	18,408	18,481
—	—	23	3,068	3,091
—	—	34	46	80
—	—	695	5,383	6,078
22,924	53	24,830	21,189	46,019
—	—	—	—	—
—	—	9	16	25
—	—	—	—	—
—	—	—	—	—
—	—	1,436	97,688	99,124
23,717	25,218	52,919	122,983	175,902
24	2,131	12,116	60,765	72,881
495,072	91,978	530,780	1,728,163	2,258,943
334,640	6,975	377,156	11,766	388,922
522,396	16,492	529,464	21,165	550,629
960	875,732	2,463	970,780	973,243
—	—	153	7,282	7,435
169,362	227,921	191,061	313,970	505,031
642	286	5,420	22,276	27,696
38,507	15,820	59,881	82,372	142,253
7,540	231	14,446	9,516	23,962
—	—	—	2	2
507	—	555	1,004	1,559
—	—	1	222	223
6,573	20,802	15,560	131,322	146,882
—	—	—	—	—
23,966	14,106	206,669	1,041,231	1,247,900
—	7,454	3,205	434,644	437,849
796	15,366	83,823	2,420,000	2,503,823
14,059	1,138,491	186,763	2,216,944	2,403,707
1,570	—	88,461	424,809	513,270
5,372	1,030	120,381	158,889	279,270
—	—	43	2,663	2,706
—	—	4	6,858	6,862
85,154	10,707	93,420	41,581	135,001
—	—	2	90	92
—	—	20	30	50
—	—	—	—	—
—	—	—	7	7
—	—	9	41	50
5,875,862	7,143,260	22,294,945	50,740,479	73,035,424

PRODUCTION OF APPELLATION CONTRÔLÉE
WINES IN FRANCE, 1976

The following tables are official French production figures supplied by the I.N.A.O. — Institut National des Appellations d'Origine. It should be kept in mind that 1976 was on the whole a very copious as well as a very good vintage and produced an above-average crop in almost all French districts.

BORDEAUX

	White	U.S. Gallons Red & Rosé	Total
Bordeaux	18,587,448	21,448,917	40,036,365
Bordeaux Supérieur	357,667	7,769,757	8,127,424
Bordeaux Clairet or Rosé	—	295,891	295,891
Entre-Deux-Mers	1,980,237	—	1,980,237
Blaye or Blayais	1,187,973	7,629	1,195,602
Côtes de Blaye	171,996	—	171,996
Premières Côtes de Blaye	2,224	2,461,219	2,463,443
Bourg, Côtes de Bourg or Bourgeais	229,231	3,806,139	4,035,370
Graves de Vayres	422,426	175,850	598,276
Sainte-Foy Bordeaux	169,012	22,915	191,927
Premières Côtes de Bordeaux	831,098	1,395,028	2,226,126
Côtes de Bordeaux-Saint Macaire	173,738	—	173,738
Bordeaux-Côtes de Castillon	—	2,216,464	2,216,464

MÉDOC

Médoc	—	2,904,158	2,904,158
Haut Médoc	—	2,644,514	2,644,514
Listrac	—	559,416	559,416
Margaux	—	1,002,460	1,002,460
Moulis	—	337,603	337,603
Pauillac	—	1,015,080	1,015,080
Saint-Estèphe	—	1,316,172	1,316,172
Saint-Julien	—	795,273	795,273

SAINT-ÉMILION

Saint-Émilion	—	6,491,311	6,491,311
Lussac-Saint-Émilion	—	1,208,697	1,208,697
Montagne-Saint-Émilion	—	1,568,661	1,568,661
Pusseguin-Saint-Émilion	—	729,326	729,326
Saint-Georges-Saint-Émilion	—	207,979	207,979
Sables-Saint-Émilion	—	792	792

POMEROL

Pomerol	—	882,948	882,948
Lalande de Pomerol	—	986,330	986,330

418

FRONSAC

	White	U.S. Gallons Red & Rosé	Total
Canon-Fronsac	—	371,870	371,870
Côtes de Fronsac	—	856,257	856,257

SAUTERNES & CERONS

	White	Red & Rosé	Total
Sauternes	689,647	—	689,647
Barsac	391,036	—	391,036
Cérons	287,179	—	287,179

GRAVES

	White	Red & Rosé	Total
Graves	1,273,615	1,524,864	2,798,479
Graves supérieures	361,891	—	361,891

RIGHT BANK

	White	Red & Rosé	Total
Cadillac	176,985	—	176,985
Loupiac	284,829	—	284,829
Sainte-Croix-du-Mont	400,435	—	400,435
BORDEAUX TOTAL	27,978,693	65,003,585	92,982,278

THE SOUTH WEST

Dordogne

	White	Red & Rosé	Total
Bergerac	1,344,895	2,973,828	4,318,723
Côtes de Bergerac	935,880	472,111	1,407,991
Côtes de Montravel	105,072	—	105,072
Haut-Montravel	31,363	—	31,363
Montravel	382,879	—	382,879
Monbazillac	1,932,189	—	1,932,189
Pécharmant	—	118,140	118,140
Rosette	69,009	—	69,009

Lot-et-Garonne

	White	Red & Rosé	Total
Côtes de Duras	778,324	402,362	1,180,686
Côtes de Buzet	14,361	577,500	591,861

Haute-Garonne, Tarn-et-Garonne

	White	Red & Rosé	Total
Côtes du Frontonnais	—	646,668	646,668

Lot

	White	Red & Rosé	Total
Cahors	—	1,333,622	1,333,622

Tarn

	White	Red & Rosé	Total
Gaillac	632,702	372,398	1,005,100

	White	U.S. Gallons Red & Rosé	Total
Béarn			
Irouléguy	—	80,203	80,203
Jurançon	651,156	—	651,156
Madiran	—	612,057	612,057
Pacherenc de Vic Bilh	23,337	—	23,337
Béarn	10,692	228,228	238,920
Aude, Hérault			
Blanquette de Limoux	1,251,016	—	1,251,016
Clairette du Languedoc	189,261	—	189,261
Fitou	—	824,868	824,868
THE SOUTH WEST TOTAL	8,352,142	8,641,987	16,994,129

BURGUNDY

	White	Red & Rosé	Total
Bourgogne	243,408	2,371,882	2,615,090
Bourgogne Aligoté	1,406,302	—	1,406,302
Bourgogne Passetoutgrain	—	1,392,653	1,392,653
Bourgogne Grand Ordinaire	161,172	377,546	538,718
Crémant de Bourgogne	228,360	2,904	231,264
Chablis			
Chablis Grand Cru	117,322	—	117,322
Chablis Premier Cru	441,434	—	441,434
Chablis	847,836	—	847,836
Petit Chablis	221,417	—	221,417
Côte de Nuits			
Chambolle-Musigny	—	146,467	146,467
Côte de Nuits-Villages	211	179,045	179,256
Fixin	—	25,898	25,898
Gevrey-Chambertin	—	399,062	399,062
Morey-Saint-Denis	713	83,503	84,216
Nuits-Saint-Georges	660	291,377	292,037
Vougeot	1,795	15,893	17,688
Vosne-Romanée	—	172,049	172,049
Bourgogne-Marsannay-la Côte	—	51,533	51,533
Bourgogne-Hautes Côtes de Nuits	5,491	114,418	119,909
Grand crus (Côte de Nuits)			
Bonne Mares	—	12,197	12,197
Chambertin	—	12,118	12,118
Chambertin Clos de Bèze	—	12,857	12,857
Chapelle-Chambertin	—	5,386	5,386
Charmes or Mazoyères-Chambertin	—	29,462	29,462
Clos de la Roche	—	11,458	11,458
Clos Saint-Denis	—	4,224	4,224
Clos de Tart	—	5,597	5,597
Échézeaux	—	42,794	42,794

	White	U.S. Gallons Red & Rosé	Total
Clos de Vougeot	—	26,849	26,849
Grands Échézeaux	—	7,788	7,788
Griotte-Chambertin	—	2,006	2,006
La Tache	—	5,016	5,016
Latricières-Chambertin	—	5,042	5,042
Mazis-Chambertin	—	8,738	8,738
Musigny	185	8,026	8,211
Richebourg	—	6,890	6,890
La Romanée	—	898	898
Romanée-Conti	—	1,795	1,795
Romanée-Saint-Vivant	—	8,633	8,633
Ruchottes-Chambertin	—	2,878	2,878
Côte de Beaune			
Aloxe-Corton	475	126,350	126,825
Auxey-Duresses	25,291	80,467	105,758
Beaune	19,061	326,964	346,025
Blagny	—	6,785	6,785
Chassagne-Montrachet	105,230	193,248	928,478
Cheilly-les-Maranges	—	5,386	5,386
Chorey-les-Beaune	528	105,415	105,943
Côte-de-Beaune	1,822	—	1,822
Côte-de-Beaune Villages	—	267,168	267,168
Ladoix	2,930	53,671	56,601
Meursault	329,076	21,727	350,803
Monthelie	1,531	83,107	84,638
Pernand-Vergelesses	13,649	101,270	114,919
Pommard	—	304,867	304,867
Puligny-Montrachet	194,990	8,738	203,728
Saint-Aubin	13,702	59,849	73,551
Saint-Romain	17,846	24,526	42,372
Santenay	3,353	303,389	306,742
Savigny-les-Beaune	8,369	282,691	291,060
Volnay	—	222,394	222,394
Bourgogne Hautes Côtes de Beaune	5,650	251,803	257,452
Grands crus (Côte de Beaune)			
Corton	1,188	73,603	74,791
Corton-Charlemagne	29,542	—	29,542
Bâtard-Montrachet	6,310	—	6,310
Bienvenues-Bâtard-Montrachet	3,802	—	3,802
Chevalier-Montrachet	3,696	—	3,696
Croits Bâtards-Montrachet	1,426	—	1,426
Montrachet	6,970	—	6,970
Côte Chalonnaise			
Givry	9,953	98,050	108,003
Mercurey	13,306	381,242	394,548
Montagny	74,527	—	74,527
Rully	32,446	30,334	62,780

| | U.S. Gallons | | |
	White	Red & Rosé	Total
Mâconnais			
Mâcon	64,706	16,025	80,731
Mâcon Supérieur	435,178	1,388,138	1,823,316
Mâcon Villages	2,081,561	38,333	2,119,894
Pouilly-Fuissé	763,277	—	763,277
Pouilly-Loché	27,720	—	27,720
Pouilly-Vinzelles	46,226	—	46,226
Saint-Véran	254,258	—	254,258
Beaujolais			
Beaujolais	90,288	10,704,989	10,795,277
Beaujolais Supérieur	14,230	498,828	513,057
Beaujolais-Villages	15,418	7,366,999	7,382,417
Brouilly	—	1,431,619	1,431,619
Chénas	—	251,724	251,724
Chiroubles	—	332,112	332,112
Côte de Brouilly	—	330,422	330,422
Fleurie	—	859,558	859,558
Julienas	—	716,417	716,417
Morgon	—	1,163,422	1,163,422
Moulin à Vent	—	710,450	710,450
Saint Amour	—	295,528	295,528
BURGUNDY TOTAL	8,395,833	35,362,457	43,758,290

RHONE VALLEY & SOUTHEAST

	White	Red & Rosé	Total
Côtes du Rhône	200,692	39,793,195	39,993,887
Côtes du Rhône-Villages	53,248	1,761,698	1,814,946
Côte Rotie	—	44,431	44,431
Condrieu	5,227	—	5,227
Chateau-Grillet	2,323	—	2,323
Chatillon en Diois	2,719	21,225	23,944
Clairette de Die	779,908	—	779,908
Crépy	102,933	—	102,933
Cassis	78,144	52,324	130,468
Clairette de Bellegarde	20,750	—	20,750
Collioure	—	24,710	24,710
Cornas	—	37,593	37,593
Crozes-Hermitage	42,741	485,575	528,316
Châteauneuf du Pape	36,669	2,427,321	2,463,990
Bandol	21,014	405,662	426,676
Bellet	4,831	8,685	16,516
Gigondas	—	732,045	732,045
Hermitage	26,030	61,195	87,225
Lirac	2,059	263,973	266,032
Roussette de Savoie	61,168	—	61,168
Palette	2,138	7,867	10,005
Saint Joseph	10,032	111,962	121,994
Saint Peray	38,200	—	38,200

	White	U.S. Gallons Red & Rosé	Total
Seyssel	51,532	—	51,532
Seyssel Mousseux	32,049	—	32,049
Tavel	—	750,446	750,446
Coteaux du Tricastin	—	1,394,712	1,394,712
Côtes du Ventoux	41,606	4,346,786	4,388,392
Vin de Savoie	1,145,628	440,088	1,585,716
RHONE VALLEY & S.E. TOTAL	2,761,651	53,171,501	55,933,152

CORSICA

	White	Red & Rosé	Total
Vin de Corse	71,280	1,029,679	1,100,959
Côteaux d'Ajaccio	4,356	178,068	182,424
Calvi	9,688	185,644	195,332
Patrimonio	27,429	433,276	460,705
Coteaux du Cap Corse	7,128	1,478	8,606
Sartène	8,976	400,039	409,015
Figari	7,418	100,452	107,870
Porto-Vecchio	15,866	1,028,860	1,044,726
CORSICA TOTAL	152,143	3,357,499	3,509,642

LOIRE VALLEY

Muscadet

	White	Red & Rosé	Total
Muscadet	1,350,703	—	1,350,703
Muscadet des Coteaux de la Loir	660,052	—	660,052
Muscadet de Sèvre et Maine	14,316,218	—	14,316,218

Anjou Saumur

	White	Red & Rosé	Total
Anjou	2,695,228	1,020,676	3,715,904
Rosé d'Anjou	—	7,465,286	7,465,286
Cabernet d'Anjou	—	4,158,528	4,158,528
Anjou Coteaux de la Loire	63,676	—	63,676
Savennières	30,518	—	30,518
Coteaux du Layon	1,484,736	—	1,484,736
Coteaux du Layon Chaume	35,692	—	35,692
Bonnezeaux	23,073	—	23,073
Quarts de Chaume	23,100	—	23,100
Coteaux de l'Aubance	77,193	—	77,193
Saumur	675,945	123,420	799,365
Cabernet de Saumur	—	2,217	2,217
Coteaux de Saumur	7,708	—	7,708
Saumur-Champigny	—	476,810	476,810
Rosé de Loir	—	555,350	555,350
Crémant de Loire	100,056	—	100,056
Saumur Mousseux	933,134	127,512	1,060,646

Touraine

	White	Red & Rosé	Total
Touraine	1,620,392	1,690,867	3,311,259
Touraine Amboise	93,720	135,115	228,835

	White	U.S. Gallons Red & Rosé	Total
Touraine Azay-le-Rideau	38,491	—	38,491
Touraine Mesland	57,525	249,823	307,348
Bourgueil	—	832,972	832,972
Saint-Nicholas-de-Bourgueil	—	428,181	428,181
Chinon	3,748	694,716	698,464
Vouvray	1,438,430	—	1,438,430
Vouvray Mousseux	561,897	—	561,897
Montlouis	279,470	—	279,470
Montlouis Mousseux	55,545	—	55,545
Sarthe			
Coteaux de Loir	3,432	7,550	10,982
Jasnières	13,516	—	13,516
Nievre Berry			
Pouilly-Fumé	470,817	—	470,817
Pouilly-sur-Loire	132,976	—	132,976
Quincy	85,008	—	85,008
Reuilly	28,300	9,636	37,936
Sancerre	1,204,764	253,888	1,458,652
Ménetou-Salon	53,697	31,389	85,086
LOIRE VALLEY TOTAL	28,618,762	18,263,942	46,882,704

FRANCHE-COMTE

	White	Red & Rosé	Total
Arbois	203,544	451,123	654,667
Chateau-Chalon	23,179	—	23,179
L'Étoile	42,451	—	42,451
Côtes du Jura	271,603	74,395	345,998
FRANCHE-COMTÉ TOTAL	540,778	525,518	1,066,296

ALSACE

	White	Red & Rosé	Total
Alsace	22,503,993	615,622	23,119,615
Crémant d'Alsace	121,757	3,907	125,664
ALSACE TOTAL	22,625,750	619,529	23,245,279

CHAMPAGNE

	White	Red & Rosé	Total
Champagne	35,774,772	226,486	36,001,258
Rosé des Riceys	—	2,218	2,218
Coteaux Champenois	5,087,174	655,802	5,742,976
CHAMPAGNE TOTAL	40,861,946	884,506	41,746,452

LANGUEDOC-ROUSILLON

	White	U.S. Gallons Red & Rosé	Total
Vins doux naturels			
Banyuls	—	779,671	779,671
Banyuls Grand Cru	—	94,089	94,089
Maury	—	1,244,047	1,244,047
Grand Rousillon	7,972	—	7,972
Rivesaltes	11,293,761	611,503	11,905,264
Muscat de Rivesaltes	2,515,128	20,116	2,535,244
Muscat de Beaumes-de-Venise	136,884	—	136,884
Muscat de Frontignan	537,741	—	537,741
Muscat de Saint-Jean-de-Minervois	26,136	—	26,136
Muscat de Lunel	163,020	—	163,020
Muscat de Mireval	94,142	—	94,142
Rasteau	60,271	2,112	537,741
Languedoc-Roussilon Total	14,835,058	2,751,540	17,586,598
Grand Total	155,122,757	188,582,064	343,704,821

NOTE: Individual figures will not add up exactly to totals because of rounding out during conversion.

BORDEAUX

THE OFFICIAL (1855) CLASSIFICATION OF
THE GREAT RED WINES OF BORDEAUX

This, except for the notations in parentheses, is the official list and the only authorized and proper one. However, wines marked (×) are no longer generally on the market or have practically ceased to exist as independent properties; those marked (+) are generally sold for a higher price than others in their class, and justifiably so; those marked (−), generally for a lower price. Thus, were a new classification to be made today, the châteaux marked (+) or (−) would probably be placed in a higher, or a lower, category.

It is interesting to note that, except for the First Growths, the wines are listed, not alphabetically, nor geographically by *commune,* but in their presumed order of merit. Thus, in 1855, Mouton Rothschild was ranked as the best of the "Seconds", Pontet-Canet as the best of the "Fifths", and so on. Note, however, that a decree of the French Minister of Agriculture effective June 21, 1973, officially raised Château Mouton-Rothschild to the rank of *Premier Cru Classé,* and alphabetized the First Growths.

All these châteaux are listed, with further details, in their proper alphabetical place in this volume.

THE MÉDOC

FIRST GROWTHS — PREMIERS CRUS

Vineyard	Commune	Approximate Cases Per Year
Château Lafite-Rothschild	Pauillac	20,000
Château Latour	Pauillac	25,000
Château Margaux	Margaux	15,000
Château Mouton-Rothschild	Pauillac	19,000
Château Haut Brion	Pessac, (Graves)	12,000

SECOND GROWTHS — DEUXIÈMES CRUS

Château Rausan-Ségla	Margaux	7,000
Château Rauzan Gassies	Margaux	11,000
Château Léoville-Las-Cases	St. Julien	25,000
Château Léoville-Poyferré	St. Julien	10,000
Château Léoville-Barton	St. Julien	10,000
Château Durfort-Vivens	Margaux	6,000
Château Gruaud-Larose	St. Julien	25,000
Château Lascombes	Margaux	18,000
Château Brane-Cantenac	Cantenac-Margaux	20,000
Château Pichon-Longueville (Baron)	Pauillac	9,000
Château Pichon-Longueville-Lalande	Pauillac	15,000
Château Ducru-Beaucaillou	St. Julien	15,000
Château Cos d'Estournel	St. Estèphe	20,000
Château Montrose	St. Estèphe	14,000

THIRD GROWTHS — *TROISIÈMES CRUS*

Vineyard	Commune	Approximate Cases Per Year
Château Kirwan (−)	Cantenac-Margaux	8,000
Château d'Issan (−)	Cantenac-Margaux	5,000
Château Lagrange (−)	St. Julien	20,000
Château Langoa-Barton	St. Julien	6,000
Château Giscours	Labarde	27,000
Château Malescot-St. Exupéry (−)	Margaux	6,000
Château Cantenac-Brown	Cantenac-Margaux	9,000
Château Boyd-Cantenac	Margaux	5,000
Château Palmer (+)	Cantenac-Margaux	10,000
Château La Lagune (+)	Ludon	25,000
Château Calon-Ségur (+)	St. Estèphe	20,000
Château Ferrière (×)	Margaux	1,500
Château Marquis d'Alesme-Becker (−)	Margaux	3,000

FOURTH GROWTHS — *QUATRIÈMES CRUS*

Vineyard	Commune	Approximate Cases Per Year
Château St. Pierre-Sevaistre / Château St. Pierre-Bontemps	St. Julien / St. Julien	7,500
Château Talbot (+)	St. Julien	30,000
Château Brainaire-Ducru	St. Julien	14,000
Château Duhart-Milon-Rothschild	Pauillac	7,000
Château Pouget (−)	Cantenac-Margaux	2,000
Château La Tour-Carnet	St. Laurent	8,000
Château Lafon-Rochet (−)	St. Estèphe	10,000
Château Beychevelle (+ +)	St. Julien	15,000
Château Le Prieuré (now called Prieuré-Lichine)	Cantenac-Margaux	7,500
Château Marquis de Terme	Margaux	15,000

FIFTH GROWTHS — *CINQUIÈMES CRUS*

Vineyard	Commune	Approximate Cases Per Year
Château Pontet-Canet (+)	Pauillac	40,000
Château Batailley	Pauillac	20,000
Château Haut-Batailley	Pauillac	7,000
Château Grand-Puy-Lacoste	Pauillac	11,000
Château Grand-Puy-Ducasse	Pauillac	8,000
Château Lynch-Bages (+)	Pauillac	15,000
Château Lynch-Moussas (−)	Pauillac	2,000
Château Dauzac (−)	Labarde	10,000
Château Mouton-Baronne-Philippe (+) (called Château Mouton d'Armailhacq until 1956)	Pauillac	15,000
Château du Tertre (−)	Arsac	10,000
Château Haut-Bages-Libéral (−)	Pauillac	4,000
Château Pédesclaux (−)	Pauillac	7,000
Château Belgrave	St. Laurent	12,000
Château Camensac	St. Laurent	3,500
Château Cos Labory	St. Estèphe	4,000
Château Clerc-Milon (−)	Pauillac	5,000
Château Croizet Bages (−)	Pauillac	6,000
Château Cantemerle (+)	Macau	7,500

427

CRUS BOURGEOIS OF THE MÉDOC

Not classified in 1855 these growths have been unofficially classified at various times. There was a classification in 1932 under the authority of the Chamber of Commerce of Bordeaux and the Chamber of Agriculture of the Gironde. In 1962 a Syndicate of Crus Bourgeois was formed and in 1966 a new list including *only* their own members was published. This list was revised December 29, 1977 as follows:

Note — Several crus are generally considered to be among the Crus Exceptionnel but since they do not belong to the Syndicate are not on its list. They are included below and marked with an asterisk (*).

GRANDS CRUS BOURGEOIS EXCEPTIONNEL

Château Agassac	Ludon
*Château Angludet	Cantenac
Château Andron Blanquet	Saint-Estèphe
Château Beausite	Saint-Estèphe
Château Capbern	Saint-Estèphe
Château Caronne Sainte-Gemme	Saint-Laurent
Château Chasse-Spleen	Moulis
Château Cissac	Cissac
Château Citran	Avensan
Château Le Crock	Saint-Estèphe
Château Dutruch-Grand-Poujeau	Moulis
Château Fourcas Dupré	Listrac
Château Fourcas Hosten	Listrac
Château Du Glana	Saint-Julien
*Château Gloria	Saint-Julien
Château Haut-Marbuzet	Saint-Estèphe
*Château Lanessan	Cussac
Château Marbuzet	Saint-Estèphe
Château Meyney	Saint-Estèphe
Château Phélan-Segur	Saint-Estèphe
Château Poujeaux-Theil	Moulis

GRANDS CRUS BOURGEOIS

Château Beaumont	Cussac
Château Bel-Orme	Saint-Seurin-de-Cadourne
Château Brillette	Moulis
Château La Cardonne	Blaignan
Château Colombier Moupelou	Pauillac
Château Coufran	Saint-Seurin-de-Cadourne
Château Coutelin-Merville	Saint-Estèphe
Château Duplessis-Hauchecorne	Moulis
Château Fontesteau	Saint-Sauveur
Château La Fleur Milon	Pauillac
Château Greysac	Bégadan
Château Hanteillan	Cissac
Château Lafon	Listrac
Château Lamarque	Lamarque
Château Lamothe	Cissac
Château Laujac	Bégadan
Château Liversan	Saint-Sauveur
Château Loudenne	Saint-Yzans

Château MacCarthy	Saint-Estèphe
Château Malleret	Le Pian
Château Morin	Saint-Estèphe
Château Moulin à Vent	Moulis
Château Le Meynieu	Vertheuil
Château Martinens	Margaux
Château Les Ormes Sorbet	Couquèques
Château Les Ormes de Pez	Saint-Estèphe
Château Patache d'Aux	Bégadan
Château Paveil de Luze	Soussans
Château Peyrabon	Saint-Sauveur
Château Pontoise Cabarus	Saint-Seurin-de-Cadourne
Château Potensac	Potensac
Château La Rose Trintaudon	Saint-Laurent
Château Reysson	Vertheuil
Château Ségur	Parempuyre
Château Sigognac	Saint-Yzans
Château Sociando Mallet	Saint-Seurin-de-Cadourne
Château Du Taillan	Le Taillan
Château La Tour de By	Bégadan
Château La Tour du Haut-Moulin	Cussac
Château Tronquoy Lalande	Saint-Estèphe
Château Verdignan	Saint-Seurin-de-Cadourne

BOURGEOIS

Château Aney	Cussac
Château Balac	Saint-Laurent-de-Médoc
Château Bellerive	Civrac
Château Belle Rose	Pauillac
Château la Bécade	Listrac
Château Bonneau	Saint-Seurin-de-Cadourne
Château le Bosq	Saint-Christoly
Château le Breuil	Cissac
Château la Bridane	Saint-Julien
Château de By	Bégadan
Château Castéra	Cissac
Château Chambert	Saint-Estèphe
Château Cap Léon Veyrin	Listrac
Château Carcannieux	Queyrac
Château Clare	Bégadan
Château la Closerie	Moulis
Château Duplessis-Fabre	Moulis
Château Fonréaud	Listrac
Château Fonpiqueyre	Saint-Sauveur
Château Fort de Vauban	Cussac
Château la France	Blaignan
Château Gallais Bellevue	Potensac
Château Grand Duroc Milon	Pauillac
Château Grand-Moulin	Saint-Seurin-de-Cadourne
Château Haut-Bages Monpelou	Pauillac
Château Haut-Canteloup	Couquèques
Château Haut-Garin	Bégadan
Château Haut-Padarnac	Pauillac

Château Houbanon	Prignac
Château Hourtin-Ducasse	Saint-Sauveur
Château de Labat	Saint-Laurent
Château Lamothe Bergeron	Cussac
Château Landon	Bégadan
Château Lassalle	Potensac
Château Lartigue de Brochon	Saint-Seurin-de-Cadourne
Château le Landat	Cissac
Château Lestage	Listrac
Château Mac Carthy Moula	Saint-Estèphe
Château Monthil	Bégadan
Château Moulin Rouge	Cussac
Château Panigon	Civrac
Château Pibran	Pauillac
Château Plantey de la Croix	Saint-Seurin-de-Cadourne
Château Pontet	Blaignan
Château Ramage la Batisse	Saint-Sauveur
Château la Roque de By	Bégadan
Château Saint-Bonnet	Saint-Christoly
Domaine de la Rose Maréchale	Saint-Seurin-de-Cadourne
Château Saransot	Listrac
Château Soudars	Avensan
Château Tayac	Soussans
Château la Tour Blanche	Saint-Christoly
Château la Tour du Mirail	Cissac
Château la Tour Haut-Caussan	Blaignan
Château la Tour Saint-Bonnet	Saint-Christoly
Château la Tour Saint-Joseph	Cissac
Domaine des Tourelles	Blaignan
Château Vieux Robin	Bégadan

SAUTERNES AND BARSAC

GREAT FIRST GROWTH — GRAND PREMIER CRU

		Approximate Cases Per Year
Château d'Yquem	Sauternes	7,000

FIRST GROWTHS — PREMIERS CRUS

Château La Tour Blanche	Bommes	5,000
Château Lafaurie-Peyraguey	Bommes	2,500
Clos Haut-Peyraguey	Bommes	2,500
Château de Rayne-Vigneau	Bommes	8,750
Château Suduiraut	Preignac	10,000
Château Coutet	Barsac	8,250
Château Climens	Barsac	8,250
Château Guiraud	Sauternes	10,000
Château Rieussec	Fargues	8,500
Château Rabaud-Promis	Bommes	10,000
Château Sigalas-Rabaud	Bommes	4,000

		Approximate Cases Per Year
Château Myrat	Barsac	5,000
Château Doisy-Daëne	Barsac	3,000
Château Doisy-Védrines	Barsac	5,000
Château D'Arche	Sauternes	5,000
Château Filhot	Sauternes	6,000
Château Broustet	Barsac	4,000
Château Nairac	Barsac	3,000
Château Caillou	Barsac	9,000
Château Suau	Barsac	1,500
Château de Malle	Preignac	5,000
Château Romer	Fargues	1,500
Château Lamothe	Sauternes	2,500

ST. ÉMILION

OFFICIAL CLASSIFICATION OF 1955

Since the wines of St. Émilion were not classified in 1855, it was decided exactly one hundred years later, in 1955, to establish a classification comparable to that of the Médoc, and a commission appointed by the *Institut National des Appellations d'Origine* carried out this difficult and thankless task.

It should be noted that Château Ausone and Château Cheval-Blanc are generally considered in a category apart, although they share the designation "First Great Growth" with ten other vineyards. Listing is alphabetic within each class.

As in the Médoc, there exist many minor châteaux producing wines of excellent quality which are not included in this official classification.

FIRST GREAT GROWTHS — PREMIERS GRANDS CRUS CLASSÉS

	Approximate Cases Per Year
Château Ausone	2,500
Château Cheval-Blanc	13,000
Château Beauséjour-Duffau	2,500
Château Beauséjour-Fagouet	4,000
Château Belair	4,000
Château Canon	8,000
Château Figeac	15,000
Château La Gaffelière	9,000
Château Magdelaine	4,000
Château Pavie	12,000
Château Trottevieille	5,000
Clos Fourtet	6,000

GREAT GROWTHS — GRANDS CRUS CLASSÉS

Château L'Arrosée	5,000
Château L'Angélus	13,000

	Approximate Cases Per Year
Château Baleau	8,000
Château Balestard-la-Tonnelle	6,000
Château Bellevue	3,000
Château Bergat	1,500
Château Cadet-Bon	2,500
Château Cadet-Piolat	2,000
Château Canon-la-Gaffelière	10,000
Château Cap-de-Mourlin	7,500
Château Chapelle-Madeleine	3,000
Château Chauvin	6,000
Château Corbin	10,000
Château Corbin-Michotte	5,000
Château Coutet	5,000
Château Croque-Michotte	6,000
Château Curé-Bon	2,500
Château Dassault	10,000
Château Faurie-de-Souchard	8,000
Château Fonplégade	5,000
Château Fonroque	8,000
Château Franc-Mayne	3,000
Château Grand-Barrail-Lamarzelle-Figeac	12,000
Château Grand-Corbin	5,000
Château Grand-Corbin-Despagne	10,000
Château Grand-Mayne	6,000
Château Grand-Pontet	5,000
Château Grandes-Murailles	1,000
Château Guadet-Saint-Julien	1,600
Château Haut-Corbin	2,000
Château Haut-Sarpe	10,000
Château Jean-Faure	8,000
Château La Carte et Le Chatalet	3,500
Château La Clotte	1,600
Château La Cluzière	1,500
Château La Couspaude	3,000
Château La Dominique	5,000
Château La Marzelle	2,500
Château Laniote	3,000
Château Larcis-Ducasse	4,000
Château Larmande	4,500
Château Laroze	10,000
Château La Serre	3,500
Château La Tour-du-Pin-Figeac	5,000
Château La Tour-du-Pin-Figeac-Moueix	5,000
Château La Tour-Figeac	10,000
Château Le Chatelet	3,500
Château Le Couvent	500
Château Le Prieuré	1,600
Château Matras	3,500
Château Mauvezin	2,000
Château Moulin-du-Cadet	2,000

	Approximate Cases Per Year
Château Pavie-Decesse	4,000
Château Pavie-Macquin	6,000
Château Pavillon du Cadet	2,500
Château Petit-Faurie-de-Soutard	5,500
Château Ripeau	5,000
Château Saint-Georges-Côte-Pavie	2,500
Château Sansonnet	3,500
Château Soutard	6,000
Château Tertre-Daugay	3,000
Château Trimoulet	6,000
Château Trois-Moulins	1,500
Château Troplong-Mondot	12,500
Château Villemaurine	7,000
Château Yon-Figeac	10,000
Clos des Jacobins	4,000
Clos La Madeleine	1,000
Clos de l'Oratoire	2,500
Clos Saint-Martin	2,000
Couvent des Jacobins	3,500

GRAVES

The châteaux of the Graves District (neglected except for Château Haut-Brion in the classification of 1855) were officially rated by the Institut National des Appellations d'Origine in 1953, although rather superficially and incompletely and this classification was revised, although still inadequately, in 1959. A number of additional vineyards producing red wines or white or both certainly deserve a place in this list and some distinctions should certainly be drawn between the various qualities of wines which they produce. Here, nevertheless, is the official classification as it exists today. Listing is alphabetic by commune and by the Château.

CLASSIFIED RED WINES — CRUS CLASSÉS (ROUGES)

		Approximate Cases Per Year
Château Bouscaut	Cadaujac	10,000
Château Haut-Bailly	Léognan	5,000
Château Carbonnieux	Léognan	7,500
Domaine de Chevalier	Léognan	3,000
Château Fieuzal	Léognan	3,000
Château Olivier	Léognan	2,000
Château Malartic-Lagravière	Léognan	5,000
Château Latour-Martillac	Martillac	4,000
Château Smith-Haut-Lafitte	Martillac	15,000
Château Haut Brion	Pessac	12,000
Château Pape-Clement	Pessac	5,000
Château La Mission-Haut-Brion	Talence	8,000
Château Latour-Haut-Brion	Talence	1,200

CLASSIFIED WHITE WINES — CRUS CLASSÉS (BLANCS)

		Approximate Cases Per Year
Château Bouscaut	Cadaujac	2,000
Château Carbonnieux	Léognan	8,000
Domaine de Chevalier	Léognan	1,500
Château Malartic-Lagravière	Léognan	1,000
Château Olivier	Léognan	10,000
Château Latour-Martillac	Martillac	1,500
Château Haut-Brion*	Pessac	1,500
Château Laville-Haut-Brion	Talence	2,000
Château Couhins	Villenave-d'Ornon	3,000

*Not classified (by request of the owner).

POMEROL

For Pomerol, directly adjoining St. Émilion, and the smallest of the great Bordeaux wine districts, no official classification of vineyards has been made. There have been a number of unofficial ones published, most of them ridiculously long for such a tiny district of small properties. An officious short list follows:

FIRST GREAT GROWTH — PREMIER GRAND CRU CLASSÉ

	Approximate Cases Per Year
Château Pétrus	5,000

GREAT GROWTHS — GRANDS CRUS CLASSÉS

Vieux Château Certan	5,500
Château La Conseillante	3,500
Château Petit-Village	4,500
Château L'Evangile	4,500
Château Trotanoy	2,500

CLASSIFIED GROWTHS — CRUS CLASSÉS

Château Lafleur	1,600
Château La Fleur-Pétrus	3,000
Château Gazin	9,000
Château Nenin	10,000
Château Beauregard	6,500
Château La Pointe	7,000

434

BURGUNDY

The vineyards of Burgundy have never been, and cannot be, classified with anything like the precision and finality of the Bordeaux châteaux, where every major vineyard has a single owner and a single name. (*See* Burgundy, Domaine, Estate-Bottling). In Chablis and on the Côte d'Or, most of the named vineyards are divided among numerous different growers: some sixty producers, for example, own vines in the Clos de Vougeot which, therefore, in any given year, is not one wine but sixty different wines.

It is, nevertheless, a mistake to imagine that the Côte d'Or vineyards have never been classified at all. An extremely careful survey and classification, no less official and no less thorough than the famous one of 1855 in Bordeaux, was published in 1861 by the *Comité d'Agriculture de l'Arrondissement de Beaune*. This eventually served as the basis of the Appellation Contrôlée regulations and, as a result, only the wines from certain specific *climats* or vineyards may legally be called Grands Crus, Premiers Crus, etc. From an overall standpoint, this old classification does have one major fault, since the Premiers Crus (or Premières Cuvées) of certain *communes*, such as Gevrey Chambertin and Vosne Romanée, are markedly superior to many Grands Crus (or Têtes de Cuvée) of lesser townships.

An attempt has been made to correct these injustices in the list which follows. Though by no means complete (there are 419 officially recognized *climats*, or vineyard names, on the Côte de Nuits, and over twice that many on the Côte de Beaune), it certainly includes almost all of those that one is likely to find on wine labels. The comparative ratings, while not official, are more or less those accepted by a majority of experts, although there will always be some differences of opinion.

WINES OF THE CÔTE D'OR

A. RED WINES

CÔTE DE NUITS Commune	Leading Vineyards	Acres
Fixin 316 acres	CLOS DE LA PERRIÈRE	11.8
	Clos du Chapitre	11.8
	Aux Cheusots (Clos Napoléon)	4.5
	Les Meix Bas	1.2
	Les Arvelets	8.2
	Les Hervelets	9.3
Gevrey-Chambertin 1,063 acres	CHAMBERTIN	34.2
	CLOS DE BÈZE	35.0
	LATRICIÉRES-CHAMBERTIN	17.1
	MAZIS-CHAMBERTIN	31.1
	CHARMES-CHAMBERTIN	31.0
	MAZOYÈRES-CHAMBERTIN	47.0
	GRIOTTE-CHAMBERTIN	13.5
	RUCHOTTES-CHAMBERTIN	7.8
	CHAPELLE-CHAMBERTIN	13.3
	CLOS SAINT JACQUES	17.3
	LES VAROILLES	14.8
	Combe aux Moines	5.4
	Cazetiers	20.0
	Etournelles	4.8
	Clos Prieur	5.6
	Lavaux	23.6

Commune	Leading Vineyards	Acres
Morey-Saint-Denis 256 acres	BONNES MARES	4.6
	(see below, Chambolle)	
	CLOS DE TART	17.8
	CLOS DE LA ROCHE	37.9
	Clos Saint-Denis	16.2
	Clos des Lambrays	21.5
	Meix Rentiers	2.9
	Clos Bussière	7.4
Chambolle-Musigny 427 acres	MUSIGNY	26.3
	BONNES MARES	33.9
	LES AMOUREUSES	13.2
	Les Charmes	23.0
	Les Baudes	8.8
	Combe d'Orveau	10.9
	Les Cras	10.4
	Derrière-la-Grange	1.8
	Les Combottes	7.2
	Les Sentiers	12.2
Vougeot 156 acres	CLOS DE VOUGEOT	124.1
	Vougeot	11.4
Flagey-Échézeaux 179 acres	GRANDS ÉCHÉZEAUX	22.6
	Les Échézeaux	74.3
Vosne-Romanée 414 acres	ROMANÉE-CONTI	4.5
	LA TÂCHE	14.9
	ROMANÉE SAINT-VIVANT	23.6
	RICHEBOURG	19.8
	LA GRANDE RUE	3.3
	LA ROMANÉE	2.1
	LES GAUDICHOTS	2.9
	AUX MALCONSORTS	14.7
	LES SUCHOTS	30.0
	LES BEAUX-MONTS	6.0
	Aux Brulées	9.6
	Aux Petits Monts	9.2
	Aux Reignots	4.2
	Clos des Réas	5.3
Nuits Saint-Georges 928 acres	LES SAINT-GEORGES	18.6
(including Prémeaux)	LES CAILLES	9.4
	CLOS DES CORVÉES	19.4
	LES VAUCRAINS	15.0
	LES PRULIERS	17.5
	LES PORRETS	17.5
	AUX THOREY	15.3
	AUX BOUDOTS	15.8
	AUX CRAS	7.7
	AUX MURGERS	12.4
	LA RICHEMONE	5.5
	Les Didiers	7.0
	La Perrière	7.6

Commune	Leading Vineyards	Acres
	Aux Perdrix	8.3
	Clos des Argilières	12.1
	Clos des Fôrets	12.4
	Clos Arlot	19.1
	Clos de la Maréchale	24.2
	Le Clos Saint-Marc	7.4
CÔTE DE BEAUNE		
Aloxe-Corton 494 acres (Approx.)	CORTON BRESSANDES	42.2
(including Ladoix and part of	CORTON CLOS DU ROI	26.0
Pernand-Vergelesses)	LE CORTON	27.9
	CORTON RENARDES	37.2
	CORTON PERRIÈRES	26.9
	CORTON LES MARÉCHAUDES	16.5
	Corton Chaumes	5.6
	Corton Languettes	18.2
	Corton La Vigne-au-Saint	5.7
	Corton Les Meix	4.9
	Corton Les Pougets	24.6
	Corton Les Grèves	4.5
	Corton Les Fiètres	3.3
	Corton en Pauland	6.6
	Les Chaillots	8.5
	Les Fournieres	15.7
	Les Valozières	15.7
Pernand-Vergelesses 354 acres	*Ile des Vergelesses*	23.0
	Les Basses Vergelesses	44.0
Savigny Les Beaune 935 acres	Vergelesses	42.0
	Lavières	45.7
	Marconnets	23.4
	Jarrons	22.7
	Dominode	—
Beaune 1,330 acres	GRÈVES	78.5
	FÈVES	10.6
	Bressandes	45.8
	Les Cent-Vignes	57.6
	Aux Cras	12.5
	Champimonts	41.0
	Marconnets	25.2
	Clos de la Mousse	8.4
	Clos des Mouches	61.4
	Les Avaux	33.1
	Aigrots	19.9
	Clos du Roi	34.3
	Les Toussaints	16.1
	Les Teurons	18.6
	Les Sizies	20.4
	En l'Orme	5.1
	A l'Écu	7.7
	Pertuisots	13.7

437

Commune	Leading Vineyards	Acres
Pommard 839 acres	RUGIENS	14.5
	ÉPENOTS	25.6
	Clos Blanc	10.6
	Pézerolles	16.0
	Rugiens-Hauts	18.8
	Petits-Epenots	50.1
	Chaponières	8.2
	Chanlins-Bas	17.7
	Boucherottes	4.1
	Platière	14.3
	Sausilles	9.4
	Jarollières	7.9
	Chanière	24.7
	Charmots	14.2
	Argillières	9.0
	Fremiers	12.9
	Bertins	9.1
	Poutures	10.9
	Arvelets	20.9
	Croix-Noires	3.1
	Clos de la Commaraine	9.8
	Clos Micot	6.7
	La Refene	6.1
	Clos de Verger	6.2
	Combes-Dessus	6.9
Volnay 530 acres	CLOS DES DUCS	6.0
	CAILLERETS	35.7
	CHAMPANS	28.0
	Fremiets	16.1
	Chevret	15.0
	Santenots	19.8
	Les Angles	8.6
	Carelle-sous-la-Chapelle	9.3
	Bousse d'Or	4.9
	Verseuil	2.0
	Clos des Chênes	40.2
	Les Mitans	9.9
	En l'Ormeau	10.7
	Pointes-d'Angles	3.1
	En Ronceret	5.0
	La Barre	3.2
Auxey 371 acres	Duresses	25.4
Monthélie 231 acres	Les Champs Fulliot	19.9
Puligny-Montrachet (*see* white wines)	CLAVOILLON	13.7
	LE CAILLERET	13.4
	Levrons	1.5
	Charmes	8.6
Chassagne-Montrachet 881 acres	*La Boudriotte*	44.3
	Clos St. Jean	35.5

438

Commune	Leading Vineyards	Acres
	La Maltroie	22.8
	Morgeot	—
	Abbaye de Morgeot	—
Santenay 940 acres	*Gravières*	72.6
	La Comme	80.1
	Clos Tavannes	—

B. WHITE WINES

Commune	Leading Vineyards	Acres
Chambolle Musigny (*See* red wines)	*Musigny Blanc*	—
Vougeot (*See* red wines)	*Clos Blanc de Vougeot*	4.6
Nuits Saint-Georges (*See* red wines)	Perrière	41.7
Aloxe-Corton (*See* red wines) (including Pernand, Ladoix)	CORTON-CHARLEMAGNE *Le Corton* *Corton Languettes* *Corton Pougets*	
Beaune (*See* red wines)	*Clos des Mouches*	
Auxey (*See* red wines)		
Meursault 1,030 acres	PERRIÈRES	42.1
	GENEVRIÈRES	41.7
	Charmes	68.4
	Poruzots	25.0
	La Pièce-sous-le-Bois	27.8
	Blagny	5.4
	Dos d'Ane	7.1
	Jennelotte	11.9
	Goutte d'Or	13.8
	Bouchères	10.5
Puligny-Montrachet 578 acres	MONTRACHET (part)	18.5
	CHEVALIER MONTRACHET	17.7
	BÂTARD MONTRACHET	29.2
	BIENVENUE-BÂTARD-MONTRACHET	5.7
	COMBETTES	16.6
	HAMEAU DE BLAGNY	10.8
	CHALUMEAUX	17.3
	FOLATIÈRES	8.5
	Pucelles	16.8
	Champ-Canet	11.4
	La Garenne	2.2
	Les Referts	32.6
	Sous-le-Puits	9.5

439

Commune	Leading Vineyards	Acres
Chassagne-Montrachet	MONTRACHET (part)	
(*See* red wines)	BÂTARD-MONTRACHET (part)	
	CRIOTS-BÂTARD-	
	MONTRACHET	4.0
	GRANDES-RUCHOTTES	7.5
	CAILLERET	15.0
	Abbaye de Morgeot	9.8
Santenay (*See* red wines)		

CHABLIS

The vineyards of Chablis, covering some 2,950 acres, have been legally defined and delimited since 1938, and their wines divided into the following categories:

1. CHABLIS GRAND CRU. Only seven small vineyards, 215 acres in all, are entitled to this, the highest ranking appellation; all seven are on the right bank of the Serein River, facing south and southwest, and six of the seven (all except Blanchots, which is in Fyé) are in the *commune* of Chablis proper. All produce wines of the highest class, but an expert might perhaps be disposed to list them in this order: *Vaudésir, Les Clos, Grenouilles, Valmur, Blanchots, Preuses* and *Bougros*. Their wines must be of at least 11% alcohol by volume, and their production may not exceed an average of 374 gallons per acre. Only the Chardonnay grape may be grown.

2. CHABLIS PREMIER CRU. Wines coming from certain other specific vineyards (862 acres in all), and usually carrying the vineyard name, and/or the important words *Premier Cru*. Until quite recently there were twenty-one such legally delimited vineyards each with its own name. They have now been grouped into eleven larger units, although the old names (marked with an asterisk * in the following list) may still be used by growers who wish to do so. Thus a Chablis Vaulorent Premier Cru may now be sold either as a Chablis Fourchaume Premier Cru or under its own name. Production is limited to an average of 427 gallons per acre, minimum alcohol 10½%.

Vineyard	Commune	Bank of Serein
The Premier Cru Vineyards and their subdivisions:		
Monts de Milieu	Fyé and Fleys	Right
Montée de Tonnerre	Fyé and Fleys	Right
*Pied d'Aloup		
*Chapelot		Right
Fourchaume	La Chapelle-Vaupelteigne,	Right
	Fontenay, Maligny and Poinchy	
*Vaulorent		
*Côte de Fontenay		
*Vaupulent		
*L'Homme Mort		
Vaucoupin	Chichée	Right

440

Vineyard	Commune	Bank of Serein
Vaillons	Chablis	Left
*Beugnons		
*Châtains		
*Séché		
*Les Lys		
Montmains	Chablis	Left
*Les Forêts		
*Butteaux		
Côte de Lechet	Milly	Left
Beauroy	Poinchy and Beines	Left
*Troesmes		
Vosgros	Chichée	Left
*Vaugiraut		
The lesser Premier Cru Vineyards:		
Les Fourneaux	Fleys	Right
*Morein		
*Côtes des Prés Girots		
Melinots	Chablis	Left
*Roncières		
*Les Eponottes		

3. CHABLIS. Wines produced on certain delimited areas of chalky soil, 1,601 acres, from the Chardonnay grape, in twenty specific *communes*. Minimum alcohol, 10%; maximum average yield, 427 gallons per acre. The *communes* are: Chablis, Beines, Béru, Chemilly-sur-Serein, Chichée, Courgis, Fleys, Fontenay, Fyé, La Chapelle-Vaupelteigne, Ligny-le-Châtel, Lignorelles, Maligny, Milly, Poilly, Poinchy, Prehy, Rameau, Villy and Viviers.

4. PETIT CHABLIS. Lesser wines from the same area (272 acres), also made from the Chardonnay grape. Minimum alcohol, 9½%; maximum average yield, 427 gallons per acre.

BEAUJOLAIS

There are nine officially-ranked *crus*, or growths, which produce the best wine of the Beaujolais. Listed alphabetically, they are: Brouilly, Chénas, Chiroubles, Côte-de-Brouilly, Fleurie, Julienas, Morgon, Moulin-à-Vent, St. Amour.

Wines from the following 39 communes may legally be labelled "Beaujolais-Villages": Arbuissonnas, *Beaujeu*, Blacé, *Cercié, Chânes, La Chapelle-de-Guinchay, Charentay, Chénas, Chiroubles, Durette, Émeringes, Fleurie, Juillé, Juliénas, Lancié*, Lantigné, *Leynes*, Montmélas, *Odénas*, Le Perréon, Pruzilly, *Quincié, Regnié*, Rivolet, *Romanèche-Thorins, St. Amour-Bellevue, St. Étienne-des-Oullières, St. Étienne-La-Varenne*, St. Julien, *St. Lager*, St. Symphorien-d'Ancelles, *St. Vérand*, Salles, Vaux, *Villié-Morgon*, Denicé, les Ardillats, Marchampt and Vauxrenard. The better are those printed in *italics*.

Maximum legal production of Beaujolais, Beaujolais Supérieur or Beaujolais Villages, 524 gallons per acre, of Beaujolais from one of the nine *crus*, 427 gallons per acre.

Total production in 1972-76 averaged twenty three million gallons, divided as follows:

Appelation	Acres	U.S. Gallons
Beaujolais	27,500	9,670,000
Beaujolais Supérieur		523,000
Beaujolais Villages	4,200	6,865,000
Brouilly	1,975	1,227,000
Chénas	450	271,000
Chiroubles	625	346,000
Côte-de-Brouilly	500	322,000
Fleurie	1,725	789,000
Juliénas	1,300	663,000
Morgon	1,350	1,121,000
Moulin-à-Vent	1,725	798,000
St. Amour	550	341,000
TOTAL	41,900	22,936,000

VINS DÉLIMITÉS DE QUALITÉ SUPÉRIEURE

V.D.Q.S. Wines listed by District and Type
R = Red   W = White   Ro = Rosé   S = Sparkling

	Types	Department
LANGUEDOC-ROUSILLON		
Cabardès	R Ro	Aude
Cabrières	Ro	Hérault
Corbières	R W Ro	Aude
Corbières Supérieures	R W Ro	Aude
Costières du Gard	R W Ro	Gard, Hérault
Coteaux du Languedoc (alone or with additional names)	R Ro	Aude, Gard, Hérault
Coteaux de la Méjanelle	R W Ro	Hérault
Coteaux de Saint-Christol	R Ro	Hérault
Coteaux de Vérargues	R Ro	Hérault
Côtes du Cabardès et de l'Orbiel	R Ro	Aude
Côtes de la Malepère	R Ro	Aude
Côtes du Roussillon	R W Ro	Pyrénées-Orientales
Côtes du Roussillon Caramany	R W Ro	Pyrénées-Orientales
Côtes du Roussillon Latour de France	R W Ro	Pyrénées-Orientales
Côtes du Roussillon-Villages	R W Ro	Pyrénées-Orientales
Faugères	R W	Hérault
La Clape	R W Ro	Aude
Minervois	R W Ro	Hérault
Montpeyroux	R Ro	Hérault
Picpoul-de-Pinet	W	Hérault
Pic-Saint-Loup	R W Ro	Hérault
Quatourze	R W Ro	Aude
Saint-Chinian	R Ro	Hérault
Saint-Drezéry	R Ro	Hérault
Saint-Georges d'Orques	R Ro	Hérault
Saint-Saturnin	R Ro	Hérault
Vin Noble du Minervois	R W Ro	Hérault

442

	Types	Department
RHÔNE and AIN		
Coteaux d'Aix-en-Provence	R W Ro	Bouches-du-Rhône, Var
Coteaux des Baux-de-Provence	R W Ro	Var
Coteaux de Pierrevert	R W Ro	Basses-Alpes
Cotes du Lubéron	R W Ro	Vaucluse
Cotes du Vivarais	R W Ro	Ardèche, Gard
Haut-Comtat	R Ro	Drôme
Rousette de Bugey	W S	Ain
Vin du Bugey (alone or with other names)	R W Ro S	Ain
Vin du Lyonnais	R W Ro	Rhone
LOIRE VALLEY		
Chateaumeillant	R Ro	Cher, Indre
Cheverny	R W Ro S	Loir et Cher
Coteaux d'Ancenis plus one of grape varieties:	R W Ro	Loire-Atlantique,
Pineau de la Loire		Maine et Loire
Chenin Blanc		
Malvoisie		
Pinot-Beurot		
Gamay		
Cabernet		
Coteaux du Vendômois	W	Loir et Cher
Côtes de Gien or Vins de Coteaux du Giennois	R W Ro	Loiret, Nièvre
Gros Plant or Gros Plant du Pays Nantais	W	Loire-Atlantique,
		Maine-et-Loire, Vendée
Valençay	R W Ro	Indre, Loir-et-Cher
Vins de Saint-Pourçain-sur-Sioule	R W Ro	Allier
LOIRE-LYONNAIS-CENTRE		
Côte-Roannaise	R Ro	Loire
Côtes d'Auvergne	R W Ro	Puy-de-Dôme
Côtes du Forez	R Ro	Loire
Vins du Haut-Poitou	R W Ro	Vienne, Deux-Sèvres
Vins de l'Orléanais	R W Ro	Loiret
Vins du Thouarsais	R W Ro	Deux-Sèvres
CHABLIS AREA		
Sauvignon de Saint-Bris	W	Yonne
LORRAINE		
Moselle	R W	Moselle
Côtes de Toul	R W Ro	Meurthe-et-Moselle
SOUTHWEST		
Cotes du Marmandais	R W	Lot-et-Garonne
Tursan	R W Ro	Landes, Gers
Vins d'Entraygues et du Fel	R W Ro	Aveyron, Cantal
Vins d'Estang	R W Ro	Aveyron
Vins de Lavilledieu	R W	Tarn-et-Garonne; Haute
		Garonne
Vins de Marcillac	R Ro	Aveyron

443

APPENDIX 5

GERMAN WINES

The geographic source is always identified on wine labels and can be specific down to an individual vineyard.

Mandatory Information

TAFELWEIN (Table Wine)
> Blends from
> Several Regions — Deutscher
> or Specific Regions — Rhein und Mosel, Main, Neckar, Oberrhein
> or Sub-Region — Rhein, Mosel, Römetor, Burgengau

QUALITÄTSWEIN (Quality Wine) — all grades
> Region — Ahr, Baden, Franken, Hessische-Bergstrasse, Mittelrhein, Mosel-Saar-Ruwer, Nahe, Rheingau, Rheinhessen, Rheinpfalz, Württemberg
> Liebfraumilch (or Liebfrauenmilch) is the one exception since by definition it must come from Nahe, Rheingau, Rheinhessen or Rheinpfalz and may be a blend from these Regions.

Optional Additional Information

> Bereich — District or Part Area within a Region; when a Bereich is mentioned a Grosslage or Einzellage may not appear.
> Gemeinde or Ortsteil — These are parishes, suburbs or sections (political and geographic communities) which are used alone or in conjunction with a Grosslage or Einzellage.
> Grosslage — General site, a group of vineyards covering various geographic communities; when used an Einzellage can not be mentioned.
> Einzellage — Individual site or vineyard usually within one political community; this is the smallest and most precise geographic designation and when used the Grosslage can not be mentioned.

QUALITÄTSWEIN AREAS

Anbaugebiete (Regions)	Grapes Type	%	Be-reiche (Dis-tricts)	Gross-lagen (General Sites)	Einzel-lagen (Individ-ual Sites)	Acres 1976	Production All German Wines Average 1973-76 '000 U.S. Gal.	%
Ahr	SF	27	1	1	43	1,193	1,203	0.5
	P	26						
	R	22						
	M	19						
Baden	M	33	7	16	327	33,008	29,783	12.7
	B	22						
	Ru	14						
	G	11						
	R	7						
	S	5						

444

Anbaugebiete (Regions)	Grapes Type	%	Be- reiche (Dis- tricts)	Gross- lagen (General Sites)	Einzel- lagen (Individ- ual Sites)	Acres 1976	Production All German Wines Average 1973–76 '000 U.S. Gal.	%
Franken	M	45	4	16	134	8,347	6,989	3.0
	S	35						
Hessische-	R	53	2	3	16	595	816	0.4
Bergstrasse	M	20						
	S	12						
Mittelrhein	R	80	3	11	112	2,125	1,848	0.8
	M	12						
Mosel-Saar-	R	66	4	·19	525	29,200	35,564	15.2
Ruwer	M	19						
	E	10						
Nahe	M	31	2	7	323	10,729	10,861	4.6
	S	28						
	R	24						
Rheingau	R	76	1	10	122	7,225	6,766	2.9
	M	11						
	S	5						
Rheinhessen	M	36	3	24	430	50,305	57,229	24.5
	S	28						
	A	6						
	R	5						
	P	5						
Rheinpfalz	M	24	2	26	333	51,204	63,537	27.2
	S	23						
	R	14						
	P	12						
Württemberg	T	25	3	15	199	18,772	18,732	8.0
	R	23						
	M	10						
	S	9						
Misc.						235	325	0.1
TOTAL			32	148*	2,568*	213,238	233,653	100.0

Notes: *Subject to change as the 1971 law is implemented.
Gemeinde or Ortsteil — Community, parish or other geographic division — 1,400 of these

White Grapes.
A — Alzeyer Scheurebe
E — Elbling
G — Gutedel (Chasselas)
M — Müller-Thurgau
R — Riesling
Ru — Ruländer
S — Silvaner

Red Grapes:
B — Blue Spätburgunder (Pinot Noir)
P — Portugieser
SF — Blue Spätburgunder and Frühburgunder
T — Trollinger

LEADING WINES OF GERMANY

Gemeinde* (Community or Parish)	Grosslage (General Site)	Einzellage (Individual Site-Vineyard)
FRANKEN		
Iphofen	Burgweg (Iphofen)	
Escherndorf	Kirchberg (Volkach)	
Würzburg		Innere Leiste
		Stein
MOSEL-SAAR-RUWER		
MOSEL		
Bernkastel	Badstube	Bratenhöfchen
		Doctor or Doktor
		Graben
		Lay
		Matheisbildchen
	Kurfürstlay	
Brauneberg	Kurfürstlay	Juffer
Dhron	Michelsberg	Hofberger
		Roterd
Erden	Schwarzlay	Busslay
		Herrenberg
		Prälat
		Treppchen
Graach	Münzlay	Abtsberg
		Domprobst
		Himmelreich
		Josephshöfer
Klusserath	Sankt Michael	Bruderschaft
		Königsberg
Kröv	Nacktarsch	
Piesport	Michelsberg	Falkenberg
		Goldtröpfchen
		Günterslay
Traben-Trarbach	Schwarzlay	
Trittenheim	Michelsberg	Altärchen
		Apotheke
Ürzig	Schwarzlay	Würzgarten
Wehlen	Münzlay	Nonnenberg
		Sonnenuhr
Zell	Schwarze Katz	
Zeltingen	Münzlay	Himmelreich
		Schlossberg
		Sonnenuhr
SAAR		
Ayl	Scharzberg	Kupp

* Wines famous in their own right and usually labeled without village name are listed in this column.

446

Gemeinde * (Community or Parish)	Grosslage (General Site)	Einzellage (Individual Site-Vineyard)
Ockfen	Scharzberg	Bockstein Geisberg Herrenberg
Scharzhofberg *	Scharzberg	
Serrig	Scharzberg	Antoniusberg Kupp Vogelsang
Wiltingen	Scharzberg	Braune Kupp
RUWER Avelsbach	Romerlay	
Eitelsbach	Romerlay	Karthäuser Hofberg- Burgberg (or) Kronenbourg (or) Sang (or) Stirn
Kasel	Romerlay	Kehrnagel Nieschen
Maximin Grünhaus *	Romerlay	Abtsberg Bruderberg Herrenberg
Waldrach	Romerlay	Hubertusberg Jesuitengarten Laurentiusberg Meisenberg
NAHE Bad Kreutznach	Kronenbourg	
Langenlonsheim	Sonnenborn	
Niederhausen	Burgweg Rosengarten	
Schlossböckelheim	Burgweg	
RHEINGAU Eltville	Steinmacher	Sonnenberg Taubenberg
Erbach	Mehrhölzchen	Hohenrain Marcobrunn or Markobrunn
Geisenheim	Burgweg	Kilzberg Klaus Klauserweg Schlossgarten
Hallgarten	Mehrhölzchen	Hendelberg Jungfer Schönhell
Hattenheim	Deutelsberg	Engelmannsberg Hassel

* Wines famous in their own right and usually labeled without village name are listed in this column.

447

Gemeinde * (Community or Parish)	Grosslage (General Site)	Einzellage (Individual Site-Vineyard)
		Mannberg Nussbrunnen Wisselbrunnen
Johannisberg	Erntebringer	Goldatzel Hansenberg Hölle Klaus Mittelhölle Schwarzenstein Vogelsang
Kiedrich	Heilegenstock	Gräfenberg Sandgrub Wasseros
Oestrich	Gottesthal	Doosberg Lenchen
Rauenthal	Steinmacher	Baiken Gehrn Rothenberg Wülfen
Rüdesheim	Burgweg	Berg Roseneck Berg Rottland Berg Schlossberg Bischofsberg
Schloss Johannisberg*		
Schloss Vollrads*		
Steinberg*		
Winkel	Honigberg	Hasensprung Jesuitengarten
RHEINHESSEN Bingen	Sankt Rochuskapelle	Scharlachberg
Nierstein	Auflangen	Glöck Heiligenbaum Kranzberg Ölberg Zehnmorgen
	Gutes Domtal Rehbach	Hipping Pettenthal
	Spiegelberg	Hölle Paterberg
Oppenheim	Güldenmorgen	Kreuz Sackträger Zuckerberg
	Krötenbrunnen	
Worms	Liebfrauenmorgen	Liebfrauenstift-Kirchenstück

*Wines famous in their own right and usually labeled without village name are listed in this column.

448

Gemeinde * (Community or Parish)	Grosslage (General Site)	Einzellage (Individual Site-Vineyard)
RHEINPFALZ		
Deidesheim	Hofstück (Deidesheim)	
	Mariengarten (Forst)	Hohenmorgen Leinhölle
	Schneppenpflug an der Weinstrasse (Forst)	
Forst	Mariengarten (Forst)	Freundstück Jesuitengarten Kirchenstück Pechstein Ungeheuer
	Schneppenpflug an der Weinstrasse (Forst)	
Ruppertsberg	Hofstück (Deidesheim)	Hoheberg Nussbien
Wachenheim	Mariengarten (Forst)	Gerümpel Goldbächel Rechbächel
	Schenkenbohl (Wachenheim) Schneppenpflug an der Weinstrasse (Forst)	

449

APPENDIX 6

ITALIAN WINES

Piedmont	116,221
Valle d'Aosta	933
Lombardy	56,841
Trentino-Alto Adige	36,425
Veneto	244,530
Fruili-Venezia-Giulia	31,129
Liguria	10,739
Emilia-Romagna	262,505
Tuscany	107,675
Umbria	20,537
Marches	58,135
Latium	122,342
Abruzzo and Molise	71,450
Campania	84,406
Apulia	275,013
Basilicata	12,786
Calabria	27,454
Sicily	227,868
Sardinia	59,050
TOTAL	1,826,039

THE CONTROLLED WINES OF ITALY

After 30 years of effort the Italian Wine Law of 1963 came into existence and since then implementing rules and regulations have been issued to bring under control all of the better wines of Italy. Once the mechanism has been set up for a particular wine it can then be labeled as such only if it meets certain standards of origin, grape variety, yield and quality.

The least strict control is for the *Denominazione di Origine Semplice* and is basically a geographic indication of wines made according to local usage from grapes typical of the production area. It is not yet in general use.

Much stricter are the requirements for *Denominazione di Origine Controllata* wines and those in effect through October 15, 1977 are listed below.

The most strict controls are for *Denominazione di Origine Controllata e Garantita* and it is expected that the first few should be the 1978 vintages of those marked with an asterisk (*).

450

D.O.C. WINES BY REGION

PIEDMONT

Asti Spumante or Asti
* Barbaresco
Barbera d'Alba
Barbera d'Asti
Barbera del Monferrato
* Barolo
Boca
Brachetto d'Acqui
Caluso Passito
Caluso Passito Liquoroso
Carema
Colli Tortonesi
Dolcetto d'Acqui
Dolcetto d'Alba
Dolcetto d'Asti
Dolcetto delle Langhe Monregalesi
Dolcetto di Diano d'Alba
Dolcetto di Dogliani

Dolcetto d'Ovada
Erbaluce di Caluso
Fara
Freisa d'Asti
Freisa di Chieri
Gattinara
Gavi or Cortese di Gavi
Ghemme
Grignolino d'Asti
Grignolini del Monferrato Casalese
Lessona
Malvasia di Casorzo d'Asti
Malvasia di Castelnuovo Don Bosco
Moscato d'Asti Spumante or Moscato d'Asti
Moscato Naturale d'Asti
Nebbiolo d'Alba
Rubino di Cantavenna
Sizzano

* DOCG — 1978 Vintage.

VALLE D'AOSTA

Donnaz

Enfer D'Arvier

LOMBARDY

Botticino
Cellatica
Colli Morenici Mantovani del Garda
Franciacorta Pinot
Franciacorta Rosso
Lugana

Oltrepò Pavese
Riviera del Garda Bresciano
Tocai di S. Martino della Battaglia
Valcalepio
Valtellina
Valtellina Superiore

TRENTINO-ALTO ADIGE

Alto Adige
Caldaro or Lago di Caldaro
Casteller
Colli di Bolzano
Meranese or Meranese di Collina
Santa Maddalena

Terlano
Teroldego Rotaliano
Trentino
Valdadige
Valle Isarco

VENETO

Bardolino
Bianco di Custoza
Breganze
Cabernet di Pramaggiore
Colli Berici
Colli Euganei
Gambellara
Merlot di Pramaggiore

Prosecco di Conegliano-Valdobbaidene
Soave
Recioto di Soave
Tocai di Lison
Valpolicella
Recioto della Valpolicella
Vini del Piave or Piace

D.O.C. WINES BY REGION (Continued)

FRIULI-VENEZIA GIULIA

Aquileia
Collio Goriziano or Collio
Colli Orientali de Friuli

Grave del Friuli
Isonzo
Latisana

LIGURIA

Cinqueterre
Cinqueterre Sciacchetra'

Rossese di Dolceacqua or Dolceacqua

EMILIA-ROMAGNA

Albana di Romagna
Bianco di Scandiano
Colli Bolognese Monte San Pietro or
  Castelli Mediovali
Gutturnio dei Colli Piacentini
Lambrusco Grasparossa di Castelvetro
Lambrusco Reggiano

Lambrusco Salamino di S. Croce
Lambrusco di Sorbara
Monterosso Val d'Arda
Sangiovese di Romagna
Trebbianino Val Trebbia
Trebbiano di Romagna

TUSCANY

Bianco della Valdinievole
Bianco di Pitigliano
Bianco Vergine Val di Chiana
* Brunello di Montalcino
Carmignano
Chianti
Elba Bianco and Rosso

Montecarlo Bianco
Montescudaio
Parrina
Rosso delle Colline Lucchesi
Vernaccia di S. Gimignano
* Vino Nobile di Montepulciano

* DOCG-1978 Vintage

MARCHES

Bianchello del Metauro
Bianco dei Colli Maceratesi
Falerio dei Colli Ascolani
Rosso Conero
Rosso Piceno

Sangiovese dei Colli Pesaresi
Verdicchio dei Castelli di Jesi
Verdicchio di Matelica
Vernaccia di Serrapetrona

UMBRIA

Colli dei Trasimeno
Orvieto

Torgiano

LATIUM

Aleatico di Gradoli
Bianco Capena
Cerveteri
Cesanese del Piglio or Piglio
Cesanese di Affile or Affile
Cesanese di Olevano Romano or
  Olevano Romano

Est! Est!! Est!!! di Montefiascone
Frascati
Marino
Merlot di Aprilia
Montecompatri Colonna or Montecompatri
  or Colonna
Sangiovese di Aprilia

452

D.O.C. WINES BY REGION (Continued)

Colli Albani
Colli Lanuvini
Cori

Trebbiano di Aprilia
Velletri
Zagarolo

ABRUZZO AND MOLISE

Montepulciano d'Abruzzo

Trebbiano d'Abruzzo

CAMPANIA

Greco di Tufo
Ischia Bianco
Ischia Rosso

Ischia Bianco Superiore
Solopaca
Taurasi

APULIA

Aleatico di Puglia
Cacc'e Mmitte di Lucera
Castel del Monte
Copertino
Locorotondo
Martina or Martina Franca
Matino
Moscato di Trani

Ostuni
Primitivo di Manduria
Rosso Barletta
Rosso di Cerignola
Salice Salentino
S. Severo
Squinzano

BASILICATA

Aglianico del Vulture

CALABRIA·

Cirò
Donnici

Pollino
Savuto

SICILY

Bianco Alcamo or Alcamo
Cerasuolo di Vittoria
Etna
Faro
Malvasia delle Lipari

Marsala
Moscato di Noto Naturale
Moscato di Pantelleria Naturale
Mascato Passito di Pantelleria
Moscato di Siracusa

SARDINIA

Campidano di Terralba or Terralba
Cannonau di Sardegna
Carignano del Sulcis
Girò di Cagliari
Malvasia di Bosa
Malvasia di Cagliari
Monica di Cagliari
Monica di Sardegna

Moscato di Cagliari
Moscato di Sorso-Sennori or Sorso or
Sennori
Nasco di Cagliari
Nuragus di Cagliari
Vermentino di Gallura
Vernaccia di Oristano

VINTAGE YEARS

CALIFORNIA

It is not true that every year is a "vintage" year in California, yet every year yields wines which bear vintage dates. There are no years when conditions are such that vintage identification on a label is not proper and a convenient guide to the age of the wine. There are, of course, variances in rainfall, temperature and sunshine which affect quality from one year to another and from one area to another. Irrigation, not permitted in the great European vineyards, makes up for lack of rain, a number of methods of fighting frost are successfully employed and technical progress in winemaking all combine to prevent disastrous years.

The great bulk of California wines are blends — various years, various climates and soil areas, various grapes (not all wine grapes). On the other hand, as true viniferas are coming more and more into vogue, the numerous smaller wineries, and some of the large ones, are producing true varietals from individual vineyards. Wine making techniques are still in flux — temperature control of fermentation, centrifuging at various stages, control of malolactic fermentation, length, type and size of wood storage, early or late bottling — all have great effect on the success of a particular "vintage".

Therefore it is impossible to draw a vintage chart or even to make meaningful vintage comments. Perhaps in the not too distant future this will come.

In the meantime, individual "vintage" wines are exciting and provide the sauce that makes California wines a great gustatory adventure.

VINTAGE YEARS OF EUROPEAN WINES

As if to console us for the problems and anxieties of modern living, the vine, man's old comforter and immemorial friend, has been exceedingly kind to us over the last two decades. Rarely in the past have we had such a remarkable succession of good vintages and bountiful harvests; we have had few disastrous years at all, none comparable to those of that hungry and bitter interregnum of 1930-32.

Possibly we have come to take our good fortune too much for granted and expect another "year of the century" to be unveiled every autumn. Yet it is unquestionably true that much of this is due, not to sheer good luck, but to a vast increase in technical knowledge and skill among both vine growers and vintners. What were catastrophes forty years ago are now problems of manageable proportions and when something odd and disquieting seems to be taking place in a vineyard or a cellar, one simply calls for the most competent nearby technical expert, as a few more enlightened vintners have been doing since the time of Pasteur. But today there are many more experts than there were, and far fewer ignorant vintners.

If this progress continues, as we all hope it will, vintage charts may become less necessary.

What follows, in any case, is something a good deal more complicated and quite different: a fairly detailed description of the wines of each major district in recent vintage years.

Ratings, 1 to 20, are based on the relative value of the wines today, not on what they were when originally produced or first marketed.

18-20 = Very Great.   *16-17 = Great*   *15 = Very Good.*
14 = Good.   *12-13 = Fair*   *11 = Poor.*

10 and Under = Very Poor. Where no ratings are given, the wines are either too old to be interesting or not on the market today.

During Frank Schoonmaker's forty years in the wine business he developed a closely knit group of associates throughout the United States, France, and Germany. The reputation his ALMANAC OF WINE has gained for its authenticity is a by product of his long-established relationships with Marquis Jacques d'Angerville, Dr. Albert Bürklin, Gunther Dünweg, Hans Josef Becker and Kenneth Onish.

The critiques of 1975 and later vintages are an assimilation of information provided by these experts who have also made current the comments on earlier vintage years written by the late Frank Schoonmaker.

The text which follows is taken largely from *The Frank Schoonmaker Report From the Wine Country* "ALMANAC OF EUROPEAN WINES."

I. FRANCE

RED BORDEAUX

1977.   Spring frosts, shortages of Merlot. Very pronounced high percentage Cabernet in Haut Médoc. Better than 1974 or 1972. Perhaps 15/20.

1976.   The long, hot summer was interrupted by rainfall during the harvest. The fortunate growers brought in both Cabernet and Melot grapes in excellent condition. In general, the Haut-Médoc was more successful than the St. Émilion or Pomerol districts. The wines are rich and fruity. Good alcohol with some weak acidity levels. These altogether charming wines will be ready far ahead of the 1975's. At this time 16/20, although some may well deserve 17/20.

1975.   If good things come in small packages, such is the case in 1975. A smaller than average crop — wines of great color and high intensity. The Médoc wines are rich in tannin and well textured. St. Émilion, Pomerol, and Graves have also produced very high quality, elegant wines. 19/20.

1974.   Coming along better than we had any right to expect after a miserably rainy late August and September. More body and color than the 1973s, although lacking in freshness. 14+/20.

1973.   An extremely copious year, surpassing even the record figures of '70 and '66. Most of the red wines are perhaps lacking a bit in body and color for the long pull, but are now good for drinking. These wines are tender, fresh, and have matured early. 14/20.

1972.   The vintage, taking place in the latter part of October, was one of the latest of this century. Hard and unattractive wines in their youth, they are now showing better. There are some better than average wines to be found, and now rate 12/20.

1971.   A very good year, far better than seemed possible in July before the harvest. Bad weather in May gravely affected the flowering of the Merlot grape. Wines a little hard but well balanced and often quite fine. 17/20.

1970.   As one of the earliest and most consistent critics of overblown propaganda, I am glad to say that I think it is possible, even probable, that the Bordeaux boys at long last have a small scale wolf by the tail. 1970 is certainly not the best year of our generation or our lifetime (frankly, I am not sure which is higher praise); almost certainly it is less good than 1961; what it has particularly to recommend it is that, contrary to all rules and expectations, it produced an enormous crop, 3½ times as much as 1961, a surprisingly small proportion of it mediocre, almost none of it bad. This is the year to watch. Surely 19/20.

1969.   If there is any justice, should go down in Bordeaux history as the Year of the Big Drum, a press agent's dream. After dismal '68, something nice *had* to happen, and by George it would! By mid-summer "another '61 was in the making", possibly "another fabulous '45". Prices were already being quoted for wines *sur souche* (in terms of grapes that had not even begun to ripen on the vine) and these were among the highest prices in the history of the Bordeaux wine trade. When the rains finally came, as they often do, as people forget, before the vintage, the fever cooled but the prices remained stubbornly as high as ever.

Had the '69s come on the market without all this fanfare, they would gladly have been accepted for what they are — very passable Clarets, a few quite good. Instead, they were ridiculously over-publicized and overpriced. Some may rate higher but 13/20 is a charitable average.

1968.   As dismal a harvest as '65 and '63. Perhaps 5/20, the 5 for effort.

1967.   A very good year, especially in St. Émilion and Pomerol, although few if any are worth laying away in a serious cellar and most of them can be drunk, if you wish, today. They are much better than the vaunted '69s, and less expensive. 14/20 for the Médoc is perhaps a shade ungenerous — you may be agreeably surprised by occasionally truly outstanding bottles. St. Émilion and Pomerol deserve 16/20 at least.

1966.   Looks better with each passing year, and most of us are having to revise upwards our already favorable opinions of its quality. The wines lack, perhaps, the power and authority of the best '64s and the splendid '61s, but they make up in balance what they lack in weight, and almost without exception they are immensely pleasing. Highly recommended, 19/20.

1965.   One of the most dismal failures of the decade. A miserable year and rainy harvest. 0/20.

1964.   A good but extremely uneven year with some admirable high spots and some disappointing lows. Rain arrived during the picking season and those who had not finished their harvest were badly hurt. This was especially the case in the Médoc, where the wines range all the way from 12/20 to 17/20. St. Émilion was luckier, a consistent 16/20. The best wines are now ready for drinking especially those from Pomerol and St. Émilion. Many of the Médoc wines are past their prime.

1963.   Disastrous in St. Émilion and Pomerol. Generally poor in the Médoc although a few châteaux produced light, early-maturing, very agreeable Clarets, now too old.

1962.   Set a record for quantity in white Bordeaux. Many of the reds have reached their peak and in any case they should be drunk shortly. 14/20.

1961.   This was an exceedingly great vintage in Bordeaux, one of the best of this century. The crop was a small one; the wines were expensive from the start and will get more so, but their quality can only be described as superb, maybe even better than 1945. The finer château-bottlings are *just beginning* to be ready to drink and they may well outlast many of us, who are now their most fervent admirers. 20/20.

1960.   Overshadowed, as was inevitable, by the highly publicized 1959s and the astonishing 1961s, the 1960s were well-balanced and agreeable Clarets from the very beginning and have always deserved more praise than they received. Those who appreciate the finesse and elegance of not-too-heavy red Bordeaux will find many of them still good and surprisingly inexpensive. They should be drunk and enjoyed, not laid away. 1960, incidentally, was the first year in which chaptalization was made legal on a wide scale in Bordeaux. 13/20.

1959.   A great year, surely, though hardly the "Year of the Century" — after all, we still have twenty-three to go, and who knows what marvels will be unveiled?

As far as older Clarets are concerned, buying them is risky, to say the least: the old vintage ratings no longer dependable. For the record, however: 1957, 1955, 1953, 1952, 1949.

These are great rarities, most of them still fine if they have been properly stored, and to drink one is a rare pleasure as well as a privilege.

WHITE BORDEAUX

Forty years ago, or a hundred and forty years ago for that matter, Château d'Yquem sold for twice as much as Château Lafite on the Bordeaux market, and in London and New York, and as it should today if actual cost of production were any criterion. But sweeter white wines are out of fashion these days, the Sauternes and all their fellow travelers; First Growth Clarets bring twice the price of Yquem, the dryest possible white wines are all the vogue, and even the dry Graves are dryer than they used to be; some producers have gone so far as to plant Cabernet grapes in delimited Barsac and attempted to make Bordeaux Rouge; even incorruptible Yquem came out with semi-dry wine called "Château Y".

There has been a tendency, in making these lighter, fresher, more *gouleyant* white Bordeaux, to depend more on the Sauvignon Blanc grape, and less on the Sémillon, and some of them actually carry this varietal grape name on their labels, as is common practice in Alsace, and recently in California. They taste, indeed, not too unlike the fruity wines of Sancerre and Pouilly-sur-Loire, and are all the better for it.

"White Bordeaux" has therefore become a sort of catch-all name, covering a multiplicity of widely differing wines, ranging from quite dry to very, very sweet, from quite cheap to very expensive, from drink-at-once to good-for-20 years. Vintage ratings in the following paragraphs are therefore set down separately, as 15/20 for Sauternes, etc., and (15/20) for the dryer, and sooner ready, Graves. Ratings for dry wines thus — (15/20) — in parentheses. Ratings for Sauternes, Barsac, Ste. Croix-du-Mont thus — 15/20 — no parentheses.

1977. Graves, good balance, lighter than 1976 and more elegant. 15/20. Sauternes a disaster. Spring frost caused great destruction in the vineyards.

1976 was a highly irregular year both in Graves as well as Sauternes. Rain during the harvest prolonged the picking process and uneven qualities of grapes were pressed even in the same vineyard. The Graves rate (14/20) and Sauternes 16/20.

1975. A very great vintage year for both dry and sweet wines. The dry wines are well balanced with fine acidity coupled with good alcohol. They will improve with an extra year's bottle age. Drink these wines in 1978/79. (17/20). The Sauternes and Barsacs are in a grand class. High sugar levels, very long after taste — filling the palate. These rich wines will need time to develop. Better than 1970 and 1967, but not quite 1962 or 1961. A well deserved 18/20.

1974 produced an extremely copious harvest in most of the Bordeaux white wine districts. The dry whites are lower than usual in alcohol. Light, with very little color, fresh and agreeable, and should be drunk promptly. (13/20). The miserable rainy weeks of September and early October played havoc in the Sauternes country and few if any of these, which depend so much on sunshine in September, will be even passable. 11/20.

1973 produced the largest crop in the history of the Bordeaux country, and the weather here unfortunately was a good deal less favorable than in Burgundy or on the Rhine. Light, pale, refreshing wines which we should drink up while they are still young. (14/20) for the dryer wines, 12/20 Sauternes, etc.

1972. Dryer wines (13/20). Sauternes, etc. 11/20.

1971. In Barsac, Sauternes and all of the other appellations for typical Bordeaux sweet wines, admirable quality. Will certainly be long-lived and already outstanding. 17/20. Dryer wines, quite full bodied, lacking perhaps in finesse and bouquet. (14/20.)

1970. Quite often over the past few years superior vintages seem to come in pairs, and so it was with Sauternes, Barsac, etc. in 1970. In sweet wines, probably the best vintage since 1962. Great, elegant, splendid sweet wines, continuing to improve. (18/20.) The dryer whites well-balanced, fine, ready to drink. 14/20.

457

1969. Certainly (as in '71) much better in white than in red Bordeaux, many Sauternes quite good, despite the September rains, at least 15/20. Spotty and uneven in Graves and the dryer whites, many too pronounced in flavor and too high in alcohol for pleasant daily drinking. Say (14/20).

1968. A disaster in Sauternes, under 10/20, but by no means as bad as in dry white Bordeaux, the best *crus* of Graves especially, as we have been led to believe: some of them have quite remarkable freshness and bouquet, and more distinction than the '69s from the same vineyards, rate (15/20). You will probably never see a shipper's white Bordeaux with 1968 on the label — the initial press reports were too unfavorable — but you will rarely be disappointed in a château-bottled white Graves of this maligned year.

1967. The first year, after four bad vintages, to produce acceptable Sauternes. They are certainly much better than 1963-'64-'65-'66, yet hardly glorious, by no means up to '61-'62, or '71-'71. Yet, if you do not expect too much you can hardly go wrong, for they are still inexpensive, deserve almost 16/20. Most of the dry whites are finished.

1966 was a very great vintage almost everywhere in Europe except, unfortunately, Sauternes, Barsac & Co., where 12/20 is almost too generous. Most of the dry wines are now over the hill.

Noteworthy older years in Sauternes:
1962-19/20.   1961-19/20.

RED BURGUNDY

1977. Surprisingly good quality better than 1974. Good color and balance, firmer than 1973, not as good as 1972. 15/20-16/20.

1976. A very great vintage year. The summer's abnormally high temperatures, coupled with near arid conditions resulted in very favorable growing conditions through all of Burgundy. As a result the harvest was one of the earliest recorded in this century (being a full three weeks early).

The wines are very deeply colored, full bodied and tannic, well balanced without an over-abundance of alcohol. This vintage has all the characteristics of a very great year, comparable to the most famous of the last three decades (1945, 1949, 1961). The 1976 wines are what the French call "Vins de Garde". They are wines that should be cellared 6-8 years to reach their maturity. The Côte de Nuits, 19/20. The Côte de Beaune, 18+/20.

1975. After a procession of six years of above average quality red wines, the balloon finally burst. Heavy rains during August and again in September took their toll in the vineyards, damaging the vegetation and causing a great deal of rot. The wines are extremely fragile, thin, and lack color. The vintage for red wine should be written off the books, perhaps a generous 10 out of 20.

1974. For those highly-skilled, quality-minded small producers who make and estate-bottle the best red wines of Burgundy, this was a disappointing, one might almost say a heart-breaking year. Until the very last days of August, conditions could hardly have been better; a very large crop (almost up to 1973) was in prospect practically everywhere. Then, one disenchanting evening, there was a violent thunderstorm, and it rained heavily all night, this was a not unwelcome break in the blue August weather. . . . but it rained the following day and the day after, out of a grey and sullen sky. And this persisted, day after day, for nearly two months.

The vintage was far from the joyous one anticipated. Glum is the better word. Nevertheless, the wines turned out to be a good deal better than any of us had believed possible. The truly scrupulous growers who had kept their production within reasonable limits, made wines which can fairly be described as "good" with some "very good", possibly a few to be rated even higher. I suggest, therefore, that you select carefully what you buy, and stick to producers who have satisfied you in the past. Do not lay too many of the '74s away. They will be, in any case, vastly better than the '68s, '65s and '63s; fruity, fresh and good, with

458

their Pinot flavor unmistakable. Say 14/20 if you are careful, with a few 15/20s if you are lucky as well.

1973. The largest crop in the modern history of Burgundy, a very good year; the fine reds will certainly be ready to drink, surprisingly enough, before the '72s and '71s and, possibly, before some '69s. Few of them seem likely to improve for as much as ten years — five or six would be a better guess — and in this they are a little like the 1959s. They have enough body, a fine true Burgundy nose, and are immediately pleasing (as some of their predecessors are still NOT, however bright their future may be). 16/20.

1972. Big and solid wines in the old Burgundy style — great quality, assuredly long life, big body. Most of them will reach their peak five or six years from now. 17/20 for the moment.

1971. An extraordinary year, one of many resounding successes and a few dismàl failures, due to the vagaries of local weather. Perhaps best on the Côte de Beaune, Corton and Beaune especially, where I cannot remember a better year; a flat 19/20. There was a good deal of hail in Gevrey-Chambertin, which did not help matters. The slow maturing Côte de Nuits wines need a couple of years more in bottle to develop properly. Few are under 17/20.

1970. A year both copious and excellent, on the order of 1966 and 1973. Except in Pommard and Chassagne-Montrachet (where there was a good deal of damage from hail), a joyous year, tender supple attractive wines, good almost from the beginning. If you buy them from a trustworthy supplier, you are most unlikely to be disappointed. The lesser appellations are now quite tired, the bigger Côte d'Or wines should be at their peak. Today 14/20.

1969. A very great year, 19/20. The first in an absolutely unprecedented series of SIX EXTRAORDINARY YEARS. The oldest vignerons on the *Côte* shake their heads and wonder whether there will be as many lean years to come like the kine in Genesis. I can only add that these vintage comments are wholly disinterested and as fair and informative as I can make them. But there has not been, since 1968 (which I called "miserable") through 1974, in red Burgundy, a year which I could in good conscience rate below 14/20. There have been any number of local disasters which I have mentioned herein — but none that affected the quality of Burgundy as a whole.

WHITE BURGUNDY

Everything that really matters in the way of white wine produced in Burgundy, from Chablis on the north to Beaujolais Blanc and St. Véran (near Mâcon) on the south, is now officially made from the Chardonnay grape alone. Twenty years ago this was more often called the "Pinot-Chardonnay" and considered a cousin of the Pinot Noir, the great redwine grape of Burgundy, and of Champagne.

Most of these fragrant, elegant and delicious wines, thanks to modern cellar technique, can now be bottled and drunk when they are not much over a year old; generally the good ones are close to their peak at three or four. Only the very best, and only in great years, will repay keeping past the age of ten.

1977. Côte d'Or—very irregular. "Villages" quality disappointing, high acidity, low sugar, short-lived, poor balance. 13/20. Good vineyard sites harvested late, better than average quality. 15/20. Chablis — Hard, high acidity, lack fruit, disappointing. Now cannot be rated higher than the 1972 Vintage. 13/20.

1976. The harvest began on August 31st due to the persistent long, dry summer. The white wines are slightly golden in color, full bodied, rich in alcohol and are already developing a wonderful bouquet. The best appellations have made a truly "grand vin". They should be enjoyed young and should reach their peak in 1979-1980. The Côte de Beaune 17/20. Chablis 18/20, some growers equate this vintage in Chablis with the great 1949.

1975. Above average quality wines were made in Meursault and Puligny, though they lack the charm and freshness of the 1973 and 1976 vintages. They have a tendency to be a

459

bit heavy and out of balance. Better in Chablis where the wines have more natural acidity. Côte de Beaune 14/20. Chablis 15+/20.

1974. Over two months of miserably rainy weather — from late August straight through the vintage and well into November — somewhat miraculously failed to undo what had already been accomplished by the sunny days of a fine summer. Again, a very large crop, especially in Chablis. There, as in the Mâconnais and on the Côte d'Or, light, fine, early-maturing wines, certainly very good (15/20), quite possible 16/20.

1973. Broke all modern records for total production, and however unlikely this may seem, the '73s are now the best white Burgundies of the present decade, especially the estate-bottlings from small producers who are quality minded. *Bouqueté,* elegant, yet with plenty of back-bone and staying power, they are eminently worth laying away except for one sad fact: they are admittedly, extravagantly expensive. Hopefully, this may change. At least 19/20, for the best Côte d'Or whites. The Mâconnais wines rate at least 17/20 in my book, and some a point more.

1972. Uneven. Some very good bottles from the Mâconnais but 15/20 is a fair average. Chablis disappointing, 13/20. On the Côte d'Or this is hardly a vintage I can recommend unreservedly for Meursault, Montrachet & Co.; rather hard wines, unpleasing slow to come round. Charitably, 14/20 at present.

1971. As was the case with red Burgundy, a year of many local disasters, yet very good wines on the whole. In the early, pre-dawn hours of April 29th, most of the best Chablis vineyards — those on the right or east bank of the Serein, all seven of the *Grands Crus,* and many of the *Premiers Crus* as well, suffered grave damage from a killing frost, and eventually produced a scant half-crop at best. The white-wine vineyards of the Côte d'Or, spared this early catastrophe, were ravaged by hail on August 19th. What was salvaged is of remarkably good quality, sometimes a bit too high in alcohol, but qhite often splendid. 16/20.

1970. These, from the very beginning, were lovely wines — fragrant and beguiling, graceful and fresh. Now they are declining after having given us many a delightful battle. Today 13/20.

1969. Seemed excellent, even extraordinary, until its prodigy of a younger brother arrived on the scene; many wine lovers may still prefer them; they are better than the '66s and '64s, far better than the fat, graceless '59s and the rest of their near contemporaries, sturdy, well-balanced, classic wines that offer few surprises and almost no disappointments.

BEAUJOLAIS

American wine drinkers, on the lookout for something less expensive than Classified Bordeaux and Vintage Burgundy, are becoming what an actor would call "quick study". We seem at least to have learned, over the last few vintages, what we really need to know about Beaujolais. This is very important and quite different, in many ways, from what a Frenchman needs to know about Beaujolais.

The new stuff, for example.

It has often been called, perhaps not inaccurately, the Frenchman's best-loved wine. In its freshness and youth, its arrival is an annual November delight and provokes in the hearts of all who have ever lived in France a sort of special nostalgia, as does *muguet,* the lilies-of-the-valley which a Frenchman buys for his sweetie on the first of May.

It inspired Léon Daudet, a famous journalist and gourmet of pre-war days, to declare that there are really three rivers, not two (the Saône and Rhône) that converge at Lyon, the third river being the Beaujolais.

This new wine can be called, progressively, *bourru* (still cloudy), *nouveau* (new), *primeur* (fresh), or *de l'année* (of the current year). It improves with keeping about as much as fresh lettuce. It is one of the exceedingly rare wines which truly cannot "travel". It is never quite as good in Lyon as in the vineyard village where it was born. It is even slightly less

460

good in Paris; decidedly less attractive in New York; and when it reaches, say, a package-store in Chicago or San Francisco, it is not at all what it was originally intended to be.

In France a great deal of it never sees a bottle at all. It arrives at one's favorite bistro in cask and it is served *en carafe* at the table or by the glass across the *"zinc"* of one's favorite bar. Before it can be shipped successfully to some place a long way from home, it has to be *travaillé*, or disciplined a little, or "stabilized" or possibly pasteurized — in any case clarified and filtered, passed through a bottling machine, given a cork and capsule, then, at a tender age, subjected to the indignity of an ocean voyage — by that time its spirit is at least subdued, and it tastes a lot less like Beaujolais and more like just any young red wine.

Geographically speaking, the Beaujolais country is part of Burgundy, but fine red Burgundy is truly a quite different and more serious wine. The Beaujolais are made from a different grape — the Gamay, or Gamay Beaujolais; true red Burgundy comes only from the Pinot Noir. If you plant the Pinot Noir on the clay and granite soil of Beujolais it rarely gives a wine of the quality expected, and the Gamay grape on the calcareous hillside of the noble Côte d'Or yields a disappointing and common wine at best. When (as occasionally happens) Beaujolais , as it matures, begins to taste like a Côte d'Or wine, the peasants say, rather contemptuously, *"il morgonne"* — begins to taste a bit like a wine from Morgon, by which they mean that it is changing its character — "like putting on airs and a foreign accent".

1977. Uneven wines from the plain, Beaujolais "tout court", barely acceptable, thin, poor balance, no fruit. 11/20. The "crus" more typical in style than 1976. Some good examples rate 15/20.

1976. An excellent vintage year. Especially high quality wines from Moulin-à-Vent and Juliénas, but even those from Beaujolis Villages and Brouilly have reached the summit of quality. Deeply colored, full bodied, concentrated flavor, long finish, and above all well balanced. The Grand Crus 19/20. Beaujolais "tout court" 16/20.

1975. A poor year for both Beaujolais "tout court" as well as the "Crus" appellations. Frequent hailstorms provoked serious rot in the vineyards, and with heavy rains in September the poor results were predictable. The wines are thin, acid, low in alcohol, and have no future. On the whole 10/20.

1974. This was by a very substantial margin the largest crop in the history of Beaujolais, and in many cases Nature seems to have been overly generous. The more conservative and careful growers produced some very good wines, fruity and pleasant, although rarely with much backbone. The best rate somewhere between 14/20 and 16/20.

1973. Another very large crop, but made on the whole in very good weather and hardly any of it bad. It should be drunk promptly or within a year or so or not at all. There are quite a few exceptions and some of these are truly remarkable examples of Beaujolais at its best. 13/20 for the common stuff, 15/20 and up for the successful.

1972. The smaller wines lacked fruit and freshness and charm, and unfortunately a large amount of this was sent to America as *primeur*. It proved short-lived and disappointing almost everywhere, deserved barely 12/20. The "big" wines from the "Nine Muses" were different indeed. At their peak, two years ago, these wines were well textured with a fine bouquet. Today they are fading rapidly and can rate only 12/20.

1971. Hardly anything less than 16/20 unless it has been mishandled or poorly stored. Quite a few of the *vins de l'année* were very good indeed, and I have the kindest possible memories of them, but they are no more. Too bad.

LOIRE VALLEY

The Loire Valley can hardly be called a wine district, in any strict geographical sense of the word. It wanders, in lazy, haphazard fashion, two-thirds of the way across France, from the western edge of Burgundy almost to the Atlantic; about a dozen different grape varieties are involved, and some twenty quite distinct and legally delimited vineyard areas, strung like a necklace of widely-spaced beads along the banks of the Loire itself and its tributaries. Together they produce more wine than Beaujolais does — a great deal of white, a great deal of *rosé,* a smaller amount of truly excellent red. Nevertheless, as far as vintage years are concerned, they can be divided into two main categories — the wines for current drinking, best when young, and the *vins de garde,* which improve with age.

Among the latter, as might be expected, are the four fine reds, all made from the Cabernet Franc grape of Bordeaux (the "breton", as Rabelais called it): Chinon, Bourgueil, St. Nicholas-de-Bourgueil, Saumur, Champigny — fragrant, lovely wines, not too expensive, even today. Then also the Vouvrays of exceptional years. Finally, the extraordinary sweet white wines of Anjou, little known in America, but comparable to the great Barsacs and Sauternes and to the *Beerenauslesen* of the Rhine.

Exceptional years are 1976, 1973, 1971 and 1969. Poor years — 1975, 1972. Unmentioned years are more or less satisfactory and should be consumed currently. Most of the wines available in restaurants and auberges of the Loire country are sold almost as soon as they are clear. As such they are inexpensive, appetizing and go exceedingly well with the Loire Valley cuisine.

COTES-DU-RHONE

For the thirsty American with a good palate and a thin pocket-book, these days about the only Happy-Hunting-Ground left in France is the Rhône Valley. This mostly for red wines, of course, but over 90% of the Côtes-du-Rhône production is red or rosé, anyway, so no matter. With three or four exceptions (Châteauneuf-du-Pape, Hermitage, Côte Rôtie and perhaps the spicy white Condrieu), they are wines that you do not really have to lay away, but if you forget a few bottles for a few years in your cellar you will be glad you did when you open them. Nor do you have to be so careful in selecting vintages — really poor years are not too frequent and the differences that separate good from very good and this from great are far less obvious than in Bordeaux and Burgundy.

This happy situation has come to exist thanks largely to the intelligent cooperation, over the past thirty years, of a number of well-informed and interested growers, a few competently managed cooperative cellars, and the I.N.A.O. (the *Appellation Contrôlée* people in Paris). Thus, when the small producers in a given district have demonstrated their ability to produce, over a period of years, a superior wine of consistent quality and special character, they end up by getting a special *Appellation Contrôlée* of their own. The most recently accorded of these is *Côtes du Ventoux,* literally "Slopes of the Windy Mountain"; the Mont Ventoux is, in fact, a famous landmark north of Avignon.

Other wines worth looking for, in the less expensive category, are those called simply "Côtes-du-Rhône" especially when followed by the word "Villages"; or the name of a specific village.

Of course, even more reassuring, is an Appellation Contrôlée which the particular wine itself has earned. There is a small constellation of such vineyards round Hermitage (Crozes-Hermitage, Cornas, St. Joseph), another group near Châteauneuf-du-Pape, farther south (Gigondas, Mont-Ventoux, etc.). Lastly Avignon, with its famous old *"Sur-le-Pont"* bridge (which, as the initiates have learned, should be *"Sous-le-Pont"*)[1]. And, beyond the Rhône, on the road to Spain, is the *Rosé* Country — Tavel, with Lirac just next door and nearly as good, and many others, sold as Côtes-du-Rhône, often with a village name appended.

Quite a number of good, dry white wines are produced, full-bodied, rather long-lived, golden. It has not been my experience that they improve greatly with keeping: white Hermitage, Crozes-Hermitage, St. Péray (also sparkling), Condrieu and Château-Grillet (both made from the Viognier grape, and doubtless the best), Châteauneuf-du-Pape Blanc, etc.

(1). The ruined Pont-St.-Bénézet, the *"Pont d'Avignon"* of the old song, originally traversed not only the two branches of the Rhône, but the green meadows of the Ile-de-la-Barthelasse which then separated them, as it still does. This broad, shady and inviting island is, even today, a favorite spot for carnivals and fairs and picnics, and it was obviously here, *"sous-le-pont"*, not *on* the narrow old bridge itself, that the dancing took place.

1977. Very good vintage from Côte Rotie to Châteauneuf du Pape. Long, rich in alcohol, good tannin and fruit. In the north 16/20. In the south 16+/20.

1976. A great vintage year from Côte Rôtie and Hermitage in the north to Châteauneuf-du-Pape and Tavel in the south. The extreme heat of the summer has produced full bodied, intense, and fiery wines in the northern vineyards. To the south the wines have a lighter balance and will develop more quickly. Perhaps equal in quality to 1970. 18+/20 in the north. 17/20 in the south.

1975. A spotty year throughout the Côtes-du-Rhône. Rains in September diluted the color, alcohol and acidity in the grapes. With not many exceptions to the rule, 13/20 in the north, 12/20 in the south.

1974. Freakish weather from the last days of August through September, yet better quality than expected in Châteauneuf-du-Pape and the Southern sector. Generally superior to 1973, but by no means great, 14/20. Hermitage, etc. disappointing, 13/20.

1973. An enormous record-breaking crop which may well bring about a few changes in the French wine regulations, some of them long overdue. Considerably better round Hermitage, etc. A good many of the lesser wines are now ready and both attractive and cheap, always providing they have had a few months in oak cooperage. Only about 12/20 in the lower valley; 15/20 in the northern half.

1972 can now be called a good to very good vintage year. The red and white wines from Hermitage are developing very well and should continue to soften in a few years. Châteauneuf-du-Pape is now ready for drinking and very attractive on the whole 16/20.

1971. These remarkable wines have now all but disappeared from the market place. Equal in quality from both the Northern and Southern Rhône Valley. For those fortunate enough to have put them away, the wines are at their best point. Easily 18/20.

1970. Excellent and bountiful vintage, almost certainly the best since 1961. The whites from Hermitage and Châteauneuf-du-Pape are beginning to fade while the red wines from these regions are at their peak. 18/20.

1969. Remarkable but uneven, clearly demonstrated the fact that in reality the Rhône Valley is not one wine district, but two. The 1969 Côte Rôtie produced splendid wines which will last for years. On the other hand, not a particularly outstanding year in Châteauneuf-du-Pape. 14/20 for the south; 18/20 for the northern part of the Rhône Valley.

CHAMPAGNE

A detailed vintage chart for Champagne cannot help being a little ridiculous: in five years out of ten the wine never even pretends to go to the consumer in an unblended state, and admittedly would be less good if it did; and what proportion of which vintage goes into a non-vintage Champagne is a well-kept trade secret.

It is certainly more sensible, therefore, to reserve comment on what might be called the "buried" years — those that disappeared into the non-vintage — and discuss only those that have been or are likely to be presented as *millésimes:* 1976, 1975, 1973, 1971, 1970 and 1969.

Although all Champagne drinkers should be aware of the fact by now, it may be just as well to say once more that although the best Champagnes improve greatly with age in bottle, even for as much as fifteen years, when stored *sur pointe* or *en masse,* cork down, before disgorging, in the cellars where they are made, hardly any Champagne improves for more than a year or two once it has been disgorged and shipped. There may well be in Epernay and Reims small reserves of undisgorged 1961 and 1962 wines of extraordinary freshness, coupled with maturity and rare quality, but the same 1961 and 1962 wines, disgorged and shipped in 1972 and 1973, are now over the hill. Whatever stories you may have been told, or however excellent your cellar, it is simply folly to buy Champagne to lay away, or to buy a Champagne over seven or eight years old unless you can be sure it has just been disgorged, and this is exceedingly unlikely.

The whole Champagne business has changed beyond all recognition over the past two decades. Before World War I, and even World War II, the French exported not far from three-quarters of what they made; the total production has greatly increased, yet the French themselves now drink nearly three-quarters of it. What is made today is largely destined for the French internal market, where it commands at least as high prices as we ourselves are prepared to pay. The French drink their Champagne young, will rarely pay a premium for a vintage, particularly an older vintage, and whether we like it or not, apart from certain selected *cuvées* and special expensive bottlings (sometimes, but not always, worth what they cost), vintage Champagne may well, before long, be a thing of the past.

Meanwhile:

1976.   While we will not see any '76 vintage until 1980, it will be one of the best since World War II. An extremely early harvest began on September 1st under ideal weather conditions. Both the Pinot Noir and the Chardonnay yielded very high sugar musts.

1975.   Another vintage year. Lighter and more elegant than the '76s with good balance and fruit.

1973.   A large crop producing wines comparable to 1970. They are a bit light, though charming.

1971 will certainly be the Vintage to drink in 1978. A distressingly small crop of remarkable quality; the wines are on the full-bodied rather than on the elegant side.

1970.   An extremely large crop, probably the largest in the long history of the Champagne country. The superior wines are light and fragrant and fine, but those of lesser origin somewhat thin and lacking in character. Can hardly be rated as a great year, but charming and acceptable and very useful.

1969.   Definitely a Vintage. About an average crop, high average quality, perhaps (as in white Burgundy) somewhat on the full-bodied side. Rather heavy-footed wines that will be quick to show their age.

ALSACE

In geography, in climate, and of course in grape varieties as well, the Alsatian wine country has much more in common with Germany than with the rest of France. Its fragrant Rieslings, its spicy Gewürztraminers, its light, fresh, rather dry Sylvaners, and its Pinot Gris (called Rülander in Germany) are basically Rhine wines, however indubitably French; vintage years in Alsace tend to follow the German rather than the French pattern.

Alsatian wines, too, are generally a good bit dryer than their German cousins; they are made above all to be drunk with food and they complement, to perfection, the bountiful and excellent cuisine of their home province.

1977.   Better than average although less good than 1976 and 1975. Will develop quickly in the bottle. 15/20.

1976.   A remarkable vintage year. The harvest began a full three weeks early. The three principal varieties, Sylvaner, Riesling, and Gewürztraminer yielded wines full bodied, rich in alcohol, and high in fruit concentration. There will be a number of great late-harvested wines which will prove superb. 18/20.

1975.   Elegant wines of fine delicacy and fruit. Less heavy than the 1976 vintage. Wines which should be enjoyed young. 17/20.

1974.   For once, decidedly better than in Germany. Wines somewhat on the dry side, but well-balanced and fine. At least 15/20.

1973.   An extremely large crop, as nearly everywhere in Europe. Surprisingly good quality. 16/20.

1972. Undistinguished; rather hard wine. Perhaps 12/20.

1971. As in Germany, a year of spectacular quality, and in the opinion of many growers the best since World War II. Most of the wines, however, are, for my palate, much too high in alcohol (rarely under 13%), assertive, heady, lacking in distinction and finesse. As I once said of the '64s, "more suited to a pleasant *kermesse* than to a gourmet's dinner." Either 18/20 or 13/20. Take your choice.

II. GERMANY

RHINE AND MOSELLE

It is now well over six years since the first German wines of the New Era — produced, bottled, labeled and shipped abroad according to the provisions of the new German wine law — reached our shores. These were the Moselles and Rhine wines of the incomparable 1971 vintage, and it is impossible to see how they could have been better, or could be now. In any case, they certainly predisposed us to look on the new regulations with a favorable eye. We shall have to forget a certain number of words and definitions which are familiar and have been helpful to us, and learn others which are perhaps more appropriate and more accurate today.

1977. The year for QbA. High acidity with careful addition of Süss Reserve will yield refreshing and fruity wines for early enjoyment. 14+/20. Kabinett wines very irregular and often less good. 13/20.

1976. Extremely hot and dry weather brought about the earliest flowering on record in both the Rhine and Moselle vineyards. The Moselle was hardest hit by the summer-long drought as most of the good vineyards produced a crop 50-60%of normal. The Rhine vineyards produced 80-90% of a normal harvest.

The quality was exceptional. The Moselle 19/20. 80% of the wine made was Spätlese and Auslese with the best vineyard sites producing almost nothing lower than Auslese quality.

The Rhine 20/20. The best vineyard sites produced 75% Spätlese and Auslese wines. Very great Beeren- and Trockenbeerenauslese wines. Better than 1971. In a class with 1921, 1937, and 1953.

1975. The fine weather in September and October permitted an exceptional harvest for the Riesling in the Moselle and Saar vineyards. The wines have a superb balance of natural fruit sugar and acidity. They are, above all, elegant and destined for a long life. The best quality Kabinett wines in many years. Spätlese and Auslese wines delicate and not overly sweet. The Moselle and Saar 19/20.

The wines from the Rheingau fared less well. Only a select few made excellent wines. For the most part, the Rieslings didn't quite have the same fruit as their Moselle brothers. Some wines slightly high in acid and will develop more slowly in bottle. 17/20.

1974. A freakish, uneven, disappointing year. The German vineyards are, of course, the northernmost of Europe, about at the latitude of Winnipeg and Labrador, and it is something of a miracle that they produce fine wines at all. They must have, in order to do so, at least two or three weeks of fine dry weather: in late May and early June, for the flowering, and again in October, for the final ripening, and the *Lese,* or harvest. Quantity depends on the first of these, quality on the second; in 1974 they got neither. Practically no great wines at all, and not even a big crop as a consolation prize. There are always exceptions in Germany, but it is hard to see how the '74s will deserve more than 13/20.

1973 on the Rhine and Moselle, as in France, was the most copious vintage in recorded history, so large, in fact, that many vintners ran short of *Fuder* and *Fässer* and had to resort to tanks and vats to lodge their wines. Some proposed using water-towers and even swimming pools, but things never quite got to that point. Others complained that the '73s were not as good as the incomparable '71s, which is indeed the case, but asking too much of God. In truth, the 1973s are excellent everywhere, 16/20 or 17/20, and most of them ready to drink.

1972.   Uneven, much better on the Rhine than on the Moselle, rather dry and lacking in bouquet and fruit. They are not likely to improve. Say 13/20.

1971.   Without question the best year since 1959 and perhaps more properly comparable to '53, that "queen of vintages" when perfect autumn weather plus a generous accession of the *noble mold* gave wines of unique elegance and bouquet. The new German wine laws therefore became effective under the most favorable circumstances imaginable, with almost no one in a mood to complain. A comparatively small crop, practically all of it deserving the new official rating of *Qualitätswein*. For the first time in decades "sugaring" (which the French call *Chaptalisation*) was completely unnecessary on the Rhine and for the most part largely on the Moselle as well; a remarkably high proportion of *Kabinett* and *Spätlese* and *Auslese* wine was produced. These are now ready to drink and some of the Auslese quality will continue to improve. 20/20.

1970.   A very large crop, better than '72, somewhat less good than '73. In general they are a bit on the dry side. They have started to fade. 13/20.

1969.   A great year, particularly on the Rhine, where some notable *Spätlesen* and *Auslesen* were produced. 16/20. Good to very good on the Moselle, the Saar Valley exceptionally good, and the village of Ürzig outstanding. 15/20.

1968.   Very poor. Now off the market. 11/20.

1967 on the Rhine was a great year, the best without much question of their decade, and many of these holding well deserve 17/20 or better. The best are noteworthy for an almost overpowering fruit, a characteristic spiciness and breed. Still fine.

As for older vintages, there are some exceptional survivors dating from '66 and '64.

III. ITALY

As the result of an extremely ambitious program undertaken by the Italian Government nearly ten years ago, more and more of the better wines of Italy are now coming forward with the words *Denominazione di Origine Controllata* printed on their main label. This is a highly laudable effort to create a system like the French *Appellations Contrôlées* in Italy — in short, to define, classify and upgrade all of the superior wines of what was known to the ancients as *Oenotria tellus*, "the Earth of Wine". This is in truth a labor of Hercules, no less than a labor of love, and those engaged in it deserve our good wishes and a fervent Godspeed.

Once these stricter standards and more precise appellations have taken effect we shall doubtless have to pay more attention to Italian vintage years than we have in the past. Yet most Italian wines are made to be drunk young, which is part of their charm; they are easy and informal and rather low in alcohol, which is to their credit, and many of them are still comparatively inexpensive, which is a blessing. It is certainly to be hoped that these, when shipped to America, will not suffer "a sea change, into something rich and strange . . ."

What is probably going to happen is that we will find increasingly available in our better Italian restaurants and local wine shops some interesting and surprisingly expensive bottles from Italy. Gattinara has appeared over the horizon, and Brunello di Montalcino; why not Ghemme and Inferno, Santa Maddalena and Cinqueterre, Vermentino, Ischia and the Vino Nobile di Montepulciano?

How many of us in America are aware that the Italians drink twice as much French wine per capita as we do?

It is about time that the Italian-Americans, who kept our interest in table wines alive after Prohibition (and may I say, without naming names, *during* Prohibition as well), who have played a major role in the progress that California has made of late, receive their just due. We can at least examine, with encouragement and tolerance, what their cousins are doing these days in the Old Country.

For the moment, let me say that *all* white and rosé Italian wines that have come my way (like all California, most French — the élite excepted — though *not* German) are as good when they are four years old as they are ever likely to be. This is even true of Soave, an old personal favorite of mine.

Red wines are another matter. The best ones made from the Nebbiolo grape in Piedmont and Lombardy in northwestern Italy and the Tuscan wines made primarily from the Sangiovese grape require time both in oak and in bottle for full enjoyment, and a few take many years to mature. The following is a list of keepers:

Lombardy
    Valtellina (Inferno, Grumello, Sassella)
        Excellent — 1964
        Good — 1975, 1973, 1971, 1970, 1967, 1961

Piedmont
    Barbaresco
        Excellent — 1974, 1971, 1964, 1961
        Good — 1973, 1970, 1969, 1968, 1967, 1965, 1962
    Barolo
        Excellent — 1974, 1971, 1964, 1961
        Good — 1973, 1970, 1969, 1968, 1967, 1965, 1962
    Gattinara
        Excellent — 1974, 1964
        Good — 1975, 1970, 1969, 1968, 1967, 1965, 1962, 1961
    Ghemme
        Excellent — 1974
        Good — 1975, 1973, 1972, 1970, 1969, 1967, 1964, 1962, 1961

Tuscany
    Brunello di Montalcino
        Excellent — 1975, 1971, 1970, 1964
        Good — 1974, 1973, 1969, 1968, 1967, 1966, 1965, 1961
    Chianti Classico Riserva
        Excellent — 1975, 1974, 1971, 1970, 1969, 1968, 1967, 1964, 1962
        Good — 1966, 1965
    Vino Nobile di Montepulciano
        Excellent — 1975, 1970, 1967
        Good — 1974, 1973, 1969, 1968, 1966, 1964, 1962, 1961

IV. SPAIN

Although California, these days, produces more than twice as much "Sherry" as Spain, the Spaniards, with the enthusiastic help of some 25 million foreign tourists, drink nearly three times as much table wine as the United States. Almost all of this is just *vino corriente*, sound and inexpensive and far from bad, rarely as much as two years old.

Only in one small corner of Spain, which is, as almost might be expected, close to the French border, are wines produced which are more or less properly vintaged and which deserve this treatment. This is the Rioja district, about a hundred miles southwest of Biarritz and San Sebastian. All too little known, the Rioja produces some more than passable white wines, and some of the most remarkable red wines of Europe. The best of these can stand comparison with all but the very best of France, and a few of them, thirty years ago, used to bring as high prices in New York as Château Margaux.

Unfortunately, there is no organized system of château or estate-bottling in Spain, almost every producer buys grapes from his neighbors to supplement his own production, and often

467

makes several quite different qualities of wine in any given vintage. The less noteworthy lots are aged and bottled and marketed normally when four or five years old, whereas the most oustanding *cuvées* are given more time in wood plus a good many years in bottle, and emerge ten or fifteen years later, as "Reservas", often under a different label and at a higher price. The following recent vintages have given wines of exceptional quality (the last six, by now, are of course in the "Reserva" class): 1971, 1969, 1966, 1964, 1962, 1961, 1959, 1958, 1955.

When it comes to all other Spanish table wines, with the most rare exceptions, buy the most recent vintage: it will be the best.

V. PORTUGAL

With the unique and splendid exception of Vintage Port, Portuguese wines hardly ever carry a vintage; when they do, this is much more in the nature of a not entirely dependable statement of age than any sort of indication of superior quality. It is one of the charms of Portuguese table wines — Vinho Verde, Dão, Colares, as well as the ever more popular *rosés* — that they do not take themselves too seriously.

When it comes to Port wine, vintage dating is a serious matter. Vintage Porto, a unique dessert wine, is finally enjoying a rebirth of interest in the United States. Like Champagne, only the highest quality years are declared a vintage year. The best from the last two decades are 1975, 1970, 1966, 1963, and 1960. These wines generally take an average of 15 to 20 years to develop properly.

However, while we are waiting for our Vintage Porto's to mature, we can drink the early maturing "Late Bottled Vintage Porto", a wine left two extra years in wood casks which should properly mature within 8 to 10 years. Recommended years — 1969, 1967, 1962, and 1961.

APPENDIX 8

SERVING WINE

ABOUT WINE GLASSES

All good wines taste better in thin, stemmed, crystal glasses, preferably uncut, and as simple in design as possible. The color of the wine can be better judged when it is so served, and the wine seems to taste better in thin rather than heavy glass.

Shown below are eight glasses of American crystal designed by Frank Schoonmaker along the traditional lines that have been used by European glass producers for generations.

Any one of the three in the first series shown below would well serve as a single, all-purpose glass, or the first and third as a pair — the larger for red wine and the smaller for white.

| 10 oz. | 9 oz. | 8 oz. |
| Red wine | Single, all-purpose | White wine |

Other recommended shapes are as follows:

| 10½ oz. | 8 oz. | 6 oz. | 5 oz. | 7 oz. |
| For great red Burgundies | For Champagnes, sparkling wines | For Rhines, Moselles, Alsatian wines, etc. | For Sherry, Port, Maderia, etc. | For fine brandy, cordials, liqueurs |

Note: These glasses, of course, are not intended to be filled to the brim — no more than one-third to one-half full.

470

THE CLASSIC WINE-AND-FOOD AFFINITIES

Millions of people drink wine daily, wherever wine is made, in the temperate zones of both hemispheres. This is mostly the inexpensive product of their own local vineyards, and as much a part of their ordinary diet as all the rest — meat, fish, vegetables, fruit and bread. Most wine-lovers and almost all true experts have a high regard for such *ordinaires,* and enjoy drinking them, always providing they are honest and well-made, which is often, but not always, the case. But such wines are staples, and apart from the general principle of moderation, they should be drunk exactly as one wishes to drink them: there are no rules. Most French and Italian peasants, lunching in the fields or vineyards, drink them straight from the bottle, and Spaniards, as often as not, out of *porrones,* or leather flasks. At home, they are sometimes served in tumblers, often diluted with water, or, in cafés, with soda water. They are generally, both red wines and white, chilled or at least cooled (in a well or a brook or a cellar) in hot weather; and, both red wines and white, served at the prevailing temperature at all other times. And this is as it should be.

Wines of superior class are another matter: they are ALWAYS the result of a special effort on the part of the producer, who has planted certain select varieties of vines on chosen hillsides where they yield less per acre, but better wine. Such producers are dedicated artisans, and in some instances true artists. It is with what they make that this volume is principally concerned.

At the risk of sounding arbitrary, or possibly even pompous, it can be said that these wines should be treated with the respect and care which the knowledge and skill and love which have gone into their production, fully merit and have copiously earned. No hard-and-fast rules govern their service, and what is given below is no more than the accumulated preferences of a good many generations of knowledgeable wine-drinkers. Much additional information will be found elsewhere in this Encyclopedia — *see* Glasses, Serving, Temperature, etc.

WITH	*SERVE*	Temperature
Caviar, smoked salmon	Champagne	Well chilled
Olives, almonds, canapés, etc. as an apéritif	Dry Sherry, Montilla, Manzanilla, dry Madeira, Champagne	Well chilled
Oysters, clams	Chablis, dry Graves, Muscadet, Pinot Blanc, Manzanilla, dry Sherry	Well chilled
Consommé or turtle soup	Dry Madeira or medium Sherry, or no wine at all	Room temperature
Bisques, and other cream soups	Whatever white wine is to follow	Chilled
Heavy, vegetable soups, *pot-au-feu*, oxtail, etc.	Whatever red wine is to follow	Room temperature
Outdoor, cold buffet in summer	Provence rosé, Gamay Beaujolais	Well chilled Cool
Barbecue: chicken	Tavel rosé, light, dry white wine	Well chilled
beef	Zinfandel, Petite Sirah	Cool
Fish: poached, grilled, sautéed Crabs, lobsters	Light white Burgundy as Pouilly-Fuissé or white Graves or Alsatian or California Riesling. Moselle, Soave.	Chilled
More complex fish or shellfish dishes Cold fowl or cold meats	Fuller white Burgundy, as Puligny-Montrachet, or California Chardonnay. White Graves, Rheingau wine, or Gewürztraminer	Chilled
Chicken or Turkey	Either fuller white wine as above or, light red Bordeaux, Cabernet Sauvignon	Chilled Room temperature
Pheasant	Champagne or light red wine (see note).	Chilled Room temperature
Roast Ham or Pork	Alsatian white, Loire-white or rosé	Chilled
Veal, sweetbreads, etc.	Lighter red Bordeaux, Beaujolais, Cabernet Sauvignon or full white wine	Room temperature Chilled
Lamb	Fine red Bordeaux, Cabernet Sauvignon	Room temperature
Beef	St. Émilion or Pomerol, lighter red Burgundy, Cabernet Sauvignon, Italian reds as Barbaresco, Barolo, Classico Chianti	Room temperature
Stews: pot roast	Beaujolais, Côtes-du Rhône, Zinfandel or Gamay	Room temperature
Stews: ragouts, prepared with wine	Full-flavored red wine — Burgundy, Rhône, Petite Sirah	Room temperature
Game, as venison, wild duck, also steak	Burgundy, Hermitage, Châteauneuf-du-Pape, Barolo	Room temperature
Salad	No wine	
Cheese	Full-bodied red wine. Big Bordeaux, Cabernet Sauvignon, Burgundy, Rhône. White Burgundy or Loire with chèvres.	Room temperature Chilled
Cheese — goat	White Burgundy	Chilled
Dessert: pastries Fruits, as pears	Sweet Sauternes, Beerenauslesen, Sweet Champagne	Well chilled
Walnuts, etc.	Port, sweet Madeira, sweet Sherry	Room temperature

Note: Choice of wines will vary with the preparation of the dish, or its sauce. For example, choose red wines for dishes with red wine sauces or brown sauces, and white wines for dishes with white wine sauces or cream sauces.

GREAT OR EXCEPTIONAL WINES

Occasions may arise when one will wish to present to fellow wine enthusiasts rare bottles of wholly extraordinary quality, and it is often better in such cases to plan the menu around the wines, rather than vice versa.

Listed below are the dishes which are likely to enable wines of different categories to be shown at their best.

	Temperature	WITH
Dry Sherry of highest quality	50° F	Slightly salted almonds and hazel nuts
Old dry Madeira	Room temp.	Turtle or Terrapin, in honor of a great tradition
Old sweet Madeira	Room temp.	Alone or with walnuts after dinner
Grand Cru Chablis	55° F	Oysters or cold fowl
Montrachet, Bâtard-Montrachet, Corton-Charlemagne, Meursault, etc.	55° F	Special fish dish or lobster, veal
Great vintage Médoc or red Graves	Room temp.	Rack or leg of lamb, rare (no mint sauce, of course)
St. Émilion, Pomerol	Room temp.	Steak, roast beef, pheasant, cheese
Great red Burgundy	60°-68° F	Guinea hen, pheasant, cheese, beef, wild duck
Exceptional red Rhône wine	60°-68° F	Wild duck, squab
Champagne	Iced — 50° F or less	Before or after a meal. All cold dishes, dishes in Champagne sauce
Great Sauternes	50° F	Pastry or soufflé carefully chosen, not too sweet
Moselles of up to and including Auslese quality	55° F	Trout *au bleu* or grilled Sole, or after dinner
Very finest Moselles of great years	60° F	Alone, before or after a light dinner
Rhine wines of up to and including Spatlese quality	50°-55° F	Fish, chicken
Very finest Rhine Auslesen, Beerenauslesen, etc.	60° F	Light pastry, soufflé, or alone after dinner
Old Barolo, Gattinara	Room temp.	Beef or game, cheese
Barbaresco, etc.	60°-68° F	Veal, cheese
Exceptional Chianti	60°-68° F	Beef or veal, cheese
Vintage Port	Room temp.	Alone or with walnuts after dinner, Stilton cheese, cigars

NOTE: Room Temperature is intended to mean 65° to 72°. No fine wine should be served at over 72° under any circumstances.